The Shorter Logical Investigations

The Shorter Logical Investigations

Edmund Husserl

Translated by J. N. Findlay
from the Second German edition of *Logische Untersuchungen*

with a new Preface by Michael Dummett
and edited and abridged with a new Introduction by
Dermot Moran

London and New York

Logische Untersuchungen first published in German
by M. Niemeyer, Halle 1900, 1901
Second German edition, Vol. I and Vol. II, Part I, first published 1913

This abridged edition first published 2001
by Routledge
11 New Fetter Lane, London EC4P 4EE

Simultaneously published in the USA and Canada
by Routledge
29 West 35th Street, New York, NY 10001

Routledge is an imprint of the Taylor & Francis Group

Translation © 1970 J. N. Findlay
Preface © 2001 Michael Dummett
Introduction and editorial matter © 2001 Dermot Moran

British Library Cataloguing in Publication Data
A catalogue record for this book is available from the British Library

Library of Congress Cataloging in Publication Data
A catalog record for this book has been requested

ISBN 978-0-415-24192-2

Dedicated to
Carl Stumpf
With Honour and in Friendship

Contents

PROLEGOMENA TO PURE LOGIC
Volume I of the German Editions   9

INVESTIGATIONS INTO PHENOMENOLOGY AND THE THEORY OF KNOWLEDGE

INVESTIGATION I
EXPRESSION AND MEANING

CHAPTER ONE
Essential distinctions

CHAPTER THREE
Fluctuation in meaning and the ideality of unities of meaning

INVESTIGATION V ω3 (CH1 & CH2)
ON INTENTIONAL EXPERIENCES AND
THEIR 'CONTENTS'   197

CHAPTER ONE
Consciousness as the phenomenological subsistence of the ego and
consciousness as inner perception   201

CHAPTER TWO
Consciousness as intentional experience   211

Third Section
Clarification of our introductory problem   377

CHAPTER NINE
Non-objectifying acts as apparent fulfilments of meaning   379

APPENDIX
External and internal perception: physical and psychical phenomena 391

Preface

Edmond Husserl's *Logical Investigations*, little known to English-speaking students of philosophy but well known to most students of the subject with a different mother tongue, is a work of the first importance in the history of philosophy. It was written at a turning point in Husserl's philosophical development, between his earlier book, *Philosophy of Arithmetic* (1891), deeply embedded in the psychologism so prevalent in German philosophy of the time, and the *Ideas towards a pure Phenomenology and phenomenological Philosophy* (1913) in which the notion of *noema* was first presented and the programme of phenomenology was first set out. In *Philosophy of Arithmetic* Husserl had criticised Gottlob Frege's *Foundations of Arithmetic* from a psychologistic standpoint. Psychologism attempts to explain concepts by reference to the inner mental operations supposedly involved in attaining them or grasping them; Frege had engaged in denouncing this methodology – the intrusion of psychological considerations into logic and the analysis of meaning – from the *Foundations of Arithmetic* onwards. Husserl, whose previous relations with Frege had been fairly cordial, was deeply affronted by his savage, and in certain respects unfair, review in 1894 of the *Philosophy of Arithmetic*, and had no further contact with him for the next twelve years. Frege's review was his most sustained attack on psychologism; and although it was resented by Husserl for its unkindness, it is widely believed to have influenced him profoundly, albeit some reject this conjecture. However this may be, Husserl had completely changed his attitude to psychologism by 1900. His arguments against it in the *Prolegomena* often coincided with those used by Frege, although he elaborated them in far more detail. Yet while Frege's objections to psychologism had made little impact, that of Husserl's assault on it was overwhelming: the *Prolegomena* came close to killing off the influence of psychologism within German philosophy, although Husserl's old teacher Brentano remained bewildered by this turn of events.

Attention to Husserl's famous book may help to correct the impression of 'German philosophy' often given by those who declare their enthusiasm for what they describe as the German tradition in the subject. This they see as originating in the work of Hegel and the idealist school generally and descending to Heidegger. Heidegger indeed began as a pupil of Husserl's, though he diverged from him so markedly; but the false impression of what the German philosophical tradition has been may be corrected by reading Husserl's disparaging remarks about Hegel, and the accompanying encomium of Bolzano, in the Appendix to Chapter 10 of the *Prolegomena*.

Frege did not see himself as the founder of a school, although he was highly conscious of his divergence from the approaches of other philosophers contemporary with him. Yet nowadays he is recognised by all analytical philosophers as the grandfather of their school of philosophy – with Bolzano, whom Husserl so greatly admired, as its great-grandfather. Husserl, on the other hand, set out to be the inaugurator of a new philosophical method; and no one could deny him the title of founder of phenomenology. They were thus progenitors of two philosophical schools that have diverged so widely from one another that communication between them has until recently been almost impossible. Yet, at the time when Husserl's *Logical Investigations* were published, no one who knew the work of both men would have thought of them as belonging to radically different schools of philosophy; they had somewhat different interests, and a markedly different literary style, but they did not then appear any great distance apart in philosophical outlook. The moment of the publication of the *Logical Investigations* was that at which the views of the founders of the rival philosophical schools approximated most closely to one another.

They even had quite similar opinions about the nature of logic. Husserl denied that logic is an essentially normative discipline; he held that any normative discipline must rest on a theoretical science. Frege is often described as having held that logic *is* essentially normative in character, and he did indeed say as much in one of his unpublished writings. He did so because, when commenting on its description as embodying the 'laws of thought', he repeatedly observed that it did not lay down laws governing the way we do think, but promulgated laws concerning how we ought to think. In fact, however, his view was essentially the same as Husserl's. He frequently described logic as concerned with the laws of truth; and in the Introduction to his *Basic Laws of Arithmetic* he says that these are laws about what *is*, independently of our judgements.

Any analytical philosopher interested in how philosophy arrived at its present state thus needs to study the *Logical Investigations* to discover how the philosophical traditions that stemmed from the work of these two innovators came to diverge so widely: one investigating intuitions of essences, the other analysing language (to which Frege himself had so ambivalent an attitude). Recent work within the analytical tradition, from the late Gareth Evans onwards, has tended to reverse the explanatory priority which that tradition has historically given to language over thought. This suggests the possibility of a *rapprochement*; at the same time it may seem to threaten a relapse into psychologism. That such a relapse has not occurred is due to the treatment of the structure of thoughts by adherents of this new tendency after the model of a Fregean semantic analysis of language. Do we have here a means of reconciling the two traditions? Or does the gulf between them remain to be bridged?

Michael Dummett
Oxford, April 2000

Introduction

The Shorter Logical Investigations

The Shorter Logical Investigations is a selection of the key sections of Edmund Husserl's two-volume *Logical Investigations*, intended to complement the longer work, now available in a paperback edition for the first time. The current revival of interest in Husserl both in connection with the project to discover the origins of analytic philosophy and also in order to understand the origins of the century-old movement known as phenomenology has drawn attention to the *Investigations*. The aim of this abridged edition is to provide an accessible introduction for professional philosophers, students and general readers alike, to a work which, although recognised as the most important foundational text of the whole phenomenological movement and as a rich source of original ideas in the philosophy of logic and in semantics, has a not undeserved reputation as a difficult, dense, impenetrable and confusing text. In fact, Husserl intended his *Investigations* to be an exhibition of his own thinking in progress, as he wrestled with difficult issues concerning logic, meaning and truth, and was always conscious that the work lacked both form and literary grace. He made several efforts to edit the book to accommodate his developing views, and even planned to replace it with something written more deliberately as an introductory text. As a result the *Logical Investigations* was progressively eclipsed by the appearance of *Ideas I*, the *Cartesian Meditations* and by the *Crisis of European Sciences*, as a basic introduction to Husserl's thought. Yet, Husserl always regarded the *Investigations* as his 'breakthrough work' and indeed his later positions are almost unintelligible unless understood in relation to his original formulations in the *Investigations*. A more compact, user-friendly version of the text, then, has long been needed. I hope this *Shorter Logical Investigations* will answer this need, and provide a convenient entry to Husserl's thought. In the long run, I can hope no better than that it will also serve as a stimulus to read the *Investigations* in the full form.

In selecting the texts, I have had to face difficult choices as Husserl's mode of writing (like Aristotle's) involves the complex dissection of problems, the consideration of the prevailing views, and then the presentation of his own position, almost as a set of asides within the exposition of the problem at hand. Nevertheless, I have attempted, within the confines of the space available, to provide as comprehensive and representative selection as could be made, while still preserving the overall structure of the work. In selecting passages, I have attempted to preserve the integrity of the individual sections Husserl himself marked out, in order not to interfere with Husserl's reasoning. I have also sought advice from Husserl scholars (my thanks to David Carr, Kevin Mulligan, Harry Reeder, Donn Welton, among many others) as to the essential passages to include. For the fuller picture, readers are urged to consult the reprint of Findlay's translation of the whole two-volume *Investigations*.

The *Logical Investigations* (1900/1901)

Edmund Husserl (1859–1938) published his *Logische Untersuchungen* (*Logical Investigations*) in two volumes in 1900 and 1901.[1] The first volume, *Prolegomena zur reinen Logik* (*Prolegomena to Pure Logic*) appeared from the publisher Max Niemeyer in July 1900.[2] The second volume, subtitled *Untersuchungen zur Phänomenologie und Theorie der Erkenntnis* ('Investigations in Phenomenology and the Theory of Knowledge'), containing six long treatises or 'Investigations', appeared in two parts in 1901. This gargantuan work – which Husserl insisted was *not* a 'systematic exposition of logic' (*eine systematische Darstellung der Logik*, LI III, Findlay II: 3; Hua XIX/1: 228),[3] but an effort at epistemological clarification and critique of the basic concepts of logical knowledge – consisted of a series of analytical inquiries (*analytische Untersuchungen*) into fundamental issues in epistemology and the philosophy of logic, and also extensive, intricate philosophical discussions of issues in semiotics, semantics, mereology (the study of wholes and parts), formal grammar (the *a priori* study of the parts of any language whatsoever in regard to their coherent combination into meaningful unities), and the nature of conscious acts, especially presentations and judgements. In fact it was these latter detailed descriptive psychological analyses of the essential structures of consciousness, in terms of intentional acts, their contents, objects and truth-grasping character, especially in the last two Investigations, which set the agenda for the emerging discipline Husserl fostered under the name *phenomenology*.

The *Prolegomena*[4] appeared as a free-standing treatise dedicated to securing the true meaning of logic as a pure, *a priori*, science of ideal meanings and of the formal laws regulating them, entirely distinct from all psychological acts, contents and procedures. The *Prolegomena* offered the strongest possible refutation to the then dominant *psychologistic* interpretation of logic, propounded by John Stuart Mill and others, which Husserl viewed as leading to a sceptical relativism that threatened the very possibility of objective knowledge. Turning instead to an older tradition of logic stemming from Leibniz, Kant, Bolzano and Lotze, Husserl defends a vision of logic as a pure theory of science – in fact, the 'science of science', in the course of which he carefully elaborates the different senses in which this pure logic can be transformed into a normative science or developed into a practical discipline or 'technology' (*Kunstlehre*).

The second volume of the *Investigations* (1901) was published in two parts: Part One contained the first Five Investigations and Part Two the long and dense Sixth Investigation, the writing of which had considerably delayed the appearance of the work as Husserl began to realise the depth of the phenomenological project he had uncovered. Whereas the *Prolegomena* was particularly influential in turning the tide against *psychologism* (Frege's efforts in the same direction being in relative obscurity at the time), it was the second volume of the *Investigations* in particular that had a major impact on philosophers interested in concrete analyses of problems of consciousness and meaning, leading to the development of phenomenology.

Phenomenology, in line with a general turn away from idealism then current, was to be a science of 'concrete' issues. According to Husserl's Introduction, phenomenology aimed to avoid speculative constructions in philosophy (exemplified, in his view, by Hegel). The *Investigations* impressed its early readers as exemplifying a radically new way of doing philosophy, focusing directly on analysis of the things themselves – the matters at issue (*die Sachen selbst*) – without the usual detour through the history of philosophy, 'merely criticising traditional philosophemes' as Husserl put it (LI VI, Intro., Findlay II: 187; Hua XIX/2: 543), or making partisan declarations in favour of some philosophical system (such as empiricism, positivism, rationalism, Hegelianism or Neo-Kantianism).

Within a decade, as Husserl's ground-breaking efforts came to be recognised, the *Investigations* had established itself as the foundational text of the nascent 'phenomenological movement' (a term Husserl himself regularly invoked) in Germany. The *Investigations'* influence subsequently spread throughout Europe, from Russia and Poland to France and Spain, such that eventually, it is no exaggeration to say that this work took on a status in twentieth-century European philosophy analogous to that of another foundational text – this time in psychoanalysis – *Die Traumdeutung (Interpretation of Dreams)*,[5] published by Husserl's contemporary Sigmund Freud (1856–1939) in 1899. The *Investigations* continues to be a necessary starting-point for anyone wanting to understand the development of European philosophy in the twentieth century, from Heidegger and Frege to Levinas, Gadamer, Sartre or Derrida.

Given that the *Logical Investigations* is such a pivotal text in twentieth-century philosophy, it remains something of a neglected masterpiece, remarkably little read, and where read, poorly understood. For some seventy years it remained untranslated into English. An American philosopher living in Europe, William B. Pitkin sought Husserl's permission to translate it into English in 1905, but he abandoned the effort when he could not get a publisher (see Hua XVIII: xxxvii; XIX/1: xxii). Seemingly, the philosopher William James, who was consulted on the project, advised the publisher not to proceed – suggesting that the last thing the world needed was another German textbook on logic, and so the project was abandoned, which grieved Husserl because he had been an admirer of James.[6] Marvin Farber, an American student of Husserl's, published a paraphrase of the *Investigations* in 1943,[7] but it was not until 1970 that John N. Findlay produced the first and only complete English translation of the Second Edition. With the hundredth anniversary of the *Investigations'* publication now upon us, it is important to make Findlay's translation available once again in an accessible form for the English-speaking reader.

The emergence of phenomenology

In the first edition of 1901, Husserl adopted the existing term 'phenomenology' (*Phänomenologie*) – a term already in currency since Lambert, Kant and Hegel, but given new vigour by Brentano and his students – in a somewhat less than fully systematic way to characterise his new approach to the conditions of the possibility of knowledge in general. Husserl wrote in his Introduction:

> *Pure* phenomenology represents a field of neutral researches, in which several sciences have their roots. It is, on the one hand, an ancillary to *psychology* conceived as an *empirical science*. Proceeding in purely intuitive fashion, it analyses and describes in their essential generality – in the specific guise of a phenomenology of thought and knowledge – the experiences of presentation, judgement and knowledge, experiences which, treated as classes of real events in the natural context of zoological reality, receive a scientific probing at the hands of empirical psychology. Phenomenology, on the other hand, lays bare the 'sources' from which the basic concepts and ideal laws of *pure* logic 'flow', and back to which they must once more be traced, so as to give them all the 'clearness and distinctness' needed for an understanding, and for an epistemological critique, of pure logic.
>
> (LI, Findlay I: 166; Hua XIX/1: 6–7)

The logician is not interested in mental acts as such, but only in objective meanings and their formal regulation, the phenomenologist on the other hand is concerned with the essential structures of cognition and their essential correlation to the things known. When Husserl says in this Introduction, 'we must go back to the things themselves' (*Wir wollen auf die 'Sachen selbst' zurückgehen*, LI, Findlay I: 168; Hua XIX/1: 10), he means particularly that the task of phenomenology is to clarify the nature of logical concepts by tracing their origins in intuition:

> Our great task is now *to bring the Ideas of logic, the logical concepts and laws (die logischen Ideen, Begriffe und Gesetze), to epistemological clarity and definiteness.* Here *phenomenological analysis* must begin.
> (LI, Findlay I: 168; Hua XIX/1: 9)

More broadly, Husserl wants to document all matters that present themselves to consciousness in their diverse modes of intuitive givenness (and not restricting the sources of intuition arbitrarily in advance, as empiricism and other theories traditionally had done). Husserl initially characterised phenomenology ambiguously as either a parallel discipline to *epistemology*, or as a more radical grounding of epistemology, that sought to *clarify* the essences of acts of cognition in their most general sense. In analysing knowledge, Husserl wanted to do justice both to the necessary *ideality* (that is: self-identity and independence of space and time) of the truths known in cognition, and at the same time properly recognise the essential contribution of the knowing acts of the subject. Thus, looking back in 1925, Husserl described the aim of the *Logical Investigations* as follows:

> In the year 1900–01 appeared my *Logical Investigations* which were the results of my ten year long efforts to clarify the Idea of pure Logic by going back to the sense-bestowing or cognitive achievements being effected in the complex of lived experiences of logical thinking.[8]

Husserl's overall aim is to lay down what he describes as the 'phenomenological founding of logic' (*die phänomenologische Fundierung der Logik*, LI, Findlay I: 175; Hua XIX/1: 22), a clarification of the essential nature of logical knowledge as a preliminary to systematic formal logic and to science in general.[9] More narrowly, his 'phenomenology of the logical experiences' (*Phänomenologie der logischen Erlebnisse*, LI, Findlay I: 168; Hua XIX/1: 10) aims to give descriptive understanding of the mental states and their 'indwelling senses' (*ihren einwohnenden Sinnes*), with the aim of fixing the meanings of key logical concepts and operations, through elaborate and careful distinctions and clarifications. 'Phenomenology', in the First Edition, then, meant the efforts to inquire, radically and consistently, back from the categories of objectivities to the subjective acts, act-structures, experiential foundations in which the objectivities of the appropriate sorts come to be objects of consciousness and to evident self-givenness, working in the domain of pure intuition, rather than being a theoretical or hypothetical construction in the manner of naturalistic psychology. As Husserl put it in 1925, this 'regressive inquiry' brings a new world to light.[10] This is the domain of the *correlation* between objectivity and subjectivity.

In particular, Husserl wants carefully to analyse the intentional subject matter of *expressive experiences (ausdrückliche Erlebnisse)* where 'expression' is understood as the articulating of meaning. His focus then is on the ideal sense of the objective intention (*ihr intentionaler Gehalt, der ideale Sinn ihrer gegenständlichen Intention*, LI, Findlay I: 174; Hua XIX/1: 21). In giving an account of the idea of meaning or expression, Husserl takes concepts apart and elaborates extensively on their many meanings before moving on to discuss other related concepts. Thus, for example, he carefully distinguishes the number of different senses of the term 'presentation' (*Vorstellung*), separating out its various psychological, logical and epistemological meanings. Likewise, he embarks on conceptual analyses of key concepts such as 'content', 'judgement' and 'consciousness'. Thus he recognises the need to sort out the many meanings of the term 'content' (*Inhalt*, sometimes *Gehalt*), a term particularly frequently invoked by logicians and psychologists of the day. In particular, the contrast between what Husserl terms in the First Edition *real* (*reell*) and *ideal* content, and later what he refers to as the distinction between *phenomenological* and *intentional* content (LI V §16). A typical example of the clarification Husserl is seeking is his differentiation in Sixth Investigation (§§30–5) of the kinds of unity and conflict of meaning contents that lay the basis for the logical laws of consistency and contradiction. It is these rigorous feats of analysis that won the admiration of early readers and, more recently, of analytic philosophers.

While Husserl's own 'concrete' analyses were initially focused primarily on the foundations of arithmetic and logic, and the structures of knowledge, gradually he and his followers broadened phenomenology to address the *a priori* structures of consciousness in general, including affective, volitional, practical, evaluative, aesthetic, religious, legal, political and other forms of conscious awareness of meaning grasping and meaning articulating. Phenomenology was to be a science of essences and as such it was a pure, *a priori* discipline, attending to the nature of things as given in 'essential seeing' (*Wesensschau*). Phenomenology would broaden the sources of intuition further than previous philosophies had allowed, and clarify the fundamental relation of thought to truth.

Quite early on, the *Investigations* attracted the attention of students of the Munich philosopher and psychologist Theodor Lipps (1851–1914), who himself had been criticised for psychologism in the *Prolegomena* and who, in consequence, altered his views to come largely into agreement with Husserl. Through Lipps's students, especially Johannes Daubert (1877–1947), the *Logical Investigations* became the leading philosophical text for a generation of German philosophers, including Alexander Pfänder (1870–1941), whose prize-winning, *Habilitation* thesis, written under Lipps at Munich, *Phenomenology of Willing. A Psychological Analysis (Phänomenologie des Wollens. Eine psychologische Analyse*, 1900), contained the word 'phenomenology' in the title, although the term does not occur elsewhere in the work.[11] Subsequently, Max Scheler (1874–1928), Adolf Reinach (1883–1917), Edith Stein (1891–1942) and Roman Ingarden (1893–1970) were all drawn to this early conception of phenomenology with its strongly realist orientation and its promise of resolving philosophy's hitherto intractable disputes.

The role of the *Investigations* in Husserl's development

Husserl himself regarded his *Logical Investigations* as a ' "break-through", not an end but rather a beginning' (*ein Werk des Durchbruchs, und somit nicht ein Ende, sondern ein Anfang,* LI Findlay I, 3; Hua XVIII: 8).[12] In it, Husserl abandoned his earlier approaches to logic and mathematics expressed in his first book, *Philosophie der Arithmetik (Philosophy of Arithmetic,* 1891),[13] which had been judged psychologist by its chief critic, Gottlob Frege (1848–1925). Husserl discovered a much more fruitful way of doing philosophy in a rigorously scientific way through the clarification of the essences of our fundamental cognitive achievements, eventually leading to his later transformation of phenomenology into a comprehensive transcendental philosophical outlook. Ever a restless innovator, he constantly reinterpreted the significance of his own contribution, and thus the *Investigations* played a singular role in his own philosophical development. Both in his lecture courses and in his private research manuscripts, he constantly reworked the ground covered in the *Logical Investigations,* for example, in his Göttingen lectures on logic (1906–7), on meaning (1907–8), on logic (1910–11), in his Freiburg lectures on logic and in *Phenomenological Psychology* (1925), in the lectures that eventually evolved into *Formal and Transcendental Logic* (1929), and even in his *Crisis of European Sciences* (1936) and the posthumously published *Experience and Judgement* (1938). Husserl's own 'breakthrough' seemed so surprising even to himself that it had to be constantly rethought.

In later years, Husserl sought to distance himself from the common understanding of the work as solely an exercise in the philosophy of logic. He complained that he was being characterised rather limitedly as a logician, whereas he saw himself more broadly as a theorist of science in general, and as the founder of a new foundational science, first philosophy or *phenomenology,* which aimed at the careful description of all forms of making *meaning* and registering *meaningfulness* and hence the whole domain of subjectivity. He even claimed (in a letter to E. Spranger, 1918, quoted in Hua XVIII: xiii) that phenomenology had 'as little to do with logic as with ethics, aesthetics, and other parallel disciplines'. In other words, Husserl would later suggest that it was simply an accident of personal biography that he happened to come to phenomenology through *logical* researches; he could just as easily have entered the field from another direction entirely. In a letter to Georg Misch of 16 November 1930, Husserl said that he lost interest in formal logic and real ontology when he made his breakthrough to the transcendental, and later concentrated on founding a theory of transcendental subjectivity and intersubjectivity.[14] Before analysing the *Investigations* in more detail, let us now turn, then, to a brief consideration of the author, Edmund Husserl.

Edmund Husserl (1859–1938): life and writings

Edmund Husserl was born in Prossnitz, Moravia (now Prostejov, Czech Republic), on 8 April 1859. He studied mathematics and physics at the universities of Leipzig and Berlin, where he was deeply influenced by the mathematician Carl Weierstrass (1815–97), before moving to the University of Vienna, where he completed his doctorate in mathematics in 1882. Following a brief period as Weierstrass' assistant and a term in the army, Husserl went back to Vienna to study philosophy with Franz Brentano from 1884 to 1886. On Brentano's recommendation, Husserl then went to the university of Halle to study with Brentano's most senior student, Carl Stumpf (1848–1936), completing his *Habilitation* thesis, *On the Concept of Number. Psychological Analyses* with him in 1887.[15] Husserl remained in Halle as a lowly, unsalaried *Privatdozent* from 1887 until 1901, the unhappiest years of his life, as he later confessed.

Although Husserl wrote research notes and manuscripts continuously and obsessively, he published few books during his lifetime.[16] His first publication at Halle came in 1891 with the *Philosophy of Arithmetic*, whose opening chapters contained a revised version of his *Habilitation* thesis. The *Logical Investigations* took another ten years of difficult labour to write, during which Husserl sacrificed many of the routines of family life. Husserl always regarded its results as provisional. Nevertheless, writing the book 'cured' him, as he later said to Dorion Cairns. Its publication facilitated a move from Halle to a new salaried position at the university of Göttingen, a renowned centre of mathematics under David Hilbert (1862–1943). It was during his years at Göttingen that he began to attract both German and international students to pursue the practice and theory of phenomenology. However, Husserl still managed only two publications between 1901 and 1916: an important long essay, *Philosophie als strenge Wissenschaft* ('Philosophy as a Rigorous Science'), commissioned by Heinrich Rickert for his new journal *Logos* in 1910/1911,[17] in which Husserl outlined his opposition to all forms of naturalism and historicism (as he understood Dilthey's *Weltanschauungsphilosophie* to be); and a major book, *Ideas Pertaining to a Pure Phenomenology and to a Phenomenological Philosophy*[18] (hereafter *Ideas* I), published in 1913, which offered an entirely new way of entering into phenomenology.

To the great shock of Husserl's earlier realist followers (such as Ingarden and Pfänder), *Ideas* I quite deliberately espoused a form of transcendental idealism (involving a radicalisation of the projects of Kant and Descartes), an outlook Husserl would continue to maintain and develop throughout his career. Husserl himself, however, insisted that he really had this orientation in mind when he was developing phenomenology in the *Investigations*. In his Introduction to *Ideas* I, he said that readers of the *Logical Investigations* had misunderstood the work as an exercise in a kind of immanent psychology, whereas he had always intended a purer and more essential phenomenological approach:

> In supposed agreement with the *Logische Untersuchungen*, phenomenology has been conceived as a substratum of empirical psychology, as a sphere comprising 'immanental' descriptions of psychical mental processes, a sphere comprising descriptions that – so the immanence in question is understood – are strictly confined within the bounds of internal *experience*. It would seem that my protest against this conception has been of little avail . . .
>
> (*Ideas* I: xviii; Hua III/1: 2)

In other words, Husserl would later claim that transcendental phenomenology as a science of pure essential possibilities was entirely distinct from psychology in all its forms, including descriptive psychology (which he now treats as a branch of empirical psychology).

In 1916, Husserl was appointed to the chair of philosophy at the University of Freiburg, which he held until his retirement in 1928. Here, as he recorded in his 1920 Foreword to the revision of the Sixth Investigation (LI, Findlay 1970: 661; Hua XIX/2: 533), he became deeply immersed in teaching and research, pursuing the ideal of a system of philosophy with phenomenology at its core, and published almost nothing, apart from an article on the renewal of philosophy in a Japanese journal *Kaizo*, a little article on Buddha, and a truncated version of his lectures on time, *On the Phenomenology of the Consciousness of Internal Time* (1928), edited by his successor to the Freiburg Chair, Martin Heidegger, more or less as a counterpoint to the latter's own *Being and Time* (1927).[19] During the last decade of his life, however, Husserl was extremely active, giving lectures in Germany, Holland and France, and publishing *Formal and Transcendental Logic* in 1929,[20] and the French version of his Paris lectures, *Méditations cartésiennes*, in 1931, translated by Gabrielle Peiffer and Emmanuel Levinas.[21] In part, Husserl's intense activity was spurred by his desire to offer a corrective to Heidegger's version of phenomenological ontology, which Husserl felt distorted and betrayed his own mission for a transcendental phenomenology.

Following the coming to power of the National Socialists in January 1933, Husserl and his family suffered under the increasingly severe anti-Semitic laws enacted in Germany, which led to the suspension of his emeritus rights and eventually (in 1935) to the withdrawal of German citizenship. While he continued to live in Freiburg, he was shunned by most of his former colleagues, apart from his assistant Eugen Fink (1905–75) and former student Ludwig Landgrebe (by then a professor in Prague). However, he set about the task of preparing his extensive research manuscripts for publication. Despite meeting with official opposition, Husserl continued to write with new vigour against the crisis of the age, producing work of astonishing scope and originality, e.g., the *Crisis of European Sciences*, developed in lectures in Vienna and Prague and published in Belgrade in 1936 (publication in Germany being denied him).[22] After a period of illness, Husserl died in Freiburg in 1938. His last work, *Erfahrung und Urteil* (*Experience and Judgement*) appeared posthumously, with the extensive editorial involvement of Ludwig Landgrebe, in 1938.[23]

Through the intervention of a young Belgian philosophy graduate and priest, Fr Hermann Van Breda (1911–74), much of Husserl's *Nachlass*, including lecture notes and research manuscripts, amounting to some 45,000 pages of hand-written material, composed in an obsolete German shorthand, the Gabelsberger system, was smuggled out of Nazi Germany and is now preserved in manuscript form in the Husserl Archives in Leuven, Belgium. Here, in cooperation with the sister archives in Cologne and Freiburg, researchers are carefully editing these manuscripts for publication in the Husserliana *Gesammelte Werke* series of which more than 30 volumes have already appeared, with more scheduled.

The genesis of the *Logical Investigations*

On his own admission, the origin of Husserl's *Logical Investigations* lay in the studies in mathematics, logic and psychology, he had been pursuing, inspired by his teachers Weierstrass, Brentano and Stumpf. As he put it, the *Investigations* originally grew out of his desire to achieve 'a philosophical clarification (*eine philosophische Klärung*) of pure mathematics' (Findlay I: 1; Hua XVIII: 5). It worried Husserl that mathematicians could produce good results and yet employ diverse and even conflicting theories about the nature of numbers and other mathematical operations. Their intuitive procedures needed philosophical grounding. In search of this grounding for mathematics, Husserl was led to consider formal systems generally, and ultimately to a review of the whole nature of meaningful thought, its connection with linguistic assertion, and its achievement of truth in genuinely evident cognitions.

Husserl suggested that the *Logical Investigations* was originally inspired by Brentano's attempts to reform traditional logic. As he put it in his 'Phenomenological Psychology' lectures of 1925:

> ... the *Logical Investigations* are fully influenced by Brentano's suggestions, as should be readily understandable in view of the fact that I was a direct pupil of Brentano.[24]

In lecture courses Husserl had attended, Brentano had proposed a reform of traditional Aristotelian syllogistic logic, restricting the range of significant logical forms, effectively reducing all forms of quantification to existential quantification, reformulating the structure of logical judgements and recasting sentences in new ways to highlight the underlying logical structure distinct from the grammatical form. Despite its promise, Husserl recognised that Brentano's project was destined to fail, since it lacked a proper clarification of the nature of meaning in general. Only a complete clarification of the 'essential phenomenological relations between expression and meaning, or between meaning-intention and meaning-fulfilment' (Findlay I: 173; Hua XIX/1: 19) could steer the proper course between grammatical analysis and meaning analysis (*Bedeutungsanalyse*), Husserl claimed.

Brentano's failed reform of logic alerted Husserl's attention to serious deficiencies in current accounts of the nature of logic, in J. S. Mill, C. Sigwart, W. Hamilton, B. Erdmann, T. Lipps, and others. Husserl's familiarity with – and deep critique of – the logical and mathematical developments of the nineteenth century are evident in his several critical reviews of logical literature, published in 1894, 1897, 1903 and 1904.[25] While he fully recognised the importance of logic understood as a calculus of classes being developed by George Boole (1815–64) and by his German contemporary, Ernst Schröder, and the attempts to interpret logical deduction as a mechanical process made by William Stanley Jevons (1835–82) and others, including Gottlob Frege, Husserl harboured worries about the limitations of formal mathematical logic, which he saw as a refinement of logical technique rather than as a genuine philosophy of logic.[26] In particular, Husserl saw a calculus purely as a formal device for mechanically transposing signs (or replacing them with equivalents) according to rules, and thus essentially different from proper logical deduction. Technical brilliance in mathematical logic still required critical theoretical insight in order to elevate it to science.

For a more positive view of logic, Husserl revived 'pure logic', a conception deriving from Leibniz and Kant, but expressed most clearly in the *Wissenschaftslehre* of the neglected Austrian logician Bernard Bolzano (1781–1848),[27] and his followers (especially Frege's teacher Rudolf Hermann Lotze, 1817–81), which saw logic as a purely formal 'science of science'. Husserl singled out Bolzano in particular as one of the greatest logicians and even as the unacknowledged forefather of modern mathematical logic:

> Logic as a science must . . . be built upon Bolzano's work, and must learn from him its need for mathematical acuteness in distinctions, for mathematical exactness in theories. It will then reach a new standpoint for judging the mathematicizing theories of logic, which mathematicians, quite unperturbed by philosophic scorn, are so successfully constructing. These theories altogether conform to the spirit of Bolzano's logic, though Bolzano had no inkling of them.
>
> (LI, *Prol.* §61; Findlay I: 143; Hua XVIII: 228)

Husserl would also credit Hermann Lotze with opening his eyes to the true nature of the ideal objectivities which logic studied, helping him to understand the domain of the ideal while avoiding Platonic hypostasization.

Of course, as Husserl set out to write the *Logical Investigations* many other philosophical issues pressed on him, leading him considerably beyond what might be considered to belong strictly to the task of laying the foundations of logic and into broader questions of epistemology, semantics and even ontology. Husserl was drawn to inquire into the conditions of meaningful utterance and expression generally, beginning with the nature of signification in general, linguistic expression, the relation between individual and species, the *a priori* laws governing the whole-part structures generally, the formal laws governing linguistic sense and non-sense, the puzzling nature of intentional content and reference, and, finally, the nature and structure of conscious acts as such, and specifically the nature and structure of judgements which aim at truth and which were traditionally considered to be the vehicles of logical thought. These themes make up the six Investigations of the second volume.

Husserl's struggle to rescue logic from psychology

As Husserl acknowledged in the Foreword to the *Investigations*, his philosophical career began from Brentano's assumption that logical issues could only be clarified by psychology. However, his initial attempts at laying a 'psychological foundation' (*psychologsiche Fundierung*, LI, Findlay I: 2; Hua XVIII: 6) for arithmetical and logical concepts and judgements quickly ran into problems. While psychology was undeniably useful for clarifying the practical procedures of human reasoning and in accounting for the origins of concepts, it failed completely to appreciate or handle the logical unity of the 'thought content' (*Denkinhalt*, Findlay I: 2; Hua XVIII: 6) involved, specifically, the complete independence of this content from all our psychical behaviour. The Pythagorean theorem stands as an independent valid truth whether anyone actually thinks it or not. Such thought contents possess an 'ideality' that allow them to be instantiated in different thought processes of the same individual (LI, Intro. §2, Findlay I: 167; Hua XIX/1: 8) or in diverse individuals' thoughts at different times. Psychological analysis could not accommodate this peculiar ideal unity of thought contents. Husserl therefore suspended his investigations into the philosophy of mathematics to grapple with the 'fundamental epistemological questions' (*die Grundfragen der Erkenntnistheorie*, Findlay I: 2; Hua XVIII: 7) thrown up by his recognition of the ideality of meanings. Mathematics and logic needed a thorough *epistemological* grounding; through a 'critique of knowledge' (*Erkenntniskritik*) to be carried out through the application of phenomenological essential insight, as Husserl would develop it.

In the *Investigations*, then, Husserl aims at the very 'Idea (*Idee*) of meaning' and the 'Idea of knowledge' – the systematic conception of the essence of meaning and knowledge, which had been completely obscured in the psychologistic approach. He employed the term 'phenomenology' to express this kind of fundamental epistemological inquiry (see LI Intro. §7), which looked at the very structure of acts of thinking and knowing as well as at the objects of knowledge in terms of their essential meanings.

Inspired by his intensive reading of Bolzano, Lotze and other logicians, and of contemporary Brentanians such as Kasimir Twardowski (1866–1938), Alois Höfler (1853–1922) and Alexius Meinong (1853–1920), Husserl came to question the idea of psychological grounding. Husserl came to reject the account in the *Philosophy of Arithmetic* of the genesis of arithmetic concepts as given which employed Brentanian descriptive psychology to trace the psychological genesis of numbers in acts of collecting and colligating. His much discussed interaction with the logician Gottlob Frege in the early 1890s may also have helped to accelerate the shift that was already occurring in his thinking.[28] It is at least clear that both philosophers separately were developing sophisticated accounts of the difference between the 'sense' (*Sinn*) of an expression and its objective reference. In Husserl's case this distinction would deepen his understanding of the structure of the intentional relation leading ultimately to his 'breakthrough' recognition of the essential correlation between thinking and its object, which he says occurred around 1898.[29]

From the outset of his career, Husserl had regarded Brentano's rediscovery of intentionality (the 'aboutness' or 'directedness' of mental acts) as hugely significant for the analysis of cognitive acts and processes (which Husserl called '*Erlebnisse*', lived experiences or mental processes), but, during the 1890s, he came to reject as unsatisfactory Brentano's account, which seemed embedded in Cartesian immanentist assumptions about the nature of ideas, and which left dangling the issue of the status of intentional objects. Husserl was dissatisfied with Brentano's characterisation of the intentional object as 'inexistent' and as 'indwelling' in the act. This characterisation seemed to repeat the impasse of the modern representationalist account of knowledge in Locke and others, with its attendant problem of the ability of the mind to get beyond its own representations. Brentano had maintained that *every* presentation related to an object, but what about presentation that appeared to have no objects? Bolzano had discussed 'objectless presentations' and the problem of the status of thoughts that involved impossible or non-actual entities (round squares, golden mountains, and so on) had been bequeathed to Brentano's pupils, especially Twardowski and Meinong. Do all thoughts refer to objects, even thoughts of impossible objects?

In a number of studies throughout the 1890s Husserl carefully clarified his own understanding of the relations between the intentional act, its content and object, in, for example, his fragments discussing the differences between 'intuition' (*Anschauung*) and 'representation' (*Repräsentation*) in terms of the kind of 'fulfilment' (*Erfüllung*) involved,[30] in his draft review of Twardowski's book *On the Content and Object of Presentations*,[31] and in the several drafts of his never completed study, *Intentionale Gegenstände* ('Intentional Objects'), probably written in 1894 and re-worked up to 1898.[32] The results of these investigations found their way into the second volume of the *Investigations*, especially the First and Fifth Investigations and the Appendix to the Sixth Investigation, where the issue of intentionality and Husserl's distance from Brentano's conception of inner perception are treated at some length.

Briefly, Husserl rejected Brentano's attempts to define psychical phenomena in distinction from physical phenomena and his account of 'immanent objectivity'. For Husserl, the main achievement of Brentano was that he identified the essential 'pointing-beyond-itself' (*über-sich-hinausweisen*) of the mental act. Twardowski's attempt to distinguish between the sensuous immanent content of the act, the act's intentional object, and the real object referred to, also suffered from a 'false duplication' of the object.[33] Husserl's answer was to distinguish between the immanent sensuous '*reelle*' contents of the mental act and the transcendent ideal meaning-content of the act, which guarantees we are speaking of the *same* meaning across repeated acts, and between these and the transcendent object of the act (and not as Twardowski considered it the *immanent* object).[34] By the late 1890s Husserl had developed the main elements of his account of the relations between signs and things signified, between intentions and their intuitive fulfilments, but it seems likely that his crucial distinction between *sensuous* acts and acts of *categorial* intuition did not emerge until he began writing the six Investigations themselves. This notion of categorial intuition, a distinct intuition of complexes founded on sensory intuition, opened up the proper domain of phenomenological viewing as Husserl would develop it after 1901.

The results of Husserl's intensive research during his most active decade of the 1890s were brought together in a remarkable way in the *Investigations*. Thus, for instance, his 1894 article, *Psychologische Studien zur elementaren Logik* ('Psychological Studies in the Elements of Logic'),[35] sketched the distinction between dependent and independent contents that inaugurated the theory of parts and wholes later incorporated into the Third Investigation. But the first real start on writing the *Investigations* came in 1896 when Husserl delivered the lectures that formed the basis of the *Prolegomena* and in 1899 began to prepare the six Investigations themselves for the press. There is some evidence, chiefly his wife Malvine's account, that Husserl was still feverishly revising when the manuscript was wrested from his hands by Stumpf and sent to the publisher.[36] Certainly, it is clear that Husserl was having difficulties containing the Sixth Investigation as it grew in length and complexity and forced him to rethink distinctions made in the earlier Investigations, including his account of the relation between demonstrative indication and fulfilment of meaning in cases of perception.

The published revisions of the *Logical Investigations* (1913, 1921)

Almost as soon as the First Edition of the *Logical Investigations* appeared, Husserl began to express dissatisfaction with some of its formulations and began to revise. In his 1902/3 lectures on epistemology, he was already clarifying the distinction between phenomenology which he characterises as a 'pure theory of essences' (*reine Wesenslehre*) and descriptive psychology.[37] But his first public opportunities came in 1903, with his reply to a critic named Melchior Palágyi[38] – where he made clear that his concept of ideality was drawn from Hermann Lotze, and that he was not opposed to the psychological explanation of concepts but only to the founding of logic upon such an explanation – and with his *Bericht über deutsche Schriften zur Logik in den Jahren 1895–1899* ('Report on German Writings in Logic from the Years 1895–1899'), where he repudiated his initial characterisation of the work as a set of investigations in 'descriptive psychology'.[39] From around 1905, as is evident from letters written to Scheler and others, Husserl clearly intended to publish a revised edition of the *Investigations* (see Hua XIX/1: xxiii). In subsequent lecture courses at Göttingen, e.g., in 1906–7,[40] 1907–8,[41] and 1910–11,[42] Husserl developed new conceptions of logic, semiotics, and semantics (including the *theory of the forms of meanings* begun in the Fourth Investigation, but which needed to be revised in the light of the Sixth), offering essential revising of aspects of the earlier tentative formulations, and leading ultimately to an entirely new theory of *phenomenological meaning*, publicly announced as the doctrine of the *noema* in *Ideas* I.

Also, from around 1905 and inspired by his reading of Kant and Descartes, Husserl was moving in a transcendental direction, embracing both Descartes' project of *prima philosophia*, first philosophy, and Kant's project of a 'critique of reason'.[43] Husserl was revising his thoughts on the nature of the flow of consciousness and on the conception of the pure ego, which he had repudiated as an unnecessary postulate in the First Edition (where he was satisfied with the empirical ego). He gradually came to see the need for a fundamental *change of attitude* (*Einstellungsänderung*) away from the 'natural attitude' as a prerequisite for the proper phenomenological seeing of the essences of cognitive acts ('noetic' acts in general) and their objects understood as pure possibilities of any consciousness whatsoever. This reorientation shed new light on the *correlation* between the intentional act and its object, understood as what is intended in the manner in which it is intended, a conception that eventually would be named as the *noema*, which made its first published appearance in *Ideas* I.

As Husserl engaged in this self-criticism and reorientation, the problem of relating these new concepts of phenomenology to his existing published work became evident. Around 1911, with the First Edition of the *Investigations* now out of print, and with misinterpretations gaining currency among his followers, Husserl began to think seriously about revising the whole work in the light of a new introduction to phenomenology and transcendental philosophy which he was planning, and which eventually appeared as *Ideas* I (1913).[44] At first, Husserl harboured ambitious plans to offer a number of new expositions of phenomenology and phenomenological philosophy that would render the old *Investigations* obsolete (see his letter of 7 July 1912 to W. E. Hocking, quoted in Hua XIX/1: xxvi). However, since *Ideas* I was a deliberately programmatic work, to complement it Husserl saw the need for examples of concrete phenomenological analyses – 'attempts at genuinely executed fundamental work on the immediately envisaged and seized things themselves' (*Versuche wirklich ausführender Fondamentalarbeit an der unmittelbar erschauten und ergriffenen Sachen*, Findlay I: 4; Hua XVIII: 9), as he puts it in the Foreword to the Second Edition. The six Investigations would remain the paradigm of these concrete phenomenological inquiries.

Husserl began revising the text of the *Logical Investigations* in March 1911, but only made real progress in spring 1913 after *Ideas* I went to press. However, even his relatively modest planned revision, done in the light of his new understanding of phenomenology (as expressed in *Ideas* I), proved too demanding, and he produced only a partially revised Second Edition in 1913.[45] This was Husserl's 'middle course' (*Mittelweg*), as he put it in his Foreword to the Second Edition, where he articulated three 'maxims' that guided the revision (Findlay I: 4–5; Hua XVIII: 10–11): namely, to leave individual errors standing as representing steps in his own path of thinking; to improve what could be improved, without altering the course and style of the original; to lift the reader level by level to newer and deeper insights.

In the revision the *Prolegomena*, which was written with a single purpose, was left largely unchanged; but those passages in the *Investigations* that specifically discussed the nature of phenomenology, and the kind of essential insight involved, were extensively altered and expanded. In general, the Second Edition highlights the central discovery of *phenomenology*, a concept that had received only tangential and incidental treatment in the First Edition, and gives surer indications about its nature. Thus, invoking his 1903 essay (quoted in Foreword to the Second Edition, Findlay I: 6; Hua XVIII: 13), Husserl claims that the chief error of the 1901 edition was to call phenomenology a 'descriptive psychology', whereas in fact, phenomenology knows nothing of personal experiences, of a self, or of others, similarly it neither sets itself questions, nor answers them, nor makes hypotheses. In 1903, Husserl had claimed that this purely immanent phenomenology was to be free of all suppositions about the nature of the psychological, and furthermore, it would actually provide a critique of knowledge that might then be used as a basis for empirical psychology or other sciences. But, in itself, phenomenology is not identical with descriptive psychology.[46] This phenomenological approach brings to evidence the general essences of the concepts and laws of logic. While both descriptive psychology and phenomenology are *a priori* disciplines, phenomenology cuts all its ties with individual minds and real psychic processes, even those understood in the most exemplary manner (LI, Intro. §3, Findlay I: 171; Hua XIX/1: 16 – added in the Second Edition).

Husserl is now more emphatic that this eidetic science relies entirely on the evidence of pure intuition, and operates within the 'sphere of immanence', bracketing all concerns with worldly existence and real psychological processes. Husserl thus imports into the text of the *Investigations* the notions of bracketing, *epoché*, and reduction, which had become central to his expositions of phenomenology only after 1905.[47] Husserl now stresses the *remoteness* and *unnaturalness* of phenomenological reflection and expands the section (LI, Intro. §3) devoted to listing various difficulties that attach to how we move from naïve to reflexive understanding. Pure phenomenological seeing (*Wesensschau*) must be purged of its inherent world-positing tendency and associated beliefs that belong to what Husserl calls 'the natural attitude' (*die natürliche Einstellung*) with its assumption of real existence (*empirisch-reales Dasein*; see LI V §2, Findlay II: 82; Hua XIX/1: 357 – paragraph added in the Second Edition). It was this purification of epistemology from the distortions imposed by the natural attitude that led Husserl to see phenomenology as essentially distinct from any psychology, including descriptive psychology. Instead, phenomenology was to be the 'universal science of pure consciousness'.[48] Husserl later stressed that the First Edition was already *de facto* 'analyses of essence', but that he gradually came to clearer self-consciousness regarding the purely eidetic nature of his inquiries.[49]

The revisions of the Second Edition constantly underscore the pure *a priori*, eidetic character of phenomenology. Consider the following typical revision to the Third Investigation. The original sentence in the First Edition, referring to the relations of dependence holding between quality and intensity of a tone, reads: 'And this is not a mere fact but a necessity'. The Second Edition reworks this sentence to read: 'Evidently this is no mere empirical fact, but an *a priori* necessity, grounded in pure essence' (LI III §4, Findlay II: 18; Hua XIX/1: 237). The pure *a priori* essential character of the laws uncovered by phenomenological insight is now sharply contrasted with the kind of empirical generalisation characteristic of the natural sciences. To clarify this further, Husserl replaced Section 12 of the Third Investigation (LI III §12), which had dealt with dependence relations between temporally coexisting and successive parts, with a completely rewritten section in the Second Edition, which specifies more exactly the nature of the distinction between analytic and synthetic propositions, whereby analytic propositions are purely formal and are not determined by their content in any way, whereas *a priori* laws which relate to contents are *synthetic a priori*.

Phenomenology focuses on the essential features of conscious states in general (akin to Kant's concern with knowledge in general, *Erkenntnis überhaupt* – a conception already elaborated in the First Edition) understood as pure possibilities rather than in terms of any empirical instantiation in animals, humans or other kinds of minds. In contrast with pure phenomenology, Husserl now more sharply characterises all psychology as empirical, as a causal science of physical organisms and their psychophysical states, e.g., 'as the empirical science of the mental attributes and states of animal realities' (*als Erfahrungswissenschaft von psychischen Eigenschaften und Zuständen animalischer Realitäten*, LI, Intro. §2, Findlay I: 169; Hua XIX/1: 12), the science which studies 'the real states of animal organisms in a real natural order' (LI Intro. §6, Findlay I: 176; Hua XIX/1: 23). Husserl distinguishes both empirical and its sub-branch descriptive psychology from pure phenomenology. While psychology is a valuable empirical science, the reduction of meanings to their psychological states, i.e., 'psychologism', is a natural, ever present temptation to the mind ('at first inevitable, since rooted in grounds of essence', LI, Intro. §2, Findlay I: 169; Hua XIX/1: 12), which can only be cured by phenomenological analysis. Only pure phenomenology, and not descriptive psychology, Husserl writes in the Second Edition, can overcome psychologism (LI, Intro. §2, Findlay I: 169; Hua XIX/1: 11–12). Furthermore, Husserl departs from Neo-Kantianism, by stressing that the grasp of the conditions for the possibility of knowledge comes from insight into the essence of knowledge, that is from phenomenological viewing.

In keeping with his new transcendental orientation, Husserl has more appreciation in the Second Edition of 'the pure ego' (*das reine Ich*, LI V §§5, 8) of the Neo-Kantians (especially Natorp), which he had originally dismissed as an unnecessary postulate for the unification of consciousness (see LI V §8, Findlay II: 352; Hua XIX/1: 374). He also endeavours to improve his initial attempts at drawing a distinction between the quality and intentional matter of acts. In particular, he was unhappy with his original characterisation of the sensuous matter of the act and the manner in which it is taken up and interpreted in the act. His later account of the *noema* was offered as a corrective (see, e.g., LI V, §16, Findlay II: 354; Hua XIX/1: 411).

In the First Edition, Husserl had characterised phenomenology as expanding or as clarifying *epistemology* (e.g., LI Intro. §1 Findlay I: 166; §2, I: 168), in that it offered a kind of 'conceptual analysis' (*Begriffsanalyse*), concerned with differentiating and disambiguating the different senses of basic epistemological concepts (such as 'presentation', *Vorstellung*). In his Introduction to the Second Edition, Husserl is now more aware of a possible misunderstanding whereby this conceptual analysis would be misunderstood purely as an investigation of language, in short as *linguistic analysis*, whereas in fact Husserl is anxious to distinguish his 'analytical phenomenology' from linguistic analysis. Reliance on language can be misleading, Husserl believes, because linguistic terms have their home 'in the natural attitude' (*in der natürlichen Einstellung*) and may mislead about the essential character of the concepts they express, whereas phenomenological thinking about consciousness takes place in the eidetic realm where all natural attitudes are bracketed. For Husserl, it is certainly true that the objects of logic – propositions or statements (*Sätze*) – are encountered only in their grammatical clothing, i.e., in linguistic assertions, and it is an obvious fact that the findings of science eventually take the form of linguistic utterances or sentences. Husserl, then, agrees with J. S. Mill that discussions of logic must begin with a consideration of language, though not issues of the nature of grammar or the historical evolution of language as such, but rather in relation to a theory of knowledge. Husserl is seeking a '*pure phenomenology of the experiences of thinking and knowing*' (Findlay I: 166; Hua XIX/1: 6), experiences not to be understood as empirical facts, but rather grasped in 'the pure generality of their essence' (ibid.). Linguistic analysis is not a substitute for a fundamental analysis of consciousness (see LI I §21). In this sense, phenomenology clarifies our linguistic practice and not the other way round.

Husserl's incomplete revisions of the Sixth Investigation

In 1913 Husserl intended to revise the Sixth Investigation in a radical fashion, but became bogged down (see his letter of 23 June 1913 to Daubert, quoted in Hua XIX/1: xxv), and eventually withheld it when he sent the revised five Investigations to press. Husserl now recognised that his original account of categorial intuition with its realist commitments did not fit comfortably with his new transcendental idealist framework. He made various attempts at a complete reworking of this Investigation in late 1913 and again in 1914, but lost enthusiasm for these revisions during the war years (1914–18), when exhaustion prevented research 'on behalf of the phenomenology of logic' (*für die Phänomenologie des Logischen*, Findlay II: 177; Hua XIX/2: 533). As he recounted, he could only 'bear the war and the ensuing "peace"' by engaging in more general philosophical reflections, specifically the elaboration of his 'Idea of a phenomenological philosophy' (*Idee einer phänomenologsiche Philosophie*, Findlay II: 177; Hua XIX/2: 533). Meanwhile, he gave the manuscripts to Edith Stein who attempted to order them into two articles for the *Jahrbuch*, but she could not get Husserl to look over her work and the project stalled.

After the war, Husserl turned again to logic and eventually was prevailed upon to publish a limited revision of the Sixth Investigation in spring 1921. In his Foreword, dated Freiburg, October 1920, Husserl regrets that he was unable to produce the radically revised Sixth Investigation promised in 1913, and acknowledges that it was the pressure of friends (including, presumably, his new assistant, Martin Heidegger) that finally forced him to produce this new edition. In fact, Husserl was never satisfied with his revision and continued to work intermittently on a full revision of this crucial Investigation, leaving some drafts that remained unpublished at his death.[50] These drafts attempt a complete rethinking of the nature of signs involving a distinction between signitive and significative intentions in attempting to specify the achievement of abstract symbolic thought.[51] Husserl was also gradually coming to recognise the contextual aspect of meaning which would lead eventually to his discovery of 'genetic' phenomenology in the early 1920s.

Husserl's 1920 Foreword is written in tones of exasperation and defensiveness regarding the many misunderstandings of his work then current. He details changes made, mainly in the second section of the Sixth Investigation, entitled *Sinnlichkeit und Verstand* (*Sensibility and Understanding*), where the concept of categorial intuition – originally introduced in the First Investigation – is treated at some length. Husserl maintains that his critics have misunderstood his talk of immediacy as relating to the immediacy of sensory intuition rather than to the nature of intuition generally. In particular he attacks the views of Friedrich Albert Moritz Schlick (1882–1936, founder of the Vienna Circle), as expressed in his *Allgemeine Erkenntnislehre* (*General Theory of Knowledge*, 1918)[52] where he had argued that Husserl's *Ideas* I relied on a bizarre notion of non-physical intuition that required a peculiarly strenuous kind of study. Husserl replies that by 'strenuous study' he means no more than the application of a mathematician. Schlick's criticism typifies a more general unease in philosophical circles with Husserl's emphasis on intuition which was seen by many as promoting an irrational *intuitionism* that could not be corrected. The Neo-Kantians voiced similar criticisms of Husserl's concept of categorial intuition, as is evident from Fink's reply to Husserl's critics.[53] How could one have *intuition* of the categorial? Husserl, on the other hand, understood by intuition, cognitive experiences which are accompanied by adequate evidence. He wants always to emphasise that acts of knowing are essentially diverse and that their respective modes of intuitive fulfilment must be appreciated and appropriately distinguished.

In his Foreword to the revision of the Sixth Investigation, Husserl also challenges an accusation – apparently widespread, but which he vehemently rejected – that he had rejected psychologism in the first volume of the *Investigations* only to fall back into it in the second (LI, Findlay II: 178; Hua XIX/2: 535).[54] Husserl believes these critics have failed to appreciate the true sense of his phenomenology, and have misunderstood it as a kind of introspectionist psychology. In order completely to separate phenomenology from introspectionism, psychology and indeed all natural sciences, Husserl emphasises the need to undertake the *epoché* and the reduction. It was only by removing all traces of the natural attitude in regard to our cognitive achievements that their true essences can come into view in an undistorted manner. This claim integrates the *Logical Investigations* into Husserl's later transcendental idealism, whose treatment is beyond the scope of this introduction. Let us now turn to examine in more detail the philosophical content of the work itself.

Husserl's *Kampfschrift*: the *Prolegomena*

In the Foreword to the Second Edition, Husserl records that the *Prolegomena* was a 'polemic on psychologism' (*Streit um den Psychologismus*, Findlay I: 6; Hua XVIII: 12), and major figures such as Paul Natorp, Wilhelm Dilthey and Wilhelm Wundt recognised it as such, so that the *Prolegomena* took on a life of its own and had an independent impact in German philosophy for its criticism of psychologism. Husserl, however, liked to emphasise its coherence with the second volume and wrote to Meinong that the critique of psychologism was central to his phenomenology of knowledge in general (letter of 27 August 1900, quoted in Hua XVIII: xvii). Others, including Wundt, could not so easily see the connection between the two volumes.

According to the Foreword, the first draft of the *Prolegomena* originated as two series of lectures delivered at Halle in the summer and autumn of 1896 (Findlay I: 5; Hua XVIII: 12) and written up in 1899. These 1896 lectures had already set out Husserl's conception of logic as a pure, formal, autonomous science of ideal meanings and the ideal laws which govern them, and offering a sharp differentiation of pure logic from the more traditional interpretation of logic as an 'art' or 'technique' (*Kunstlehre*) of thinking well. The Halle lectures, however, do not contain some of the more important parts of the *Prolegomena*, namely, the discussion of relativism (*Prol.* §§32–7), and the detailed criticisms of Mill, Spencer, Sigwart and Erdmann, and the discussion of 'thought-economy' associated with Mach and Avinarius (*Prol.* §§52–6). As the *Prolegomena* was written entirely in one cast of mind, Husserl did not feel the need to make major revisions in the Second Edition.

Husserl's negative aim was to demonstrate that the psychologistic interpretation of logic was a self-defeating, self-contradictory absurdity:

> the correctness of the theory presupposes the irrationality of its premises, the correctness of the premises the irrationality of the theory.
>
> (*Prol.* §26, Findlay I: 61; Hua XVIII: 95)

Furthermore, whereas the study of traditional logic should have given a clear understanding of the 'rational essence of deductive science' and indeed be the 'science of science', in fact the logic of his time was not adequate to that task. Husserl's positive aim was to find out 'what makes science science' (*Prol.* §62, Findlay I: 144; Hua XVIII: 230), but the unclarity and confusion surrounding logical concepts put the whole project of exact scientific knowledge at risk:

> In no field of knowledge is equivocation more fatal, in none have confused concepts so hindered the progress of knowledge, or so impeded insight into its true aims, as in the field of pure logic.
>
> (*Prol.* §67, Findlay I: 154; Hua XVIII: 246)

In his 1900 *Selbstanzeige* ('Author's Report') to the *Prolegomena* Husserl announced that he was defending logic as a pure, *a priori*, independent, theoretical science, reviving the older Bolzanian idea of a pure logic against the prevailing psychologistic misinterpretation of logic that leads to contradictions and absurdities, and ultimately to sceptical relativism. Husserl argues that logical laws and concepts belong to the realm of the ideal, being purely formal, that is, applied in general to every kind of content. In the *Prolegomena* Husserl makes an important distinction between empirical *generalisation* and the kind of *formalisation* required for idealisation in science and mathematics. He contrasts this pure theoretical logic with applied logic, understood as an art of thinking (*Kunstlehre*), drawing an analogy with the contrast between pure geometry and the art of land surveying (*Feldmesskunst*). Thus, in the *Selbstanzeige* Husserl defines pure logic as

> ... the scientific system of ideal laws and theories which are purely grounded in the sense of the ideal categories of meaning; that is, in the fundamental concepts which are common to all sciences because they determine in the most universal way which makes sciences objective sciences at all: namely, unity of theory.[55]

Science as such is for Husserl a regulated interconnection of ideal truths expressed in propositions. Logic deals with these propositions and their component meanings in their utmost generality, understood as pure categories. According to Husserl, following in the Kantian tradition, all logical distinctions are 'categorial' (LI II §1) and belong to 'the pure form of possible objectivities of consciousness as such' (LI II, Findlay I: 240; Hua XIX/1: 115). Furthermore, knowledge can be about many kinds of different things, there are multifarious objects of knowledge, not just real things, but ideal entities, relations, events, values. The conception of scientific knowledge must be sufficiently broad to accommodate this diversity of objects of knowledge. Husserl, then, wants a new account of logic as a pure *a priori* science, a *mathesis universalis* in the manner of Leibniz. It must be balanced with a new theory of the nature of objects in general, formal ontology, developed in the Third Investigation. In other words, pure logic has a counterpart, the pure theory of objects.

Husserl's encounter with Frege – the issue of psychologism

Since the rejection of psychologism and the defence of the ideal objectivity of logical laws is now more usually credited to Gottlob Frege rather than to Husserl, it is appropriate at this point to examine the relations between these two logicians. In fact, they corresponded with one another on various issues in mathematics and semantics in 1891 (and again in 1906). Husserl was one of the first philosophers in Germany to recognise Frege's work, and, although he had criticised Frege's account of the nature of identity in the *Philosophy of Arithmetic* in 1891, relations between the two were collegial and mutually respectful. But, in 1894, Frege published an acerbic review of Husserl's *Philosophy of Arithmetic*, in which he accused Husserl of making a number of fundamental errors.[56] According to Frege, Husserl treated numbers naïvely as properties of things or of aggregates rather than as the extensions of concepts (the *extension* of a concept is the set of objects the concept picks out).[57] Husserl had seen number as deriving from our intuition of groups or multiplicities and since neither one nor zero is a multiple, strictly speaking they were not positive numbers for Husserl. Frege criticised Husserl's account of zero and one as negative answers to the question: 'how many?' Frege states that the answer to the question, 'How many moons has the earth?', is hardly a negative answer, as Husserl would have us believe. Furthermore, Frege believed, Husserl seemed to be confusing the numbers themselves with the *presentations* of number in consciousness, analogous to considering the moon as generated by our act of thinking about it. Crucially for Frege, in identifying the objective numbers with subjective acts of counting, Husserl was guilty of *psychologism*, the error of tracing the laws of logic to empirical psychological laws. If logic is defined as the study of the laws of thought, there is always the danger that this can be interpreted to mean the study of how people actually think or ought to think; understanding necessary entailment, for example, as that everyone is so constituted psychologically if he believes *p* and if he believes that *p* implies *q* then he cannot help believing that *q* is true. For Frege, Husserl has collapsed the logical nature of judgement into private psychological acts, collapsing together truth and judging something as true.

According to the journal kept by W. R. Boyce-Gibson, who studied with Husserl in Freiburg in 1928, Husserl later acknowledged that Frege's criticisms had 'hit the nail on the head'. On the other hand, there is considerable evidence that Husserl was already moving away from his own earlier psychologism when Frege's review was published, especially in his critique of Schröder's *Algebra of Logic*.[58] Husserl was already embracing Bolzano's *Wissenschaftslehre*[59] with its doctrine of 'states of affairs' and 'truths in themselves', whose precise nature he then came to understand through his reading of Hermann Lotze's account of the Platonic Ideas, as he had reported in his reply to Melchior Palágyi in 1903. Given the supposedly crucial importance of Frege's review of Husserl, it is surprising that Frege receives only one mention in the *Prolegomena* in a footnote (*Prol.* §45, Findlay I: 318; Hua XVIII: 172 n. **) where Husserl writes: 'I need hardly say that I no longer approve of my own fundamental criticisms of Frege's anti-psychologistic position set forth in my *Philosophy of Arithmetic*'. Husserl now cites both Frege's *Die Grundlagen der Arithmetik* (*Foundations of Arithmetic*, 1884) and the Preface to his *Grundgesetze der Arithmetik* (*Fundamental*

Laws of Arithmetic, 1893) as anti-psychologistic statements of which Husserl can now approve.

In fact, Husserl had abandoned the approach of the *Philosophy of Arithmetic* almost as soon as it was published in 1891. He realised that the cardinal numbers were not the basis of all numbers, and in particular that the psychological approach could not handle the more complex numbers (e.g., the imaginary numbers). In the *Prolegomena* Husserl explicitly denies that numbers themselves are to be understood in terms of acts of counting although they can only be accessed through acts of counting:

> The number Five is not my own or anyone else's counting of five, it is also not my presentation or anyone else's presentation of five.
> (LI, *Prol.* §46, Findlay I: 109; Hua XVIII: 173–4)

While it is only by counting that we encounter numbers, numbers are not simply products of the mind. This would deny objective status to mathematics. The psychological origin of arithmetic concepts does not militate against the independent ideal existence of these concepts as species quite distinct from 'the contingency, temporality and transience of our mental acts' (LI, *Prol.* §46, Findlay I: 110; Hua XVIII: 175). Two apples can be eaten but not the number two, Husserl says in his 1906/7 lectures. For Husserl, logical concepts contain nothing of the process by which they are arrived at, any more than number has a connection with the psychological act of counting. Numbers and propositions, such as the Pythagorean theorem, are ideal 'objectivities' (*Gegenständlichkeiten*, Findlay: 'objective correlates'), which are the substrates of judgements just as much as any real object is. In contrast to 'real' entities that bear some relation to time, if not to space, the pure identities of logic are 'irreal' or 'ideal'. Husserl characterised them as 'species' in the Aristotelian sense, along side other 'unities of meaning', for example the meaning of the word 'lion', a word which appears only once in the language despite its multiple instantiations in acts of speaking and writing. What is logically valid is *a priori* applicable to all worlds. In the *Prolegomena*, then, Husserl, holds a view similar to Wittgenstein in the *Tractatus* – logic says nothing about the real world, the world of facts. It is a purely formal *a priori* science. Husserl, however, integrates logic into a broader conception of the theory of science.

Whereas Husserl had begun in 1887 with the assumption that psychology would ground all cognitive acts, he ends the Foreword to his *Investigations* by quoting Goethe to the effect that one is against nothing so much as errors one has recently abandoned, in order to explain his 'frank critique' (*die freimütige Kritik*) of psychologism (LI, Findlay I: 3; Hua XVIII: 7). While in agreement with Frege concerning the dangers of psychologism for logic, Husserl was not persuaded by Frege's project for mathematical logic as, in general, he was, as we have seen, suspicious of the purely formal turn to symbolic logic, exemplified in his day by the logical programmes of George Boole (see Hua XXIV: 162), William Stanley Jevons and Ernst Schröder, which for him contained theoretical flaws and confusions. That is not to say that Husserl thought of formalisation as unnecessary; in fact, he saw it as the only purely scientific way of advancing logic (LI, *Prol.* §71, Findlay I: 158–9; Hua XVIII: 254). Thus he praised the elegance with which mathematicians were expanding and transforming the domain of traditional logic, and he criticised those who refused to recognise the proper role of mathematics in these matters. However, Husserl believed that this mathematical tendency was manifesting itself as a kind of technical ability that had not reflected on the nature of its founding concepts. Philosophy must try to think through the essential meanings of logical procedures:

> The philosopher is not content with the fact that we find our way about in the world, that we have legal formulae which enable us to predict the future course of things, or to reconstruct its past course: he wants to be able to clarify the essence of a thing, an event, a cause, an effect, of space, of time, etc., as well as that wonderful affinity which this essence has with the essence of thought, which enables it to be thought, with the essence of knowledge, which makes it knowable, with meaning which make it capable of being meant etc.
>
> (*Prol.* §71, Findlay I: 159; Hua XVIII: 255)

As Husserl put it in his 1906/7 lectures, 'Introduction to Logic and Theory of Knowledge', one must distinguish between mathematical logic and philosophical logic (Hua XXIV: 163). Towards the end of his life Husserl would repeat this criticism in *The Crisis of European Sciences*, where he would criticise this 'idolization of a logic which does not understand itself' and claim that a formal deductive system is not in itself an explanatory system (*Crisis*, §55, Carr: 189; Hua VI: 193). For Husserl, purely extensionalist logic or calculus could never be more than a brilliant technique. From the *Prolegomena* onwards, Husserl offered a complex account of the full nature of what he called 'formal logic', utilising a much wider conception than is now current. In some respects his account of logic is quite traditional, being centred on the notion of judgement or assertion (Greek: *apophansis*) and hence is, following Aristotle, characterised as 'apophantic logic' (see LI, IV §14, Findlay II: 72; Hua XIX/1: 344). On the other hand, in *Formal and Transcendental Logic* (§§12–15) Husserl articulated this mature vision of this 'formal logic', which for him included formal grammar or what he called 'the pure theory of forms of meaning' that laid down the conditions of meaning combination as such; then a second level of 'consequence-logic' or the logic of validity which is concerned with inference; and finally a 'logic of truth', which recognised that logic aims not only at formal validity but seeks to articulate truth. In the *Prolegomena* Husserl also saw the need for a general 'theory of manifolds' or the theory of the possible forms of theories to complete his account of the nature of logic in general. We cannot deal with the complexities of Husserl's vision of logic here, except to note that in the *Investigations* Husserl was not pursuing an objectivist account of logic as his exclusive aim. Husserl recognised the essential 'two-sidedness' of the acts which are aimed at logical meanings, on the one hand there are the laws governing the meanings themselves, but there are also the judgings, inferrings, and other acts, which are oriented towards the subjective side, that need to be treated by phenomenology (*Formal and Transcendental Logic* §8). In other words, the aim of phenomenology is to study the essential *correlations* between acts of knowing and the objects known, something that became clearer to Husserl after he wrote the *Investigations*.

The structure of the six Investigations

While the *Prolegomena* was written with a single purpose and, by Husserl's standards, remains a relatively straightforward piece of writing, the six Investigations of the second volume at first sight seem much less unified and coherent, with most commentators testifying to their uneven, fragmentary and sprawling character. Husserl himself warned that the work could not be considered as a finished exposition of scientific results or as '*one* book or work in the literary sense' (LI, Findlay I: 5; Hua XVIII: 11), but rather should be seen as a 'systematically bound chain of investigations', 'a series of analytical investigations' (*eine Reihe analyticher Untersuchungen*, I, Findlay I: 173; Hua XIX/1: 20), which would need further elaboration through 'resolute cooperation among a generation of research-workers' (I, Findlay I: 171; Hua XIX/1: 16–17). It had to be seen as a living development of philosophical ideas, a journal of philosophical discovery.

A recent commentator, Kit Fine, has remarked (referring specifically to the Third Investigation but applicable with justice to the whole): 'Such is the range of the work that it is with a growing sense of excitement that one discovers the riches that lie beneath its rough and seemingly impenetrable exterior'.[60] David Bell has identified a threefold structure to the work, with the *Prolegomena* establishing the need for ideal unities in logic and knowledge generally, the first four Investigations clarifying issues of linguistics, semantics, formal ontology and formal grammar, while the final two Investigations were properly phenomenological, studying the nature of conscious acts and their claim to knowledge and truth.[61] The *Investigations*, then, is more united than its outward appearance suggests, and rich in sophisticated philosophical insights, albeit embedded in Husserl's wordy and labyrinthine presentation. In part, the progressive structure of the work is obscured by Husserl's tendency to enter into exhaustive critiques of other positions in order to arrive at his own view in circuitous manner, and then set out again circumspectly and tentatively, warning always of the need for further analyses and distinctions to be borne in mind.[62] One always has the sense of philosophising in progress rather than of a completed system, of listening to a great mind communing with itself. According to the author, the *Investigations* proceed by lifting the reader from lower to higher levels, moving in a 'zig-zag' manner (*im Zickzack*, I, Findlay I: 175; Hua XIX/1: 22), forced to employ concepts that would be clarified later in a reflective 'turning back' (*zurückkehren*). Indeed, Husserl's whole approach has the character of such 'backward questioning' (*Rückgrafen*).

The six lengthy Investigations of the second volume are concerned with analysing elements of the form of knowledge, such notions as meaning, concept, proposition, truth (LI *Prol.* §71, Findlay I: 159–60; Hua XVIII: 236–7). Husserl begins with the general structure of signs and meaningful expressions; then moves to analyse the status of universals (which he calls *species*) and the nature of abstraction; followed by a treatise on the laws governing the relations of dependence between parts and wholes; another mini-treatise on the relation between logic and grammar as *a priori* disciplines; the nature of consciousness, including the meaning of intentionality and the ambiguities surrounding the associated notions of content, object, presentation, and finally the nature of the identifying syntheses involved in judgement and its relation to truth. Along the way, he offers sharp criticisms of prevailing views, including a critique of J. S. Mill's account of connotation and denotation, a refutation of sensationalism, a rebuttal of empiricist theories of abstraction (Locke, Berkeley, Hume, Mill), a sharpened definition of the *a priori* including a new distinction between the formal (analytic) and material (synthetic) *a priori* which claims to be an advance on Kant, and careful discussions of Bolzano, Mill, Brentano and others, in terms of their views on logic, psychology and the nature of judgements and their contents.

A basic assumption of Husserl's understanding of knowledge is that knowledge is essentially understood and communicated in the form of expressive statements, where a statement is a unified whole with a single, possibly complex, meaning, that says something *about* something. It refers to an object (whether an individual thing or a state of affairs) through a 'sense' or 'meaning' (Husserl employs both *Sinn* and *Bedeutung* for 'meaning'). Of course, in the *Logical Investigations*, and indeed since 1891, Husserl was fully aware of Frege's distinction between *Sinn* ('sense') and *Bedeutung* ('reference' or 'meaning'), but he does not observe it since it is at variance with ordinary German usage. Husserl prefers to use the terms *Sinn*, *Bedeutung* and also *Meinung* more or less as equivalent notions (see LI II §2, Findlay I: 240; Hua XIX/1: 115) although later, in *Ideas* I §124, he will restrict '*Bedeutung*' to linguistic meaning only and use '*Sinn*' more broadly to include all meanings, including non-conceptual contents (e.g., perceptual sense). Both Frege and Husserl agree that the *sense* of a statement is an ideal unity not affected by the psychic act grasping it, nor by the psychic stuff (mental imagery, feelings, and so on) that accompanies the psychological episode. Logic (and mathematics and the other formal sciences) is concerned to process the laws governing these abstract ideal unities which Husserl characterises as having 'being in itself' (*An-sich-sein*, translated by Findlay as 'intrinsic being') as unities in manifolds (Findlay I: 169; Hua XIX/1: 12) as well as a 'being for' (*Für-sich-sein*) the thinker. In themselves, they are pure identities, remaining unchanged irrespective of their being counted, judged, or otherwise apprehended in psychic acts. As Husserl says in the *Prolegomena*, truths are what they are irrespective of whether humans grasp them at all (*Prol.* §65, Findlay I: 150; Hua XVIII: 240). Despite the fact that the objects of logic are ideal and transtemporal, nevertheless, they must also be accessible and graspable by the human mind, as Husserl later explains:

> . . . it is unthinkable that such ideal objects could not be apprehended in appropriate subjective psychic acts and experiences.[63]

We can imagine any such ideal meaning or *Sinn* being entertained or judged or considered in some way by a mind. It is simply a fact that these ideal meanings (*Sinne*) present themselves to us as something that is subjectively grasped: '. . . ideal objects confront us as subjectively produced formations in the lived experiencing and doing of the forming'.[64] This is their 'being-for'. They are always truths *for* some possible mind, subjective acts are 'constituting acts' for these ideal objectivities. The question then becomes: how are these hidden psychic experiences *correlated* to the 'idealities'? Frege had answered in a naïve manner: our minds simply *grasp* ideal thoughts. But Husserl wants to give an account that does justice to the essential two-sidedness of our cognitive achievements by analysing the structure of this expressing and grasping of meaning.

For Husserl, the primary interest of what he calls 'phenomenology' in the second volume of the *Investigations* does not lie in identifying the ideal nature of the idealities (numbers, logical entities, pure meanings) that are the focus of mathematics, logic, semantics and other sciences. Rather, Husserl is primarily interested in the mental acts *correlated* with these ideal objectivities and the laws governing these essential intentional correlations (see Hua XXIV: 172). Initially, he tended to understand these acts as psychological realities which instantiate pure essences in a kind of token/type relation. To get at their essential natures he initially thought he could use Brentanian descriptive psychology. After 1901 Husserl realised he was mistaken to characterise in psychological terms what were the essences of cognitive acts and their correlative objects. Psychic acts, like physical objects, are parts of the natural world and are governed by temporal relations, and other features of our contingent universe. The essential structures of acts of cognition, on the other hand, were not parts of the world, and hence could not be treated by psychology. Thus it was some four years after the *Inves-*

tigations, as Husserl recalled in the *Crisis* §70 (Carr: 243; Hua VI: 246), that he arrived at self-consciousness regarding the true nature of the phenomenological method uncovered in 1901. He then realised that pure or transcendental phenomenology has essentially to replace descriptive psychology and that real/ideal distinction had to be replaced by a purely essential study of the noetic/noematic structure of intentional experiences. Husserl thinks the intentional acts themselves can be isolated as true for all possible consciousnesses. Phenomenology does not discuss states of animals, but rather perceptions *as such*, willings *as such*, just as pure arithmetic deals with pure number and geometry deals with pure shapes, and not actual shapes as encountered in nature. For Husserl, it was the task of phenomenology to delineate in advance the possible forms of each intentional act and its limits. This is why phenomenology despite its descriptive rigour is actually an *a priori* science, not an empirical one.

Husserl is aware that one cannot just assume one has a grasp of the *concepts* just because one understands the *meanings* of the words that express the concepts. There are concealed ambiguities in the linguistic expressions, and so it is necessary to fix our concepts through clear self-sustaining intuitions:

> We desire to render self-evident in fully-fledged intuitions that what is here given in actually performed abstractions is what the word-meanings in our expression of the law really and truly stand for.
>
> (LI, Findlay I: 168; Hua XIX/1: 10)

The aim is to achieve clarity and distinctness in concepts by making whatever appropriate disambiguations as can be brought to intuitive clarity.

For Husserl, questions concerning the relation of the objective to the subjective acts of the mind, questions of the meaning of the so-called *adequatio rei ad intellectus*, cannot be separated from issues in pure logic. Such questions as how these ideal objectivities come to be presented to the mind and grasped by it and so end up becoming something subjective must be addressed:

> How can the ideality of the universal *qua* concept or law enter the flux of real mental states and become an epistemic possession of the thinking person?
>
> (LI, Intro. §2, Findlay I: 169; Hua XIX/1: 13)

How is there an *adequatio rei et intellectus* in the case of the relation between ideal concepts and human psychical acts? We have to pass over from a naïve performance of acts to an *attitude of reflection* (*Einstellung der Reflexion*). Husserl wants to discover the *a priori* relations between meaning and its expression, and he sets out the basis of this in the First Investigation.

The First Investigation: the nature of meaningful expression

Although, at first glance, the First Investigation appears to be an essay on *signs* (*Zeichen*), clearly influenced by Mill's *Logic* (LI I §16), and by linguistic studies by Brentanists such as Twardowski and Anton Marty, in fact Husserl intended it to have a 'merely preparatory character' (LI, Findlay I: 6–7; Hua XVIII: 13), aiming correctly to identify the elements of the meaning function (*Bedeutungsfunktion*) in conscious life. Although it contains discussions of proper names, common names, collective terms, demonstratives, speech acts, and so on, Husserl's interest was not in philosophy of language as such, but rather in specifying the structure of meaningful assertion, separating out the acts which go to make up the intentional expression and fulfilment of meaning. In this First Investigation (§9) Husserl develops his crucial distinction (held from early in his career) between meaning-intending and meaning-fulfilling acts and the 'unity of coincidence' or 'covering' (*Deckungseinheit*) between meant and fulfilled senses in those situations where a concrete intuition fills out the intending sense. As Husserl's conception of signification became more nuanced, this Investigation was considerably reworked in the Second Edition.

Husserl begins from Mill's claim that, since all thought is expressed in language, a study of linguistic forms is a prerequisite to the clarification of logical forms. He departs from Mill, however, in his account of the manner in which proper names ('Schulze', 'Socrates') signify their referents. Drawing on and refining some traditional distinctions in then current semantics (e.g., Marty), Husserl distinguishes between the function of an expression to *intimate* (*die kundgebende Funktion*) something to someone, and its expression of an ideal *sense* or *meaning* (*Sinn* or *Bedeutung*) which is the same in different performances of the assertion or in acts of understanding it. Moreover, normally an act of expressing is directed *beyond* its meaning to its associated object or objectivity (*zugehörige Gegenständlichkeit*), through a specific manner of intentional reference (*intentionale Beziehung*). Finally, Husserl has a brief introductory discussion of the different kinds of 'objectivities' to which things can be directed, distinguishing between simple and categorial objectivities (LI I §12) – the focus of the Sixth Investigation.

Husserl begins by distinguishing between signs functioning as *indications* (*Anzeichen*), which operate through linking one *extant* thing with another without a mediating meaning, e.g., smoke indicating fire, flag is a sign of a nation, a brand that marks a slave, chalk that marks out a house, and *expressions* (*die Ausdrücke*), in his specific sense, that require the mediation of a meaning or sense and refer to some object regardless of its existential status. As Husserl says: 'It is part of the notion of an expression to have a meaning' (LI I §15). A meaningless expression, e.g., 'abracadabra', would not be an expression at all. This is not meant to be an exhaustive treatment of signs and signification, but merely a distinction between different *functions* of signs. Husserl is interested in the mental act of meaningful *expression*, irrespective of whether it is uttered, written, or simply thought to oneself. His account is a semantics of speaker intention. Communication is not Husserl's concern, because, for him, logic is concerned only with the *expression* of ideal meanings. The pragmatics of communication or reception of meaning is a secondary matter, a concern for the philosopher of language.

An expression may have a set of physical sounds or written marks or merely imagined utterance, but what makes it an *expression* (and not just a reproduction of sounds like a parrot) is the mental state (or act) that 'enlivens' or 'ensouls' it. Normally, in any expressive act, the inner fused unity (*eine innig verschmolzene Einheit*, LI I §10) of sign and thing signified, of word and object, is experienced. Our interest usually focuses on the object intended and not on either the meaning or any associated verbal chain (unless our interest is, let us say, in assonance or in grammar, e.g., if someone says, 'I done that', the speaker's attention may be directed at confirming having done something and not towards the poor grammatical form). This is not to say that the thought exists apart from its expression. Thoughts *come to form* in a linguistic way.

There are many other features entwined with the act of expression. Husserl further distinguishes between what expression 'shows forth', conveys, or *intimates* (*kundgibt*) and what it *means*, and between what it *means* and what *object* it names (LI I §6). Typically, Husserl recognises the inherent complexities (even if he here does not focus on them), for instance, in communication, an expression both expresses a meaning and indicates something to the hearer. An expression functions as an indication when, for example, it indicates to the hearer the meaning intentions of the speaker (LI I §7). Through this intimating function other aspects of the communicative situation may be picked up, e.g., that the speaker is angry or is making a judgement. Expressions, then, have a communicative function in relation to others. A speaker endows a certain word-chain with a sense that can be understood by a hearer, with certain 'sense-giving acts' (*sinnverleihende Akte*, LI I §7). This, Husserl says, makes mental commerce (*geistige Verkehr*) possible. But besides their function in communication with others, expressions play a role in our individual, solitary, mental life, where communicating has no role, and therefore the act of meaning (*Akt des Bedeutens*) must be strictly distinguished from its 'intimation achievement' (*die kundgebende Leistung*, LI I §8). When an expression is articulated it normally directs interest away from itself towards what it intends to convey, but this directing away is not a form of indicating (§8). In silent soliloquy we may use imagined words rather than spoken words, we may even imagine the sounds of the words. Here we express our meanings although we do not intimate them to others. The expression of meaning, therefore, remains an issue even for the solitary thinker (LI I §8), where no indicative function is required.

Husserl distinguishes between expressions which function solely to *name* (*nennen*) and other more complicated forms, which Husserl calls 'predicatively formed complexes' which are essentially predicates. Husserl thinks that the referential power of proper names has been misunderstood by Mill, who views a proper name as non-connotative and directly *denoting* its 'subject' (in Mill's terminology) without the mediation of an abstract meaning (or 'attribute').[65] Names do pick out their objects directly, but not through *indication*, rather they have an expressive function that allows the name to *mean* the object in different sentential formations.

According to Husserl's fundamental distinction between meaning intentions and meaning fulfilments, 'meaning intentions' (*Bedeutungsintentionen*) or 'meaning-conferring acts' (*die bedeutungsverleihenden Akte*) include all those acts involved in *confirming, corroborating, illustrating* (*erfüllen, bestätigen, bekräftigen, illustrieren*, LI I §9). An expression has to be consciously endowed with meaning to be a vehicle of meaning. The content or meaning of the thought expressed is furthermore an ideal unity, e.g., 'three perpendiculars of a triangle intersect in a point' (LI I §11). This meaning is something identical (*das Identische*), whose precise identity is preserved in repetition (*Wiederholung*) of the expression. In assertion, we are asserting that state of affairs 'holds' or 'obtains'. We commit ourselves to the 'objective validity' of the state of affairs, even though the state of affairs is what it is, whether we maintain its validity or not. It is a 'validity-unity in itself' (*eine Geltungseinheit an sich*). We judge that the state of affairs obtains because we see it to be so.

Every expression says something 'of' or 'about' (*über*) something (LI I §11), but the object does not usually coincide with the meaning. Different names, e.g., 'victor of Jena', 'vanquished at Waterloo', or 'London', 'Londres', can refer to the same object (Napoleon, the city of London). Expressions may have different meanings but the same objective reference. Similarly, expressions with the same meaning may have different objective references, e.g., the expression 'horse' as applied to different horses, to both the individual 'Bucephalus' and to the type, the carthorse (§12). Proper names are 'equivocal' for Husserl in that they can name something different only if they mean something different, they have multiple senses (§15). On the other hand, general names, words like 'horse' can have many different values but have the one meaning (§15). In general, Husserl wants to distinguish between the *meaning* (*Bedeutung*) of an expression and its power to *name*, that is, to direct itself to something objective (*ein Gegenständliches*). An expression names its object *through* (*mittels*) its meaning (LI I §13).

In the First Investigation, Husserl distinguishes between objective expressions and those 'subjective' expressions whose meaning shifts with the occasion. This broad category, which includes pronouns ('I', 'you'), demonstratives ('this', 'that'), temporal adverbs like 'now', he terms 'essentially occasional expressions' (*wesentlich okkasionelle Ausdrücke*, LI I §26). These depend on the context for their specific meaning and yet also seem to have a fixed sense of their own. 'Now' means 'the present time'; 'I' means 'the person who is currently speaking'. But Husserl recognises that one cannot simply replace the word 'I' with 'the person who is currently speaking' in all contexts and preserve meaning (LI I §26). The term, however, is not wholly equivocal, but has layered elements, one of which depends on the context in which it is used (the 'indicated meaning'), and the other meaning which shows an act of indicating or pointing is being performed (the 'indicative meaning', LI I §26; Findlay I: 219; Hua XIX/1: 89).[66] In the First Edition, indexicals are treated as non-normal or derivative forms of meaning (unlike words like 'lion'), which could, at least in theory, be replaced by non-indexical expressions (LI I §28), although Husserl recognises this may be practically impossible. Husserl saw the need to broaden this account in the Sixth Investigation (LI VI §5), so that indexicals stand at the basis of all empirical predication, a change of mind Husserl notes in the Second Edition (LI, Findlay I: 7; Hua XVIII: 13). In a sense, every statement must be located in a context before its precise meaning can be understood (e.g., referring to the 'birth of Christ', or 'the sun' requires a certain *deixis*; see Husserl's notes, Hua XIX/2: 817). In 1929, in *Formal and Transcendental Logic* (§80; Hua XVII: 207), Husserl says that in the First Edition of the *Investigations* he had not understood the 'horizonal intentionality' at work whereby the understanding of a statement requires attention to its horizoning context. A formal system needs the support of context-relative elements.

Husserl also discusses another kind of expression where the mental act the speaker is performing is announced in the expression itself, for example, in speech acts where the speaker promises, wishes, and so on. Husserl here identifies the class of speech acts, subsequently studied by his student, Adolf Reinach. Interest in speech acts was revived by John Austin and systematised by John Searle.[67]

An important part of the discussion in the First Investigation concerns Husserl's vigorous attempts to distinguish between the meaning of an expression and the various accompanying images, feelings and illustrations that intertwine with it. Husserl's aim is to distinguish the logical content of meaning from all accompanying psychological content (he remarks that even Descartes had distinguished the imaginative representation of a chiliagon from its conceptual meaning, LI I §18). A central issue of this Investigation is the distinction between expressions based on intuition and those which function through some kind of symbolisation. Seeing something in the case of perceiving an object and seeing it symbolically are different act functions for Husserl (LI I §20). Husserl was not satisfied with his account of expression in this Investigation and his advances in the Sixth Investigation forced him to rethink the very basis of his account in the years after 1901. His 1908 lectures on meaning, for example, offer the basis for a revised account, which has a more sophisticated treatment of the relation between expressive act, meaning and empty or filled intention. In later years, Husserl would constantly return to the essential nature of meaning intending in its various forms.

The Second Investigation: abstraction and the grasp of universals

The Second Investigation treats of the nature of universal meanings or *species* (*Spezies*) as Husserl calls them. Understanding the true nature of abstraction is important for the foundations of logic, since logic utilises the crucial distinction between *individual* and *general* or *universal* objects (*allgemeine Gegenstände*). Husserl wants to develop empiricism by defending the need to recognise universal objects also, a view which is best understood as a kind of Aristotelianism. Some critics, however, accused Husserl of Platonism. In a remark added in the Second Edition, he concedes that his view may be termed *idealism* (LI II, Findlay I: 238; Hua XIX/1: 112), understood as a purely epistemological doctrine, which recognises the proper domain of the ideal (*das Ideale*) against psychologism. Husserl in fact thinks that the 'excesses of extreme conceptual realism' (*Begriffsrealismus*, LI II §2) have led philosophers to challenge not just the reality of general concepts but also their 'objectivity'.

In this Investigation Husserl offers primarily a historical critique of Locke, Berkeley, Hume and of abstractionist representationalism in general, with the overall aim of understanding the relation between meaning as an ideal unity and the *act* of meaning (*das Bedeuten*) expressing it. In the *Prolegomena* Husserl had already established that meanings are ideal unities, now he wants to specify the relation between this ideal unity of meaning and the expression which 'means' it, the significant or 'meaning consciousness' (*Bedeutungsbewusstsein*). Husserl's claim (developed from Lotze) in the First Edition is that this relation is the same as that between species and individuals. Indeed, for Husserl, meaning is a kind of 'species' (*Spezies*) which is instantiated in a particular act. The traditional account says that we intend the species (e.g., 'horse' as opposed to an individual horse) by abstraction from the individual, but there are different accounts of the nature of this abstraction. One view he rejects is that abstraction is a kind of selective attention on one aspect of an object. In opposition to this view, Husserl wants to develop a proper concept of abstraction, freed from the distortions of the modern philosophical and psychological tradition. He calls this 'ideation' but revises his views in the Second Edition since, in *Ideas* I, Husserl had developed a new account of ideation now understood as essential seeing or essence inspection (*Wesenserschauung, Ideas* I §3).

For Husserl, the difference between an act that intends an individual and one that intends the species becomes clear in reflecting on the manner in which evidence is fulfilled for such presentations (LI II §1). Husserl insists that intending the species is essentially different in kind from intending the individual *qua* individual. In both acts, the same concrete object (*das Konkretum*) may be given, with the same sense contents interpreted in exactly the same way (LI II §1), but we *mean* 'red' not 'red house', the species not the individual. In the act of individual reference, we intend this thing or property or part of the thing, whereas in the specific act we intend the species, that is, we intend not the thing or a property understood in the here and now, but rather the 'content' (*Inhalt*), the 'idea' (*die Idee*), that is 'red' as opposed to the individual 'red-moment' (LI II §1). As Husserl adds in the Second Edition (referring forward to the Sixth Investigation), this specific act is a *founded* (*fundierte*) act, involving a new 'mode of apprehension' (*Auffassungsweise*), which sets the species before us as a general object. When we mean the species we perform a distinct act which is oriented towards the species as such and not towards the individual thing or part.

Husserl understands this relation between general and individual as that between *species* and individual *instance* (*Einzelfall* §1), between 'red' in general and this red 'moment' of an object. Husserl goes on to insist (§2) on an important difference between individual singular items, *Einzelheiten* (things of experience) and *specific singulars* (e.g., the number 2). He makes a parallel distinction between individual and specific universals, whereby individual universal judgements, e.g., 'all men are mortal', are distinguished from specific universal judgements, e.g., 'all propositions of logic are *a priori*'.

Husserl offers deep criticisms of the prevailing empiricist and nominalist accounts of the process by which universals are distinguished in our knowledge. Husserl ends by introducing his notions of abstract, dependent parts and concrete, independent parts, as a way of beginning to understand the true nature of abstraction in a phenomenological manner. This leads him to the theory of parts and wholes.

The Third Logical Investigation – parts and wholes

Husserl himself stressed the importance of the Third Investigation as offering the proper way into his thought, and, in his 1913 revision, was already lamenting its neglect. This Investigation sketches a 'pure theory of wholes and parts', called, in the Second Edition, 'formal ontology' (LI III, Findlay II: 3; Hua XIX/1: 228), inaugurating a discipline now known as *mereology*. With the specific view of clarifying the relations holding between the parts of meaningful acts of *expression* (in the Fifth and Sixth Investigations), Husserl here attempts to specify the *a priori* possibilities inherent in part-whole relations in general, i.e., the precise forms part-whole relations can take in advance of all empirical instances (LI III §1).

Husserl is interested in the different ways in which something can be a part, and the laws governing the relation of parts to the whole, and of parts to other parts. Every object either is or can be a part. Wholes can be parts of larger wholes, and parts can have parts. Not all parts can be wholes however. Wholes and parts stand in various relations of *dependency* (*Unselbstständigkeit*) such that one part is *founded* on another. Husserl gives a strict sense to foundation (a notion already present in Meinong): when part **A** cannot be presented without a part **B**, **A** is said to be founded on **B** (LI III §14).

Husserl's account recapitulates his studies of the early 1890s. His starting point (LI III §3) is his mentor Carl Stumpf's work on the relations between parts and wholes in psychological acts, specifically in relation to sensory concepts such as colour and extension, or the quality and intensity of sounds. Stumpf situated his discussion of part/whole relations specifically in relation to *psychology*, whereas Husserl wants to formalise to a pure theory of wholes and parts in the most general sense. Stumpf was influenced by Brentano's reflections on the subject in his lectures on *Descriptive Psychology*,[68] and Husserl also acknowledges the independent investigations of Christian von Ehrenfels on 'form qualities' (*Gestaltqualitäten*, LI III §4), where items are grouped in specific ways, e.g., flocks, points seen against a background, and so on.[69] Husserl even discovers whole/part analysis in the 'phenomenology of inner experience' of George Berkeley in his critique of Locke (LI III §2).

Husserl begins somewhat misleadingly by discussing the different ways parts are presented and are differentiated in *experience*, but in fact wants a formal analysis of the manner in which parts and wholes of any *objects* whatsoever cohere or co-exist together. Anything that can be distinguished in an object is a *part* (*Teil*). Parts may be divided into 'independent' (*selbstständig*) and 'dependent' (*unselbtständig*), according as they can stand on their own or whether they require inherence in the whole of which they are a part. A part may be independently presented, e.g., head of a horse, and these Husserl terms 'pieces' (*Stücke*, LI III §2), e.g., the segments of an orange which can stand apart from one another and from the whole. But some parts are inseparable (*untrennbar*), e.g., colour and extension, and these Husserl calls 'moments' and which he sometimes characterises as 'abstract' parts in that they can only appear in the context of a larger whole. A *dependent* moment is one that *depends*, or, in Husserl's language, is *founded* on another whole or part. Thus, to give an example, Husserl will constantly repeat, the act-quality of a conscious experience is an abstract moment of the act (LI III §20), unthinkable detached from all matter. Of course, one can isolate parts within parts, so that the whole notions of dependence and independence are relativised (LI III §13). Husserl goes on to lay down six laws concerning parts and wholes (LI III §14), which have since been modified and expanded in a whole formal mereological theory. These laws include, for example, the law that: if **a** is dependent part of a whole **W** then it is also a dependent part of any other whole that has **W** as a part. In later writings (e.g., *Experience and Judgement* and *Formal and Transcendental Logic*), Husserl returns to part-whole relations in a somewhat different analysis but his part-whole analysis always remains central to his philosophy.

The Fourth Investigation: formal grammar

The Fourth Investigation, extensively revised and expanded in the Second Edition, is a study of what Husserl terms 'pure grammar' (Second Edition: 'pure logical grammar'), i.e., of the formal laws governing the combining or binding of meanings (*Bedeutungen*) into a senseful unity rather than simply yielding a nonsensical string of words, and is, generally speaking, an application of his part-whole theory to the field of semantics. He speaks of the 'pure theory of forms of meaning' (*die reine Formenlehre der Bedeutungen*, LI IV §14). The aim is to provide a pure morphology of meaning that lays the basis by providing possible forms of logical judgements, whose objective validity is the focus of formal logic proper. Husserl is explicitly reviving the old idea of an *a priori* grammar against both the psychological interpretations of grammar dominant in his day and the empirical theorists who were imprisoned in a false paradigm (e.g., assuming Latin grammar as the paradigm, LI IV §14).

Just as simple objects can be combined to produce complex objects, *simple* meanings combine to produce *complex* meanings (LI IV §2). Moreover, meaning-parts need not mirror parts of the object, and vice versa. Meaning has its own parts and wholes. Husserl maintains that all combinations are governed by laws; his aim is to find the least number of independent elementary laws (LI IV §13). It must be possible to identify the rules of all such possible valid combinations *a priori*, combinations that produce well-formed expressions as opposed to nonsense (such as 'This careless is green', LI IV §10). Husserl famously distinguished (LI I §15 and LI IV §12) between *nonsense* (*Unsinn*) and *countersense* or absurdity (*Widersinn*). The concept of 'square circle' is not senseless or non-sensical, but constitutes an absurdity, a contradiction in terms, a 'counter-sense' that cannot be realised. Formal grammar, on Husserl's account, can eliminate only nonsense not absurdity and is therefore not yet formal logic in the sense of specifying what can be objectively valid.[70] In later writings, notably the *Formal and Transcendental Logic* and *Experience and Judgment*, Husserl continued to maintain that formal grammar provided the bedrock rules for meaningfulness which made possible formal logic, and is the basis for both the logic of inference (*Konsequenzlogik*) and what Husserl calls the 'logic of truth'. He is more careful in later writings to emphasise that he is dealing with formal combinations of meanings (e.g., 'A and B not if') rather than material combinations of meanings (e.g., 'round square'), whereas in the Fourth Investigation he tends misleadingly to employ examples drawn from the material sphere.[71] The laws of formal meaning are purely analytic laws as opposed to synthetic *a priori* laws which govern such areas as geometry or mechanics. The core of Husserl's analysis is his use of a traditional distinction (but specifically developed by Anton Marty) between *syncategorematic* words (e.g., words like 'but', 'and', 'to', 'if'), and *categorematic* words, e.g., nouns, verbs (but not complete expressions) and his analysis of these in terms of independence and dependence relations. Husserl treats *syncategorematic* expressions as meaningful but dependent, incomplete parts of wholes, which in this case are well-formed expressions which are complete or 'closed' (*geschlossen*). Verbal parts can be distinguished in terms of those that are separately meaningful (like particles, e.g., 'bi-' as in 'bi-sexual') or meaningless ('bi' as in 'bite'). Husserl focuses on proper names and the manner in which they name the object in a 'single ray'. The formal theory of meanings will lay down the formal laws that regulate how adjectives can become substantives, how a subject can shift to the predicate position and so on, and other rules of combination and 'modification' (a concept drawn from Twardowski, who studied the manner certain adjectives modify the noun, e.g., a *false friend* is not a *friend* at all.

This Investigation had a profound influence on the work of the linguist Roman Jakobson (1896–1982), especially on his notion of phonemes as complex unities.[72] It also influenced the Polish logician Stanislaw Lesniewski (1886–1939) in his account of categorial grammar, and indeed finds echoes in Noam Chomsky's project of a 'universal grammar' (a term Husserl himself invokes with approval, LI IV §14). For Husserl, however, the meaningfulness of linguistic combinations is distinct from the structural laws governing conscious acts and their contents, to which he turns in the Fifth Investigation.

The Fifth Investigation: intentional experiences and their contents

The Fifth Logical Investigation, subtitled 'Intentional Experiences and their "Contents"', is Husserl's attempt to sort out ambiguities in Brentano's descriptive psychological analysis of conscious acts, their contents and objects (in the Second Edition, these are restricted to 'pure immanence'). Husserl begins by specifying what he means by 'consciousness', bracketing discussion of the relation of conscious acts to an ego, and focusing exclusively on the intentional character of conscious experiences deriving from Brentano's rediscovery of intentionality. However, Husserl regards Brentano's characterisation of intentionality as misleading and inadequate, trapped inside the old Cartesian dualism of subject and object and with all the problems inherent in that representationalist account. Under the notion of 'objectifying act' he offers a more precise account of what Brentano called 'presentation', and goes on to address what he calls 'cardinal problem of phenomenology', namely, the doctrine of judgement (LI, Findlay I: 7; Hua XVIII: 14), which is further treated in the Sixth Investigation. Husserl is especially critical of the many unresolved ambiguities in Brentano's foundational concept of 'presentation' (*Vorstellung*) and carefully differentiates between the many senses of the term (LI V §44), stressing however that logic must decide which meaning of 'presentation' is most appropriate for its own needs. Logic does not follow linguistic usage as logical definition is a kind of artifice (LI IV §3).

In *Psychology from an Empirical Standpoint* (1874), Brentano had held that all psychic acts are characterised by 'directedness' or 'aboutness':

> Every mental phenomenon is characterized by what the Scholastics of the Middle Ages called the intentional (or mental) inexistence of an object, and what we might call, though not wholly unambiguously, reference to a content, direction towards an object (which is not to be understood here as meaning a thing), or immanent objectivity.[73]

In a general sense, every psychic act intends an object, though not necessarily something existent. Husserl paraphrases: 'in perception something is perceived, in imagination, something imagined, in a statement something stated, in love something loved, in hate hated, in desire desired etc.' (LI V §10, Findlay II: 95; Hua XIX/1: 380). Brentano himself came to realise that his expression 'intentional inexistence', which he claimed he had used to express the concept of inherence or *inesse* of the Scholastics, had been misunderstood as a special kind of subsistence. In his later writings, he claimed he never intended to say that the intentional object is merely some kind of object in our minds, some purely immanent thing. Husserl rejects Brentano's attempt to distinguish between 'psychical' and 'physical' phenomena, but sees his discovery of intentionality as having independent value (LI V §9). Husserl is cautious about using Brentano's term 'act' without qualification, but, above all, wants to avoid misleading talk of 'immanent' objectivity. He insists that all objects of thought – including the objects of fantasy and memory – are *mind-transcendent*. Even when I am imagining something non-existent, e.g., if I am thinking of the mythical god Jupiter the God Jupiter is not *inside* my thought in any sense, it is not a real element or real part of the experience (LI V §11). Rather, even fictional objects are *transcendent* above our mental experiences; intentional experience always transcends itself towards the object, its character is a 'pointing beyond itself towards' (*über sich hinausweisen*) something.

Drawing on the older logical tradition, Husserl offers a new global distinction between the *matter* and the *quality* of intentional acts. Acts of different quality (judgings, wishings, questionings) may have the same matter. Not all our experiences are intentional in the sense of presenting something to our attention. According to Husserl, *sensations* in themselves are not intentional, they are not the object which we intend, rather they accompany the intentional act and fill it out. Sensations belong to the 'matter' (and are grasped as such only in reflection), whereas the act quality provides the form of the act.

With an eye to distinctions made by Brentano's followers, especially Kasimir Twardowski, Husserl goes on to develop the differences between the contents of experience and the properties of the mind-transcendent object. When I see an object, I only ever see it from one side, in a certain kind of light, from a certain angle and so on. As I walk around the box for example, I see different 'profiles' (*Abschattungen*) or 'aspects' of the box, and yet I know I am getting glimpses of the same object in the different perceptual acts. The same object is presenting itself to me in different modes. Husserl's distinction in the Fifth Investigation (LI V §17) between the object which is intended and the particular mode under which it is intended forms the basis for his later distinction between *noesis* and *noema* in *Ideas* I. Furthermore, Husserl regards it as an *a priori* law that physical objects are displayed in *Abschattungen*.

Whereas Brentano recognised only three basic classes of psychical acts (namely, *presentations, judgements*, and what he called '*phenomena of love and hate*'), Husserl recognises myriad forms of intentional structure. He more carefully differentiates the fundamental structure of *judgements* in a manner opposed to Brentano, who had challenged the traditional notion of judgement as a synthesis of subject and predicate, and had interpreted the judgement 'the cat is black' as an asserting or positing of 'black cat'. Husserl denies that judgements can be treated as nominal acts, as simply *naming* complex states of affairs (LI V §17). We can, of course, turn a judgement into a nominal act, by nominalising the content of the judgement. This belongs as an *a priori* essential possibility to judgements (LI V §36). So, to the judgement 'the cat is black' corresponds the nominalisation 'the cat's being black' which can then function as the basis for further judgements. But this internal relation between judging and nominalising does not mean that they are essentially the same kind of act. Husserl, following Bolzano, declares judgements to be essentially different from presentations. Judgements *assert* something to be the case (LI V §33). A judgement *articulates* and specifies in a 'many-rayed act' the parts of the situation that a nominalising act presents in a 'single-rayed act', as Husserl puts it.[74] The relation between presentation and judgement is not as described by Brentano.

Rather than operating with Brentano's simple and rather naïve distinction between the presenting act and presented content of an intention, or even using the broader notion of a 'nominal act', Husserl suggests that we ought to speak more generally of 'objectivating acts' (LI V §37) which include both the nominal and the judgemental act. Husserl thinks that the claim that all acts either are or are founded on objectifying acts is a more accurate reformulation of Brentano's basic law that all psychic acts are either presentations or founded on presentations. Husserl's clarification of the nature of presentation and judgement leads to his discussion of the manner in which these acts find intuitive fulfilment in the Sixth Investigation.

The Sixth Logical Investigation: towards the phenomenology of knowledge

The Sixth Investigation – by far the longest and most difficult – attempts to connect the previous analyses of the act of meaning to the notion of truth through a deeper exploration of the relations between the acts that intend meaning and the various levels of possible fulfilment, as they feature in different kinds of conscious act, e.g., perceptions, imaginings, and acts of what Husserl calls 'signitive intention' where meanings are handled in a purely symbolic way without intuitive fullness. Husserl's target is knowledge and the connection with truth. In earlier Investigations Husserl had recognised a new class of categorial acts or acts of categorial intuition, founded on sensuous acts but with essentially different objects. The Sixth Investigation is the first full analysis of the nature of these categorial acts, including reviewing the relation of sensory matter to the content of the act as a whole. Husserl wants a 'phenomenology of the varying degrees of knowledge' (LI VI, Findlay II: 184; Hua XIX/2: 539), carefully discriminating between the many different senses in which something can be realised or fulfilled for us in an act of perception or imagination, the relation between concept and intuition, e.g., in the act of seeing a blackbird.

Husserl sees the paradigm case of a successful intentional act as an act where the meaning is fulfilled by the *presence* in intuition of the intended object with full 'bodily presence' (*Leibhaftigkeit*). Thus, when I actually see something before my eyes, I have a fulfilled intuition. Later, I can relive this intuition but it is now a memory, still oriented to the object, but not presented with the same presence or immediacy. In memory or in other forms of 'calling to mind' or 're-presenting' (*Vergegenwärtigung*) we still may have a full intuition of the object, but now no longer with the distinctive bodily presence that characterises perception. There are other forms of intending which are merely 'empty' (*Leermeinen*), e.g., when I use words in a casual way without really thinking about what I am saying, when I talk about something without really thinking about it and so on. Empty or 'signitive' intendings, of course, constitute the largest class of our conscious acts, and, from the beginning of his career, Husserl had been fascinated as to how these kinds of intentions can function as knowledge.

Husserl's interest in the manner in which meaning is expressed in different acts leads him to revise the account of meaning as species which was employed in the earlier Investigations. I can utter different sentences with different senses or meanings based on the same act of perceiving (LI VI §4). Furthermore, a listener can understand the meaning with enacting the act of perception or indeed re-enacting it in imagination. The listener can understand it as a *report* of my act of perceiving, i.e., 'he says that he sees a blackbird'. In the expression 'I see a blackbird' the sense or meaning of that expression is not carried by the perceptual act alone. For Husserl the *sense* of the statement can survive the elimination of the act of perception, in other words, I do not have actually to enact the act of seeing to grasp the meaning of the statement. The act of perception somehow anchors the meaning but does not embody it completely. This leads Husserl to revise his earlier discussion of 'essentially occasional expressions' (§5), recognising that meaning is not simply instantiated in an act, but that the act has its own specific form of intending where the meaning appears with its own mode of givenness which the instantiation model did not adequately handle.

According to Kant, our experience has two components: a receptive element of sensory intuition and an element of reflective conceptuality (which Kant called 'spontaneity'). But Kant explicitly denied that humans had the capacity to *intuit* concepts. Husserl agrees with Kant concerning the sensory matter of most of our concepts, but holds that in higher order intuitions we do have the capacity to intuit ideal 'categorial' entities, from the 'mixed category' of the concept of colour, to pure categories, and at the highest level, logical categories such as unity, plurality and existence. Husserl treats 'categorial intuition' (*kategoriale Anschauung*) as akin to a kind of perception. The first attempt to express it comes in the second section of the Sixth Investigation entitled 'Sense and Understanding' (§§40–66). Categorial intuition involves a broadening of the concepts of perception and intuition. According to Husserl my intuition of a 'state of affairs' (*Sachverhalt*), e.g., 'I see *that* the paper is white', involves categorial intuition, a complex intuition that something is the case. In a judgement of this kind I intuit *what is going on*, as it were. How is this 'being the case' intuited? Husserl agrees with Kant that being is not a predicate, that is, that the existing situation is not a property of the individual object (the white paper). Saying that something *is* does not give us an intuition of a new property in a manner similar to learning 'something is red'. But this shows for Husserl that assertion of the category of being does not involve grasping a property or the object itself. Nor does it emerge from reflecting on the act of consciousness as some had thought, rather the categorial structure belongs to the ideal structure of the object, to the objectivity as such. Categorial acts yield up the grasp of the pure categorial concepts, 'if . . . then', 'and', 'or' and so on, which have no correlates in the objects of the perceptual acts themselves. For Husserl, moreover, categorial acts are *founded* on the sensory acts of perceiving, but do not *reduce* to them. For Husserl, categorial acts grasp states of affairs and in fact constitute them in the very categorial act. Thus it is not the case that I grasp sensuously the components of the judgement and synthesise them using some kind of subjective rules of the understanding as Kant suggests (according to Husserl's interpretation), rather we apprehend the state of affairs of which the non-sensuous categorial elements are necessary constituents.

In the course of this complex investigation Husserl outlines a new conception of truth, re-thinking the classical correspondence account. It was this discussion of truth which attracted the interest of Heidegger and others (e.g., Ernst Tugendhat), but unfortunately we cannot treat it further here.

The influence of the *Logical Investigations*

Although, as the young Heidegger recognised, the *Logical Investigations* did not have an immediate impact on mainstream philosophy in Germany, within a decade it was recognised as a major philosophical achievement by leading figures such as Paul Natorp, Wilhelm Dilthey, Wilhelm Wundt and Heinrich Rickert.[75] Husserl suspected that much of Meinong's work after 1901 owed a direct – but unacknowledged – debt to the *Investigations*, but Brentano ignored the work.

In particular, the *Prolegomena* was credited with refuting psychologism. In a 1905 study, the elder statesman of German philosophy, Wilhelm Dilthey praised Husserl's *Investigations* as 'epoch-making' for its use of description in epistemology.[76] The psychologist Wilhelm Wundt, too, accepted the *Prolegomena*'s arguments against psychologism, but criticised Husserl's second volume as proposing an extreme 'logicism' and demanding a complete reform of psychology. Husserl rejected Wundt's criticism as a complete misunderstanding of the work, saying he neither advocated logicism (in Wundt's sense), nor said a word about the reform of psychology.[77] In line with the Neo-Kantian tradition in general, Paul Natorp had been an early critic of psychologism. Indeed, Husserl had written to Natorp in 1897 announcing that he was working on a book to dispel the 'subjective-psychologising tendency' from logic. Natorp reviewed the *Prolegomena* favourably in *Kant Studien* in 1901, portraying Husserl as broadening the essentially Kantian inquiry into the necessary conditions of the possibility of experience.[78] Natorp predicted that Husserl would move towards Kant as he came to overcome his naïve opposition between the empirical psychological realm and the realm of abstract idealities.[79] Husserl, however, always kept his distance from Neo-Kantianism, claiming that phenomenology was more radical.

As we have seen, in his Göttingen years (1901–16), Husserl attracted many brilliant students, e.g., Johannes Daubert (1877–1947), Moritz Geiger (1880–1937), Adolf Reinach (1883–1917), Max Scheler (1874–1928), Hedwig Conrad-Martius (1888–1966), Roman Ingarden and Edith Stein, all drawn to Husserl's new way of approaching logical and epistemological problems which broke with the tradition. Around 1909, the young Freiburg seminarian Martin Heidegger encountered the *Logical Investigations* and poured over the work without being certain what it was that fascinated him.[80] He later recalled:

> ... both volumes of Husserl's *Logical Investigations* lay on my desk in the theological seminary ever since my first semester there ... I had learned from many references in philosophical periodicals that Husserl's thought was determined by Franz Brentano. ... From Husserl's *Logical Investigations*, I expected a decisive aid in the questions stimulated by Brentano's dissertation.[81]

Heidegger himself initially began reading Husserl to understand Brentano's account of the nature of being and was drawn especially to the Fifth and Sixth Investigations, especially Husserl's original accounts of categorial intuition and of truth. Heidegger saw in Husserl's account of categorial intuition not only a method for articulating the nature of the existential judgement but also the basis of a new way of thinking about the notion of truth and the meaning of being. Heidegger went on to read the *Investigations* in the seminars of Heinrich Rickert and Emil Lask, a young scholar who also worked on categorial intuition. Heidegger discussed the *Logical Investigations* in one of his first publications, a review of recent logical research published in 1912, where he recognises that Husserl had drawn out the theoretic incoherence of psychologism and its relativistic consequences. For Heidegger, Husserl had not only enlarged the scope of logic, but had made central the problematics of judgement and the nature of evidence.[82] Indeed, it was Heidegger who, as Husserl's assistant at Freiburg from 1919, repeatedly urged Husserl to reprint the Sixth Investigation, to which Husserl finally agreed in 1920.

News of the *Logical Investigations* spread outside Germany also, being translated into Russian as early as 1909, which version had a major influence on Roman Jacobson's conception of a formal science of language. Through Roman Ingarden, who reviewed it in Polish, the *Investigations* played an important role in Polish philosophy, influencing Stanislaw Lesniewski's development of mereology, for instance. It was translated into Spanish in 1929. A French translation of the Second Edition appeared in three volumes between 1959 and 1963,[83] but Husserl's influence on French philosophy had begun much earlier through the efforts of his earlier Göttingen students, Jean Héring and later through the writings of Emmanuel Levinas, Jean-Paul Sartre, Maurice Merleau-Ponty, Paul Ricoeur and Jacques Derrida, all of whom began their philosophical careers with critical studies of Husserl. Derrida, for instance, has acknowledged that his whole philosophical impetus arises out of his studies on Husserl, e.g., his study of Husserl's concept of genesis, written as a part of his doctoral research project in 1953–4.[84] Since the publication of Derrida's influential interpretations and critique of Husserl's account of signs in the First Investigation, an argument has raged as to whether Derrida has misinterpreted – even wilfully distorted – Husserl's account.[85]

During his Freiburg years (1916–38), Husserl became a philosopher of international renown, in contact with prominent philosophers of his day, including Ernst Cassirer, Bertrand Russell, Rudolf Carnap, Charles Hartshorne and William Kneale, among others. Among his own brilliant Freiburg students were Oskar Becker (1889–1964) and Fritz Kaufmann (1891–1958). Husserl's phenomenology also had a stimulating influence on philosophers who later came to be associated with the Frankfurt School, including Herbert Marcuse, Hannah Arendt, Theodor Adorno and Max Horkheimer (the latter of whom both wrote dissertations on Husserl). Husserl of course has been a major influence on both Ernst Tugendhat's and Karl-Otto Apel's philosophies of language, and his work in the *Investigations* has been compared with the equally original breakthroughs of Ludwig Wittgenstein.

In contrast to the situation in continental Europe, the *Logical Investigations* was somewhat slower to gain recognition in the English-speaking world. Bertrand Russell wrote to Husserl on 19 April 1920 saying that he had taken a copy of his *Logical Investigations* with him to jail, with the intent of reviewing it for *Mind*, but the review never appeared. However, in 1924, Russell recognised the *Logical Investigations* as a 'monumental work', listing it alongside his own *Principles of Mathematics* (1903) and works by William James, Frege and G. E. Moore (who, incidentally, also admired Husserl's book),[86] for their efforts in the refutation of German idealism.[87] Indeed, as Findlay noted, the *Logical Investigations* have much in common with the practice of philosophy as understood by Bertrand Russell. Richard Rorty in his *Philosophy and the Mirror of Nature* has remarked: 'Russell joined Husserl in denouncing the psychologism which had infected the philosophy of mathematics, and announced that logic was the essence of philosophy.'[88] Indeed, one can find many themes in the *Logical Investigations* which are also treated in analytic philosophy, e.g., Husserl offers his own version of a solution to the problem of definite descriptions, famously treated by Russell.[89]

Husserl himself visited England in 1922 intent on establishing relations with English philosophers (Husserl being the first German philosopher to visit England since the Great War). He delivered a number of lectures which were attended by Gilbert Ryle among others, but the lectures were not a success, despite his meeting well-known figures such as Broad, Stout and G. Dawes Hicks. The *Logical Investigations* has been discussed in relation to the history of analytic philosophy by Michael Dummett, David Bell and others.[90] The logician Kurt Gödel studied the *Logical Investigations* after 1959 and was especially impressed by the treatment of categorial intuition in the Sixth Investigation which he recommended to other logicians.[91]

The contemporary relevance of the *Logical Investigations*

The six Investigations stand as a vast resource of philosophical ideas, some tentatively sketched, others more confidently laid out. Of primary significance are Husserl's discussions of the meanings of key philosophical terms. He carefully differentiates between logical and psychological content, empty and filled intuitions, the difference between generalisation and formalisation, the meanings of signification and reference, the nature of nominal and categorial acts, and so on.

Husserl's *Prologemena* is still of interest for its original conception of the nature and scope of pure logic and its discussion of the self-refuting character of psychologism, relativism (including 'anthropologism'). Husserl's critique of psychologism later expanded to a wide-ranging critique of naturalism, specifically the 'naturalisation of consciousness', in his 1911 essay 'Philosophy as a Rigorous Science', and these anti-naturalist arguments are still relevant to the contemporary debate between naturalists (e.g., Quine, Dennett, Churchland) and anti-naturalists (e.g., Hilary Putnam, John McDowell, Robert Brandom). Indeed, Putnam regularly cites Husserl's critique of naturalism, especially as formulated in the *Crisis*, but which has its origins in the *Investigations*.

The *Investigations* are an important resource for discussions of consciousness and other issues discussed in contemporary philosophy of mind. In particular, Husserl's account of intentionality in the Fifth Investigation has been hugely influential, but his views on the nature of perceptual content are also important and relevant to the work of Peacocke and others. Husserl has been seen as a strong defender of the subjective point of view and the ineliminability of consciousness from any full account of the nature of knowledge, themes which have more recently been treated by John Searle, Colin McGinn, Thomas Nagel and others.[92] Indeed, John Searle's account of intentionality strongly resembles Husserl's, although Searle himself denies any direct influence. Other contemporary philosophers, e.g., Peter Simons, Barry Smith, Kevin Mulligan, are interested in developing morely precisely the formal ontology or descriptive metaphysics of the *Investigations*.

The *Investigations* are also of crucial interest as a source text for anyone wishing to understand the nature of phenomenology as it was developed both by Husserl and by his followers. Heidegger's phenomenological writings of the period between 1919 and 1928 would not be comprehensible without a thorough understanding of Husserl's breakthrough work. As the meaning of the phenomenological tradition comes once more to be interrogated, a return to the *Investigations* to attempt to understand the precise nature of the phenomenology that appeared therein seems inevitable.

John N. Findlay's translation

Finally some words on the present translation. The publication of J. N. Findlay's translation of the *Investigations* helped to correct a view of Husserl which, up to 1970, had been based primarily on the availability of Gibson's translation of *Ideas* I. Findlay has produced a powerful and much admired translation, based on the Second Edition. In keeping with the nature of that edition, he does not usually indicate where the text departs from the First Edition. It is important to bear in mind that this (and subsequent editions up to the fourth) were the ones Husserl himself authorised and a critical edition did not appear in the Husserliana series until 1984, and thus was not available to Findlay.[93]

Inevitably, given both the size of the book and the need to find suitable English terms to render Husserl's many technical distinctions and innovations,

Findlay's translation has its limitations. There is some sloppiness, with words, phrases, and even whole sentences being omitted. Some footnotes have been dropped (e.g., LI IV §10; Hua XIX/1: 328), while others are incorporated into the main text. There are some unhappy construals (*Gehalt* as 'substance' rather than 'content'), some misunderstandings (e.g., *ein Gewaltsreich* rendered as '*tour de force*' rather than 'act of violence', Hua XVIII: 13), but in the main, the translation is serviceable and the prose smooth, clear, even elegant. While a new translation is certainly desirable, it will take some years, and in the meantime, students of Husserl need something in their hands right now. Given the limitations of a reprint of this kind, I have corrected only the more egregious errors, and do not claim to have identified them all. Although not all agreed with the project of reprinting Findlay, nevertheless I must record my gratitude to the following Husserl scholars for their assistance: Rudolf Bernet, Iain Lyne, Sebastian Luft, Ullrich Melle, Kevin Mulligan, Karl Schuhmann, Peter Simons, Claire Ortiz Hill and Donn Welton.

DERMOT MORAN

Dublin, December 2000

Notes

1 E. Husserl *Logische Untersuchungen*, 2 vols, (1900–1), Halle: Max Niemeyer. Four editions appeared in Husserl's lifetime: a revised Second Edition of the *Prolegomena* and first five Investigations in 1913, a revised edition of the Sixth Investigation in 1921, a Third Edition with minor changes in 1922, and a Fourth Edition in 1928. A critical edition, which includes Husserl's written emendations and additions to his own copies (*Handexemplar*), has appeared in the Husserliana series in two volumes: Volume XVIII, *Logische Untersuchungen*, Vol. I: *Prolegomena zur reinen Logik*, text of the First and Second Edition, ed. Elmar Holenstein (The Hague: Martinus Nijhoff, 1975), and Volume XIX, *Logische Untersuchungen*, Vol. II: *Untersuchungen zur Phänomenologie und Theorie der Erkenntnis*, in two volumes, ed. Ursula Panzer (Dordrecht: Kluwer, 1984). The only English translation is: Edmund Husserl, *Logical Investigations*, 2 volumes, trans. J. N. Findlay (London/New York: Routledge & Kegan Paul/Humanities Press, 1970). Findlay translates from the Second Edition. Hereafter, the *Investigations* will be cited as 'LI' followed by the relevant Investigation number, section number, volume and page number of the present Routledge edition; followed by volume number and page number of the Husserliana (abbreviated to 'Hua') edition of the German text.

2 Husserl had originally contracted with another publisher, Verlag Veit & Co., Leipzig, and indeed some sample copies had already been printed before Niemeyer took over. Husserl, in his *Selbstanzeige* ('Author's Report'), claims some copies were available from the end of November 1899 ('Selbstanzeige', *Vierteljahrschrift für wissenschaftliche Philosophie* 24 (1900), 511; reprinted Hua XVIII: 262), but Karl Schuhmann thinks it is unlikely that any copies were available to the author before May 1900. The book did not appear from Niemeyer until July 1900, and the Foreword is dated Halle, 21 May 1900. See K. Schuhmann, *Husserl-Chronik. Denk- und Lebensweg Edmund Husserls*, Husserliana Dokumente 1 (The Hague: Martinus Nijhoff, 1977), p. 61. Hereafter cited as '*Chronik*'.

3 While not offering a 'system of logic' Husserl hoped (in the First Edition) at least to be able to lay the ground-work for a 'future construction (*Aufbau*) of logic', see LI, Intro., §5; Hua XIX/1: 21 A edition. Findlay translates the emended Second Edition version, where Husserl says he hopes to lay the ground-work 'for a philosophical logic which will derive clearness from basic phenomenological sources' (Findlay I: 174).

4 See Edmund Husserl, 'Selbstanzeige', pp. 511–12, reprinted in Hua XVIII: 261–2, trans. in Edmund Husserl, *Introduction to the Logical Investigations. A Draft of a Preface to the Logical Investigations (1913)*, ed. Eugen Fink, trans. Philip Bossert and Curtis Peters (The Hague: Martinus Nijhoff, 1975), pp. 3–4. Hereafter cited as '*Draft Preface*'.

5 Sigmund Freud, *Die Traumdeutung* (Leipzig/Vienna, 1899), now *Gesammelte Werke* vols 2–3 (London: Imago, 1952), new trans. by Joyce Crick, *The Interpretation of Dreams* (Oxford: Oxford University Press, 1999). This work first appeared in November 1899.

6 See Schuhmann, *Chronik*, p. 363. But Pitkin's version has been contested, see H. Spiegelberg, 'What William James Knew About Husserl. On the Credibility of Pitkin's Testimony', in Lester E. Embree (ed.), *Life-World and Consciousness. Essays for Aron Gurwitsch* (Evanston, IL: Northwestern University Press, 1972), pp. 407–22. It now seems likely that Pitkin never even began the translation.

7 Marvin Farber, *The Foundation of Phenomenology* (Albany, NY: SUNY Press, 1943).

8 Husserl, 'Task and Significance of the *Logical Investigations*', text taken from Husserl's 1925 lectures on *Phänomenologische Psychologie*, Hua IX (The Hague: Martinus Nijhoff, 1962), p. 20, trans. John Scanlon, *Phenomenological Psychology. Lectures, Summer Semester 1925* (The Hague: Martinus Nijhoff, 1977), p. 14. Hereafter cited as '*Phenomenological Psychology*'.

9 Husserl has various formulas to express the aim: 'a philosophical laying down of the foundations of pure logic' (*eine philosophische Grundlegung der reinen Logik*, Findlay I: 237; Hua XIX/1: 112), the laying down of the 'phenomenological foundations of pure logic' (*phänomenologische Fundamentierung der reinen Logik*, LI VI §34, Findlay II: 257; Hua XIX/2: 643).

10 *Phenomenological Psychology*, p. 20; Hua IX: 28.

11 Alexander Pfänder, *Phänomenologie des Wollens. Eine psychologische Analyse* (Leipzig: Johan Ambrosius Barth Verlagsbuchhandlung, 1900), 3rd edition reprinted in *Alexander Pfänders gesammelte Schriften*, Vol. 1 (Munich, 1963), the introduction to this work is translated in A. Pfänder, *Phenomenology of Willing and Motivation and Other Phaenomenologica*, trans. Herbert Spiegelberg (Evanston, IL: Northwestern University Press, 1967).

12 See also Husserl, *Draft Preface*, p. 32.

13 The critical edition is published in Husserliana, Volume XII, *Philosophie der Arithmetik. Mit ergänzenden Texten (1890–1901)*, ed. L. Eley (The Hague: Martinus Nijhoff, 1970).

14 Reprinted in E. Husserl, *Briefwechsel*, ed. Karl Schuhmann and Elizabeth Schuhmann. 10 vols (Dordrecht: Kluwer, 1994), Vol. VI, p. 282.

15 E. Husserl, *Über den Begriff der Zahl, Psychologische Analysen*, reprinted in *Philosophie der Arithmetik: Mit ergänzenden Texten (1890–1901)*, op. cit.

16 Husserl, in his letter of 3 January 1905 to Brentano, says that he was not a typical ambitious lecturer who sought to publish extensively.

17 E. Husserl, 'Philosophie als strenge Wissenschaft', *Logos* 1 (1911), 289–341, now collected in Husserl, *Aufsätze und Vorträge 1911–1921*, ed. H. R. Sepp and Thomas Nenon, Hua XXV (Dordrecht: Kluwer, 1986), pp. 3–62, trans. as *Philosophy as*

a Rigorous Science, in Quentin Lauer, *Edmund Husserl. Phenomenology and the Crisis of Philosophy* (New York: Harper & Row, 1964), pp. 71–147.

18 The critical edition is published in Husserliana Vol. III/1 as *Ideen zu einer reinen Phänomenologie und phänomenologischen Philosophie.* Book 1: *Allgemeine Einführung in die reine Phänomenologie*, First part: *Text der 1-3. Auflage*, ed. Karl Schuhmann (The Hague: Martinus Nijhoff, 1977), trans. by F. Kersten as *Ideas Pertaining to a Pure Phenomenology and to a Phenomenological Philosophy, First Book* (Dordrecht: Kluwer, 1983). Hereafter cited as '*Ideas* I' followed by page number of English translation and Husserliana volume number and pagination of German.

19 E. Husserl, *Zur Phänomenologie des inneren Zeitbewusstseins (1893–1917)*, ed. R. Boehm, Hua X (The Hague: Martinus Nijhoff, 1966; 2nd edn, 1969), trans. J. B. Brough, *On the Phenomenology of the Consciousness of Internal Time*, Collected Works IV (Dordrecht: Kluwer, 1990). Husserl expressed dissatisfaction with Heidegger's edition of these time lectures more or less from their publication.

20 Now Husserliana Vol. XVII: Edmund Husserl, *Formale und transzendentale Logik. Versuch einer Kritik der logischen Vernunft. Mit ergänzenden Texten*, ed. Paul Janssen (The Hague: Martinus Nijhoff, 1974), trans. by D. Cairns as *Formal and Transcendental Logic* (The Hague: Martinus Nijhoff, 1969).

21 E. Husserl, *Méditations cartésiennes: introduction à la phénoménologie*, trans. G. Peiffer and E. Levinas (Paris: Almand Colin, 1931). The German text was not published until 1950 as *Cartesianische Meditationen und Pariser Vorträge*, ed. Stephan Strasser, Husserliana I (The Hague: Martinus Nijhoff, 1950), trans. D. Cairns as *Cartesian Meditations. An Introduction to Phenomenology* (Dordrecht: Kluwer, 1993). Hereafter '*CM*', followed by page number of English translation, Hasserliana volume and page number.

22 Edmund Husserl, *Die Krisis der europäischen Wissenschaften und die transzendentale Phänomenologie. Eine Einleitung in die phänomenologische Philosophie*, ed. W. Biemel, Husserliana VI (The Hague: Martinus Nijhoff, 1962), trans. David Carr, *The Crisis of European Sciences and Transcendental Phenomenology. An Introduction to Phenomenological Philosophy* (Evanston, IL: Northwestern University Press, 1970). Hereafter '*Crisis*' followed by page number of English translation, Husserlian volume and page number.

23 E. Husserl, *Erfahrung und Urteil: Untersuchungen der Genealogie der Logik*, ed. L. Landgrebe (Hamburg: Meiner, 1999), trans. James S. Churchill and Karl Ameriks as *Experience and Judgment. Investigations in a Genealogy of Logic* (Evanston, IL: Northwestern University Press, 1973).

24 E. Husserl, 'The Task and the Significance of the *Logical Investigations*', in J. N. Mohanty (ed.), *Readings on Edmund Husserl's Logical Investigations* (The Hague: Martinus Nijhoff, 1977), p. 207.

25 These reports are collected in E. Husserl, *Aufsätze und Rezensionen (1890–1910)*, ed. B. Rang, Hua Vol. XXII (The Hague: Martinus Nijhoff, 1979), trans. Dallas Willard in Edmund Husserl, *Early Writings in the Philosophy of Logic and Mathematics*, Collected Works V (Dordrecht: Kluwer, 1994), pp. 171–96 and 207–302. Hereafter cited as '*Early Writings*' followed by English pagination and then Husserliana volume and page number.

26 See Dallas Willard, 'Husserl's Critique of Extensionalist Logic: "A Logic That Does Not Understand Itself"', *Idealistic Studies* 9, 2 (May 1979), 143–64.

27 B. Bolzano, *Wissenschaftslehre* (1837; reprinted Sulzbach: Seidel), abridged and trans. by Rolf George as *Theory of Science* (Oxford: Basil Blackwell, 1972).

28 See J. N. Mohanty, *Husserl and Frege* (Indiana: Indiana University Press, 1982), and Claire Ortiz Hill and Guillermo Rosado Haddock, *Husserl or Frege? Mean-*

ing, Objectivity and Mathematics (La Salle, IL: Open Court, 2000), and Michael Dummett, *Frege: Philosophy of Mathematics* (London: Duckworth, 1991), pp. 141–540.

29 See *Crisis* §48, trans. Carr, p. 166n; Hua VI: 169 n1.

30 E.g., 'Intuition and *Repräsentation*, Intention and Fulfilment', Hua XXII: 269–302, trans. *Early Writings*, pp. 313–44.

31 K. Twardowski, *Zur Lehre vom Inhalt und Gegenstand der Vorstellungen. Eine psychologische Untersuchung* (Vienna: Hölder, 1894; reprinted Munich: Philosophia Verlag), trans. R. Grossmann, *On the Content and Object of Presentations. A Psychological Investigation* (The Hague: Martinus Nijhoff, 1977).

32 See E. Husserl, 'Intentional Objects', *Early Writings*, pp. 345–87; Hua XXII: 303–48. See also the draft translated by Robin Rollinger in his *Husserl's Position in the School of Brentano* (Utrecht: University of Utrecht Publications, 1996), pp. 195–222.

33 E. Husserl, 'Intentional Objects', *Early Writings*, p. 350; Hua XXII: 308.

34 For a further discussion of these issues, see Dermot Moran, 'Heidegger's Critique of Husserl's and Brentano's Accounts of Intentionality', *Inquiry* 43 (2000), 39–66.

35 E. Husserl, 'Psychologische Studien zur elementaren Logik', *Philosophische Monatshefte* 30 (1894), 159–91, reprinted in Hua XXII: 92–123, trans. Dallas Willard, 'Psychological Studies in the Elements of Logic', in Husserl, *Early Writings*, pp. 139–79.

36 Schuhmann, *Chronik*, p. 58.

37 Two quotations (Ms. F I 26/83b and F I 26/12a) from the manuscript of Husserl's lectures on *Erkenntnistheorie* are reproduced in the Editor's Introduction to Hua XIX/1: xxx–xxxi.

38 See E. Husserl's review of Melchior Palágyi's *Der Streit der Psychologisten und Formalisten in der modernen Logik*, *Zeitschrift für Psychologie und Physiologie der Sinnesorgane* 31 (1903), 287–94, reprinted in Hua XXII: 151–61, trans. Dallas Willard, 'Review of Melchior Palágyi's *Der Streit der Psychologisten und Formalisten in der modernen Logik*', *Early Writings*, pp. 197–206.

39 E. Husserl, 'Bericht über deutsche Schriften zur Logik in den Jahren 1895–1899', *Archives für systematische Philosophie* 9 (1903) and 10 (1904), reprinted Hua XXII: 162–258, trans. D. Willard, 'Report on German Writings in Logic from the Years 1895–1899', *Early Writings*, pp. 207–302.

40 See E. Husserl, *Einleitung in die Logik und Erkenntnistheorie. Vorlesungen 1906/07*, ed. Ullrich Melle, Hua XXIV (Dordrecht: Kluwer, 1985).

41 See E. Husserl, *Vorlesungen über Bedeutungslehre. Sommersemester 1908*, ed. Ursula Panzer, Hua XXVI (Dordrecht: Kluwer, 1986).

42 See E. Husserl, *Logik und allgemeine Wissenschaftstheorie. Vorlesungen 1917/18, mit ergänzenden Texten aus der ersten Fassung 1910/11*, ed. Ursula Panzer, Hua XXX (Dordrecht: Kluwer, 1996).

43 Husserl, XXIV 445; *Early Writings*, p. 493; see also Husserl, *Die Idee der Phänomenologie. Fünf Vorlesungen*, ed. W. Biemel, Hua II (The Hague: Martinus Nijhoff, 1973), p. 22, trans. Lee Hardy as *The Idea of Phenomenology*. Husserl Collected Works VIII (Dordrecht: Kluwer, 1999), p. 18.

44 See Husserl's letter of 15 January 1911 to W. Windelband, and his letter to Daubert, 4 March 1911, both quoted in Hua XIX/1: xxiii.

45 In his Foreword to the Second Edition, dated Göttingen, October 1913, Husserl records that the book had been out of print for some years, and he expresses uncertainty about the form in which it should now appear.

46 E. Husserl, 'A Report on German Writings in Logic (1895–1899)', in *Early Writings*, p. 251; Hua XXII: 206–7.

47 Husserl explicitly laid out the method of *epoché* and reduction in his 1907 lectures, *Die Idee der Phänomenologie. Fünf Vorlesungen*, Hua II, *op. cit.*, trans. by Lee Hardy as *The Idea of Phenomenology*, op. cit.

48 See Husserl's 1906–7 *Introduction to Logic and the Theory of Knowledge*, Hua XXIV: 217–20.

49 See E. Husserl, 'Entwurf einer "Vorrede" zu den *Logischen Untersuchungen* (1913)', ed. E. Fink, *Tijdschrift voor Filosofie* 1, 1 (Feb. 1939), 107–33 and ibid., No. 2 (May 1939), 319–39 (hereafter 'Fink, *Entwurf*'), trans. Philip Bossert and Curtis Peters, *Draft Preface*. See especially, Fink, *Entwurf* §11, p. 329.

50 Ullrich Melle of the Husserl-Archief, Leuven, is currently editing the manuscripts Husserl left of his 1913 and 1914 revisions of the Sixth Investigation for publication in Volume XX of the Husserliana series.

51 I am grateful to Ullrich Melle for providing me with the typescript of his paper 'Husserl's Unfinished Revision of the Sixth Logical Investigation', presented in Copenhagen, May 2000.

52 M. Schlick, *Allgemeine Erkenntnislehre*, Vol. 1 (Berlin, 1918), 2nd edn trans. A. Blumberg, *General Theory of Knowledge* (La Salle, IL: Open Court, 1974).

53 E. Fink, 'The Phenomenological Philosophy of Edmund Husserl and Contemporary Criticism', in R. O. Elveton (ed.), *The Phenomenology of Husserl. Selected Critical Readings*, 2nd edn (Seattle: Noesis Press, 2000), esp. pp. 79–80.

54 Husserl seems particularly stung by this criticism which he returned to several times, including in *Formal and Transcendental Logic* §56, p. 152; Hua XVII: 160–1.

55 *Selbstanzeige* ('Author's Report') to the *Prolegomena*, trans. in Husserl, *Draft Preface*, ed. Fink, p. 4; Hua XVIII: 262.

56 G. Frege, 'Rezension von: E. G. Husserl, *Philosophie der Arithmetik* I', *Zeitschrift für Philosophie und philosophische Kritik* (1894), 313–32, reprinted in Frege, *Kleine Schriften*, ed. I. Angelelli (Hildesheim: Georg Olms, 1967), trans. by E. W. Kluge as 'Review of Dr. E. Husserl's *Philosophy of Arithmetic*', in *Husserl. Expositions and Appraisals*, ed. Frederick Elliston and Peter McCormick (Notre Dame: University of Notre Dame Press, 1981), pp. 314–24.

57 More accurately, Frege defines numbers as follows: 'the Number which belongs to the concept F is the extension of the concept "equal to the concept F"', Frege, *Die Grundlagen der Arithmetik* (Breslau: Koebner, 1884), trans. J. L. Austin, *The Foundations of Arithmetic*, 2nd rev. edn (Evanston, IL: Northwestern University Press, 1994), pp. 79–80.

58 W. R. Boyce-Gibson, 'From Husserl to Heidegger: Excerpts from a 1928 Diary by W. R. Boyce-Gibson', ed. H. Spiegelberg, *Journal of the British Society for Phenomenology* 2 (1971), 58–83. For a full account of the debate regarding the supposed influence of Frege on Husserl, see Mohanty, *Husserl and Frege*.

59 Ernest Hocking, a student of Husserl's from the early Göttingen days, reports how Husserl recommended his students to read Bolzano's *Wissenschaftslehre*. See W. E. Hocking, 'From the early days of the "Logische Untersuchungen"', in H. L. Van Breda and J. Taminiaux (eds), *Edmund Husserl. 1859–1959. Recueil commémoratif à l'occasion du centenaire de la naissance du philosophe* (The Hague: Martinus Nijhoff, 1959), p. 3.

60 K. Fine, 'Part-Whole', in Barry Smith and David Woodruff Smith (eds), *The Cambridge Companion to Husserl* (Cambridge: Cambridge University Press, 1995), p. 464.

61 David Bell, *Husserl* (London: Routledge, 1991), pp. 85–6.

62 Robert Sokolowski, 'The Structure and Content of Husserl's *Logical Investigations*', *Inquiry* 14 (1971), 318–50, esp. p. 319.

63 Husserl, 'Task and Significance of the *Logical Investigations*', *Phenomenological Psychology*, p. 18; Hua IX: 25.

64 Husserl, *Phenomenological Psychology*, p. 18; Hua IX: 25.

65 J. S. Mill, *A System of Logic* (London: John W. Parker, 1843), Vol. 1, Bk 1, Ch. 2, §5, p. 40.

66 See K. Mulligan and B. Smith, 'A Husserlian Theory of Indexicality', *Grazer Philosophische Studien* 28 (1996), 133–63. See also K. Schuhmann, 'Husserl's Theories of Indexicals', in F. M. Kirkland and D. P. Chattopadhyaya (eds), *Phenomenology – East and West* (Dordrecht: Kluwer, 1993), pp. 111–27.

67 John R. Searle, *Speech Acts: An Essay in the Philosophy of Language* (Cambridge: Cambridge University Press, 1969). On Reinach, see K. Mulligan (ed.), *Speech Act and Sachverhalt. Reinach and the Foundations of Realist Phenomenology* (Dordrecht: Martinus Nijhoff, 1987).

68 F. Brentano, *Descriptive Psychology*, trans. B. Müller (London: Routledge, 1995). In the background also is Bolzano's discussion of parts and wholes in his *Wissenschaftslehre*.

69 See Barry Smith and K. Mulligan, 'Husserl's Third Logical Investigation: The Formal Ontology of the Part-Whole Relation', in B. Smith and K. Mulligan (eds), *Parts and Moments. Studies in Logic and Formal Ontology* (Munich: Philosophia Verlag, 1992), pp. 35–45.

70 A similar point is made by Rudolf Carnap, who may have been directly influenced by Husserl whose seminars he attended in 1924. See Y. Bar-Hillel, 'Remarks on Carnap's Logical Syntax of Language', in Paul Schilpp (ed.), *The Philosophy of Rudolf Carnap* (La Salle, IL: Open Court, 1963), pp. 519–43.

71 See Suzanne Bachelard, *A Study of Husserl's Formal and Transcendental Logic*, trans. Lester Embree (Evanston, IL: Northwestern University Press, 1968), p. 7.

72 Roman Jakobson acknowledges the importance of Husserl's work for linguistics in his essays, 'Zur Struktur des Phonems' (1939) and in his *Main Trends in the Science of Language* (London: Allen & Unwin, 1973), pp. 13–16. See Elmar Holenstein, 'Jakobson's Contribution to Phenomenology', in *Roman Jakobson: Echoes of His Scholarship*, ed. David Armstrong and C. H. Van Schooneveld (Lisse: Peter De Ridder Press, 1977), pp. 145–62.

73 F. Brentano, *Psychology from an Empirical Standpoint*, trans. A. C. Rancurello, D. B. Terrell and L. L. McAlister, 2nd edn with new Introduction by Peter Simons (London: Routledge, 1995), p. 88.

74 Nominalisation makes possible the shift from formal apophantics to formal ontology.

75 For an account of some of the immediate reactions to Husserl's *Investigations* in Germany, see Farber, *The Foundation of Phenomenology*, op. cit., pp. 147–69.

76 Wilhelm Dilthey, *Studien zur Grundlegung der Geisteswissenschaften*, Gesammelte Schriften VII (Stuttgart: B. G. Teubner, 1968), p. 14n: 'Suche ich nun hier diese meine Grundlegung einer realistisch oder kritisch objektiv gerichteten Erkenntnistheorie fortzubilden, so muss ich ein für allemal im ganzen darauf hinweisen, wie vieles ich den in der Verwertung der Deskription für die Erkenntnistheorie epochemachenden "Logische Untersuchungen" von Husserl (1900.1901) verdanke.' [If I am now seeking to develop further my foundation of a theory of knowledge with a realistically or critically objective orientation, I must first and foremost and in general mention how much I owe to the *Logical Investigations* of Husserl, which are epoch-making in the use of description for the theory of knowledge.]

77 See W. Wundt, 'Psychologismus und Logizismus', in *Kleine Schriften*, Vol. 1 (Leipzig, 1910) and Husserl's reply in his draft Preface of 1913 (in the new edition of Ullrich Melle), 'Zwei Fragmente zum Entwurf einer Vorrede zur zweiten

Auflage der *Logischen Untersuchungen*', to appear in Husserliana series. Husserl is very critical of Wundt's misreading: exclaiming at one point: 'One cannot read the *Logical Investigations* like a newspaper'.

78 Paul Natorp, 'Zur Frage der logischen Methode. Mit Beziehung auf Edmund Husserls Prolegomena zur reinen Logik', *Kant Studien* 6 (1901), 270ff., reprinted in H. Noack (ed.), *Husserl* (Darmstadt: Wissenschaftliche Buchgesellschaft, 1973), pp. 1–15, trans. as 'On the Question of Logical Method in Relation to Edmund Husserl's Prolegomena to Pure Logic', by J. N. Mohanty, in J. N. Mohanty (ed.), *Readings on Edmund Husserl's Logical Investigations* (The Hague: Martinus Nijhoff, 1977), pp. 55–66.

79 See Natorp, 'Zur Frage der logischen Methode', pp. 270ff, and Iso Kern, *Husserl und Kant* (The Hague: Martinus Nijhoff, 1964), p. 31.

80 Martin Heidegger, *Zur Sache des Denkens* (Tübingen: Niemeyer, 1969), trans. as 'My Way to Phenomenology', by Joan Stambaugh, in M. Heidegger, *On Time and Being* (New York: Harper & Row, 1972), pp. 74–82.

81 Ibid., pp. 74–5.

82 Martin Heidegger, 'Neuere Forschungen über Logik', *Literarische Rundschau für das katholische Deutschland* 38, 10 (1 Oct. 1912), cols 465–72; 11, cols 517–24; No. 12, cols 565–70, reprinted in M. Heidegger, *Frühe Schriften (1912–1916)*, ed. F.-W. Von Hermann (Frankfurt: Klostermann, 1978), pp. 17–43.

83 E. Husserl, *Recherches logiques*, trans. from the German by Hubert Elie, Arion L. Kelkel and René Schérer, 3 vols (Paris: Presses Universitaires de France, 1959–63).

84 J. Derrida, *Le Problème de la genèse dans la philosophie de Husserl* (Paris: Presses Universitaires de France, 1990).

85 See J. Derrida, *La Voix et le phénomène* (Paris: Presses Universitaires de France, 1967), ed. and trans. David Allison as *Speech and Phenomena and Other Essays on Husserl's Theory of Signs* (Evanston, IL: Northwestern University Press, 1973). For a critique of Derrida's interpretation see J. Claude Evans, *Strategies of Deconstruction. Derrida and the Myth of the Voice* (Minneapolis: University of Minnesota Press, 1991).

86 W. R. Boyce-Gibson records in his diary that Moore admired the *Investigations*, see his 'From Husserl to Heidegger', ed. Spiegelberg, p. 66.

87 B. Russell, *Skeptical Essays* (New York: W. W. Norton, 1928), pp. 70–1.

88 Richard Rorty, *Philosophy and the Mirror of Nature* (Oxford: Basil Blackwell, 1980), p. 166.

89 An indication of this recent analytic interest in Husserl is to be seen in Woodruff Smith (ed.), *Cambridge Companion to Husserl*.

90 Michael Dummett, *Origins of Analytic Philosophy* (London: Duckworth, 1993), pp. 43–56; Bell, *Husserl*.

91 See Richard Tieszen, 'Gödel's Path from the Incompleteness Theorems (1931) to Phenomenology (1961)', *Bulletin of Symbolic Logic* 4, 2 (June 1998), 181–203.

92 See John R. Searle, *The Mystery of Consciousness* (London: Granta, 1997), p. 5: 'Consciousness so defined is an inner, first-person, qualitative phenomenon'; Colin McGinn, *The Subjective View* (Oxford: Oxford University Press, 1983), and Thomas Nagel, *The View From Nowhere* (Oxford: Oxford University Press, 1986), whose central problem is the relation between the perspective of a person within the world and the objective view of the world which includes that person and his or her viewpoint. For Husserl's defence of the first-person, see David Carr, *The Paradox of Subjectivity* (New York: Oxford University Press, 1999), p. 77: '[Husserl's] phenomenology is not just about experiences but about the first-person standpoint itself'.

93 See note 1 above. Even the critical edition has been criticised for not retaining
   Husserl's own particular orthographical conventions, and for taking the Second
   Edition (B text) as basic and showing the First Edition (A text) only in footnotes.
   Findlay began his translation of the Fifth and Sixth Investigations before the
   Second World War but was unable to gain the publishing permissions until 1961.

Select bibliography

Primary Sources

Husserl, Edmund (1956–) *Gesammelte Werke*. Husserliana. Dordrecht: Kluwer.
Husserl, Edmund (1996) *Gesammelte Schriften*. Hamburg: Meiner.
Husserl, Edmund (1999) *Erfahrung und Urteil: Untersuchungen der Genealogie der Logik*, hrsg. L. Landgrebe. Hamburg: Meiner.

Husserl in Translation

Husserl, Edmund (1964) *Philosophy as a Rigorous Science*, 1911, in Quentin Lauer, *Edmund Husserl. Phenomenology and the Crisis of Philosophy*, New York: Harper & Row.
Husserl, Edmund (1967) *Cartesian Meditations*, trans. Dorion Cairns, The Hague: Martinus Nijhoff.
Husserl, Edmund (1969) *Formal and Transcendental Logic*, trans. Dorion Cairns, The Hague: Martinus Nijhoff.
Husserl, Edmund (1970) *The Crisis of European Sciences and Transcendental Phenomenology. An Introduction to Phenomenological Philosophy*, trans. David Carr, Evanston, IL: Northwestern University Press.
Husserl, Edmund (1973) *Experience and Judgment: Investigations in a Genealogy of Logic*, trans. J. S. Churchill and Karl Ameriks, Evanston, IL: Northwestern University Press.
Husserl, Edmund (1975) *Introduction to the Logical Investigations. Draft of a Preface to the Logical Investigations*, ed. E. Fink, trans. P. J. Bossert and C. H. Peters, The Hague: Martinus Nijhoff.
Husserl, Edmund (1977) *Phenomenological Psychology. Lectures, Summer Semester 1925*, trans. J. Scanlon, The Hague: Martinus Nijhoff.
Husserl, Edmund (1981) *Husserl. Shorter Works*, trans. and ed. Frederick Elliston and Peter McCormick, Notre Dame: University of Notre Dame Press.
Husserl, Edmund (1983) *Ideas pertaining to a Pure Phenomenology and to a Phenomenological Philosophy, First Book*, trans. F. Kersten, Dordrecht: Kluwer.
Husserl, Edmund (1989) *Ideas pertaining to a Pure Phenomenology and to a Phenomenological Philosophy, Second Book*, trans. R. Rojcewicz and A. Schuwer, Dordrecht: Kluwer.

Husserl, Edmund (1990) *On the Phenomenology of the Consciousness of Internal Time*, trans. J.B. Brough, Collected Works IV, Dordrecht: Kluwer.
Husserl, Edmund (1994) *Early Writings in the Philosophy of Logic and Mathematics*, trans. Dallas Willard, Collected Works V, Dordrecht: Kluwer.
Husserl, Edmund (1997) *Thing and Space: Lectures of 1907*, trans. R. Rojcewicz, Collected Works VII, Dordrecht: Kluwer.
Husserl, Edmund (1999) *The Idea of Phenomenology*, trans. Lee Hardy. Dordrecht: Kluwer.
Husserl, Edmund (1999) *The Essential Husserl*, ed. Donn Welton, Bloomington, IN: Indiana University Press.

Further Reading

Bell, David (1990) *Husserl*, London: Routledge.
Bernet, Rudolf, Iso Kern and Eduard Marbach (1993) *An Introduction to Husserlian Phenomenology*. Evanston, IL: Northwestern University Press.
DeBoer, Theodor (1978) *The Development of Husserl's Thought*. The Hague: Martinus Nijhoff.
Derrida, Jacques (1973) *Speech and Phenomena and Other Essays on Husserl's Theory of Signs*, ed. and trans. David Allison, Evanston, IL: Northwestern University Press.
Dreyfus, Hubert L. (ed.) (1982) *Husserl, Intentionality and Cognitive Science*, Cambridge, MA: MIT Press.
Dummett, Michael (1991) *Frege: Philosophy of Mathematics*, London: Duckworth.
Dummett, Michael (1991) *Frege and Other Philosophers*, Oxford: Oxford University Press.
Dummett, Michael (1993) *Origins of Analytic Philosophy*, London: Duckworth.
Elveton, R. O. (ed.) (2000) *The Phenomenology of Husserl. Selected Critical Readings*, 2nd edn, Seattle: Noesis Press.
Farber, Marvin (1943) *The Foundation of Phenomenology*, Albany, NY: State University of New York Press.
Levinas, Emmanuel (1973) *The Theory of Intuition in Husserl's Phenomenology*, trans. A. Orianne, Evanston, IL: Northwestern University Press.
Mohanty, J. N. (ed.) (1977) *Readings on Husserl's Logical Investigations*, The Hague: Martinus Nijhoff.
Mohanty, J. N. (1982) *Husserl and Frege*, Bloomington, IN: Indiana University Press.
Moran, Dermot (2000) *Introduction to Phenomenology*. London and New York: Routledge.
Moran, Dermot (2000) 'Heidegger's Critique of Husserl's and Brentano's Accounts of Intentionality', *Inquiry* 43: 39–66.
Mulligan, Kevin and Smith, Barry (1986) 'Husserl's Logical Investigations', *Grazer Philosophische Studien* 27: 199–207.
Ricoeur, Paul (1967) *Husserl. An Analysis of his Philosophy*, Evanston, IL: Northwestern University Press.
Schérer, René (1967) *La Phénoménologie des 'Recherches Logiques' de Husserl*, Paris: Presses Universitaires de France.

Schuhmann, Karl (1977) *Husserl-Chronik. Denk- und Lebensweg Edmund Husserls*, Husserliana Dokumente 1, The Hague: Martinus Nijhoff.

Sepp, Hans Rainer (ed.) (1988) *Edmund Husserl und die phänomenologische Bewegung. Zeugnisse in Text und Bild*, Freiburg/Munich: Karl Alber Verlag.

Smith, Barry and Woodruff Smith, David (eds) (1995) *The Cambridge Companion to Husserl*, Cambridge: Cambridge University Press.

Sokolowski, Robert (1971) 'The Structure and Content of Husserl's *Logical Investigations*', *Inquiry* 14: 318–50.

Sokolowski, Robert (2000) *Introduction to Phenomenology*, Cambridge: Cambridge Univesity Press.

Spiegelberg, Herbert (1994) *The Phenomenological Movement. A Historical Introduction*, 3rd revised and enlarged edition with the assistance of Karl Schuhmann, Dordrecht: Kluwer.

Ströker, Elizabeth (1993) *Husserl's Transcendental Phenomenology*. Stanford, CA: Stanford University Press.

Taminiaux, Jacques (1985) 'Heidegger and Husserl's *Logical Investigations*', in *Dialectic and Difference*, New Jersey: Humanities Press, 91–114.

Translator's Introduction
(Abridged)

I have been largely, but not absolutely uniform, in my translation of the key-terms, since my aim has been to render their sense, which demands adaptation to their German or English context, rather than to provide a code from which the German can be uniformly inferred from the English. The German text is, after all, again available, even if, regrettably it was long out of print. And Husserl, despite his prolixity and technicality, conforms to the Keynesian description of a Cambridge philosopher as 'a prose writer, hoping to be understood'; he is not a hierophant, requiring a word-for-word translation of his dark locutions in the hope that some of their doubtful sense will be preserved. I have translated *Vorstellung* almost uniformly by 'presentation', recognizing that the latter is not really an English word: the concept expressed by Husserl's (and Brentano's) term is not an English concept either. 'Idea' is required for other purposes, and is in any case ambiguous, and 'representation', if anyone can tolerate it, is required for the cases where Husserl uses *Repräsentation, Darstellung* etc. *Anschauung* (*anschaulich* etc.) I have rendered by 'intuition' ('intuitive' etc.) since this is the traditional rendering of the term in translations of Kant, and since the word has no proper equivalent in English. I have occasionally varied this use by substituting or adding such terms as 'envisage', 'illustrate', 'picture', 'see', and their derivatives. *Einsicht* etc., which more properly means 'intuition' as understood in English, I have translated by 'insight' etc., though sometimes I have talked of 'perspicuity' etc. I have translated *Idee* by 'Idea' and *Spezies* by 'Species', capitalizing both terms where ideal entities are in question. I have sometimes capitalized terms, e.g. 'Perception', where ideal notions were intended, but in general I have been inconsistently sparing with capitals, as I believe that they readily become tyrannous and obfuscate sense. I have translated *Erlebnis* (*erleben* etc.) by 'experience', though I have sometimes substituted 'lived experience', 'live through' etc.; I have not devised a separate word for *Erfabhung*, since Husserl often uses the words interchangeably, and since the English word is used in two ways, clear in the context, and is in fact practically two words. 'Having an experience' and 'learning by experience' obviously involve two distinct, though cognate, uses of the word 'experience'. I have translated *psychisch* by 'mental' in informal contexts like the Prolegomena where 'psychical' would be strained, but I have used 'psychical' where Brentano's technical use, and its contrast with *physisch*, was in question. I have indicated the difference between *real* and *reell* (meaning 'in the world of natural things' and 'actually part of' respectively) by putting the German word in brackets after an English use of 'real'. I am not convinced that Husserl meant much by his solemn distinction of these two terms, and I regret the necessity of translating *wirklich* by 'actual', when 'real' is often more suitable. It is curious that Husserl should have used the word *real* of a thing-like status which need not involve 'reality' in the sense of genuine existence, and which he came afterwards to hold *never* involved 'reality' in the English sense. I have translated *schlicht* by 'straightforward', and *eigentlich* (in technical contexts) by 'authentic', and I have translated *unselbständig* by 'non-independent', since the English word 'dependent' has less negativity and more relativity than *unselbständig*. Sometimes I have also had traffic with 'self-sufficient' for *selbständig*, instead of 'independent'. *Inhalt* I have, of course, translated by 'content', but this makes difficulties in the case of other words for which 'content' alone seems suitable: *Gehalt*, e.g. has been badly translated by 'substance'. *Fundieren, fundierte* etc., are of course 'found', 'founded' (though sometimes I have yielded to the charms of 'basing', 'based' etc.) but *fundierend* has varied from 'foundational' to 'underlying' according to context or euphony. *Moment* I have usually translated as 'moment', but sometimes, in less technical contexts, as 'side' or 'aspect'. *Bedeutung* in the sense of significant content I have translated by 'meaning', less commonly by 'sense': Husserl does not follow Frege in keeping the two words distinct, and neither ever means the *object* of a reference. The word *bedeuten* I have translated by 'act of meaning' or simply by the verb 'to mean', though I have sometimes used 'refer', 'reference' as an equivalent. Husserl in the main tends to say that we mean *objects, not meanings, by way of* the meanings which words *have* rather than *mean*, and I have followed his usage in English, with which it on the whole agrees, rather than trying to introduce distinctions into my translation which have only recently been thought necessary. *Wahrnehmen, Wahrnehmung* etc., I have translated by 'perceive', 'perception', the established equivalents, though when a *Wahrnehmung* means an individual act, I have, for the sake of shortness, translated it by 'percept'. *Innere Wahrnehmung* has been translated by 'inner', 'inward' or 'internal perception' quite without principle, and the same holds *mutatis mutandis* of *aüssere Wahrnehmung*. *Erkennen, Erkenntnis* I have generally translated by 'know', 'knowledge', though there are contexts, particularly in the Sixth Investigation where 'cognize', 'cognition', 'recognize', 'recognition' seemed more suitable. *Evidenz* and its derivatives I have rendered by 'self-evidence', 'inward evidence' according to context: there are cases of *Evidenz*, e.g. those of *innere Wahrnehmung*, which have no *self*-evidence in the English sense. The adjective *evident* I have sometimes translated by 'evident', but in general I have found that the forensic and documentary associations of the English word 'evidence' are fatal to understanding. Many students are permanently bewildered by these associations. That a similar thing holds of 'reflection', 'reflective' etc., used to translate the German word where it has to do with introspection, and not with 'reflection' as we ordinarily understand it, has not led me to depart from the use in question. After all, Locke's similar use of 'reflection' has misled, and always will mislead, countless incautious and forgetful students. I have translated *begründen, Begründung* etc., by 'grounding' etc., also by 'prove' ('proof'), 'demonstrate' ('demonstration'), 'validate' ('validation'). It expresses a reversed view of argument more usual to Continental than to British intellectuals. With these explanations, it is to be hoped that Husserl can speak for himself.

J. N. FINDLAY

Yale University

Foreword

(First German Edition, Volume I, 1900)

The Logical Investigations whose publication begins with these *Prolegomena*, have arisen out of unavoidable problems which have constantly hindered, and finally interrupted, the progress of my efforts, spread over many years, at achieving a philosophical clarification of pure mathematics. Together with questions regarding the origin of the basic concepts and insights of mathematics, these efforts were especially concerned with difficult questions of mathematical theory and method. The expositions of the traditional logic, so often reformulated, should have succeeded in providing us with an intelligible and perspicuous account of the rational essence of deductive science, with its formal unity and symbolic methodology. A study of the actually given deductive sciences, however, left all these things problematic and obscure. The deeper that my analyses penetrated, the more conscious I became that the logic of our time was not adequate to that actual science which it was none the less its function to elucidate.

I was plunged into peculiar difficulties by my logical researches into formal arithmetic and the theory of manifolds, a discipline and method which stretches far beyond all peculiarities of the special forms of number and extension. They forced me into discussions of a very general sort, which lifted me above the narrow sphere of mathematics, and pushed me towards a universal theory of formal deductive systems. There were many sets of problems that then bore down upon me, of which I shall here mention only a single one.

There were evidently possibilities of generalizing (transforming) formal arithmetic, so that, without essential alteration of its theoretical character and methods of calculation, it could be taken beyond the field of quantity, and this made me see that quantity did not at all belong to the most universal essence of the mathematical or the 'formal', or to the method of calculation which has its roots in this essence. I then came to see in 'mathematicizing logic' a mathematics which was indeed free from quantity, while remaining none the less an indefeasible discipline having mathematical form and method, which in part dealt with the old syllogisms, in part with new forms of inference quite alien to tradition. Important problems then loomed before me regarding the universal essence of the mathematical as such, and the natural connection, or the possible boundaries, between systems of quantitative and non-quantitative mathematics, and especially, e.g., regarding arithmetical and logical formality. Naturally, I also had to go on from this point to more fundamental questions regarding the essence of the form of knowledge in contradistinction to its matter, and the sense of the distinction between formal (pure) and material properties, truths and laws.

But in another quite different direction I also found myself involved in problems of general logic and epistemology. I began work on the prevailing assumption that psychology was the science from which logic in general, and the logic of the deductive sciences, had to hope for philosophical clarification. For this reason psychological researches occupy a very large place in the first (the only published) volume of my *Philosophy of Arithmetic*. There were, however, connections in which such a psychological foundation never came to satisfy me. Where one was concerned with questions as to the origin of mathematical presentations, or with the elaboration of those practical methods which are indeed psychologically determined, psychological analyses seemed to me to promote clearness and instruction. But once one had passed from the psychological connections of thinking, to the logical unity of the thought-content (the unity of theory), no true continuity and unity could be established. I became more and more disquieted by doubts of principle, as to how to reconcile the objectivity of mathematics, and of all science in general, with a psychological foundation for logic. In this manner my whole method, which I had taken over from the convictions of the reigning logic, that sought to illuminate the given science through psychological analyses, became shaken, and I felt myself more and more pushed towards general critical reflections on the essence of logic, and on the relationship, in particular, between the subjectivity of knowing and the objectivity of the content known. Logic left me in the lurch wherever I hoped it would give me definite answers to the definite questions I put to it, and I was eventually compelled to lay aside my philosophical-mathematical investigations, until I had succeeded in reaching a certain clearness on the basic questions of epistemology and in the critical understanding of logic as a science.

If I now publish these essays, the product of many years of work, *on a new foundation of pure logic and epistemology*, I do so in the conviction that I shall not be misunderstood for independently choosing a path remote from that of prevailing logical trends, in view of the grave, factually based motives that have inspired me. The course of my development has led to my drawing apart, as regards basic logical convictions, from men and writings to whom I owe most of my philosophical education, and to my drawing rather closer to a group of thinkers whose writings I was not able to estimate rightly, and whom I consulted all too little in the course of my labours. I have had, however, unfortunately to abstain from any subsequent insertion of comprehensive literary and critical references to researches having an affinity with my own. As regards my frank critique of the psychologistic logic and epistemology, I have but to recall Goethe's saying: There is nothing to which one is more severe than the errors that one has just abandoned.

E. HUSSERL

Halle a. d. S. May 21st 1900

(Second German Edition, Volume I, 1913)

The question as to the form in which I should undertake to republish the present work, out of print for some years, has caused me no little concern. My *Logical Investigations* were my 'break-through', not an end but rather a beginning. When the work had been printed, my studies continued forthwith. I tried to give a fuller account of the meaning, the method and the philosophical scope of phenomenology, to pursue the woven threads of my problems further in every direction, and to track down and tackle parallel problems in all ontic and phenomenological fields. Understandably, as the horizon of my research widened, and as I became better acquainted with the intentional 'modifications' so perplexingly built on one another, with the multiply interlacing structures of consciousness, there came a shift in many of the conceptions formed in my first penetration of the new territory. Remaining obscurities were cleared up, ambiguities removed, isolated observations to which at the start no special importance could be given, gained fundamental meaning as one passed over into larger contexts. Everywhere, in brief, there were not merely supplementations but transvaluations in one's original field of research, and from the point of view of one's widened, deepened knowledge, even the arrangement of one's treatments no longer seemed quite adequate. The sense and the extent of these forward steps, and their widening effect on one's field of research comes out in the recently published First Book of my *Ideas towards a pure Phenomenology and Phenomenological Philosophy*, printed in the first volume of the *Jahrbuch für Philosophie und phänomenologische Forschung* (1913), and the publication of the two remaining Books, which will follow immediately, will show this still better.

I originally cherished the hope that, after discovering and exploring the radical problems of pure phenomenology and phenomenological philosophy, I should be able to present a series of systematic expositions that would render a reprinting of the old work unnecessary, in so far as its content, not at all jettisoned, but purged and divided according to subject, would come into its own in association with the new work. But when execution began, a serious objection at once raised itself. Many years would be needed for the carrying out of the extensive, difficult task of imposing literary unity on our

Investigations: though they stood there complete and concrete, they would have for the most part to be expounded anew and to have their difficulties ironed out. I therefore decided first of all to plan my *Ideas*. They were to give a universal, yet contentful presentation of the new phenomenology, based throughout on actually executed work, a presentation of its method, of its systematic field of problems, of its function in making possible a strictly scientific philosophy, as well as a reduction to rational theory of empirical psychology. After all this, the *Logical Investigations* would be republished, and that in a better form, adapted to the standpoint of the *Ideas*, and so helping to introduce the reader to the nature of genuinely phenomenological and epistemological *work*. For if these Investigations are to prove helpful to those interested in phenomenology, this will be because they do not offer us a mere programme (certainly not one of the high-flying sort which so encumber philosophy) but that they are attempts at genuinely executed fundamental work on the immediately envisaged and seized things themselves. Even where they proceed critically, they do not lose themselves in discussions of standpoint, but rather leave the last word to the things themselves, and to one's work upon such things. The *Ideas* ought in effect to rest on the work of the *Logical Investigations*. If, through the latter, the reader has been brought openly to investigate and concern himself with a group of fundamental questions, then the *Ideas*, with their policy of illuminating method from ultimate sources by putting a sketch of the main structures of pure consciousness before one, by systematically locating one's work-problems in the latter, could assist him to a further, independent advance.

The carrying out of the first part of my plan was relatively easy, though the unexpected length of the first two Books of the *Ideas*, essential for my purposes and undertaken by me in one piece, forced me to divide their publication, so that the First Book alone had to suffice provisionally. But the fulfilment of my second aim was far harder. Anyone who knows the old work, will see the impossibility of lifting it entirely on to the level of the *Ideas*. That would mean a complete recasting of the work, and a postponement to the Greek kalends. It seemed to me, on the other hand, to be a comfortable rather than a conscientious decision, in view of the aims justifying a new edition, to abandon all revision and merely reprint the work mechanically. Was I entitled to mislead the reader once more, through all my omissions, waverings and self-misunderstandings, which, however unavoidable and pardonable in the first edition of such a work, would yet put unnecessary difficulties in the way of a clear grasp of essentials?

All that remained possible was to attempt a middle course, and in a manner to let myself go in attempting it. It meant leaving untouched certain unclarities, and even errors, which were part and parcel of the unified style of the work. The following maxims guided my revision:

1. To allow nothing into the new edition regarding which I was not fully persuaded that it deserved thorough study. In this respect single errors could

be left standing, since I could allow them to count as natural steps towards a truth that would transform their good intentions. I could say to myself in all this: Readers who stem from general philosophical drifts of the present – which are in essence the same as those in the decade of this work's origin – can, like the work's author, only at first gain access to what are mere steps towards certain phenomenological (logical) positions. Only when they have gained sure mastery over the style of phenomenological research, do they see the fundamental meaning of certain distinctions which appeared previously to be insignificant nuances.

2. To improve all that could be improved, without altering the course and style of the old work, and, above all, to bring to most definite expression the new thought-motives that had their 'break-through' in the old work, but which had, in the first edition, been at times sharply stressed, at times blurred, by the hesitant and timid author.

3. To lift the reader gradually, in the course of the expositions, to a relatively rising total level of insight, following in this the original peculiarity of the work. We must here voice the reminder that the work was a systematically bound *chain of investigations* but not, properly speaking, *one* book or work in a literary sense. There is in it a regular ascent from a lower to a higher level, and a working of oneself into ever new logical and phenomenological insights, which never leave the previously achieved ones quite untouched. Ever new phenomenological strata swim into our view and add determination to our conceptions of the earlier ones. This character of the old work made a kind of revision seem possible, which consciously leads the reader onward and upward, in such a way that, in the final Investigation, the level of the *Ideas* is in essentials reached, so that the previous unclearnesses and half-truths, that we had to put up with, appear perspicuously clarified.

I went ahead in the sense of these maxims, and have the impression as regards both provisionally published pieces (the *Prolegomena* and the first part of the Second Volume) that the big efforts I made have not been wasted. I have naturally had to add here, and strike out there, at times to rewrite single sentences, and at times whole paragraphs and chapters. The thought-content has become more packed and full in extent: the total extent of the work, more specifically that of the Second Volume, has grown unavoidably, despite all suppression of critical supplementation, so that this volume has had to be divided.

Regarding the individual Investigations and their reconstructed form, the following should be said. The *Prolegomena to Pure Logic* is, in its essential content, a mere reworking of two complementary series of lectures given at Halle in the summer and autumn of 1896. To this the greater liveliness of the exposition is due, which has assisted its influence. The piece is, moreover, written in one cast of thought, and I therefore thought I ought not to revise it radically. But I found I could, on the other hand, from about the middle on, carry out many quite large improvements in presentation, could expunge slips and put main points into sharper light. Some very essential, if partial, insufficiencies – such as the concept of a 'truth in itself' which is too one-sidedly oriented to *vérités de raison* – had to be left, since they were part of the unified level of the piece. The Sixth Investigation (now the Second Part of the Second Volume) brings in necessary clarification in this respect.

To burden the polemic on psychologism with new criticisms and counter-criticisms (which would not have introduced the least new thought-motive) did not seem very appropriate to me. I must emphasize the relation of this piece to 1899, the precise date at which I merely rewrote it. (The printing of the *Prolegomena*, minus the Foreword, was already complete in November 1899. See my self-reference in the *Vierteljahrschr. f. wiss. Philosophie*, 1900, p. 512 *f.*) Since its appearance, some authors that I looked on as represent-ing logical psychologism have essentially changed their position. Th. Lipps, e.g., in his extremely significant, original writings, has since 1902 not at all been the man that is here quoted. Other authors have, in the meantime, sought different foundations for their psychologistic position, a point not to be ignored, since my presentation takes no account of it.

As regards the Second Volume of the new edition, the hesitant Introduc-tion, so little true to the essential sense and method of the actually written Investigations, was radically revised. I felt its defects immediately after its appearance, and also found immediate occasion (in a review in the *Archiv f. system. Philos.* XI (1903), p. 397 *ff.*) to object to my misleading account of phenomenology as descriptive psychology. Some of the main points of principle are there briefly but sharply characterized. The psychological de-scription performed in inner experience appears as put on a level with the description of external events in nature performed in external description, but it is, on the other hand *opposed* to phenomenological description, from which all transcendent interpretations of immanent data, even those of psychical acts and states of a real ego, are entirely excluded. The descriptions of phenomenology are said (p. 399) 'to deal neither with lived experiences nor classes of lived experiences of empirical persons ... phenomenology knows nothing of persons, of my experiences or those of others, and surmises nothing regarding them: it raises no questions in regard to such matters, attempts no determinations, constructs no hypotheses'. The complete reflec-tive clarity that I had achieved in these and following years regarding the essence of phenomenology, which led gradually to the systematic doctrine of 'phenomenological reduction' (cf. *Ideas*, I, Section 2), was of use in the rewriting of this Introduction, and also in the text of all the following In-vestigations, thereby raising the whole work to an essentially higher level of clarity.

Of the five Investigations which occupy the First Part of the Second Volume, the first, *Expression and Meaning*, retains its merely preparatory character in the new edition. It stimulates thought, it directs the gaze of the phenomenological beginner to the initial, already most difficult problems of the consciousness of meaning, without doing full justice to them. The manner in which it deals with occasional meanings (to which, however, in strictness, all empirical predications belong) is an act of violence – the enforced consequence of the imperfect conception of the essence of 'truth in itself' in the *Prolegomena.*

As a further defect of this Investigation, only understood and corrected at the end of the volume, we must note that it has no regard to the distinction and parallelism between the 'noetic' and the 'noematic': the fundamental role of this distinction in *all* fields of consciousness is first fully laid bare in the *Ideas*, but comes through in many individual arguments in the last Investigation of the old work. For this reason, the essential ambiguity of 'meaning' as an Idea is not emphasized. The noetic concept of meaning is one-sidedly stressed, though in many important passages the noematic concept is principally dealt with.

The Second Investigation concerning *The Ideal Unity of the Species and Modern Theories of Abstraction*, had a style and limitation of theme, a certain completeness, which made a few detailed amendments, but no thoroughgoing reconstructions, desirable. As before, there is no discussion of the various types of Ideas, with their demand for a deep separation of essence, to which naturally Ideations, as deeply and essentially separate, correspond. All that this Investigation is concerned with, is the fact that one can learn to see Ideas, represented, e.g. by the Idea Red, and that one can become clear as to the essence of such 'seeing'.

The Third Investigation *On the Doctrine of Wholes and Parts* has undergone very thorough revision, though in its case no unsatisfactory compromises needed to be made, and no subsequent corrections or deepenings were necessary. All that was here needed was to assist the inner sense of the Investigation, and what I thought were its important results, to better operation and to remove numerous imperfections of statement. I have the impression that this Investigation is all too little read. I myself derived great help from it: it is also an essential presupposition for the full understanding of the Investigations which follow.

The position of the Fourth Investigation, *On the Distinction between independent and non-independent Meanings and the Idea of Pure Grammar*, is similar to that of the Third. My position in this case is also unaltered. I not only amended, but also in many places enriched, the content of the text, changes which point to future publications from my lectures on logic.

The Fifth Investigation, *On intentional Experiences and their 'Contents'*, had to undergo deep-going revision. In it cardinal problems of phenomenology (those in particular of the phenomenological doctrine of judgement) were tackled: in these it was possible to achieve a considerably higher level of clarity and insight without needing to alter the structure and essential content of the Investigation. I no longer approve of the rejection of the pure ego, but left the arguments in question in a shortened and formally improved form, as being the basis of P. Natorp's interesting polemic in his new *Allgemeine Psychologie*, volume 1, 1912. I have completely excised the much cited, very unclear, and, in the context, quite dispensable §7, 'Reciprocal Demarcation of Psychology and Natural Science'. I was perhaps all too conservative in retaining the quite unsuitable term 'nominal presentation': I was afraid in general of tampering with the terminology of the old work.

The revised version of the Sixth Investigation, now in the press, is designed as the Second Part of the Second Volume: it is the most important Investigation from a phenomenological point of view. In this case I soon persuaded myself that it would not be enough to revise the old content, following the original content paragraph by paragraph. Its fund of problems still were my pace-setter, but I had advanced considerably in regard to them, and the sense of my 'maxims' would not permit a further use of compromises in regard to them. I accordingly went along quite freely, and, in order to give scientific treatment to the great themes so imperfectly dealt with in the first edition, I added whole series of new chapters, which increased the bulk of this Investigation very considerably.

As in the *Prolegomena* I did not, in my second volume (my Fourth Investigation made a small exception) go into the many criticisms which rest, I am sorry to say, almost exclusively on misunderstandings of the *sense* of my positions. I therefore thought it more useful to discuss in universal form, and in their historical position, the *typical* misunderstandings of my philosophical endeavours, and that at the end of the Second Volume, in an epilogue, so to say. It will be a good thing if the reader has a look at this Appendix immediately after reading the *Prolegomena*, so as to guard himself in time against such apparently natural misunderstandings.

A full index will be added to the work, prepared with great care by my doctoral candidate Rudolf Clemens. I must express my heartfelt thanks for much friendly assistance, and, in the first place, to the Privatdozent Dr Adolf Reinach, who helped me with his zeal and knowledge when, two years ago, I first went thoroughly into deliberations concerning the possibilities of revision. The labours of correction were greatly lightened by the help of Dr Hans Lipps and by the doctoral candidate Jean Hering.

E. HUSSERL

Göttingen October 1913

Prolegomena to
pure logic

Introduction

§1 The controversy regarding the definition of logic and the essential content of its doctrines

'There is accordingly as much difference of opinion in regard to the definition of logic as there is in the treatment of the science itself. This was only to be expected in the case of a subject, in regard to which most writers have only employed the same words to express different thoughts' (John Stuart Mill, *Logic*, Introduction, §1). Many decades have passed since John Stuart Mill introduced his valuable work on logic with these sentences, and important thinkers here and beyond the Channel have devoted their best powers to logic and have enriched its literature with ever new presentations. But even today these sentences could serve as a suitable expression of the state of logical science, even today we are very far from complete agreement as to the definition of logic and the content of its essential doctrines. Contemporary logic, of course, wears quite a different face from the logic of the mid-century. Owing particularly to the influence of the distinguished thinker just mentioned, the first of the three main tendencies that we find in logic, the psychological, has definitely come to prevail over the formal and the metaphysical tendencies, both as regards the number and the importance of its exponents. But the other two tendencies are still carried on, and the disputed questions of principle, reflected in different definitions of logic, are still disputed, while it is still true, and perhaps more true than ever, that different writers merely employ the same words to express different thoughts. This is not merely true of expositions stemming from different philosophical 'camps'. The side on which most life is to be found, that of psychological logic, manifests unity of conviction only in regard to the demarcation of the discipline, its essential aims and methods. But one could scarcely be blamed for exaggerating if one applied the phrase *bellum omnium contra omnes* to the doctrines put forth, and, in particular, to the opposed interpretations of traditional formulae and doctrines. It would be vain to seek to delimit a sum total of substantial propositions or theories in which one might see the hard core of our epoch's logical science and the heritage bequeathed by it to the future.

§2 Necessity of a renewed discussion of questions of principle

In this state of the science, which does not permit one to separate individual conviction from universally binding truth, a reversion to questions of principle remains a task that must ever be tackled anew. This holds particularly as regards the questions which play a decisive role in the dispute among logical 'tendencies' and, together with this, in the dispute as to the correct demarcation of the science. The interest in just these questions has certainly cooled off in the last decades. After Mill's brilliant attacks on the logic of Hamilton, and the no less famous, but not so fruitful, logical investigations of Trendelenburg, these questions seemed to have been fully dealt with. But with the great resurgence of psychological studies, the psychologistic tendency in logic also gained dominance, and all effort centred in the systematic building up of the discipline upon principles presumed valid. The fact, however, that so many attempts made by such important thinkers to put logic on the sure path of a science, have not led to any shattering success, suggests that the ends in view have perhaps not been sufficiently clarified to allow successful investigation.

One's conception of the aims of a science find expression in its definition. We naturally do not think that successful work on a discipline demands a prior conceptual demarcation of its field. The definitions of a science mirror the stages of that science's development; knowledge of the conceptual character of a science's objects, of the boundaries and place of its field, follow the science and progress with it. None the less, the degree of adequacy of such definitions, or of the views of the field they express, react on the progress of the science itself, and, according to the direction in which such definitions depart from truth, such a reaction can have a slight, or a very important influence on the development of the science. The field of a science is an objectively closed unity: we cannot arbitrarily delimit fields where and as we like. The realm of truth is objectively articulated into fields: researches must orient themselves to these objective unities and must assemble themselves into sciences. There is a science of numbers, a science of spatial figures, of animal species etc., but there are no special sciences of prime numbers, of trapezia, or of lions, nor of all three taken together. Where a group of discoveries and problems impresses us as 'belonging together', and leads to the setting up of a science, inadequate demarcation can consist merely in the fact that the field-concept is at first too narrow for what is given, and that concatenations of grounding connections stretch beyond the delimited field, and only draw together in a closed unity over a much wider field. Such limitations of horizon need not be prejudicial to the flourishing progress of the science. It may be that theoretical interest finds its first satisfaction in the narrower field, and that work that can be done without regard to deeper and wider logical ramifications, is what is needed in the first instance.

There is another, much more dangerous fault in field-delimitation: the confusion of fields, the mixture of heterogeneous things in a putative field-unity, especially when this rests on a complete misreading of the objects whose investigation is to be the essential aim of the proposed science. Such an unnoticed μετάβασις εἰς ἄλλο γένος can have the most damaging consequences: the setting up of invalid aims, the employment of methods wrong in principle, not commensurate with the discipline's true objects, the confounding of logical levels so that the genuinely basic propositions and theories are shoved, often in extraordinary disguises, among wholly alien lines of thought, and appear as side-issues or incidental consequences etc. These dangers are considerable in the philosophical sciences. Questions as to range and boundaries have, therefore, much more importance in the fruitful building up of these sciences than in the much favoured sciences of external nature, where the course of our experiences forces territorial separations upon us, within which successful research can at least be provisionally established. It was Kant who uttered the famous special words on logic which we here make our own: 'We do not augment, but rather subvert the sciences, if we allow their boundaries to run together.' The following Investigation hopes to make plain that all previous logic, and our contemporary, psychologically based logic in particular, is subject, almost without exception, to the above-mentioned dangers: through its misinterpretation of theoretical principles, and the consequent confusion of fields, progress in logical knowledge has been gravely hindered.

§3 Disputed questions. The path to be entered

The traditionally disputed questions which concern the demarcation of logic are the following:

1. Is logic a theoretical or a practical discipline (a 'technology')?

2. Is it independent of other sciences, and, in particular, of psychology and metaphysics?

3. Is it a formal discipline? Has it merely to do as usually conceived, with the 'form of knowledge', or should it also take account of its matter?

4. Has it the character of an *a priori*, a demonstrative discipline or of an empirical, inductive one?

All these disputed questions are so intimately bound up together, that to take up a stance on one of them, is to some extent at least to be determined, or factually influenced, in the stance one takes up on the others. There are really only two parties. Logic is a theoretical discipline, formal and demonstrative, and independent of psychology: that is one view. For the other it counts as a technology dependent on psychology, which of course excludes the possibility of its being a formal, demonstrative discipline like the other side's paradigm arithmetic.

Since we do not really mean to become involved in these traditional disputes, but rather to clarify the differences of principle at work in them, and to work towards a clarification of the essential aims of a pure logic, we shall proceed as follows: we shall start from the almost universally accepted contemporary treatment of logic as a technology, and shall pin down its sense and its justification. This will naturally lead on to the question of the theoretical foundations of this discipline, and of its relations, in particular, to psychology. This question coincides in essence, in the main if not entirely, with the cardinal question of epistemology, that of the objectivity of knowledge. The outcome of our investigation of this point will be the delineation of a new, purely theoretical science, the all-important foundation for any technology of scientific knowledge, and itself having the character of an *a priori*, purely demonstrative science. This is the science intended by Kant and the other proponents of a 'formal' or 'pure' logic, but not rightly conceived and defined by them as regards its content and scope. The final outcome of these discussions is a clearly circumscribed idea of the disputed discipline's essential content, through which a clear position in regard to the previous mentioned controversies will have been gained.

Chapter 1

Logic as a normative and, in particular, as a practical discipline

§4 The theoretical incompleteness of the separate sciences

It is a common experience that the excellence of an artist's mastery over his material, and the decisive certainty with which he judges and assesses works in his art, is only quite exceptionally based on a theoretical knowledge of the rules which prescribe direction and order to his practice, and determine the standards of value on which the perfection or imperfection of the complete work must be assessed. Normally the practising artist is not the man who can who can inform us rightly regarding the principles of his art. He follows principles neither in his creation nor his evaluation. In his creation he follows the inner activity of his harmoniously trained powers, in his judgement his finely formed artistic taste and feeling. This is not merely so in the case of fine art, of which one may first have thought, but in that of the arts generally, in the widest sense of the word. It therefore holds for the activities of scientific creation and the theoretical evaluation of their results, for the scientific demonstrations of facts, laws, theories. Even the mathematician, the physicist and the astronomer need not understand the ultimate grounds of their activities in order to carry through even the most important scientific performances. Although their results have a power of rational persuasion for themselves and others, yet they cannot claim to have demonstrated all the last premises in their syllogisms, nor to have explored the principles on which the success of their methods reposes. The incomplete state of all sciences depends on this fact. We do not here mean the mere incompleteness with which the truths in a field have been charted, but the lack of inner clarity and rationality, which is a need independently of the expansion of the science. Even mathematics, the most advanced of all sciences, can in this respect claim no special position. Though often still treated as the ideal of all science as such, how little it really is such is shown by the old, yet never finally composed disputes as to the foundations of geometry, or as to the justification of the method of imaginaries. The same thinkers who sustain marvellous mathematical methods with such incomparable mastery, and who add new methods to them, often show themselves incapable of accounting satisfactorily for their logical validity and for the limits of their right use. Though the sciences have grown great despite these defects, and have helped us to a formerly undreamt of mastery over nature, they cannot satisfy us theoretically. They are, as theories, not crystal-clear: the function of all their concepts and propositions is not fully intelligible, not all of their presuppositions have been exactly analysed, they are not in their entirety raised above all theoretical doubt.

§5 The theoretical completion of the separate sciences by metaphysics and theory of science

To reach this theoretical goal we first need, as is fairly generally admitted, a type of investigation which belongs to the metaphysical realm.

Its task is to pin down and to test the untested, for the most part not even noticed, yet very significant metaphysical presuppositions that underlie at least all those sciences that are concerned with actual reality. Such presuppositions are, e.g., that an external world exists, that it is spread out in space and time, its space being, as regards its mathematical character, three-dimensional and Euclidean, and its time a one-dimensional rectilinear manifold; that all process is subject to the causal principle etc. These presuppositions, all to be found in the framework of Aristotle's First Philosophy, are at present ranked under the quite unsuitable rubric of 'epistemology'.

Such a metaphysical foundation is not, however, sufficient to provide the desired theoretical completion of the separate sciences. It concerns, moreover, only such sciences as have to do with actual reality, which does not include all sciences, certainly not the purely mathematical sciences whose objects are numbers, manifolds etc., things thought of as mere bearers of ideal properties independent of real being or non-being. The case is different in regard to another class of investigations whose theoretical completion is plainly an indispensable postulate in our quest for knowledge, investigations which concern all sciences equally, since they concern, in brief, whatever makes sciences into sciences. This names the field of a new, and, as we shall see, complex discipline, whose peculiarity it is to be the science of science, and which could therefore be most pointedly called theory of science (*Wissenschaftslehre*).

§6 The possibility and justification of logic as theory of science

The possibility and justification of such a discipline – a normative and practical discipline relating to the Idea of science – can be shown by the following considerations.

Science is concerned, as its name indicates, with knowing, but this does not mean that it itself consists of a sum or tissue of acts of knowing. Science exists objectively only in its literature, only in written work has it a rich relational being limited to men and their intellectual activities: in this form it is propagated down the millennia, and survives individuals, generations and nations. It therefore represents a set of external arrangements, which, just as they arose out of the knowledge-acts of many individuals, can again pass over into just such acts of countless individuals, in a readily understandable manner, whose exact description would require much circumlocution. For us it is here sufficient that science provides, or should provide, certain more immediate preconditions of acts of knowing, real possibilities of knowing, whose realization by the 'normal' or 'suitably endowed' individual in well-known, 'normal' circumstances can be looked on as an attainable goal of his endeavour. In this sense, therefore, science aims at knowledge.

In knowledge, however, we possess truth. In actual knowledge, to which we see ourselves ultimately referred back, we possess truth as the object of a correct judgement. But this alone is not enough, since not every correct judgement, every affirmation or rejection of a state of affairs that accords with truth, represents *knowledge* of the being or non-being of this state of affairs. Rather we may say that, if it is to be called 'knowledge' in the narrowest, strictest sense, it requires to be evident, to have the luminous certainty that what we have acknowledged *is*, that what we have rejected *is not*, a certainty distinguished in familiar fashion from blind belief, from vague opining, however firm and decided, if we are not to be shattered on the rocks of extreme scepticism. Common talk does not, however, stay put in this strict concept. We also speak, e.g. of an act of knowing where the judgement we pass is associated with a clear memory that we previously passed a judgement of precisely the same content accompanied with inner evidence. This happens particularly where our memory also concerns a demonstrative thought-process out of which this inner evidence grew, and that we are sure we can reproduce *with* such evidence. ('I know that the Pythagorean theorem is true – I can prove it': instead of the second half, one can of course also say 'but I have forgotten the proof'.)

We therefore conceive 'knowledge' in a wider, but not wholly loose sense: we separate it off from baseless opinion, by pointing to some 'mark' of the presumed state of affairs or for the correctness of the judgement passed by us. The most perfect 'mark' of correctness is inward evidence, it counts as an immediate intimation of truth itself. In the vast majority of cases we lack such absolute knowledge of truth, in whose place we make use – one need *only* think how memory functions in the above examples – of the inner evidence for a higher or lower degree of probability for our state of affairs, with which, if probability-levels become high enough, a firm judgement is usually associated. The inward evidence of the probability of a state of affairs A will not serve to ground the inward evidence of its truth, but it will serve to ground those comparative, inwardly evident value-assessments, through which, in accordance with positive or negative probability-values, we can distinguish the reasonable from the unreasonable, the better-founded from the worse-founded assumptions, opinions and surmises. Ultimately, therefore, all genuine, and, in particular, all scientific knowledge, rests on inner evidence: as far as such evidence extends, the concept of knowledge extends also.

There is none the less a remaining duality in the concept of knowing or knowledge. Knowledge in the narrowest sense of the word is the being inwardly evident that a certain state of affairs is or is not, e.g. that S is P or that it is not P. If it is evident that a certain state of affairs is probable to this or that degree, then we have knowledge in the strictest sense of such a probability, but, in regard to the being of the state of affairs itself, and not of its probability, we only have knowledge in a wider, modified sense. It is in this latter sense, with an eye to degrees of probability, that one speaks of a greater or lesser degree of knowledge. Knowledge in the pregnant sense – its being quite evident that S is P – then counts as the absolutely fixed, ideal limit which the graded probabilities for the being-P of S approach asymptotically.

But the concept and task of science covers more than mere knowledge. If we live through and recognize the presence of inner percepts, singly or in groups, we have knowledge, but are far removed from science: the same applies generally to all incoherent groups of acts of knowing. A group of isolated bits of chemical knowledge would certainly not justify talk of a science of chemistry. More is plainly required, i.e. *systematic coherence in the theoretical sense*, which means finding grounds for one's knowing, and suitably combining and arranging the sequence of such groundings.

The essence of science therefore involves unity of the foundational connections: not only isolated pieces of knowledge, but their grounded validations themselves, and together with these, the higher inter-weavings of such validations that we call theories, must achieve systematic unity. The aim is not merely to arrive at knowledge, but knowledge in such degree and form as would correspond to our highest theoretical aims as perfectly as possible.

That we look upon, and practically strive after, systematic form as the purest embodiment of the Idea of science, does not evince some merely aesthetic trait in our nature. Science neither wishes nor dares to become a field for architectonic play. The system peculiar to science, i.e. to true and correct science, is not our own invention, but is present in things, where we simply find or discover it. Science seeks to be a means towards the greatest possible conquest of the realm of truth by our knowledge. The realm of truth is, however, no disordered chaos, but is dominated and unified by law. The investigation and setting forth of truths must, therefore, likewise be systematic, it must reflect the systematic connections of those truths, and must use the latter as a ladder to progress and penetrate from the knowledge given to, or already gained by us to ever higher regions of the realm of truth.

Science can never do without this helpful ladder. The inward evidence on which all knowledge ultimately reposes, is no gift of nature, appearing together with the mere idea of states of affairs without any methodically artful set-up. People would otherwise never have thought of building up sciences. The longueurs of method would lose their sense if to intend meant to succeed. Why should one search into relations of entailment or construct proofs, if one shared in truth through immediate intimation? The inward evidence, moreover, which stamps one presented state of affairs as having real being, or the absurdity which stamps it as having no being at all (and the same, likewise, in regard to probability and improbability) is, in fact, only immediately felt in the case of a relatively quite limited group of primitive facts. Countless true propositions are only grasped by us as true when we methodically validate them. In their case, a mere regard to our propositional thought, will not induce inward evidence, even if it does induce judgemental decision. Both are, however, induced, certain circumstances being normal, where we set forth from certain known truths, and tread a certain path in thought to our intended proposition. There may be many ways of establishing the same proposition, starting from these or those bits of knowledge. It is, however, a characteristic and essential circumstance that there are infinitely many truths which could never be transformed into knowledge without such methodical procedures.

That this is the case, that we need grounded validations in order to pass beyond what, in knowledge, is immediately and therefore trivially evident, not only makes the sciences possible and necessary, but with these also a *theory of science*, a *logic*. All sciences proceed methodically in the pursuit of truth, employ more or less artificial aids in order to bring to knowledge truths or probabilities that would otherwise remain hidden, and in order to use the obvious or the already established as a lever for achieving what is remote and only mediately attainable. The comparative treatment of these methodical aids, in which the insights and experiences of countless generations of thinkers are stored up, should provide the means for setting up general norms for such procedures and likewise rules for their inventive construction in various classes of cases.

§10 The ideas of theory and science as problems of the theory of science

Something more must be added. The theory of science, as here shown up, is not merely concerned to investigate the forms and laws of isolated validations, and the auxiliary devices which go with these. Isolated validations also occur beyond the boundaries of science: clearly, therefore, isolated validations – and loosely piled heaps of such validations – do not make up science. Science requires, as said above, a certain unity of validatory interconnection, a certain unity in the stepwise ascent of its validatory arguments, and this form of unity has itself a lofty teleological meaning in the attainment of the highest goal of knowledge for which all science strives: to advance as far as possible in the research into truth, i.e. not in the research into separate truths, but into the realm of truth or its natural provinces.

The task of the theory of science will therefore also be to deal with the sciences as *systematic unities of this or that sort* in other words, with the formal features that stamp them as sciences, with the features that determine their mutual boundaries and their inner articulation into fields, into relatively closed theories, with the features which fix their essentially different species or forms etc.

This systematic tissue of validatory arguments can in fact be subordinated to the concept of method, so that science's task is not merely to deal with the methods of knowledge in the sciences, but also with such methods as are themselves styled sciences. Its task is not merely to separate off valid from invalid demonstrations, but also valid from invalid theories and sciences. The task thus assigned it is plainly not independent of the one previously mentioned, but to a considerable extent presupposes a prior carrying out of the former. Research into the sciences as systematic unities is unthinkable without prior research into their validatory procedures. Both at least enter into the notion of a science of science as such.

§11 Logic or theory of science as normative discipline and as technology

From our discussions up to this point logic – in the sense of the theory of science here in question – emerges as a *normative discipline*. Sciences are creations of the spirit which are directed to a certain end, and which are for that reason to be judged in accordance with that end. The same holds of theories, validations and in short of everything that we call a 'method'. Whether a science is truly a science, or a method a method, depends on whether it accords with the aims that it strives for. Logic seeks to search into what pertains to genuine, valid science as such, what constitutes the Idea of Science, so as to be able to use the latter to measure the empirically given sciences as to their agreement with their Idea, the degree to which they approach it, and where they offend against it. In this logic shows itself to be a normative science, and separates itself off from the comparative mode of treatment which tries to conceive of the sciences, according to their *typical* communities and peculiarities, as concrete cultural products of their era, and to explain them through the relationships which obtain in their time. For it is of the essence of a normative science that it establishes general propositions in which, with an eye to a normative standard, an Idea or highest goal, certain features are mentioned whose possession guarantees conformity to that standard, or sets forth an indispensable condition of the latter. A normative science also establishes cognate propositions in which the case of non-conformity is considered or the absence of such states of affairs is pronounced. Not as if one had to state general marks in order to say what an object should be to conform to its basic norm: a normative discipline never sets forth universal criteria, any more than a therapy states universal symptoms. Special criteria are what the theory of science particularly gives us, and what it alone can give us. If it maintains that, having regard to the supreme aim of the sciences and the human mind's actual constitution, and whatever else may be invoked, such and such methods M_1, M_2 . . . arise, it states general propositions of the form: 'Every group of mental activities of the sorts AB . . . which realize the combinatory form M_1 (or M_2 . . .) yield a case of correct method', or, what amounts to the same 'Every (soi-disant) methodical procedure of the form M_1 (or M_2 . . .) is a correct one.' If one could really formulate all intrinsically possible valid propositions of this and like sort, our normative science would certainly possess a measuring rod for every pretended method, but then also only in the form of special criteria.

Where the basic norm is an end or can become an end, the normative discipline by a ready extension of its task gives rise to a technology. This occurs in this case too. If the theory of science sets itself the further task of investigating such conditions as are subject to our power, on which the realization of valid methods depends, and if it draws up rules for our procedure in the methodical tracking down of truth, in the valid demarcation and construction of the sciences, in the discovery and use, in particular, of the many methods that advance such sciences, and in the avoidance of errors in all of these concerns, then it has become a _technology of science._ This last plainly includes the whole normative theory of science, and it is therefore wholly appropriate, in view of the unquestionable value of such a technology, that the concept of logic should be correspondingly widened, and should be defined in its sense.

§12 Relevant definitions of logic

The definition of logic as a technology was much favoured by tradition, but closer determinations of it left much to be desired. Definitions such as 'technology of judgement, of reasoning, of knowing, of thinking' (_l'art de penser_) are misleading, and in any case too narrow. If we restrict the vague meaning of the word 'thinking' in the last-mentioned definition (in use to this day) to the concept of correct judgement, our definition reads: 'the technology of correct judgement'. But that this definition is too narrow is plain from the fact that the aim of scientific knowledge does not follow from it. If one says that 'the aim of thinking is first perfectly fulfilled in science', this is without doubt right, but it concedes that not thought or knowledge is really the end of the technology in question, but that towards which thought itself is a means.

Other definitions are open to similar objections. They are open to the objection recently revived by Bergmann that the technology of an activity, e.g. painting, singing, riding, would be expected above all 'to show what one must do to perform the relevant activity correctly, e.g. how one must hold and wield the brush in painting, how one must use the chest, throat and mouth in singing, how one must pull and relax the reins in riding and press with one's legs'. This would admit into the field of logic doctrines wholly alien to it.[1]

Schleiermacher's definition of logic as the technology of scientific knowledge certainly comes closer to the truth. For obviously in a discipline so defined one would have to consider only what is peculiar to scientific knowledge, and to probe its possible demands: the further preconditions which in general favour the emergence of knowledge would be left to pedagogy, hygiene etc. But Schleiermacher's definition does not plainly say that this technology should also set up rules for the demarcation and construction of the sciences, whereas this aim, on the other hand, includes the aim of scientific knowledge. Excellent thoughts towards the circumscription of our discipline are to be found in Bolzano's *Wissenschaftslehre*, but rather in his preliminary critical searchings than in the definition he himself espouses. This last sounds oddly enough: the theory of science (or logic) is 'the science which shows us how to present the sciences in convenient textbooks'.[2]

Chapter 2

Theoretical disciplines as the foundation of normative disciplines

§14 The concept of a normative science. The basic standard or principle that gives it unity

We begin by concentrating on a proposition that is of decisive importance for our further investigation: that every normative and likewise every practical discipline rests on one or more theoretical disciplines, inasmuch as its rules must have a theoretical content separable from the notion of normativity (of the 'shall' or 'should'), whose scientific investigation is the duty of these theoretical disciplines.

To clear up this point, let us first discuss the concept of a normative science in its relation to that of a theoretical science. The laws of the former tell us (it is usually held) what shall or should be, though perhaps, under the actual circumstances, it neither is nor can be. The laws of the latter, contrariwise, merely tell us what is. We must now ask what is meant by such a 'shall be' or 'should be' as opposed to what is.

The original sense of 'shall' or 'should', which relates to a certain wish or will, a certain demand or command, is plainly too narrow, e.g. You shall listen to me, *X* shall come to me. As we speak in a wider sense of a demand, where there is no one who demands, and perhaps no one on whom demand is made, so we frequently speak of a 'shall' or a 'should' which is independent of anyone's wishing or willing. If we say 'A soldier should be brave', this does not mean that we or anyone else are wishing or willing, commanding or requiring this. One might rather suppose that a corresponding wishing and requiring would be generally justified, i.e. in relation to every soldier, though even this is not quite right, since it is surely not necessary that we should here be really evaluating a wish or a demand. 'A soldier should be brave' rather means that only a brave soldier is a 'good' soldier, which implies (since the predicates 'good' and 'bad' divide up the extension of the concept 'soldier') that a soldier who is not brave is a 'bad' soldier. *Since* this value-judgement holds, everyone is entitled to demand of a soldier that he should be brave, the same ground ensures that it is desirable, praiseworthy etc., that he should be brave. The same holds in other instances. 'A man should practise neighbourly love', i.e. one who omits this is no longer a 'good' man, and therefore *eo ipso* is (in this respect) a 'bad' man. 'A drama should not break up into episodes' – otherwise it is not a 'good' drama, not a 'true' work of art. In all these cases we make our positive evaluation, the attribution of a positive value-predicate, depend on a condition to be fulfilled, whose non-fulfilment entails the corresponding negative predicate. We may in general, take as identical or at least as equivalent the forms 'An *A* should be *B*' and 'An *A* that is not *B* is a bad *A*', or 'Only an *A* which is a *B* is a good *A*'.

The term 'good' naturally functions in the widest sense of what is in any way valuable: in the concrete propositions ranged under our formula it is to be understood in the specific sense of the valuations it presupposes, e.g. as useful, beautiful, moral etc. There are as many ways of speaking of a 'should' as there are different species of valuations, as there are, in consequence, actual or presumed values.

Negative statements of what should not be are not to be taken as negations of the corresponding affirmative statements, as, too, in the ordinary sense, the denial of a demand does not amount to a prohibition. 'A soldier should not be cowardly' does not mean that it is false that a soldier should be cowardly, but that a cowardly soldier also is a bad one. The following forms are therefore equivalent: 'An *A* should not be *B*', and 'An *A* which is *B* is in general a bad *A*' or 'Only an *A* which is not *B* is a good *A*'.

That 'should' and 'should not' are mutually exclusive follows formally from their interpretations, and the same holds of the proposition that judgements regarding what should be entail no assertion regarding what correspondingly is.

The just clarified judgements of normative form are plainly not the only ones that one would allow to count as such, even if the word 'should' or 'shall' does not occur in their expression. It is inessential if, instead of saying '*A* should (or should not) be *B*' we also are able to say '*A* must (or may not) be *B*'. We touch more substance if we point to the two new formulae '*A* need not be *B*' and '*A* may be *B*', which are in contradictory opposition to the above forms. 'May not' is therefore the negation of 'should', or, what is the same, of 'must'; 'may' the negation of 'should not' or, what is the same, of 'may not', as can readily be seen from the interpreting value-judgements: 'An *A* need not be *B*' = 'An *A* that is not *B* is not therefore a bad *A*'; 'An *A* may be *B*' = 'An *A* that is *B* is not therefore a bad *A*'.

There are yet other propositions that must be reckoned with here, e.g. 'For an *A* to be a good *A* it suffices (or does not suffice) that it is *B*'. Whereas our former propositions are about certain *necessary* conditions for attributing or denying positive or negative value-predicates, our concern in the present proposition is with *sufficient* conditions. Other further propositions aim at stating what are at once necessary and sufficient conditions.

We have thus run through the essential forms of general normative propositions. To them of course correspond forms of particular and singular value-judgement which contribute nothing of importance to our analysis, and of which the latter at least do not count for our purposes. They have always a nearer or remoter relation to certain normative generalities: in abstract normative disciplines, they can only occur in relation to their governing generalities. Such disciplines are as such located beyond all individual existence, their generalities are 'purely conceptual', they have a lawlike character in the strict sense of the word 'law'.

We see from these analyses that each normative proposition presupposes a certain sort of valuation or approval through which the concept of a 'good' or 'bad' (a value or a disvalue) arises in connection with a certain class of objects: in conformity with this, objects divide into good and bad ones. To be able to pass the normative judgement 'A soldier should be brave', I must have some conception of a 'good' soldier, and this concept cannot be founded on an arbitrary nominal definition, but on a general valuation, which permits us to value soldiers as good or bad according to these or those properties. Whether or not this valuation is in any sense 'objectively valid', whether we can draw any distinction between the subjectively and objectively 'good', does not enter into our determination of the sense of should-propositions. It is sufficient that something is held valuable, that an *intention* is effected having the content that something is valuable or good.

If, conversely, a pair of value-predicates has been laid down for an appropriate class, following upon a certain general valuation, then the possibility of normative judgements is given: all forms of normative proposition have then definite sense. Every constitutive property B of the 'good' A yields, e.g. a proposition of the form 'An A should be B', every property incompatible with B, a proposition 'An A may not (should not) be B' etc.

Finally, as regards the *concept of the normative judgement* we can, following our analysis, describe it as follows: In relation to a general underlying valuation, and the content of the corresponding pair of value-predicates determined by it, every proposition is said to be 'normative' that states a necessary, or a sufficient, or a necessary and sufficient condition for having such a predicate. If we have once drawn a distinction between 'good' and 'bad' in our valuations in a particular sense, and so in a particular sphere, we are naturally concerned to decide the circumstances, the inner or outer properties that are or are not guarantees that a thing is good or bad in this sense: what properties may not be lacking if an object from that sphere is to be accorded the value of 'good'.

Where we speak of good and bad, we also usually make comparative valuational distinctions between *better* and best or between *worse* and worst. If pleasure is our good, then the more intense, and again the more enduring, pleasure is better. If knowledge counts as our good, not every piece of knowledge will therefore count as 'equally good'. We value the knowledge of laws more highly than the knowledge of singular facts: the knowledge of more general laws, e.g. 'Every equation of the nth degree has n roots', more highly than the knowledge of the special laws that fall under them – 'Every equation of the fourth degree has four roots'. There are therefore normative questions relating to relative value-predicates just as there are in the case of absolute value-predicates. If the constitutive content of what is to be esteemed good or bad is fixed, one must ask what, in comparative valuation, will count constitutively as better or worse, and, further, what are the nearer and the more remote, the necessary and the sufficient conditions for the relative predicates, laying down the content of the better and worse, and ultimately of the relatively best. The constitutive contents of positive and relative value-predicates are, so to say, the metric units in terms of which objects of the relevant sphere are measured.

The sum total of these norms plainly forms a closed group, determined by our fundamental valuation. The normative proposition which demands generally of the objects of a sphere that they should measure up to the constitutive features of the positive value-predicate to the greatest extent possible, has a central place in each group of mutually coherent norms, and can be called their *basic norm*. This role is, e.g., played by the categorical imperative in the group of normative propositions which make up Kant's Ethics, as by the principle of the 'greatest possible happiness of the greatest possible number' in the Ethics of the Utilitarians.

The basic norm is the correlate of the definition of 'good' and 'bad' in the sense in question. It tells us on what basic standard or basic value all normativization must be conducted, and does not therefore represent a normative proposition in the strict sense. The relationship of the basic norm to what are, properly speaking, normative propositions, is like the relation between so-called definitions of the number-series and the arithmetical theorems about the relations of numbers which are always referred back to these. The basic norm could also be called a 'definition' of the standard conception of good – e.g. of the morally good – but this would mean departing from the ordinary logical concept of definition.

If, in relation to such a 'definition', or fundamental and universal valuation, we make it our aim to conduct scientific researches into a sum total of mutually relevant normative propositions, we come upon the Idea of a Normative Discipline. Each such discipline is therefore unambiguously characterized by its basic norm, or by the definition of what shall count as 'good' in such a discipline. If, e.g. the production, maintenance, increase and intensification of pleasure counts as our good, we shall ask by what objects, or in what subjective and objective circumstances, pleasure is excited. We shall enquire generally into the necessary and sufficient conditions for the emergence, maintenance, increase etc., of pleasure. These questions taken as targets for our scientific discipline yield a *hedonic*: this hedonic is normative ethics in the sense of the hedonists. The valuation directed to the arousal of pleasure yields the basic norm which determines the unity of the discipline and distinguishes it from every other normative discipline. Every normative discipline therefore has its own basic norm which is in each case its unifying principle. *Theoretical disciplines* do not have this central reference of all researches to a fundamental valuation as the source of a dominant normative interest. The unity of their researches, and the coordination of what they know, is determined exclusively by a theoretical interest directed to investigating matters that really belong together theoretically, in virtue of the inner laws of things, and which must therefore be investigated together in their mutual coherence.

§15 Normative disciplines and technologies

A normative interest is naturally dominant in the case of *real* (*realen*) objects, as the objects of *practical* valuations. Hence the undeniable tendency to identify the notion of a normative discipline with that of a practical discipline or a *technology*. It is easy to see, however, that such an identification cannot be sustained. Schopenhauer, e.g., who is led by his doctrine of inborn character to reject in principle all practical moralizing, has an ethics in the sense of a normative science, which he himself works out. For he does not at all abandon distinctions in moral value. A technology represents a particular case of a normative discipline which arises when the basic norm consists in achieving a universal practical aim. Plainly, therefore, every technology includes in itself an entire normative discipline, which is not itself a practical discipline. For its task presupposes that, altogether apart from everything relating to practical attainment, the narrower task of fixing norms has first been carried out, norms by which we can assess the adequacy to the general notion of the end to be achieved, or the possession of the properties characteristic of the class of values in question. Every normative discipline, conversely, whose fundamental valuation is transformed into a corresponding teleological prescription, widens out into a technology.

§16 Theoretical disciplines as the foundation of normative disciplines

It is now easy to see that each normative, and, *a fortiori*, each practical discipline, presupposes one or more theoretical disciplines as its foundations, in the sense, namely, that it must have a theoretical content free from all normativity, which as such has its natural location in certain theoretical sciences, whether these are already marked off or yet to be constituted.

The basic norm (or basic value, or ultimate end) determines, we saw, the unity of the discipline: it also is what imports the thought of normativity into all its normative propositions. But alongside of this general thought of measurement in terms of a basic norm, these propositions have their own theoretical content, which differs from one case to another. Each expresses the thought of a measuring relation between norm and what it is a norm for, but this relation is itself objectively characterized – if we abstract from valuational interest – as a relation between condition and conditioned, which relation is set down as existent or non-existent in the relevant normative propositions. Every normative proposition of, e.g., the form 'An *A* should be *B*' implies the theoretical proposition 'Only an *A* which is *B* has the properties *C*', in which '*C*' serves to indicate the constitutive content of the standard-setting predicate 'good' (e.g. pleasure, knowledge, whatever, in short, is marked down as good by the valuation fundamental to our given sphere). The new proposition is purely theoretical: it contains no trace of the thought of normativity. If, conversely, a proposition of the latter form is true, and thereupon a novel valuation of a *C* as such emerges, and makes a normative relation to the proposition seem requisite, the theoretical proposition assumes the normative form 'Only an *A* which is *B* is a good *A*', i.e. 'An *A* should be *B*'. Normative propositions can therefore make an appearance even in theoretical contexts: our theoretical interest in such contexts attaches value to the being of a state of affairs of a sort – to the equilateral form, e.g., of a triangle about to be determined – and then assesses other states of affairs, e.g. one of equiangularity, in relation to this: If the triangle is *to be* equilateral, it must be equiangular. Such a modification is, however, merely passing and secondary in theoretical sciences, since our last intention is here directed to the theoretical coherence of the things themselves. Enduring results are not therefore stated in normative form, but in the forms of this objective coherence, in the form, that is, of a general proposition.

It is now clear that the theoretical relations which our discussion has shown to lie hidden in the propositions of normative sciences, must have their logical place in certain theoretical sciences. If the normative science is to deserve its name, if it is to do scientific work on the relations of the facts to be normatively considered to their basic norms, it must study the content of the theoretical nucleus of these relations, and this means entering the spheres of the relevant theoretical sciences. In other words: Every normative discipline demands that we know certain non-normative truths: these it takes from certain theoretical sciences, or gets by applying propositions so taken to the constellation of cases determined by its normative interest. This naturally holds, likewise, in the more special case of a technology, and plainly to a greater extent. The theoretical knowledge is there added which will provide a basis for a fruitful realization of ends and means.

One point should be noted in the interest of what follows. Naturally these theoretical sciences may share in very different degrees in the scientific foundation and elaboration of the normative discipline in question. Their significance for it can also be greater or less. It may become plain that, to satisfy the interests of a normative discipline, the knowledge of certain sorts of theoretical connection has a prime urgency, and that the development and bringing closer of the theoretical field of knowledge to which they belong therefore plays a decisive part in making such a normative discipline possible. In building up such a discipline, it may be that certain sorts of theoretical knowledge play a useful and perhaps very weighty role, but none the less are of secondary significance, since their removal would only narrow, but not wholly destroy, the field of the discipline. One may think, e.g., of the relation between merely normative and practical ethics (see above, §15). All the propositions which have to do with making practical realization possible, do not effect the sphere of the pure norms of ethical valuation. If these norms, or the theoretical knowledge underlying them, were to fall away, ethics would vanish altogether. If the former propositions were to drop out, there would be no possibility of ethical practice (or no possibility of a technology of ethical conduct).

It is in relation to such distinctions that talk of the *essential* foundations of a normative science must be understood. We mean thereby the theoretical sciences that are absolutely essential to its construction, perhaps also the relevant groups of theoretical propositions which are of decisive importance in making the normative discipline possible.

Chapter 3

Psychologism, its arguments and its attitude to the usual counter-arguments

§17 The disputed question as to whether the essential theoretical foundations of normative logic lie in psychology

If we now apply the general results arrived at in the last chapter to logic as a normative discipline, a first, very weighty question arises: Which theoretical sciences provide the essential foundations of the theory of science? And to this we forthwith add the further question: Is it correct that the theoretical truths we find dealt with in the framework of traditional and modern logic, and above all those belonging to its essential foundations, have their theoretical place in the sciences that have been already marked off and independently developed?

Here we encounter the disputed question as to the relation between psychology and logic, since one dominant tendency of our time has a ready answer to the questions raised: The essential theoretical foundations of logic lie in psychology, in whose field those propositions belong – as far as their theoretical content is concerned – which give logic its characteristic pattern. Logic is related to psychology just as any branch of chemical technology is related to chemistry, as land-surveying is to geometry etc. This tendency sees no need to mark off a new theoretical discipline, and, in particular, not one that would deserve the name of logic in a narrower and more pointed sense. Often people talk as if psychology provided the sole, sufficient, theoretical foundation for logical technology. So we read in Mill's polemic against Hamilton: 'Logic is not a science separate from and coordinate with psychology. To the extent that it is a science at all, it is a part or branch of psychology, distinguished from it on the one hand as the part is from the whole, and on the other hand as the art is from the science. It owes all its theoretical foundations to psychology, and includes as much of that science as is necessary to establish the rules of the art' (*An Examination of Sir William Hamilton's Philosophy*, p. 461). According to Lipps it even seems that logic is to be ranked as a mere constituent of psychology for he says: 'The fact that logic is a specific discipline of psychology distinguishes them satisfactorily from one another' (Lipps, *Grundzüge der Logik* (1893), §3).

§18 The line of proof of the psychologistic thinkers[1]

If we ask for the justification of such views, a most plausible line of argument is offered, which seems to cut off all further dispute *ab initio*. However one may define logic as a technology – as a technology of thinking, judging, inferring, knowing, proving, of the courses followed by the understanding in the pursuit of truth, in the evaluation of grounds of proof etc. – we find invariably that mental activities or products are the objects of practical regulation. And just as, in general, the artificial working over of a material presupposes the knowledge of its properties, so this will be the case here too, where we are specially concerned with psychological material. The scientific investigation of the rules according to which this stuff should be worked over, naturally leads back to the scientific investigation of these properties. Psychology therefore provides the theoretical basis for constructing a logical technology, and, more particularly, the psychology of cognition.[2]

Any glance at the contents of logical literature will confirm this. What is being talked of throughout? Concepts, judgements, syllogisms, deductions, inductions, definitions, classifications etc. – all psychology, except that they are selected and arranged from normative and practical points of view. Draw the bounds of pure logic as tightly as one likes, it will not be possible to keep out what is psychological. This is implicit in the concepts constitutive for logical laws: truth and falsehood, affirmation and negation, universality and particularity, ground and consequent etc.

§19 The usual arguments of the opposition and the psychologistic rejoinder

Remarkably enough, the opposition believes that it can base a sharp separation of the two disciplines on precisely the normative character of logic. Psychology, it is said, deals with thinking as it is, logic with thinking as it should be. The former has to do with the natural laws, the latter with the normative laws of thinking. It reads in this sense in Jäsche's version of Kant's Lectures on Logic: 'Some logicians presuppose psychological principles for logic, but to introduce such principles into logic, is as absurd as to derive morality from Life. If we take principles from psychology, i.e. from observations of our understanding, we shall only see how thought proceeds, and what happens under manifold subjective hindrances and conditions. Those would only lead to a knowledge of merely *contingent* laws. Logic does not however ask after *contingent*, but after *necessary* laws – not how we think but how we ought to think. The rules of logic must therefore be taken, not from the *contingent*, but from the *necessary* use of reason, which one finds in oneself apart from all psychology. In logic we do not wish to know what the understanding is like and how it thinks, nor how it has hitherto proceeded in its thinking, but how it ought to proceed in its thinking.

It should teach us the correct use of the understanding, the use in which it is consistent with itself' (Introduction, I. Concept of Logic. Kant's *Werke*, ed. Hartenstein, 1867, VIII, p. 14). Herbart takes up a similar position when he objects to the logic of his time and 'the would be psychological stories about understanding and reason with which it starts', by saying that this is as badly in error as a moral theory which tried to begin with the natural history of human tendencies, urges and weaknesses, and by pointing to the normative character of logic as of ethics (Herbart, *Psychologie als Wissenschaft*, II, §119, original ed. II, p. 173).

Such arguments do not dismay the psychologistic logicians. They answer: A necessary use of the understanding is none the less a use of the understanding, and belongs, with the understanding itself, to psychology. Thinking as it should be, is merely a special case of thinking as it is. Psychology must certainly investigate the natural laws of thinking, the laws which hold for all judgements whatever, whether correct or false. It would, however, be absurd to interpret this proposition as if such laws only were psychological as applied with the most embracing generality to *all* judgements whatever, whereas special laws of judgement, like the laws of correct judgement, were shut out from its purview. (Cf., e.g. Mill, *An Examination*, p. 459 f.) Or does one hold a different opinion? Can one deny that the normative laws of thinking have the character of such special laws? This also will not do. Normative laws of thought, it is said, only try to say how one must proceed *provided* one wants to think *correctly*. 'We think correctly, in the material sense, when we think of things as they are. But for us to say, certainly and indubitably, that things are like this or like that, means that the nature of our mind prevents us from thinking of them otherwise. For one need not repeat what has been so often uttered, that one can obviously not think of a thing as it is, without regard to the way in which one must think of it, nor can one make of it so isolated an object of knowledge. The man, therefore, who compares his thought of things with the things themselves can in fact only measure his contingent thinking, influenced by custom, tradition, inclination and aversion, against a thinking that is free from such influences, and that heeds no voice but that of its own inherent lawfulness.'

'The rules, therefore, on which one must proceed in order to think rightly are merely rules on which one must proceed in order to think as the nature of thought, its specific lawfulness, demands. They are, in short, identical with the natural laws of thinking itself. Logic is a physics of thinking or it is nothing at all.' (Lipps, 'Die Aufgabe der Erkenntnistheorie', *Philos. Monatshefte*, XVI (1880), p. 530 f.)

It may perhaps be said from the antipsychologistic side:[3] Of course the various kinds of presentations, judgements, syllogisms etc., also have a place in psychology as mental phenomena and dispositions, but psychology has a different task in regard to them than logic. Both investigate the laws of these activities, but 'law' means something quite different in the two cases.

The task of psychology is to investigate the laws governing the real connections of mental events with one another, as well as with related mental dispositions and corresponding events in the bodily organism. 'Law' here means a comprehensive formula covering coexistent and successive connections that are without exception and necessary. Such connections are causal. The task of logic is quite different. It does not enquire into the causal origins or consequences of intellectual activities, but into their truth-content: it enquires what such activities *should* be like, or how they *should* proceed, in order that the resultant judgements should be true. Correct judgements and false ones, evident ones and blind ones, come and go according to natural laws, they have causal antecedents and consequences like all mental phenomena. Such natural connections do not, however, interest the logician; he looks rather for ideal connections that he does not always find realized, in fact only exceptionally finds realized in the actual course of thoughts. He aims not at a physics, but an ethics of thinking. Sigwart therefore rightly stresses the point that, in the psychological treatment of thought, 'the opposition of true and false has as little part to play as the opposition of good or bad in human conduct is a psychological matter'.[4]

We cannot be content – such will be the psychologistic rejoinder – with such half-truths. The task of logic is of course quite different from that of psychology: who would deny it? It is a technology of knowledge, but how could such a technology ignore questions of causal connection, how could it look for ideal connections without studying natural ones? 'As if every "ought" did not rest on an "is", every ethics did not also have to show itself a physics.' (Lipps, 'Die Aufgabe der Erkenntnistheorie', *op. cit.* p. 529.) 'A question as to what should be done always reduces to a question as to what must be done if a definite goal is to be reached, and this question in its turn is equivalent to a question as to how this goal is *in fact reached*' (Lipps, *Grundzüge der Logik*, §1). That psychology, as distinct from logic, does not deal with the opposition of true and false 'does not mean that psychology treats these different mental conditions on a like footing, but that it renders both intelligible in a like manner' (Lipps, *op. cit.* §3, p. 2). Theoretically regarded, Logic therefore is related to psychology as a part to a whole. Its main aim is, in particular, to set up propositions of the form: Our intellectual activities must, either generally, or in specifically characterized circumstances, have such and such a form, such and such an arrangement, such and such combinations and no others, if the resultant judgements are to have the character of evidence, are to achieve knowledge in the pointed sense of the word. Here we have an obvious causal relation. The psychological character of evidence is a causal consequence of certain antecedents. What sort of antecedents? This is just what we have to explore.[5]

The following often repeated argument is no more successful in shaking the psychologistic ranks: Logic, it is said, can as little rest on psychology as on any other science; since each science is only a science in virtue of its harmony with logical rules, it presupposes the validity of these rules. It would therefore be circular to try to give logic a first foundation in psychology.[6]

The opposition will reply: That this argument cannot be right, is shown by the fact that it would prove the impossibility of all logic. Since logic itself must proceed logically, it would itself commit the same circle, would itself have to establish the validity of rules that it presupposes.

Let us, however, consider more closely what such a circle could consist in. Could it mean that psychology presupposes the validity of logical laws? Here one must notice the equivocation in the notion of 'presupposing'. That a science presupposes the validity of certain rules may mean that they serve as premises in its proofs: it may also mean that they are rules in accordance with which the science must proceed in order to be a science at all. Both are confounded in our argument for which reasoning *according* to logical rules, and reasoning *from* logical rules, count as identical. There would only be a circle if the reasoning were *from* such rules. But, as many an artist creates beautiful works without the slightest knowledge of aesthetics, so an investigation may construct proofs without ever having recourse to logic. Logical laws cannot therefore have been premises in such proofs. And what is true of single proofs is likewise true of whole sciences.

§20 A gap in the psychologistic line of proof

In these and similar arguments the anti-psychologistic party seem undoubtedly to have got the worst of it. Many think the battle quite at an end, they regard the rejoinders of the psychologistic party as completely victorious. One thing only might arouse our philosophical wonder, that there was and is such a battle at all, that the same arguments have repeatedly been adduced while their refutations have not been acknowledged as cogent. If everything really were so plain and clear as the psychologistic trend assures us, the matter would not be readily understandable, since there are unprejudiced, serious and penetrating thinkers on the opposite side as well. Is this not again a case where the truth lies in the middle? Has each of the parties not recognized a valid portion of the truth, and only shown incapacity for its sharp conceptual circumscription, and not even seen that they only had part of the whole? Is there not perhaps an unresolved residuum in the arguments of the anti-psychologists – despite much unclearness and error in detail which has made refutation easy; are they not informed by a true power, which always re-emerges in unbiased discussion? I for my part would answer 'Yes'. It seems to me that the greater weight of truth lies on the anti-psychologistic side, but that its key-thoughts have not been properly worked out, and are blemished by many mistakes.

Let us go back to the question we raised above regarding the essential foundations of normative logic. Have the arguments of psychologistic thinkers really settled this? Here a weak point at once appears. The argument only proves one thing, that psychology *helps* in the foundation of logic, not that it has the only or the main part in this, not that it provides logic's *essential foundation* in the sense above defined (§16). The possibility remains open that another science contributes to its foundation, perhaps in a much more important fashion. Here may be the place for the 'pure logic' which on the other party's view, has an existence independent of all psychology, and is a naturally bounded, internally closed-off science. We readily grant that what Kantians and Herbartians have produced under this rubric does not quite accord with the character that our suggested supposition would give it. For they always talk of normative laws of thinking and particularly of concept-formation, judgement-framing etc. Proof enough, one might say, that their subject-matter is neither theoretical nor wholly unpsychological. But this objection would lose weight if closer investigation confirmed the surmise suggested to us above in §13 (excised from this edition), that these schools were unlucky in defining and building up the intended discipline, yet none the less approached it closely, in so far as they discerned an abundance of interconnected theoretical truths in traditional logic, which did not fit into psychology, nor into any other separate science, and so permitted one to divine the existence of a peculiar realm of truth. And if these were the truths to which all logical regulation in the last resort related, truths mainly to be thought of when 'logical truths' were in question, one could readily come to see in them what was essential to the whole of logic, and to give the name of 'pure logic' to their theoretical unity. That this hits off the true state of things I hope actually to prove.

Chapter 4

Empiricistic consequences of psychologism

§22 The laws of thought as supposed laws of nature which operate in isolation as causes of rational thought

Here is also the place to take up an attitude towards a widely held conception of logical law, which characterizes correct thought by its conformity with certain laws of thought (however we may formulate them), but is disposed at the same time to interpret such conformity in the following psychologistic manner: The laws of thought count as natural laws characterizing the peculiarity of our mind *qua* thinking, and the essence of the conformity, as definitory of correct thinking, lies in the *pure* operation of these laws, their non-disturbance by alien mental influences (such as custom, inclination, tradition). (Cf. the citations above in §19 from Lipps' article on the task of epistemology.)

We need only instance one of the grave consequences of this doctrine. Laws of thought, as causal laws governing acts of knowledge in their mental interweaving, could only be stated in the form of probabilities. On this basis, no assertion could be *certainly* judged correct, since probabilities, taken as the standard of all certainty, must impress a merely probabilistic stamp on all knowledge. We should stand confronted by the most extreme probabilism. Even the assertion that all knowledge was merely probable would itself only hold probably: this would hold of this latter assertion, and so on *in infinitum*. Since each successive step reduces the probability level of the previous one a bit, we should become gravely concerned about the worth of all knowledge. One may hope, however, that, with some luck, the probability-levels of these infinite series may always have the character of a Cantorian 'fundamental series', of such a sort that the final limiting value or the probability of the knowledge to be judged is a real number > 0. Sceptical awkwardnesses would of course vanish if one looked on the laws of thought as matters of direct insight. But how should one have insight into causal laws?

Even if this difficulty were removed, we could still ask: Where on earth is the proof that the pure operation of these laws (or any other laws) would yield correct laws of thinking? Where are the descriptive and genetic analyses which entitle us to explain the phenomena of thought by two sorts of natural law, one exclusively determining such causal sequences as allow logical thought to emerge, whereas others help to determine alogical thought? Does the assessment of thoughts by logical laws amount to a proof of their causal origin in these same laws as laws of nature?

It seems that certain ready confusions have here opened the way to psychologistic errors. Logical laws have first been confused with the judgements, in the sense of acts of judgement, in which we may know them: the laws, as '*contents of judgement*' have been confused with the *judgements themselves*. The latter are real events, having causes and effects. Judgements whose contents are laws are, in particular, frequently operative as *thought-motives*, directing the course of our thought-experience, as those contents, the laws of thinking, prescribe. In such cases the real order and connection of our thought-experiences conforms to that which we think generally in our governing knowledge of the law: it is a concrete individual instance of that general law. If, however, the law is confused with the judgement or knowledge of the law, the ideal with the real, the law appears as a *governing power* in our train of thought. With understandable ease a second confusion is added to the first: we confuse a law as a *term in causation with a law as the rule of causation*. In other fields, too, we familiarly employ mythic talk of natural laws as presiding powers in natural events – as if the rules of causal connection could themselves once more significantly function as causes, i.e. as terms in just such connections. The serious confusion of things so essentially dissimilar has plainly been favoured in the case before us by the previous confusion of a law with the knowledge of a law. Logical laws already appeared as motive powers in thinking. They presided causally, it was imagined, over the course of our thoughts – they were accordingly causal laws of thinking. They expressed how we must think in consequence of the nature of *our* mind, they characterized the human mind as a thinking mind in the pointed sense. If at times we think otherwise than these laws require, we are not, properly speaking, 'thinking' at all, we are not judging as the natural laws of thinking, or the *nature of our mind qua* thinking, requires, but as other laws determine (once more causally). We are following the disturbing leads of custom, passion etc.

Other motives of course may have suggested the same conception. The empirical fact that persons performing normally in a given sphere, e.g. scientists in their fields, usually judge in a logically correct manner, seems to demand, as a natural explanation, that the logical laws by means of which the correctness of thinking is assessed, also determine the course of thinking, in the manner of causal laws, while isolated deviations from the norm may readily be put to the account of the troubling influences stemming from other psychological sources.

Against this the following argument should suffice. Let us imagine an ideal person, in whom *all* thinking proceeds as logical laws require. Naturally the fact that this occurs must have its explanatory ground in certain psychological laws, which govern the course of the mental experiences of this being, starting from certain initial 'collocations'. I now ask: Would the natural laws and the logical laws in this assumed situation be one and the same? Obviously the answer is 'No'. Causal laws, according to which thought must proceed in a manner which the ideal norms of logic might justify, are by no means identical with those norms. If a being were so constituted as never to be able to frame contradictory judgements in a unified train of thought, as never to be able to perform inferences which defy the syllogistic moods, this would not mean that the law of contradiction, the *Modus Barbara* etc., were laws of nature explanatory of this being's constitution. The example of a computer makes the difference quite clear. The arrangement and connection of the figures which spring forth is regulated by natural laws which accord with the demands of the arithmetical propositions which fix their meanings. No one, however, who wants to give a physical explanation of the machine's procedures, will appeal to arithmetical instead of mechanical laws. The machine is no thought-machine, it understands neither itself nor the meaning of its performances. But our own thought-machine might very well function similarly, except that the real course of one kind of thought would always have to be recognized as correct by the insight brought forward in another. This latter thinking could be the product of the same or other thought-machines, but ideal evaluation and causal explanation would none the less remain disparate. The 'initial collocations' should also not be forgotten: indispensable in causal explanation, they are senseless for ideal evaluation.

The psychologistic logicians ignore the fundamental, essential, never-to-be-bridged gulf between ideal and real laws, between normative and causal regulation, between logical and real necessity, between logical and real grounds. No conceivable gradation could mediate between the ideal and the real. It is characteristic of the low state of logical insights in our time, that a thinker of Sigwart's stature should dare, in connection with the fiction of an intellectually ideal being like that discussed above, to maintain that, for such a being, 'logical necessity would also be a real necessity that engenders real thinking', or that he should make use of the concept of thought-compulsion to elucidate the notion of 'logical ground' (Sigwart, *Logik*, I, p. 259 f.). The same holds of Wundt when he sees in the law of sufficient reason the 'basic law of the dependence of our thought-acts on one another' (Wundt, *Logik*, I, p. 573). That one is really concerned in these connections with basic errors in logic will, one hopes, become a certainty, even to the prejudiced, in the course of further investigations.

§23 A third consequence of psychologism, and its refutation

A third consequence (see §21 above (excised from this edition)) for the psychologistic logician is that, if the laws of logic have their epistemological source in psychological matter of fact, if, e.g., as our opponents generally say, they are normative transformations of such facts, they must themselves be psychological in content, both by being laws for mental states, and also by presupposing or implying the existence of such states. This is palpably false. No logical law implies a 'matter of fact', not even the existence of presentations or judgements or other phenomena of knowledge. No logical law, properly understood, is a law for the facticities of mental life, and so not a law for presentations (as experiences), nor for judgements (experiences of judging), nor for our other mental experiences.

Most psychologistic thinkers are too deeply enthralled by their general prejudice even to try to verify it in the case of the definitely acknowledged logical laws. If such laws *must* be psychological, why try to show in detail that they really are so? No one sees that a consistent psychologism would force one to interpret logical laws in a manner quite alien to their true sense. One fails to see that these laws, naturally understood, presuppose nothing mental, no facts of psychic life, whether in their establishment or their content. They do so no more than the laws of pure mathematics do so.

If psychologism were on the right track, one should, in treating of syllogisms, expect only rules of the following type: It is an empirical fact that, in circumstances *X*, conclusions of the form *C*, stamped with apodeictically necessary consequence, attend upon premisses of the form *P*. To syllogize 'correctly', i.e. to achieve judgements of this distinctive stamp through syllogizing, one must proceed in this manner, one must see that the circumstances really are *X*, and the premisses *P*. Mental matters of fact would then be the matters regulated, the existence of such matters would be presupposed in the grounding of such laws, and would be part of their content. But no single syllogistic rule is of such a type. What, e.g., does the mood *Barbara* tell us? Only this: that, if in the case of any class-terms *A*, *B*, *C* all *A*'s are *B*'s and all *B*'s *C*'s, then all *A*'s will be *C*'s. The *Modus Ponens*, likewise, written out in full, reads: It is a valid law for any propositions *P*, *Q*, that if *P* is the case, and it also is the case that if *P* is the case *Q* is so, then *Q* also is the case. These and all similar laws are as little psychological as they are empirical. They were of course set up by traditional logic to serve as norms for our judging activities. But do they implicitly say anything about a single actual judgement, or about any other mental phenomenon? If anyone thinks they do let him prove it. Whatever a proposition implicitly asserts can be inferred from it in a valid syllogism. But what forms of syllogism permit us to deduce facts from a pure law?

It is irrelevant to object that talk of logical laws never could have arisen had we not actually experienced presentations and judgements, and abstracted the relevant, basic logical concepts from them, or that, wherever we understand and assert such laws, the existence of presentations and judgements is implied, and can therefore be inferred. We need hardly observe that this does not follow from our law, but from the fact that we understand and assert such a law, and that a like consequence could be inferred from every assertion. One ought not, further, to confuse the psychological presuppositions or components of the *assertion* of a law, with the logical 'moments' of its *content*.

'Empirical laws' have, *eo ipso*, a factual content. Not being true laws, they merely say, roughly speaking, that certain coexistences or successions obtain generally in certain circumstances, or may be expected, with varying probability, in varying circumstances. But even the strict laws of the natural sciences are not without factual content. They do not merely concern facts, but also imply their existence.

We must, however, be more precise. Exact laws, as normally formulated, are pure laws: they exclude all factual content. But, if we consider the proofs to which they owe their scientific justification, it is at once clear that we cannot justify them as pure laws, in their normal formulation. The law of gravitation, as formulated in astronomy, has never really been proved. What has been proved is a proposition of the form: Our knowledge up to date serves to found a probability of the highest theoretical dignity to the effect that, in so far as experience yields to the instruments on hand, either Newton's law, or one of the endlessly many conceivable mathematical laws whose differences from Newton's law lie within the limits of unavoidable experimental error is true. This truth carries its big load of factual content, and is not at all a law in the strict sense of the word. It also plainly includes several vaguely delimited concepts.

All laws of fact in the exact sciences are accordingly genuine laws, but, epistemologically considered, no more than idealizing fictions with a *fundamentum in re*. They fulfil the task of rendering those theoretical sciences possible, which bring the ideal of science as near as may be to actuality, and so realize, to the extent that this can be within the unsurmountable limits of human knowledge, the ideal of explanatory theory, of law-governed unity, the highest theoretical aim of all scientific research into facts. Instead of the absolute knowledge that is denied us, we use our insight on individual and general facts of experience, and from these first work out those apodeictic probabilities (so to speak) in which all attainable knowledge of the real is comprehended. We then reduce these probabilities to certain exact thoughts having the genuine form of laws, and so succeed in building up formally perfect systems of explanatory theory. Such systems as theoretical mechanics, theoretical acoustics, theoretical optics, theoretical astronomy etc., really only hold as ideal possibilities with a *fundamentum in re*; they do not exclude countless other possibilities, but even include these within limits. This, however, concerns us no further, nor are we concerned to discuss the practical functions in knowledge of these ideal theories, their feats of successfully predicting future facts or reconstructing past ones, and their technical feats of enabling us to master nature practically. We return to the case we were considering.

If, as we have shown, pure law remains a mere ideal in the realm of factual knowledge, it is realized in the realm of 'purely conceptual' knowledge. In this sphere our purely logical laws belong, as well as the laws of *mathesis pura*. Their origin, or, rather, their justifying proof, is not an inductive one, and so they are free from that existential content which attaches to all probabilities as such, even to such as are the highest and most valuable. What they say has entire validity: they themselves in their absolute exactness are evident and proven, and not, in their stead, certain other assertions of probability of obviously vague constitution. The law we have is not one of countless theoretical possibilities within a certain factually delimited sphere. It is the single, sole truth which excludes all other possibilities and which, being established by *insight*, is kept pure from fact in its content and mode of proof.

The above considerations show how intimately the two halves of the psychologistic case hang together: that logical laws do not merely entail existential assertions of mental facts, but are also laws *for* such facts. We have just refuted the first half of their case. But the following argument suggests that our refutation also covers the second half. For just as each law established empirically and inductively from singular facts, is a law *for* such facts, so, conversely, each law *for* facts is a law established empirically and inductively, and from such a law, as has been shown, assertions with existential content are inseparable.

We ought of course to exclude from factual laws such general assertions as merely apply pure conceptual propositions – which state universally valid relations on a basis of pure concepts – to matters of fact. If 3 > 2, then the three books on this table also exceed the two books in this cupboard, and so for any things whatever. But our pure proposition of number does not refer to things, but to numbers in their pure generality – it is *the* number 3 that is greater than *the* number 2 – and it applies not merely to individual, but to 'general' objects, e.g. to species of colour or sound, to types of geometrical figure and to suchlike timeless generalities.

If all this is admitted, it is of course impossible to regard logical laws (considered in their purity) as the laws either of mental activities or of mental products.

§24 Continuation

Many would perhaps try to evade our conclusion by objecting: Not every law for facts has an empirico-inductive origin. We should rather draw a distinction. All knowledge of law rests on experience, but not all such knowledge arises out of experience inductively, by the well-known logical process which goes from singular facts, or empirical generalities of lower level, to general laws. The laws of logic are, in particular, empirical, but not inductive laws. The basic notions of logic are abstracted from psychological experience together with the purely conceptual relations given with them. What we find true in the individual case, we recognize at a glance to be true universally, since based upon abstracted contents. Experience accordingly yields an immediate awareness of the law-governed character of our mind.

And since we have no need of induction, our conclusion is likewise free from inductive imperfection: it has no mere character of probability, but one of apodeictic certainty. It is not vague, but precise in sense, it in no way includes assertions having existential content.

What is here objected will not, however, do. Undoubtedly our knowledge of logical laws, considered as an act of mind, presupposes an experience of individuals, has its basis in concrete intuition. But one should not confuse the *psychological* 'presuppositions' and 'bases' of the *knowledge* of a law, with the *logical* presuppositions, the grounds and premisses, of that *law*: we should also, therefore, not confuse psychological dependence (e.g. dependence of origin) with logical demonstration and justification. The latter conforms to an insight into the objective relation of ground and consequence, whereas the former relates to mental links of coexistence and succession. No one can seriously hold that the concrete singular cases before us, on which our insight into a law is 'grounded', really function as logical grounds or premisses, as if the mere existence of such singulars entailed the universality of law. Our intuitive grasp of the law may require two psychological steps: one glance at the singulars of intuition, and a related insight into law. Logically, however, only one step is required. The content of our insight is not inferred from singulars.

All knowledge 'begins with experience', but it does not therefore 'arise' from experience. What we assert is that each law for facts arises *from* experience, which means that it can only be inductively based on individual experiences. If there are laws known by insight, these cannot (immediately) be laws for facts. Where in the past immediate self-evidence has been claimed for factual laws, it is clear that men have been confusing genuine factual laws, i.e. laws of coexistence and succession, with ideal laws to which a reference to definite times is alien, or that they have been confusing the lively persuasive force of familiar empirical generalities, with the insight only found in the realm of pure concepts.

Should such an argument not seem decisive, it can none the less serve to strengthen other arguments. Another such argument will be here added.

Hardly anyone would deny that all laws of pure logic are of one and the same character. If we can show, in the case of some of them, that they cannot possibly be regarded as laws for facts, the same must hold for all of them. Among logical laws there are, however, some which concern truths, which have truths as their regular 'objects'. It is the case, e.g., that for every truth A, its contradictory opposite is no truth. It is the case, for each pair of truths A, B, that their conjunctions and disjunctions[1] are truths, and that if three truths A, B, C are so related that A is a ground for B, B for C, that A is also a ground for C. It is, however, absurd to treat laws which hold for truths as such, as laws for facts. No truth is a fact, i.e. something determined as to time. A truth can indeed have as its meaning that something is, that a state exists, that a change is going on etc. The truth itself is, however, raised above time: i.e. it makes no sense to attribute temporal being to it, nor to say that it arises or perishes. This absurdity is clearest in the case of the laws of truth themselves. If they were 'real' laws, they would be rules for the coexistence and succession of facts, i.e. of such facts as are truths, and to these facts, which they govern, they themselves as truths would belong. A law would therefore ascribe a 'coming and going' to certain facts called truths, among which, as one among others, the law would itself be found. The law would arise and perish in conformity with the law, a patent absurdity. The case is similar if we treat the law of truth as a law of coexistence, as temporally singular and yet fixing a general rule for each and every existence in time. Such absurdities[2] are unavoidable if the fundamental distinction between ideal and real objects, and the corresponding distinction between ideal and real laws, is disregarded or misunderstood. We shall see repeatedly how this distinction settles the disputes which divide psychologistic logic from pure logic.

Chapter 7

Psychologism as a sceptical relativism

§32 The ideal conditions for the possibility of a theory as such. The strict concept of scepticism

The worst objection that can be made to a theory, and particularly to a theory of logic, is that it goes against *the self-evident conditions for the possibility of a theory in general.* To set up a theory whose content is explicitly or implicitly at variance with the propositions on which the sense and the claim to validity of all theory rests, is not merely wrong, but basically mistaken.

There are two respects in which one can here talk of the self-evident 'conditions of the possibility' of any theory whatever. One can talk of these in a *subjective* respect. Here one's concern is with the *a priori* conditions upon which the possibility of immediate and mediate *knowledge*[1] depends, as also the possibility of rationally *justifying* any theory. The theory which validates knowledge is itself a piece of knowledge: its possibility depends on certain conditions, rooted, in purely conceptual fashion, in knowledge and its relation to the knowing subject. It is, e.g. part of the notion of knowledge, in the strict sense, that it is a judgement that does not merely claim to state truth, but is also certain of this claim's justification, and actually possesses the justification in question. If the judging person were never in a position to have direct personal experience and apprehension of his judgement's self-justifying character, if all his judgements lacked that inner evidence which distinguishes them from blind prejudices, and yields him luminous certainties, it would be impossible to provide a rational account and a foundation for knowledge, or to discourse on theory and science. A theory therefore violates the subjective conditions of its *own* possibility as a theory, when, following our example, it in no way prefers an inwardly evident judgement to a blind one. It thereby destroys the very thing that distinguishes it from an arbitrary, unwarranted assertion.

It is plain that, by the subjective conditions of possibility, we do not here mean real conditions rooted in the individual judging subject, or in the varied species of judging beings (e.g. of human beings), but ideal conditions whose roots lie in the form of subjectivity as such, and in its relation to knowledge. We shall distinguish them by speaking of *noetic* conditions.

In an *objective* respect, talk of the conditions for the possibility of any theory do not concern the theory as a subjective unity of items of knowledge, but theory as an objective unity of truths or propositions, bound together by relations of ground and consequent. The conditions here are all the *laws* whose foundation lies purely in the notion of theory, or more specifically, in the notions of truth, of proposition, of object, of property, of relation etc., the notions, i.e. which enter *essentially into the concept of theoretical unity*. To deny these laws amounts to an assertion that all such terms – theory, truth, object, property etc. – lack a *coherent sense*. A theory is self-destroying, in this logico-objective respect, if its content offends against the laws without which theory as such can have no rational, no coherent sense.

The logical offences of such a theory can lie in its *presuppositions*, in its forms of *theoretic connection*, or in the *thesis that it sets forth*. The violation of logical conditions is at its grossest when the *sense* of the theoretic thesis involves a rejection of those laws on which the rational possibility of any thesis, and the proof of any thesis, depend. The same holds of noetic conditions and of theories which violate them. We may distinguish (without attempting a classification) between false, nonsensical, logically and noetically absurd, and finally *sceptical theories*. The last cover all theories whose theses either plainly say, or analytically imply, that the logical or noetic conditions for the possibility of any theory are false.

The term 'scepticism' is thus connected with a clear concept and is clearly divided into logical and noetic scepticism. The concept of such scepticism applies to the ancient forms of scepticism with theses such as: There is no truth, no knowledge, no justification of knowledge etc. Our previous treatments have shown[2] that empiricism, whether moderate or extreme, is an instance of our pregnant concept of scepticism. That it is of the essence of a sceptical theory to be *nonsensical*, is at once plain from its definition.

§33 Scepticism in the metaphysical sense

The term 'scepticism' is commonly used with some vagueness. Ignoring its popular sense, we find that philosophical theories are called 'sceptical' if they try to limit human knowledge considerably and on principle, and especially if they remove from the sphere of possible knowledge wide fields of real being, or such especially precious sciences as metaphysics, natural science, or ethics as a rational discipline.

Among such inauthentic forms of scepticism there is one which is readily confused with the purely epistemic scepticism here defined, which would limit knowledge to mental existence, and would deny the existence or knowability of 'things in themselves'. Such theories are plainly *metaphysical*, they have no connection with scepticism proper, their thesis is free from logical and noetic *absurdity*, their claim to validity is a mere question of arguments and proofs. Confusions and genuinely sceptical modifications then only arise from the paralogistic influence of tempting ambiguities or of sceptical convictions elsewhere fostered. If, e.g., a metaphysical sceptic states his view in the form 'There is no *objective* knowledge' (i.e. no knowledge of things in themselves), or 'All knowledge is *subjective*' (i.e. all factual knowledge is merely the knowledge of facts of consciousness), there is a great temptation to yield to the ambiguity of the subject-object terminology, and to transform the original sense which suits our metaphysical standpoint into a noetic-sceptical sense. The proposition 'All knowledge is subjective' becomes the totally new assertion 'All knowledge as a conscious phenomenon is subject to the laws of human consciousness: the so-called forms and laws of knowledge are merely functional forms of consciousness, or laws governing such functional forms, i.e. psychological laws'. When metaphysical scepticism thus wrongly favours epistemological scepticism, the latter, contrariwise, if taken to be self-evident, seems to provide powerful arguments for the former. People reason, e.g.:

> Logical laws, as laws for our functions of knowing, lack 'real meaning'; we can at least never know if they agree with things in themselves. To assume a 'preformation-system' is wholly gratuitous. If the comparison of an item of knowledge with its object (needed to establish an *adaequatio rei et intellectus*) is excluded by the notion of the thing-in-itself, this applies also to the comparison of the subjective laws of our conscious functions with the objective being of things and their laws. If there are things in themselves, we can know nothing whatever about them.

Metaphysical questions do not concern us here. We have mentioned them only to have before us at an early stage, an instance of the confusion between metaphysical and logico-noetic scepticism.

§34 The concept of relativism and its specific forms

In order to criticize psychologism we have yet to discuss the concept of *subjectivism* or *relativism* which also is part of the above-mentioned metaphysical theory. One of its original forms is caught in the Protagorean formula: 'Man is the measure of all things', provided this last is interpreted as saying 'The individual man is the measure of all truth.' For each man that is true which seems to *him* true, one thing to one man and the opposite to another, if that is how he sees it. We can therefore also opt for the formula 'All truth (and knowledge) is relative – relative to the contingently judging subject'. If, however, instead of such a subject, we make some contingent *species* of judging beings the pivot of our relations, we achieve a new form of relativism. Man as *such* is then the measure of all human truth. Every judgement whose roots are to be found in what is *specific* to man, in the constitutive laws of man as species – is a true judgement, for us human beings. To the extent that such judgements belong to the form of common human subjectivity, the term 'subjectivism' is in place here too (in talk of the subject as the ultimate source of knowledge etc.). It is best to employ the term 'relativism', and to distinguish *individual* from *specific* relativism. The restriction of the latter to the human species, stamps it as *anthropologism*. We turn to criticism. Our interests demand that it should be very careful.

§35 Critique of individual relativism

Individual relativism is such a bare-faced and (one might almost say) 'cheeky' scepticism, that it has certainly not been seriously held in modern times. It is a doctrine no sooner set up than cast down, though only for one who recognizes the objectivity of all that pertains to logic. One cannot persuade the subjectivist any more than one can the open sceptic, a man simply lacking the ability to see that laws such as the law of contradiction have their roots in the mere meaning of truth, that from these it follows that talk of a subjective truth, that is one thing for one man and the opposite for another, must count as the purest nonsense. He will not bow to the ordinary objection that in setting up his theory he is making a claim to be convincing to others, a claim presupposing that very objectivity of truth which his thesis denies. He will naturally reply: My theory expresses my standpoint, what is true for me, and need be true for no one else. Even the subjective fact of his thinking, he will treat as true for himself, and not as true in itself.[3] That we should, however, be able to convince the subjectivist personally, and make him admit his error, is not important: what is important is to refute him in an objectively valid manner. Refutation presupposes the leverage of certain self-evident, universally valid convictions. Such are those trivial insights on which every scepticism must come to grief, insights which show up sceptical doctrines as in the strictest, most genuine sense nonsensical. The content of such assertions rejects what is part of the sense or content of every assertion and what accordingly cannot be significantly separated from any assertion.

§36 Critique of specific relativism and, in particular, of anthropologism

In the case of subjectivism, it is doubtful whether anyone seriously holds it. Modern and recent philosophy leans, however, so strongly towards specific relativism, and, in particular, towards anthropologism, that it is quite rare to encounter a thinker free from the taint of such erroneous doctrines. But such doctrines are, however, sceptical in the sense defined above, and so suffer from the grossest absurdities conceivable in a theory: we find in them, too, slightly masked, an evident contradiction between the sense of their thesis, and that which cannot be separated from the sense of any thesis *qua* thesis. It is not hard to show this in detail:

1. Specific relativism makes the assertion: Anything is true for a given species of judging beings that, by their constitution and laws of thought, must count as true. This doctrine is absurd. For it is part of its sense that the same proposition or content of judgement can be true for a subject of the species *homo*, but may be false for another subject of a differently constituted species. The same content of judgement cannot, however, be both true and false: this follows from the mere sense of 'true' and 'false'. If the relativist gives these words their appropriate meaning, his thesis is in conflict with its own sense.

It is plainly a vain evasion to plead that the words of the adduced principle of contradiction were incomplete, but that, when we unfolded the sense of the words 'true' and 'false', it was the humanly true and false that were in question. For the ordinary subjectivist could likewise plead that talk about the true and the false was inexact, and that truth (or falsehood) for the individual were what was really meant. And one would of course answer him by saying: An evidently valid law cannot have a plainly absurd meaning, and talk of what is true *for* this one or that one is absurd. It is absurd to regard it as an open possibility that the same judged content – with dangerous ambiguity we say 'the same judgement' – should be alike true and false, as one or other judges it. There will be a corresponding answer to specific relativism: 'Truth for this or that species', e.g. for the human species, is, as here meant, an absurd mode of speech. It can no doubt be used in a good sense, but it then means something wholly different, i.e. the circle of truths to which man as such has access. What is true is absolutely, intrinsically true: truth is one and the same, whether men or non-men, angels or gods apprehend and judge it. Logical laws speak of truth in this ideal unity, set over against the real multiplicity of races, individuals and experiences, and it is of this ideal unity that we all speak when we are not confused by relativism.

2. We saw that the principles of contradiction and excluded middle tell us what pertains to the mere sense of the words 'true' and 'false'. In this regard it is possible to restate our objection in the words: If the relativist says that there could be beings not bound by these principles – this assertion is easily seen as equivalent to the relativistic formula stated above – he *either* means that there could be propositions or truths, in the judgements of such beings, which do not conform to these principles, *or* he thinks that the course of judgement of such beings is not *psychologically* regulated by these principles. If he means the latter, his doctrine is not at all peculiar, since we ourselves are such beings. (One need only recall our objections to the psychologistic interpretation of logical principles.) But if he means the former, we may simply reply: Either such beings understand the words 'true' and 'false' in our sense, in which case it is irrational to speak of logical principles not holding, since they pertain to the mere sense of these words as understood by us. We should never dream of *calling* anything true or false, that was at

variance with them. Alternatively, such beings use the words 'true' and 'false' in some different sense, and the whole dispute is then one of words. If, e.g., they call those things 'trees' which we call 'propositions', then the statements in which the logical laws are expressed of course do not hold, but they will also have lost the sense in which we asserted them. It therefore comes out that the sense of the word 'truth' has been totally altered by relativism, which yet pretends to talk of truth in the sense laid down by the logical laws, which is the only sense we all employ when we talk of truth. In a single sense there is only a single truth, in an equivocal sense there are naturally as many 'truths' as there are equivocal uses.

3. The constitution of a species is a fact: from a fact it is only possible to derive other facts. To base facts relativistically on the constitution of the species therefore means to give it a factual character. This is absurd. Every fact is individually and therefore temporally determinate. In the case of truth, talk of temporal determination only makes sense in regard to a fact posited by a truth (provided, that is, that it is a truth about facts): it makes no sense in regard to the truth itself. It is absurd to think of truths as being causes or effects, as we have already indicated. If someone wished to argue from the fact that a true judgement, like any judgement, must spring from the constitution of the judging subject in virtue of appropriate natural laws, we should warn him not to confuse the 'judgement', *qua* content of judgement, i.e. as an ideal unity, with the individual, real act of judgement. It is the former that we mean when we speak of the judgement $2 \times 2 = 4$, which is the same whoever passes it. One should likewise not confuse the true judgement, as the correct judgement in accordance with truth, with the *truth* of this judgement or with the true content of judgement. My act of judging that $2 \times 2 = 4$ is no doubt causally determined, but this is not true of the truth $2 \times 2 = 4$.

4. If, as anthropologism says, all truth has its source in our common human constitution, then, if there were no such constitution, there would be no truth. The thesis of this hypothetical assertion is absurd, since the proposition 'There is no truth' amounts in sense to the proposition 'There is a truth that there is no truth'. The absurdity of the thesis entails the absurdity of the hypothesis, but, since the hypothesis represents the negation of a valid proposition, having factual content, it admits of falsehood but not of absurdity. No one has in fact ever thought of rejecting as *absurd* those geological and physical theories which give the human race a beginning and an end in time. The stigma of absurdity therefore taints the whole hypothetical statement, since it connects an antecedent having a coherent ('logically possible') sense with an absurd ('logically impossible') consequent. The same stigma then taints anthropologism, and extends naturally, *mutatis mutandis*, to the wider form of relativism.

5. On a relativistic view the constitution of a species might yield the 'truth', valid for the species, that no such constitution existed. Must we then say that there is in reality no such constitution, or that it exists, but only for us? But

what if all men, and all species of judging beings, were destroyed, with the exception of the species in question? We are obviously talking nonsense. The notion that the non-existence of a certain constitution should be based on this very constitution, is a flat contradiction: that the truth-conditioning, and therefore existent constitution should condition the truth (among other truths) of its own non-existence. The absurdity is not greatly lessened if we substitute existence for non-existence, and apply our arguments, not to an imaginary species, which from a relativistic standpoint is possible, but to our human species. Our contradiction then vanishes, but not the absurdity associated with it. The relativity of truth means that, what we call truth, depends on the constitution of the species *homo* and the laws which govern this species. Such a dependence will and can only be thought of as causal. The truth that such a constitution and such laws subsist must then have its real explanation in the fact of this subsistence: the principles of our explanation must be identical with such laws – again mere nonsense. Our constitution would be *causa sui* in respect of laws, which would cause themselves in virtue of themselves etc.

6. The relativity of truth entails the relativity of cosmic existence. For the world is merely the unified objective totality corresponding to, and inseparable from, the ideal system of all factual truth. One cannot subjectivize truth, and allow its object (which only exists as long as truth subsists) to count as absolutely existent, or as existent 'in itself'. There would therefore be no world 'in itself', but only a world for us, or for any other chance species of being. This may suit some, but it becomes dubious once we point out that the ego and its conscious contents also pertain to the world. That I am, and that I am experiencing this or that, might be false if my specific constitution were such as to force me to deny these propositions. And there would be absolutely no world, not merely no world for this or that one, if no actual species of judging beings in the world was so constituted as to have to recognize a world (and itself in that world). If we confine ourselves to the only species actually known to us, animal species, then a change in their constitution would mean a change in the world, and that although animal species are thought to be evolutionary products of the world. We are playing a pretty game: man evolves from the world and the world from man; God creates man and man God.

The essential core of this objection lies in the self-evident conflict between relativism and the inner evidence of immediately intuited existence, i.e. with the evidence of 'inner observation' in the legitimate, indispensable sense. The inner evidence of judgements resting on intuition is rightly contested when such judgements intentionally transcend the content of the actual data of consciousness. They have true inward evidence when their intention rests on this content itself, and finds fulfilment in it, just as it is. This inner evidence is not attainted by the vagueness of all such judgements: one need only think of the ineliminable vagueness of the determination of time, and perhaps also of place, in any immediate judgement of intuition.

§37 General observation. The concept of relativism in an extended sense

Our two forms of relativism are special cases of relativism in the widest sense of the word, as a doctrine which somehow derives the pure principles of logic from facts. Facts are 'contingent': they might very well not have been the case, they might have been different. If the facts then differ, logical principles also will differ; they will also be contingent, with a being relative to the facts on which they are founded. I do not wish to counter this by merely bringing in the apodeictic inner evidence of logical laws, points argued for in former chapters: I wish to bring in another point which is more important in this context (cf. §32 of the present chapter). Anyone can see from my statements up to this point that for me the pure truths of logic are all the ideal laws which have their whole foundation in the 'sense', the 'essence' or the 'content', of the concepts of Truth, Proposition, Object, Property, Relation, Combination, Law, Fact etc. More generally stated, they have their whole foundation in the sense of the concepts which make up the heritage of *all* science, which represent the categories of constituents out of which science as such is essentially constituted. Laws of this sort should not be violated by any theoretical assertion, proof or theory, not because such a thing would render the latter false – so would conflict with any truth – but because it would render them inherently absurd. An assertion, e.g., whose content quarrels with the principles whose roots lie in the *sense* of truth as such, is self-cancelling. For to assert, is to maintain the truth of this or that content. A proof whose content quarrels with the principles rooted in the *sense* of the relation of ground and consequent, is self-cancelling. For to prove, is to state that there is such and such a relation of ground and consequent etc. That an assertion is 'self-cancelling', is 'logically absurd', means that its particular content (sense, meaning) contradicts the general demands of its own, pertinent meaning-categories, contradicts what has its general root in the general meaning of those categories. It is now clear that, in this pregnant sense, any theory is logically absurd which deduces logical principles from any matters of fact. To do so is at variance with the general sense of the concepts of 'logical principle' and 'fact', or, to speak more precisely and more generally, of the concepts of 'truth based on the mere content of concepts' and 'truth concerning individual existence'. It is easy to see that the objections against the above discussed relativistic theory are, in the main, objections to relativism in the most general sense.

§38 Psychologism in all its forms is a relativism

In our attacks on relativism, we have of course had psychologism in mind. Psychologism in all its subvarieties and individual elaborations is in fact the same as relativism, though not always recognized and expressly allowed to be such. It makes no difference whether, as a formal idealism, based on a 'transcendental psychology', it seeks to save the objectivity of knowledge, or whether, leaning on empirical psychology, it accepts relativism as its ineluctable fate.

Every doctrine is *ipso facto* relativistic, a case of specific relativism, if, with the empiricists, it treats the pure laws of logic as empirical, psychological laws. It is likewise relativistic, if, with the apriorists, it deduces these laws, in more or less mythic fashion, from certain 'original forms' or 'modes of functioning' of the (human) understanding, from consciousness as such, conceived as generic (human) reason, from the psycho-physical constitution of man, from the *intellectus ipse* which, as an innate (generically human) disposition, precedes all actual thought and experience. All the objections we have made to specific relativism also affect such doctrines. One must of course take the somewhat shifting key-words of apriorism, e.g. 'understanding', 'reason', 'consciousness', in the natural sense which gives them an essential connection with the human species. It is the curse of the theories under consideration that they at one time give these words a real, at another time an ideal sense, and so weave an inextricable tangle of true and false statements. Aprioristic theories, to the extent that they yield to relativistic motives, must be counted as relativistic. Such relativism is no doubt restricted, i.e., to the realm of mathematics and natural science, when, as in the case of some Kantian thinkers, certain logical principles are set aside as principles of 'analytic' judgements, but sceptical absurdities are not thereby avoided. For, in their narrower field, they still deduce truth from generic human nature, the ideal from the real, or, more precisely, the necessity of laws from the contingency of facts.

We are, however, more interested in the extreme, consistent psychologism which permits no such restrictions. To such a psychologism the main English empiricists, as well as the more recent German logicians, belong, i.e. thinkers such as Mill, Bain, Wundt, Sigwart, Erdmann and Lipps. To criticize all such works is neither possible nor desirable. In view, however, of the reformatory aims of these Prolegomena, I do not wish to pass over the main works of modern German logic, and especially not the important work of Sigwart, which, more than any other, has pushed logic in the last decades into psychological channels.

Chapter 8

The psychologistic prejudices

So far our attack has been mainly upon the consequences of psychologism. We now turn against its arguments: we shall try to show that what it regards as obvious truths are in fact delusive prejudices.

§41 First prejudice

A first prejudice runs: Prescriptions which regulate what is mental must obviously have a mental basis. It is accordingly self-evident that the normative principles of knowledge must be grounded in the psychology of knowledge.

One's delusion vanishes as soon as one abandons general argumentation and turns to the 'things themselves'.

We must first put an end to a distorted notion which both parties share, by pointing out that logical laws, taken in and for themselves, are not normative propositions at all in the sense of prescriptions, i.e. propositions which tell us, as part of their *content*, how one *should* judge. One must always distinguish between laws that *serve as norms* for our knowledge-activities, and laws which include normativity in their thought-content, and *assert* its universal obligatoriness.

Let us take as an example the well-known syllogistic principle we expressed in the words: A mark of a mark is also a mark of the thing itself. This statement would be commendably brief if its expression were not also an obvious falsehood.[1] To express it concretely, we shall have to adjust ourselves to a few more words. 'It is true of every pair of characters A, B, that if every object which has the character A also has the character B, and if any definite object S has the character A, then it also has the character B.' That this proposition contains the faintest thought of normativity must be strongly denied. We can employ our proposition for normative purposes, but it is not therefore a norm. Anyone who judges that every A is also B, and that a certain S is A, ought also to judge that this S is B. Everyone sees, however, that this proposition is not the original proposition of logic, but one that has been derived from it by bringing in the thought of normativity.

The same obviously holds of all syllogistic laws, as of all laws of pure logic as such.[2] But not of such laws alone. A capacity for normative use is shared by the truths of other theoretical disciplines, and above all by those of pure mathematics, which are usually kept separate from logic.[3] The well-known principle

$$(a + b)\,(a - b) = a^2 - b^2$$

tells us, e.g. that the product of the sum and the difference of any two numbers equals the difference of their squares. Here there is no reference to our judging and the manner in which it *should* be conducted; what we have before us is a theoretical law, not a practical rule. If, however, we consider the corresponding practical proposition: 'To arrive at the product of the sum and difference of two numbers, one should find the difference of their squares', we have conversely uttered a practical rule and not a theoretical law. Here, too, the transformation of law into rule involves a bringing in of the notion of normativity; the rule is the obvious, apodeictic consequence of the law, but it none the less differs from it in thought-content.

We can even go further. It is clear that *any* theoretical truth belonging to *any* field of theory, can be used in a like manner as the foundation for a universal norm of correct judgement. The laws of logic are not at all peculiar in this respect. In their proper nature, they are not normative but theoretical truths, and as such we can employ them, as we can the truths of all other disciplines, as norms for our judgement.

We cannot, however, treat the general persuasion that the laws of logic are norms of thinking as quite baseless, nor the obviousness with which it impresses us as a mere delusion. These laws must have some intrinsic *prerogative* in the regulation of our thought. But does this mean that the idea of regulation, or of an 'ought', must therefore form part of the content of such laws? Can it not *follow* from that content with self-evident necessity? In other words: May not the laws of logic and pure mathematics have a distinctive meaning-content which gives them a *natural right* to regulate our thought?

This simple treatment shows us how both sides have made their mistakes.

The anti-psychologists went wrong by making the regulation of knowledge the 'essence', as it were, of the laws of logic. The purely theoretical character of formal logic, and its identity of character with formal mathematics, were thereby insufficiently recognized. It was correctly seen that the set of laws treated in traditional syllogistic theory were remote from psychology. Their natural right to regulate knowledge was recognized, for which reason they must be made the kernel of all practical logic. The difference between the proper content of these laws, and their function, their practical application, was, however, ignored. Men failed to see that so-called basic laws of logic were not in themselves norms, though they could be used normatively. Concern with this normative use had led men to speak of such laws as laws of thought, and so it appeared that these laws, too, had a psychological content, and that their only difference from what are ordinarily called psychological laws lay in this normative function, not possessed by other psychological laws.

The psychologistic thinkers, on the other hand, went wrong in putting forward a presumed axiom whose invalidity we may expose in a few words: It is entirely obvious that each general truth, whether psychological or not, serves to found a rule for correct judgement, but this not only assures us of the meaningful possibility, but even of the actual existence of rules of judgement which do not have their basis in psychology.

Not all rules which set standards for correct judgement are on that account *logical* rules. It is, however, evident that, of the genuinely logical rules which form the nucleus of a technology of scientific thinking, only one set permits and demands a psychological establishment: the technical precepts specifically adapted to human nature concerning the acquisition and criticism of scientific knowledge. The remaining, much more important group consists of normative transformations of laws, which belong solely to the objective or ideal content of the science. Psychological logicians, even such as are of the stature of a Mill or a Sigwart, treat science from its subjective side (as a methodology of the specifically human acquisition of knowledge), rather than from its objective side (as the Idea of the theoretical unity of truth), and therefore lay one-sided stress on the methodological tasks of logic. In doing so they ignore the *fundamental difference between the norms of pure logic and the technical rules of a specifically human art of thought.* These are totally different in character in their content, origin and function. The laws of logic, seen in their original intent, concern only what is ideal, while these methodological propositions concern only what is real. If the former spring from immediately evident axioms, the latter spring from empirical facts, belonging mainly to psychology. If the formulation of the former promotes our purely theoretical interests, and gives only subsidiary practical help, the latter, on the other hand, have an immediate practical aim, and they only give indirect help to our theoretical interests, in so far as they aim at the methodical progress of scientific knowledge.

§44 Second prejudice

To confirm his first prejudice that rules for cognition must rest on the psychology of cognition, the psychologistic party appeals to the actual content of logic (cf. the arguments of §15 above). What is logic about? Everywhere it concerns itself with presentations and judgements, with syllogisms and proofs, with truth and probability, with necessity and possibility, with ground and consequent, and with other closely related or connected concepts. But what can be thought of under such headings but mental phenomena and formations? This is obvious in the case of presentations and judgements. Syllogisms, however, are proofs of judgements by means of judgements, and proof is plainly a mental activity. Talk of truth, probability, necessity, possibility etc., likewise concerns judgements: what they refer to can only be manifested or experienced in judgements. Is it not, therefore, strange that one should wish to exclude from psychology propositions and theories which relate to psychological phenomena? In this regard the distinction between purely logical and methodological propositions is pointless, the objection affects both equally. Every attempt, therefore, to extrude even a part of logic from psychology, on ground of its pretended 'purity', must count as radically mistaken.

§45 Refutation. Pure mathematics would likewise be made a branch of psychology

Obvious as all this may seem, it *must* be mistaken. This is shown by the absurd consequences which, as we know, psychologism cannot escape. There is, however, another reason for misgiving: the natural affinity between purely logical and mathematical doctrine, which has often led to an assertion of their theoretical unity.

We have already mentioned by the way that even Lotze taught that mathematics must be regarded as 'an independently developed branch of general logic'. 'Only a practically motivated division of teaching' can, he thinks, blind us to the fact that mathematics 'has its whole home-ground in the general field of logic' (*Logik*, ed. 2, §18, p. 34 and §112, p. 138). To which Riehl adds that 'one could well say that logic coincides with the general part of purely formal mathematics (taken in the sense of H. Hankel)' (A. Riehl, *Der philosophische Kritizismus und seine Bedeutung für die positive Wissenschaft*, vol. II, Part I, p. 226). However this may be, an argument that is correct for logic must be approved in the case of arithmetic as well. Arithmetic sets up laws for numbers, for their relations and combinations: numbers, however, are the products of colligation and counting, which are mental activities. Relations arise from relating activities, combinations from acts of combination. Adding and multiplying, subtracting and dividing – these are merely mental processes. That they require sensuous supports makes no difference, since this is true of any and every act of thinking. Sums, products, differences and quotients, and whatever may be determined in arithmetical propositions, are merely mental processes, and must as such obey mental laws. It may be highly desirable that modern psychology with its earnest pursuit of exactness should be widened to include mathematical theories, but it would hardly be much elevated by the inclusion of mathematics itself as one of its parts. For the heterogeneity of the two sciences cannot be denied. The mathematician, on the other hand, would merely smile if psychological studies were pressed upon him as supposedly providing a better and deeper grounding for his theoretical pronouncements. He would rightly say that mathematics and psychology belong to such different worlds, that the very thought of interchange among them was absurd: here, if anywhere, talk of a μετάβασις εἰς ἄλλο γένος is applicable.[4]

§46 The research domain of pure logic is, like that of mathematics, an ideal domain

These objections may have taken our argument far afield, but, when we attend to their content, they help us to state the basic errors of our opponents' position. *The comparison of pure logic with pure mathematics*, its mature sister discipline, which no longer needs fight for its right to independent existence, provides us with a reliable *Leitmotiv*. We shall first glance at mathematics.

No one regards the theories of pure mathematics, e.g. the pure theory of numbers, as 'parts or branches of psychology', though we should have no numbers without counting, no sums without addition, no products without multiplication etc. The patterns of all arithmetical operations refer back to certain mental acts of arithmetical operation, and only in reflection upon these can we 'show' what a total, sum, product etc., is. In spite of the 'psychological origin' of arithmetical concepts, everyone sees it to be a fallacious μετάβασις to demand that mathematical laws should be psychological. How is this to be explained? Only *one* answer is possible. Counting and arithmetical operation as *facts*, as mental acts proceeding in time, are of course the concern of psychology, since it is the empirical science of mental facts in general. Arithmetic is in a totally different position. Its domain of research is known, it is completely and exhaustively determined by the familiar series of ideal species 1, 2, 3 ... In this sphere there can be no talk of individual facts, of what is temporally definite. Numbers, Sums and Products and so forth are not such casual acts of counting, adding and multiplying etc., as proceed here and there. They also differ obviously from *presentations* in which they are given. The number Five is not my own or anyone else's counting of five, it is also not my presentation or anyone else's presentation of five. It is in the latter regard a possible *object* of acts of presentation, whereas, in the former, it is the ideal *species* of a form whose concrete *instances* are found in what becomes objective in certain acts of counting, in the collective whole that these constitute. In no case can it be regarded without absurdity as a *part* or *side* of a mental experience, and so not as something real. If we make clear to ourselves what the number Five truly is, if we conceive of it adequately, we shall first achieve an articulate, collective presentation of this or that set of five objects. In this act a collection is intuitively given in a certain formal articulation, and so as an instance of the number-species in question. Looking at this intuited individual, we perform an 'abstraction', i.e. we not only isolate the non-independent moment of collective form in what is before us, but we apprehend the Idea in it: the number Five as the species of the form swims into our conscious sphere of reference. What we are now meaning is not this individual instance, not the intuited object as a whole, not the form immanent in it, but still inseparable from it: what we mean is rather the *ideal form-species*, which is absolutely one in the sense of arithmetic, in whatever mental act it may be individuated for us in an intuitively constituted collective, a species which is accordingly untouched by the contingency, temporality and transience of our mental acts. Acts of counting arise and pass away and cannot be meaningfully mentioned in the same breath as numbers.

Arithmetical propositions are concerned with such ideal unities ('lowest species' in a heightened sense quite different from that of empirical classes), and this holds both of numerical propositions (arithmetical singulars) and of algebraic propositions (arithmetical generalizations). They tell us nothing about what is real, neither about the real things counted, nor about the real acts in which they are counted, in which such and such indirect numerical characteristics are constituted for us. Concrete numbers and numerical propositions belong in the scientific fields to which the relevant concrete units belong: propositions about arithmetical thought-processes belong in psychology. In strict propriety, arithmetical propositions say nothing about 'what is contained in our mere number-presentations': as little as they speak of other presentations, do they speak of ours. They are rather concerned with absolute numbers and number-combinations in their abstract purity and ideality. The propositions of universal arithmetic – the nomology of arithmetic we may call it – are laws rooted *in the ideal essence of the genus Number*. The *ultimate* singulars which come within the range of these laws, are *ideal singulars*: they are the determinate numbers, i.e. the lowest specific differences of the genus number. It is to these singulars that arithmetically singular propositions relate, propositions which belong to the arithmetic of definite numbers. These arise through the application of universal arithmetical laws to numerically specific numbers, they express what is purely part of the ideal essence of these numbers. None of these propositions reduces to one that has empirical generality, not even to the widest case of such generality, one that applies without exception to the entire real world.

What we have here said in regard to pure arithmetic carries over at all points to *pure* logic. In the latter case too, we accept as obvious the fact that logical concepts have a psychological origin, but we deny the psychologistic conclusion to which this seems to lead. In consideration of the domain that must be granted to logic in the sense of a *technology* of scientific knowledge, we naturally do not doubt that logic is to a large extent concerned with our mental states. Naturally the methodology of scientific research and proof must take full cognizance of the nature of the mental states in which research and proof take their course. Logical terms such as 'presentation', 'concept', 'judgement', 'syllogism', 'proof', 'theory', 'necessity', 'truth' etc., may therefore, and must therefore, come up as general names for psychical experiences and dispositions. We deny, however, that this ever occurs in the purely logical parts of logical technology. We deny that the theoretical discipline of pure logic, in the independent separateness proper to it, has any concern with mental facts, or with laws that might be styled 'psychological'. We saw that the laws of pure logic, e.g. the primitive 'laws of thought', or the syllogistic formulae, totally lose their basic sense, if one tries to interpret them as psychological. It is therefore clear from the start *that the concepts which constitute these and similar laws have no empirical range.* They cannot, in other words, have the character of those mere universal notions whose range is that of individual singulars, but they must be notions truly *generic, whose range is exclusively one of ideal singulars, genuine species.* It is clear, for the rest, that the terms in question, and all such as function in purely logical contexts, must be *equivocal*; they must, on the one hand, stand for class-concepts of mental states such as belong in psychology, but, on the other hand, for generic concepts covering ideal singulars, which belong in a sphere of pure law.

§49 Third prejudice. Logic as the theory of evidence

We shall state a third prejudice – one particularly to the fore in the arguments of chapter 11, §19 in this volume – in the following words: All truth pertains to judgement. Judgement, however, is only recognized as true when it is *inwardly evident*. The term 'inner evidence' stands, it is said, for a peculiar mental character, well-known to everyone through his inner experience, a peculiar feeling which guarantees the truth of the judgement to which it attaches. If logic is the technology which will assist us to know the truth, logical laws are obviously psychological propositions. They are, in fact, propositions which cast light on the psychological conditions on which the presence or absence of this 'feeling of inner evidence' depends. Practical prescriptions are naturally connected with such propositions, and help us to achieve judgements having this distinctive character. Such psychologically based rules of thought must surely be meant where we speak of logical laws or norms.

Mill hits on this conception when he attempts to draw a line between logic and psychology, and says: 'The properties of thought which concern logic are some of its contingent properties, those namely on the presence of which depends good thinking as distinguished from bad' (*An Examination of Sir William Hamilton's Philosophy*, p. 462). In his further statements, he repeatedly calls logic the (psychologically conceived) 'theory' or 'philosophy of evidence' (op. cit. pp. 473, 475–6, 478) he was of course not immediately concerned with the propositions of pure logic. In Germany this point of view occasionally crops up in Sigwart. 'Logic', he says, 'can only proceed by becoming conscious of the way this subjective feeling of necessity [the 'inner feeling' of the evident of our previous paragraph] makes its appearance, and then expressing these conditions in a general manner' (*Logik*, 1, ed. 2, p. 16).

Many statements of Wundt's tend in a similar direction. We read, e.g., in his *Logik* that 'the properties of self-evidence and universal validity involved in certain thought-connections, permit us to derive the logical from the psychological laws of thought'. The normative character of the former 'has its sole foundation in the fact that certain psychological thought-connections actually *do* have self-evidence and universal validity, without which it would not be possible for us to approach thought with the demand that it *should* satisfy the conditions of the self-evident and universally valid'. 'The conditions that must themselves be fulfilled if we are to have self-evidence and universal validity are called the logical laws of thought.' But Wundt emphasizes that 'psychological thinking is always the more comprehensive form of thinking'.[5]

In the logical literature at the end of last century the interpretation of logic as a practically applied psychology of the inwardly evident certainly became more penetrating and more widely entertained. The *Logik* of Höfler and Meinong here deserves special mention, since it may be regarded as the first properly carried out attempt to make a thorough, consistent use of the notion of the psychology of inward evidence over the whole field of logic. Höfler says that the main task of logic is the investigation of 'those laws, primarily psychological, which express the dependence of emergent inward evidence on the particular properties of our presentations and judgements' (*Logik*, Vienna 1890, p. 16). 'Among all actually given thought-phenomena, or even such as we can conceive possible, logic must pick out the types or forms of thinking to which inner evidence attaches directly, or which are necessary conditions for the emergence of inner evidence' (op. cit. p. 17). The seriousness of such psychologism is shown by the rest of the treatment. Thus the method of logic, in its concern with the theoretical groundwork of correct thinking, is said to be the same method that psychology applies to *all* mental phenomena: it must *describe* such phenomena, in this case those of correct thinking, and reduce them as far as may be to simple laws, i.e. explain more complex laws by way of simple ones (op. cit. p. 18). Further on, one reads that the logical doctrine of the syllogism is given the task of 'formulating the laws, which tell us what features in our premises determine whether a certain judgement can be deduced from them with inward evidence'. Etc. etc.

§50 Transformation of logical propositions into equivalent propositions about the ideal conditions for evidence of judgement. The resultant propositions are not psychological

We turn to criticism. We are far from regarding as unobjectionable the nowadays commonplace, but far from clear assumption with which the argument starts, that all truth lies in our judgements. We do not of course doubt that to know truth and to utter it justifiably, presupposes the prior seeing of it. Nor do we doubt that logic as a technology must look into the psychological conditions in which inner evidence illuminates our judgements. We may even go a further step in the direction of the conception we are refuting. While we seek to preserve the distinction between purely logical and methodological propositions, we expressly concede that the former have a relation to the psychological datum of inner evidence, that they in a sense state its psychological conditions.

Such a relation must, however, be regarded as purely ideal and indirect. The pure laws of logic say absolutely nothing about inner evidence or its conditions. We can show, we hold, that they only achieve this relation through a process of application or transformation, the same sort of process, in fact, through which every purely conceptual law permits application to a generally conceived realm of empirical cases. The propositions about inner evidence which arise in this manner keep their *a priori* character, and the conditions of inner evidence that they assert bear no trace of the psychological or the real. They are purely conceptual propositions, transformable, as in every like case, into statements about *ideal* incompatibilities or possibilities.

A little reflection will make matters clear. Every law of pure logic permits of an (inwardly evident) transformation, possible *a priori*, which allows one to read off certain propositions about inward evidence, certain conditions of inward evidence, from it. The combined principles of contradiction and excluded middle are certainly equivalents to the proposition: One and only *one* of two mutually contradictory judgements *can* manifest inner evidence.[6] The mood *Barbara* is likewise certainly equivalent to the proposition: The inner evidence of the necessary truth of a proposition of the form *All A's are C's* (more precisely, its truth as a necessary consequence), may appear in a syllogizing act whose premises are of the forms *All A's are B's* and *All B's are C's*. The like holds of every proposition of pure logic. Understandably so, since there evidently is a general equivalence between the proposition *A is true* and *It is possible for anyone to judge A to be true in an inwardly evident manner*. The propositions, therefore, whose sense lies in stating what necessarily is involved in the notion of truth, that the truth of propositions of certain forms determines the truth of propositions of corresponding other forms, can certainly be transformed into equivalent propositions which connect the possible emergence of inner evidence with the forms of our judgements.

Our insight into such connections will, however, provide us with the means to refute the attempt to swallow up pure logic in a psychology of inner evidence. In itself, plainly, the proposition *A is true* does not state the same thing as the equivalent proposition *It is possible for anyone and everyone to judge that A is the case*. The former says nothing about anyone's judgement, not even about judgements of anyone in general. The position here resembles that of propositions of pure mathematics. The statement that $a + b = b + a$ states that the numerical value of the sum of two numbers is independent of their position in such a sum, but it says nothing about anyone's acts of counting or addition. The latter first enters the picture in an inwardly evident, equivalent transformation. It is an *a priori* truth that no number can be given *in concreto* unless we count, and no sum unless we add.

But even when we abandon the original forms of the propositions of pure logic, and turn them into corresponding equivalents regarding inward evidence, nothing results which psychology could claim as its own. Psychology is an empirical science, the science of mental facts, and psychological possibility is accordingly a case of real possibility. Such possibilities of inner evidence are, however, real ones, and what is psychologically impossible may very well be ideally possible. The solution of the generalized '3-body problem', or *n*-body problem' may transcend all human cognitive capacity, but the problem *has* a solution, and the inner evidence which relates to it is therefore possible. There are decimal numbers with trillions of places, and there are truths relating to them. No one, however, can actually imagine such numbers, nor do the additions, multiplications etc., relating to them. Inward evidence is here a psychological impossible, yet, *ideally* speaking, it undoubtedly represents a possible state of mind.

The turning of the notion of truth into the notion of the possibility of evident judgement has its analogue in the relation of the concepts *Individual Being* and *Possibility of Perception*. The equivalence of these concepts, if by 'perception' we mean adequate perception, is undeniable. A perception is accordingly *possible*, in which the whole world, with the endless abundance of its bodies, is perceived at *one* glance. But this ideal possibility is of course no real possibility, we could not attribute it to any empirical subject, particularly since such a vision would be an endless continuum of vision: unitarily conceived, it would be a Kantian Idea.

Though we stress the ideality of the possibilities of evident judgement which can be derived from logical principles, and which we see to reveal their *a priori* validity in cases of apodeictic self-evidence, we do not deny their *psychological utility*. If we take the law that, out of two contradictory propositions, one is true and one is false, and deduce from it the truth that, one only out of every pair of possible contradictory judgements can have the character of inward evidence, we may note this to be a self-evidently correct deduction, if self-evidence be defined as the experience in which the correctness of his judgement is brought home to a judging subject, the new proposition utters a truth about the compatibilities or incompatibilities of certain *mental experiences*. In this manner, however, every proposition of pure mathematics tells us something about possible and impossible happenings in the mental realm. No empirical enumeration or calculation, no mental act of algebraical transformation or geometrical construction, is possible which conflicts with the ideal laws of mathematics. These laws accordingly have a psychological use. We can read off from each of them *a priori* possibilities and impossibilities relating to certain sorts of mental acts, acts of counting, of additive and multiplicative combination etc. These laws are not thereby made into psychological laws. Psychology, the natural science concerned with what we mentally live through, has to look into the *natural conditions* of our experience. In its field are specifically to be found the empirically real relationships of our mathematical and logical activities, whose *ideal* relations and laws make up an independent realm. This latter realm is set up in purely universal propositions, made up out of 'concepts' which are not class-concepts of mental acts, but ideal concepts of essence, each with its concrete foundation in such mental acts or in their objective correlates. The number Three, the Truth named after Pythagoras etc., are, as our discussion showed, neither empirical singulars nor classes of singulars: they are ideal objects ideationally apprehended in the correlates of our acts of counting, of inwardly evident judging etc.

In relation to inner evidence, psychology has therefore merely the task of tracking down the *natural* conditions of the experiences which fall under this rubric, of investigating the real contexts in which, as experience shows, inward evidence arises and perishes. Such natural conditions are concentration of interest, a certain mental freshness, practice etc. Their investigation does not lead to knowledge which is exact in its content, to inwardly evident, truly lawlike generalizations, but only to vague, empirical generalizations. The inward evidence of our judgements does not merely depend on such psychological conditions, conditions that one might also call external and empirical, since they are rooted not purely in the specific form and matter of our judgement, but in its empirical context in mental life: it depends also on *ideal* conditions. Each truth stands as an ideal unit over against an endless, unbounded possibility of correct statements which have its form and its matter in common. Each actual judgement, which belongs to this ideal manifold, will fulfil, either in its mere form or in its matter, the ideal conditions for its own possible inward evidence. The laws of pure logic are truths rooted in the concept of truth, and in concepts essentially related to this concept. They state, in relation to possible acts of judgement, and on the basis of their mere form, the ideal conditions of the possibility or impossibility of their inner evidence. Of these two sorts of conditions of the inwardly evident, the former relates to the special constitution of the sorts of psychical being which the psychology of the period recognizes, psychological induction being limited by experience. The other conditions, however, have the character of ideal laws, and hold generally for every possible consciousness.

§51 The decisive points in this dispute

A final clearing-up of our present dispute depends likewise on a correct discernment of the most fundamental of epistemological distinctions, the distinction between the real and the ideal, or the correct discernment of all the distinctions into which this distinction can be analysed. We are here concerned with the repeatedly stressed distinctions between real and ideal truths, laws, sciences, between real and ideal (individual and specific) generalities and also singularities etc. Everyone, no doubt, has some acquaintance with these distinctions: even so extreme an empiricist as Hume draws a fundamental distinction between 'relations of ideas' and 'matters of fact', a distinction which the great idealist Leibniz drew before him, using the rubrics *vérités de raison* and *vérités de fait*. To draw an epistemologically important distinction does not, however, mean that one has as yet grasped its epistemological essence. One must clearly grasp what the ideal is, both intrinsically and in its relation to the real, how this ideal stands to the real, how it can be immanent in it and so come to knowledge. The basic question is whether ideal objects of thought are – to use the prevailing jargon – mere pointers to 'thought-economies', verbal abbreviations whose true content merely reduces to individual, singular experiences, mere presentations and judgements concerning individual facts, or whether the idealist is right in holding that such an empiricistic doctrine, nebulous in its generality, can indeed be uttered, but in no wise thought out, that all attempts to reduce ideal unities to real singulars are involved in hopeless absurdities, that its splintering of concepts into a range of singulars, without a concept to unify such a range in our thought, cannot be thought etc.

The understanding of our distinction between the real and the ideal 'theory of inner evidence' presupposes, on the other hand, correct concepts of *inner evidence* and *truth*. In the psychologistic literature of the last decades we have seen inner evidence spoken of as a casual feeling which attends on certain judgements, and is absent from others, which at best has a universally human linkage with certain judgements and not with others, a linkage in every normal human being in normal circumstances of judgement. There are certain normal circumstances in which every normal person feels self-evidence in connection with the proposition $2 + 1 = 1 + 2$, just as he feels pain when he gets burnt. One might then well ask what gives such a special feeling authority, how it manages to guarantee the truth of our judgement, 'impress the stamp of truth' on it, 'proclaim its truth', or whatever other metaphor one cares to use. One might also ask what such vague talk of normal endowment and normal circumstances precisely covers, and might point to the fact that even this recourse to normality will not make inwardly evident judgements coincide with true ones. It is in the last resort undeniable that even the normal man in normal circumstances must pass, in an unnumbered majority of cases, possible correct judgements which lack inner evidence. One would surely not wish to conceive the 'normality' in question in such a way that no actual human being, and no possible human being living in our finite natural conditions, could be called 'normal'.

Empiricism altogether misunderstands the relation between the ideal and the real: it likewise misunderstands the relation between truth and inner evidence. Inner evidence is no accessory feeling, either casually attached, or attached by natural necessity, to certain judgements. It is not the sort of mental character that simply lets itself be attached to any and every judgement of a certain class, i.e. the so-called 'true' judgements, so that the phenomenological content of such a judgement, considered in and for itself, would be the same whether or not it had this character. The situation is not at all like the way in which we like to conceive of the connection between sensations and the feelings which relate to them: two persons, we think, have the same sensations, but are differently affected in their feelings. Inner evidence is rather nothing but the 'experience' of truth. Truth is of course only experienced in the sense in which something ideal can be an experience in a real act. Otherwise put: *Truth is an Idea, whose particular case is an actual experience in the inwardly evident judgement.* The inwardly evident judgement is, however, an experience of primal givenness: the non-self-evident judgement stands to it much as the arbitrary positing of an object in imagination stands to its adequate perception. A thing adequately perceived is not a thing merely meant in some manner or other: it is a thing primarily given in our act, and as what we mean it, i.e. as itself given and grasped without residue. In like fashion what is self-evidently judged is not merely judged (meant in a judging, assertive, affirmative manner) but is given in the judgement-experience as itself present – present in the sense in which a state of affairs, meant in this or that manner, according to its kind, whether singular or general, empirical or ideal etc., can be 'present'. The analogy which connects all experiences of primal givenness, then leads to analogous ways of speaking, and inner evidence is called a seeing, a grasping of the self-given (true) state of affairs, or, as we say with tempting equivocation, of the truth. And, as in the realm of perception, the unseen does not at all coincide with the nonexistent, so lack of inward evidence does not amount to untruth. *The experience of the agreement* between meaning and what is itself present, meant, between the actual *sense of an assertion* and the self-given *state of affairs*, is inward evidence: the *Idea* of this agreement is truth, whose ideality is also its objectivity. It is not a chance fact that a propositional thought, occurring here and now, agrees with a given state of affairs: the agreement rather holds between a self-identical propositional meaning, and a self-identical state of affairs. 'Validity' or 'objectivity', and their opposites, do not pertain to an assertion as a particular temporal experience, but to the assertion *in specie*, to the pure, self-identical assertion $2 \times 2 = 4$ etc.

This conception alone accords with the fact that it makes no difference whether we perform a judgement (a judgement with the content, the meaning *J*) insightfully, or whether we have insight into the truth, the being of *J*. We accordingly also have insight into the fact that no one's insight can be at variance with our own (to the extent that either of us really has insight). This has its source in the essential relation between the experience of truth and truth. Our conception alone escapes the doubt which the conception of inner evidence as a casually connected feeling never can escape, and which plainly amounts to a complete scepticism: the doubt whether, when we have insight that J is the case, another might not have the insight that J', incompatible with J, is the case, that insights in general might not clash with insights, without a hope of settlement. We understand, accordingly, why the 'feeling' of inner evidence has no other essential precondition but the truth of the judged content in question. It is obvious that where there is nothing, nothing can be seen, but it is no less obvious that where there is no truth, there can be no seeing something to be true, i.e. no inward evidence (cf. *Investigation* vi, chapter 5).

Chapter 10

End of our critical treatments

§61 Need for special investigations to provide an epistemological justification and partial realization of the Idea of pure logic

The authority of Leibniz must, however, count even less for us than that of Kant or Herbart, since he could not give to his great intentions the weight of completed achievements. He belongs to a past age, beyond which modern science feels that it has travelled a long way. Authorities do not in fact carry much weight as opposed to the broad advance of a science supposedly rich and secure in its results. Their influence must be less, in so far as they lack a sufficiently clarified, positively elaborated concept of the discipline in question. Clearly, if we do not want to stick half way, and to run the risk that our critical reflections may be barren, we must take up the task of *constructing the Idea of pure logic on a sufficiently broad basis*. Only in a series of meaty individual treatments, which will provide a more precise idea of the content and character of the essential logical researches, and which will work out the notion of logic more definitely, can one remove the prejudice which sees logic as an insignificant field of more or less trivial statements. As against this, we shall see that our discipline extends far and wide, not merely in respect of its content of systematic theories, but above all in regard to the difficult and important investigations needed for its philosophical foundation and assessment.

But even the putative triviality of the field of purely logical truths, would in itself be no argument for its treatment as a mere aid towards a logical technology. The interests of pure theory require us to treat what constitutes a unified whole of theory in a theoretically closed manner, and not as a mere aid towards external ends. Our investigations so far have, we hope, made plain that a correct grasp of the essence of pure logic, and of its unique position in relation to all other sciences, is one of the most important questions in the whole of epistemology. If this is plain, it is likewise of vital interest to this fundamental philosophical science, that pure logic should be fully expounded in purity and independence. Epistemology must, of course, not be taken to be a discipline following upon or coinciding with metaphysics, but one which precedes metaphysics, as it precedes psychology and all other disciplines.

Appendix

References to F. A. Lange and B. Bolzano

Wide as is the gulf which divides my logic from F. A. Lange's, I am in agreement with him, and regard him as having done the discipline a service, in that, in a period when pure logic was mainly despised, he definitely stood out for the view that 'science may expect important advances from attempts at a separate treatment of the purely formal elements of logic' (*Logische Studien*, p. 1). Our agreement extends further: in the most general features it also applies to the Idea of the discipline, which Lange could not indeed bring to essential clarity. He has good grounds for regarding the hiving off of pure logic as the hiving off of the doctrines which he calls 'the apodeictic element in logic', i.e. 'the doctrines which, like mathematical theorems, can be developed in an absolutely cogent manner'. His next remarks are well worth remembering:

> The mere fact of the *presence of cogent truths* is so important, that every trace of such truths must be carefully followed up. To omit such an investigation on account of the small value of formal logic, or its inadequacy as a theory of human thought, would have to be rejected from this point of view as a confusion of theoretical with practical aims. Such an objection would be as if a chemist refused to analyse a compound because in its compounded state it was very valuable, whereas its single constituents were unlikely to have any value.
>
> (*op. cit.* p. 7 *f.*)

He is just as right in another passage: 'Formal logic as an apodeictic science, has a value totally independent of its validity: every system of truths which hold *a priori*, deserves the highest respect' (*op. cit.* p. 127).

While Lange warmly supported the Idea of a purely formal logic, he had no notion that this Idea had already been realized to a relatively high degree. I am of course not referring to the many expositions of formal logic, which flourished especially in the schools of Kant and Herbart, and which did so little to live up to their own claims. I am referring to Bernhard Bolzano's *Wissenschaftslehre*, published in 1837, a work which, in its treatment of the logical 'theory of elements', far surpasses everything that world-literature has to offer in the way of a systematic sketch of logic. Bolzano did not, of course, expressly discuss or support any independent demarcation of pure logic in our sense, but he provided one *de facto* in the first two volumes of his work, in his discussions of what underlay a *Wissenschaftslehre* or theory of science in the sense of his conception; he did so with such purity and scientific strictness, and with such a rich store of original, scientifically confirmed and ever fruitful thoughts, that we must count him as one of the greatest logicians of all time. He must be placed historically in fairly close proximity to Leibniz, with whom he shares important thoughts and fundamental conceptions, and to whom he is also philosophically akin in other respects. Even he, however, did not quite exhaust the rich inspiration of Leibniz's logical intuitions, especially not in regard to mathematical syllogistics and to *mathesis universalis*. Too few of Leibniz's posthumous writings were, however, known at the time, and there was no 'formal' mathematics or theory of manifolds to provide a key to their understanding.

In each line of his wonderful book, Bolzano shows himself to be an acute mathematician, who lets the same spirit of scientific strictness rule in logic which he himself first introduced into the theoretical treatment of the basic concepts and propositions of mathematical analysis, which thereby acquired a new foundation. For this the history of mathematics has *not* forgotten to grant him a famous place. Of the ambiguous profundity of that systematic philosophy, which rather aimed at thinking out world-conceptions and a world-wisdom, and which hindered the progress of scientific philosophy so badly by its unholy blend of discordant intentions, Bolzano – the contemporary of Hegel – shows no trace. His thought-patterns are of mathematical straightforwardness and plainness, but also of mathematical clearness and strictness. Only when one has gone more deeply into the sense and aim of these patterns throughout the whole discipline, does one find what great mental work and achievement lie hidden behind plain statements and formularized expositions. To philosophers bred in the prejudices, in the thought- and speech-habits of the idealistic schools – not all of us have completely outgrown such influences – such a scientific approach readily seems shallow and void of ideas, as well as ponderous and pedantic. Logic as a science must, however, be built upon Bolzano's work, and must learn from him its need for mathematical acuteness in distinctions, for mathematical exactness in theories. It will then reach a new standpoint for judging the mathematicizing theories of logic, which mathematicians, quite unperturbed by philosophic scorn, are so successfully constructing. These theories altogether conform to the spirit of Bolzano's logic, though Bolzano had not an inkling of them. It will at least be impossible for a future historian of logic to be so wrong as the otherwise thorough Ueberweg, who treats a work of the rank of the *Wissenschaftslehre* on a level with – Knigge's *Logic for Females (Logik für Frauenzimmer)*.[1]

Much as Bolzano's achievement is 'cast in one piece', it cannot be regarded (as such a deeply honest thinker would be the first to admit) as in any way final. To mention only one point, one particularly feels his defects in epistemological directions. There are either no investigations, or else only quite insufficient ones, which give genuine philosophical intelligibility to logical thought-achievements, and so provide a philosophical estimate of logic as a discipline. Such questions can be evaded by a thinker who, like a mathematician, is building theories upon theories, without having to bother himself about questions of underlying principle. They cannot be evaded by someone who undertakes to make clear, to those who either fail to see or to admit a discipline's validity, or who mix up essential tasks with quite heterogeneous ones, what the inherent justification of such a discipline really is, and what the nature of its tasks and objects may be. Our comparison of these present *Logical Investigations* with Bolzano's work is meant to make clear, not that our *Investigations* are in any sense mere commentaries upon, or critically improved expositions of, Bolzano's thought-patterns, but that they have been crucially stimulated by Bolzano (as also by Lotze).

Chapter 11

The idea of pure logic

Wishing to gain a provisional image, sketched with a few characteristic touches, of the goal aimed at by the individual discussions which follow these Prolegomena, we shall now try to bring conceptual clarity to that idea of pure logic, for which our critical discussions up to this point have more or less prepared us.

§62 The unity of science. The interconnection of things and the interconnection of truths

Science is, in the first place a unified item in anthropology: it is a unity of acts of thinking, of thought-dispositions, as well as of certain external arrangements pertinent thereto. What makes this unified whole anthropological, and what especially makes it psychological, are not here our concern. We are rather interested in what makes science science, which is certainly not its psychology, nor any real context into which acts of thought are fitted, but a certain objective or ideal interconnection which gives these acts a unitary objective relevance, and, in such unitary relevance, an ideal validity.

More definiteness and clearness are, however, needed at this point. Two meanings can be attached to this objective interconnection which ideally pervades scientific thought, and which gives 'unity' to such thought, and so to science as such: it can be understood as an *interconnection of the things* to which our thought-experiences (actual or possible) are intentionally directed, or, on the other hand, as an *interconnection of truths*, in which this unity of things comes to count objectively as being what it is. These two things are given together *a priori*, and are mutually inseparable. Nothing can be without being thus or thus determined, and that it is, and that it is thus and thus determined, is the self-subsistent truth which is the necessary correlate of the self-subsistent being. What holds of single truths, or single states of affairs, plainly also holds of interconnections of truths or of states of affairs. This self-evident inseparability is not, however, identity. In these truths or interconnections of truths the actual existence of things and of interconnections of things finds expression. But the interconnections of truths differ from the interconnections of things, which are 'truly' in the former; this at once appears in the fact that truths which hold of truths do not coincide with truths that hold of the things posited in such truths.

To forestall misunderstandings, I must expressly emphasize the fact that I use the words 'objectivity', 'object', 'thing' etc., always in the widest sense, in accordance, therefore, with my preferred sense of the term 'knowledge'. An object of knowledge may as readily be what is real as what is ideal, a thing or an event or a species of a mathematical relation, a case of being or of what ought to be. This applies automatically to expressions like 'unified objectivity', 'interconnection of things' etc.

Both sorts of unity are given to us, and can only by abstraction be thought apart, in judgement or, more precisely, in *knowledge* – the unity of objectivity, on the one hand, and of truth, on the other. The expression 'knowledge' is wide enough to cover both simple acts of knowing, as well as logically unified interconnections of knowledge, however complicated: either of these, considered as a whole, is a cognitive act. If now we perform an act of cognition, or, as I prefer to express it, live in one, we are 'concerned with the object' that it, in its cognitive fashion, means and postulates. If this act is one of knowing in the strictest sense, i.e. if our judgement is inwardly evident, then its object is *given* in primal fashion (*originär*). The state of affairs comes before us, not merely putatively, but as actually before our eyes, and in it the object itself, *as* the object that it is, i.e. just as it is intended in this act of knowing and not otherwise, as bearer of such and such properties, as the term of such relations etc. It is not merely putatively, but actually thus, and *as* actually thus it is given to our knowledge, which means that it is not merely thought (judged) but known to be such. Otherwise put, its being thus is a truth actually realized, individualized in the experience of the inwardly evident judgement. If we reflect on this individualization, we perform an ideational abstraction, and the truth itself, instead of our former object, becomes our apprehended object. We hereby apprehend the truth as the ideal correlate of the transient subjective act of knowledge, as standing opposed in its unity to the unlimited multitude of possible acts of knowing, and of knowing individuals.

To the interconnections of knowledge there ideally correspond interconnections of truths. Suitably understood, these are not merely complexes *of* truths, but complex truths, which therefore themselves in their totality fall under the concept of truth. There also the *sciences* belong, the word understood objectively in the sense of unified truth. In the general correlation which subsists between truth and objectivity, there is a unitary objectivity which corresponds to the unity of truth in one and the same science: this is the unity of the *scientific field*. In relation to this, all the singular truths of the same science *belong together in their subject-matter*, an expression which, as we shall see later, seems to be here used in a wider sense than usual.

§63 Continuation. The unity of theory

We may now ask what constitutes the *unity of a science*, and therewith the unity of its field. For not every putting of truths together in a single association of truths, which might remain an entirely external one, constitutes a science. To a science, as we said in our first chapter,[1] a certain unified interconnection of demonstration pertains. This too, however, is not enough: it points to demonstration, to proof as something essentially pertaining to the Idea of Science, but fails to say what sort of unity of proof constitutes a science.

To reach clearness, we begin by making certain general pronouncements.

Scientific knowledge is, as such, *grounded knowledge*. To know the ground of anything means to see the necessity of its being so and so. Necessity as an objective predicate of a truth (which is then called a necessary truth) is tantamount to the law-governed validity of the state of affairs in question. To see *a state of affairs as a matter of law* is to see *its truth as necessarily obtaining*, and to have knowledge of the *ground of the state of affairs* or of its truth: all these are equivalent expressions.[2] A natural equivocation, of course, leads us to call every general truth that itself utters a law, a necessary truth. Corresponding to our first defined sense, it would have been better to call it the explanatory ground of a law, from which a class of necessary truths follows.

Truths divide into *individual* and *general* truths. The former contain (whether explicitly or implicitly) assertions regarding the actual existence of individual singulars, whereas the latter are completely free from this, and only permit us to infer (purely from concepts) the *possible* existence of what is individual.

Individual truths are as such *contingent*. If in their case one speaks of a grounded explanation, one is concerned with a proof of their necessity under certain presupposed *circumstances*. If the interconnection of one fact with others is one of law, then its existence, resting on the laws which govern interconnections of the sort in question, and on the assumption of the pertinent circumstances, is determined as a *necessary existence*.

If we are not dealing with the proof of a factual, but of a *general* truth (which again has the character of a law in respect of its possible application to facts falling under it) we are referred to certain general laws, which, by way of specialization (not individualization) and deductive consequence yield the proposition to be proved. The proof of general laws necessarily leads to certain laws which in their essence, i.e. intrinsically, and not merely subjectively or anthropologically, are not further provable. These are called *basic laws*. The systematic unity of the ideally closed sum total of laws resting on *one* basic legality (*Gesetzlichkeit*) as their final ground, an arising out of it through systematic deduction, is the *unity of a systematically complete theory*. This basic legality may here either consist of one basic law or a conjunction of *homogeneous* basic laws.

We possess theories in this strict sense in universal arithmetic, in geometry, in analytical mechanics, in mathematical astronomy etc. Our concept of theory is usually a relative one, i.e. a theory is relative to a multiplicity of single items that it governs, for which it provides the explanatory grounds. Universal arithmetic gives us an explanatory theory for numerical and concrete number-propositions, analytical mechanics for mechanical facts, mathematical astronomy for the facts of gravitation etc. The possibility of taking on the function of explanation is an obvious consequence of the essence of a theory in our absolute sense. In a looser sense, we mean by a theory a deductive system in which the last grounds are not basic laws in the strict sense of the word, but, as genuine grounds, take us closer to these. In the gradations of a closed theory, a theory in this relaxed sense forms a step.

We also note the following difference: every explanatory interconnection is deductive, but not every deductive interconnection is explanatory. All grounds are premisses, but not all premisses are grounds. Every deduction is indeed necessary, i.e. it obeys laws: but that its conclusions follow *according to* laws (the laws of inference) does not mean that they follow *from* laws which in a pregnant sense serve to 'ground' them. One tends, indeed, to call every premiss, and especially a universal one, a 'ground' for the consequences which flow from it, a noteworthy equivocation.

§65 The question as to the ideal conditions of the possibility of science or of theory in general. A. The question as it relates to actual knowledge

We now raise an important question as to the 'conditions of the possibility of science in general'. Since the essential aim of scientific knowledge can only be achieved through theory, in the strict sense of the nomological sciences, we replace our question by a question as to the *conditions of the possibility of theory in general*. A theory as such consists of truths, and its form of connection is a deductive one. To answer our question is therefore also to answer the more general question as to the conditions of the possibility of *truth in general*, and again of *deductive unity* in general. The historical echoes in the form of our question are of course intentional. We are plainly concerned with a quite necessary generalization of the question as to the 'conditions of the possibility of experience' (*Erfahrung*). The unity of an experience is for Kant the unity of objective legality: it falls, therefore, under the concept of theoretical unity.

The sense of our question needs, however, to be more precisely fixed. It might very well be at first understood in the *subjective* sense, in which case it would be better expressed as a question as to the conditions of the possibility of *theoretical knowledge* in general, or, more generally, of inference in general or knowledge in general, and in the case of any *possible* human being. Such conditions are in part *real*, in part *ideal*. We shall ignore the former, the psychological conditions. Naturally the possibility of knowledge in a psychological regard embraces all the causal conditions on which our thinking depends. *Ideal* conditions for the possibility of knowledge may, as said before,[3] be of two sorts. They are either *noetic* conditions which have their grounds, *a priori*, in the Idea of Knowledge as such, without any regard to the empirical peculiarity of human knowledge as psychologically conditioned, or they are purely *logical* conditions, i.e. they are grounded purely in the 'content' of our knowledge. It is evident *a priori*, as regards the former, that thinking subjects must be in general able to perform, e.g., all the sorts of acts in which theoretical knowledge is made real. We must, in particular, as thinking beings, be able to see propositions as truths, and to see truths as consequences of other truths, and again to see laws as such, to see laws as explanatory grounds, and to see them as ultimate principles etc. But it is also, on the other hand, inwardly evident that truths are what they are, and that, in particular, laws, grounds, principles are what they are, whether we have insight into them or not. Since they do not hold in so far as we have insight into them, but we can only have insight into them in so far as they hold, they must be regarded as objective or ideal conditions of the possibility of our knowledge of them. *A priori* laws, accordingly, relating to truth as such, to deduction as such and to theory as such (i.e. to the universal essence of these ideal unities) must be characterized as laws which express the conditions for knowledge in general, or for deductive and theoretical knowledge in general, conditions which have their 'pure' foundation is the 'content' of knowledge.

Plainly we are here concerned with *a priori* conditions of knowledge, which can be discussed and investigated apart from all relation to the thinking subject and to the Idea of Subjectivity in science. The laws in question have a meaning-content which is quite free from such relation, they do not talk, even in ideal fashion, of knowing, judging, inferring, representing, proving etc., but of truth, concept, proposition, syllogism, ground and consequent etc., as we fully said above (§47 excised). Obviously these laws may undergo self-evident transformations through which they acquire an express relation to knowledge and the knowing subject, and now themselves pronounce on real possibilities of knowledge. Here as elsewhere, *a priori* assertions regarding ideal possibilities arise through the transferred application of ideal relationships (expressed in purely general propositions) to empirical instances (cf. the arithmetical example in §23 above).

The ideal conditions of knowledge which we have called 'noetic' as opposed to those which are logically objective, are, basically, no more than such modifications of the insights, the laws which pertain to the pure content of knowledge, as render them fruitful for the criticism of knowledge, and, by further modifications, for practical, logical normativity. For the *normative* modifications of the laws of pure logic, which we spoke of above, also come in here.

§66 B. The question as it relates to the content of knowledge

Our treatment has shown that questions as to the ideal conditions of the possibility of *knowledge* in general, and of theoretical knowledge in particular, ultimately lead us back to certain *laws*, whose roots are to be found purely in the content of knowledge, or of the categorial concepts that it falls under, and which are so abstract that they contain no reference to knowledge as an act of a knowing subject. These laws (or the categorial concepts which enter into them) are what are to be understood as constituting the conditions of the possibility of *theory* in general, in the objectively ideal sense. For it is possible to raise questions as to the conditions of possibility, not only in regard to theoretical knowledge, as we have so far done, but also in regard to its *content*, i.e. we can raise them directly in regard to theory itself. We then understand by 'theory', let us again stress, a certain *ideal content* of possible knowledge, just as in the case of 'truth', 'law' etc. There is a single truth, which corresponds to the multitude of individual acts of knowledge having the same content, which is just their ideally identical content. In like manner, the ideally identical content of a theory corresponds to the multitude of individual knowledge-combinations, in each of which – whether occurring now or then, in these subject or in those – the *same* theory comes to be known. It is accordingly not *made up of acts* but of purely *ideal* elements, of truths, and that in purely ideal forms, those of *ground and consequent*.

If we now directly relate our question as to conditions of possibility, to theory in the objective sense and to theory in general, such a possibility can only have the sense which applies to other objects of pure conception. From such objects, we are led back to concepts, and 'possibility' means no more than the 'obtaining' (*Geltung*) or rather essentiality (*Wesenhaftigkeit*) of the concepts in question. This is what is often called the 'reality' as opposed to the 'imaginariness' of concepts, which latter could better be called 'essencelessness'. In such a sense, one speaks of real definitions which guarantee the possibility, the 'obtaining', the reality of the defined concept, and again of the opposition between real and imaginary numbers, geometrical figures etc. Talk of possibility in regard to concepts becomes equivocal through a transfer. What is in an authentic sense possible is the existence of objects falling under the relevant concepts, a possibility guaranteed *a priori* through knowledge of conceptual essence, which flashes upon us, e.g., as the result of such an object's being intuitively presented. The essentiality of the concept is then likewise spoken of as a possibility in a transferred sense.

In this connection questions as to the *possibility* of a theory as such, and as to the conditions on which such possibility depends, gain an easily grasped sense. The possibility or essentiality of a theory in general is assured by our perspicuous knowledge of some definite theory. The wider question will however be: What are the universal, law-governed conditions of this possibility of theory in general? *What therefore constitutes the ideal essence of theory as such*? What are the primitive 'possibilities' out of which the possibility of theory is constituted, or, what is the same, what are the *primitive essential concepts* out of which the concept of theory, itself an essential concept, is constituted? And further: What are the pure laws which, rooted in these concepts, impart unity to all theory as such, laws which pertain to the form of theory as such, and which determine, in *a priori* fashion, the possible (essential) modifications or species of theory?

If these ideal concepts or laws delimit the possibility of theory in general, if, in other words, they express what essentially pertains to the Idea of Theory, it immediately follows that each putative theory only is a theory to the extent to which it accords with these concepts or laws. The logical justification of a concept, i.e. of its ideal possibility, is achieved by going back to its intuitive or deducible essence. Logical justification of a given theory as such, i.e. justification in virtue of its pure form, demands that we go back to the essence of its form, and so to the *concepts and laws which are ideal constituents of theory in general* (the 'conditions of its possibility'), which regulate, in *a priori*, deductive fashion, all specialization of the Idea of Theory in its possible kinds. Things are here as they are in the wider field of deduction, e.g. in the case of simple syllogisms. Though they may be intrinsically illuminated by insight, they none the less receive their final, deepest justification by recourse to the formal, syllogistic law which imparts insight into the *a priori* ground of syllogistic interconnection. The same holds in the case of any deduction, however complicated, and especially in the case of a theory. In perspicuous, theoretical thought we gain insight into the grounds of some state of affairs explained: but the deeper-going insight into the essence of the theoretical linkage which itself constitutes the theoretical content of such thought, and the *a priori* laws on which such thought-achievement depends, are first reached when we track down the form, the law, and the interweavings of theory, at the quite different level of knowledge to which they belong.

To point to profounder insights and justifications, serves to bring out the supreme value of the theoretical investigations which help to solve our suggested problem. We are dealing with *systematic theories which have their roots in the essence of theory*, with an *a priori, theoretical, nomological science which deals with the ideal essence of science as such*, and which accordingly has parts relating to systematic theories whose empirical, anthropological aspect it excludes. In a profound sense, we are dealing with the theory of theory, with the science of the sciences. Its achievement in enriching our knowledge must, of course, be kept separate from its problems themselves, and from the proper content of their solution.

§67 The tasks of pure logic. First: the fixing of the pure categories of meaning, the pure categories of objects and their law-governed combinations

Having provisionally fixed the Idea of the *a priori* discipline whose deeper understanding will be the goal of our efforts, we may now summarize the tasks that we shall assign to it. Three sets of tasks must be distinguished.

We must, *first* of all, lay down the more important concepts, in particular all the *primitive* concepts which 'make possible' the interconnected web of knowledge as seen objectively, and particularly the web of theory. We must also clarify these concepts scientifically. We are, in other words, concerned with the concepts which constitute the Idea of unified theory, or with the concepts which are connected with these through ideal laws. Into such a constitution second-order concepts, i.e. concepts of concepts and of other ideal unities, naturally enter. A given theory is a certain deductive combination of given propositions which are themselves certain sorts of combinations of given concepts. The Idea of the pertinent 'form' of the theory arises if we substitute variables for these given elements, whereby concepts of concepts and of other Ideas, replace straightforward concepts. Here belong the concepts: Concept, Proposition, Truth etc.

The concepts of the *elementary connective forms* naturally play a constitutive role here, those connective forms, in particular, which are quite generally constitutive of the deductive unity of propositions, e.g. the conjunctive, disjunctive, hypothetical linkage of propositions to form new propositions. Such a role is also played by the forms of connection of inferior elements of meaning into one simple proposition, which in their turn lead to the varied subject-forms, predicate-forms, forms of conjunctive and disjunctive connection, plural forms etc. Fixed laws govern the gradual complications through which an unending multiplicity of ever new forms emerges out of our primitive set. These *laws of complication* make possible a sweeping oversight of the concepts derivable from the primitive concepts and forms; these naturally belong, together with this sweeping oversight itself, in the field of research dealt with here. (Cf. Investigation IV in vol. II.)

In close connection with the concepts so far mentioned, i.e. the categories of meaning, and married to them by ideal laws, are other correlative concepts such as Object, State of Affairs, Unity, Plurality, Number, Relation, Connection etc. These are the pure, the formal *objective categories*. These too must be taken into account. In both cases we are dealing with nothing but concepts, whose notion makes clear that they are independent of the particularity of any material of knowledge, and under which all the concepts, propositions and states of affairs that specially appear in thought, must be ordered. They arise therefore solely in relation to our varying thought-functions: their concrete basis is solely to be found in possible acts of thought, as such, or in the correlates which can be grasped in these. (See §62 above and Investigation VI, §44 in vol. II.)

All these concepts must now be pinned down, their 'origin' must in each case be investigated. Not that psychological questions as to the origin of the conceptual presentations or presentational dispositions here in question, have the slightest interest for our discipline. This is not what we are enquiring into: we are concerned with a *phenomenological origin* or – if we prefer to rule out unsuitable talk of origins, only bred in confusion – we are concerned with *insight into the essence* of the concepts involved, looking methodologically to the fixation of unambiguous, sharply distinct verbal meanings. We can achieve such an end only by *intuitive representation* of the essence in adequate Ideation, or, in the case of complicated concepts, through knowledge of the essentiality of the elementary concepts present in them, and of the concepts of their forms of combination.

All these are seemingly trivial, preparatory tasks. To a large extent they are necessarily clothed in the form of discussions of terminology, and readily seem to the layman to be barren, pettifogging word-exercises. But as long as concepts are not distinguished and made clear to ideational intuition, by going back to their essence, further effort is hopeless. In no field of knowledge is equivocation more fatal, in none have confused concepts so hindered the progress of knowledge, or so impeded the insight into its true aims, as in the field of pure logic. The critical analyses of these Prolegomena have everywhere shown this.

It is impossible to overestimate the importance of this first group of problems; it is doubtful whether they do not in fact involve the greatest difficulties in the whole discipline.

§68 Secondly: the laws and theories which have their grounds in these categories

Our *second* group of problems lies in the search for the *laws* grounded in the two above classes of categorial concepts, which do not merely concern possible forms of complication and transformation of the theoretical items they involve (see Investigation IV), but rather the *objective validity* of the formal structures which thus arise: on the one hand, the truth or falsity of *meanings* as such, purely on the basis of their categorial formal structure, on the other hand (in relation to their *objective* correlates), the being and not being of objects as such, of states of affairs as such, again on the basis of their pure, categorial form. These laws, which concern meanings and objects as such, with the widest universality conceivable, the universality of logical categories, are in themselves theories. (See Investigation I, §29.) We have, on the *one* side, the side of meaning, theories of inference, e.g. syllogistics, which is however only one such theory. On the other side, the side of the correlates, we have the pure theory of pluralities, which has its roots in the concepts of a plurality, the pure theory of numbers, which has its roots in the concept of a number – each an independently rounded-off theory. All the laws here belonging lead to a limited number of primitive or basic laws, which have their immediate roots in our categorial concepts. They must, in virtue of their homogeneity, serve to base an all-comprehensive theory, which will contain the separate theories just mentioned, as relatively closed elements in itself.

We are here concerned with the territory of those laws, which in formal universality span all possible meanings and objects, under which every particular theory or science is ranged, which it must obey if it is to be valid. Not that every such theory presupposes every such law as the ground of its possibility and validity. The ideal completeness of the categorial theories and laws in question, rather yields the all-comprehensive fund from which each particular valid theory derives the ideal grounds of essential being appropriate to its form. These are the laws to which it conforms, and through which, as a theory validated by its form, it can be ultimately justified. In so far as theory is an all-embracing unity built out of single, interwoven truths, it is plain that the laws governing the concept of truth, as well as the laws governing the possibility of single combinations of this or that form, will be included in the delimited territory. In spite of, or rather on account of, the fact that theory is the narrower notion, the task of exploring the conditions of its possibility, comprehends more content than the corresponding task in the case of truth in general, and in the case of the primitive forms of propositional combinations (cf. above, §65).

§69 Thirdly: the theory of the possible forms of theories or the pure theory of manifolds

When all these investigations have been concluded, we shall have done justice to the Idea of a science of the conditions of the possibility of theory in general. We see at once, however, that this science points beyond itself to a completing science, which deals *a priori* with the *essential sorts (forms) of theories and the relevant laws of relation*. The Idea therefore arises, all of this being taken together, of a more comprehensive science of theory in general. In its fundamental part, the essential concepts and laws which pertain constitutively to the Idea of Theory will be investigated. It will then go over to differentiating this Idea, and investigating *possible theories* in *a priori* fashion, rather than the possibility of theory in general.

The tasks mentioned have been carried out to a sufficient extent, and it is possible to construct, out of purely categorial concepts, many definite concepts of possible theories or pure 'forms' of theories, whose essential status has been deduced from laws. These distinct forms are not mutually unrelated. There will be a definite, ordered procedure which will enable us to construct the possible forms of theories, to survey their legal connections, and to pass from one to another by varying their basic determining factors etc. There will be universal propositions, if not for the forms of theory generally, then at least for forms of theory belonging to defined classes, which will govern the legal connection, the transformation and the mutual interchange of these forms.

The propositions that must here be affirmed will plainly be of a different content and character from the basic propositions and theorems of theories of the second group, from, e.g., syllogistic or arithmetical laws. It is, however, clear from the start that the deduction of such propositions (for there can be no true basic laws in this case) must have their entire basis in the previously mentioned theories.

This is a last, highest goal for a theoretical science of theory in general. It is also not indifferent from the point of view of the practical side of knowledge. To fit a theory into its formal class may rather be of the greatest methodological importance. For, with the extension of the deductive, theoretical sphere, the liveliness and freedom of theoretical research also increases: there is increased richness and fruitfulness of method. The solution of problems raised within a theoretical discipline, or one of its theories, can at times derive the most effective methodical help from recourse to the categorial type or (what is the same) to the form of the theory, and perhaps also by going over to a more comprehensive form or class of forms and to its laws.

Investigations into phenomenology and the theory of knowledge

Introduction

§I The necessity of phenomenological investigations as a preliminary to the epistemological criticism and clarification of pure logic

The necessity that we should begin logic with linguistic discussions has often been acknowledged from the standpoint of a logical technology. 'Language', we read in Mill, 'is evidently one of the principal instruments or helps of thought; and any imperfection in the instrument, or in the mode of employing it, is confessedly liable, still more than in almost any other art, to confuse and impede the process, and destroy all ground of confidence in the result. For a mind not previously versed in the meaning and right use of the various kinds of words, to attempt the study of methods of philosophizing, would be as if some one should attempt to become an astronomical observer, having never learnt to adjust the focal distance of his optical instruments so as to see distinctly.'[1] A deeper ground for this necessity of beginning logic with linguistic analysis is, however, seen by Mill in the fact that it would not otherwise be possible to investigate the meaning of propositions, a matter which stands 'at the threshold' of logical science itself.

This last remark of our distinguished thinker indicates a point of view regulative for *pure* logic, and, be it noted, for *pure* logic treated as a *philosophical* discipline. I assume accordingly that no one will think it enough to develop pure logic merely in the manner of our mathematical disciplines, as a growing system of propositions having a naïvely factual validity, without also striving to be philosophically clear in regard to these same propositions, without, that is, gaining insight into the essence of the modes of cognition which come into play in their utterance and in the ideal possibility of applying such propositions, together with all such conferments of sense and objective validities as are essentially constituted therein. Linguistic discussions are certainly among the philosophically indispensable preparations for the building of pure logic: only by their aid can the true *objects* of logical research – and, following thereon, the essential species and differentiae of such objects – be refined to a clarity that excludes all misunderstanding. We are not here concerned with grammatical discussions, empirically conceived and related to some historically given language: we are concerned with discussions of a most general sort which cover the wider sphere of an objective *theory of knowledge* and, closely linked with this last, the *pure phenomenology of the experiences of thinking and knowing.* This phenomenology, like the more inclusive *pure phenomenology of experiences in general,* has, as its exclusive concern, experiences intuitively seizable and analysable in the pure generality of their essence, not experiences empirically perceived and treated as real facts, as experiences of human or animal experients in the phenomenal world that we posit as an empirical fact. This phenomenology must bring to pure expression, must *describe* in terms of their essential concepts and their governing formulae of essence, the essences which directly make themselves known in intuition, and the connections which have their roots purely in such essences. Each such statement of essence is an *a priori* statement in the highest sense of the word. This sphere we must explore in preparation for the epistemological criticism and clarification of pure logic: our investigations will therefore all move within it.

Pure phenomenology represents a field of neutral researches, in which several sciences have their roots. It is, on the one hand, an ancillary to *psychology* conceived as an *empirical science.* Proceeding in purely intuitive fashion, it analyses and describes in their essential generality – in the specific guise of a phenomenology of thought and knowledge – the experiences of presentation, judgement and knowledge, experiences which, treated as classes of real events in the natural context of zoological reality, receive a scientific probing at the hands of empirical psychology. Phenomenology, on the other hand, lays bare the 'sources' from which the basic concepts and ideal laws of *pure* logic 'flow', and back to which they must once more be traced, so as to give them all the 'clearness and distinctness' needed for an understanding, and for an epistemological critique, of pure logic. The epistemological or phenomenological groundwork of pure logic involves very hard, but also surpassingly important researches. To revert to what we set forth as the tasks of pure logic in the first volume of these *Investigations,* we have taken it upon us to give firm clarity to notions and laws on which the objective meaning and theoretical unity of all knowledge is dependent.[2]

§2 Elucidation of the aims of such investigations

All theoretical research, though by no means solely conducted in acts of verbal expression or complete statement, none the less terminates in such statement. Only in this form can truth, and in particular the truth of theory, become an abiding possession of science, a documented, ever available treasure for knowledge and advancing research. Whatever the connection of thought with speech may be, whether or not the appearance of our final judgements in the form of verbal pronouncements has a necessary grounding in essence, it is at least plain that judgements stemming from higher intellectual regions, and in particular from the regions of science, could barely arise without verbal expression.

The objects which pure logic seeks to examine are, in the first instance, therefore given to it in grammatical clothing. Or, more precisely, they come before us embedded in concrete mental states which further function either as the *meaning-intention* or *meaning-fulfilment* of certain verbal expressions – in the latter case intuitively illustrating, or intuitively providing evidence for, our meaning – and forming a *phenomenological unity* with such expressions.

In these complex phenomenological unities the logician must pick out the components that interest him, the characters of the acts, first of all, in which logical presentation, judgement and knowledge are consummated: he must pursue the descriptive analysis of such act-types to the extent that this helps the progress of his properly logical tasks. We cannot straightway leap, from the fact that theory 'realizes' itself in certain mental states, and has instances in them, to the seemingly obvious truth that such mental states must count as the primary object of our logical researches. The pure logician is not primarily or properly interested in the psychological judgement, the concrete mental phenomenon, but in the logical judgement, the identical asserted meaning, which is one over against manifold, descriptively quite different, judgement-experiences.[3] There is naturally, in the singular experiences which correspond to this ideal unity, a certain pervasive common feature, but since the concern of the pure logician is not with the concrete instance, but with its corresponding Idea, its abstractly apprehended universal, he has, it would seem, no reason to leave the field of abstraction, nor to make concrete experiences the theme of his probing interest, instead of Ideas.

Even if phenomenological analysis of concrete thought-experiences does not fall within the true home-ground of pure logic, it none the less is indispensable to the advance of purely logical research. For all that is logical must be given in fully concrete fashion, if, as an object of research, it is to be made our own, and if we are to be able to bring to self-evidence the *a priori* laws which have their roots in it. What is logical is first given us in imperfect shape: the concept as a more or less wavering meaning, the law, built out of concepts, as a more or less wavering assertion. We do not therefore lack logical insights, but grasp the pure law with self-evidence, and see how it has its base in the pure forms of thought. Such self-evidence depends, however, on the verbal meanings which come alive in the actual passing of the judgement regarding the law. Unnoticed equivocation may permit the subsequent substitution of other concepts beneath our words, and an appeal on behalf of an altered propositional meaning may quite readily, but wrongly, be made on the self-evidence previously experienced. It is also possible, conversely, that a misinterpretation based on equivocation may distort the sense of the propositions of pure logic (perhaps turning them into empirical, psychological propositions), and may tempt us to abandon previously experienced self-evidence and the unique significance of all that belongs to pure logic.

It is not therefore enough that the Ideas of logic, and the pure laws set up with them, should be given in such a manner. Our great task is now *to bring the Ideas of logic, the logical concepts and laws, to epistemological clarity and definiteness.*

Here *phenomenological analysis* must begin. Logical concepts, as valid thought-unities, must have their origin in intuition: they must arise out of an ideational intuition founded on certain experiences, and must admit of indefinite reconfirmation, and of recognition of their self-identity, on the reperformance of such abstraction. Otherwise put: we can absolutely not rest content with 'mere words', i.e. with a merely symbolic understanding of words', such as we first have when we reflect on the sense of the laws for 'concepts', 'judgements', 'truths' etc. (together with their manifold specifications) which are set up in pure logic. Meanings inspired only by remote, confused, inauthentic intuitions – if by any intuitions at all – are not enough: we must go back to the 'things themselves'. We desire to render self-evident in fully-fledged intuitions that what is here given in actually performed abstractions is what the word-meanings in our expression of the law really and truly stand for. In the practice of cognition we strive to arouse dispositions in ourselves which will keep our meanings unshakably the same, which will measure them sufficiently often against the mark set by reproducible intuitions or by an intuitive carrying out of our abstraction. Intuitive illustration of the shifting meanings which attach to the same term in differing propositional contexts likewise convinces us of the fact of equivocation: it becomes evident to us that what a word means in this or that case has its fulfilment in essentially different intuitive 'moments' or patterns, or in essentially different general notions. By distinguishing among concepts confounded by us, and by suitably modifying our terminology, we then likewise achieve a desired 'clearness and distinctness' for our logical propositions.

The phenomenology of the logical experiences aims at giving us a sufficiently wide descriptive (though not empirically-psychological) understanding of these mental states and their indwelling sense, as will enable us to give fixed meanings to all the fundamental concepts of logic. Such meanings will be clarified both by going back to the analytically explored connections between meaning-intentions and meaning-fulfilments, and also by making their possible function in cognition intelligible and certain. They will be such meanings, in short, as the interest of pure logic itself requires, as well as the interest, above all, of epistemological insight into the essence of this discipline. Fundamental logical and noetic concepts have, up to this time, been quite imperfectly clarified: countless equivocations beset them, some so pernicious, so hard to track down, and to keep consistently separate, that they yield the main ground for the very backward state of pure logic and theory of knowledge.

We must of course admit that many conceptual differentiations and circumscriptions of the sphere of pure logic can become evident to the natural attitude without phenomenological analysis. The relevant logical acts are carried out and adequately fitted to their fulfilling intuitions, though there is no reflection on the phenomenological situation itself. What is most completely evident can, however, be confused with something else, what it apprehends can be misconstrued, its assured directives can be rejected. Clarifying researches are especially needed to explain our by no means chance inclination to slip unwittingly from an objective to a psychological attitude, and to mix up two bodies of data distinguishable in principle however much they may be essentially related, and to be deceived by psychological misconstructions and misinterpretations of the objects of logic. Such clarifications can, by their nature, only be achieved within a phenomenological theory of the essences of our thought- and knowledge-experiences, with continuous regard to the things essentially meant by, and so belonging to the latter (in the precise manners in which those things are *as such* 'shown forth', 'represented' etc.). Psychologism can only be radically overcome by a pure phenomenology, a science infinitely removed from psychology as the empirical science of the mental attributes and states of animal realities. In our sphere, too, the sphere of pure logic, such a phenomenology alone offers us all the necessary conditions for a finally satisfactory establishment of the totality of basic distinctions and insights. It alone frees us from the strong temptation, at first inevitable, since rooted in grounds of essence, to turn the logically objective into the psychological.

The above mentioned motives for phenomenological analysis have an obvious and essential connection with those which spring from *basic questions of epistemology*. For if these questions are taken in the *widest* generality, i.e. in the 'formal' generality which abstracts from all matter of knowledge – they form part of a range of questions involved in the full clarification of the Idea of pure logic. We have, on the one hand, the fact that all thought and knowledge have as their aim *objects* or *states of affairs*, which they putatively 'hit' in the sense that the 'being-in-itself' of these objects and states is supposedly shown forth, and made an identifiable item, in a multitude of actual or possible meanings, or acts of thought. We have, further, the fact that all thought is ensouled by a thought-form which is subject to ideal laws, laws circumscribing the objectivity or ideality of knowledge in general. These facts, I maintain, eternally provoke questions like: How are we to understand the fact that the intrinsic being of objectivity becomes 'presented', 'apprehended' in knowledge, and so ends up by becoming subjective? What does it mean to say that the object has 'being-in-itself', and is 'given' in knowledge? How can the ideality of the universal *qua* concept or law enter the flux of real mental states and become an epistemic possession of the thinking person? What does the *adaequatio rei et intellectus* mean in various cases of knowledge, according as what we apprehend and know, is individual or universal, a fact or a law etc.? These and similar questions can, it is plain, not be separated from the above-mentioned questions regarding the clarification of pure logic, since the task of clarifying such logical Ideas as Concept and Object, Truth and Proposition, Fact and Law etc., inevitably leads on to these same questions. We should in any case have to tackle them so that the essence of the clarification aimed at in phenomenological analyses should not itself be left obscure.

§3 The difficulties of pure phenomenological analysis

The difficulties of clearing up the basic concepts of logic are a natural consequence of the extraordinary difficulties of strict phenomenological analysis. These are in the main the same whether our immanent analysis aims at the *pure* essence of experiences (all empirical facticity and individuation being excluded) or treats experiences from an empirical, psychological standpoint. Psychologists usually discuss such difficulties when they consider introspection as a source of our detailed psychological knowledge, not properly however, but in order to draw a false antithesis between introspection and 'outer' perception. The source of all such difficulties lies in the unnatural direction of intuition and thought which phenomenological analysis requires. Instead of becoming lost in the performance of acts built intricately on one another, and instead of (as it were) naïvely positing the existence of the objects intended in their sense and then going on to characterize them, or of assuming such objects hypothetically, of drawing conclusions from all this etc., we must rather practise 'reflection', i.e. make these acts themselves, and their immanent meaning-content, our objects. When objects are intuited, thought of, theoretically pondered on, and thereby given to us as actualities in certain ontic modalities, we must direct our theoretical interest away from such objects, not posit them as realities as they appear or hold in the intentions of our acts. These acts, contrariwise, though hitherto not objective, must now be made objects of apprehension and of theoretical assertion. We must deal with them in new acts of intuition and thinking, we must analyse and describe them in their essence, we must make them objects of empirical or ideational thought. Here we have a direction of thought running counter to deeply ingrained habits which have been steadily strengthened since the dawn of mental development. Hence the well-nigh ineradicable tendency to slip out of a phenomenological thought-stance into one that is straightforwardly objective, or to substitute for mental acts, or for the 'appearances' or 'meanings' immanent in them, characters which, in a naïve performance of such acts, were attributed to their objects. Hence, too, the tendency to treat whole classes of genuinely subsistent objects, e.g. Ideas – since these may be evidently given to us in ideating intuitions – as phenomenological constituents of presentations *of* them.

A much discussed difficulty – one which seems to threaten in principle all possible immanent description of mental acts or indeed all phenomenological treatment of essences – lies in the fact that when we pass over from naïvely performed acts to an attitude of reflection, or when we perform acts proper to such reflection, our former acts necessarily undergo change. How can we rightly assess the nature and extent of such change? How indeed can we know anything whatever about it, whether as a fact or as a necessity of essence?

In addition to this difficulty of reaching firm results, capable of being self-evidently reidentified on many occasions, we have the further difficulty of *stating such results*, of *communicating them to others*. Completely self-evident truths of essence, established by the most exact analysis, must be expounded by way of expressions whose rich variety does not compensate for the fact that they only fit familiar natural objects, while the experiences in which such objects become constituted for consciousness, can be directly referred to only by way of a few highly ambiguous words such as 'sensation', 'perception', 'presentation' etc. One has, further, to employ expressions which stand for what is intentional in such acts, for the object to which they are directed, since it is, in fact, impossible to describe referential acts without using expressions which recur to the things to which such acts refer. One then readily forgets that such subsidiarily described objectivity, which is necessarily introduced into almost all phenomenological description, has undergone a change of sense, in virtue of which it now belongs to the sphere of phenomenology.

If we ignore such difficulties, others emerge concerned with the persuasive communication of our resultant insights to others. These insights can be tested and confirmed only by persons well-trained in the ability to engage in pure description in the unnatural attitude of reflection, trained in short to allow phenomenological relations to work upon them *in full purity*. Such purity means that we must keep out the falsifying intrusion of all assertions based on the naïve acceptance and assessment of objects, whose existence has been posited in the acts now receiving phenomenological treatment. It likewise prohibits any other going beyond whatever is essential and proper to such acts, any application to them of naturalistic interpretations and assertions. It forbids us, i.e., to set them up as psychological realities (even in an indefinitely general or exemplary fashion), as the states of 'mind-endowed beings' of any sort whatsoever. The capacity for such researches is not readily come by, nor can it be achieved or replaced by, e.g., the most elaborate of trainings in experimental psychology.

Serious as are the difficulties standing in the way of a pure phenomenology in general, and of the phenomenology of the logical experiences in particular, they are by no means such as to make the whole attempt to overcome them appear hopeless. Resolute cooperation among a generation of research-workers, conscious of their goal and dedicated to the main issue, would, I think, suffice to decide the most important questions in the field, those concerned with its basic constitution. Here we have a field of *attainable* discoveries, fundamentally involved in the possibility of a *scientific* philosophy. Such discoveries have indeed nothing dazzling about them: they lack any obviously useful relation to practice or to the fulfilment of higher emotional needs. They also lack any imposing apparatus of experimental methodology, through which experimental psychology has gained so much credit and has built up such a rich force of cooperative workers.

§4 It is essential to keep in mind the grammatical side of our logical experiences

Analytic phenomenology, needed by the logician in his preparatory laying of foundations, is concerned, among other things, with 'presentations' and with them primarily; it is, more precisely, concerned with those presentations to which *expression* has been given. In the complex objects of its study, its primary interest attaches to the experiences lying behind 'mere expressions', experiences which perform roles either of meaning-intention or of meaning-fulfilment. It cannot, however, quite ignore the sensuous-linguistic side of its complex objects (the element of 'mere expression' in them) nor the way in which this element is associated with the meaning that 'ensouls' it. Everyone knows how readily and how unnoticeably an analysis of meaning can be led astray by grammatical analysis. Since the direct analysis of meaning is, however, difficult, we may welcome each aid, however imperfect, that indirectly anticipates its results, but grammatical analysis is even more important in virtue of the errors its use promotes when it replaces a *true analysis of meaning*, than for any positive aid. Rough reflection on our thoughts and their verbal expression, conducted by us without special schooling, and often needed for the practical ends of thinking, suffice to indicate a certain parallelism between thinking and speaking. We all know that words mean something, and that, generally speaking, different words express different meanings. If we could regard such a correspondence as perfect, and as given *a priori*, and as one particularly in which the essential categories of meaning had perfect mirror-images in the categories of grammar, a phenomenology of linguistic forms would include a phenomenology of the meaning-experiences (experiences of thinking, judging etc.) and meaning-analysis would, so to speak, coincide with grammatical analysis.

Deep reflection is not, however, needed to show that a parallelism satisfying such far-reaching demands has as little foundation in grounds of essence as it obtains in fact. *Grammatically relevant distinctions of meaning* are at times *essential*, at times *contingent*, according as the practical aims of speech dictate peculiar forms for essential or contingent differences of meaning. (The latter are merely such as have a frequent occurrence in human intercourse.)

It is well-known, however, that differentiation of expressions does not merely depend on differences of meaning. I need point only to 'shades' of meaning, or to aesthetic tendencies which fight against any bare uniformity of expression, or against discord in speech-sound or rhythm, and so demand an abundant store of available synonyms.

The rough concomitances among verbal and thought-differences, and particularly among *forms* of words and thoughts, makes us naturally tend to seek logical distinctions behind expressed grammatical distinctions. It is, therefore, *an important matter for logic that the relation between expression and meaning should be made analytically clear.* We should perceive clearly that, in order to decide whether a distinction should, in a given case, count as logical or merely grammatical, we must go back from *vague* acts of meaning to the correspondingly clear, articulate ones, acts saturated with the fulness of exemplary intuition in which their meaning is fulfilled.

It is not enough to have the common knowledge, easily garnered from suitable examples, that grammatical differences need not coincide with logical ones. The common knowledge that such distinctions do not always go hand in hand – that languages, in other words, express material differences of meaning, widely used in communication, in forms as pervasive as the fundamental logical differences having their *a priori* roots in the general essence of meanings – such common knowledge may open the way to a dangerous radicalism. The field of logical forms may be unduly restricted. A wide range of logically significant forms may be cast forth as merely grammatical: only a few may be kept, such as suffice to leave some content to traditional syllogizing. Brentano's attempted reform of formal logic, valuable as it no doubt still is, plainly suffered from this exaggeration. Only a complete clearing-up of the essential phenomenological relations between expression and meaning, or between meaning-intention and meaning-fulfilment, can give us a firm middle stance, and can enable us to give the requisite clearness to the relations between grammatical and meaning-analysis.

§5 Statement of the main aims of the following analytical investigations

We accordingly pass to a series of analytic investigations which will clear up the constitutive Ideas of a pure or formal logic, investigations which relate in the first place to the pure theory of logical forms. Starting with the empirical connection between meaning-experiences and expressions, we must try to find out what our variously ambiguous talk about 'expressing' or 'meaning' really amounts to. We must try to see what essential phenomenological or logical distinctions apply *a priori* to expressions, and how we may in essence describe, and may place in pure categories, the experiences – to deal first with the phenomenological side of expressions – that have an *a priori* fitness for the meaning-function. We must find out how the 'presenting' and 'judging' achieved in such experiences stand to their corresponding 'intuition', how they are 'illustrated', or perhaps 'confirmed' or 'fulfilled', in the latter, or rendered 'evident' by it etc. It is not hard to see that investigations of such matters must precede all clarifications of the basic concepts and categories of logic. Among our introductory investigations we shall have to raise fundamental questions as to the acts, or, alternatively, the ideal meanings, which in logic pass under the name of 'presentations' (*Vorstellungen*). It is important to clarify and prise apart the many concepts that the word 'presentation' has covered, concepts in which the psychological, the epistemological and the logical are utterly confused. Similar analyses deal with the concept of *judgement* in the sense in which logic is concerned with it. So-called 'judgement-theory' neglects this task: it is in the main, in respect of its essential problems, a theory of presentation. We are naturally not interested in a psychological theory, but in a phenomenology of presentation- and judgement-experiences as delimited by our epistemological interests.

As we probe the essence of the expressive experiences, we must also dig more deeply into their *intentional subject-matter*, their objective intention's ideal sense, i.e. into the unity of its meaning and the unity of its object. We must, above all, dwell upon the enigmatic double sense or manner, the two-sided context, in which the same experience has a 'content', and the manner in which in addition to its real (*reell*) and proper content, an ideal, intentional content must and can dwell in it.

Here also belong questions relating to the 'object-directedness' or 'object-lessness' of logical acts, to the sense of the distinction between intentional and true objects, to the clarification of the Idea of truth in relation to the Idea of judgemental self-evidence, to the clarification of the remaining, closely connected logical and noetic categories. These investigations in part cover the same ground as those dealing with the constitution of logical forms, to the extent, of course, that we settle questions as to the acceptance or rejection of putative logical forms, or doubts as to their logical or merely grammatical distinctness from forms already recognized, in the course of our clarification of form-giving, categorial concepts.

We have thus vaguely indicated the range of problems to which the ensuing investigations will be oriented. These investigations make no claim to be exhaustive. Their aim is not to provide a logical system, but to do the initial spadework for a philosophical logic which will derive clearness from basic phenomenological sources. The paths taken by such an analytic investigation will also naturally differ from those suitable to a final, systematic, logically ordered statement of established truth.

§6 Additional Notes

Note 1 Our investigations will often inevitably take us beyond the narrow phenomenological sphere whose study is really required for giving direct evidence to the Ideas of logic. This sphere is itself not given to us initially, but becomes delimited in the course of our investigation. We are, in particular, forced beyond this sphere of research when we prise apart the many confused concepts obscurely confounded in our understanding of logical terms, and when we find which of them are truly logical.

Note 2 The phenomenological founding of logic involves the difficulty that we must, in our exposition, make use of all the concepts we are trying to clarify. This coincides with a certain wholly irremovable defect which affects the systematic course of our basic phenomenological and epistemological investigations. If a type of thought requires prior clarification, we should not make uncritical use of its terms or concepts in that clarification itself. But one should not expect that one should only be required to analyse such concepts critically, when the actual interconnection of one's logical materials has led up to them. Or, put differently, systematic clarification, whether in pure logic or any other discipline, would in itself seem to require a stepwise following out of the ordering of things, of the systematic interconnection in the science to be clarified. Our investigation can, however, only proceed securely, if it repeatedly breaks with such systematic sequence, if it removes conceptual obscurities which threaten the course of investigation *before* the natural sequence of subject-matters can lead up to such concepts. We search, as it were, in zig-zag fashion, a metaphor all the more apt since the close interdependence of our various epistemological concepts leads us back again and again to our original analyses, where the new confirms the old, and the old the new.

Note 3 If *our* sense of phenomenology has been grasped, and if it has not been given the current interpretation of an ordinary 'descriptive psychology', a part of natural science, then an objection, otherwise justifiable, will fall to the ground, an objection to the effect that all theory of knowledge, conceived as a systematic phenomenological clarification of knowledge, is built upon psychology. On this interpretation pure logic, treated by us as an epistemologically clarified, *philosophical* discipline, must in the end likewise rest upon psychology, if only upon its preliminary descriptive researches into intentional experiences. Why then so much heated resistance to psychologism?

We naturally reply that if psychology is given its old meaning, phenomenology is not descriptive psychology: its peculiar 'pure' description, its contemplation of pure essences on a basis of exemplary individual intuitions of experiences (often freely *imagined* ones), and its descriptive fixation of the contemplated essences into pure concepts, is no empirical, scientific description. It rather excludes the natural performance of all empirical (naturalistic) apperceptions and positings. Statements of descriptive psychology regarding 'perceptions', 'judgements', 'feelings', 'volitions' etc., use such names to refer to the real states of animal organisms in a real natural order, just as descriptive statements concerning physical states deal with happenings in a nature not imagined but real. All general statements have here a character of empirical generality: they hold for *this* nature. Phenomenology, however, does not discuss states of animal organisms (not even as belonging to a possible nature as such), but perceptions, judgements, feelings *as such*, and what pertains to them *a priori* with unlimited generality, as *pure* instances of *pure* species, of what may be seen through a purely intuitive apprehension of essence, whether generic or specific. Pure arithmetic likewise speaks of numbers, and pure geometry of spatial shapes, employing pure intuitions in their ideational universality. Not psychology, therefore, but phenomenology, underlies all clarifications in pure logic (and in all forms of rational criticism). Phenomenology has, however, a very different function as the necessary basis for every psychology that could with justification and in strictness be called scientific, just as pure mathematics, e.g. pure geometry and dynamics, is the necessary foundation for all exact natural science (any theory of empirical things in nature with their empirical forms, movements etc.). Our essential insights into perceptions, volitions and other forms of experience will naturally hold also of the corresponding empirical states of animal organisms, as geometrical insights hold of spatial figures in nature.

Translator's Additional Note 4 The above Note 3 is a typical account of what Husserl had come to mean by 'phenomenology' by the time that the Second Edition of the *Logical Investigations* was published in 1913. It replaces the following Note, which indicates what he meant by the term when the First Edition was published in 1901:

> Phenomenology is descriptive psychology. Epistemological criticism is therefore in essence psychology, or at least only capable of being built on a psychological basis. Pure logic therefore also rests on psychology – what then is the point of the whole battle against psychologism?
>
> The necessity of *this* sort of psychological foundation of pure logic, i.e. a strictly descriptive one, cannot lead us into error regarding the mutual independence of the two sciences, logic and psychology. For pure description is merely a preparatory step towards theory, not theory itself. One and the same sphere of pure description can accordingly serve to prepare for very different theoretical sciences. It is *not the full science of psychology that serves as a foundation for pure logic*, but certain classes of descriptions which are the step preparatory to the theoretical researches of psychology. These in so far as they describe the empirical objects whose genetic connections the science wishes to pursue, also form the substrate for those fundamental abstractions in which logic seizes the essence of its ideal objects and connections with inward evidence. Since it is epistemologically of unique importance that we

should separate the purely descriptive examination of the knowledge-experience, disembarrassed of all theoretical psychological interests, from the truly psychological researches directed to empirical explanation and origins, it will be good if we rather speak of 'phenomenology' than of descriptive psychology. It also recommends itself for the further reason that the expression 'descriptive psychology', as it occurs in the talk of many scientists, means the sphere of scientific psychological investigation, which is marked off by a methodological preference for inner experience and by an abstraction from all psychophysical explanation.

§7 'Freedom from presuppositions' as a principle in epistemological investigations

An epistemological investigation that can seriously claim to be scientific must, it has often been emphasized, satisfy the *principle of freedom from presuppositions*. This principle, we think, only seeks to express the strict exclusion of all statements not permitting of a comprehensive *phenomenological* realization. Every epistemological investigation that we carry out must have its pure foundation in phenomenology. The 'theory' that it aspires to, is no more than a thinking over, a coming to an evident understanding of, thinking and knowing as such, in their pure generic essence, of the specifications and forms that they essentially have, of the immanent structures that their objective relations involve, of the meaning of 'validity', 'justification', 'mediate' and 'immediate evidence', and their opposites, as applied to such structures, of the parallel specifications of such Ideas in relation to varying regions of possible objects of knowledge, of the clarified sense and role of the formal and material 'laws of thought' seen in their *a priori* structural connections with the knowing consciousness etc. If such a 'thinking over' of the meaning of knowledge is itself to yield, not mere opinion, but the evident knowledge it strictly demands, it must be a pure intuition of essences, exemplarily performed on an actual *given* basis of experiences of thinking and knowing. That acts of thought at times refer to transcendent, even to non-existent and impossible objects, is not to the case. For such direction to objects, such presentation and meaning of what is not really (*reell*) part of the phenomenological make-up of our experiences, is a descriptive feature of the experiences in question, whose sense it should be possible to fix and clarify by considering the experiences themselves. In no other way would it be possible.

We must keep apart from the pure theory of knowledge questions concerning the justifiability of accepting 'mental' and 'physical' realities which transcend consciousness, questions whether the statements of scientists regarding them are to be given a serious or unserious sense, questions whether it is justifiable or sensible to oppose a second, even more emphatically 'transcendent' world, to the phenomenal nature with which science is correlated, and other similar questions. The question as to the existence and nature of 'the external world' is a metaphysical question. The theory of knowledge, in generally clearing up the ideal essence and valid sense of cognitive thought, will of course deal with general questions regarding the possibility and manner of a knowledge or rational surmise about 'real' objective things, things in principle transcending the experiences which know them, and regarding the norms which the true sense of such a knowledge requires: it will not enter upon the empirically oriented question as to whether we as men really can arrive at such knowledge from the data we actually have, nor will it attempt to realize such knowledge. On our view, theory of knowledge, properly described, is no theory. It is not science in the pointed sense of an explanatorily unified theoretical whole. *Theoretical explanation* means an ever increased rendering intelligible of singular facts through general laws, and an ever increased rendering intelligible of general laws through some fundamental law. In the realm of facts, our task is to know that what happens under given groups of circumstances, happens *necessarily*, i.e. according to *natural laws*. In the realm of the *a priori* our task is to understand the *necessity* of specific, lower-level relationships in terms of comprehensive general necessities, and ultimately in terms of those most primitive, universal relational *laws* that we call axioms. The theory of knowledge has nothing to explain in this theoretical sense, it neither constructs deductive theories nor falls under any. This is clear enough if we consider the most general, the so-to-say formal theory of knowledge that came before us in our *Prolegomena* as the philosophical completion of pure mathematics conceived in absolute width as including all *a priori*, categorial knowledge in the form of systematic theories. This theory of theories goes together with, and is illuminated by, a formal theory of knowledge which precedes all empirical theory, which precedes, therefore, all empirical knowledge of the real, all physical science on the one hand, and all psychology on the other, and of course all metaphysics. Its aim is not to *explain* knowledge in the psychological or psychophysical sense as a *factual* occurrence in objective nature, but to *shed light* on the *Idea* of knowledge in its constitutive elements and laws. It does not try to follow up the real connections of coexistence and succession with which actual acts of knowledge are interwoven, but to understand the *ideal* sense of the *specific* connections in which the objectivity of knowledge may be documented. It endeavours to raise to clearness the pure forms and laws of knowledge by tracing knowledge back to an adequate fulfilment in intuition. This 'clearing up' takes place in the framework of a phenomenology of knowledge, a phenomenology oriented, as we saw, to the essential structures of pure experiences and to the structures of sense (*Sinnbestände*) that belong to these. From the beginning, as at all later stages, its scientific statements involve not the slightest reference to real existence: no metaphysical, scientific and, above all, no psychological assertions can therefore occur among its premisses.

A purely phenomenological 'theory' of knowledge naturally has an application to all naturally developed, and (in a good sense) 'naïve' sciences, which it transforms into 'philosophical' sciences. It transforms them, in other words, into sciences which provide us with clarified, assured knowledge in every sense in which it is possible to desire the latter. As regards the sciences of 'reality', such epistemological clarification can as much be regarded as a 'scientific' as a 'metaphysical' evaluation.

The investigations which follow aspire solely to such freedom from metaphysical, scientific and psychological presuppositions. No harm will of course be done by occasional side-references which remain without effect on the content and character of one's analyses, nor by the many expository devices addressed to one's public, whose existence (like one's own) is not therefore presupposed by the content of one's investigations. Nor does one exceed one's prescribed limits if one starts, e.g., from existent languages and discusses the merely communicative meaning of their many forms of expression, and so on. It is easily seen that the sense and the epistemological worth of the following analyses does not depend on the fact that there really are languages, and that men really make use of them in their mutual dealings, or that there really are such things as men and a nature, and that they do not merely exist in imagined, possible fashion.

The real premises of our putative results must lie in propositions satisfying the requirement that what they assert permits of an *adequate phenomenological justification*, a fulfilment through *evidence* in the strictest sense. Such propositions must not, further, ever be adduced in some other sense than that in which they have been intuitively established.

Expression and meaning

Chapter 1

Essential distinctions

§1 An ambiguity in the term 'sign'

The terms 'expression' and 'sign' are often treated as synonyms, but it will not be amiss to point out that they do not always coincide in application in common usage. Every sign is a sign for something, but not every sign has 'meaning', a 'sense' that the sign 'expresses'. In many cases it is not even true that a sign 'stands for' that of which we may say it is a sign. And even where this can be said, one has to observe that 'standing for' will not count as the 'meaning' which characterizes the expression. For signs in the sense of indications (notes, marks etc.) *do not express* anything, unless they happen to fulfil a significant as well as an indicative function. If, as one unwillingly does, one limits oneself to expressions employed in living discourse, the notion of an indication seems to apply more widely than that of an expression, but this does not mean that its content is the genus of which an expression is the species. To mean is *not a particular way of being a sign in the sense of indicating something.* It has a narrower application only because meaning – in communicative speech – is always bound up with such an indicative relation, and this in its turn leads to a wider concept, since meaning is also capable of occurring without such a connection. *Expressions* function meaningfully even in *isolated mental life, where they no longer serve to indicate anything.* The two notions of sign do not therefore really stand in the relation of more extensive genus to narrower species.

The whole matter requires more thorough discussion.

§2 The essence of indication

Of the two concepts connected with the word 'sign', we shall first deal with that of an *indication*. The relation that here obtains we shall call the *indicative relation*. In this sense a brand is the sign of a slave, a flag the sign of a nation. Here all marks belong, as characteristic qualities suited to help us in recognizing the objects to which they attach.

But the concept of an indication extends more widely than that of a mark. We say the Martian canals are signs of the existence of intelligent beings on Mars, that fossil vertebrae are signs of the existence of prediluvian animals etc. Signs to aid memory, such as the much-used knot in a handkerchief, memorials etc., also have their place here. If suitable things, events or their properties are deliberately produced to serve as such indications, one calls them 'signs' whether they exercise this function or not. Only in the case of indications deliberately and artificially brought about, does one speak of standing for, and that both in respect of the action which produces the marking (the branding or chalking etc.), and in the sense of the indication itself, i.e. taken in its relation to the object it stands for or that it is to signify.

These distinctions and others like them do not deprive the concept of indication of its essential unity. A thing is only properly an indication if and where it in fact serves to indicate something to some thinking being. If we wish to seize the pervasively common element here present we must refer back to such cases of 'live' functioning. In these we discover as a common circumstance the fact that certain objects or states of affairs *of whose reality someone has actual knowledge* indicate to him *the reality of certain other objects or states of affairs*, in the sense that *his belief in the reality of the one is experienced* (though not at all evidently) *as motivating a belief or surmise in the reality of the other*. This relation of 'motivation' represents a *descriptive unity* among our acts of judgement in which indicating and indicated states of affairs become constituted for the thinker. This descriptive unity is not to be conceived as a mere form-quality founded upon our acts of judgement, for it is in their unity that the essence of indication lies. More lucidly put: the 'motivational' unity of our acts of judgement has itself the character of a unity of judgement; before it as a whole an objective correlate, a unitary state of affairs, parades itself, is meant in such a judgement, appears to be in and for that judgement. Plainly such a state of affairs amounts to just this: that certain things *may* or *must* exist, *since* other things have been given. This 'since', taken as expressing an objective connection, is the objective correlate of 'motivation' taken as a descriptively peculiar way of combining acts of judgement into a single act of judgement.

§5 Expressions as meaningful signs. Setting aside of a sense of 'expression' not relevant for our purpose

From indicative signs we distinguish *meaningful* signs, i.e. *expressions*. We thereby employ the term 'expression' restrictively: we exclude much that ordinary speech would call an 'expression' from its range of application. There are other cases in which we have thus to do violence to usage, where concepts for which only ambiguous terms exist call for a fixed terminology. We shall lay down, for provisional intelligibility, that each instance or part of *speech*, as also each sign that is essentially of the same sort, shall count as an expression, whether or not such speech is actually uttered, or addressed with communicative intent to any persons or not. Such a definition excludes facial expression and the various gestures which involuntarily accompany speech without communicative intent, or those in which a man's mental states achieve understandable 'expression' for his environment, without the added help of speech. Such 'utterances' are not expressions in the sense in which a case of speech is an expression, they are not phenomenally one with the experiences made manifest in them in the consciousness of the man who manifests them, as is the case with speech. In such manifestations one man communicates nothing to another: their utterance involves no intent to put certain 'thoughts' on record expressively, whether for the man himself, in his solitary state, or for others. Such 'expressions', in short, have properly speaking, *no meaning*. It is not to the point that another person may interpret our involuntary manifestations, e.g. our 'expressive movements', and that he may thereby become deeply acquainted with our inner thoughts and emotions. They 'mean' something to him in so far as he interprets them, but even for him they are without meaning in the special sense in which verbal signs have meaning: they only mean in the sense of indicating.

In the treatment which follows these distinctions must be raised to complete conceptual clarity.

§6 Questions as to the phenomenological and intentional distinctions which pertain to expressions as such

It is usual to distinguish two things in regard to every expression:

1. The expression physically regarded (the sensible sign, the articulate sound-complex, the written sign on paper etc.).

2. A certain sequence of mental states, associatively linked with the expression, which make it be the expression of something. These mental states are generally called the 'sense' or the 'meaning' of the expression, this being taken to be in accord with what these words ordinarily mean. But we shall see this notion to be mistaken, and that a mere distinction between physical signs and sense-giving experiences is by no means enough, and not at all enough for logical purposes.

The points here made have long been observed in the special case of names. We distinguish, in the case of each name, between what it 'shows forth' (i.e. mental states) and what it means. And again between what it means (the sense or 'content' of its naming presentation) and what it names (the object of that presentation). We shall need similar distinctions in the case of all expression, and shall have to explore their nature precisely. Such distinctions have led to our distinction between the notions of 'expression' and 'indication', which is not in conflict with the fact that an expression in living speech also functions as an indication, a point soon to come up for discussion. To these distinctions other important ones will be added which will concern the relations between meaning and the intuition which illustrates meaning and on occasion renders it evident. Only by paying heed to these relations, can the concept of meaning be clearly delimited, and can the fundamental opposition between the symbolic and the epistemological function of meanings be worked out.

§7 Expressions as they function in communication

(they operate, indicatively)

Expressions were originally framed to fulfil a communicative function: let us, accordingly, first study expressions in this function, so that we may be able to work out their essential logical distinctions. The articulate sound-complex, the written sign etc., first becomes a spoken word or communicative bit of speech, when a speaker produces it with the intention of 'expressing himself about something' through its means; he must endow it with a sense in certain acts of mind, a sense he desires to share with his auditors. Such sharing becomes a possibility if the auditor also understands the speaker's intention. He does this inasmuch as he takes the speaker to be a person, who is not merely uttering sounds but *speaking to him*, who is accompanying those sounds with certain sense-giving acts, which the sounds reveal to the hearer, or whose sense they seek to communicate to him. What first makes mental commerce possible, and turns connected speech into discourse, lies in the correlation among the corresponding physical and mental experiences of communicating persons which is effected by the physical side of speech. Speaking and hearing, intimation of mental states through speaking and reception thereof in hearing, are mutually correlated.

If one surveys these interconnections, one sees at once that all expressions in *communicative* speech function as *indications*. They serve the hearer as signs of the 'thoughts' of the speaker, i.e. of his sense-giving inner experiences, as well as of the other inner experiences which are part of his communicative intention. This function of verbal expressions we shall call their *intimating function*. The content of such intimation consists in the inner experiences intimated. The sense of the predicate 'intimated' can be understood more narrowly or more widely. The *narrower* sense we may restrict to *acts which impart sense*, while the *wider* sense will cover *all* acts that a hearer may introject into a speaker on the basis of what he says (possibly because he tells us of such acts). If, e.g., we state a wish, our judgement concerning that wish is what we intimate in the narrower sense of the word, whereas the wish itself is intimated in the wider sense. The same holds of an ordinary statement of perception, which the hearer forthwith takes to belong to some actual perception. The act of perception is there intimated in the wider sense, the judgement built upon it in the narrower sense. We at once see that ordinary speech permits us to call an experience which is intimated an experience which is *expressed*.

To understand an intimation is not to have conceptual knowledge of it, not to judge in the sense of asserting anything about it: it consists simply in the fact that the hearer *intuitively* takes the speaker to be a person who is expressing this or that, or as we certainly can say, *perceives* him as such. When I listen to someone, I perceive him as a speaker, I hear him recounting, demonstrating, doubting, wishing etc. The hearer perceives the intimation in the same sense in which he perceives the intimating person – even though the mental phenomena which make him a person cannot fall, for what they are, in the intuitive grasp of another. Common speech credits us with percepts even of other people's inner experiences; we 'see' their anger, their pain etc. Such talk is quite correct, as long as, e.g., we allow outward bodily things likewise to count as perceived, and as long as, in general, the notion of perception is not restricted to the adequate, the strictly intuitive percept. If the essential mark of perception lies in the intuitive persuasion that a thing or event is itself before us for our grasping – such a persuasion is possible, and in the main mass of cases actual, without verbalized, conceptual apprehension – then the receipt of such an intimation is the mere perceiving of it. The essential distinction just touched on is of course present here. The hearer perceives the speaker as manifesting certain inner experiences, and to that extent he also perceives these experiences themselves: he does not, however, himself experience them, he has not an 'inner' but an 'outer' percept of them. Here we have the big difference between the real grasp of what is in adequate intuition, and the putative grasp of what is on a basis of inadequate, though intuitive, presentation. In the former case we have to do with an experienced, in the latter case with a presumed being, to which no truth corresponds at all. Mutual understanding demands a certain correlation among the mental acts mutually unfolded in intimation and in the receipt of such intimation, but not at all their exact resemblance.

§8 Expressions in solitary life

So far we have considered expressions as used in communication, which last depends essentially on the fact that they operate indicatively. But expressions also play a great part in uncommunicated, interior mental life. This change in function plainly has nothing to do with whatever makes an expression an expression. Expressions continue to have meanings as they had before, and the same meanings as in dialogue. A word only cases to be a word when our interest stops at its sensory contour, when it becomes a mere sound-pattern. But when we live in the understanding of a word, it expresses something and the same thing, whether we address it to anyone or not.

It seems clear, therefore, that an expression's meaning, and whatever else pertains to it essentially, cannot coincide with its feats of intimation. Or shall we say that, even in solitary mental life, one still uses expressions to intimate something, though not to a second person? Shall one say that in soliloquy one speaks to oneself, and employs words as signs, i.e. as indications, of one's own inner experiences? I cannot think such a view acceptable. Words function as signs here as they do everywhere else: everywhere they can be said to point to something. But if we reflect on the relation of expression to meaning, and to this end break up our complex, intimately unified experience of the sense-filled expression, into the two factors of word and sense, the word comes before us as intrinsically indifferent, whereas the sense seems the thing aimed at by the verbal sign and meant by its means: the expression seems to direct interest away from itself towards its sense, and to point to the latter. But this pointing is not an indication in the sense previously discussed. The existence of the sign neither 'motivates' the existence of the meaning, nor, properly expressed, our belief in the meaning's existence. What we are to use as an indication, must be perceived by us as existent. This holds also of expressions used in communication, but not for expressions used in soliloquy, where we are in general content with imagined rather than with actual words. In imagination a spoken or printed word floats before us, though in reality it has no existence. We should not, however, confuse imaginative presentations, and the image-contents they rest on, with their imagined objects. The imagined verbal sound, or the imagined printed word, does not exist, only its imaginative presentation does so. The difference is the difference between imagined centaurs and the imagination of such beings. The word's non-existence neither disturbs nor interests us, since it leaves the word's expressive function unaffected. Where it *does* make a difference is where intimation is linked with meaning. Here thought must not be merely expressed as meaning, but must be communicated and intimated. We can only do the latter where we actually speak and hear.

One of course speaks, in a certain sense, even in soliloquy, and it is certainly possible to think of oneself as speaking, and even as speaking to oneself, as, e.g., when someone says to himself: 'You have gone wrong, you can't go on like that.' But in the genuine sense of communication, there is no speech in such cases, nor does one tell oneself anything: one merely conceives of oneself as speaking and communicating. In a monologue words can perform no function of indicating the existence of mental acts, since such indication would there be quite purposeless. For the acts in question are themselves experienced by us at that very moment.

§9 Phenomenological distinctions between the physical appearance of the expression, and the sense-giving and sense-fulfilling act

If we now turn from experiences specially concerned with intimation, and consider expressions in respect of distinctions that pertain to them equally whether they occur in dialogue or soliloquy, two things seem to be left over: the expressions themselves, and what they express as their meaning or sense.

Several relations are, however, intertwined at this point, and talk about 'meaning', or about 'what is expressed', is correspondingly ambiguous. If we seek a foothold in pure description, the concrete phenomenon of the sense-informed expression breaks up, on the one hand, into the *physical phenomenon* forming the physical side of the expression, and, on the other hand, into the *acts* which give it *meaning* and possibly also *intuitive fulness*, in which its relation to an expressed object is constituted. In virtue of such acts, the expression is more than a merely sounded word. It *means* something, and in so far as it means something, it relates to what is objective. This objective somewhat can either be actually present through accompanying intuitions, or may at least appear in representation, e.g. in a mental image, and where this happens the relation to an object is realized. Alternatively this need not occur: the expression functions significantly, it remains more than mere sound of words, but it lacks any basic intuition that will give it its object. The relation of expression to object is now unrealized as being confined to a mere meaning-intention. A *name*, e.g., names its object whatever the circumstances, in so far as it *means* that object. But if the object is not intuitively before one, and so not before one as a named or meant object, mere meaning is all there is to it. If the originally *empty* meaning-intention is now fulfilled, the relation to an object is realized, the naming becomes an actual, conscious relation between name and object named.

Let us take our stand on this fundamental distinction between meaning-intentions void of intuition and those which are intuitively fulfilled: if we leave aside the sensuous acts in which the expression, *qua* mere sound of words, makes its appearance, we shall have to distinguish between two acts or sets of acts. We shall, on the one hand, have acts essential to the expression if it is to be an expression at all, i.e. a verbal sound infused with sense. These acts we shall call the *meaning-conferring acts* or the *meaning-intentions.* But we shall, on the other hand, have acts, not essential to the expression as such, which stand to it in the logically basic relation of *fulfilling* (confirming, illustrating) it more or less adequately, and so actualizing its relation to its object. These acts, which become fused with the meaning-conferring acts in the unity of knowledge or fulfilment, we call the *meaning-fulfilling* acts. The briefer expression 'meaning-fulfilment' can only be used in cases where there is no risk of the ready confusion with the *whole* experience in which a meaning-intention finds fulfilment in its correlated intuition. In the realized relation of the expression to its objective correlate,[1] the sense-informed expression becomes one with the act of meaning-fulfilment. The sounded word is first made one with the meaning-intention, and this in its turn is made one (as intentions in general are made one with their fulfilments) with its corresponding meaning-fulfilment. The word 'expression' is normally understood – wherever, that is, we do not speak of a 'mere' expression – as the *sense-animated* expression. One should not, therefore, properly say (as one often does) that an expression *expresses its meaning* (its intention).

One might more properly adopt the alternative way of speaking according to which the *fulfilling act* appears as *the act expressed by the complete expression*: we may e.g., say, that a statement 'gives expression' to an act of perceiving or imagining. We need not here point out that both meaning-conferring and meaning-fulfilling acts have a part to play in intimation in the case of communicative discourse. The former in fact constitute the inmost core of intimation. To make them known to the hearer is the prime aim of our communicative intention, for only in so far as the hearer attributes them to the speaker will he understand the latter.

§10 The phenomenological unity of these acts

The above distinguished acts involving the expression's appearance, on the one hand, and the meaning-intention and possible meaning-fulfilment, on the other, do not constitute a mere aggregate of simultaneously given items in consciousness. They rather form an intimately fused unity of peculiar character. Everyone's personal experience bears witness to the differing weight of the two constituents, which reflects the asymmetry of the relation between an expression and the object which (through its meaning) it expresses or names. Both are 'lived through', the presentation of the word and the sense-giving act: but, while we experience the former, we do not live *in* such a presentation at all, but solely in enacting its sense, its meaning. And in so far as we do this, and yield ourselves to enacting the meaning-intention and its further fulfilment, our whole interest centres upon the object intended in our intention, and named by its means. (These two ways of speaking have in fact the same meaning.) The function of a word (or rather of an intuitive word-presentation) is to awaken a sense-conferring act in ourselves, to point to what is intended, or perhaps given intuitive fulfilment in this act, and to guide our interest exclusively in this direction.

Such pointing is not to be described as the mere objective fact of a regular diversion of interest from one thing to another. The fact that two presented objects A and B are so linked by some secret psychological coordination that the presentation of A regularly arouses the presentation of B, and that interest is thereby shifted from A to B – such a fact does not make A the expression of the presentation of B. To be an expression is rather a descriptive aspect of the *experienced unity* of sign and thing signified.

What is involved in the descriptive difference between the physical sign-phenomenon and the meaning-intention which makes it into an expression, becomes most clear when we turn our attention to the sign *qua* sign, e.g. to the printed word as such. If we do this, we have an external percept (or external intuitive idea) just like any other, whose object loses its verbal character. If this object again functions as a word, its presentation is wholly altered in character. The word (*qua* external singular) remains intuitively present, maintains its appearance, but we no longer intend it, it no longer properly is the object of our 'mental activity'. Our interest, our intention, our thought – mere synonyms if taken in sufficiently wide senses – point exclusively to the thing meant in the sense-giving act. This means, phenomenologically speaking, that the intuitive presentation, in which the physical appearance of the word is constituted, undergoes an essential phenomenal modification when its object begins to count as an *expression*. While what constitutes the object's appearing remains unchanged, the intentional character of the experience alters. There is constituted (without need of a fulfilling or illustrative intuition) an act of meaning which finds support in the verbal presentation's intuitive content, but which differs in essence from the intuitive intention directed upon the word itself. With this act, the new acts or act-complexes that we call 'fulfilling' acts or act-complexes are often peculiarly blended, acts whose object coincides with the object meant in the meaning, or named through this meaning.

In our next chapter (excised from this edition) we shall have to conduct additional researches into the question as to whether the 'meaning-intention', which on our view characteristically marks off an expression from empty 'sound of words' consists in the mere association of mental imagery of the intended object with the sounded words, or at least necessarily involves such an act of fancy, or whether, on the other hand, mental imagery lies outside of the essence of an expression, and rather performs a fulfilling role, even if only of a partial, indirect or provisional character. In order not to blur the main outlines of our thought, we shall not here enter more deeply into phenomenological questions. In this whole investigation, we need only do as much phenomenology as is required to establish essential, primary distinctions.

The provisional description so far given will have shown how complex is the correct description of a phenomenological situation. Such complexity appears inevitable once we clearly see that all objects and relations among objects only are what they are for us, through acts of thought essentially different from them, in which they become present to us, in which they stand before us as unitary items that we *mean*. Where not the phenomenological, but the naïvely objective interest dominates, where we live in intentional acts without reflecting upon them, all talk of course becomes plain sailing and clear and devoid of circumlocution. One then, in our case, simply speaks of 'expression' and of 'what is expressed', of name and thing named, of the steering of attention from one to the other etc. But where the phenomenological interest dominates, we endure the hardship of having to describe phenomenological relationships which we may have experienced on countless occasions, but of which we were not normally conscious as objects, and we have also to do our describing with expressions framed to deal with objects whose appearance lies in the sphere of our normal interests.

§11 The ideal distinctions: firstly, between expression and meaning as ideal entities

We have so far considered 'the well-understood expression' as a concrete experience. Instead of considering its two types of factor, the expression's appearance and the sense-conferring or sense-fulfilling experience, we wish to consider what is, in a certain fashion, given 'in' these: the expression itself, its sense and its objective correlate. We turn therefore from the real relation of acts to the ideal relation of their objects or contents. A subjective treatment yields to one that is objective. The ideality of the relationship between expression and meaning is at once plain in regard to both its sides, inasmuch as, when we ask for the meaning of an expression, e.g. 'quadratic remainder', we are naturally not referring to the sound-pattern uttered here and now (*hic et nunc*), the vanishing noise that can never recur identically: we mean the expression *in specie*. 'Quadratic remainder' is the same expression by whomsoever uttered. The same holds of talk about the expression's meaning, which naturally does not refer to some meaning-conferring experience.

Every example shows that an essential distinction must here be drawn.

If I sincerely say – we shall always presume sincerity – 'The three perpendiculars of a triangle intersect in a point', this is of course based on the fact that I judge so. If someone hears me and understands my assertion, he likewise knows this fact; he 'apperceives' me as someone who judges thus. But is the judging here *intimated* the meaning of my assertion, is it what my assertion asserts, and in that sense expresses? Plainly not. It would hardly occur to anyone, if asked as to the sense or meaning of my assertion, to revert to my judgement as an inner experience. Everyone would rather reply by saying: What this assertion asserts is *the same* whoever may assert it, and on whatever occasion or in whatever circumstances he may assert it, and what it asserts is precisely this, *that the three perpendiculars of a triangle intersect in a point*, no more and no less. One therefore repeats what is in essence 'the same' assertion, and one repeats it because it is the one, uniquely adequate way of expressing the same thing, i.e. its meaning. In this selfsame meaning, of whose identity we are conscious whenever we repeat the statement, nothing at all about judging or about one who judges is discoverable. We thought we were sure that a state of affairs held or obtained objectively, and what we were sure of we expressed by way of a declarative sentence. The state of affairs is what it is whether we assert that it obtains or not. It is intrinsically an item, a unity, which is capable of so obtaining or holding. But such an obtaining is what appeared before us, and we set it forth as it appeared before us: we said 'So the matter is'. Naturally we could not have done this, we could not have made the assertion, if the matter had not so appeared before us, if, in other words, we had not so judged. This forms part of an assertion as a psychological fact, it is involved in its intimation. But only in such intimation; for while what is intimated consists in inner experiences, what we assert in the judgement involves nothing subjective. My act of judging is a transient experience: it arises and passes away. But what my assertion asserts, the content *that the three perpendiculars of a triangle intersect in a point*, neither arises nor passes away. It is an identity in the strict sense, one and the same geometrical truth.

It is the same in the case of all assertions, even if what they assert is false and absurd. Even in such cases we distinguish their ideal content from the transient acts or affirming and asserting it: it is the meaning of the assertion, a unity in plurality. We continue to recognize its identity of intention in evident acts of reflection: we do not arbitrarily attribute it to our assertions, but discover it in them.

If 'possibility' or 'truth' is lacking, an assertion's intention can only be carried out symbolically: it cannot derive any 'fulness' from intuition or from the categorial functions performed on the latter, in which 'fulness' its value for knowledge consists. It then lacks, as one says, a 'true', a 'genuine' meaning. Later we shall look more closely into this distinction between intending and fulfilling meaning. To characterize the various acts in which the relevant ideal unities are constituted, and to throw light on the essence of their actual 'coincidence' in knowledge, will call for difficult, comprehensive studies. It is plain, however, that each assertion, whether representing an exercise of knowledge or not – whether or not, i.e., it fulfils or can fulfil its intention in corresponding intuitions, and the formative acts involved in these – involves an intention, in which intention, as its unified specific character, its meaning is constituted.

It is this ideal unity men have in mind when they say that 'the' judgement is the meaning of 'the' declarative sentence. Only the fundamental ambiguity of the word 'judgement' at once tends to confuse the evidently grasped ideal unity with the real act of judging, to confuse what the assertion intimates with what it asserts.

What we have here said of complete assertions readily applies also to actual or possible parts of assertions. If I judge *If the sum of the angles in a triangle does not equal two right angles, the axiom of parallels does not hold*, the hypothetical antecedent is no assertion, for I do not say that such an inequation holds. None the less it says something, and what it says is once more quite different from what it intimates. What it says is not my mental act of hypothetical presumption, though I must of course have performed this in order to speak sincerely as I do. But it is rather the case that, when this subjective act is intimated, something objective and ideal is brought to expression: the hypothesis whose conceptual content can appear as the same intentional unity in many possible thought-experiences, and which evidently stands before us in its unity and identity in the objectively-ideal treatment characteristic of all thinking.

The same holds of the other parts of our statements, even of such as do not have the form of propositions.

§12 Continuation: the expressed objectivity

Talk of *what an expression expresses* has, in the discussion so far, several essentially different meanings. It relates, *on the one hand*, to intimation in general, and especially in that connection to sense-giving acts, at times also to sense-fulfilling acts (if these are present at all). In an assertion, e.g., we express our judgement (we intimate it), but we also express percepts and other sense-fulfilling acts which illustrate our assertion's meaning. *On the other hand*, such talk relates to the 'contents' of such acts, and primarily to the meanings, which are often enough said to be 'expressed'.

It is doubtful whether the examples analysed, in our last section, would suffice even to lend provisional intelligibility to the notion of meaning, if one could not forthwith introduce a new sense of 'expression' for purposes of comparison. The terms 'meaning', 'content', 'state of affairs' and all similar terms harbour such powerful equivocations that our intention, even if expressed most carefully, still can promote misunderstanding. The third sense of 'being expressed', which we must now discuss, concerns the *objective correlate* meant by a meaning and expressed by its means.

Each expression not merely says something, but says it *of* something: it not only has a meaning, but refers to certain *objects*. This relation sometimes holds in the plural for one and the same expression. But the object never coincides with the meaning. Both, of course, only pertain to an expression in virtue of the mental acts which give it sense. And, if we distinguish between 'content' and object in respect of such 'presentations', one's distinction means the same as the distinction between what is meant or said, on the one hand, and what is spoken of, by means of the expression, on the other.

The necessity of distinguishing between meaning (content) and object becomes clear when a comparison of examples shows us that several expressions may have the same meaning but different objects, and again that they may have different meanings but the same object. There is of course also the possibility of their differing in both respects and agreeing in both. The last occurs in the cases of synonymous expressions, e.g. the corresponding expressions in different languages which mean and name the same thing ('London', 'Londres'; 'zwei', 'deux', 'duo' etc.).

Names offer the plainest examples of the separation of meaning from the relation to objects, this relation being in their case usually spoken of as 'naming'. Two names can differ in meaning but can name the same object, e.g. 'the victor at Jena' – 'the vanquished at Waterloo'; 'the equilateral triangle' – 'the equiangular triangle'. The meaning expressed in our pairs of names is plainly different, though the same object is meant in each case. The same applies to names whose indefiniteness gives them an 'extension'. The expressions 'an equilateral triangle' and 'an equiangular triangle' have the same objective reference, the same range of possible application.

It can happen, conversely, that two expressions have the same meaning but a different objective reference. The expression 'a horse' has the same meaning in whatever context it occurs. But if on one occasion we say 'Bucephalus is a horse', and on another 'That cart-horse is a horse', there has been a plain change in our sense-giving presentation in passing from the one statement to the other. The expression 'a horse' employs the same meaning to present Bucephalus on one occasion and the cart-horse on the other. It is thus with all general names, i.e. names with an 'extension'. 'One' is a name whose meaning never differs, but one should not, for that reason, identify the various 'ones' which occur in a sum: they all mean the same, but they differ in objective reference.

The case of proper names is different, whether they name individual or general objects. A word like 'Socrates' can only name different things by meaning different things, i.e. by becoming *equivocal*. Wherever the word has *one* meaning, it also names *one* object. The same holds of expressions like 'the number two', 'redness' etc. We therefore distinguish equivocal names that have *many meanings* from general or class-names that have *many values*.

The same holds of other types of expression, though in their case talk of objective reference involves certain difficulties in virtue of its manifoldness. If we consider, e.g., statements of the form 'S is P' we generally regard the subject of the statement as the object about which the statement is made. Another view is, however, possible, which treats the *whole* state of affairs which corresponds to the statement as an analogue of the object a name names, and distinguishes this from the object's meaning. If this is done one can quote as examples pairs of sentences such as 'a is bigger than b' – 'b is smaller than a', which plainly say different things. They are not merely grammatically but also 'cogitatively' different, i.e. different in meaning-content. But they express the same state of affairs: the same 'matter' is predicatively apprehended and asserted in two different ways. Whether we define talk of the 'object' of a statement in one sense or the other – each has its own claims – statements are in either case possible which differ in meaning while referring to the same object.

§13 Connection between meaning and objective reference

Our examples entitle us to regard the distinction between an expression's meaning and its power to direct itself as a name to this or that objective correlate – and of course the distinction between meaning and object itself – as well-established. It is clear for the rest that the sides to be distinguished in each expression are closely connected: an expression only refers to an objective correlate *because* it means something, it can be rightly said to signify or name the object *through* its meaning. An act of meaning is the determinate manner in which we refer to our object of the moment, though this mode of significant reference and the meaning itself can change while the objective reference remains fixed.

A more profound phenomenological clarification of this relation can be reached only by research into the way expressions and their meaning-intentions function in knowledge. This would show that talk about *two distinguishable sides* to each expression, should not be taken seriously, that the essence of an expression lies solely in its meaning. But the same intuition (as we shall show later) can offer fulfilment of different expressions: it can be categorially apprehended in varying ways and synthetically linked with other intuitions. Expressions and their meaning-intentions do not take their measure, in contexts of thought and knowledge, from mere intuition – I mean phenomena of external or internal sensibility – but from the varying intellectual forms through which intuited objects first become intelligibly determined, mutually related objects. And so expressions, even when they function outside of knowledge, must, as symbolic intentions, point to cat-egorially *formed* unities. Different meanings may therefore pertain to the same intuitions regarded in differing categorial fashion, and may therefore also pertain to the same object. But where a whole range of objects corresponds to a single meaning, this meaning's own essence must be *indeterminate*: it must permit a sphere of possible fulfilment.

These indications may suffice for the moment. They must guard in advance against the error of seriously thinking that sense-giving acts have two distinct sides, one which gives them their meaning, while the other gives them their determinate direction to objects.[2]

§14 Content as object, content as fulfilling sense and content as sense or meaning simpliciter

Relational talk of 'intimation', 'meaning' and 'object' belongs *essentially* to every expression. Every expression intimates something, means something and names or otherwise designates something. In each case, talk of 'expression' is equivocal. As said above, relation to an actually given objective correlate, which fulfils the meaning-intention, is *not* essential to an expression. If this last important case is also taken into consideration, we note that there are two things that can be said to be expressed in the realized relation to the object. We have, on the one hand, the *object itself*, and the object as meant in this or that manner. On the other hand, and more properly, we have the object's ideal correlate in the acts of meaning-fulfilment which constitute it, *the fulfilling sense*. Wherever the meaning-intention is fulfilled in a corresponding intuition, i.e. wherever the expression actually serves to name a given object, there the object is constituted as one 'given' in certain acts, and, to the extent that our expression really measures up to the in-tuitive data, as given *in the same manner* in which the expression *means* it. In this unity of coincidence between meaning and meaning-fulfilment, the essence of the meaning-fulfilment corresponds with, and is correlative, to the essence of meaning: the essence of the meaning-fulfilment is the *fulfilling* sense of the expression, or, as one may also call it, the sense expressed by the expression. One says, e.g., that a statement of perception expresses a perception, but also that it expresses the *content* of a perception. We distinguish, in a perceptual statement, as in every statement, between *content* and *object*; by the 'content' we understand the self-identical meaning that the hearer can grasp even if he is not a percipient. We must draw the same distinction in the case of fulfilling acts, in the case, therefore, of perceptions and their categorial formations. Through these acts the objective correlate of our act of meaning stands before us intuitively as the very object we mean. We must, I say, distinguish again, in such fulfilling acts, between their *content*, the meaning-element, as it were, in the categorially formed percept, and the *object* perceived. In the unity of fulfilment, the fulfilling content coincides with the intending content, so that, in our experience of this unity of coincidence, the object, at once intended and 'given', stands before us, not as two objects, but as *one* alone. The ideal conception of the act which *confers meaning* yields us the Idea of the *intending meaning*, just as the ideal conception of the correlative essence of the act which *fulfils* meaning, yields the *fulfilling meaning*, likewise *qua* Idea. This is the *identical content* which, in perception, pertains to the totality of possible acts of perception which intended the same object perceptually, and intend it actually as the same object. This content is therefore the ideal correlate of this *single* object, which may, for the rest, be completely imaginary.

The manifold ambiguities in talk about what an expression expresses, or about an *expressed content*, may therefore be so ordered that one distinguishes between a content in a *subjective*, and a content in an *objective* sense. In the latter respect we must distinguish between:

> The content as intending sense, or as sense, *meaning simpliciter*,
> the content as fulfilling sense, and
> the content as object.

§15 The equivocations in talk of meaning and meaninglessness connected with these distinctions

The application of the terms 'meaning' and 'sense', not merely to the content of the meaning-intention inseparable from the expression, but also to the content of the meaning-fulfilment, engenders a most unwelcome ambiguity. It is clear from previous indications, where we dealt with the fact of fulfilment, that the acts on either side, in which intending and fulfilling sense are constituted, need not be the same. What tempts us to transfer the same terms from intention to fulfilment, is the peculiar way in which the unity of fulfilment is a unity of identification or coincidence: the equivocation which one hoped a modifying adjective might render innocuous, can scarcely be avoided. We shall continue, of course, to understand by 'meaning' *simpliciter* the meaning which, as the identical element in our intention, is essential to the expressions as such.

'Meaning' is further used by us as synonymous with 'sense'. It is agreeable to have parallel, interchangeable terms in the case of this concept, particularly since the sense of the term 'meaning' is itself to be investigated. A further consideration is our ingrained tendency to use the two words as synonymous, a circumstance which makes it seem rather a dubious step if their meanings are differentiated, and if (as G. Frege has proposed)[3] we use one for meaning in our sense, and the other for the objects expressed. To this we may add that both terms are exposed to the same equivocations, which we distinguished above in connection with the term 'expression', and to many more besides, and that this is so both in scientific and in ordinary speech. Logical clarity is much impaired by the manner in which the sense or meaning of an expression is, often in the same thought-sequence, now looked upon as the acts intimated by it, now as its ideal sense, now as the objective correlate that it expresses. Since fixed terminological landmarks are lacking, the concepts themselves run confusedly into one another.

Fundamental confusions arise from these facts. General and equivocal names are, e.g., repeatedly lumped together, since both can be predicatively referred to a plurality of objects. Lacking fixed concepts, men did not know how to distinguish the *multiple senses* of the equivocal names from the *multiple values* of the general ones. Here we also meet with the frequent unclearness as to the true essence of the difference between collective and general names. For, where collective meanings are fulfilled, we intuit a plurality of items: fulfilment is articulated into a plurality of individual intuitions, and so, if intention and fulfilment are not kept apart, it may well seem that the collective expression in question has many meanings.

It is more important for us to set forth precisely the most detrimental equivocations in talk which concerns *meaning* and *sense*, on the one hand, or *meaningless* or *senseless* expressions, on the other. If we separate the blurred concepts, the following list emerges:

1. It is part of the notion of an expression to have a meaning: this precisely differentiates an expression from the other signs mentioned above. A meaningless expression is, therefore, properly speaking, no expression at all: it is at best something that claims or seems to be an expression, though, more closely considered, it is not one at all. Here belong articulate, word-like sound-patterns such as 'Abracadabra', and also combinations of genuine expressions to which no unified meaning corresponds, though their outer form seems to pretend to such a meaning, e.g. 'Green is or'.

2. In meaning, a relation to an object is constituted. To use an expression significantly, and to refer expressively to an object (to form a presentation of it), are one and the same. It makes no difference whether the object exists

or is fictitious or even impossible. But if one gives a very rigorous interpretation to the proposition that an expression, in so far as it has meaning, relates to an object, i.e. in a sense which involves the existence of the object, then an expression has *meaning* when an object corresponding to it exists, and it is *meaningless* when no such object exists. Meanings are often spoken of as signifying the *objects* meant, a usage that can scarcely be maintained consistently, as it springs from a confusion with the genuine concept of meaning.

3. If the meaning is identified with the objective correlate of an expression, a name like 'golden mountain' is meaningless. Here men generally distinguish objectlessness from meaninglessness. As opposed to this, men tend to use the word 'senseless' of expressions infected with contradiction and obvious incompatibilities, e.g. 'round square', or to deny them meaning by some equivalent phrase. Sigwart,[4] e.g., says that a self-contradictory formula such as 'square circle' expresses no concept we can think, but that it uses words to set up an insoluble task. The existential proposition 'There is no square circle', on his view denies the possibility of connecting a concept with these words, and by a concept he expressly wants us to understand (if we get him right) the 'general meaning of a word', which is just what we mean by it. Erdmann[5] has similar opinions in regard to the instance 'A square circle is frivolous'. We should, in consistency, have to apply the word 'senseless', not merely to expressions immediately absurd, but to those whose absurdity is mediate, i.e. the countless expressions shown by mathematicians, in lengthy indirect demonstrations, to be objectless *a priori*. We should likewise have to deny that concepts like *regular decahedron* etc., are concepts at all.

Marty raises the following objection to the thinkers just mentioned. 'If the words are senseless, how could we understand the question as to whether such things exist, so as to answer it negatively? Even to reject such an existence, we must, it is plain, somehow form a presentation of such contradictory material'[6] . . . 'If such absurdities are called senseless, this can only mean that they have no rational sense'.[7] These objections are clinching, in so far as these thinkers' statements suggest that they are confusing the true meaninglessness mentioned above under 1, with another quite different meaninglessness, i.e. *the* a priori *impossibility of a fulfilling sense*. An expression has meaning in this sense if a possible fulfilment, i.e. the possibility of a unified intuitive illustration, corresponds to its intention. This possibility is plainly meant ideally. It concerns no contingent acts of expression or fulfilment, but their ideal contents: meaning as an ideal unity, here to be called 'intending meaning', on the one hand, and fulfilling meaning, standing to it in a certain relation of precise adequacy, on the other. We apprehend this ideal relation by ideative abstraction based on an act of unified fulfilment. In the contrary case we apprehend the real impossibility of meaning-fulfilment through an experience of the incompatibility of the partial meanings in the intended unity of fulfilment.

The phenomenological clarification of these relationships calls for long, difficult analyses, as will appear in a later investigation.

4. If we ask what an expression means, we naturally recur to cases where it actually contributes to knowledge, or, what is the same, where its meaning-intention is intuitively fulfilled. In this manner the 'notional presentation', i.e. the meaning-intention, gains clarity, it shows itself up as 'correct', as 'really' capable of execution. The draft it makes on intuition is as it were cashed. Since in the unity of fulfilment the act of intention coincides with the fulfilling act, and fuses with it in the most intimate fashion – if indeed there is any difference left over here at all – it readily seems as if the expression first got its meaning here, as if it drew meaning from the act of fulfilment. The tendency therefore arises to treat the *fulfilling intuitions* – categorially formative acts are here in general passed over – as meanings. But fulfilment is often imperfect – we shall have to devote closer study to all such possibilities – and expressions often go with remotely relevant, only partially illustrative intuitions, if with any at all. Since the phenomenological differences of these cases have not been closely considered, men have come to locate the significance of expressions, even of such as could make no claim to adequate fulfilment, in accompaniments of intuitive imagery. This naturally led to a total denial of meaning to absurd expressions.

The new concept of meaning therefore originates in a confusion of meaning with fulfilling intuition. On this conception, an expression has meaning if and only if its intention – we should say its 'meaning-intention' – is in fact fulfilled, even if only in a partial, distant and improper manner. The understanding of the expression must be given life through certain 'ideas of meaning' (it is commonly said), i.e. by certain *illustrative* images.

The final refutation of highly attractive, opposed notions is an important task which requires lengthy discussions. These we shall postpone to the next chapter, and here go on enumerating different concepts of meaning.

Chapter 3

Fluctuation in meaning and the ideality of unities of meaning

§24 Introduction

In our last chapter (excised from this edition) we dealt with the act of meaning. But among the conclusions of our first chapter was a distinction between the act of meaning, on the one hand, and meaning itself, on the other, the ideal unity as against the multiplicity of possible acts. This distinction, like the others which go along with it – the distinction between expressed content taken in a subjective, and the same taken in an objective sense, and, in the latter respect, the distinction between content as significatum and content as nominatum – are in countless cases undoubtedly clear. This holds of all expressions which occur in the context of an adequately expounded scientific theory. There are, however, cases where the situation is different, which require particular consideration if they are not to plunge all our hard-won distinctions back into confusion. Expressions whose meaning shifts, especially such as are occasional or vague, here raise serious problems. To solve these problems by distinguishing between shifting acts of meaning, on the one hand, and ideal units of meaning, on the other, is the theme of the present chapter.

§25 Relations of coincidence among the contents of intimation and naming

Expressions may relate to the contemporary mental state of the person using them as much as they relate to other objects. They accordingly divide into those that also *intimate what they name* (or what they generally stand for), and those in whose case *named and intimated contents fall asunder*. Instances of the former class are interrogative, optative and imperative sentences, of the latter, statements relating to external things, to one's own past experiences, to mathematical relationships etc. If someone utters the wish 'I should like a glass of water', this serves to indicate to the hearer the speaker's wish, which is also the object of the statement. What is intimated and what is named here coincide in part. I say 'in part', since the intimation obviously goes further. It extends to the judgement expressed in the words 'I should like etc.'. The like naturally holds of statements about the ideas, judgements, and surmises of the speaker which are of the forms 'I imagine that . . .', 'I am of the opinion that . . .', 'I judge that . . .', 'I conjecture that . . .'. A case even of total coincidence seems at first sight possible, in, e.g., the words 'the state of mind intimated by the words I am now uttering', though the interpretation of our example breaks down on closer examination. But intimation and the state of affairs asserted fall quite apart in statements such as '$2 \times 2 = 4$'. This statement does not say what is said by 'I judge that $2 \times 2 = 4$'. They are not even equivalent statements, since the one can be true when the other is false.

One must of course stress that if the notion of 'intimation' is given the *narrower* sense defined above, the objects named in the above examples are *not* among the experiences they intimate. A man saying something about his contemporary mental state, communicates its presence through a judgement. Only as intimating such a judgement (whose content is that he wishes, hopes etc., this or that) is the man apperceived by the hearer as one who wishes, hopes etc. The meaning of such a statement lies in this judgement, whereas the inner experiences in question are among the objects judged *about*. If we limit intimation in the narrower sense to experiences which carry an expression's meaning, the contents of intimation and naming remain as distinct here as they are generally.

§26 Essentially occasional and objective expressions

The expressions which name the momentary content of intimation belong to a wider class of expressions whose meaning varies from case to case. This happens, however, in so peculiar a manner, that one hesitates to speak of 'equivocation' in this case. The same words 'I wish you luck' which express my wish, can serve countless other persons to express wishes having 'the same' content. Not only do the wishes themselves differ from case to case, but the meanings of the wish-utterances do so too. At one time a person *A* confronts a person *B*, at another time a person *M* confronts a person *N*. If *A* wishes *B* 'the same' that *M* wishes *N*, the sense of the wish-utterances, which includes the idea of the confronting persons, is plainly different. This ambiguity is, however, quite different from that of the word 'dog' which at one time means a type of animal, and at another a foot or a grate.[1] The class of ambiguous expressions illustrated by this last example are what one usually has in mind when one speaks of 'equivocation'. Ambiguity in such cases does not tend to shake our faith in the ideality and objectivity of meanings. We are free, in fact, to limit our expression to a *single* meaning. The ideal unity of each of the differing meanings will not be affected by their attachment to a common designation. But how do things stand in the case of the other expressions? Can we there still stick to self-identical meaning-unities, elsewhere made clear in their opposition to varying persons and their experiences, when here our meanings must vary *with* such persons and their experiences? Obviously we are here dealing with a case of unavoidable rather than chance ambiguity, one that cannot be removed from our language by an artificial device or convention.

To promote clearness we shall define the following distinction between *essentially subjective and occasional* expressions, on the one hand, and *objective* expressions, on the other. For simplicity's sake we shall deal only with expressions in their normal use.

We shall call an expression *objective* if it pins down (or can pin down) its meaning merely by its manifest, auditory pattern, and can be understood without necessarily directing one's attention to the person uttering it, or to the circumstances of the utterance. An objective expression may be in varying ways equivocal: it may stand in the stated relation to several meanings, so that it depends on the psychological context (on the chance drift of the hearer's thoughts, on the tenor of the talk already in progress and the tendencies it arouses etc.) which of these meanings it arouses and means. It may be that a glance at the speaker and his situation may help all this. But whether or not the word *can* be understood in one or other of such meanings does not depend on this glance as a *sine qua non*.

On the other hand, we call an expression essentially subjective and occasional, or, more briefly, *essentially occasional*, if it belongs to a conceptually unified group of possible meanings, in whose case it is essential to orient actual meaning to the occasion, the speaker and the situation. Only by looking to the actual circumstances of utterance can one definite meaning out of all this mutually connected class be constituted for the hearer. Since we regularly understand such expressions in normal circumstances, the very idea of these circumstances, and of their regular relation to the expression, involves the presence of generally graspable, sufficiently reliable clues to guide the hearer to the meaning intended in the case in question.

Among objective expressions we have, e.g., all expressions in theory, expressions out of which the principles and theorems, the proofs and theories of the 'abstract' sciences are made up. What, e.g., a mathematical expression means, is not in the least affected by the circumstances of our actual use of it. We read and understand it without thinking of a speaker at all. The case is different with expressions which serve the practical needs of ordinary life and with expressions which, in the sciences, prepare the way for theoretical results. I mean by the latter expressions with which the investigator accompanies his own thought, or acquaints others with his considerations and endeavours, with his methodical preparations and his provisional beliefs.

Every expression, in fact, that includes a *personal pronoun* lacks an objective sense. The word 'I' names a different person from case to case, and does so by way of an ever altering meaning. What its meaning is at the moment, can be gleaned only from the living utterance and from the intuitive circumstances which surround it. If we read the word without knowing who wrote it, it is perhaps not meaningless, but is at least estranged from its normal sense. Certainly it strikes us differently from a wanton arabesque: we know it to be a word, and a word with which whoever is speaker designates himself. But the conceptual meaning thus evoked in not what the word 'I' means, otherwise we could simply substitute for it the phrase 'whatever speaker is designating himself'. Such a substitution would lead to expressions, not only unusual, but also divergent in sense, if, e.g., instead of saying 'I am pleased' I said 'Whatever speaker is now designating himself is pleased'. It is the universal *semantic function* of the word 'I' to designate whoever is speaking, but the notion through which we express this function is not the notion immediately constitutive of its meaning.

In solitary speech the meaning of 'I' is essentially realized in the immediate idea of one's own personality, which is also the meaning of the word in communicated speech. Each man has his own I-presentation (and with it his individual notion of I) and this is why the word's meaning differs from person to person. But since each person, in speaking of himself, says 'I', the word has the character of a universally operative indication of this fact. Through such *indication* the hearer achieves understanding of the meaning, he takes the person who confronts him intuitively, not merely as the speaker, but also as the immediate object of this speaker's speech. The word 'I' has not itself directly the power to arouse the specific I-presentation; this becomes fixed in the actual piece of talk. It does not work like the word 'lion' which can arouse the idea of a lion in and by itself. In its case, rather, an indicative function mediates, crying as it were, to the hearer 'Your *vis-à-vis* intends himself'.

We must, however, add something to what has been said. Properly speaking, we should not suppose that the immediate presentation of the speaker sums up the entire meaning of the word 'I'. The word is certainly not to be regarded as an equivocal expression, with meanings to be identified with all possible proper names of persons. Undoubtedly the idea of self-reference, as well as an implied pointing to the individual idea of the speaker, also belong, *after a certain fashion*, to the word's meaning. We shall have to admit that two meanings are here built upon one another in peculiar fashion. The one, relating to the word's general function, is so connected with the word that its indicative function can be exercised once something is actually presented: this indicative function is, in its turn, exercised *for* the other, singular presentation, and, by subsumption, makes the latter's object known as what is here and now meant. The former meaning can be called the *indicating* meaning, the latter the meaning *indicated*.

What is true of personal pronouns is of course also true of demonstratives. If someone says 'this', he does not directly arouse in the hearer the idea of what he means, but in the first place the idea or belief that he means something lying within his intuitive or thought-horizon, something he wishes to point out to the hearer. In the concrete circumstances of speech, this thought is an adequate guide to what is really meant. 'This' read in isolation likewise lacks its proper meaning, and is understood only to the extent that it arouses the notion of its demonstrative function (which we call its indicating meaning). In each case of normal use, its full, actual meaning can only grow out of the prominent presentation of the thing that it makes its object.

We must grant, of course, that a demonstrative often works in a manner that can claim equivalence with an objective use. A 'this' in a mathematical context points to something determined in a conceptually fixed manner, that is understood as meant in this manner, without our needing to regard the actual utterance. A mathematical exposition, after expressly stating a proposition, may go on to say 'This follows from the fact that . . .'. Here the proposition in question could itself have been substituted for the word 'this' without greatly altering the sense; this follows from the exposition's objective sense. One must of course attend to the continuous exposition since, not the intended meaning, but only the thought of an indication, belongs to the demonstrative considered by itself. Mediation by indicating meanings merely promotes brevity and increases mastery over the main drift of one's thought-intentions. The same plainly does not apply in the common case where the demonstrative 'this' and similar forms stand for the house confronting the speaker, for the bird flying up before him etc. Here individual intuition, varied from case to case, must do duty: it is not enough to look back to previously uttered objective thoughts.

In the sphere of essentially occasional expressions one has also the subject-bound determinations 'here', 'there', 'above', 'below', 'now', 'yesterday', 'tomorrow', 'later' etc. 'Here' (to think out a last example) designates the speaker's vaguely bounded spatial environment. To use the word is to refer to one's place on the basis of an intuitive, believing presentation of one's own person and location. This changes from case to case, and changes likewise from person to person, though each can say 'here'. It is again the general function of the word to name the spatial environment of the speaker, so that the genuine meaning of the word is first constituted in the variable presentation of this place. The meaning of 'here' is in part universal and conceptual, inasmuch as it always names a place as such, but to this universal element the direct place-presentation attaches, varying from case to case. In the given circumstances of speech, it acquires heightened intelligibility by subsumption under the conceptual indicating presentation of 'here'.

An essentially indicating character naturally spreads to all expressions which include these and similar presentations as parts: this includes all the manifold speech-forms where the speaker gives normal expression to something concerning himself, or which is thought of in relation to himself. All expressions for percepts, beliefs, doubts, wishes, fears, commands belong here, as well as all combinations involving the *definite article*, in which the latter relates to something individual and merely pinned down by class- or property-concepts. When we Germans speak of *the* Kaiser we of course mean the present German Kaiser. When we ask for *the* lamp in the evening, each man means his own.

Note. Expressions with essentially occasional meaning, as dealt with in this section, do not fit into Paul's useful division of expressions into those of usual and those of occasional meaning. His division is based on the fact 'that the meaning which a word has in each application need not coincide with what usage accords in it in and for itself' (H. Paul, *Prinzipien der Sprachgeschichte*, p. 68). Paul has, however, included our essentially occasional expressions in his treatment, for he says: 'There are some words in occasional use which are essentially framed to designate the concrete, but which none the less lack their own relation to a definite concretum till individual application gives them one. Here belong personal pronouns, possessive and demonstrative adjectives, demonstrative adverbs, also words like "now", "today", "yesterday".'[2] It seems to me that occasional expressions in this sense fall outside of Paul's definitory antithesis. For it pertains to the *usual* sense of this class of expressions, that they owe their determinate meaning to the occasion, and are therefore occasional in a somewhat *different* sense. Expressions of usual meaning (in Paul's sense) can be divided into those usually univocal and those usually equivocal, and the latter into expressions usually varying among definite meanings assignable in advance (such as the casual equivoca 'cock', 'bear' etc.) and those in which this is not so, since their meaning is oriented in each case to the individual instance, though the manner of this orientation is a matter of usage.

§29 Pure logic and ideal meanings

Pure logic, wherever it deals with concepts, judgements, and syllogisms, is exclusively concerned with the *ideal* unities that we here call 'meanings'. If we take the trouble to detach the ideal essence of meanings from their psychological and grammatical connections, if we try, further, to clear up their *a priori* relations of adequacy, founded in this essence, to the objective correlates that they mean, we are already within the domain of pure logic.

This is clear from the start if we *first* think of the position logic takes up to the many sciences, the position of nomological science, concerned with the ideal essence of science as such, or, what is the same, the position of nomological science, of scientific thought in general, taken purely in its theoretic content and connection. It is clear, *secondly*, when we note that the theoretic content of a science is no more than the meaning-content of its theoretical statements, disembarrassed of all contingent thinkers and occasions of judgement, and that such statements are given *unity* by the theory's pattern, which in its turn acquires objective validity through the ideally guaranteed adequacy of its unified meaning to the objective correlate meant by it (which is 'given' to us in self-evident knowledge). Undeniably what we call 'meaning' in this sense covers only ideal unities, expressed through manifold expressions, and thought of in manifold act-experiences, but none the less clearly separable from such chance expressions and from such chance experiences of thinking subjects.

If all given theoretic unity is in essence a unity of meaning, and if logic is the science of theoretic unity in general, then logic evidently is the science of meanings as such, of their essential sorts and differences, as also of the ideal laws which rest purely on the latter. Among such essential differences we have those between meanings which have, and meanings which have no objects, between true and false meanings, and, among such laws, we have the pure 'laws of thought', which express the *a priori* connection between the categorial form of meanings and their objectivity or truth.

This notion of logic as a science of meanings is of course at odds with the mode of speech and treatment of the traditional logic, which operates with psychological or psychologically slanted terms such as 'idea', 'judgement', 'affirmation', 'denial', 'presupposition', 'inference' etc., and which thinks it is really only establishing differences of psychology and tracking down psychological laws relating to these. After the critical investigations of our *Prolegomena* we can no more be taken in by all this. It only shows how far logic still is from a proper understanding of the objects which make up its own true field of research, and how much it has still to learn from the objective sciences, whose essence it none the less claims to make theoretically intelligible.

Where the sciences unfold systematic theories, when they no longer merely communicate the progress of personal research and proof, but set forth the objectively unified, ripe fruit of known truth, there is absolutely no talk of judgements, ideas and other mental acts. The objective researcher of course *defines* his expressions. He says: By '*vis viva*', by 'mass', by an 'integral', by a 'sine' etc., this or that is meant. But he only points thereby to the *objective meaning* of his expressions, he indicates what 'contents' he has in mind, which play their part as constitutive moments in the truths of his field. He is not interested in understanding, but in the concepts, which are for him ideal unities of meaning, and also in the truths, which themselves are made up out of such concepts.

The investigator then propounds propositions, and naturally, in so doing, he asserts or judges. But he has no wish to speak of his own or of anyone else's judgements, but of the correlated *states of affairs*, and when his critical discussions concern propositions, he means by the latter the ideal meanings of statements. He does not say that judgements are true or false, but that propositions are so: his premises are propositions, and so are his conclusions. Propositions are not constructed out of mental acts of presentation or belief: when not constructed out of other propositions, they ultimately point back to concepts.

Propositions are themselves the elements of *inferences*. Here too there is a distinction between acts of inferring and their unified contents, syllogisms, i.e. the self-identical *meanings* of certain complex statements. The relation of necessary consequence in which the form of an inference consists, is not an empirical-psychological connection among judgements as experiences, but an ideal relation among possible statement-meanings, among propositions. It 'exists' or 'subsists', i.e. it is valid, and such validity is something without essential relation to an empirical thinker. If a natural scientist deduces a machine's working from the laws of the lever, gravitation etc., he no doubt experiences all sorts of subjective acts. What, however, he thinks of, and what he knits together in unity, are concepts and propositions together with their objective relations. An objective unity of meaning, i.e. one adequate to the objectivity which is self-evidently 'given', thereby corresponds to his subjective thought-connections: this is whatever it is, whether anyone realizes this in thought or not.

This holds in general. Though the scientific investigator may have no reason to draw express distinctions between words and symbols, on the one hand, and meaningful thought-objects, on the other, he well knows that expressions are contingent, and that the thought, the ideally selfsame meaning, is what is essential. He knows, too, that he does not *make* the objective validity of thoughts and thought-connections, of concepts and truths, as if he were concerned with contingencies of his own or of the general human mind, but that he *sees* them, *discovers* them. He knows that their ideal being does not amount to a psychological 'being in the mind': the authentic objectivity of the true, and of the ideal in general, suspends *all* reality, including such as is subjective. If some scientists at times think differently on this point, they do so, not in their professional scientific settings, but on subsequent reflection. If, with Hume, we may hold that men's true beliefs are better documented by their deeds than by their words, then we may twit such thinkers with not understanding themselves. They pay no unprejudiced heed to what they think in their unreflective enquiries and demonstrations, but are led astray by the supposed authority of logic, with its psychologistic fallacies and subjectively distorted terminology.

All theoretical science consists, in its objective content, of *one* homogeneous stuff: it is an ideal fabric of *meanings*. We can go even further and say that the whole, indefinitely complex web of meanings that we call the theoretical unity of science, falls under the very category that covers all its elements: it is itself a unity of meaning.

If meaning, rather than the act of meaning, concept and proposition, rather than idea and judgement, are what is essential and germane in science, they are necessarily the general object of investigation in the science whose theme is the essence of science. Everything that is logical falls under the two correlated categories of *meaning* and *object*. If we speak in the plural of *logical categories*, we have only to do with the pure species distinguishable *a priori* within the genus of meaning, or with the correlated forms of *categorially considered objectivity*. In such categories the laws formulable in logic have their foundation. We have, on the one hand, such laws as abstract from the ideal relations between meaning-intention and meaning-fulfilment, and so from any possible knowledge-use of meanings, and consider only how meanings can be compounded to form novel meanings (whether 'real' or 'imaginary').[3] We have, on the other hand, *logical laws*, in the more emphatic sense, which consider meanings in respect of their having or not having objects, in respect of their truth or their falsity, their consistency or their absurdity, to the extent that such things are merely determined by the categorial form of such meanings. Corresponding with these latter laws, we have equivalent, correlated *laws for objects in general, objects determined in thought by mere categories*. All valid assertions regarding existence and truth, that are capable of being framed in abstraction from all material of knowledge on a mere foundation of meaning-forms, find their place among such laws.

The ideal unity of the species and modern theories of abstraction

Introduction

Following the discussions of the last investigation, we grasp the ideal unity of a meaning in the light of the act-character of signification; this signification's peculiar 'tincture' distinguishes the meaning-consciousness of a given expression from that of one which differs in meaning. This does not of course mean that this act-character is the concrete reality upon whose basis the meaning as Species is constituted for us. The relevant concrete reality is rather the total experience of the understood expression, which is informed by this act-character as its animating 'tincture'. The relation between the meaning and the significant expression (or its 'meaning-tincture') is the same as the relation, e.g., between the Species Red and a red object of intuitive experience (or the 'moment' of red which appears in this object). When we mean Red *in specie*, a red object appears before us, and in this sense we look towards the red object to which we are nevertheless not referring. The moment of red is at the same time emphasized in this object, and to that extent we can again say that we are looking towards this moment of red. But we are not referring to this individually definite trait in the object, as we are referring to it when, e.g., we make the phenomenological observation that the red moments in the separate portions of the apparent object's surface are themselves separate. While the red object and its emphasized red moment appear before us, we are rather 'meaning' the single identical Red, and are meaning it in a novel conscious *manner*, though which precisely the Species, and not the individual, becomes our object. The same would apply also to a meaning in its relation to an expression, and an expression's meaningful orientation, whether this expression relates to a corresponding intuition or not.

Meaning as a Species therefore arises out of the above-mentioned background through *abstraction*, but not through abstraction in that improper sense by which empiricist psychology and epistemology are dominated, a sense which altogether fails to seize what is specific, and whose inability to do so is even counted as a virtue. The issue of abstraction has a twofold relevance to a philosophical laying down of the foundations of pure logic. It is relevant in the first place since among the categorial distinctions of meanings which pure logic must essentially consider, we find a distinction which corresponds to the opposition between individual and universal objects. But it also has, in the second place, a particular relevance, since meanings as such, i.e. meanings in the sense of specific unities, constitute the domain of pure logic, so that to misread the essence of the Species must in each case be to strike at the very essence of logic. It will accordingly not be unsuitable to tackle the problem of abstraction even at this early point in our introductory series of investigations, so as to assure the basic foundations of pure logic and epistemology by defending the intrinsic right of specific (or ideal) objects to be granted objective status alongside of individual (or real) objects. This is the point on which relativistic, empiricistic psychologism differs from idealism, which alone represents the possibility of a self-consistent theory of knowledge.

To talk of 'idealism' is of course not to talk of a metaphysical doctrine, but of a theory of knowledge which recognizes the 'ideal' as a condition for the possibility of objective knowledge in general, and does not 'interpret it away' in psychologistic fashion.

Chapter 1

Universal objects and the consciousness of universality

§1 We are conscious of universal objects in acts which differ essentially from those in which we are conscious of individual objects

Our own position has been indicated above in a few words; its justification should require few additional explanations. All that we maintain – the validity of the distinction between specific and individual objects, and the difference of the manner in which each type of objects is present to us, is brought clearly before our consciousness – has the guarantee of self-evidence. This self-evidence automatically emerges as soon as the relevant presentations are clarified. We need only refer to cases where individual or specific presentation are intuitively 'fulfilled', to be utterly clear as to the sorts of objects 'meant' by such presentations, and as to what counts as an essential homogeneity or disparity in their sense. Reflection on both classes of acts simply makes plain whether or not there are essential differences in the manner in which they are performed.

In the latter regard comparison shows that the act in which we mean the Species, is in fact essentially different from the act in which we mean the individual, whether, in this later case, we refer to a whole concrete thing, or to an individual piece or property attaching to it. There is, of course, certain phenomenal commonality in either case. In either case the same concrete thing makes its appearance, and to the extent that it does so, the same sense-contents are given and interpreted in an identical manner, i.e. the same course of actually given sense and image-contents serves as a basis for the same 'conception' or 'interpretation', in which the appearance of the *object* with the *properties* presented by those contents is constituted for us. But the same appearance sustains different acts in the two cases. In the first case it provides the presentative basis for an act of *individual* reference, i.e. for an act in which we apply ourselves to the apparent thing itself, and 'mean' this thing or this feature, this part of the thing. In the latter case it provides the presentative basis for an act of conception and reference directed to a Species: i.e. while the thing appears, or rather the feature in the thing, it is not this objective feature, this feature here and now, that we mean. We mean its *content*, its 'Idea'; we mean, not this aspect of red in the house, but Red as such. This act of meaning is plainly an act 'founded' on underlying apprehensions (see Investigation VI, §45); a new mode of apprehension has been built on the intuition of the individual house or of its red aspect, a mode of apprehension constitutive of the intuitive presence of the Idea of Red. And as the character of this mode of apprehension sets the Species before us as a universal object, so too there develop, in intimate connection with such an object, formations like 'red thing' (thing containing an instance of red), 'this case of red' (the red of this house) etc. The primitive relation between Species and Instance emerges: it becomes possible to look over and compare a range of instances, and perhaps to judge with self-evidence: 'In all these cases individual moments differ, but in each the same Species is realized: this Red is the same as that – specifically treated it is the same colour – and yet again this red differs from that one – i.e. individually treated, it is a different objective individual feature'. This distinction, like all fundamental logical distinctions, is categorial. It pertains to the pure form of possible objects of consciousness as such. (See also Investigation VI, ch. 6*f*.)

§2 The indispensability of talk about universal objects

The excesses of conceptual realism have led men to dispute, not merely the reality, but the objectivity of the Species. This is certainly quite wrong. The question as to whether it is possible or necessary to treat Species as objects can plainly only be answered by going back to the meaning (the significance, the sense) of the names standing for Species, and to the meaning of the assertions claiming to hold for Species. If these names and assertions can be interpreted as making the true objects of our intention individual, if the intention of the nominal and propositional thoughts which give them meaning can be thus understood, then we must yield to our opponents' doctrine. But if this is not so, if the semantic analysis of such experiences, shows that their direct, true intention is plainly not directed upon individual objects, and if in particular their universal relation to a range of individual objects is plainly shown up as merely an indirect pointing to logical connections whose content (sense) will first be unfolded in new thoughts, or which will require new expressions – then our opponents' doctrine is evidently false. Now in fact we cannot at all help distinguishing between *individual* singulars, like the 'things' of experience, and *specific* singulars, like the numbers and manifolds of mathematics, or like the presentations and judgements (the concepts and propositions) of pure logic. *Number* is a concept which, as has often been stressed, has 1, 2, 3 . . . as its subordinate singulars. *A* number is, e.g., the number 2, not any group of two individual objects. If we mean these, even quite indefinitely, we should also say so; our thought will then at least march with our expression.

The difference between individual and specific singulars corresponds to the no less essential difference between individual and specific universals (or between individual and specific universality). These differences at once carry over into the field of judgement, and run through the whole of logic. Singular judgements divide into *individually singular* judgements such as *Socrates is a man*, and *specifically singular* judgements such as *Two is an even number*, or *A Round Square is a nonsensical concept*. Universal judgements divide into *individually* universal judgements such as *All men are mortal*, and *specifically universal* judgements such as *All analytic functions can be differentiated*, or *All propositions of pure logic are* a priori.

These distinctions and others like them are quite irremovable. We are not merely dealing with abbreviated expressions: we cannot eliminate such differences through any elaboration or circumscription.

Inspection of each instance will, for the rest, yield the conviction that a Species really becomes an object in knowledge, and that judgements of the same logical forms are possible in relation to it, as is the case with individual objects. We may choose an instance from the group that concerns us particularly. Logical ideas, unitary meanings as such, are, as we said, ideal objects, whether they present what is universal or what is individual, e.g. *the city of Berlin* as an identical sense which recurs in talk and reference, or the direct idea of the theorem of Pythagoras (whose explicit utterance need not be carried out), or this very idea *the theorem of Pythagoras*.

We, from our point of view, would point out that each such meaning certainly counts as a unit in our thought and that on occasion we pass evident judgements upon it as a unit: it can be compared with other meanings and distinguished from them. It can be an identical subject for numerous predicates, an identical term in numerous relations. It can be summed together with other meanings and can be counted as a unit. As self-identical, it can in its turn serve as the object for many new meanings. All these things are the same in its case as in the case of other objects, e.g. horses, stones, mental acts etc., that are not meanings. A meaning can be treated as self-identical only because it is self-identical. This argument we find unassailable: it applies of course to all specific unities, even to such as are not meanings.

§3 Must the unity of the Species be regarded as a spurious unity? Identity and exact likeness

We wish to follow tradition in upholding a strict view of the identity of the Species, in contrast with prevailing doctrines which pin their faith on the wide diffusion of improper uses of 'identity'. Very often we speak of *the same* thing in the case of exactly like things. We speak, e.g., of 'the same cupboard', 'the same dress', 'the same hat' in the case of exactly similar products framed on the same pattern, products, i.e., exactly like one another in such respects as interest us in connection with such things. We speak in this sense of 'the same conviction', 'the same doubt', 'the same question', 'the same wish' etc. etc. Such impropriety of usage is thought likewise to be present in talk of the 'same Species' and, in particular, in talk of the 'same meaning'. We speak of 'the same meaning' ('the same concept', 'the same proposition') in relation to a pervasively like meaning-experience, we speak of 'the same red' (red in general) 'the same blue' etc., in respect to a pervasively like colouring.

Against this argument I object, that an improper use of identity in the case of like things, refers us back, through its very impropriety, to a proper use of the same term, i.e. to an identity. We find in fact that wherever things are 'alike', an identity in the strict and true sense is also present. We cannot predicate exact likeness of two things, without stating the respect in which they are thus alike. Each exact likeness relates to a Species, under which the objects compared, are subsumed: this Species is not, and cannot be, merely 'alike' in the two cases, if the worst of infinite regresses is not to become inevitable. If we specify the respect of our comparison, we point by way of a more general class-term to the range of specific differences among which the one which appears in our compared members is to be found. If two things are 'alike' as regards form, then the Form-Species in question is the identical element, if they are 'alike' as regards colour, the Colour-Species is this element etc. etc. Not every Species has of course an unambiguous verbal expression, and so at times a suitable expression for a 'respect' is lacking, and to state it clearly might be difficult. We none the less keep it in view, and it governs our talk of 'alikeness'. It would of course appear as a total inversion of the true state of things, were one to try to define identity, even in the sensory realm, as being essentially a limiting case of 'alikeness'. Identity is wholly indefinable, whereas 'alikeness' is definable: 'alikeness' is the relation of objects falling under one and the same Species. If one is not allowed to speak of the identity of the Species, of the respect in which there is 'alikeness', talk of 'alikeness' loses its whole basis.

§4 Objections to the reduction of ideal unity to dispersed multiplicity

We now direct attention to another point. Should anyone wish to reduce talk about a single attribute to a subsistence of certain relations of exact likeness, we ask him to consider the difference which comes out in the following opposition. We make a comparison between:

1. Our intention, when we grasp any group of intuitively like objects in unitary fashion, or when we recognize their exact likeness *at a single glance*, or when in single acts of *comparison* we recognize the likeness of one definite object to certain others and ultimately to all objects in the group,[1] and

2. Our intention when, possibly basing ourselves on the same intuitive foundations, we apprehend as an *ideal unity* the attribute which constitutes the respect in which the things are alike or are compared.

It is plain that, in our two cases, the target of our intention, the object meant and named as subject of our assertion, is quite different. However many like objects may float before us in intuition or comparison, they and their 'alikenesses' are certainly not what we mean in our second case. What we mean is the 'universal', the ideal unity, and not these units and pluralities.

The two intentional situations are utterly different, not merely logically, but also psychologically. In the second case no intuition of likeness, not even a comparison, is at all needed. I recognize this paper as paper and as white, and thereby make clear to myself the general sense of the expressions 'paper' and 'white as such', but I need not carry out any intuitions of likeness nor any comparisons. One can say for the rest, no doubt, that these conceptual ideas would never have arisen had like objects never appeared together, nor been intuitively related by their likeness. This psychological fact is, however, totally irrelevant here, where the question weighed concerns what an attribute counts as in knowledge, and what it should count as in the full light of 'evidence'.

It is clear, further and lastly, that when we try to make plain an intention to a Species by somehow presenting singulars as belonging to groups of exact similars, such presented singulars only comprise a few members of such groups, and can never exhaust their total range. One may then well ask what will give unity to this range, what will make it a possible object for awareness and knowledge, if the unity of the Species altogether lapses, and together with it the thought-form of 'allness', which gives the Species a bearing on the whole host of *A*'s represented in our thought, which we refer to through the sense of the expression 'the totality of *A*'s'. To point to the 'same' universally shared moment will of course not help us at all. It is numerically present as often as there are single objects represented within the range of the Species. How can anything unify if it must itself first be unified?

We can also derive no assistance from the objective possibility of recognizing all members of the range to be *like* one another: it cannot give unity to this range for our thought and knowledge. For, as a possibility, it is nothing for our consciousness, unless we think of it and grasp it. But such a grasp would, on the one hand, presuppose the thought of the unity of the range, and this range would itself also confront us as an ideal unity. Each attempt to transform the being of what is ideal into the possible being of what is real, must obviously suffer shipwreck on the fact that possibilities themselves are ideal objects. Possibilities can as little be found in the real world, as can numbers in general, or triangles in general.

The empiricistic attempt to dispense with Species as objects by having recourse to their extensions can therefore not be carried out. It cannot tell us what gives unity to such extensions. The following objection makes this particularly clear. The conception we are criticizing operates with 'circles of similars', but makes too much light of the difficulty that each object belongs to a plurality of 'circles of similars', and that we must be in a position to say what distinguishes these 'circles of similars' among themselves. It is plain that, in default of a previously given Specific Unity, we cannot avoid a regress *in infinitum*. An object *A* is similar to other objects, to one object in the respect *a*, to another in the respect *b* etc. But such 'respects' do not imply that a Species is there, which effects unity. What then unifies the circle of similars determined, e.g., by Redness, as against the circle determined by Triangularity? The empiricistic conception only says: These are differing similarities. If *A* and *B* are similar in respect of red, and *A* and *C* in respect of triangularity, these similarities must differ *in kind*. But here we again come up against kinds. Similarities are compared, and form genera and species, just as their absolute members do. We should then have to have recourse to similarities of such similarities, and so on *in infinitum*.

§6 Transition to the following chapters

We have, in our last treatment, been forced to react critically to conceptions opposed to ours. In this we encountered a line of thought common to all forms of empiricistic theories of abstraction, however much they may otherwise differ in content. It seems necessary, however, to grant greater play to such criticism, so as to draw more profit from our conception of the essence of universal objects and universal presentations, in analysing and testing the various main types of modern theories of abstraction. Critically to point out errors in other thinkers' views will provide an opportunity to round off and complete our own conception, and at the same time to test its reliability.

The empiricistic 'theory[2] of abstraction', like most parts of modern epistemological theory, suffers from the mixture of two essentially different scientific interests, one concerned with the psychological *explanation of experiences*, the other with the 'logical' *classification* of their *thought-content* or *sense*, and the criticism of their possible achievement as acts of knowing. In the former regard we seek to establish empirical bonds tying the thought-experiences in question to other facts in the flux of real happenings, facts responsible for them causally, or on which they exert effects. In the latter regard we are intent upon the 'origin of the concepts' which pertain to our words: we seek to clarify their 'true meaning' or significance through plainly establishing their intention in the sense of their *fulfilments*, which are first realized when suitable intuitions are adduced. To study the essence of these phenomenological connections is to lay bare the indispensable foundation for an epistemological clarification of the 'possibility' of knowledge. It is also, in our case, to give essential clearness to the possibility of making valid assertions regarding universal objects (or regarding individual objects *as* objects of corresponding universal concepts) and, in connection therewith, to set forth in self-evident fashion the correct sense in which a universal counts as an 'entity', and an individual as a thing ranged under universal predicates. If a theory of abstraction is to have an epistemological function, if it is to clarify knowledge, it must set forth the immediate descriptive situation in which a Species comes to consciousness, it must through this clarify the sense of names of attributes, and thence go on to resolve perspicuously the many misinterpretations that the essence of the Species has suffered. It will go astray from the start if it loses itself in empirical-psychological analyses of the abstractive process and its cause and effects, and if, rapidly dismissing the descriptive content of the abstractive consciousness, it directs its main concern to unconscious dispositions and hypothetical associative linkages. What generally happens in such cases is that the essential immanent content of the consciousness of universality, which could have been classified properly without more ado, goes disregarded and unmentioned.

And, even if a theory of abstraction aims at the field of what is immanently discoverable in all true (and therefore intuitive) abstraction, and steers clear of the misguided confusion between essential (i.e. epistemologically clarifying) and empirical (i.e. psychologically explanatory) analysis, it will still go astray from the start if it falls into the other confusion (strongly suggested by ambiguous talk of 'general representation') between *phenomenological* and *objective* analysis. What our acts of meaning merely assign to their objects, will be assigned to these acts themselves as their real (*reelles*) constituent. Here the regulative field of consciousness and its immanent essence are again covertly abandoned, and all given over to confusion.

The following analyses will show that our sketchy characterization fits the most influential modern theories of abstraction, and that these really go astray for reasons that we have just summarily stated.

Chapter 2

The psychological hypostatization of the universal

§7 The metaphysical and psychological hypostatization of the universal. Nominalism

Two misunderstandings have dominated the development of doctrines concerning universal objects:

First: the metaphysical hypostatization of the universal, the assumption that the Species really exists *externally* to thought.

Secondly: the *psychological hypostatization* of the universal, the assumption that Species really exists *in* thought.

The older nominalism, whether of an extreme or a conceptualistic type, attacked the first misunderstanding, the misunderstanding which underlies Platonic realism (in the sense in which this is traditionally conceived). To combat the second misunderstanding, especially in the form of Locke's abstract ideas, has inspired the development of the modern theory of abstraction since Berkeley's time, and has given it its definite trend towards extreme nominalism (which is now usually called 'nominalism' *simpliciter*, and opposed to conceptualism). It was thought needful, to avoid the absurdities of Locke's abstract ideas, altogether to reject universal objects as peculiar thought-unities, and universal presentations as peculiar acts of thought. Ignoring the difference between universal intuitions on the one hand – among which not only such abstract ideas, but the general images of traditional logic belong – and universal meanings on the other, men rejected 'conceptual presentations', with their peculiar presentative intentions, if not in word, then at least in the sense of these words, and replaced them by individual presentations merely functioning in an extraordinary manner.

Nominalism therefore adds itself, as a third misunderstanding, to our previous two: in various forms it seeks to transform what is universal in object and act of thought, into what is individual.

These misunderstandings, in so far as they are still of actual interest, must be gone through in order. It lies in the nature of our subject-matter, as our discussions up to this point have made plain, that we cannot separate vexed issues regarding the essence of universal objects from issues regarding the essence of universal presentations. It is vain to seek to make out a persuasive case validating talk about universal objects, if one does not also remove doubts as to how such objects can be presented, and if one does not further refute theories apparently proving, by scientific psychological analysis, that only individual presentations exist, that only individual objects therefore can be, and ever have been brought to consciousness, and that talk about universal objects can only be understood as fictitious or as gravely improper.

We may leave aside, as long disposed of, the misunderstandings of Platonic realism. But the thought-motives pressing towards a psychologizing realism are obviously still operative, as appears particularly in the manner in which Locke tends to be criticized. We must go deeper into such motives in this chapter.

§8 A deceptive line of thought

The following line of thought might be opposed to our conception, not so much out of serious conviction, as in order to give an apagogic proof of the untenability of talk about Species as universal objects:

If Species are nothing real (*reales*), and if they are also nothing in thought, then they are nothing at all. How can we talk about something if it does not at least exist *in our thought*? The being of the ideal is therefore obviously a being in consciousness; the name 'content of consciousness' rightly applies to it. As opposed to this, real being (*reales Sein*) is no mere being in consciousness, or being-a-content: it is being-in-itself, transcendent being, being outside of consciousness.

We do not wish to lose ourselves in the erring paths of such a metaphysics. For us what is 'in' consciousness counts as real (*real*) just as much as what is 'outside' of it. What is real (*real*) is the individual with all its constituents: it is something here and now. For us temporality is a sufficient mark of reality. Real being and temporal being may not be identical notions, but they coincide in extension. We do not, of course, suppose that psychical experiences are in a metaphysical sense 'things'. But even they belong to a thinglike unity, if the traditional metaphysical conviction is right in holding that all temporal existents must be things, or must help to constitute things. Should we wish, however, to keep all metaphysics out, we may simply define 'reality' in terms of temporality. For the only point of importance is to oppose it to the timeless 'being' of the ideal.

It is further clear that the universal, as often as we speak of it, is a thing thought of by us: it is not therefore a thought-content in the sense of a real (*realen*)[1] constituent in our thought-experiences, and likewise not a thought-content in the sense of an intension, but is rather an object that we think of. Is it not obvious that an object, even when real (*real*) and truly existent, cannot be conceived as a real part of the act which thinks it? And isn't even the fictitious and the absurd, whenever we speak of it, something we think of?

It is naturally not our intention to put the *being of what is ideal* on a level with the *being-thought-of which characterizes the fictitious of the nonsensical.*[2] The latter does not exist at all, and nothing can properly be predicated of it: if we none the less speak of it as having its own, 'merely intentional' mode of being, we see on reflection that this is an improper way of speaking. There are, in fact, merely certain necessary and valid connections among 'objectless ideas', whose analogy with truths governing ideas having objects, has prompted this talk of objects merely presented which do not genuinely exist. Ideal objects, on the other hand, exist genuinely. Evidently there is not merely a good sense in speaking of such objects (e.g. of the number 2, the quality of redness, of the principle of contradiction etc.) and in conceiving them as sustaining predicates: we also have insight into certain categorial truths that relate to such ideal objects. If these truths hold, everything presupposed as an object by their holding must have being. If I see the truth that 4 is an even number, that the predicate of my assertion actually pertains to the ideal object 4, then this object cannot be a mere fiction, a mere *façon de parler*, a mere nothing in reality.

This does not exclude the possibility that the sense of this being, and the sense also of this predication, does not coincide exactly with their sense in cases where a real (*reales*) predicate, a *property* is asserted or denied of a real subject. Otherwise put: we do not deny but in fact emphasize, that there is a fundamental categorial split in our unified conception of being (or what is the same, in our conception of an object as such); we take account of this split when we distinguish between ideal being and real being; between being as Species and being as what is individual. The conceptual unity of predication likewise splits into two essentially different sub-species according as we affirm or deny properties of individuals, or affirm or deny general determinations of Species. This difference does not, however, do away with a supreme unity in the concept of an object, nor with the correlated concept of a categorial propositional unity. In either case something (a predicate) pertains or does not pertain to an object (a subject), and the sense of this most universal pertinence, together with the laws governing it, also determines the most universal sense of being, or of an object, as such; exactly as the more special sense of generic predication, with its governing laws, determines (or presupposes) the sense of an ideal object. If everything which has being is rightly recognized as having being, and as having such and such a being, in virtue of the evidence with which, in thought, we apprehend it as being, then without doubt we may not reject the self-justifying claims of ideal being. No interpretative skill in the world can in fact eliminate ideal objects from our speech and our thought.

Chapter 3

Abstraction and attention

§14 Objections to any and every form of nominalism. (*a*) The lack of a descriptive fixation of aims

We see from the above, and from similar expositions, how, despite great elaboration, no attempt has really been made to pin down what is descriptively given and what demands clarification, and to relate the two to one another. Let us once more run through our own undoubtedly clear, natural train of thought. What we are *given* are certain differences in the field of names: among others, the difference between such names as name what is individual, and such as name what is specific. If we confine ourselves, for the sake of simplicity to direct names ('proper names' in an extended sense of the word), names like 'Socrates' or 'Athens', on the one hand, stand opposed to names like 'Four' (the number-Four as a *single* member of the number-series), '*C*' (the note *C* as *one member* of the musical scale), 'Red' (as the name of *one* colour), on the other. To these names certain meanings correspond, and through these we refer to objects. What these named objects are can, one would imagine, not be in doubt. In the one case it is the person Socrates, the city of Athens, or any other *individual* object, in the other case the Number Four, the note *C*, the colour Red, or any other *ideal* object. What we mean by the significant use of words, what objects we name by them, and what these objects count as when we name them, this no one can dispute with us. It is accordingly *evident* that when I say 'Four' in the generic sense, as, e.g., in the statement 'Four is a prime number relatively to seven', I am meaning the Species *Four*, I have *it* as object before my logical regard, and am passing judgement on it, and not on anything individual. I am not judging about any individual group of four things, nor about any constitutive moment, piece or side of such a group, for each part, *qua* part of what is individual, is itself likewise individual. But to make an object of something, to make it a subject of predications or attributions, merely differs in name from having a presentation of it, and having a presentation in a sense which, while not the only one, is none the less the standard one for logic. We therefore assert with self-evidence: There are 'universal presentations', i.e. presentations of what is specific, just as there are presentations of what is individual.

We spoke of self-evidence, but self-evidence in respect of objective differences of meanings implies that we go beyond the merely symbolic use of expressions and refer ourselves to corresponding intuitions for final correction. Basing ourselves on intuitive presentations, we carry out the fulfilments of meanings corresponding to our merely significant intentions, we realize their 'genuine' purport. If we do this in our present case, some individual group of four units certainly floats pictorially before us, and to that extent underlies our presentation and our judgement. But we do not pass judgement on this group of four, we do not mean *it* in the subject-idea of our above example. Not the pictured group, but the number Four, the Specific Unity is our subject, and it is of *this* that we say that it is prime relatively to Seven. Strictly speaking, this Specific Unity is likewise nothing in, or attached to, the apparent group, for, if it were, it would be something individual, a thing here and now. But our reference, though itself existing now, refers to nothing less than what is now, it refers to Four, the ideal, timeless unity.

Reflecting on our experiences of individual and specific meaning – whether purely intuitive, purely symbolic, or at once a symbolic and a fulfilled significant intention – we must now carry out further phenomenological descriptions. Their task would be to lay bare the relations, fundamental to a clarification of knowledge, which hold between blind (or pure symbolic reference) and intuitive (or authentic) reference, and in the case of the latter to show the varying manner in which individual images function in consciousness, according as we intend what is individual or what is specific. This would enable us, e.g., to answer questions as to how, and in what case, the universal is brought to subjective awareness in the individual act of thought, and perhaps achieves self-evident givenness, and how it can acquire a connection with the boundless sphere of individual cases ranged under it, of which we can of course form no adequate pictorial presentation.

In Mill's exposition, as in all similar expositions, there is no question of simply recognizing evident data and consequently proceeding on the path we have just sketched. What should have been a fixed point in reflective clarification, is pushed aside unnoticed; the theory therefore misses its target, which it had lost sight of before, or rather never clearly seen. What it tells us may be informative in regard to this or that psychological precondition or component of our intuitively achieved consciousness of universality, or in regard to the psychological role of signs in directing unitary trains of thought etc. etc. This has, however, no immediate relevance to the objective use of universal meanings, and to the undoubted truth enshrined in talk about universal objects (subjects, singulars) and in predications which relate to these; that it has mediate relevance must first be established. Mill's conception, like all empiricistic conceptions, can indeed not appeal to such evident starting-points or goals, since its whole concern is to prove the nullity of what such self-evidence shows to have genuine subsistence, namely universal objects and the universal presentations in which such objects are constituted for consciousness. Expressions such as 'universal object', 'universal presentation' certainly arouse memories of old, burdensome errors. But, however much they may have been historically misinterpreted, they must still have a normal interpretation which justifies them. Empirical psychology cannot teach us this normal meaning: we can learn it only by going back to the self-evident sense of propositions which are built upon general presentations and which relate to general objects as subjects of their predications.

§15 (b) The origin of modern nominalism as an exaggerated reaction to Locke's doctrine of general ideas. The essential character of this nominalism, and of the theory of abstraction in terms of attention

The theory of abstraction held by Mill and his empiricist followers, like the theories of abstraction held by Berkeley and Hume, gets stuck in its attack on the error of 'abstract ideas'. It gets stuck by allowing itself to be misled by the chance circumstance that Locke, in his interpretation of general ideas, hit on his absurd general triangle: it thinks that serious talk of such ideas necessarily demands Locke's absurd interpretation. The fact is overlooked that this error is especially due to the unclarified ambiguity of the word 'idea' (and of the German word *Vorstellung*), and that what is absurd for one concept of 'idea' is possible and justifiable for another. How could this fact be apparent to Locke's opponents, when their notion of an 'idea' remained in the same obscurity that had misled Locke? In consequence of this fact, men fell into that *modern nominalism*, whose essence no longer lies in the rejection of realism, but of what is, properly speaking, conceptualism. Not only did men reject the absurd general ideas of Locke, but also general concepts in the full, true sense of the word, in the sense, that is, that is evidently revealed by an analysis of the objective meaning-content of our thinking as constitutive of the Idea of what is a unity-for-thought (*Denkeinheit*).

Such a view is fostered by wrongly interpreted psychological analyses. We tend naturally to turn our gaze among logical phenomena to whatever has primary intuitive palpability; we are then misled into taking the inner pictures which are found to accompany our names as the meanings of those names. If we become clear, however, that a meaning is merely what we mean, or what we understand by an expression, we cannot maintain such a conception. For if meaning consisted in the intuitive individual presentations which 'illustrate' the sense of general names, the objects of such presentation, precisely as they are intuitively presented, would be just what we meant by those names, and each name would be an equivocal proper name. To cope with such differences, intuitive individual presentations are said to sustain new psychological functions when they occur in association with general *names*: they determine other trains of ideas, they fit otherwise into the course of our thoughts, they influence this course in a different fashion.

All this is quite irrelevant to the phenomenological facts. Here and now, at the very moment that we significantly utter a general name, we mean what is general, and our meaning differs from our meaning when we mean what is individual. This difference must be pinned down *in the descriptive content of the isolated experience*, in the individually and actually performed general assertion. What things are causally connected with such an experience, what psychological consequences may follow from it, all this does not concern us. Such things concern the psychology of abstraction, not its phenomenology.

The nominalistic currents of our time have certainly threatened to change our notion of conceptualism so that the nominalism of John Stuart Mill, avowed by him so decisively, has lately been disputed.[1] We should not, however, see it as the essence of nominalism that, in its attempted clarification of the sense and theoretical achievement of universals, it loses itself in a blind associative play of names as mere verbal noises; its essence lies in the fact that its attempted clarifications overlook the *peculiar consciousness* exemplified in our living sense of the meaning of signs, in our actual understanding of them, in the grasped sense of our assertions, and also exemplified in correlative acts of fulfilment, which yield us the 'true' Idea of the universal, the wholly evident ideation in which the universal 'itself' is given to us. This consciousness means what it means to us, whether or not we know anything about psychology, or about mental antecedents and consequences, associative dispositions, etc. If the nominalist wishes to give an empirical explanation of this consciousness of the universal, as a fact of our human nature, if he wishes to connect it causally with such and such factors, such and such previous experiences, such and such unconscious dispositions, we should not object in principle. We should merely deny the interest, for pure logic and epistemology, of such empirical psychological facts. Instead of this, however, the nominalist says that to differentiate general ideas from individual ones, and to oppose the former to the latter, is really to talk senselessly. He denies that there is abstraction in the sense of a peculiar consciousness of the universal which lends evidence to general names and meanings: in reality only individual intuitions exist, some with an interplay of conscious and unconscious happenings, which never take us beyond the sphere of what is individual, nor constitute, i.e. bring to awareness and perhaps to self-presentation, any essentially new sort of objectivity.

Each thought-experience, like every mental state, has, empirically treated, its descriptive content, as well as its causal antecedents and consequents; it makes itself felt in the rush of life, and exercises its productive functions. But in the field of *phenomenology* and, above all, in the sphere of *epistemology* – the phenomenological clarification of ideal thought- and knowledge-unities – only essence and sense matter: what we mean when we make assertions, what object is set up for us by our act of meaning as such, in virtue of its sense, what partial meanings enter essentially into the make-up of our act of meaning, what essential forms and differences it exhibits, and so on. What is of interest to epistemology, must be shown up exclusively in the *content* of the *meaning-experiences and the fulfilment-experiences themselves*, and be shown up as essential. If we also find, in the range of what can be thus evidently shown up, the distinction between universal presentations and individual, intuitive presentations (which we undoubtedly do), then no talk of genetic functions and associations can be relevant to such a distinction, or contribute a jot to its clarification.

It carries the matter no further and fails to remove our objections, if, like Mill, we look on *exclusive attention* to some single attribute (or dependent feature) of the intuited object, as being the act which, in our actual consciousness, in the supposed genetic situation, gives the name its 'generic' meaning. Though recent thinkers, who share Mill's ideas without sharing his extreme empiricist tendencies, may call themselves 'conceptualists', thinking that the interest which turns 'attributes' into objects will also guarantee the existence of general meanings – their doctrine is and remains essentially nominalistic.

Generality remains for them a matter of the associative function of signs, it consists in the psychologically regulated association of 'the same sign' with 'the same' objective feature – or rather with the feature which always recurs in the same determinate form and is at times emphasized by attention. This *generality of a psychological function* is, however, quite removed from the *generality which belongs to the intentional content of the logical experiences themselves*, or which, described objectively and ideally, belongs to our *meanings and our meaning-fulfilments*. This last generality escapes nominalism entirely.

§16 (c) Generality of psychological function and generality as a meaning-form. Different senses of the relation of a universal to an extension

To bring complete clearness to this important distinction between generality of psychological function, and generality as pertaining to a significant content itself, we must pay heed to the differing logical functions of general names and meanings, and in connection therewith to the differing senses of talk of their generality, or of their relation to a range of particulars.

Let us set the following three forms side by side: *an A, all A, A in general*, e.g. *a triangle, all triangles, the triangle*, the last taken as in the sentence 'The triangle is a species of figure'.[2]

The expression 'an *A*' can function predicatively as the predicate of innumerable categorical assertions, and the aggregate of the true, or intrinsically possible assertions of this sort, determines all the possible subjects to which being an *A* either actually pertains, or could without contradiction pertain, in other words the actual or possible 'range' ('extension') of the 'concept' *A*. This universal concept *A*, or the universal predicate 'an *A*', applies to all the objects in this range – we take for the sake of simplicity the range to which it applies truly – i.e., the assertions in the aggregate in question are all true: there are, phenomenologically speaking, as possibilities, self-evident judgements with a corresponding content. This generality belongs, therefore, to the logical function of the predicate; it is not represented in the individual act, the single case where the meaning *an A* is enacted, or where we mean the corresponding adjectival predicate. It appears in these only as a form of indefiniteness; the word 'A' expresses a form, which evidently pertains to our meaning-intention or our meaning-fulfilment, and is connected with *what* either intends. This form is a wholly irreducible moment; its peculiarity can only be recognized, not explained away by any sort of psychological-genetic treatment. Ideally put: the word 'A' expresses a primitive logical form. The same plainly holds of the formation 'an *A*', which likewise represents a primitive logical structure.

The generality of which we are here speaking, belongs, we say, to the *logical* function of predicates, it consists in the *logical possibility* of propositions of a certain sort. We stress the logical character of this possibility, to show that we are concerned with a possibility that can be seen *a priori* to belong to meanings as Specific Unities, not to psychologically contingent acts. If we see that Red is a universal predicate, one associable with many possible subjects, our meaning no longer relates to something whose existence is in a real (*realen*) sense governed by those natural laws which govern the coming and going of experiences in time. We are not talking of experiences at all, but of the single self-identical predicate Red, and of the possibility of certain sentences, each single in the same sense, in which this same predicate occurs.

If we now pass to the form 'all *A*'s', generality pertains to the form of the act itself. We expressly mean *all A's*, to all such *A*'s our presentation and predication relates in the universal judgement, though perhaps no single *A* is 'itself' 'directly' presented. This idea of a range, is however, no complex of the ideas of the members of this range; so little is this the case, that such individual presentations as perhaps float before us have nothing at all to do with the significant intention to *all A's*. Here also the word 'all' points to a peculiar semantic form: we leave aside the question whether it can be resolved into simpler forms or not.

If we deal finally with the form *the A (in specie)*, generality again pertains to our significant content itself. Here, however, we encounter a wholly different sort of universality, the universality of the Species, which, while it may have the closest *logical* relations to universality of range, none the less evidently differs from the latter. The forms *the A* and *all A's* – likewise *any A, no matter which* are not the same in meaning: theirs is no mere grammatical difference, determined in the end by mere verbal noise. They are *logically* distinct forms, giving expression to essential differences of meaning. The consciousness of Specific Generality must count as an essentially new mode of 'presentation', as one, namely, that does not merely present individual singulars in a new manner, but makes us aware of a new sort of singulars, i.e. Singular Species. What sort of singulars these are, and how they stand *a priori* to individual singulars, or how they differ from these latter, must of course be gleaned from the logical truths which, grounded in pure forms, govern both sorts of singulars and their mutual *a priori* relations (i.e. their relations of essence or Idea). Here there is no obscurity or possible error as long as one keeps to the straight sense of these truths, or, what is the same, to the straight sense of the meaning-forms in question, whose self-evident interpretations are called truths of logic. Only an erroneous sideslip into psychologistic and metaphysical trains of thought produces obscurity; it creates pseudo-problems and frames pseudo-theories to solve them.

§17 (*d*) Application to the critique of nominalism

If we now look back on the nominalistic theory of abstraction, we see from the above that its main error lies in quite ignoring the irreducible peculiarities of the forms of consciousness (of the forms of our intentions and of their correlative fulfilments). Its defective descriptive analysis makes it blind to the fact that the forms of logic are no more than these forms of significant intention which have themselves been made objects of a consciousness which treats them as unities, and so turns them into Ideal Species. Generality is also to be found among these forms. Nominalism further confuses the various concepts of generality that we have separated above. It one-sidedly prefers the generality which belongs to concepts in their predicative function, as a possibility of associating the same concept predicatively with several subjects. Being blind to the logically ideal character of this possibility, with its roots in semantic form, it puts psychological associations in its place, associations necessarily alien to, even incommensurable with, the predicates and propositions in question. Since it claims to have completely cleared up the nature of general meanings through such psychological analyses, its confusions grossly distort the generality of universal and specific presentations; this generality we saw belonged to the semantic essence of the individual act as such, as an indwelling meaning-form. What belongs phenomenologically to the immanent essence of the individual act, is turned into a psychological play of events, that throw no light, whether as causes or effects, on the individual act in which the entire total consciousness of universality comes alive.

§21 The difference between attending to a non-independent moment of an intuited object and attending to the corresponding attribute *in specie*

It will not be profitless to explore the difficulties of our contested theory a little further. Our own conception will become clearer when its whole contrast with this theory has been worked out.

Concentrated attention to an attributive moment is looked on as intuitively fulfilling (as yielding the 'true sense') of the general meaning attaching to the name of the corresponding attribute. To mean the Species intuitively, and to perform an act of concentrated attention, are looked on as one and the same. But how do things stand, we may ask, in cases where *we expressly refer to the individual moment*? What differentiates the two types of case? If we are struck by an individual trait of an object, by its peculiar colouring, e.g., or by its noble form etc., we pay special attention to this trait, and yet have no general presentation. The same question applies to complete concrete things. What is the difference between exclusive attention to the individually apparent statue, and the intuitive grasp of the corresponding Idea, that could be realized in countless real statues?

Our opponents might reply: in individual treatment, individualizing moments enter our sphere of interest, in specific treatment, they are shut out. Our interest is confined to what is general, i.e. to a content which in itself provides no individual distinctions. Instead of pressing our previous objection – whether attention to individuating determinations creates individuality, while inattention destroys it – we ask rather whether, in individual treatment, we also necessarily *mean* the individuating moments, which it is held must be concurrently noticed? Does an individual proper name also implicitly name individuating determinations, those, e.g., of time and place? Here is my friend Hans and I call him 'Hans'. He is no doubt individually determined, he is always at a particular point in space and time. If these determinations were, however, concurrently meant, the name 'Hans' would change its meaning with every step that my friend takes, on every occasion that I address him by name. Such a thing can scarcely be maintained, nor would one care to take refuge in saying that a proper name is really general. For the peculiar generality in respect of the varied times, positions, situations of the same individual thing differs in form from the specific generality of the thing's attribute or of the generic Idea 'thing in general'.

Often enough, at least, we are indifferent to the here and the now in attending to some part or characteristic trait of an object. We do not therefore consider it *in specie*, as we certainly do not mean to perform an 'abstraction' in the sense of a general presentation.

Perhaps one might here have recourse to the assumption that individuating determinations are *marginally* noticed. This cannot give much help. A great deal is marginally noticed, but is not for that reason really meant. Where the consciousness of the universal is intuitively achieved, as a true and genuine abstraction, the individual object of the underlying intuition certainly has a subsidiary place in consciousness, but is not at all meant. Mill's talk about our unconsciousness of the determinations that we abstract from is a useless, strictly speaking an absurd fiction.[3] In the numerous cases where, looking to some singular intuitive fact, we utter the corresponding generality, the singular element stays before our eyes, we do not suddenly become blind to what is individual in our case; this certainly does not happen when, e.g., we look at this jasmine in bloom, and inhaling its scent, say 'Jasmine has a heady scent'.

If finally one grasps at a new evasion and admits that the individuating element is not specially picked out like the preferred point of our interest, not even marginally noticed, as are objects lying outside of our main interest, but that it is rather *subsidiarily* noticed (*mitbeachtet*), as being part of our main interest and peculiarly implied in its intention – then the whole ground of the theory is abandoned. For the theory claimed to make do with the mere emphasis of regard towards the concrete given object, or a peculiar feature given in it, and it now ends by postulating a variety of forms of consciousness that it should surely have dispensed with.

§22 Fundamental deficiencies in the phenomenological analysis of attention

This leads us at once to the weakest point of the theory; which is to be found in the question 'What is attention?' We are of course not reproaching the theory for failing to offer us a perfected phenomenology and psychology of attention, but for failing to clear up the nature of attention to an extent absolutely required by its aims. It should have ascertained what gives the word 'attention' its unitary sense, in order to see how far its range of application extends, or what the objects in each case are that we can (in a normal sense) claim to attend to. Above all, it should have inquired into the relation of attention to the meaning or reference which gives names and other expressions their significance. The sort of theory of abstraction just disputed, is possible only through the Lockean prejudice according to which the objects to which consciousness in its acts is immediately and properly directed, and the objects, particularly, of attention, must necessarily be mental contents, real occurrences in consciousness. It seems perfectly obvious that an act of consciousness can immediately act only on what is actually (*wirklich*) given in consciousness, i.e. on contents that it *really* (*reell*) includes among its elements. What is outside consciousness can only be the mediate object of a conscious act; and this occurs simply when the immediate content of the act, its primary object, serves as a representation, an image, a sign, of what is beyond consciousness.

Once accustomed to this mode of approach, one readily tries to clear up the objective relations and forms inherent in the intention of acts, by looking predominantly to their present conscious contents as their supposedly immediate objects, and, misled by the seeming intelligibility of talk about representations and signs, entirely ignores the true, supposedly mediate objects of the acts. Unthinkingly one credits to *contents* everything which acts, in their straightforward reference, place in the *object*; its attributes, its colours, forms etc., are forthwith called 'contents' and actually interpreted as contents in the psychological sense, e.g. as sensations.

How far this whole conception is at odds with the plain phenomenological situation, and how thoroughly it has debauched epistemology, we shall yet have many opportunities to observe. Here it may suffice to point out that when, e.g., we have a presentation or judgement about a horse, it is a horse, not our sensations of the moment, that is presented and judged about. Our sensations are only presented and judged about in psychological reflection, whose modes of conception should not be read into the immediate situation. That an appropriate train of sensations or images is *experienced*, and is in this sense conscious, does not and cannot mean that this is the *object* of an act of consciousness, in the sense that a perception, a presentation or a judgement is directed upon it.

This mistaken conception has further had a detrimental effect on the theory of abstraction. Led astray by the seemingly obvious, one takes experienced contents to be the normal objects to which one pays attention. The concrete phenomenal thing is treated as a complex of contents, i.e. of attributes grown together in a single intuitive image. And it is then said of these attributes, taken as experienced mental contents, that their non-independence precludes their separation from the concretely complete image: they can only be noticed in the latter. How could such a theory of abstraction intelligibly account for the formation of abstract ideas of that class of attributive determinations which are indeed perceived, but which by their nature never are adequately perceived, which cannot be given in the form of a mental content? I need only mention three-dimensional spatial shapes, in particular closed surfaces of solids or complete solids, such as the sphere and the cube. And how does the matter stand with the myriads of conceptual presentations, perhaps realized with the help of sensuous intuition, but which no intuitive aspect, even from the sphere of inner sense, instantiates? Here one can certainly not talk of a mere heeding of what is given in (sensuous) intuition, nor of a heeding of experienced contents.

Our own point of view inclines us first to draw a distinction in the sphere of sensuous abstraction – the sphere usually stressed for simplicity's sake – between acts in which an attributive aspect is intuitively 'given', and acts built upon these, which are not mere acts of attention to such an aspect, but rather acts of a new kind, referring in general fashion to the corresponding Species. Whether intuition presents the attributive aspect adequately or inadequately, is beside the point. We should then draw the further distinction between cases of sensuous abstraction, i.e. of an abstraction straightforwardly and perhaps adequately adjusted to sensuous intuition, and cases of non-sensuous or of at most partially sensuous abstraction, i.e. cases where the realized consciousness of the universal is at most only partially built on acts of sensuous intuition, and for the rest on non-sensuous acts, and accordingly related to thought-forms or categories whose nature does not permit of sensuous fulfilment. Suitables examples of the former, are unmixed concepts from outer or inner sense, such as colour, noise, pain, judgement, will, of the latter, concepts such as series, sense, disjunctive member, identity, being etc. etc. This difference will again seriously engage us in future investigations.

§23 Significant talk of attention embraces the whole sphere of thinking and not merely the sphere of intuition

The unitary sense to talk of 'attending' so little calls for 'contents' in the psychological sense (as the objects to which we attend), that it ranges beyond the sphere of intuition, and embraces the whole sphere of thinking. It makes no difference how thought is conducted, whether on an intuitive basis or in pure symbols. If we are theoretically concerned with *the culture of the Renaissance*, with *ancient philosophy*, with *the development of astronomical ideas*, with *elliptical functions*, with *curves of the nth order*, with *laws of algebraic operations* etc., we attend to all these matters. If our judgement is of the form *All A's are B's*, our attention is given to this universal state of affairs, we are concerned with allness, and not with this or that single matter. And so in general. Each thought, or at least each consistent thought, can no doubt become intuitive, to the extent that it is built in a certain fashion on 'corresponding' intuition. But the attention performed on such an intuition, whether of inner or outer sense, does not amount to attention to that intuition's phenomenological content, and just as little to attention to the object apparent in it. The *a certain*, or the *any*, the *all* and the *each*, the *and*, the *or*, the *not*, the *if* and the *then* etc., are not things we can point to in an object of basic sensuous intuition, that can be 'had' sensationally or externally represented or painted. Certain acts naturally correspond to all of them. The words have their meaning; in understanding them we realize certain forms pertaining to our objective intention. But these acts are not the *objects* that we mean: they are the activity of meaning or presenting, which only becomes objective to psychological reflection. The *object* we mean is variously the universal state of affairs *All A's are B's*, or the generic state of affairs *The A (in specie) is a B*, or the indefinitely singular state of affairs *Any A is a B* etc. We do not attend to the individual intuition, which perhaps accompanies our thought-presentations, and on which their evidence is founded: we do not attend to those act-characters which either give our intuition form, or which find their fulfilment in formed intuition. What we attend to are the *objects of our thinking*, the objects and states of affairs seen by thought in this or that manner, which are revealed to our insight when we perform such acts on such a foundation. And an abstraction in which we seize some point of conception or meaning, where we do not merely look to what is individual and intuitive (perceiving it attentively and what not), means no more than that we perform certain thought-acts with insight, acts sometimes of one form and sometimes of another.

The range of the unitary notion of attention is therefore so wide that it doubtless embraces the whole field of intuitive and cogitative *reference* (*Meinens*), the field of presentation (*Vorstellens*) in a well-defined but sufficiently wide sense, which comprehends both intuition and thought. Ultimately it extends as far as the concept: Consciousness of something. To talk distinctively of attention, as of a certain selectivity in the sphere of consciousness, takes account therefore of a certain difference which is not dependent on the species of our mode of consciousness (on the manner of our consciousness). We have certain 'presentations' while not 'concentrating' on their objects, but upon the objects of other presentations.

Attending is thus represented as a straightforward, not further describable *way* in which contents, otherwise lost in the undivided flow of consciousness, achieve separate consciousness, in which they are 'emphasized' or 'discovered' by us. If, in a similar sense, all differences in the manner of presentation are denied, attention is then seen as an illuminating and indicative function operating within *this* field. But all this involves an extreme narrowing of concepts whose wider meanings cannot be eliminated, and to which one must unavoidably have recourse. Dazed by the confusion between object and mental content, one forgets that the objects of which we are 'conscious', are not simply *in* consciousness as in a box, so that they can merely be found in it and snatched at in it; but that they are first *constituted* as being what they are for us, and as what they count as for us, in varying forms of objective intention. One forgets that, from the mere finding of a mental content, i.e. the pure immanent intuition of such a content, up to the external perception and imagination of objects neither found immanently in consciousness, nor capable of being so found, and from these on to the loftiest thought-formations with their manifold categorial forms and appropriately correlated semantic forms, an *essentially* single concept runs continuously: in all cases, whether we *intuit* in perceptual, fancying or remembering fashion, or whether we think in empirical and logico-mathematical forms, an intending, or reference (*Vermeinen*) is present, that *aims* at an object, a consciousness is present that is the consciousness *of* this object. The mere existence of a content in the psychic interplay is, however, not at all this being-meant or being-referred-to. This first arises when this content is 'noticed', such notice being a look directed towards it, a presentation of it. To define the presentation of a content as the mere fact of its being experienced, and in consequence to give the name 'presentations' to all experienced contents, is one of the worst conceptual distortions known to philosophy. It is without doubt responsible for an untold legion of epistemological and psychological errors. If we stick to the intentional concept of presentation, which alone sets a standard for epistemology and logic, we shall be unable to judge that all differences between presentations reduce to differences in their presented 'contents'. It is clear, on the contrary, and particularly in the field of pure logic, that *to each primitive logical form a peculiar 'manner of consciousness', a peculiar 'manner of presentation'*, corresponds. In so far, of course, as *each new mode of intentional reference always in a manner also concerns objects*, i.e. constitutes novel forms with which the object is brought to consciousness, one can no doubt say that all difference in presentation lies in what is presented. One must carefully note, however, that there are *two sorts of differences in the object, in what is presented*, differences of *categorial form* and differences in the *'thing itself'*; this 'thing' can be brought to consciousness *as* the same in a variety of forms. More will be said on these heads in later Investigations.

Chapter 4

Abstraction and representation

§24 The general idea as a device for economizing thought

There is an error originating from mediaeval nominalism which likes to represent general concepts and names as *mere devices* in an economy of thinking, devices which will spare us the individual consideration and naming of all individual things. The function of concepts, it is said, is to enable the thinking mind to transcend the limits set it by the unsurveyable multiplicity of individual singulars; their economizations of thinking enable the mind to reach its goal of knowledge indirectly, as it could never have reached it directly. General concepts make it possible for us to treat things in bundles as it were, to make assertions about whole classes of objects at a single 'go'; we can therefore talk about countless objects, instead of conceiving and judging each object 'on its own'.

Locke brings this thought into modern philosophy when he says, e.g., in the last part of Book III, chapter III of his *Essay* . . . 'that men making abstract ideas, and settling them in their minds with names annexed to them, do thereby enable themselves to consider things, and discourse of them as it were in bundles, for the easier and readier improvement and communication of their knowledge; which would advance but slowly were their words and thoughts confined only to particulars'.[1]

This exposition reveals itself as nonsensical if one reflects that, without general meanings, one can make no assertions at all, not even such as are singular, and that one cannot talk of thinking, judging or knowing, in a sense relevant to logic, on a mere foundation of the direct presentations of individuals. The most ideal adaptation of the human mind to the multiplicity of individual things, the genuine, effortless realization of adequate individual conceptions, would not render thought superfluous. For performances attainable in this manner are not performances of thinking.

Along intuitive pathways, e.g., no laws come to light. A knowledge of laws may very well promote the survival of thinking beings, it may usefully govern the formation of forward looking intuitive presentations, and may be much more useful in this respect than the natural pull of association. But the relation of the function of thought to the preservation of thinking beings, i.e. of human beings, has its place in psychological anthropology, not in the theory of knowledge. What is performed by a law as an ideal unity, its *logical* embrace of innumerable instances in a general propositional meaning, is something that no intuition can perform, not even the universal intuition of a God. For to intuit is plainly not to think. The perfection of thought lies doubtless in intuitive, i.e. in 'authentic' thinking, in that knowledge in which our thought-intention is 'satisfied' (as it were) by passing over into intuition. Even the brief discussions of the previous chapter permit us, however, to speak of a grave misinterpretation of this fact, when intuition – understood in the usual sense of acts of external or internal sense – is regarded as the proper intellectual function, and when the true role of conceptual thought is taken to be its use of indirect devices which economize intuition, and overcome the all too narrow limits of the latter. Certainly we are accustomed to using an all-seeing mind as a logical ideal, but only because we quietly add to its all-seeing capacities, capacities for knowing and thinking all. We imagine this mind as one not merely active in mere intuitions, i.e. in intuitions perhaps adequate but none the less unthinking, but as also casting these intuitions into categorial forms and combining them synthetically, and finding in such formed, combined intuitions the ultimate fulfilment of its thought-intentions, thereby realizing the ideal of all-inclusive knowledge. We shall, therefore have to say: Not mere intuition, but adequate, categorially formed intuitions, completely accommodated to thought, or conversely, thought which draws its evidence from intuition, constitute the goal of true knowledge. The 'economy of thought' only makes sense, and has its rich field within the sphere of thought and knowledge: it is in fact really an economy of knowledge.[2]

On the theory of wholes and parts

Introduction[1]

The difference between 'abstract' and 'concrete' contents, which is plainly the same as Stumpf's distinction between *dependent* (non-independent) and *independent* contents, is most important for all phenomenological investigations; we must, it seems, therefore, first of all submit it to a thorough analysis. As said in my previous Investigation, this distinction, which first showed up in the field of the descriptive psychology of sense-data, could be looked on as a special case of a universal distinction. It extends beyond the sphere of conscious contents and plays an extremely important role in the field of *objects as such*. The systematic place for its discussion should therefore be in the *pure (a priori) theory of objects as such*, in which we deal with ideas pertinent to the *category of object*, ideas such as Whole and Part, Subject and Quality, Individual and Species, Genus and Species, Relation and Collection, Unity, Number, Series, Ordinal Number, Magnitude etc., as well as the *a priori* truths which relate to these. Here again we cannot allow our analytic investigation to wait on the systematic development of our subject-matter. Difficult notions employed by us in our clarificatory study of knowledge, and made to work rather in the manner of a lever, cannot be left unexamined, till they spontaneously emerge in the systematic fabric of the logical realm. For we are not here engaged on a systematic exposition of logic, but on an epistemological clarification, as well as on the prolegomena to any future exposition of logic.

To plumb the difference between dependent and non-independent contents, therefore, points so directly to the fundamental questions of the Pure Theory of Wholes and Parts (which is a part of formal ontology) that we cannot avoid going into these questions in some detail.

Chapter 1

The difference between independent and non-independent objects

§1 Complex and simple, articulated and unarticulated objects

Since the Investigation which follows mainly concerns relations of Parts, we start off with a wholly general discussion of such relations.

Objects can be related to one another as Wholes to Parts, they can also be related to one another as coordinated parts of a whole. These sorts of relations have an *a priori* foundation in the Idea of an object. Every object is either actually or possibly a part, i.e. there are actual or possible wholes that include it. Not every object, on the other hand, need perhaps have parts, and we have therefore the ideal division of objects into the *simple* and the *complex*.

The terms 'complex' and 'simple' are therefore defined by the qualification of having parts or not having parts. They may, however, be understood in a second, possibly more natural sense, in which complexity, as the word's etymology suggests, points to a plurality of disjoined parts in the whole, so that we have to call *simple* whatever cannot be 'cut up' into a plurality of parts, i.e. that in which not even two *disjoined* parts can be distinguished. In the unity of a sensory phenomenon we can perhaps discover a wholly determinate 'moment' of redness as well as the generic 'moment' of colour. Colour and determinate redness are not, however, disjoined 'moments'. Redness on the other hand, and the extension that it covers, are such disjoined moments, since they have no community of content. They have, we may say, a mutual association in the widest sense of the word; we have here a general relation of parts which is that of disjoined parts in a whole, an association of such parts. It now seems appropriate to call the associated parts *members* of the association: but to give so wide a sense to talk about members of a whole, means to count colour and shape as the associated parts of a coloured expanse. That goes against linguistic usage. For in such wholes the parts have relative dependence as regards one another: we find them so closely united as to be called 'interpenetrating'. It is quite different in the case of wholes which are broken up, or could be broken up, into *pieces*: in their case talk of members or of articulated structure alone comes natural. The parts are here not merely disjoined from each other, but relatively independent, they have the character of mutually-put-together *pieces*.

Even at the start of our discussion, we see that the relations of parts fall under characteristically different *forms*: these forms, we suspect, depend on the cardinal difference between independent and non-independent objects, which is our theme in the present section.

§2 Introduction of the distinction between independent and non-independent objects (contents)

We interpret the word 'part' in the *widest* sense: we may call anything a 'part' that can be distinguished 'in' an object, or, objectively phrased, that is 'present' in it. Everything is a part that is an object's real possession, not only in the sense of being a real thing, but also in the sense of being something really in something, that truly helps to make it up:[1] an object in itself, considered in abstraction from all contexts to which it is tied, is likewise a part. Every non-relative 'real' (*reale*) predicate therefore points to a part of the object which is the predicate's subject: 'red' and 'round', e.g., do so, but not 'existent' or 'something'. Every 'real' (*reale*) mode of association, e.g. the moment of spatial configuration, likewise counts as a proper part of the whole.

The term 'part' is not used so widely in ordinary discourse. If we now try to pin down the limitations which mark off this ordinary, from *our* notion of part, we come up against the fundamental distinction called by us that of *independent* and *non-independent* parts. Where one talks of 'parts' without qualification, one generally has the *independent* parts (those referred to as 'pieces') in mind. Since each part can be made the specific object (or, as we also have frequently said, 'content') of a presentation directed upon it, and can therefore be called an object or 'content', the distinction of parts just mentioned points to a distinction in objects (or contents) as such. The term 'object' is in this context always taken in its widest sense.

In ordinary talk of objects or of parts, one of course involuntarily thinks of independent objects. The term 'content' is less restricted in this respect since 'abstract contents' are also commonly talked of. But talk of 'contents' tends to move in a purely psychological sphere, a limitation with which we may start investigating our distinction, but which must be dropped as we proceed.[2]

As a matter of history the distinction between independent and non-independent contents arose in the psychological realm, more specifically in the field of the phenomenology of inner experience. In a polemic against Locke, Berkeley[3] said: We have the ability to recall individual things previously seen, or to put them together or break them down in imagination. We can imagine a man with two heads, the trunk of a man tied to the body of a horse, or isolated pieces such as a separated head, nose, ear etc. As opposed to this, it is impossible to form 'abstract ideas', to separate the idea, e.g., of a movement from that of a moving body. We can only abstract, in the Lockean separative sense, such parts of a presented whole as are in fact unified with other parts, but as could also exist without them. Since *esse* for Berkeley here always means the same as *percipi*, this inability to exist means no more than an inability to be perceived. We must note, further, that for Berkeley ideas are the things perceived, i.e. contents of consciousness in the sense of things we really (*reell*) live through.

We may now make a statement that brings out the essential point of Berkeley's distinctions, making use of a readily understandable verbal change.[4]

Seen in their mutual interrelations, contents presented together on any occasion fall into two main classes: independent and non-independent contents.[5] We have independent contents wherever the elements of a presentational complex (complex of contents) by their very nature *permit their separated presentation*; we have dependent contents wherever this is not the case.

§3 The inseparability of non-independent contents

To be more precise in regard to this ability or inability-to-be-separately-presented, we make use of some of Stumpf's observations – quite insufficiently noticed – and assert the following:[6]

It is self-evident, in regard to *certain* contents, that the modification or elimination of at least *one* of the contents given with them (but not contained in them), must modify or eliminate those contents themselves. In the case of *other* contents, this is not at all self-evident; it is not absurd to suppose them remaining unaffected despite the modification or elimination of all coexistent contents. Contents of the former sort can *only* be conceived as parts of more comprehensive wholes, whereas the latter appear possible, even if nothing whatever exists beside them, nothing therefore bound up with them to form a whole.

In the sense just laid down every phenomenal thing and piece of a thing is *separably presentable*. The head of a horse can be presented 'on its own' or 'cut off', i.e. we can hold it in our fancy, while we allow the other parts of the horse, and its whole intuited setting, to alter and vanish at will. Strictly speaking, the phenomenal thing or its piece, i.e. the sensuous phenomenon as such, the spatial shape filled with sensuous qualities, never stays just the same in descriptive content: but the content of such a 'phenomenon' does not at least involve anything entailing a self-evident, necessary, functional dependence of its changes on those of coexistent phenomena. This holds, we may say, of phenomenal objects as such, as well as of the 'appearances', in the sense of the *experiences*, in which these things appear, as also in respect of the sensational complexes which are given an objective 'interpretation' in such experiences. Good examples in this field are the phenomena of tones and chords, of smells and other experiences, that we can readily think of apart from all relation to existent thinghood.

§4 Analyses of examples following Stumpf

Let us now consider some instances of inseparable contents, e.g. the relation of *visual quality* to *extension*, or the relation of both to the *figure* which bounds them. It is doubtless true in a certain sense that these moments can be *independently* varied. Extension can stay the same while colour varies indefinitely, colour stay the same while extent and figure vary indefinitely. But, strictly speaking, such independent variability affects only the *kinds* of the 'moments' in their various genera. While the moment of colour remains constant in respect of its specific shade, extension and shape may vary indefinitely in their sub-species, and vice versa. Specifically the same quality, and nuance of quality, may be stretched or spread out over every extension, and, conversely, the same extension may be covered by every quality. Scope, however, remains for relations of functional dependence among the changes of such moments, which, be it noted, are not exhausted by the ideal content of their Species. The moment of colour, as immediate part-content of the intuited concrete thing, is not the same in the two concrete intuitions, even when the quality, the lowest differentiation of the genus colour, remains the same. Stumpf has made the powerful observation:

> Quality shares after a fashion in changes of extension. We express this verbally when we say that colour diminishes, becomes smaller, even to the vanishing point. Increase and diminution are names for quantitative changes.
> Quality is indeed affected in sympathy with changes in extent, although its own peculiar manner of change is independent of extent. It does not thereby become less green or less red: it has itself no degrees, only kinds, and can in itself neither increase nor diminish, only alter. But none the less, when we leave quality quite unchanged as regards its peculiar manner of change, e.g. let it stay green, it still is affected by quantitative change. And that this is perhaps not an improper or misleading verbal transfer, is shown by the fact that a quality can *decrease to nothing*, that in the end *mere change of quantity can bring it to nought*.[7]

We accept Stumpf's observation, only adding that it is not really the quality that is affected, but the immediate intuitive 'moment' falling under it. Quality must be looked on as a second-order abstraction, just like the figure and magnitude of an extension. But just on account of the law here under discussion, the moment in question can only be named by way of concepts determined by the genera of Quality and Extension. Quality is differentiated to the qualitative 'moment' now under consideration, by something not contained in the Genus Colour, since we rightly treat the quality, e.g. the determinate shade of red, as the *Infima Species* within this genus. Just so, a determinate figure is the last difference of the Genus Figure, though the corresponding immediate, intuitive 'moment' is further differentiated. But the combinations among the various last differences of the Genera Figure and Colour fully determine the 'moments' in question, determine whatever else may be like or unlike them. The dependence of the immediate 'moments' therefore means a certain necessary relationship among them, which is determined purely by their abstracta at the level just above them.

Stumpf adds the following valuable remarks:

> From this (i.e. the above described functional dependence of the 'moments' of Quality and Extension), it follows that both are *in their nature inseparable*, that they in some manner *compose a total content*, of which they are merely part-contents. Were they merely items in a sum, one might possibly think that, absolutely treated, disappearance of Extension might mean the concomitant disappearance of Quality, that they did not exist apart; but that Quality should gradually diminish and vanish through the mere diminution and vanishing of Quantity, without changing in its own fashion *as* Quality, would be unintelligible . . . they can in any case not be independent contents. *Their nature forbids them to have an isolated and mutually independent existence in our ideas.*[8]

The same sort of thing could be said of the relation of Intensity to Quality. The intensity of a tone is not something indifferent or so-to-speak alien to its quality. We cannot keep the intensity just as it is, while the quality varies at will, or is allowed to vanish. Eliminate quality and you unavoidably eliminate intensity, and vice versa. Evidently this is no mere empirical fact, but an *a priori* necessity, grounded in pure essence. In the response to change we have a further analogy to the previously mentioned case: if intensity steadily approaches the zero-limit, we feel our qualitative impression likewise reduced, even though the quality as such remains specifically unaltered.

Further examples fully illustrate the *'moments' of unity* in the intuitive contents, 'moments' built on the elements that we primarily distinguish, by which such elements are similarly or dissimilarly *associated into sensuous intuitive wholes*. The use of such examples gives us our first narrower concepts of a whole, of an association etc., and, further, our distinctive concepts of various kinds and sorts of wholes, whether present to outer or inner sense.

These 'moments of unity' are of course the same as the contents called 'form-qualities' by von Ehrenfels, 'figural' moments by myself, and 'founded contents' by Meinong.[9] But one needs here a supplementary distinction between the *phenomenological* moments of unity, which give unity to the experiences or parts of experiences (the real phenomenological data), and the *objective* moments of unity, which belong *to the intentional objects and parts of objects, which in general* transcend the experiential sphere. The expression 'moment of unity', incidentally recommended to me by Riehl, has such obvious advantages in virtue of its immediate intelligibility, that it might well be universally adopted.

§10 The multiplicity of laws governing the various sorts of non-independent contents

Our discussions so far have shown that there is always an *a priori* law governing what is non-independent, having its conceptual roots in what is universal in the whole and part in question. But this law can be interpreted and expressed with more or less definiteness. To pin down the concept of non-independence, it is enough to say that a non-independent object can only be what it is (i.e. what it is in virtue of its essential properties) in a more comprehensive whole. At times, however, a non-independent object can vary in Species: this entails varying the kind of supplementation it requires for existence. If we say, for example, that the 'moment' of sensory quality, e.g. of sensory colour, is non-independent, and requires a whole in which it may be embodied, we have only laid down *one* side of our governing law, the side of a part which belongs to the Genus Sensory Quality. We have not, however, laid down the character of the whole, the manner in which such a 'quality' is its part, nor the sort of supplement it needs to achieve existence. It is different when we say that a sensory quality can only exist in a sense-field, and a sensory colour in a visual sense-field, or that it can only exist as qualifying an extension. Here the law lays down the other sides as well; the notion of a visual sense-field is given; and it means a particular, definite sort of whole among various possible sorts of whole. Just so, the notion of 'qualifying an extension' points to quite specific possibilities of law-governed inherence that a non-independent 'moment' may have to a whole. The specific character of this inherence is fixed in general fashion both by the essence of Sensory Quality and the essence of Extension, but each is contained in its *own* manner in the essential unity of visual sensation, or of the visual field in which all such unities find their place. This manner cannot be further described. If we ask what differentiates the generic feature of *being a sensory 'moment'*, so as to yield the specific feature of *being a sensory quality*, we can give no answer that helps us; we can point to no additional feature in which the concept of quality is not included. Just so, if we are asked what must be added to *Colour* to produce its Species Redness we can only answer 'Redness'.

The notion of what is non-independent, with its indirectly, generally characterized definitory lawfulness, points to many factually determined, variable laws of essence. It is not a peculiarity of certain sorts of parts that they should only be parts in general, while it remains quite indifferent what they are conglomerated with, and into what sorts of connection they are fitted. There are fixed, necessary connections, pure laws definite in content, which vary with the pure Species of non-independent contents, and accordingly prescribe one sort of completion to one of them, another sort of completion to another. The Species associated in these laws, which mark off the spheres of contingent individuality presupposed by these laws – are occasionally, but not always, lowest specific differences. A law, for instance, may prescribe to contents of the Species Colour a connection with contents of the Species Extension, but it does not prescribe a definite extension to a definite colour, or vice versa. The values of the lowest differences are accordingly not functionally interrelated. The law only refers to lowest Species, i.e. Species having the multiplicity of ultimate specific differences *immediately* beneath them. On the other hand, if we consider the dependence of qualitative remoteness on the qualities on which it rests, we find it unambiguously determined by the lowest specific differences of these qualities, and so again determined as a lowest difference.

The concept of non-independence accordingly amounts to that of ideal *lawfulness in unified combinations.* If a part stands in an ideally law-bound and not merely factual combination, it *must* lack independence; since such a law-bound combination merely means that a part whose pure essence is of one sort, can exist lawfully only in association with certain other parts of these or those suitable sorts. And even where a law tells us of the impossibility, rather than the necessity *of an association*, where it says, e.g., that the existence of a part *A* excludes the existence of a part *B* as incompatible with *A*, our case still reduces to one of non-independence. For an *A* can only exclude a *B*, if both exclusively require the same thing. A colour excludes another colour, but only if both aim to cover an identical piece of surface, and both cannot do so completely. To each essential, law-bound exclusion of a determinate characterization, there corresponds a positive law-bound requirement of a corresponding characterization and vice versa.

§11 The difference between these 'material' laws and 'formal' or 'analytic' laws

The necessities or laws which serve to define given types of non-independent contents rest, as we often have emphasized, on the specific essence of the contents, on their peculiar nature. More precisely, they rest on the pure Genera, Species, differentiae under which, as contingent singulars, non-independent contents as well as their supplementing contents, fall. If we conceive of the totality of such ideal objects, we have with them the totality of pure essences, the essences of all ideally possible individual objects (existences). To these essences correspond the concepts or propositions which have content, which we sharply distinguish from purely formal concepts and propositions, which lack all 'matter' or 'content'. To the latter belong the categories of formal logic and the formal ontological categories mentioned in the last chapter of the *Prolegomena*, which are essentially related to these, as well as to all syntactical formations they engender. Concepts like Something, One, Object, Quality, Relation, Association, Plurality, Number, Order, Ordinal Number, Whole, Part, Magnitude etc., have a basically different character from concepts like House, Tree, Colour, Tone, Space, Sensation, Feeling etc., which for their part express genuine content. Whereas the former group themselves round the empty notion of Something or Object as such, and are associated with this through formal ontological axioms, the latter are disposed about various highest material Genera or Categories, in which *material ontologies* have their root. This cardinal division between the 'formal' and the 'material' spheres of Essence gives us the true distinction between the *analytically a priori* and the *synthetically a priori* disciplines (or laws and necessities). The next section will make systematic pronouncements on these matters.

It is now immediately plain, that all the laws or necessities governing different sorts of *non-independent* items fall into the spheres of the *synthetic a priori*: one grasps completely what divides them from merely formal, contentless items. Laws of the type of the law of causation, which lay down the non-independence of changes in what is thinglike and real, or the laws – generally imperfectly formulated – which assert the non-independence of mere qualities, intensities, extensions, boundaries, relational forms etc. – would not be put on a level with a purely 'analytic' generalization such as 'A whole cannot exist without parts' or with analytic necessities such as 'There cannot be a king (master, father) without subjects (servants, children) etc.'. We may say in general: correlatives mutually entail one another, they cannot be thought of, or cannot be, without each other. If we set beside these any definite propositions of the opposite sort, e.g., 'A colour cannot exist without something coloured' or 'A colour cannot exist without some space that it covers' etc. – the difference leaps into view. 'Colour' is not a relative expression, whose meaning includes the idea of a relation to something else. Though colour is 'unthinkable' without something coloured, the existence of the latter, and more definitely that of a space, is not 'analytically' founded on the notion of colour.

The following discussion clears up the essence of the difference.

A part *as such* cannot exist at all without a whole whose part it is. On the other hand we say, with an eye to *independent* parts: A part often *can* exist without a whole whose part it is. Obviously this involves no contradiction. What we mean is that, if the part is treated in respect of its *internal content*, its own essence, then a thing having this same content can exist without a whole *in* which it exists; it can exist by itself, not associated with anything else, and will not then be a part. Change in, or complete elimination of associations, does not here affect the part's own, peculiarly qualified content, and does not eliminate its existence: only its relations fall away, the fact that it *is* a part. The contrary holds of other sorts of parts: without any association, as non-parts, they are unthinkable, *in virtue of their very content.* These impossibilities or possibilities are rooted in the essential specificity of the contents. The case is quite different in regard to the analytic triviality that a part as such cannot exist without a whole whose part it is. It would be a 'contradiction', i.e. a 'formal', 'analytical' absurdity, to call *X* a part where there was no whole belonging to *X*. Here the inner content of the part is irrelevant, the underlying 'formal' lawfulness of our case has nothing in common with the material lawfulness of our above cases, and can accordingly not disturb them.

That correlatives as such mutually condition one another certainly points to certain mutually requiring 'moments', it points to the mutually 'belonging' relationships and relative properties which we find in the case of every relation. But it does so only with formal indefiniteness. The legality which here obtains is one and the same for all relations as such: it is in fact a merely formal legality, rooted in mere analytic essences, here in fact in the essence of relation as a formal category. It takes over none of the material specificity of relations and of their members, and discourses merely of 'certain' relations and members. It will perhaps say in the simple case of dyadic relations: If a *certain A* stands in a *certain* relation to a certain *B*, this same *B* stands in a certain *corresponding* (converse) relation to that *A*; *A* and *B* are here *quite freely variable.*

§12 Basic determinations in regard to analytic and synthetic propositions

We may give the following general definitions:

Analytic Laws are unconditionally universal propositions, which are accordingly free from all explicit or implicit assertions of individual existence; they include none but formal concepts, and if we go back to such as are primitive, they contain only formal categories. Analytic Laws stand opposed to their *specifications*, which arise when we introduce concepts *with content*, and thoughts perhaps positing individual existence, e.g. *this, the Kaiser.* The specification of laws always yields necessary connections: specifications of analytic laws therefore yield *analytically necessary connections.* What are called 'analytic propositions' are in general analytically necessary connections. When they imply existential assertions (e.g. *If this house is red, then redness pertains to this house*) such analytic necessity relates to that content of the proposition in virtue of which it empirically specifies the analytic law, not to its empirical assertion of existence.

We may define *analytically necessary propositions* as propositions whose truth is completely independent of the peculiar content of their objects (whether thought of with definite or indefinite universality) and of any possible existential assertions. They are propositions which permit of a *complete 'formalization'* and can be regarded as special cases or empirical applications of the formal, analytic laws whose validity appears in such formalization. In an analytic proposition it must be possible, without altering the proposition's logical form, to replace all material which has content, with an empty formal *Something*, and to eliminate every assertion of existence by giving all one's judgements the form of universal, unconditional laws.

It is, e.g., an analytic proposition that *the existence of this house includes that of its roof, its walls and its other parts.* For the *analytic* formula holds that the existence of a whole $W(A, B, C...)$ generally includes that of its parts $A, B, C...$ This law contains no meaning which gives expression to a material Genus or Species. The assertion of individual existence, implied by the *this* of our illustration, is seen to fall away by our passage into the pure law. This is an analytic law: it is built up exclusively out of formal–logical categories and categorial forms.

Having formed the concept of an analytic law and of an analytic necessity, we also have *eo ipso* formed the concept of a *synthetic a priori* law, and of a *synthetic a priori* necessity. Each pure law, which includes material concepts, so as not to permit of a formalization of these concepts *salva veritate* – each such law, i.e., that is not analytically necessary – is a *synthetic a priori* law. Specifications of such laws are synthetic necessities: empirical specifications of course are so also, e.g. *This red is different from this green.*

What we have said should be enough to make plain the essential distinction between laws grounded in the specific nature of the contents to which non-independent factors belong, and analytic and formal laws, which, being founded purely on formal 'categories', are unaffected by all 'material of knowledge'.

Note 1 The points here made may be compared with those of Kant, which in our view do not deserve to be called 'classical'. It seems to us that these points satisfactorily dispose of one of the most important problems in the theory of knowledge, and make a first, decisive step in the division of *a priori* ontologies. Future publications will carry the enquiry further.

Note 2 It is readily seen that the main concepts dealt with by us in this section: *Whole and Part, Independence and Non-independence, Necessity* and *Law*, are essentially changed in sense when they are not understood in the sense of *purely conceptual matters of essence*, but are given an empirical interpretation. For the purpose of the investigations which follow, it is not, however, necessary fully to discuss these empirical concepts and their relation to the pure ones.

Chapter 2

Thoughts towards a theory of the pure forms of wholes and parts

§14 The concept of Foundation and some relevant theorems

The law stated and applied in the last paragraph of the previous section (excised from this edition) is not an empirical proposition, and yet not an immediate law of essence. Like many similar laws, it permits of *a priori* proof. Nothing can show up the worth of a strict statement more clearly than the possibility of giving a deductive proof of such propositions as are familiar to us in another guise. In view of the great scientific interest that the constitution of a deductive theoretical transformation claims in every field, we wish to linger here a little.

Definitions. If a law of essence means that an A cannot as such exist except in a more comprehensive unity which connects it with an M, we say that an *A as such requires foundation by an M* or also that *an A as such needs to be supplemented by an M*. If accordingly A_0, M_0 are determinate instances of the pure kinds A or M, actualized in a single whole, and standing in the relations mentioned, we say that *A_0 is founded upon M_0*, and that it is *exclusively* founded on M_0, if A_0's need for supplementation is satisfied by M_0 alone. This terminology can of course be carried over to the Species, by a quite harmless equivocation. We say further, more indefinitely, that the two contents or two pure Species, stand in a *foundational relationship* or in a relationship of *necessary connection*. This indeed leaves it open which of the two possible but not mutually exclusive relationships is meant. The indefinite expression: *A_0 requires supplementation by, is founded upon a certain moment*, plainly means the same as the expression: '*A_0 is non-independent*'.

Proposition 1 If an A as such requires to be founded on an M, every whole having an A, but not an M, as a part, requires a similar foundation.

This proposition is axiomatically self-evident. If an A cannot *be* except when completed by M, a whole including an A but no M cannot satisfy A's need for supplementation and must itself share it.

As a corollary we can assert the following, making use of the definition of our previous section.

Proposition 2 A whole which includes a non-independent 'moment', without including, as its part, the supplement which that 'moment' demands, is likewise non-independent, and is so relatively to every superordinate independent whole in which that non-independent 'moment' is contained.

Proposition 3 If W is an independent part of (and so[1] also relatively to) F, then every independent part w of W also is an independent part of F.

If w needed a supplement M relatively to F, and so had a foundation M_0 in the range of F, this foundation would necessarily be included in W. For, if this were not so, W would require supplementation in respect of M in conformity with Prop. 1, and since M_0 is a part of F, it would, on Prop. 2, be non-independent relatively to F, which contradicts the assumption. But in accordance with this assumption, w is an independent part of W, and so also independent relatively to W: there can therefore be nothing in the range of W which could serve as a foundation for w, and so also nothing in the whole range of F.

The proposition before us can also, with suitable changes in symbolization, be expressed as follows:

If A is an independent part of B, and B an independent part of C, A is also an independent part of C or more briefly: An independent part of an independent part is an independent part of a whole.

Proposition 4 If C is a non-independent part of a whole W, it is also a non-independent part of every other whole of which W is a part.

C is non-independent relatively to W, i.e. it possesses a foundation in an M_0 belonging to the range of W. This M_0 must naturally also appear in the range of every whole superordinate to W, i.e. every whole which includes W as a part. C must therefore also be non-independent relatively to each such whole. (On the other hand, we add, C may very well be independent relatively to a subordinate whole: we need only so draw its boundaries that the required supplement M is excluded therefrom. A 'piece' of an extended phenomenon *in abstracto*, but taken as a 'moment', is independent relatively to such extension; this, however, itself lacks independence relatively to the concrete wholes of the occupied extension.)

Our proposition permits an expression analogous to the previous one, i.e. if A is a non-independent part of B, and B a non-independent part of C, then A too is a non-independent part of C.

A non-independent part of a non-independent part is a non-independent part of a whole.

Proposition 5 A relatively non-independent object also is absolutely non-independent, whereas a relatively independent object may be non-independent in an absolute sense.

For a proof see the previous section (excised from this edition).

Proposition 6 If A and B are independent parts of some whole W, they are also independent relatively to one another. For if A required supplementation by B, or any part of B, there would be, in the range of parts determined by W, certain parts (those of B) in which A would be founded. A would therefore not be independent relatively to its whole W.

§21 Exact pinning down of the pregnant notions of Whole and Part, and of their essential Species, by means of the notion of Foundation

Our interest in the foregoing treatments was directed to the most general relations of essence between wholes and parts, or between parts among one another (i.e. of contents that combine into a whole). In our definitions and descriptions on these matters the notion of Whole was presupposed. It is however possible to *dispense* with this notion *in all cases:* for it can be substituted the simple *coexistence* of the contents that were denominated parts. One could, e.g., define as follows:

A content of the species A is founded upon a content of the species B, if an *A* can by its essence (i.e. legally, in virtue of its specific nature) not exist, unless a *B* also exists: this leaves open whether the coexistence of a *C,* a *D* etc. is needed or not.

One can proceed similarly with the other definitions. If all is taken thus generally, one could then give the following noteworthy definition of the *pregnant concept of Whole* by way of the *notion of Foundation:*

By a Whole we understand a range of contents which are all covered *by a single foundation* without the help of further contents. The contents of such a range we call its parts. Talk of the *singleness of the foundation* implies that *every content is foundationally connected, whether directly or indirectly, with every content.* This can happen in that all these contents are immediately or mediately founded on each other without external assistance, or in that all together serve to found a new content, again without external assistance. In the latter case the possibility remains open that this unitary content is built up out of partial contents, which in their turn are founded on partial groups from the presupposed range of contents, just as the Whole content is founded on its total range. Intermediate cases are finally also possible, where the unity of foundation is so formed, e.g., that *A* founds a new content together with *B, B* one together with *C, C* one together with *D* etc. In such cases the formation of new unities is in short concatenated.

One sees at once how such differences determine *essential divisions of the whole*. In the cases first referred to, the 'parts' (defined as members of the range in question) 'interpenetrated', in the other cases they were 'mutually external', but, whether taken all together, or concatenated in pairs, they embodied real forms of association. Where one speaks of connections, associations etc. in the narrower sense, one means wholes of the second sort, i.e. wholes where contents relatively independent as regards one another – where the whole falls apart into its *pieces* – serve to found *new* contents as their 'combinatory forms'. Talk of wholes and parts tends in general to be oriented exclusively to such cases.

The same whole can be interpenetrative in relation to certain parts, and combinatory in relation to others: the sensuous, phenomenal thing, the intuitively given spatial shape clothed with sensuous quality, is (just as it appears) interpenetrative in respect of reciprocally founded 'moments' such as colour and extension, and combinatory in respect of its 'pieces'.

§23 Forms of categorial unity and wholes

In the sense in which we are here trying to pin down the notion of a whole, *a mere aggregate* or mere coexistence of any contents is not to be called a *whole*, as little as a likeness (the being of the same sort) or a difference (the being of *another sort, or, in another sense, the not being identical*) are *wholes.*[2] 'Aggregate' is an expression for a categorial unity corresponding to the mere form of thought, it stands for the correlate of a certain *unity of reference* relating to all relevant objects. The objects themselves, being only held together in thought, do not succeed in founding a new content, whether taken as a group or together; no material form of association develops among them through this unity of intuition, they are possibly 'quite disconnected and intrinsically unrelated'. This is shown in the fact that the form of the aggregate is quite indifferent to its matter, i.e. it can persist in spite of wholly arbitrary variation in its comprised contents. A 'founded' content, however, depends on the specific 'nature' of its 'founding' contents: there is a pure law which renders the Genus of the 'founded' content dependent on the definitely indicated Genera of the 'founding' contents. A whole in the full and proper sense is, in general, a combination determined by the lowest Genera of the parts. A law corresponds to each material unity. There are different sorts of whole corresponding to these different laws, or, otherwise put, to the different sorts of contents that are to serve as parts. We cannot at will make the same content at one time part of one sort of whole, at another time part of another sort. To be a part, and, more exactly, to be a part of some determinate sort (a metaphysical, physical or logical part or whatever) is rooted in the pure generic nature of the contents in question, and is governed by laws which in our sense are *a priori* laws or 'laws of essence'. This is a fundamental insight whose meaning must be respected in all our treatments and formulations. And with this insight we have the foundation for a systematic theory of the relations of wholes and parts as regards their pure forms, the categorially definable types which abstract from the 'sensuous' material of such wholes.

Before we pursue these thoughts, we must remove a further difficulty. The form of an aggregate is a purely categorial form, in opposition to which the form of a whole, of a unity due to foundation, appeared to be a material form. But did we not say in the previous section that unity (and we were talking specifically of a unity based on foundation) was a categorial predicate? Here we must note that, on our doctrine, the Idea of unity or the Idea of a whole is based on the idea of 'Founding', and the latter Idea upon the Idea of a Pure Law; the Form of a Law is further as such categorial – a law is not thinglike, not therefore perceptible – and that *to this extent* the notion of a Founded Whole is a categorial notion. But the *content* of the law governing each such whole is determined by the material specificity of the 'founding' contents and consequently of the 'founded' types of content, and it is this law, definite in its content, which gives the whole its unity. For this reason we rightly call each ideally possible specification of the Idea of such unity a material or also a real (*reale*) unity.

According to our previous assertions,[3] the laws constitutive of the various sorts of whole are *synthetically a priori*, as opposed to laws which are analytically *a priori*, such as those governing pure categorial forms, e.g. the Form-Idea of a whole as such, and all merely formal specifications of this Idea. We prefer to dwell in what follows, on such formal specifications.

§24 The pure formal types of wholes and parts. The postulate of an *a priori* theory

The pure forms of *wholes and parts* are determined by the *pure forms of law*. Only what is *formally* universal in the foundational relation, as expressed in our definition, is then relevant, together with the *a priori* combinations that it permits. We rise, in the case of any type of whole, to its pure form, its categorial type, by abstracting from the specificity of the sorts of content in question. More clearly expressed, this *formalizing abstraction* is something quite different from what is usually aimed at under the title of 'abstraction': it is a quite different performance from the one which sets in relief the universal Redness in a concrete visual datum, or the generic 'moment' of Colour in the Redness previously abstracted. In formalization we replace the names standing for the sort of content in question by indefinite expressions such as *a certain sort of content, a certain other sort of content etc.* At the same time, on the semantic side, corresponding substitutions of purely categorial for material thoughts take place.[4]

The distinctions between abstract parts and 'pieces' are purely formal, being in this sense drawn in purely categorial fashion, as can be seen at once from our pronouncements above. These pronouncements had however to be suitably interpreted in accordance with our present leaning towards final formalization: the pure concept of the whole, in the sense of our last definition, had to be made their basis. The distinction likewise between nearer and remoter parts that we merely explained, in descriptive fashion,[5] by means of illustrations, can now be reduced to the mere form of certain foundational relations, and so formalized.

In our examples we saw above that, in the case of many intuitive wholes, a graded series of fragmentations of such wholes always results in fragments of these wholes themselves, fragments all equally close to the whole, and which could with equal justice count as results of a *first* fragmentation. The sequence of the 'piecings' was in these instances not prescribed by the essence of the wholes. What is here relevant is first the proposition that *pieces of pieces of a whole are themselves pieces of the whole* – a proposition that we formally proved above[6] (in different words). But we were there dealing with 'pieces', for which the sequence of fragmentations was meaningless, since it corresponded to no graded series of *'foundations'*. All pieces always stood to the whole in the same relation of 'foundation'. There were no differences in the *form* of the relation to the whole, all parts were 'contained in the whole' in the same fashion. The matter would be quite different were we to fragment aesthetic unities, e.g. a star-shape built out of star-shapes, which in their turn are composed of stretches and ultimately of points. The points serve to 'found' stretches, the stretches serve to 'found', as new aesthetic unities, the individual stars, and these in their turn serve to 'found' the star-pattern, as the highest unity in the given case. The points, stretches, stars and the final star-pattern are not now coordinated as are partial stretches in a stretch. There is, in their case, a fixed order of 'foundations', in which what is founded at one level serves to 'found' the level next above, and in such a manner that at each level new forms, only reachable at that level, are involved. We may here add the universal proposition:

'Pieces' are essentially mediate or remote parts of a whole whose 'pieces' they are, if combinatory forms unite them with other 'pieces' into wholes which in their turn constitute wholes of higher order by way of novel forms.

The difference between the parts nearer or further in regard to the whole has accordingly its essential ground in the formally expressible diversity of foundational relations.

The case is similar in regard to non-independent 'moments', if we take account of the essential formal distinction between such 'moments' as can only satisfy their need for supplementation in the *complete whole*, and such as can satisfy this need in *pieces* of this whole. This makes a difference to the mode of belonging, to the *form of foundation*: by it certain parts, e.g. the total extent of the intuited thing, belong exclusively to the thing as a whole, while other parts, e.g. the extent of a 'piece', belong specifically to this 'piece', and only more remotely to the whole. This mediacy is no longer inessential, as is that of second-level 'pieces' in the division of a stretch, but is an essential mediacy, to be characterized in terms of the formal nature of the relationship. Obviously similar reasons place *'pieces' of non-independent 'moments' which pertain directly to the whole, further from the whole than the 'moments' are*: this at least is the case if the rule holds that we found valid in the field of intuition, that such 'pieces' can have their immediate foundation only in a 'piece' of the whole. The wider proposition also can be formally expressed: *Abstract parts are further from the whole, are in essence mediate parts, if their need for supplement is satisfied in the sphere of a mere part.* This part can then well either be a 'piece' of the whole, or be in need of further completion. The mediacy in the latter case consists in the fact that the law of supplementation in which the form of foundation resides, points, in the case of the originally mentioned abstract part, to a whole which, in virtue of a new law of supplementation is, and must be, a part of a more comprehensive whole, i.e. of the complete whole, which accordingly only includes the first part mediately. This permits us also to say that *abstract parts of the whole that are not abstract parts of its 'pieces', are nearer to the whole than the abstract parts of the 'pieces'*.

These thoughts can only be meant, and are only meant, to count as mere indications of a future treatment of the theory of Wholes and Parts. A proper working out of the pure theory we here have in mind, would have to define all concepts with mathematical exactness and to deduce all theorems by *argumenta in forma*, i.e. mathematically. Thus would arise a complete law-determined survey of the *a priori* possibilities of complexity in the form of wholes and parts, and an exact knowledge of the relations possible in this sphere. That this end can be achieved, has been shown by the small beginnings of purely formal treatment in our present chapter. In any case the progress from vaguely formed, to mathematically exact, concepts and theories is, here as everywhere, the precondition for full insight into *a priori* connections and an inescapable demand of science.

The distinction between independent and non-independent meanings and the idea of pure grammar

Introduction

In the following discussions we wish to turn our gaze to a fundamental difference in the field of meanings, a difference which lies hidden behind insignificant grammatical distinctions, such as those between categorematic and syncategorematic expressions, or between closed and unclosed expressions. To clear up such distinctions will enable us to apply our general distinction between independent and non-independent objects in the special field of meanings, so that the distinction treated in our present Investigation may be called that of independent and non-independent meanings. It yields the necessary foundation for the essential categories of meaning on which, as we shall briefly show, a large number of *a priori* laws of meaning rest, laws which abstract from the objective validity, from the real (*real*) or formal truth, or objectivity of such meanings. These laws, which govern the sphere of complex meanings, and whose role it is to divide sense from nonsense, are not yet the so-called laws of logic in the pregnant sense of this term: they provide pure logic with the *possible meaning-forms*, i.e. the *a priori* forms of complex meanings significant as wholes, whose 'formal' *truth* or '*objectivity*' then depends on these pregnantly described 'logical laws'. The former laws guard against *senselessness* (*Unsinn*), the latter against formal or analytic *nonsense* (*Widersinn*) or formal absurdity. If the laws of pure logic establish *what an object's possible unity requires in virtue of its pure form*, the laws of complex meanings set forth the requirements of merely *significant unity*, i.e. the *a priori* patterns in which meanings belonging to different semantic categories can be united to form one meaning, instead of producing chaotic nonsense.

Modern grammar thinks it should build exclusively on psychology and other empirical sciences. As against this, we see that the old idea of a universal, or even of an *a priori grammar*, has unquestionably acquired a foundation and a definite sphere of validity, from our pointing out that there are *a priori* laws which determine the possible forms of meaning. The extent to which there may be other discoverable fields of the grammatical *a priori* goes beyond our present field of interest. Within pure logic, there is a field of laws indifferent to all objectivity to which, in distinction from 'logical laws' in the usual pregnant sense, the name of 'logico-grammatical laws' can be justifiably given. Even more aptly we can oppose *the pure theory of semantic forms* to *the pure theory of validity* which presupposes it.

§1 Simple and complex meanings

We start from the immediately obvious division of meanings into *simple* and *complex*, which corresponds to the grammatical distinction between simple and complex expressions or locutions. A complex expression is an expression, to the extent that it has *one* meaning; as a complex *expression* it is made up of parts which are themselves expressions, and which as such have their own meanings. If we read of 'a man of iron' or 'a king who wins the love of his subjects' etc., we are impressed by such part-expressions or part-meanings as those of *man, iron, king, love* etc.

If we now find further part-meanings in such part-meanings, meanings may again come forward as parts of these, but this can obviously not go on *in infinitum*. Continued division must ultimately lead to simple, elementary meanings. That there really are such simple meanings is shown by the indubitable case of *something*. The presentative experience we have when we understand this word is undoubtedly complex, but its meaning shows no sign of complexity.

§4 The question of the meaningfulness of 'syncategorematic' components of complex expressions

The treatment of complex meanings leads at once to a new and fundamental division. Such meanings are, in general, only given to us as meanings of articulate word-complexes. Regarding these one may, however, ask whether each word in such a complex has its own correlated meaning, and whether all verbal articulation and form counts as expressing a corresponding semantic articulation and form. According to Bolzano, 'each word in speech stands for its own presentation, while some stand for entire propositions'.[1] He therefore, without further ado, attributes a peculiar meaning to every conjunction or preposition. On the other hand, one frequently hears of words and expressions that are merely 'synsemantic', i.e. that have no meaning by themselves, but acquire this only in conjunction with other meanings or expressions. One distinguishes between complete and incomplete expressions of presentations, and likewise between complete and incomplete expressions of judgements and of the phenomena of feeling and will, and one bases on such a distinction the notion of the *categorematic* or *syncategorematic* sign. Marty applies the expression 'categorematic sign' (or 'name') to 'all verbal means of designation, that are not merely synsemantic (as, e.g., "the father's", "around", "nonetheless" etc.) but which yet do not themselves completely express a judgement (an assertion), or a feeling or voluntary decision etc. (requests, commands, questions etc.), but merely express a presentation. "The founder of ethics", "a son who has insulted his father" are names.'[2] Since Marty and other writers employ the terms 'syncategorematic' and 'synsemantic' in the same sense of signs 'which only have complete significance together with other parts of speech, whether they help to arouse concepts as mere parts of a name, or contribute to the expression of a judgement (i.e. to a statement) or to that of an emotion or act of will (i.e. to a request or command-sentence) etc.',[3] it would have been more consistent to interpret the notion of categorematic expression equally widely. This notion should have been made to cover all *independently significant* or complete expressions of any intentional experience (any 'psychic phenomenon' in Brentano's sense), and a division should have been made then between the categorematic expressions of presentations (i.e. names), the categorematic expressions of judgements (i.e. statements) etc. Whether such a coordination is justified, whether names, e.g., express presentations in the same sense that request-sentences express requests, wish-sentences express wishes etc., and likewise whether the things that names and sentences are said to 'express' are themselves experiences of meaning, or how they stand to meaning-intentions and meanings – all these are questions to which we shall have to devote earnest thought. However this may be, the distinction between categorematic and syncategorematic expressions, and the pleas for its introduction, certainly have justification, and so we are led to conceive syncategorematic words in a manner at variance with the above-mentioned doctrine of Bolzano. Since the distinction between categorematic and syncategorematic words is grammatical, it might seem that the situation underlying it is likewise 'merely grammatical'. We often use several words to express a 'presentation' – this, one might think, depends on chance peculiarities of one's language. The articulation of one's expression may bear no relation to the articulation of meaning. The syncategorematic words which help to build up this expression are, properly speaking, quite meaningless: only the whole expression really has a meaning.

The grammatical distinction, however, permits another interpretation, provided one decides to view the completeness or incompleteness of expressions as reflecting a certain completeness or incompleteness of meanings, the grammatical distinction as reflecting a certain essential semantic distinction.[4] Language has not been led by chance or caprice to express presentations by names involving many words, but by the need to express suitably a plurality of mutually cohering part-presentations, and dependent presentational forms, within the enclosed self-sufficiency of a presentational unity.[5] Even a non-independent moment, an intentional form of combination through which, e.g., two presentations unite in a third, can find semantic expression, it can determine the peculiar meaning-intention of a word or complex of words. Clearly we may say that if presentations, expressible thoughts of any sort whatever, are to have their faithful reflections in the sphere of meaning-intentions, then there must be a semantic form which corresponds to each presentational form. This is in fact an *a priori* truth. And if the verbal resources of language are to be a faithful mirror of all meanings possible *a priori*, then language must have grammatical forms at its disposal which give distinct expression, i.e. sensibly distinct symbolization, to all distinguishable meaning-forms.

§5 Independent and non-independent meanings. The non-independence of the sensory and expressive parts of words

This conception is plainly the only right one. We must not merely distinguish between categorematic and syncategorematic expressions but also between categorematic and syncategorematic *meanings*.[6] It is more significant to speak of *independent* and *non-independent* meanings. It is of course possible that meaning may so shift that an unarticulated meaning replaces one that was originally articulated, so that nothing in the meaning of the total expression now corresponds to its part-expressions. But in this case the expression has ceased to be genuinely complex, and tends, in developed speech, to be telescoped into one word. We no longer count its members as syncategorematic expressions, since we do not count them as expressions at all. We only call significant signs expressions, and we only call expressions complex when they are compounded out of expressions. No one would call the word 'king' a complex expression since it consists of several sounds and syllables. As opposed to this, many-worded expressions are admittedly complex, since it is part of the notion of a word to express something; the meaning of the word need not, however, be independent. Just as non-independent meanings may occur only as 'moments' of certain independent ones, so the linguistic expression of non-independent meanings may function only as formal constituents in expressions of independent meanings: they therefore become linguistically non-independent, i.e. 'incomplete' expressions.

Our first purely external impression of the difference between categorematic and syncategorematic expressions ranks the syncategorematic parts of expressions on a level with quite different parts of expressions, with the letters, sounds and syllables which are in general meaningless. I say 'in general', since there are many genuine syncategorematic expressions even among these, such as the prefixes and suffixes used in inflexion. But, in the vast majority of cases, they are not parts of an expression *qua* expression, i.e. not its significant parts; they are only parts of the expression as a sensuous phenomenon. Syncategorematic expressions are therefore understood, even when they occur in isolation; they are felt to carry definite 'moments' of meaning-content, 'moments' that look forward to a certain completion which, though it may be indeterminate materially, is formally determined together with the content in question, and is circumscribed and governed by it. But where a syncategorematic expression functions normally, and occurs in the context of an independently complete expression, it has always, as illustration will testify, a *determinate* meaning-relation to our total thought; it has as its meaning a certain non-independent part of this thought, and so makes a definite contribution to the expression as such. That we are right becomes clear when we consider that the same syncategorematic expression can occur in countless compounds in which it always plays the same semantic role. For this reason, in cases of syncategorematic ambiguity, we can reasonably consider, doubt and dispute whether the same conjunction, predicate or relational expression has the same meaning in two contexts or not. To a conjunction like 'but', or to a genitive like 'father's', we can significantly attribute a meaning, but not to a verbal fragment like 'fu'. Both come before us as needing completion, but their needs of completion differ essentially: in the one case the need principally affects the thought rather than the mere expression, in the other case it affects the expression alone or rather the fragmentary expression. The hope is it may *become* an expression, a possible spur to thought. In the successive formation of a complex verbal structure its total meaning gradually gets built up,[7] in the successive formation of a word, the word alone gets built up; only when the word is completed does it house the fleeting thought. In its own way, of course, the verbal fragment evokes thoughts: that it is, e.g., a verbal fragment, and how it may be completed; these are not, however, its meaning. And according as we complete it in differing ways (fu–futile, fuming, fugitive, furry, refuge etc.) the meaning alters, without thereby revealing an element common to this multitude of meanings, that could be taken to be *the* meaning of this common fragment. We search in vain also for a structuring of the individual word-meaning which might in part depend upon the significance of this verbal fragment. It is quite meaningless.

§7 The conception of non-independent meanings as founded contents

We have recognized that the seemingly indifferent distinction between categorematic and syncategorematic expressions corresponds to a fundamental division in the realm of meanings. We took the former as our starting-point, but the latter revealed itself as basic, as the prime foundation of the grammatical distinction.

The concept of the *expression*, or of the difference between the merely audible, or sensuous parts of an expression and its partial expressions in the true sense of the word, or, as we may say more pointedly, its *syntactical parts* (roots, prefixes, suffixes,[8] words, conjoined complexes of words), can only be fixed by recurring to a distinction among meanings. If these divide into simple and complex meanings, the expressions which fit them must also be simple or complex, and *this* complexity necessarily leads back to final significant parts, to syntactical parts and so once more to expressions. On the other hand, the analysis of expressions as mere sensuous phenomena also always yields mere sensuous parts, ones that no longer signify. The same is true of the superimposed distinction of expressions into categorematic and syncategorematic. It can at least be described by holding the former to be capable of serving as complete expressions, finished locutions by themselves, whereas the latter cannot. But if one wishes to limit the vagueness of this characterization, and to pin down the sense that is here relevant, as well as the inner ground that enables some expressions, and not others, to stand as finished locutions, one must, as we saw, go back to the semantic realm, and point out there the need of completion that attaches to certain non-independent meanings.

Having called syncategorematic meanings 'non-independent', we have already said where we think the essence of such meanings lies. In our enquiries into non-independent contents in general, we have given a general determination of the concept of non-independence: it is this same non-independence that we have to recognize in the field of meaning. Non-independent contents, are contents not able to exist alone, but only as parts of more comprehensive wholes. This inability has its *a priori* governing ground in the specific essences of the contents in question. Each non-independence points to a law to the effect that a content of the sort in question, e.g. sort A, can exist only in the context of a whole $W(AB...M)$, where $B...M$ stand for *determinate* sorts of content. 'Determinate', we said, since no law merely asserts connection between the sort A, and any other sorts whatever, that an A only needs some completion, no matter what. Law involves specific determinateness of context: dependent and independent variables have spheres limited by fixed generic or specific characters. We have mainly employed as examples the concrete things of sensuous intuition. We could, however, have brought in other fields, those of act-experiences and their abstract contents.

Here we are only interested in meanings. We conceived these as ideal unities, but our distinction naturally passed over from the real (*real*) to the ideal realm. In the concrete act of meaning something, there is a moment which corresponds to the meaning which makes up the essential character of this act, i.e. necessarily belongs to each concrete act in which the same meaning is 'realized'. In regard to the division of acts into simple and complex, a concrete act can involve several acts; such partial acts can live in the whole, whether as independent or non-independent parts. An act of meaning, in particular, can *as such* be complex, be made up of acts of meaning. A total meaning then belongs to the whole act, and to each partial act a partial meaning (a part of the meaning that is itself a meaning). A meaning, accordingly, may be called 'independent' when it can constitute the *full, entire meaning of a concrete act of meaning*, 'non-independent', when this is not the case. It can then only be realized in a non-independent part-act in a concrete act of meaning, it can only achieve concreteness in relation to certain other complementary meanings, it can only exist in a meaningful whole. The non-independence of meaning *qua* meaning thus defined determines, in our view, the essence of the syncategorematica.

§8 Difficulties of this conception. (*a*) Whether the non-independence of the meaning does not really only lie in the non-independence of the object meant

We must now consider the difficulties of our conception. We shall first discuss the relation between independence and non-independence of meanings, and independence and non-independence of objects meant. One might for the moment think the former distinction reducible to the latter.[9] Acts which lend meaning refer as 'presentations', as 'intentional' experiences, to objects. If some constituent of an object is non-independent, it cannot be 'presented' in isolation; the corresponding meaning therefore demands a completion, it is itself non-independent. The seemingly obvious principle emerges: categorematic expressions are directed to independent objects, syncategorematic expressions to non-independent ones.

Such a conception is readily seen to be erroneous. The very expression *non-independent moment* provides a decisive counter-example. It is a categorematic expression and yet presents a non-independent object. *Every non-independent object whatever can be made the object of an independent meaning*, and that directly, e.g. *Redness, Figure, Likeness, Size, Unity, Being.* These examples show that independent meanings correspond, not merely to *material* moments of objects, but also to their *categorial forms*, meanings peculiarly directed to these forms and making them their objects: the latter are not for that reason self-existent in the sense of being independent. The possibility of independent meanings directed to non-independent 'moments' is not at all remarkable, when we reflect on the fact that a meaning 'presents' an object, but does not therefore have the character of picturing it, that its essence consists rather in a certain intention, which can be intentionally 'directed' to anything and everything, to what is independent as much as what is non-independent. Anything, everything can be objectified as a thing meant, i.e. can become an intentional object.

§10 *A priori* laws governing combinations of meanings

If we relate the distinction between independent and non-independent meanings to the more general distinction between independent and non-independent objects, we are really covering one of the most fundamental facts in the realm of meaning: *that meanings are subject to* a priori *laws regulating their combination into new meanings.* To each case of non-independent meaning, a law of essence applies – following the principle discussed by us in relation to all non-independent objects whatever – a law regulating the meaning's need of completion by further meanings, and so pointing to the forms and kinds of context into which it must be fitted. Since meanings cannot be combined to form new meanings without the aid of connective forms, which are themselves meanings of a non-independent sort, there are obviously *a priori* laws of essence governing all meaning-combinations. The important fact here before us is not peculiar to the realm of meaning: it plays its part wherever combination occurs. All combinations whatever are subject to pure laws; this holds particularly of all material combinations limited to a single sphere of fact, where the results of combination must occupy the same sphere as the combining members. (This case is opposed to that of formal, 'analytic' combinations, e.g. collections, which are not bound up with the peculiarities of a sphere of fact, nor with the factual essence of their combining members.) In no sphere is it possible to combine items of any and every kind by way of any and every form: the sphere of items sets *a priori* limits to the number of combinatorial forms, and prescribes the general laws for filling them in. That this fact is general should not lessen our obligation to point out such general laws in each given field, and to pursue their unfolding into special laws.

As regards the field of meaning, the briefest consideration will show up our unfreedom in binding meanings to meanings, so that we cannot juggle at will with the elements of a significantly given, connected unity. Meanings only fit together in antecedently definite ways, composing other significantly unified meanings, while other possibilities of combination are excluded by laws, and yield only a heap of meanings, never a single meaning. The impossibility of their combination rests on a law of essence, and is by no means merely subjective. It is not our mere factual incapacity, the compulsion of our 'mental make-up', which puts it beyond us to realize such a unity. In the cases we here have in mind, the impossibility is rather objective, ideal, rooted in the pure essence of the meaning-realm, to be grasped, therefore, with apodictic self-evidence. The impossibility attaches, to be more precise, not to what is singular in the meanings to be combined, but to the essential *kinds*, the *semantic categories*, that they fall under. This or that meaning is, of course, itself a species, but, relative to a meaning-category, it only counts as an individual specification. In arithmetic, likewise, relatively to numerical forms and laws a numerically definite number is an individual specification. Wherever, therefore, we see the impossibility of combining given meanings, this impossibility points to an unconditionally general law to the effect that meanings belonging to corresponding meaning-categories, and conforming to the same pure forms, should lack a unified result. We have, in short, an *a priori* impossibility.

What we have just said holds of course of the *possibility* of significant combinations as it holds of their impossibility.

To consider an example. The expression 'This tree is green' has unified meaning. If we formalize this meaning (the independent logical proposition) and proceed to the corresponding pure form of meaning, we obtain 'This

S is *P*', an ideal form whose range of values consists solely of independent (propositional) meanings. It is now plain that what we may call the 'materialization' of this form, its specification in definite propositions, is possible in infinitely many ways, but that we are not completely free in such specification, but work confined within definite limits. We cannot substitute any meanings we like for the variables '*S*' and '*P*'. Within the framework of our form we can change our example 'This tree is green' into 'This gold . . .', 'This algebraic number . . .', 'This blue raven etc., is green': any nominal material – in a wide sense of 'nominal material' – can here be inserted, and so plainly can any adjectival material replace the '*P*'. In each case we have once more a meaning unified in sense, i.e. an independent proposition of the prescribed form, but if we depart from the categories of our meaning-material, the unitary sense vanishes. Where nominal material stands, any nominal material can stand, but not adjectival, nor relational, nor completed propositional material. But where we have materials from such other categories, other material of the same kind can be put, i.e. always material from the same category and not from another. This holds of all meanings whatsoever, whatever the complexity of their form.

In such free exchange of materials within each category, false, foolish, ridiculous meanings – complete propositions or elements of propositions – may result, but such results will necessarily be unified meanings, or grammatical expressions whose sense can be unitarily realized. When we transgress the bounds of categories, this is no longer true. We can string together words like 'This careless is green', 'More intense is round', 'This house is just like'; we may substitute 'horse' for 'resembles' in a relational statement of the form '*a* resembles *b*', but we achieve only a word-series, in which each word is as such significant, or points to a complete, significant context, but we do not, in principle, achieve a closed unity of sense. This is above all the case when we seek arbitrarily to exchange parts which are themselves formed units within an articulated unit of meaning, or when we replace such parts by others taken at random from other meanings, as, e.g., when we try to replace the antecedent in a hypothetical proposition (a mere element in the total unity that we call '*the* hypothetical proposition') by a nominal element, or one of the members of a disjunction by a hypothetical consequent. Instead of doing this in the concrete, we may also attempt it in the corresponding pure forms of meaning, i.e. propositional forms. We are at once made aware, through *a priori* insight into law, that such intended combinations are ruled out by the very nature of the constituents of the pure patterns in question, that such constituents can only enter into definitely constituted meaning-patterns.

It is plain, finally, that the pure elements of form in a concrete unity of meaning can never change places with the elements to which they give form, and which also give our meaning its relation to things. The specification of unified meaning-forms such as 'An *S* is *p*', 'If *S* is *p*, *Q* is *r*' etc., cannot, in principle, so proceed that abstracted elements of form take the place of the 'terms', i.e. the materials in the meaning-pattern which relate to things. We can construct verbal strings such as 'if the or is green', 'A tree is and' etc., but such strings have no graspable single meanings. It is an analytic truth that the forms in a whole cannot function as its materials, nor vice-versa, and this obviously carries over into the sphere of meanings.

In general we recognize, as we construct and think over such examples, that every concrete meaning represents a fitting together of materials and forms, that each such meaning falls under an ideal pattern that can be set forth in formal purity, and that to each such pattern an *a priori* law of meaning corresponds. This law governs the formation of unitary meanings out of syntactical materials falling under definite categories having an *a priori* place in the realm of meanings, a formation according to syntactical forms which are likewise fixed *a priori*, and which can be readily seen to constitute a fixed system of forms. Hence arises the great task equally fundamental for logic and for grammar, of setting forth the *a priori* constitution of the realm of meanings, of investigating the *a priori* system of the formal structures which leave open all material specificity of meaning, in a 'theory of the forms'.

§12 Nonsense and absurdity

One must, of course, distinguish the law-governed incompatibilities to which the study of syncategorematica has introduced us, from the other incompatibilities illustrated by the example of 'a round square'. As said in our *First Investigation*,[10] one must not confound the senseless (or nonsensical) with the absurd (or 'counter-sensical'), though we tend to exaggerate and call the latter 'senseless', when it is rather a sub-species of the significant. The combination 'a round square' really yields a unified meaning, having its mode of 'existence' or being in the *realm of ideal meanings, but it is apodictically evident* that no existent object can correspond to such an existent meaning. But if we say 'a round or', 'a man and is' etc., there exist no meanings which correspond to such verbal combinations as their expressed sense. The coordinated words give us the indirect idea of *some* unitary meaning they express, but it is apodictically clear that no such meaning can exist, that significant parts of these sorts, thus combined, cannot consist with each other in a unified meaning. This indirect notion would not itself be accepted as the meaning of such verbal complexes. When an expression functions normally, it evokes its meaning: when understanding fails, its sensuous similarity to understood, meaningful speech will evoke the inauthentic notion of a 'certain' pertinent meaning, since the meaning itself is what is precisely missing.

The difference between the two incompatibilities is plain. In the *one* case certain partial meanings fail to assort together in a unity of meaning as far as the objectivity or truth of the total meaning is concerned. An object (e.g. a thing, state of affairs) which unites all that the unified meaning conceives as pertaining to it by way of its 'incompatible' meanings, neither exists nor can exist, though the meaning itself exists. Names such as 'wooden iron' and 'round square' or sentences such as 'All squares have five angles' are names or sentences as genuine as any. In the *other* case the possibility of a unitary meaning itself excludes the possible coexistence of certain partial meanings in itself. We have then only an indirect idea, directed upon the synthesis of such partial meanings in a single meaning, and at the same time see that no object can ever correspond to such an idea, i.e. that a meaning of the intended sort cannot exist. The judgement of incompatibility is in one case connected with presentations, in another with objects; presentations of presentations enter the former unity of judgement, whereas plain presentations enter the latter.

The *grammatical* expression of the *a priori* incompatibilities and compatibilities here in question, as of the pertinent laws governing meaning-combinations, must in part be found in the grammatical rules governing the parts of speech. If we ask why our language allows certain verbal combinations and disallows others, we are to a large extent referred to contingent linguistic habits, to matters of mere fact concerning language, which develop in one way in one speech-community and another way in another. In part, however, we encounter the essential difference of independent and non-independent meanings and, closely involved therewith, the *a priori* laws of the combination and transformation of meanings, laws which must be more or less revealed in every developed language, both in its grammar of forms and in the related class of grammatical incompatibilities.

§13 The laws of the compounding of meanings and the pure logico-grammatical theory of forms

The task of an accomplished science of meanings would be to investigate the law-governed, essence-bound structure of meanings and the laws of combination and modification of meaning which depend upon these, also to reduce such laws to the least number of independent elementary laws. We should obviously also need to track down the primitive meaning-patterns and their inner structures, and, in connection with these, to fix the pure categories of meaning which circumscribe the sense and range of the indeterminates – the 'variables' in a sense quite close to that of mathematics – that occur in such laws. What formal laws of combination may achieve, can be made fairly plain by arithmetic. There are definite forms of synthesis, through which, quite in general or in certain definite conditions, two numbers give rise to new numbers. The 'direct operations' $a + b$, ab, a^b yield resultant numbers unrestrictedly, the 'inverse operations, $a - b$, a/b, $b\sqrt{a}$, $^b\log a$, only in certain conditions. That this is the case must be laid down by an *assertion* or rather a *law of existence*, and perhaps proved from certain primitive axioms. The little we have so far been able to indicate has made plain that there are similar laws governing the existence or non-existence of meanings in the semantic sphere, and that in these laws meanings are not free variables, but are bound down to the range of varying categories, all arising out of the nature of the sphere in question.

In the pure logic of meanings, whose higher aim is the laws of objective validity for meanings (to the extent that such validity depends purely on semantic form), the theory of the essential meaning-structures, and the laws of their formal constitution, provide the needed foundation. Traditional logic, with its theories of concepts and judgements, offers us a few isolated starting-points, without being clear as to the end to be aimed at, either in general or in respect of the pure Idea of meaning. Plainly the theory of the elementary structures and the concrete patterns of 'judgement' – here understood as 'propositions' – will comprise the whole form-theory of meanings, each concrete meaning-pattern being either a proposition or a possible element in propositions. We must note that the exclusion of the 'material of knowledge', to which pure logic is by its very sense committed, obliges us to keep out everything which could give semantic forms (types, patterns) a definite relation to factual spheres of being. Everywhere indefinitely general presentations of factual material, definitely determined only in respect of semantic category, e.g. nominal, adjectival, propositional etc., must do duty for contentful concepts and even for the highest of such concepts, e.g. physical thing, spatial thing, mental thing etc.

Our first task, therefore, in a purely logical form-theory of meanings, is to lay down the *primitive* forms of meaning with the requisite purity just described. *We must fix the primitive forms of independent meanings, of complete propositions with their internal articulations, and the structures contained in such articulations.* We must fix, too, the primitive forms of *compounding* and *modification* permitted by the essence of different categories of possible elements. (We must note that complete propositions can become members of other propositions.) After this, we must systematically survey a boundless multitude of further forms, all derivable by way of repeated compounding or modification.

The forms to be established are naturally 'valid', which here means that, however specified, they will yield real meanings, meanings real as meanings. To each such primitive form there belongs, therefore, *an a priori law of existence*, to the effect that each meaning-combination conforming to such a form genuinely yields a unified meaning, provided only that its terms, the Form's indeterminates or variables, belong to certain semantic categories. The *deduction of derived forms* must also *pro tanto* be a deduction of their validity, and laws of existence will, therefore, also relate to these, but they will be deduced from those relating to the primitive forms. Any two propositions yield, when combined in the form *M and N*, another proposition, any two adjectives another adjective (again one meaning that can stand as a complex but unitary attribute or predicate). To any two propositions, *M*, *N*, there belong, likewise, the primitive connective forms *If M then N, M or N*, so that the result again is a proposition. To any nominal meaning *S*, and any adjectival meaning *p*, there belongs the primitive form *Sp* (e.g. *red house*), the result being a new meaning fixed by law in the category of nominal meaning. We could in this manner give many other examples of primitive connective forms. We must remember, in stating all the laws that hold here, and in conceiving categorial Ideas of *proposition, nominal presentation, adjectival presentation*, which determine the variables of the laws, to abstract from the changing syntactical forms that such meanings have in given cases, and that they have to have in some determinate form. We speak of the same name, whether it occupies the subject-position or serves as a correlated object, of the same adjective, whether used predicatively or attributively, of the same proposition, whether used as a free unit or as a conjunctive, disjunctive, or hypothetical antecedent or consequent, or whether occupying this or that place as a member in a complex propositional unity. We thus fix plainly the much used, but never scientifically clarified, talk about *terms* in traditional logic. In the formal laws which enter the purview of this logic,[11] as in our own laws of structures, such 'terms' function as variables; the categories circumscribing the range of their variability are categories of terms. The scientific pinning down of these categories is plainly one of the first tasks of our doctrine of forms.

If we now make gradual substitutions in the primitive forms set forth, and for a simple term repeatedly substitute a combination exemplifying the same forms, and if we always reapply our primitive existential law, we arrive at ever new forms, of deductively proven validity, encapsulated in one another with any degree of complexity. Thus for the conjunctive combination of propositions one can substitute:

> (*M* and *N*) and P
> (*M* and *N*) and (P and *Q*)
> {(*M* and *N*) and P} and *Q*

etc., etc., and so for the disjunctive and hypothetical combination of propositions, and for other modes of combinations in any other semantic categories. We see at once that the compoundings go on *in infinitum*, in a manner permitting comprehensive oversight, that each new form remains tied to the same semantic category, the same field of variability as its terms, and that, as long as we stay in this field, all framable combinations of meanings necessarily *exist*, i.e. must represent a unified sense. We see also that the relevant existential propositions are obvious deductive consequences of an existential proposition with the primitive form. Instead of constantly reapplying the same mode of combination, we can plainly vary our procedure at will, and combine different forms of combination in our construction, always within legally allowed limits, and so conceive an infinity of complex forms legally engendered. As we formulate these facts in consciousness, we gain insight *into the* a priori *constitution of the meaning-realm in respect of all those forms which have their* a priori *origin in its basic forms.*

This insight, and the final comprehensive insight into the formal constitution of the *whole* semantic realm, is, of course, the one aim of such investigations. It would be stupid to hope for worthwhile rules for the compounding of meanings (or rules for the grammatical compounding of expressions) from the formulation of semantic types, and the existential laws relating to them. There is no temptation here to depart from the line of correctness, hence no practical interest in determining it scientifically. *Nonsense* stands so immediately revealed, with each deviation from normal forms, that we hardly fall into such deviations in the practice of thought and speech. The theoretical interest of the systematic investigation of all possible meaning-forms and primitive structures, is all the greater. We, in fact, rise to the insight that all possible meanings are subject to a fixed *typic* of categorial structures built, in *a priori* fashion, into the general Idea of meaning, that *a priori* laws govern the realm of meaning, whereby all possible concrete meaning-patterns systematically depend on a small number of primitive forms, fixed by laws of existence, out of which they flow by pure construction. This last generalization, through its *a priori*, purely categorial character, brings to scientific awareness a basic chapter in the constitution of 'theoretical reason'.

Additional note. I talked above of compounding and *modification*. The rules of modification also have a place in the sphere we must define. What we mean is shown by the analogue of *suppositio materialis* considered above. Other instances are differences of contextual functioning, of *a priori* syntactical position, as when a name functioning as subject shifts to the object-place. These differences are not easy to elucidate: they are mixed up with empirical factors, and terminate in case-forms and syntactical forms of grammar. The difference between the attributive and predicative functioning of adjectival meanings, as well as similar matters, have here their place. (The investigations of the form-doctrine of meanings announced in our First Edition, and since expounded with many improvements in my lectures at Göttingen since 1901, will shortly, I hope, be laid before a wider public in my *Jahrbuch für Philosophie und phänomenologische Forschung*.)

On intentional experiences and their 'contents'

Introduction

In our Second Investigation we clarified the general sense of the ideality of the Species and, together with it, the sense of the ideality of meanings with which pure logic is concerned. As with all ideal unities, there are here real possibilities, and perhaps actualities, which correspond to meanings: to meanings *in specie* correspond acts of meaning, the former being nothing but ideally apprehended aspects of the latter. New questions now arise regarding the kind of experiences in which the supreme genus Meaning has its originative source, and likewise regarding the various sorts of experiences in which essentially different sorts of meaning unfold. We wish to enquire into the originative source of the concept of Meaning and its essential specifications, so as to achieve a deeper-going, more widely ranging answer to our question than our investigations have so far given us. In very close connection with this question, certain other questions arise: meanings have to be present in meaning-intentions that can come into a certain relation to intuition. We have often spoken of the *fulfilment* of a meaning-intention through a corresponding intuition, and have said that the highest form of such fulfilment was that of self-evidence. It is therefore our task to describe this remarkable phenomenological relationship, and to lay down its role, and so to clarify the notions of knowledge which presuppose it. For an analytical investigation these tasks are not really separable from our earlier work on the essence of meaning (particularly as this last relates to the logical presentation and the logical judgement).

The present investigation will not yet embark on these tasks, since we cannot enter upon them without first performing a much more general phenomenological investigation. Experiences of meaning are classifiable as 'acts', and the meaningful element in each such single act must be sought in the act-experience, and not in its object; it must lie in that element which makes the act an 'intentional' experience, one 'directed' to objects. The essence of the fulfilling intuition likewise consists in acts, for thinking and intuiting must be different *qua* acts. Naturally, too, self-fulfilment must be reckoned a relation especially bound up with the characters of acts. No term in descriptive psychology is, however, more controversial than the term 'act', and doubt, if not quick rejection, may have been aroused by all passages in our previous Investigations where we made use of the notion of 'act' to characterize or express our conception. It is therefore important, and a precondition for carrying out all our tasks, that this concept should be clarified before all others. It will appear that the concept of act, *in the sense of an intentional experience*, circumscribes an important generic unity in the sphere of experiences (apprehended in its phenomenological purity), and that to put meaning-experiences into this genus enables us to characterize them in a truly worthwhile manner.

It is of course part of phenomenological research into the essence of acts as such, that we should clear up the difference between the *character* and the *content* of acts, and that, as regards the latter, we should point out the fundamentally different senses in which the 'content' of an act has been talked about.

The nature of acts as such cannot be satisfactorily discussed unless one goes fairly fully into the phenomenology of 'presentations'. The intimate relevance of this topic is recalled by the well-known statement, that every act is either a presentation or is founded upon presentations. We must, however, ask which of the very many concepts of 'presentation' is here the required one: to separate the closely confused phenomena underlying the ambiguities of this word thus becomes an essential part of our task.

The treatment of the problems thus roughly outlined (to which certain others will be intimately linked) is suitably connected by us with the many concepts of consciousness which are always being distinguished, and are always shading into one another in descriptive psychology. Mental acts are often called 'activities of consciousness', 'relations of consciousness to a content (object)', and 'consciousness' is, in fact, at times defined as a comprehensive expression covering mental acts of all sorts.

Consciousness as the phenomenological subsistence of the ego and consciousness as inner perception

§1 Varied ambiguity of the term 'consciousness'

In psychology there is much talk of 'consciousness', and likewise of 'conscious contents' and 'conscious experiences': the latter are generally abbreviated to 'contents' and 'experiences'. This talk is mainly connected with the division between psychical and physical phenomena; the former being those phenomena which belong to the sphere of psychology, the latter to the sphere of the natural sciences. *Our* problem, that of circumscribing the concept of 'mental act' in its phenomenological essence, is closely connected with *this* problem of division, since the concept arose precisely in this context, as supposedly marking off the psychological sphere. *One* concept of consciousness is justifiably employed in effecting this demarcation correctly, *another* yields us the definition of a mental act. We must, in either case, distinguish between several thematically cognate, and so readily confounded, notions.

We shall, in what follows, discuss three concepts of consciousness, as having interest for our purposes:

1. Consciousness as the entire, real (*reelle*) phenomenological being of the empirical ego, as the interweaving of psychic experiences in the unified stream of consciousness.
2. Consciousness as the inner awareness of one's own psychic experiences.
3. Consciousness as a comprehensive designation for 'mental acts', or 'intentional experiences', of all sorts.

It need hardly be said that we have not exhausted *all* ambiguities of the term in question. I particularly recall, e.g., modes of speech current in non-scientific parlance such as 'entering consciousness', 'coming to consciousness', 'heightened' or 'reduced' self-consciousness, the 'awakening of self-consciousness' (the last expression quite differently used in psychology from the sense given it in ordinary life), and so forth.

Since *all* terms at all relevant for terminological differentiation are ambiguous, an unambiguous fixing of the concepts which here distinguish themselves can only be done indirectly: we must put together equivalent expressions, and oppose them to expressions to be kept apart from them, and we must employ suitable paraphrases and explanations. We shall therefore have to make use of these aids.

§2 First sense: Consciousness as the real phenomenological unity of the ego's experiences. The concept of an experience

We begin with the following summary statement. The modern psychologist defines (or could define) his science as the science of 'psychic individuals' considered as concrete conscious unities, *or* as the science of the conscious experiences of experiencing individuals; the juxtaposition of these terms in this context determines a certain concept of consciousness and, at the same time, certain concepts of experience and content. These latter terms, 'experience' and 'content', mean for the modern psychologist the real occurrences (Wundt rightly calls them 'events') which, in flux from one moment to the next, and interconnected and interpenetrating in manifold ways, compose the real unity-of-consciousness of the individual mind. In this sense, percepts, imaginative and pictorial presentations, acts of conceptual thinking, surmises and doubts, joys and griefs, hopes and fears, wishes and acts of will etc., are, just as they flourish in our consciousness, 'experiences' or 'contents of consciousness'. And, with these experiences in their total and concrete fulness, their component parts and abstract aspects are also *experienced*: they are real contents of consciousness. Naturally, it is irrelevant whether these parts are in some manner inwardly articulated, whether they are marked off by special acts directed upon themselves, and whether, in particular, they are themselves objects of an 'inner' perception, which seizes them as they are in consciousness, and even whether they can be such objects or not.

We may now point out that *this concept of consciousness can be seen in a purely phenomenological manner*, i.e. a manner which *cuts out all relation to empirically real existence* (to persons or animals in nature): experience in the descriptive-psychological or empirically-phenomenological sense then becomes experience in the sense of pure phenomenology.[1] The clarifying illustrations that we now append may and must lead to the conviction that the required exclusion lies always in our power, and that the descriptive-psychological treatments that we have first applied or might first apply to such illustrations, are to be interpreted 'purely' in the manner sketched above, and to be understood in what follows as pure, *a priori* insights into essence. The same, of course, holds in all parallel cases.

The sensational moment of colour, e.g., which in outer perception forms a real constituent of my concrete seeing (in the phenomenological sense of a visual perceiving or appearing) is as much an 'experienced' or 'conscious'

[handwritten margin note: for the modern psychologist]

content, as is the character of perceiving, or as the full perceptual appearing of the coloured object. As opposed to this, however, this object, though perceived, is not itself experienced nor conscious, and the same applies to the colouring perceived in it. If the object is non-existent, if the percept is open to criticism as delusive, hallucinatory, illusory etc., then the visually perceived colour, that of the object, does not exist either. Such differences of normal and abnormal, of veridical and delusive perception, do not affect the internal, purely descriptive (or phenomenological) character of perception. While the seen colour, i.e. the colour appearing upon and with the appearing object of visual perception, and seen as its property, and one with it in its present being – while this colour certainly does not exist as an experience, there is a real part (*reelles Bestandstück*) of our experience, of this appearing to perception, which corresponds to it. Our colour-sensation corresponds to it, that qualitatively determinate phenomenological colour-aspect, which receives an 'objectifying interpretation' in perception, or in an intrinsic aspect of such perception (the 'appearance of the object's colouring'). These two, the colour-sensation and the object's objective colouring, are often confounded. In our time people have favoured a form of words according to which both are the same thing, only seen from a different standpoint, or with a different interest: psychologically or subjectively speaking, one has a sensation, physically or objectively speaking, one has a property of an external thing. Here it is enough to point to the readily grasped difference between the red of this ball, objectively seen as uniform, and the indubitable, unavoidable projective differences among the subjective colour-sensations in our percept, a difference repeated in *all* sorts of objective properties and the sensational complexes which correspond to them.

What we have said about single properties carries over to concrete wholes. It is phenomenologically false to say that the difference between a conscious content in perception, and the external object perceived (or perceptually intended) in it, is a mere difference in mode of treatment, the *same appearance* being at one time dealt with in a subjective connection (in connection with appearances which relate to an ego), and at another time in an objective connection (in connection with the things themselves). We cannot too sharply stress the equivocation which allows us to use the word '*appearance*' *both of the experience in which the object's appearing consists* (the concrete perceptual experience, in which the object itself seems present to us) and of *the object which appears as such.* The deceptive spell of this equivocation vanishes as soon as one takes phenomenological account as to how little of the object which appears is as such to be found in the experience of its appearing. The appearing of the thing (the experience) is not the thing which appears (that seems to stand before us *in propria persona*). As belonging in a conscious connection, the appearing of things is experienced by us, as belonging in the phenomenal world, things appear before us. The appearing of the things does not itself appear to us, we live through it.

If we ourselves appear to ourselves as members of the phenomenal world,[2] physical and mental things (bodies and persons) appear in physical and mental relation to our phenomenal ego. *This relation of the phenomenal object* (that we also like to call a 'conscious content') *to the phenomenal subject* (myself as an empirical person, a thing) must naturally be *kept apart from the relation of a conscious content, in the sense of an experience, to consciousness in the sense of a unity of such conscious contents* (the phenomenological subsistence of an empirical ego). There we were concerned with the relation of two appearing things, here with the relation of a single experience to a complex of experiences. Just so, conversely, we must of course distinguish the relation of the appearing person I to the externally appearing thing, from *the relation of the thing's appearing ('qua' experience) to the thing which appears*. If we speak of the latter relation, we only make clear to ourselves that the experience is not itself what is intentionally present 'in' it: we can, e.g., make plain that what is predicated of a thing's appearing is not also predicated of the thing that appears in it. And yet another relation is the *objectifying relation* ascribed by us to the *sense-complex experienced by us when something appears to us, a relation in which the complex stands to the object which appears to us*. We concede that such a complex is experienced in the act of appearing, but say that it is in a certain manner 'interpreted' or 'apperceived', and hold that it is in the phenomenological character of such an animating interpretation of sensation that what we call the appearing of the object consists.[3]

Similar distinctions of essence to those needed by us in the case of perception, when we sought to separate off what is really 'experience' in it and really composes it, from what is only 'in' it in an 'improper' or intentional sense, will have soon to be drawn in the case of other 'acts' as well. We shall soon have to deal with such distinctions more generally. Here it is only important to guard from the start against certain misleading thought-tendencies, which might obscure the plain sense of the notions to be elucidated.

§4 The relation between experiencing consciousness and experienced content is no phenomenologically peculiar type of relation

The foregoing exposition has made clear that the relation in which experiences are thought to stand to an experiencing consciousness (or to an experiencing 'phenomenological ego')[4] points to *no peculiar phenomenological situation.* The ego in the sense of common discourse is an empirical object, one's own ego as much as someone else's, and each ego as much as any physical thing, a house or a tree etc. Scientific elaboration may alter our ego-concept as much as it will, but, if it avoids fiction, the ego remains an individual, thinglike object, which, like all such objects, has phenomenally no other unity than that given it through its unified phenomenal properties, and which in them has its own internal make-up. If we cut out the ego-body from the empirical ego, and limit the purely mental ego to its phenomenological content, the latter reduces to a unity of consciousness, to a real experiential complex, which we (i.e. each man for his own ego) find in part evidently present, and for the rest postulate on good grounds. The phenomenologically reduced ego is therefore nothing peculiar, floating above many experiences: it is simply identical with their own interconnected unity. In the nature of its contents, and the laws they obey, certain forms of connection are grounded. They run in diverse fashions from content to content, from complex of contents to complex of contents, till in the end a unified sum total of content is constituted, which does not differ from the phenomenologically reduced ego itself. These contents have, as contents generally have, their own law-bound ways of coming together, of losing themselves in more comprehensive unities and, in so far as they thus become and are one, the phenomenological ego or unity of consciousness is already constituted, without need of an additional, peculiar ego-principle which supports all contents and unites them all once again. Here as elsewhere it is not clear what such a principle would effect.[5]

§5 Second sense. 'Inner' consciousness as inner perception

Our sense of the terms 'consciousness', 'experience', 'content', has been fixed in the treatments of the last three sections, a descriptive-psychological sense which, with phenomenological 'purification', becomes *purely* phenomenological. We wish to adhere to this sense in future, but only when other concepts have been expressly indicated.

A second concept of consciousness is expressed by talk of 'inner consciousness'. This is that 'inner perception' thought to accompany actually present experiences, whether in general, or in certain classes of cases, and to relate to them as its objects. The 'self-evidence' usually attributed to inner perception, shows it to be taken to be an *adequate* perception, one ascribing nothing to its objects that is not intuitively presented, and given as a real part (*reell*) of the perceptual experience, and one which, conversely, intuitively presents and posits its objects just as they are in fact experienced in and with their perception. Every perception is characterized by the intention of grasping its object as present, and *in propria persona*. To this intention perception corresponds with complete perfection, achieves *adequacy*, if the object in it is itself actually present, and in the strictest sense present *in propria persona*, is exhaustively apprehended as that which it is, and is therefore itself a real (*reell*) factor in our perceiving of it. It is accordingly clear, and evident from the mere essence of perception, that adequate perception can only be 'inner' perception, that it can only be trained upon experiences simultaneously given, and belonging to a single experience with itself. This holds, precisely stated, only for experiences in the purely phenomenological sense. One cannot, however, at all concur with the converse opinion and say, in psychological language, that each percept directed upon one's own inner experience (which would be called an 'inner' percept in the natural sense of the word) need be adequate. In view of the just exposed ambiguity of the expression 'inner perception', it would be best to have different terms for inner perception, as the perception of one's own experiences, and adequate or evident perception. The epistemologically confused and psychologically misused distinction of inner and outer perception would then vanish; it has been put in the place of the genuine contrast between *adequate* and *inadequate* perception which has its roots in the *pure* phenomenological essences of such experiences. [On this point, see the Appendix on internal and external perceptions.]

Many thinkers, as, e.g., Brentano, are led to posit a close connection between the two concepts of consciousness so far discussed, because they think that they may regard the consciousness, or the being-experienced, of contents, in the first sense, as at the same time a consciousness in the second sense. The equivocation which pushes us to treat consciousness as a sort of knowing, and in fact of intuitive knowing, may here have recommended a conception fraught with too many grave difficulties. I recall the infinite regress which sprung from the circumstance that inner perception is itself another experience, which requires a new percept, to which the same again applies etc., a regress which Brentano sought to avoid by distinguishing between a primary and a secondary direction of perception. Since our concern is here with purely phenomenological asseverations, we must leave theories of this sort on one side, so long, that is, as the need to assume the unbroken activity of inner perception cannot be phenomenologically demonstrated.

§6 Origin of the first concept (empirical ego) of consciousness out of the second (phenomenological ego)

Undeniably the second concept of consciousness is the more 'primitive': it has an 'intrinsic priority'. The following considerations would enable us to pass in scientific order from this last narrower concept to our former, broader one. If we consider the self-evidence of the *Cogito, ergo sum*, or rather of its simple *sum*, as one that can be sustained against all doubts, then it is plain that what here passes as ego cannot be the empirical ego. But since, on the other hand, we cannot allow the self-evidence of the proposition 'I am' to depend on the knowledge and acceptance of philosophical ideas about the ego which have always remained questionable, we can at best say: In the judgement 'I am' self-evidence attaches to a certain central kernel of our empirical ego-notion which is not bounded by a perfectly clear concept. If we now ask what could belong to this conceptually undemarcated and therefore unutterable kernel, what may constitute the self-evidently certain, given element in the empirical ego at each moment, it comes easy to refer to judgements of inner (i.e. adequate) perception. Not only is it self-evident that I am: self-evidence also attaches to countless judgements of the form *I perceive this or that*, where I not merely think, but am also self-evidently assured, that what I perceive is given as I think of it, that I apprehend the thing itself, and for what it is – this pleasure, e.g., that fills me, this phantasm of the mind that float before me etc. All these judgements share the lot of the judgement 'I am', they elude complete conceptualization and expression, they are evident only in their living intention, which cannot be adequately imparted in words. What is adequately perceived, whether expressed thus vaguely or left unexpressed, constitutes the epistemologically primary, absolutely certain focus yielded by the reduction, at any given moment, of the phenomenal empirical ego to such of its content as can be grasped by the pure phenomenologist. It is also true, conversely, that in the judgement 'I am', it is the kernel of what is adequately perceived which, ranged under the ego, first makes possible and provides a ground for this 'I am's' evidence.[6] To this primary focus more territory is added when we reduce to its past phenomenological content all that retention, essentially attached to perception, reports as having been recently present, and also all that recollection reports as having belonged to our earlier actual experience, and when we then go back through reflection to what 'in' retention and remembrance is reproductively phenomenological. We proceed similarly with what can be assumed on empirical grounds to coexist with what at each instant we adequately perceive, or with what can be assumed to have coexisted with what now forms the reflective substance of retention and recollection, and can be assumed to have cohered continuously with it in unity. When I say 'cohered continuously with it in unity', I refer to the unity of the concrete phenomenological whole, whose parts are either *abstract aspects*, mutually founded upon, and requiring each other in their coexistence, or *pieces* from whose nature spring forms of coexistent unity, forms which actually contribute to the content of the whole as real indwelling aspects. These 'unities of coexistence' pass continuously into one another from one moment to the next, composing a unity of change, of the stream of consciousness, which in its turn demands the continuous persistence, or no continuous change, of at least one aspect essential for its total unity, and so inseparable from it as a whole. This part is played by the presentative form of *time* which is immanent in the stream of consciousness, which latter appears as a unity in time (not in the time of the world of things, but in the time which appears together with the stream of consciousness itself, and in which the stream flows). Each instant of this time is given in a continuous projective series of (so-to-speak) 'time-sensations'; in each actual phase of the stream of consciousness the *whole* time-horizon of the stream is presented, and it thereby possesses a form overreaching all its contents, which remains the same form continuously, though its content steadily alters.

This accordingly forms the phenomenological content of the ego, of the empirical ego in the sense of the psychic subject. Phenomenological reduction yields the really self-enclosed, temporally growing unity of the stream of experience. The notion of experience has widened out from what is inwardly perceived, and that is in *this* sense conscious, to the notion of the 'phenomenological ego', by which the empirical ego is intentionally constituted.

§8 The pure ego and awareness ('*Bewusstheit*')

We have not so far referred to the pure ego (the ego of 'pure apperception') which for many Kantians, and likewise for many empirical investigators, provides the unitary centre of relation, to which all conscious content is as such referred in a wholly peculiar fashion. To the fact of 'subjective experience' or consciousness, this pure ego is accordingly held to pertain essentially. 'Consciousness is relation to the ego', and whatever stands in this relation is a content of consciousness. 'We *call* anything content if it is related to an ego in consciousness: its other properties are irrelevant.' 'This relation is plainly one and the same despite manifold variation of content: it constitutes, in fact, what is common and specific to consciousness. We mark it off', says Natorp (whom we are continuously quoting),[7] 'by the special expression "awareness" (*Bewusstheit*) to distinguish it from the total fact of consciousness.'

> *The ego as subjective centre of relation* for all contents in my consciousness, cannot be compared to what are contrasted with it, it is not relative to them as they are to it, it is not consciously given to its contents as they are given *to* it. It reveals itself as *sui generis* in its incapacity to be in anything else's consciousness, while other things are in *its* consciousness. It cannot itself be a content, and resembles nothing that could be a content of consciousness. For this reason, it can be no further described, since all descriptive terms we might seek to employ, could be drawn only from the content of consciousness, and could not therefore hit off the ego, or a relation to the ego. Otherwise put: each *idea* we could make of the ego would turn it into an *object*, but we have ceased to think of it as an ego, if we think of it as an object. To be an ego is not to be an object, but to be something opposed to all objects, for which they are objects. The same holds of their relation to the ego. Being-in-consciousness means being-objective for an ego: such being-objective cannot in its turn be made into an object.
>
> The fact of awareness, while it is the basic fact of psychology, can be acknowledged and specially emphasized, but it can neither be defined nor deduced from anything else.

These statements are impressive, but closer consideration fails to substantiate them. How can we assert such a 'basic fact of psychology', if we are unable to think it, and how can we think it, if not by making the ego and consciousness, both subject-matters of our assertion, into 'objects'? This might be done if we thought of this fact only in indirect, symbolic fashion. Natorp, however, wants it to be a 'basic fact', which must as such surely be given in direct intuition. He in fact tells us that it 'can be acknowledged and specially emphasized'. Surely what is acknowledged or emphasized will be content? Surely it will be made into an object? Perhaps, indeed, some narrower concept of object is excluded, but the wider concept is here relevant. A taking note of a thought, a sensation, a stirring of displeasure etc., makes these experiences objects of inner perception, without making them objects in the sense of things, just so, the ego as relational centre, and any particular relation of the ego to some content, will, if taken note of, be objectively given.

I must frankly confess, however, that I am quite unable to find this ego, this primitive, necessary centre of relations.[8] The only thing I can take note of, and therefore perceive, are the empirical ego and its empirical relations to its own experiences, or to such external objects as are receiving special attention at the moment, while much remains, whether 'without' or 'within', which has no such relation to the ego.

I can only clarify this situation by subjecting the empirical ego, with its empirical relation to objects, to phenomenological analysis, from which the above conception necessarily results. We excluded the body-ego, whose appearances resemble those of any other physical thing, and dealt with the mind-ego, which is empirically bound up with the former, and appears as belonging to it. Reduced to data that are phenomenologically actual, this yields us the complex of reflectively graspable experiences described above, a complex which stands in the same sort of relation to the mental ego as the side of a perceived external thing open to perception stands to the whole thing. The conscious intentional relation of the ego to its objects means for me simply that intentional experiences whose intentional objects are the ego-body, the personal ego-mind and therefore the entire empirical ego-subject or human person, are included in the total phenomenological being of a unity of consciousness, and that such intentional experiences also constitute an essential phenomenological kernel in the phenomenal ego.

This brings us to our *third* concept of consciousness, defined in terms of 'acts' or 'intentional experiences', which will be analysed in our next chapter. If the peculiar character of intentional experiences is contested, if one refuses to admit, what for us is most certain, that being-an-object consists phenomenologically in certain acts in which something appears, or is thought of as our object, it will not be intelligible how being-an-object can itself be objective to us. For us the matter is quite clear: there are acts 'trained upon' the character of acts in which something appears, or there are acts trained upon the empirical ego and its relation to the object. The phenomenological kernel of the empirical ego here consists of acts which bring objects to its notice, acts in which the ego directs itself to the appropriate object.

I am unable, further, to grasp the view that the relation of the ego to conscious content is bare of all difference. For if by 'content' we mean the *experience* which forms the real side of the phenomenological ego, surely the way in which contents enter the unity of experience will depend throughout on their specific nature, which is true of all parts that enter into wholes? But, if by 'content' we mean some object upon which consciousness 'directs itself', whether perceivingly, imaginingly, retrospectively, expectantly, conceptually or predicatively etc., then it plainly involves many differences, obvious even in running through the expressions just used.

Objection may be raised to our previous assertion that the ego appears to itself, enjoys a consciousness and, in particular, a perception of itself. Self-perception of the empirical ego is, however, a daily business, which involves no difficulty for understanding. We perceive the ego, just as we perceive an external thing. That the object does not offer all its parts and sides to perception is as irrelevant in this case as in that. For perception is essentially the presumptive apprehension of some object, not its adequate intuition. Perception itself, though part of the ego's phenomenological being, naturally falls, like so much else in consciousness that evades notice, beyond the glance of perception, much as ungrasped, yet apparent, aspects of a perceived external thing are not themselves perceived. Ego and thing are in either case said to be perceived, and perceived they indeed are, and in full, 'bodily' presence.

Additional Note to the Second Edition. I must expressly emphasize that the attitude here taken up to the question of the pure ego – an attitude I no longer endorse, as remarked before – *is irrelevant to the investigations of this volume.* Important as this question may be, phenomenologically or in other respects, there remain wide fields of phenomenological problems, relating more or less generally to the real content of intentional experiences, and to their relation of essence to intentional objects, which can be systematically explored without taking up any stance on the ego-issue. The present investigations are entirely confined to such problems. But since such an important work as volume I of P. Natorp's Second Edition of his *Einleitung in die Psychologie* concerns itself with what I have said above, I have not simply struck it out.

Chapter 2

Consciousness as intentional experience

We must now embark upon a fuller analytic discussion of our third concept of consciousness, which ranges over the same phenomenological field as the concept of 'mental act'. In connection with this, talk of conscious contents, talk in particular concerning contents of presentations, judgements etc., gains a variety of meanings, which it is all-important to sort out and to subject to the sharpest scrutiny.

§9 The meaning of Brentano's demarcation of 'psychic phenomena'

Among the demarcations of classes in descriptive psychology, there is none more remarkable nor more important philosophically than the one offered by Brentano under his title of 'psychical phenomena', and used by him in his well-known division of phenomena into psychical and physical. Not that I can approve of the great thinker's guiding conviction, plain from the very terms that he uses, that he had achieved an exhaustive classification of 'phenomena' through which the field of psychological research could be kept apart from that of natural science, and through which the vexed question of the right delimitation of the fields of these disciplines could be very simply solved. Possibly a good sense can be given to defining psychology as the science of psychical phenomena, and to the coordinated definition of natural science as the science of physical phenomena, but there are good reasons for disputing the view that the concepts which occur in Brentano's division are those found under like names in the definitions in question. It can be shown that not all 'psychical phenomena' in the sense of a possible definition of psychology, are psychical phenomena (i.e. mental acts) in Brentano's sense, and that, on the other hand, many genuine 'psychical phenomena' fall under Brentano's ambiguous rubric of 'physical phenomena'.[1] The value of Brentano's conception of a 'psychical phenomenon' is, however, quite independent of the aims that inspired it. A sharply defined class of experiences is here brought before us, comprising all that enjoys mental, conscious existence in a certain *pregnant* sense of these words. A real being deprived of such experiences, merely having[2] contents inside it such as the experiences of sensation, but unable to interpret these objectively, or otherwise use them to make objects present to itself, quite incapable, therefore, of referring to objects in further acts of judgement, joy, grief, love, hatred, desire and loathing – such a being would not be called 'psychical' by anyone. If one doubts whether it is at all possible to conceive of such a being, a mere complex of sensations, one has but to point to external phenomenal things, present to consciousness through sensational complexes, but not appearing as such themselves, and called by us 'bodies' or 'inanimate things', since they lack all psychical experiences in the sense of our examples. Turning aside from psychology, and entering the field of the philosophical disciplines proper, we perceive the fundamental importance of our class of experiences, since only its members are relevant in the highest ranks of the normative sciences. They alone, seized in their phenomenological purity, furnish concrete bases for abstracting the fundamental notions that function systematically in logic, ethics and aesthetics, and that enter into the ideal laws of these sciences. Our mention of logic recalls the particular interest which has inspired our whole probing into such experiences.

§10 Descriptive characterization of acts as 'intentional' experiences

We must now dig down to the essence of Brentano's demarcation of phenomenal classes, of his concept of consciousness in the sense of psychical act. Moved by the interest in classification just mentioned, Brentano conducts his enquiry in the form of a two-edged separation of the two main classes of 'phenomena' that he recognizes, the psychical and the physical. He arrives at a sixfold differentiation in which only two heads are relevant for our purpose, since in all the others misleading ambiguities do their destructive work, rendering untenable his notion of 'phenomenon' in general and of 'physical phenomenon' in particular, as well as his concepts of internal and external perception.[3]

Of his two principal differentiations, one directly reveals the *essence* of psychical phenomena or acts. This strikes us unmistakably in any illustration we choose. In perception something is perceived, in imagination, something imagined, in a statement something stated, in love something loved, in hate hated, in desire desired etc. Brentano looks to what is graspably common to such instances, and says that 'every mental phenomenon is characterized by what the mediaeval schoolmen called the intentional (or mental) inexistence of an object, and by what we, not without ambiguity, call the relation to a content, the direction to an object (by which a reality is not to be understood) or an immanent objectivity. Each mental phenomenon contains something as object in itself, though not all in the same manner.'[4] This 'manner in which consciousness refers to an object' (an expression used by Brentano in other passages) is presentative in a presentation, judicial in a judgement etc. etc. Brentano's attempted classification of mental phenomena into presentations, judgements and emotions ('phenomena of love and hate') is plainly based upon this 'manner of reference', of which three basically different kinds are distinguished (each admitting of many further specifications).

Whether we think Brentano's classification of 'psychical' phenomena successful, and whether we think it basically significant for the whole treatment of psychology, as Brentano claims it is, does not matter here. Only one point has importance for us: that there are essential, specific differences of intentional relation or intention (the generic descriptive character of 'acts'). The manner in which a 'mere presentation' refers to its object, differs from the manner of a judgement, which treats the same state of affairs as true or false. Quite different again is the manner of a surmise or doubt, the manner of a hope or a fear, of approval or disapproval, of desire or aversion; of the resolution of a theoretical doubt (judgemental decision) or of a practical doubt (voluntary decision in the case of deliberate choice); of the confirmation of a theoretical opinion (fulfilment of a judgemental intention), or of a voluntary intention (fulfilment of what we mean to do). Most, if not all, acts are complex experiences, very often involving intentions which are themselves multiple. Emotional intentions are built upon presentative or judging intentions etc. We cannot, however, doubt that to resolve such complexes is always to come down on primitive intentional characters whose descriptive essence precludes reduction into other types of experience, and that the unity of the descriptive genus 'intention' ('act-character') displays specific differences, flowing from its pure essence, which take *a priori* precedence over empirical, psychological matters-of-fact. There are essentially different species and subspecies of intention. We cannot, in particular, reduce all differences in acts into differences in the presentations or judgements they involve, with help only from elements not of an intentional kind. Aesthetic approval or disapproval, e.g., is evidently and essentially a peculiar mode of intentional relation as opposed to the mere presentation or theoretical assessment of the aesthetic object. Aesthetic approval and aesthetic predicates may be asserted, and their assertion is a judgement, and as such includes presentations. But the aesthetic intention and its objects are then *objects* of presentations and judgements: it remains essentially distinct from these theoretical acts. To evaluate a judgement as valid, an emotional experience as elevated etc., presupposes analogous, closely related, not specifically identical intentions. Just so in comparisons of judgemental with voluntary decisions etc.

We take intentional relation, understood in purely descriptive fashion as an inward peculiarity of certain experiences, to be the essential feature of 'psychical phenomena' or 'acts', seeing in Brentano's definition of them as 'phenomena intentionally containing objects in themselves' a circumscription of essence, whose 'reality' (in the traditional sense) is of course ensured by examples.[5] Differently put in terms of pure phenomenology: Ideation performed in exemplary cases of such experiences – and so performed as to leave empirical-psychological conception and existential affirmation of being out of account, and to deal only with the real phenomenological content of these experiences – yields us the pure, phenomenological generic Idea of *intentional experience* or *act*, and of its various pure species.[6] That not all experiences are intentional is proved by sensations and sensational complexes. Any piece of a sensed visual field, full as it is of visual contents, is an experience containing many part-contents, which are neither referred to, nor intentionally objective, in the whole.

The discussions which follow will give precision and clarity to the fundamentally different uses of the word 'content'. Everywhere it will appear that what one grasped in the analysis and comparison of instances of the two sorts of contents, can be ideationally seen as a pure distinction of essence. The phenomenological assertions we aim at, are all meant by us (even without special pointing) as assertions of essence.

A second characterization of mental phenomena by Brentano that has value for us is the formula 'that they are either presentations or founded upon presentations'.[7] 'Nothing can be judged about, nothing can likewise be desired, nothing can be hoped or feared, if it is not presented.'[8] In this characterization the term 'presentation' does not of course mean the presented content or object, but the act of presenting this.

This characterization does not seem a suitable starting-point for our researches, since it presupposes a concept of 'presentation' that has yet to be worked out: it is hard to draw distinctions among the word's highly ambiguous uses. The discussion of the concept of 'act' will lead us naturally on to this. But the characterization is an important utterance, whose content prompts further investigations: we shall have to come back to it later.

§11 Avoidance of verbally tempting misunderstandings. (*a*) The 'mental' or 'immanent' object

While we adhere to Brentano's essential characterization, our departures from his opinions force us to abandon his terminology. It will be as well to drop talk of 'psychical phenomena', or of 'phenomena' at all, where we are dealing with experiences of the class in question. 'Psychical phenomena' is a justifiable phrase only on Brentano's view that it fairly circumscribes the psychological field of research: on our view all experiences are in this respect on a level. The term 'phenomenon' is likewise fraught with most dangerous ambiguities, and insinuates a quite doubtful theoretical persuasion, expressly professed by Brentano, that each intentional experience is a phenomenon. As 'phenomenon' in its dominant use (which is also Brentano's) means an appearing object as such, this implies that each intentional experience is not only directed upon objects, but is itself the object of certain intentional experiences. One thinks here, mainly, of the experiences in which things 'appear' in the most special sense, i.e. perceptions: 'every psychical phenomenon is an object of inner consciousness'. We have already mentioned the grave misgivings that keep us from assenting to this.

Further objections surround the expressions used by Brentano as parallel with, or roughly circumscribing, his term 'psychical phenomenon', and which are also in general use. It is always quite questionable, and frequently misleading, to say that perceived, imagined, asserted or desired objects etc., 'enter consciousness' (or do so in perceptual, presentative fashion etc.), or to say conversely that 'consciousness', 'the ego' enters into this or that sort of relation to them, or to say that such objects 'are taken up into consciousness' in this or that way, or to say, similarly, that intentional experiences 'contain something as their object in themselves' etc. etc.[9] Such expressions promote *two misunderstandings*: first, that we are dealing with a real (*realen*) event or a real (*reales*) relationship, taking place between 'consciousness' or 'the ego', on the one hand, and the thing of which there is consciousness, on the other; secondly, that we are dealing with a relation between two things, both present in equally real fashion (*reell*) in consciousness, an act and an intentional object, or with a sort of box-within-box structure of mental contents. If talk of a *relation* is here inescapable, we must avoid expressions which tempt us to regard such a relation as having psychological reality (*Realität*), as belonging to the real (*reellen*) content of an experience.

Let us first discuss our *second* misunderstanding more closely. It is particularly suggested by the expression 'immanent objectivity' used to name the essential peculiarity of intentional experiences, and likewise by the equivalent scholastic expressions 'intentional' or 'mental inexistence' of an object. Intentional experiences have the peculiarity of directing themselves in varying fashion to presented objects, but they do so in an *intentional* sense. An object is 'referred to'[10] or 'aimed at' in them, and in presentative or judging or other fashion. This means no more than that certain experiences are present, intentional in character and, more specifically, presentatively, judgingly, desiringly or otherwise intentional. There are (to ignore certain exceptions) not two things present in experience, we do not experience the object and beside it the intentional experience directed upon it, there are not even two things present in the sense of a part and a whole which contains it: only one thing is present, the intentional experience, whose essential descriptive character is the intention in question. According to its particular specification, it constitutes the full and sole presentation, judgement etc. etc., of this object. If this experience is present, then, *eo ipso* and through its own essence (we must insist), the intentional 'relation' to an object is achieved, and an object is 'intentionally present'; these two phrases mean precisely the same. And of course such an experience may be present in consciousness together with its intention, although its object does not exist at all, and is perhaps incapable of existence. The object is 'meant', i.e. to 'mean' it is an experience, but it is then merely entertained in thought, and is nothing in reality.

If I have an idea of the god Jupiter, this god is my presented object, he is 'immanently present' in my act, he has 'mental inexistence' in the latter, or whatever expression we may use to disguise our true meaning. I have an idea of the god Jupiter: this means that I have a certain presentative experience, the presentation-of-the-god-Jupiter is realized in my consciousness. This intentional experience may be dismembered as one chooses in descriptive analysis, but the god Jupiter naturally will not be found in it. The 'immanent', 'mental object' is not therefore part of the descriptive or real make-up (*deskriptiven reellen Bestand*) of the experience, it is in truth not really immanent or mental. But it also does not exist extramentally, it does not exist at all. This does not prevent our-idea-of-the-god-Jupiter from being actual, a particular sort of experience or particular mode of mindedness (*Zumutesein*), such that he who experiences it may rightly say that the mythical king of the gods is present to him, concerning whom there are such and such stories. If, however, the intended object exists, nothing becomes phenomenologically different. It makes no essential difference to an object presented and given to consciousness whether it exists, or is fictitious, or is perhaps completely absurd. I think of Jupiter as I think of Bismarck, of the tower of Babel as I think of Cologne Cathedral, of a regular thousand-sided polygon as of a regular thousand-faced solid.[11]

These so-called immanent contents are therefore merely intended or intentional, while truly *immanent contents*, which belong to the real make-up (*reellen Bestande*) of the intentional experiences, are *not intentional*: they constitute the act, provide necessary *points d'appui* which render possible an intention, but are not themselves intended, not the objects presented in the act. I do not see colour-sensations but coloured things, I do not hear tone-sensations but the singer's song, etc. etc.[12]

What is true of presentations is true also of other intentional experiences that are built upon them. To represent an object, e.g. the Schloss at Berlin, to oneself, is, we said, to be minded in this or that descriptively determinate fashion. To *judge* about this Schloss, to delight in its architectural beauty, to cherish the wish that one could do so etc. etc., are new experiences, characterized in novel phenomenological terms. All have this in common, that they are modes of objective intention, which cannot be otherwise expressed than by saying that the Schloss is perceived, imagined, pictorially represented, judged about, delighted in, wished for etc. etc.

We shall need more elaborate investigation to determine the justification of talking figuratively about the object presented in a presentation, judged in a judgement etc., as well as the full sense of talk about the relation of acts to objects. It is clear, at least, as far as we now have penetrated, that it will be well to avoid all talk of immanent objectivity. It is readily dispensed with, since we have the expression 'intentional object' which is not exposed to similar objections.

As regards misleading talk of the intentional 'containment' of objects in acts, it is undeniable that the parallel, equivalent locutions – 'the object is a conscious datum', 'is in consciousness', 'is immanent in consciousness' etc. – suffer from a most damaging ambiguity; 'being conscious' (*bewusst*) here means something quite different from the possible senses given to it in the two previously discussed meanings of 'consciousness'. All modern psychology and epistemology have been confused by these and similar equivocations. With psychological thought and terminology as influential as they are now, it would be ill-advised to set up our own terms in opposition to those of contemporary psychology. Our first concept of consciousness, given an empirical-psychological slant, covers the whole stream of experience which makes up the individual mind's real unity, together with all aspects that enter into the constitution of this stream. This conception shows signs of spreading to psychology, and we therefore decided in our last chapter to give the preference to it, though we did so in phenomenological purity and not from a properly psychological angle. We must therefore exercise some necessary care in talking of consciousness as inner perception, or in talking of it as intentional relation, even if we do not altogether avoid such 'uses', which would scarcely be practicable.

§12 (*b*) The act and the relation of consciousness or the ego to the object

The situation is similar as regards the first misunderstanding we mentioned, where it is imagined that consciousness, on the one hand, and the 'matter in consciousness' on the other, become related to one another in a real sense. ('The ego' is here often put in the place of 'consciousness'.) In *natural reflection*, in fact, it is not the single act which appears, but the ego as one pole of the relation in question, while the other pole is the object. If one then studies an act-experience, which last tempts one to make of the ego an essential, selfsame point of unity in every act. This would, however, bring us back to the view of the ego as a relational centre which we repudiated before.

But if we simply 'live' in the act in question, become absorbed, e.g., in the perceptual 'taking in' of some event happening before us, in some play of fancy, in reading a story, in carrying out a mathematical proof etc., the ego as relational centre of our performances becomes quite elusive. The idea of the ego may be specially *ready* to come to the fore, or rather to be recreated anew, but only when it is really so recreated, and built into our act, do *we* refer to the object in a manner to which something descriptively ostensible corresponds. We have here, in the actual experience described, a correspondingly complex act which presents the ego, on the one hand, and the presentation, judgement, wish etc., of the moment, with its relevant subject-matter, on the other. From an *objective* standpoint (and so, too, from the standpoint of natural reflection) it is doubtless the case that in each act the ego is intentionally directed to some object. This is quite obvious since the ego is either no more than the 'conscious unity', or contemporary 'bundle', of experiences, or, in a more natural empirically-real (*realer*) perspective, the continuous thing-like unity, constituted in the unity of consciousness as the personal subject of our experiences, the ego whose mental states these experiences are, that performs the intention, percept, or judgement in question. If such and such an intentional experience is present, the ego *eo ipso* has the corresponding intention.

The sentences 'The ego represents an object to itself', 'The ego refers presentatively to an object', 'The ego has something as an intentional object of its presentation' therefore mean the same as 'In the phenomenological ego, a concrete complex of experiences, a certain experience said, in virtue of its specific nature, to be a presentation of object *X*, is really (*reell*) present.' Just so the sentence 'The ego judges about the object' means the same as 'such and such an experience of judging is present in the ego' etc. etc. In our *description* relation to an experiencing ego is inescapable, but the experience described is not itself an experiential complex having the ego-presentation as its part. We perform the description after an objectifying act of reflection, in which reflection on the ego is combined with reflection on the experienced act to yield a relational act, in which the ego appears as itself related to its act's object through its act. Plainly an essential descriptive change has occurred. The original act is no longer simply there, we no longer live in it, but *we attend to it and pass judgement on it*.

We must therefore avoid the misunderstanding which our present discussion has just ruled out, that of treating relation to an ego as of the essence of an intentional experience itself.[13]

§13 The fixing of our terminology

After these critical prolegomena, we shall now fix our own terminology, excluding as far as we can, and in their light, all conflicting assumptions and confusing ambiguities. We shall avoid the term 'psychical phenomenon' entirely, and shall talk of 'intentional experiences' wherever accuracy requires it. 'Experience' must be understood in the phenomenological sense fixed above. The qualifying adjective 'intentional' names the essence common to the class of experiences we wish to mark off, the peculiarity of *intending*, of referring to what is objective, in a presentative or other analogous fashion. As a briefer expression, in harmony with our own and foreign verbal usage, we shall use the term 'act'.

These expressions certainly have their defects. We speak of 'intending' [not, of course, in English: *Trans.*] in the sense of specially noticing, or attending to something. *An intentional object need not, however, always be noticed or attended to.* Several acts may be present and interwoven with one another, but attention is emphatically active in one of them. We experience them all together, but we 'go all out' (as it were) in this particular one. But it is not unfitting, in view of the traditional use of the term 'intentional object', to which Brentano has given renewed currency, to speak in a correlative sense of 'intention', especially when we have the term 'attending' to do the work of 'intention' in the other sense; we shall find reason to hold that attention does not involve a peculiar act.[14] Another ambiguity, however, confronts us. The term 'intention' hits off the peculiarity of acts by imagining them to *aim* at something, and so fits the numerous cases that are naturally and understandably ranked as cases of theoretical aiming. But the metaphor does not fit all acts equally, and if we study the examples enumerated in §10, we cannot avoid distinguishing a *narrower* and a *wider* concept of intention. In our metaphor an act of *hitting the mark* corresponds to that of aiming, and just so certain acts correspond as 'achievements' or 'fulfilments' to other acts as 'intentions' (whether of the judging or the desiring sort). The image therefore fits these latter acts quite perfectly; fulfilments are, however, themselves acts, i.e. 'intentions', though they are not intentions – at least not in general – in that narrower sense *which points to corresponding fulfilments.* This ambiguity, once recognized, becomes harmless. But of course, where the narrower concept is wanted, this must be expressly stated. The equivalent term 'act-character' will also help to avoid misunderstandings.

In talking of 'acts', on the other hand, we must steer clear of the word's original meaning: *all thought of activity must be rigidly excluded.*[15] The term 'act' is so firmly fixed in the usage of many psychologists, and so wellworn and loosed from its original sense that, after these express reservations, we can go on using it without concern. If we do not wish to introduce artificial novelties, strange alike to our living speech-sense and to historical tradition, we can hardly avoid inconvenience of the just-mentioned sort.

§14 Difficulties which surround the assumption of acts as a descriptively founded class of experiences

In all these terminological discussions, we have gone deep into descriptive analyses of a sort required by our interests in logic and epistemology. Before we go deeper, however, we shall have to consider some objections which affect the bases of our descriptions.

There are a group of thinkers who absolutely reject any marking-off of a class of experiences which have been described by us as 'acts' or 'intentional experiences'. In this connection Brentano's original introduction of the distinction, and his aims in introducing it, have, with some surreptitious misunderstandings, produced confusion: they have kept the distinction's extraordinarily valuable descriptive content from being rightly assessed. Natorp, e.g., rejects it decisively. But when this distinguished thinker objects by saying that[16] 'I can deal with a tone by itself or in relation to other contents of consciousness, without also paying regard to its being for an ego, but I cannot deal with myself and my hearing by themselves, without thinking of the tone', we find nothing in this that could confuse. Hearing certainly cannot be torn out of the hearing of a tone, as if it were something apart from the tone it hears. But this does not mean that two things are not to be distinguished: the tone heard, the object of perception, and the hearing of the tone, the perceptual act. Natorp is quite right in saying of the former: 'Its existence for me is my consciousness of it. If anyone can catch his consciousness in anything else than the existence of a content for him, I am unable to follow him.' It seems to me, however, that the 'existence of something for me', is a thing both permitting and requiring further phenomenological analysis. Consider, first, differences in the mode of attention. A content is differently present to me, according as I note it implicitly, not relieved in some whole, or see it in relief, according as I see it marginally, or have specially turned my focussing gaze upon it. More important still are differences between the existence of a content in consciousness in the sense in which a sensation so exists, without being itself made a perceptual object, and of a content which *is* made such an object. The choice of a tone as an instance slightly obscures the distinction without altogether removing it. 'I hear' can mean in psychology 'I am having sensations': in ordinary speech it means 'I am perceiving'; I hear the adagio of the violin, the twittering of the birds etc. Different acts can perceive the same object and yet involve quite different sensations. The same tone is at one moment heard close at hand, at another far away. The same sensational contents are likewise 'taken' now in this, and now in that manner. What is most emphasized in the doctrine of apperception is generally the fact that consistency of stimulus does not involve constancy of sensational content; what the stimulus really provokes is overlaid by features springing from actualized dispositions left behind them by previous experiences. Such notions are, however, inadequate and, above all, phenomenologically irrelevant. Whatever the origin of the experienced contents now present in consciousness, we can think that the same sensational contents should be present with a differing interpretation, i.e. that the same contents should serve to ground perceptions of different objects. Interpretation itself can never be reduced to an influx of new sensations; it is an act-character, a mode of consciousness, of 'mindedness' (*Zumuteseins*). We call the experiencing of sensations in this conscious manner the perception of the object in question. What has here been made plain, in a context of natural existence, and by methods appropriate to psychology and natural science, will yield up its phenomenological substance if we abstract from the empirically real (*Realen*). If we consider pure experiences and their own essential content, we form Ideas of pure species and specific situations, in this case the pure species of Sensation, Interpretation, Perception in relation to its *perceptum*, and the relations of essence among these. We then see it to be a fact of essence that the being of a sensational content differs from that of the perceived object presented by it, which is not a reality in consciousness (*reell bewusst*).[17]

All this becomes clear if we change our field of illustration for that of vision. Let us lay the following considerations before a sceptic. I see a thing, e.g. this box, but I do not see my sensations. I always see *one and the same box*, however *it* may be turned and tilted. I have always the *same* 'content of consciousness' – if I care to call the perceived object a content of consciousness. But each turn yields a *new* 'content of consciousness', if I call experienced contents 'contents of consciousness', in a much more appropriate use of words. Very different contents are therefore experienced, though the same object is perceived. The experienced content, generally speaking, is not the perceived object. We must note, further, that the object's real being or non-being is irrelevant to the true essence of the perceptual experience, and to its essence as a perceiving of an object as thus and thus appearing, and as thus and thus thought of. In the flux of experienced content, we imagine ourselves to be in perceptual touch with one and the same object; this itself belongs to the sphere of what we experience. For we experience a 'consciousness of identity', i.e. a claim to apprehend identity. On what does this consciousness depend? Must we not reply that different sensational contents are given, but that we apperceive or 'take' them 'in the same sense', and that *to take them in this sense is an experienced character through which the 'being of the object for me' is first constituted*. Must we not say, further, that the consciousness of identity is framed on a basis of these two sorts of experienced characters, as the immediate consciousness that they *mean the same*? And is this consciousness not again an act in our defined sense, whose objective correlate lies in the identity it refers to? These questions, I think, call for an affirmative and evident answer. I find nothing more plain than the distinction here apparent between contents and acts, between perceptual contents in the sense of presentative sensations, and perceptual acts in the sense of interpretative intentions overlaid with various additional characters. Such intentions, united with the sensations they interpret, make up the full concrete act of perception. Intentional characters and complete intentional acts are, of course, contents of consciousness in the widest descriptive sense of experiences: all differences predicable at all, are in this sense *eo ipso* differences of content. But within this widest sphere of what can be experienced, we believe we have found an evident difference between intentional experiences, in whose case *objective intentions* arise through *immanent characters* of the experiences in question, and experiences in whose case this does not occur, contents that may serve as the building-stones of acts *without being acts themselves*.

Examples that will serve to elucidate this distinction, and also to show up various characters of acts, are provided by comparing perception with memory, or comparing either with presentations by means of physical images

(paintings, statues etc.), or of signs. Verbal expressions yield the best examples of all. Let us imagine[18] that certain arabesques or figures have affected
us aesthetically, and that we then suddenly see that we are dealing with
symbols or verbal signs. In what does this difference consist? Or let us take
the case of an attentive man hearing some totally strange word as a sound-
complex without even dreaming it is a word, and compare this with the case
of the same man afterwards hearing the word, in the course of conversation,
and now acquainted with its meaning, but not illustrating it intuitively?
What in general is the surplus element distinguishing the understanding of a
symbolically functioning expression from the uncomprehended verbal sound?
What is the difference between simply looking at a concrete object *A*, and
treating it as representative of 'any *A* whatsoever'? In this and countless
similar cases it is act-characters that differ. All logical differences, and differences in categorial form, are constituted in logical acts in the sense of
intentions.

In analysing such cases the inadequacies of the modern theory of apperception become plain: it overlooks points decisive from a logical or epistemological standpoint. It does not do justice to phenomenological fact; it
does not even attempt to analyse or describe it. Differences of interpretation
are above all *descriptive* differences, and these alone, rather than obscure,
hypothetical events in the soul's unconscious depths, or in the sphere of
physiological happenings, concern the epistemologist. These alone permit of
a purely phenomenological treatment, excluding all transcendent affirmations,
such as the critique of knowledge presupposes. Apperception is our surplus,
which is found in experience itself, in its descriptive content as opposed to the
raw existence of sense: it is the act-character which as it were ensouls sense,
and is in essence such as to make us perceive this or that object, see this tree,
e.g., hear this ringing, smell this scent of flowers etc. etc. *Sensations*, and the
acts 'interpreting' them or apperceiving them, are alike experienced, *but they
do not appear as objects*: they are not seen, heard or *perceived* by any sense.
Objects on the other hand, appear and are perceived, but they are not
experienced. Naturally we exclude the case of adequate perception.

The same holds in other cases: it holds, e.g., in the case of the 'sensations'
(or however we choose to call contents serving as bases to interpretation)
which are found in acts of simple or representative imagining. It is an imaging
interpretation that sets an imagined rather than a perceptual appearance
before us, where experienced sensations mediate the appearance of a pictorially presented object (e.g. a centaur in a painting).[19] One sees at once that
the very same thing which, in relation to the intentional object, is called its
presentation, i.e. the perceiving, remembering, picturing, symbolizing intention directed towards it, is also called an *interpretation, conception, apperception* in relation to the sensations really present in this act.

I also regard it as relevantly evident, in regard to the examples just cited, that
there are different 'manners of consciousness', different intentional relations

to objects: the character of our intention is specifically different in the case of perceiving, of direct 'reproductive' recall, of pictorial representation (in the ordinary sense of the interpretation of statues, pictures etc.), and again in the case of a presentation through signs. Each logically distinct way of entertaining an object in thought corresponds to a difference in intention. To me it seems irrefragable that we only know of such differences because we envisage them in particular cases (apprehend them adequately and immediately), can then compare them and range them under concepts, and can thus make them into objects of varying acts of intuition and thought. From such 'seeing' we can, through abstract Ideation, progress toward an adequate grasp of the pure species they exemplify, and of the connections of essence among these latter. When Natorp remarks that 'all richness, all multiplicity of consciousness pertains rather to contents alone. Consciousness of a simple sensation does not differ, *qua* consciousness, from consciousness of a world: the "being in consciousness" is entirely the same in both; their difference lies solely in their content', he seems to me not to be keeping apart quite distinct notions of consciousness and content, and to be erecting his identification into an epistemological principle. We have explained the sense in which we too teach that all multiplicity of consciousness depends on content. Content must mean experience, a real part of consciousness: consciousness itself must be the complex formed by experiences. The world, however, never is a thinker's experience. To refer to the world may be an experience, but the world itself is the object intended. It is immaterial, from the point of view of our distinction, what attitude one takes up to the question of the make-up of objective being, of the true, real inner being of the world or of any other object, or of the relation of objective being, as a 'unity', to our 'manifold' thought-approaches, or of the sense in which one may metaphysically oppose immanent to transcendent being. The distinction in question is prior to all metaphysics, and lies at the very gates of the theory of knowledge: it presupposes no answers to the questions that this theory must be the first to provide.

§15 Whether experiences of one and the same phenomenological kind (of the genus Feeling in particular) can consist partly of acts and partly of non-acts

A new difficulty arises in regard to the generic unity of intentional experiences.

It might be thought that the standpoint from which we divide experiences into intentional and non-intentional, is a merely external one, that the same experiences, or experiences of the same phenomenological class, may at times have an intentional relation to some object, and at times have none. The examples used to attest either concept, and also, in part, the attempted solutions of the problem, have already been discussed in literary fashion in regard to the debated issue as to whether the 'intentional relation' suffices to demarcate 'psychical phenomena' (the domain of psychology) or not. The debate centred chiefly in phenomena from the sphere of *feeling*. Since the intentionality of other feelings seemed obvious, two doubts were possible: one wondered whether intentionality might not perhaps attach loosely to the *acts* of feeling in question, belonging really to the presentations fused with them, or whether intentionality could be essential to the class of feelings, since one allowed it to some feelings while denying it to others. The connection between this commonly debated question and our present question has thus been made clear.

We must first see whether any sorts of feeling-experience are essentially intentional, and then whether other sorts of feeling-experience lack this property.

(a) Are there any intentional feelings?

Many experiences commonly classed as 'feelings' have an undeniable, real relation to something objective. This is the case, e.g., when we are pleased by a melody, displeased at a shrill blast etc. etc. It seems obvious, in general, that every joy or sorrow, that is joy or sorrow *about* something we think of, is a directed act. Instead of joy we can speak of pleased delight in something, instead of sorrow we can speak of displeased or painful dislike of it, aversion from it etc. etc.

Those who question the intentionality of feeling say: Feelings are mere states, not acts, intentions. Where they relate to objects, they owe their relation to a complication with presentations.

No intrinsic objection is involved in this last position. Brentano who defends the intentionality of feelings, also maintains without inconsistency that feelings, like all acts that are not themselves presentations, have presentations as their foundations.[20] We can only direct ourselves feelingly to objects that are presented to us by inwoven presentations. No difference emerges between the disputing parties until someone is really prepared to maintain that feeling, considered in itself, involves nothing intentional, that it does not point beyond itself to a felt object, that only its union with a presentation gives it a certain relation to an object, a relation only intentional by way of *this* connection and not intrinsically so. This is just what the other party disputes.

Brentano thinks we have here two intentions built on one another: the underlying, founding intention gives us the *presented* object, the founded intention the *felt* object. The former is separable from the latter, the latter inseparable from the former. His opponents think there is only *one* intention here, the presenting one.

If we subject the situation to a careful phenomenological review, Brentano's conception seems definitely to be preferred. Whether we turn with pleasure to something, or whether its unpleasantness repels us, an object is presented.

But we do not merely have a presentation, with an added feeling *associatively* tacked on to it, and not intrinsically related to it, but pleasure or distaste *direct* themselves to the presented object, and could not exist without such a direction. If two psychical experiences, e.g. two presentations, are associated in an objective-psychological sense, there is a phenomenologically discernible type of associative unity among the reproduced experiences which corresponds to the objective dispositions which govern them. Side by side with the intentional elation which each has to its object, there is also a phenomenological mode of connection: one idea, e.g. that of Naples, carries with it the idea of Vesuvius, the one is peculiarly bound up with the other, so that we say in regard to the objects presented – the mode of their presentation here essentially requires further description – that the one reminds us of the other. (This sentence is being used to express a phenomenological situation.) It is easily seen, however, that though all this in a sense constitutes a new intentional relationship, it does not turn each associated member into an object of the other's intention. The intentional relationships remain unconfused in their association. How indeed could they furnish an object, borrowed from an associated intention, to something not itself intentional? It is clear, further, that such a phenomenologically associative relation is extrinsic, not at all to be put on a level with the relation of pleasure to the pleasant. The presentation which reproduces is quite possible without such a reproductive function. But pleasure without anything pleasant is unthinkable. And it is unthinkable, not because we are here dealing with correlative expressions, as when we say, e.g., that a cause without an effect, or a father without a child, is unthinkable, but because *the specific essence of pleasure demands a relation to something pleasing.* Just so the feature known as conviction is unthinkable apart from something of which we are convinced. There is, similarly, no desire whose specific character can do without something desired, no agreement or approval without something agreed on or approved etc. etc. These are all intentions, genuine acts in our sense. They all 'owe' their intentional relation to certain underlying presentations. But it is part of what we mean by such 'owing' that they themselves really now *have* what they owe to something else.

It is plain, too, that the relation between founding (underlying) presentation and founded act cannot be correctly described by saying that the former *produces* the latter. We say that the object arouses our pleasure, just as we say in other cases that some circumstance inspires doubt, compels agreement, provokes desire etc. But the result of such apparent causation, the pleasure, doubt or agreement provoked, is itself through and through intentional. We are not dealing with an external causal relation where the effect conceivably could be what it intrinsically is without the cause, or where the cause brings something forth that could have existed independently.

Closer consideration shows it to be absurd in principle, here or in like cases, to treat an intentional as a causal relation, to give it the sense of an empirical, substantial-causal case of necessary connection. For the intentional object, here thought of as ' provocative', is only in question as an intentional, not as an external reality, which really and psycho-physically determines my mental life. A battle of centaurs, seen in a picture or framed in fancy, 'provokes' my approval just like some beautiful, real landscape: if I look on the latter psycho-physically as the real cause of my mentally provoked state of pleasure, this 'causation' is altogether different from the causation we have when we see the visible landscape – in virtue of such and such a mode of appearing and such and such pictured colours and forms – as the 'source', 'ground' or 'cause' of my pleasure. Pleasantness or pleasure do not belong as effect to this landscape considered as a physical reality, but only to it *as appearing in this or that manner*, perhaps as thus and thus judged of or as reminding us of this or that, in the conscious act here in question: it is as such that the landscape 'demands', 'arouses' such feelings.[21]

(b) Are there non-intentional feelings? Distinction between feeling-sensations and feeling-acts

We may now ask more generally whether, in addition to the intentional varieties of feeling, there are not other *non*-intentional species. It may seem at first that an obvious 'Yes' is the right answer. In the wide field of so-called sensory feelings, no intentional characters can be found. The sensible pain of a burn can certainly not be classed beside a conviction, a surmise, a volition etc. etc., but beside sensory contents like rough or smooth, red or blue etc. If we recall such pains, or any sensory pleasures (the fragrance of a rose, the relish of certain foods etc. etc.), we find that our sensory feelings are blended with the sensations from the various sense-fields, just as these latter are blended with one another.

Every sensory feeling, e.g. the pain of burning oneself or of being burnt, is no doubt after a fashion referred to an object: it is referred, on the one hand, to the ego and its burnt bodily member, on the other hand, to the object which inflicts the burn. In all these respects there is conformity with other sensations: tactual sensations, e.g., are referred in just this manner to the bodily member which touches, and to the external body which is touched. And though this reference is realized in intentional experiences, no one would think of calling the referred sensations intentional. It is rather the case that our sensations are here functioning as presentative contents in perceptual acts, or (to use a possibly misleading phrase) that our sensations here receive an objective 'interpretation' or 'taking-up'. They themselves are not acts, but acts are constituted through them, wherever, that is, intentional characters like a perceptual interpretation lay hold of them, and as it were animate them. In just this manner it seems that a burning, piercing, boring pain, fused as it is from the start with certain tactual sensations, must itself count as a sensation. It functions at least as other sensations do, in providing a foothold for empirical, objective interpretations.

All this seems unobjectionable, and the whole question disposed of. We seem to have shown that *some* feelings are to he reckoned among intentional experiences, while others are non-intentional.

But we are led to doubt, then, whether two such sorts of 'feelings' really form a single class. We spoke previously of 'feelings' of liking and dislike, of approval and disapproval, of valuation and disvaluation – experiences obviously akin to theoretical acts of assent and rejection, of taking something to be probable or improbable, or to deliberative acts of judgemental or voluntary decision etc. Here we have a *kind*, a plain unity of essence, which included nothing but acts, where such sensations of pain and pleasure have no place: descriptively the latter belong, in virtue of their specific essence, among tactual, gustatory, olfactory and other sensations. Being at best presentative contents of objects of intention, but not themselves intentions, they manifest descriptive differences so essential, that we cannot seriously believe in the unity of a genuine class. In both cases of course, we speak of 'feelings', i.e. in the case of the above-mentioned acts of liking as in the case of the above-mentioned sensations. This fact need not perplex, any more than our ordinary talk of 'feeling', in the sense of touching, need lead us astray in the case of tactile sensations.

Brentano has already pointed to the ambiguity here dealt with, in discussing the intentionality of feelings. He draws a distinction, in sense if not in words, between *sensations* of pain and pleasure (feeling-sensations) and pain and pleasure in the sense of *feelings*. The contents of the former – or, as I should simply say, the former[22] – are in this terminology 'physical', while the latter are 'psychical phenomena', and they belong therefore to essentially different genera. This notion I regard as quite correct, but only doubt, whether the meaning of the word 'feeling' does not lean predominantly towards 'feeling-sensation', and whether the many acts we call 'feelings' do not owe their name to the feeling-sensations with which they are essentially interwoven. One must of course not mix up questions of suitable terminology with questions regarding the factual correctness of Brentano's distinction.

Our distinction should constantly be kept in mind and fruitfully applied in analysing all complexes of feeling-sensations and feeling-acts. Joy, e.g., concerning some happy event, is certainly an act. But this act, which is not merely an intentional character, but a concrete and therefore complex experience, does not merely hold in its unity an idea of the happy event and an act-character of liking which relates to it: a sensation of pleasure attaches to the idea, a sensation at once seen and located as an emotional excitement in the psycho-physical feeling-subject, and also as an objective property – the event seems as if bathed in a rosy gleam. The event thus pleasingly painted now serves as the first foundation for the joyful approach, the liking for, the being charmed, or however one's state may be described. A sad event,

likewise, is not merely seen in its thinglike content and context, in the respects which make it an event: it seems clothed and coloured with sadness.
The same unpleasing sensations which the empirical ego refers to and locates
in itself – the pang in the heart – are referred in one's emotional conception
to the thing itself. *These* relations are purely presentational: we first have an
essentially new type of intention in hostile repugnance, in active dislike etc.
Sensations of pleasure and pain may continue, though the act-characters
built upon them may lapse. When the facts which provoke pleasure sink
into the background, are no longer apperceived as emotionally coloured,
and perhaps cease to be intentional objects at all, the pleasurable excitement
may linger on for a while: it may itself be felt as agreeable. Instead of
representing a pleasant property of the object, it is referred merely to the
feeling-subject, or is itself presented and pleases.

Much the same holds in the sphere of desire and volition.[23] If difficulty
is felt in the fact that desire does not always seem to require conscious
reference to what is desired, that we are often moved by obscure drives or
pressures towards unrepresented goals, and if one points especially to the
wide sphere of natural instinct, where goal-consciousness is at least absent
at the start, one may say: This is a case of mere sensations – we may speak
analogically of 'desire-sensations' – without needing to affirm the existence
of an essentially new class of sensations – i.e. of experiences really lacking
intentional reference, and so also remote in kind from the essential character of intentional desire. Alternatively one may say: Here we are dealing
with intentional experiences, but with such as are characterized by indeterminateness of objective direction, an 'indeterminateness' which does
not amount to a privation, but which stands for a descriptive character of
one's presentation. The idea we have when 'something' stirs, when there is
a rustling, a ring at the door, etc., an idea had before we give it verbal
expression, has indeterminateness of direction, and this indeterminateness is
of the intention's essence, it is determined as presenting an indeterminate
'something'.

Our one concept of desire might fit many cases, and our other concept
others, and we might have to allow, not a relation of generic community
between intentional and non-intentional urges or desires, but one of mere
equivocation.

We must observe, also, that our classification is oriented to the concretely
complex, and that the total character of such unities may at one time seem
to depend on sensational features (e.g. pleasure on urge-sensations), at
another on act-intentions which rest on these. The formation and use of
our expressions will at times therefore point to sensory contents, at times to
act-intentions, so giving rise to the equivocations in question.

Additional Note. The obvious tendency of our conception is to attribute
primary, genuine differences in intensity to underlying sensations, and to
concrete acts only in a secondary manner, in so far as their concrete total

character involves differences of intensity in their sensational basis. *Act-intentions*, the inseparable aspects which give acts their essential distinctive peculiarities, or which characterize them severally as judgements, feelings etc., *must be without intrinsic intensity*. Deeper analyses are, however, required here.

§16 Distinction between descriptive and intentional content

We have buttressed our notion of the essence of acts against objection, and given them a generic unity of essence in their character as intentions, as consciousnesses in the unique descriptive sense. We now introduce an important phenomenological distinction, obvious after our previous discussions, between the *real (reellen)*[24] and the *intentional* content of an act.

By the real phenomenological content of an act we mean the sum total of its concrete or abstract parts, in other words, the sum total of the *partial experiences* that really constitute it. To point out and describe such parts is the task of pure descriptive psychological analysis operating from an empirical, natural-scientific point of view. Such analysis is in all cases concerned to dismember what we inwardly experience as it in itself is, and as it is really *(reell)* given in experience, without regard either to genetic connections, or to extrinsic meaning and valid application. Purely descriptive psychological analysis of an articulated sound-pattern finds only sounds and abstract parts or unifying forms of sounds, it finds no sound-vibrations or organs of hearing etc.; it also never finds anything that resembles the ideal sense that makes the sound-pattern to be a name, nor the person to whom the name may apply. Our example suffices to make our intention clear. The real *(reell)* contents of acts are of course only known through descriptive analyses of this kind. That obscurities of intuition or inadequacies of descriptive conception – faults, in short, of method – may lead to much 'manufacture' of sensations (to use Volkelt's phrase) cannot be denied. This, however, only concerns the legitimacy of particular cases of descriptive analysis. It is clear, if anything is clear, that intentional experiences contain distinguishable parts and aspects, and this alone is of importance here.

Let us now shift from our natural-scientific, psychological standpoint to an ideal-scientific, phenomenological one. We must exclude all empirical interpretations and existential affirmations, we must take what is inwardly experienced or otherwise inwardly intuited (e.g. in pure fancy) as pure experiences, as our exemplary basis for acts of Ideation. We must ideate universal essences and essential connections in such experiences – ideal Species of experiencing of differing levels of generality, and ideally valid truths of essence which apply *a priori*, and with unlimited generality, to possible experiences of these species. We thus achieve insights in a pure phenomenology which is here oriented to *real (reellen)* constituents, whose descriptions are in every way 'ideal' and free from 'experience', i.e. from presupposition of real *existence*. When we speak simply of the real (*reellen*), and in general of the phenomenological analysis and description of experiences, the tie-up of our discussions to psychological material is (we must keep on stressing) merely transitional, since none of its empirically real (*reellen*) conceptions and assertions of existence (e.g. of experiences as states of animal beings having experiences in a real (*realen*), space-time world) are at all operative, that *pure* phenomenological validity of essence is aimed at and claimed.[25]

Content in the real (*reellen*) sense is the mere application of the most general notion of content, valid in all fields to intentional experiences. If we now oppose *intentional*[26] to real (*reell*) content, the word shows that the peculiarity of intentional experiences (or acts) is now in question. Here, however, there are several concepts, all grounded in the *specific* nature of acts, which may be equally covered by the rubric 'intentional content', and are often so covered. We shall first have to distinguish *three* concepts of the intentional content: the *intentional object* of the act, its *intentional material* (as opposed to its *intentional quality*) and, lastly its *intentional essence*. These distinctions will become familiar in the course of the following very general analyses, which are also essential to the more restricted aim of clarifying the essence of knowledge.

§17 The intentional content in the sense of the intentional object

Our first concept of intentional content needs no elaborate preliminaries. It concerns the intentional object, e.g. a house when a house is presented. That the intentional object does not generally fall within the real (*reellen*) content of an act, but rather differs completely from this, has been already discussed. This is not only true of acts pointing intentionally to 'outer' things; it is also true in part of acts that point to our own present experiences, as when I speak of, e.g., my actually present, but 'background' conscious experiences. Partial coincidence is only found where an intuition actually points to something 'lived through' in the intentional act itself, as, e.g., in acts of adequate perception.

We must distinguish, in relation to the intentional content taken as object of the act, between *the object as it is intended*, and the *object* (period) *which* is intended. In each act an object is presented as determined in this or that manner, and as such it may be the target of varying intentions, judgemental, emotional, desiderative etc. Known connections, actual or possible, entirely external to the reality of the act, may be so cemented with it in intentional unity as to be held to attribute objective properties to the same presented object, properties not in the scope of the intention in question. Many new presentations may arise, all claiming, in virtue of an objective unity of knowledge, to be presenting the same object. In all of them the object *which* we intend is the same, but in each our intention differs, each means the object in a different way. The idea, e.g., of the German Emperor, presents its object as an Emperor, and as the Emperor of Germany. The man himself is the son of the Emperor Frederick III, the grandson of Queen Victoria, and has many other properties neither named nor presented. One can therefore quite consistently speak of the intentional and extra-intentional content of the object of some presentation, and one can use many other suitable, non-technical expressions, e.g. what we intend in the object, that would not lead to misunderstandings.

Another, yet more important, distinction goes with the distinction just drawn, that between *the objective reference of the act, taken in its entirety*, and the *objects to which its various partial, constituent acts refer*. Each act has its own appropriate, intentional, objective reference: this is as true of complex as of simple acts. *Whatever the composition of an act out of partial acts way be, if it is an act at all, it must have a single objective correlate*, to which we say it is 'directed', in the *full, primary* sense of the world. Its partial acts (if they really are acts entering the complex act as parts, and not mere parts *of* this act) likewise point to objects, which will, in general, not be the same as the object of the whole act, though they may occasionally be the same. In a *secondary* sense, no doubt, the whole act may be said to refer to these objects also, but its intention only terminates on them inasmuch as its constituent acts primarily intend them. Or, seen from the other side, they are only the act's objects in so far as they help to make up its true object, in the manner in which this is intended. They function as terms of relations in which the primary object is seen as the correlated term. The act, e.g., corresponding to the name 'the knife on the table' is plainly complex: the object of the whole act is a knife, of one of its part-acts, a table. But, as the whole nominal act refers to the knife as on the table, presents it in this relative position to the latter, one can say that the table is in a secondary sense an intentional object of the whole act. Again, to illustrate another important class of cases, the knife is the object *about* which we judge or make a statement, when we say that the knife is on the table; the knife is not, however, the primary or full object of the judgement, but only the object of its subject. The full and entire object corresponding to the whole judgement is the *state of affairs* judged: the same state of affairs is presented in a mere presentation, wished in a wish, asked after in a question, doubted in a doubt etc. The wish that the knife were on the table, which coincides (in object) with the judgement, is concerned with the knife, but we don't in it wish the knife, but that the knife should be on the table, that this should be so. The state of affairs must obviously not be confused with the judging of it, nor with the presentation of this judgement: I plainly do not wish for a judgement, nor for any presentation. Just so there is a corresponding question regarding the knife, but the knife is not (nonsensically) what we ask; we ask regarding the knife's position on the table, whether this actually is the case.

So much for the first sense in which we speak of intentional contents. Since such talk is so highly ambiguous, we shall do well never to speak of an intentional content where an intentional object is meant, but to call the latter the intentional object of the act in question.

§18 Simple and complex, founding and founded acts

We have so far only learnt to attach one meaning to the term 'intentional contents'. Further meanings will develop in our ensuing investigations, where we shall attempt to seize on certain important peculiarities of the phenomenological essence of acts, and to throw light on the ideal unities rooted in these.

We start with the difference, previously noted, between simple and compound acts. Not every unitary experience compounded out of acts is for that reason a *compound* act, just as every concatenation of machines is not a compound machine. Our comparison illuminates our further requirements. A compound machine is a machine compounded out of machines, but so compounded, that it has a total performance into which the performances of the partial machines flow, and the like is the case in regard to compounded acts. Each partial act has its particular intentional reference, each its unitary object, and its way of referring to it. These manifold part-acts are, however, summed up in one total act, whose total achievement lies in the unity of its intentional reference. To this the individual acts contribute their individual performances: the unity of what is objectively presented, and the whole manner of the intentional reference to it, are not set up *alongside* of the partial acts, but *in* them, in the way in which they are combined, a way which realizes a unity of *act*, and not merely a unity of experience. The object of this total act could not appear as it does, unless the partial acts presented their objects in their fashion: their general function is to present parts, or to present externally related terms, or to present relational forms of the object etc. The same is true of the non-presentative aspects of the act that make out of the unified qualities in the partial acts the quality of whole acts, and so determine the specifically different ways in which the objects concerned in either sort of act are 'taken up into consciousness'.

We may take as an example the unity of categorical or hypothetical predication, where the total acts are plainly put together out of partial acts. The subject-member of a categorical assertion is an underlying act, a positing of a subject, on which the positing of a predicate, its attribution or denial, reposes. Just so the antecedent of a hypothetical assertion is constituent in a clearly demarcated part-act, upon which the conditional assertion is built. The total experience is in each case plainly one act, one judgement, whose single, total object is a single state of affairs. As the judgement does not exist alongside of, or between, the subject-positing and the predicating acts, but exists in them as their dominant unity, so, on the correlative side, the objective unity is the state of affairs judged, an appearance emergent out of subject and predicate, or out of antecedent and consequent.

The situation may be yet more complex. On such a structured act (whose members may themselves be further structured) a new act may be built, e.g. a joy may be built on the assertion of a state of affairs, a joy *in* that state of affairs. The joy is not a concrete act in its own right, and the judgement an act set up beside it: the judgement rather underlies the joy, fixes its content, realizes its abstract possibility for, without some such foundation, there could be no joy at all.[27] Judgements may similarly serve as foundations for surmises, doubts, questions, wishes, acts of will etc., and the latter acts may likewise serve to found other acts in their turn. There are therefore manifold ways in which acts may be combined into total acts. The briefest consideration makes plain that there are deep differences in the ways in which acts are concretely woven into other acts, or based upon underlying acts, and made possible by such concretion: the systematic investigation of such ways, even in descriptive, psychological fashion, is as yet hardly in its beginnings.

§20 The difference between the quality and the matter of an act

We now turn from the distinction between the acts in which we 'live' and the acts which proceed 'on the side', to another extremely important, seemingly plain distinction lying in a quite different direction. This is the distinction between the general act-character, which stamps an act as merely presentative, judgemental, emotional, desiderative etc., and its 'content' which stamps it as presenting *this*, as judging *that* etc. etc. The two assertions '2 × 2 = 4' and 'Ibsen is the principal founder of modern dramatic realism', are both, *qua* assertions, of one kind; each is qualified as an assertion, and their common feature is their *judgement-quality*. The one, however, judges one content and the other another content. To distinguish such 'contents' from other notions of 'content' we shall speak here of the *matter* (material) of judgements. We shall draw similar distinctions between *quality* and *matter* in the case of all acts.

Under the rubric of 'matter' we shall not divide, and then reassemble in unity, constituents of an act such as the subject-act, the predicate-act etc.: this would make the unified total content the act itself. What we here have in mind is something totally different. Content in the sense of 'matter' is a component of the concrete act-experience, which it may share with acts of quite different quality. It comes out most clearly if we set up a series of identical utterances, where the act-qualities change, while the matter remains identical. All this is not hard to provide. We recall familiar talk to the effect that *the same content* may now be the content of a mere presentation, now of a judgement, now of a question, now of a doubt, a wish etc. etc. A man who frames the presentation 'There are intelligent beings on Mars' frames the same presentation as the man who asserts 'There are intelligent beings on Mars', and the same as the man who asks 'Are there intelligent beings on Mars?', or the man who wishes 'If only there are intelligent beings on Mars!' etc. etc. We have deliberately written out the closely correspondent expressions in full. To be alike in 'content', while differing in act-quality has its visible grammatical expression; the harmony of grammatical forms points the way to our analysis.

What do we mean by the 'same content'? Plainly the intentional objectivity of the various acts is the same. One and the same state of affairs is presented in the presentation, put as valid in the judgement, wished for in the wish, asked about in the question. This observation does not, however, go far enough, as we shall now show. In real (*reell*) phenomenological treatment, objectivity counts as nothing: in general, it transcends the act. *It makes no difference what sort of being we give our object, or with what sense or justification we do so, whether this being is real* (real) *or ideal, genuine, possible or impossible, the act remains 'directed upon' its object.* If one now asks how something non-existent or transcendent can be the intentional object in an act in which it has no being, one can only give the answer we gave above, which is also a wholly sufficient one. The object is an intentional object: this means there is an act having a determinate intention, and determinate in a way which makes it an intention towards this object. This 'reference to an object' belongs peculiarly and intrinsically to an act-experience, and the experiences manifesting it are by definition intentional experiences or acts.[28] *All differences in mode of objective reference are descriptive differences in intentional experiences.*

We must note, however, that this peculiarity revealed in the phenomenological essence of acts, of directing themselves to a *certain* object and not another, will not exhaust the phenomenological essence in question. We spoke of differences in mode of objective reference, but this lumps together totally distinct, independently variable differences. Some are differences in *act-quality*, as when we speak of such different ways of being intentional as being presented, being judged, being asked etc. Such variation intersects with the *other*, wholly independent variation in objective reference: one act may point to this, another to that object, regardless as to whether the acts are alike or different in quality. *Every quality can be combined with every objective reference.* This second variation therefore points to a second *side in the phenomenological content of acts, differing from their quality.*

In the case of this latter variation, which concerns the changing direction to objects, one does not speak of different 'manners of objective reference', though the differentia of this direction lies in the act itself.

Looking more closely, we see another possibility of variation independent of quality which certainly prompts talk of different ways of referring to objects. We see, too, that the twofold variation just distinguished is not quite in a position to effect a neat separation of what must be defined as 'matter' from quality. Our distinction posited two sides in every act: its quality, which stamped it as, e.g., presentation or judgement, and its matter, that lent it direction to an object, which made a presentation, e.g., present *this* object and no other. This is quite right, and yet is to some extent misleading. For one is at first tempted to interpret the situation simply: matter is that part of an act which gives it direction to this object and no other. Acts are therefore unambiguously determined by their quality, on the one hand, and by the object they will intend, on the other. This seeming obviousness is, however, delusive. One can readily see, in fact, that *even if quality and objective direction are both fixed at the same time, certain variations remain possible.* Two identically qualified acts, e.g. two presentations, may appear directed, and evidently directed, to the same object, without full agreement in intentional essence. The ideas *equilateral triangle* and *equiangular triangle* differ in content, though both are directed, and evidently directed, to the same object: they present the same object, although 'in a different fashion'. The same is true of such presentations as *a length of a + b units* and *a length of b + a units*; it is also true of statements, in other respects synonymous, which differ only in 'equivalent' concepts. The same holds if we compare other types of equivalent assertions, e.g. *We shall have rain* and *The weather is becoming rainy.* If we consider a series of acts like the judgement *It will rain today*, the surmise *It may well rain today*, the question *Will it rain today?* and the wish *Oh that it would rain today!*, we see that it exemplified identity not only as regards objective reference in general, but also *as regards a new sense of objective reference*, a sense not fixed by the quality of the act.

Quality only determines whether what is already presented *in definite fashion* is intentionally present as wished, asked, posited in judgement etc. The matter, therefore, must be *that element in an act which first gives it reference to an object, and reference so wholly definite that it not merely fixes the object meant in a general way, but also the precise way in which it is meant.*[29] The matter – to carry clearness a little further – is that peculiar side of an act's phenomenological content that not only determines *that* it grasps the object but also *as what* it grasps it, the properties, relations, categorial forms, that it itself attributes to it. It is the act's matter that makes its object count as this object and no other, it is *the objective, the interpretative sense (Sinn der gegenständlichen Auffassung, Auffassungssinn)* which serves as basis for the act's quality (while indifferent to such qualitative differences). Identical matters can never yield distinct objective references, as the above examples prove. Differences of equivalent, but not tautologically equivalent expressions, certainly affect matter. Such differences must not be thought to correspond to any fragmentation of matter: there is not one piece of matter corresponding to an identical object, another to the differing mode of presenting it. Reference to objects is possible *a priori* only as being a definite manner of reference: it arises only if the matter is fully determined.

To this we may add an observation: act-quality is undoubtedly *an abstract aspect of acts*, unthinkable apart from all matter. Could we hold an experience possible which was a judging without definite subject-matter? This would take from the judgement its character as intentional experience, which is evidently part of its essence.

The same holds of matter. A matter that was not matter for presentation, nor for judgement, nor for . . . etc. etc., would be held to be unthinkable.

Talk about the manner of objective reference is ambiguous: at times it points to differences of quality, at times to differences of matter. We shall henceforth counteract such ambiguity by suitable locutions involving the terms 'quality' and 'matter'. That such talk has yet other important meanings will appear in due course. [Cf. the enumeration in *Inv* VI, §27 below.]

§21 The intentional and the semantic essence

We shall postpone investigation of the difficult problems here involved, to treat of a new distinction, in which a new concept of intentional content arises, which has to be separated off from the full descriptive content of the act.

In each act's descriptive content we have distinguished quality and matter as two mutually dependent aspects. If both are taken together, it would at first seem, the act in question will merely have been reconstituted. Looked at more closely, however, another conception distinguishes itself from whose point of view *the two aspects, brought to unity, do not make up the concrete, complete act*. Two acts may in fact agree in respect of their quality and their matter, and yet differ descriptively. In so far as quality and matter now count for us (as will be shown later) as the wholly essential, and so never to be dispensed with, constituents of an act, it would be suitable to call the union of both, forming one part of the complete act, the act's *intentional essence*. To pin down this term, and the conception of the matter it goes with, we simultaneously introduce a second term. To the extent that we deal with acts, functioning in expressions in sense-giving fashion, or capable of so functioning – whether all acts are so capable must be considered later – we shall speak more specifically of the *semantic essence* of the act. The ideational abstraction of this essence yields a 'meaning' in our ideal sense.

In justification of our conceptual ruling, we may point to the following new series of identifications. We may say generally, and with good sense, that a man may, at different times, and that several men may, at the same or different times, have the same presentation, memory, expectation, perception, utter the same assertion or wish, cherish the same hope etc. etc.[30]

To have the same presentation means, but does not mean as much as, having a presentation of the same object. The presentation I have of Greenland's icy wastes certainly differs from the presentation Nansen has of it, yet the object is the same. Just so the ideal objects *straight line* and *shortest line* are identical, but the presentations – 'straight' being suitably defined – different.

Talk about the same presentation, judgement etc. points to no individual sameness of acts, as if my consciousness were in some way conjoined with someone else's. It also means no relation of perfect likeness, of indiscernibility as regards inner constituents, as if the one act merely duplicated the other. We have the same presentation of a thing, when we have presentations in which the thing is not merely presented, but presented as exactly the same: following our previous treatment we may add 'presented with the same interpretative sense' or 'based on the same matter'. In our 'essence' we really have the same presentation despite other phenomenological differences. Such essential identity comes out most clearly when we reflect how presentations function in forming higher acts. For essential identity can be equivalently defined if we say: Two presentations are in essence the same, if exactly the same statements, and no others, can be made on the basis of either regarding the presented thing (either presentation being taken alone, i.e. analytically). The same holds in regard to other species of acts. Two judgements are essentially the same judgement when (in virtue of their content alone) everything that the one judgement tells us of the state of affairs judged, would also be told us by the other, and nothing more is told us by either. Their truth-value is identical, and this is clear to us when 'the' judgement, the intentional essence uniting judgement-quality and judgement-matter, is the same.

Let us now be quite clear that *the intentional essence does not exhaust the act phenomenologically*. An imaginative presentation, qualified *as* merely imaginative, is unessentially altered in manner, if the fullness and vividness of the sensuous contents helping to build it up is increased or decreased, or, objectively put, if the object now appears with greater clearness and definiteness, now becomes lost in a mist, now becomes paler in colour etc. Whether or not one here assumes intensive differences, whether one concedes or denies a basic likeness between the sensory phantasms here present and the sensational elements in perception, all this makes little difference to the absolute qualities, forms etc. of the act, in so far as the act's intention, its *meaning*, stays unchanged, identically determined (identity of matter). We attribute these changes, not to the object, but to its 'appearance'; we 'mean' the object as constant and persistent, and we 'mean' this in merely 'feigning' fashion (identity of quality). As opposed to this, the *matter* of a unitary presentation changes if its object is given as changing (despite any overreaching form of unity to which the intentional object's identity-in-variety corresponds). The same is true when new features enrich our conception of an object, which is constantly before consciousness, features not previously part of the object's intentional content, of the object of our presentation as such.

The case of perception is similar. If many persons share the 'same' percept, or repeat a previous one, we have merely an identity of matter, of intentional essence, which does not at all exclude change in the descriptive content of the experience. The same holds of the variable part played, or that can be played, by imagination in perception, in the putting of a perceived object before us. Whether or not images of the back of the cigarette-box float in front of me, with this or that degree of fulness, steadiness and vividness, is quite irrelevant to the essential content, the interpretative sense of my percept, to that side of it, in short which, suitably understood, explains and justifies talk of the 'same percept' in opposition to a multiplicity of phenomenologically distinct perceptual acts. In each of such cases the object is presupposed as identical, is seen clothed with the same array of properties: it is 'meant' or 'apprehended' and posited in perceptual fashion.

A percept may, further, have the same matter as a flight of fancy: the latter may present an object or state of affairs in imagination as being 'just the same' as it is perceptually apprehended in the percept. Nothing may be objectively ascribed in the one case which is not likewise ascribed in the other. Since the *quality* of the presentation may be identical (e.g. in the case of memory), we see that the specific differences of intuitive acts do not depend on their intentional essence.

Much the same may be said of any sort of act. Many persons cherish the *same* wish, when their optative intention is the same. This wish may in one person be fully expressed, in another unexpressed, in one person it may bring to full intuitive clarity its basic presentative content, in another it may be more or less 'notional' etc. In each case the identity of essence plainly lies in the two aspects distinguished above, in an identity of act-quality and of matter. The same may be claimed for expressive acts, for the acts in particular which *lend meaning* to expressions: as said above by anticipation, their *semantic essence*, i.e. the really present (*reell*) phenomenological correlate of their meaning, coincides with their intentional essence.

We may confirm our notion of semantic essence (the act of meaning *in concreto*) by recalling the series of identities used above in Investigation I (§12) in order to draw a distinction between a unity of meaning and a unity of object, and the numerous examples of expressive experience which there illustrated our general notion of intentional essence. The identity of 'the' judgement or of 'the' statement consists in an identity of meaning repeated *as* the same in the many individual acts, and represented in them by their semantic essence. This leaves room for important descriptive difference in regard to other constituents of these acts, as we have pointed out in detail.[31]

Appendix to §11 and §20

Critique of the 'image-theory' and of the doctrine of the 'immanent' objects of acts

There are two fundamental, well-nigh ineradicable errors that have to be guarded against in the phenomenological interpretation of the relationship between act and subject:

1. The erroneous *image-theory*, which thinks it has sufficiently explained the fact of presentation – fully present in each act – by saying that: '*Outside the thing itself is there (or is at times there); in consciousness there is an image which does duty for it.*'

To this notion we must object that it entirely ignores a most weighty point: that in a representation by images the *represented* object (the original) is *meant*, and meant by way of its image as an apparent object. This representative character is, however, no 'real predicate', no intrinsic character of the object which functions as image: an object is not representative as, e.g., it is red and spherical. What therefore enables us to go beyond the image which alone is present in consciousness, and to refer to the latter *as* an image to a certain extraconscious object? To point to the resemblance between image and thing will not help. It is doubtless present, as an objective matter-of-fact, when the thing actually exists. But for consciousness, which is assumed only to possess the image,[32] this fact means nothing: it can throw no light on the essence of the representative relation to the object, to the original, which is external to itself. Resemblance between two objects, however precise, does not make the one be an image of the other. Only a presenting ego's power to use a similar as an image-representative of a similar – the first similar had intuitively, while the second similar is nonetheless *meant* in its place – makes the image *be* an image. This can only mean that the constitution of the image as image takes place in a peculiar intentional consciousness, whose *inner* character, whose *specifically* peculiar mode of apperception, not only constitutes what we call image-representation as such, but also, through its particular inner determinateness, constitutes the image-representation of this or that *definite* object. The reflective, relational opposition of image to original does not, however, point to two genuinely apparent objects in the imaginative act itself, but rather to possible cognitive consummations, which new acts must realize, both fulfilling the imaginal intention and achieving a synthesis between the image and the thing it represents. Inaccurate oppositions of inner likenesses to outer objects cannot be allowed in a descriptive psychology, and much less in a pure phenomenology. A painting only is a likeness for a likeness-constituting consciousness, whose imaginative apperception, basing itself on a percept, first gives to its primary, perceptually apparent object the status and meaning of an image. Since the interpretation of anything as an image presupposes an object intentionally given to consciousness, we should plainly have a *regressus in infinitum* were we again to let this latter object be itself constituted through an image, or to speak seriously of a 'perceptual image' immanent in a simple percept, *by way of which* it refers to the 'thing itself'. We must come to see, moreover, the general need for a constitution of presented objects *for* and *in* consciousness, in consciousness's own circle of essential being. We must realize that a transcendent object is not present to consciousness merely because a content rather similar to it simply somehow *is* in consciousness –

a supposition which, fully thought out, reduces to utter nonsense – but that all relation to an object is part and parcel of the phenomenological essence of consciousness, and can in principle be found in nothing else, even when such a relation points to some 'transcendent' matter. This pointing is 'direct' in the case of a straightforward presentation: it is mediate in the case of a 'founded' presentation, e.g. one by way of images.

One should not talk and think as if an image stood in the same relation to consciousness as a statue does to a room in which it is set up, or as if the least light could be shed on the matter by inventing a hotch-potch of two objects. One must rise to the fundamental insight that one can only achieve the understanding one wants through a phenomenological analysis of the essences of the acts concerned, which are acts of the 'imagination' in the wide, traditional sense of Kant and Hume. The essential and *a priori* peculiarity of such acts consists in the fact that in them 'an object appears', sometimes straightforwardly and directly, and sometimes as 'counting' as a 'representation by images' of an object that resembles it. Here we must not forget that the representative image, like any apparent object, is itself constituted in an act in which the prime source of its representative character is to be sought.

Our exposition extends, *mutatis mutandis*, to the theory of representation in the wider sense of a *theory of signs*. To be a sign, likewise, is no real (*real*) predicate; it requires a founded conscious act, a reference to certain novel characters of acts, which are all that is phenomenologically relevant and, in consequence of this last predicate, all that is really (*reell*) phenomenological.

2. It is a serious error to draw a real (*reell*) distinction between 'merely immanent' or 'intentional' objects, on the one hand, and 'transcendent', 'actual' objects, which may correspond to them on the other. It is an error whether one makes the distinction one between a sign or image really (*reell*) present in consciousness and the thing it stands for or images, or whether one substitutes for the 'immanent object' some other real (*reelles*) datum of consciousness, a content, e.g., as a sense-giving factor. Such errors have dragged on through the centuries – one has only to think of Anselm's ontological argument – they have their source in factual difficulties, but their support lies in equivocal talk concerning 'immanence' and the like. It need only be said to be acknowledged *that the intentional object of a presentation is the same as its actual object, and on occasion as its external object, and that it is absurd to distinguish between them.* The transcendent object would not be the object of *this* presentation, if it was not *its* intentional object. This is plainly a merely analytic proposition. The object of the presentation, of the 'intention', *is* and *means* what is presented, the intentional object. If I represent God to myself, or an angel, or an intelligible thing-in-itself, or a physical thing or a round square etc., I mean the transcendent object named in each case, in other words my intentional object: it makes no difference whether this object exists or is imaginary or absurd. 'The object is

merely intentional' does not, of course, mean that it exists, but only in an intention, of which it is a real (*reelles*) part, or that some shadow of it exists. It means rather that the intention, the reference[33] to an object so qualified, exists, but not that the object does. If the intentional object exists, the intention, the reference, does not exist alone, but the thing referred to exists also. But enough of these truisms, which so many philosophers still manage to obfuscate so completely.

What we have said above does not, of course, stop us from distinguishing, as we said previously, between the object *tout court* which is intended on a given occasion, and the object *as* it is then intended – what interpretative slant is put upon it and with what possible fulness of intuition – and in the latter case peculiar analyses and descriptions will be appropriate.

Chapter 3

The matter of the act and its underlying presentation

§22 The question of the relation between the matter and quality of an act

We wind up our general probe into the phenomenological structure of intentional experience with a discussion which throws important light on the main problems in our special field of meaning. It deals with the relation of *quality* to *matter*, and so with the sense in which each act both needs and also includes in itself a presentation which serves as its basis. We here at once come up against fundamental difficulties, scarce noticed before[1] and certainly not put into words. The gap in our phenomenological knowledge is all the more grievous since, while it remains unfilled, we can have no real insight into the essential make-up of intentional experiences, and none therefore into meanings.

Quality and matter were distinguished by us as two 'moments', two inner constituents of all acts. We did so quite properly. If, e.g., we call an experience one of 'judgement', there must be some inner determination, not some mere outwardly attached mark, that distinguishes it as a judgement from wishes, hopes and other sorts of acts. This determination it shares with all judgements: what distinguishes it from all other judgements (i.e. judgements other *in essence*) is above all its matter (disregarding certain other 'moments' to be investigated later). This matter also is an inner moment of the act. This is not so much directly apparent – quality and matter are not readily prised apart in the analysis of, e.g., an isolated judgement – but appears when we set qualitatively different acts side by side, and compare them in respect of certain correspondent identities, when we find an identical matter as a moment common to them all, much as in the sensory realm we come upon like intensities or colours. *What we only have to ask is what this identical element is and how it stands to the moment of quality.* Are we dealing with two *separate albeit abstract constituents of acts,* such as colour and shape in sensuous intuition, or are they otherwise related, as, e.g., *genus* and *differentia* etc.? This question is all the more weighty since the matter of acts is that aspect of them which gives them their *determinate objective reference*. To be as clear as one can in regard to the nature of such reference is of fundamental interest for epistemology, since all thinking takes place in acts.

§23 The view of 'matter' as a founding act of 'mere presentation'

The first answer to our question is furnished by the well-known proposition, used among others by Brentano to circumscribe his 'psychical phenomena', that each such phenomenon – in our terminology and definition *each intentional experience – is either a presentation or based upon underlying presentations*. More precisely, this remarkable proposition means that in each act the intentional object is *presented in an act of presentation*, and that, whenever we have no case of 'mere' presentation, we have a case of presentation so peculiarly and intimately inwoven with one or more further acts or rather act-characters, that the presented objects become the object judged about, wished for, hoped for etc. Such plurality of intentional reference is not achieved in a linked concomitance or sequence of acts, in each of which the object has a novel, i.e. a recurrent, intentional presence, but in a single strictly unitary act, in which a single object is only *once* apparent, but is in this single appearance the target of a complex intention. We can, in other words, interpret our proposition as saying that an intentional experience only gains objective reference by incorporating an experienced act of presentation in itself, through which *the object is presented to it*. The object would be nothing to consciousness if consciousness did not set it before itself as an object, and if it did not further permit the object to become an object of feeling, of desire etc.

These added intentional characters are plainly not to be regarded as *complete* and *independent acts*: they cannot be conceived apart from the act of objectifying presentation, on which they are accordingly based. That an object or state of affairs should be desired, without being presented in and with such desire, is not merely not the case in fact, but is entirely inconceivable, and the same holds in every similar case. The matter before us therefore claims to be *a priori*, and the proposition asserting it is a self-evident *law of essence*. The addition of, e.g., desire to some underlying presentation, is not the addition of something that exists independently, with its own independent direction to some object: we must see it as the addition of a non-independent factor, intentional no doubt as having real reference to an object, and unthinkable *a priori* without it, but only able to develop or gain such reference through intimate *liaison* with a presentation. But *this last is more than a mere act-quality*: unlike the quality of desire based upon it, it is quite capable of independent existence as a concrete intentional experience, as an act of 'mere' presentation.

We round off these explanations with an observation which must be kept in mind in future discussions: that among cases of 'mere presentation' we must include, following Brentano, all cases of mere imagination, where the apparent object has neither being nor non-being asserted of it, and where no further acts concern it, as well as all cases where an expression, e.g. a statement, is well understood without prompting us either to belief or disbelief. It is mainly by contrast with such a 'belief-character', whose addition perfects judgement, that the notion of mere presentation can be elucidated. It is well-known how important a part this contrast plays in the modern theory of judgement.

Returning to our proposition, we are tempted (as said at the beginning) to apply the principle there expressed and here set forth, to explain the relation between matter and quality. Identity of matter accompanying change of quality rests, we may say, on the 'essential' identity of the underlying presentation. Or otherwise put: acts having the same 'content', and differing only in intentional essence, inasmuch as one judges, one wishes, one doubts etc., this same content, have 'in essence' the same presentation as their basis. If this presentation underlies a judgement, it yields (in its present sense as 'matter') the content of a judgement. If it underlies a desire, it yields the content of a desire etc. etc.

We spoke of *'essentially* the same presentation'. We are not to be taken as saying that matter and underlying presentation are actually one and the same, since 'matter' is merely an abstract 'moment' in an act. In talking of 'essentially the same presentation' we rather meant, following previous discussion, presentations with one and the same matter, which may, of course, be phenomenologically differentiated by further 'moments' which have nothing to do with matter. Since quality is also the same, all these presentations have the same 'intentional essence'.

The following is the outcome: that, while every other intentional essence is a complex of quality and matter, the intentional essence of a presentation is pure matter – or is pure quality, however one may choose to call it. Otherwise put, it is only because all other acts have a complex intentional essence, and necessarily include a presentative factor among their essential constituents, that talk of the difference between quality and matter arises. The word 'matter' refers to the necessary, basic presentative constituent. In the case of simple acts, which are also *eo ipso* presentative, the whole distinction necessarily falls away. One should then say: the difference between quality and matter represents no basic difference among the kinds of abstract moments found in acts. *Matters*, treated in and for themselves, *do not differ from qualities*: they are *qualities of presentation*. What we call the intentional essence of an act is its total qualitative being: this is what is essential to it, as opposed to what varies accidentally.

The matter could also be put in the following manner:

If an act is simple, i.e. is a pure presentation, its quality coincides with what we have called its intentional essence. If it is complex – and all acts that are not mere presentations, as well as all complex presentations, belong here – its complex intentional essence is merely a complex of qualities brought together in unity, from which a unitary total quality emerges, in such a way, however, that each primitive or complex quality in the pattern, which is not itself a presentative quality, rests upon such a presentative quality, which in this function yields, or is called, the corresponding matter, or the total matter in relation to the complex total act.

§27 The testimony of direct intuition. Perceptual presentation and perception

We close our argument with the 'testimony of inner perception', which should come first in exploring controversial questions of description, though we see reason to prefer speaking of immediate intuitive analysis of the essences of intentional experiences. Such a reversal of *expository* order is permitted and in certain circumstances necessary. We wish in epistemology to render all due honour to the evidence of a rightly understood, immanent inspection of essence which is falsely credited to 'internal perception'. But this testimony, when appealed to, must be conceptually apprehended and asserted, and will thereby lose much authority and permit of well-founded doubts. Different people all appeal to such 'internal perception', and come to quite opposite results: they read different things into it or out of it. This is true in the case before us. The analyses just done enable us to recognize this fact, and to distinguish and appraise various illusions which arise in interpretations of the data of phenomenological inspections of essence. The same holds in regard to the evidence of general principles based on our inner intuition of individual cases, based on this evidence, i.e., and not on interpretative interpolations.

We said above that it was wrong to talk of 'internal perception' instead of 'immanent inspection of essences' in making the usual appeals to the 'evidence of internal perception'. For, if one examines the matter, all such appeals either serve to establish facts of essence belonging to the pure phenomenological sphere, or mere transfers of such facts to the sphere of psychological reality. Assertions of phenomenological fact can never be epistemologically grounded in *psychological experience (Erfahrung)*, nor in *internal perception* in the ordinary sense of the word, but only in *ideational, phenomenological inspection of essence*. The latter has its illustrative start in inner intuition, but such inner intuition need not be actual internal perception or other inner experience (*Erfahrung*), e.g. recollection: its purposes are as well or even better served by any free fictions of inner imagination provided they have enough intuitive clarity. Phenomenological intuition, however, as often stressed, fundamentally excludes all psychological apperception and real (*reale*) assertion of existence, all positings of psycho-physical nature with its actual things, bodies and persons, including one's own empirical ego, as well as all that transcends pure consciousness. This exclusion is achieved *eo ipso*, since the phenomenological inspection of essence, in its turning of immanent ideation upon our inner intuitions, only turns its ideating gaze on what is *proper* to the real (*reellen*) or intentional being of the experiences inspected, and only brings to an adequate focus the specific modes of experience which such individual experiences exemplify, and the *a priori* ideal laws which relate to them. It is of the greatest importance to be quite clear on this matter. Men are misled by a mere illusion when they think, in conducting epistemological discussions, or in psychological discussions which base general principles of conscious data on apodictic evidence, that the source of such evidence lies in inner experience (*Erfahrung*), and in particular in internal perception, i.e. in acts which *assert existence*. This cardinal error infects that style of psychologism which thinks it has satisfied the requirements of pure logic, ethics and epistemology and that it has gone beyond extreme empiricism, merely because it speaks of 'apodictic evidence' and even of '*a priori* insights', without ever leaving the ground of internal experience (*Erfahrung*) and psychology. It is in principle impossible to go beyond Hume in this manner, since he too acknowledges the *a priori* in the form of 'relations of ideas', and yet is so far from distinguishing in principle between inner experience (*Erfahrung*) and Ideation, that he interprets the latter nominalistically as a set of contingent facts. [Second Edition comment. *Trans.*]

Going into more detail, it is, of course, evident that each intentional experience has its basis in a presentation. It is evident that we cannot judge if the state of affairs about which we judge is not present to our minds, and the same is true of enquiring, doubting, surmising, desiring etc. But does a 'presentation' here mean what it means in other contexts? May we not be thralls to an equivocation when we expand this evidence into the principle: 'Each act-experience is either a mere presentation, or has its basis in presentations'. We are put on our guard by the fact that, if we confront our experiences in sternly descriptive fashion, we do not by any means always find it possible to analyse the acts which are not 'mere presentations' into the partial acts which supposedly make them up. Let us contrast a case where intentional reference is plainly compound, and in relation to the same matter, with one or other of our dubious cases. I cannot rejoice in anything unless what I rejoice in stands before me in the hues of existence, in the perceptual, the reminiscent, possibly also the judgemental and assertive manner. Here the compounding is indubitable. If, e.g., I see and rejoice, the act-character of my joy has its basis in a percept with its own act-character, which makes its matter into matter for my joy. The character of my joy may fall away while my percept remains unaltered. Without doubt, therefore, it forms part of the concretely complete experience of joy.

Perception offers an example of the dubious compounding of acts. Here as in all acts we distinguish between quality and matter. Comparison with a corresponding mere presentation, one, e.g., of mere imagination, shows how the same object can be present *as* the same (with the same 'interpretative sense'), and yet present in an entirely different 'manner'. In perception the object seemed to achieve full-bodied presence, to be there *in propria persona*. In the imaginative presentation it merely 'floats before us', it is 'represented' without achieving full-bodied presence. This is not, however, the difference that concerns us: ours is a difference of mere 'moments', involving neither matter nor quality, just like, e.g., the difference between perceiving and recollecting one selfsame object which is present to mind with the same interpretative sense etc. Let us therefore compare a percept with a mere presentation that corresponds to it, while *abstracting* from all such differences. On our conception, a 'matter' is abstractly common to both cases, given in each case in different fashion, and with a differing act-quality. On the other conception which we were questioning, the matter which underlies perception is itself a second act-quality, that of an underlying act of mere presentation. Does analysis reveal anything of the sort? Can we look on a percept as a compound act in which an independent act of mere presentation can be really isolated?

Perhaps someone will here point to the possibility of an exactly correspondent illusion, and will hold that, once exposed as illusion, it can be seen as the isolated mere presentation, inwrought without change into our percept and providing it with its matter. Illusion, while not recognized as illusion, was simple perception. But, later, its perceptual character, the act-quality of belief, fell away, and the mere perceptual presentation remained. The same compounding must be assumed to obtain in all percepts: everywhere the underlying perceptual presentation – whose quality forms the matter of perception – will be completed by a belief-character.

Let us discuss the matter more closely in the light of a concrete example. Wandering about in the Panopticum Waxworks we meet on the stairs a charming lady whom we do not know and who seems to know us, and who is in fact the well-known joke of the place: we have for a moment been tricked by a waxwork figure. As long as we *are* tricked, we experience a perfectly good percept: we see a lady and not a waxwork figure. When the illusion vanishes, we see exactly the opposite, a waxwork figure that only *represents* a lady. Such talk of 'representing' does not of course mean that the waxwork figure is modelled on a lady as in the same waxworks there are figure-models *of* Napoleon, *of* Bismarck etc. The percept of the wax-figure as a thing does not therefore underlie our awareness of the same figure as representing the lady. The lady, rather, makes her appearance together with the wax-figure and in union with it. Two perceptual interpretations, or two appearances of a thing, interpenetrate, coinciding as it were in part in their perceptual content. And they interpenetrate in conflicting fashion, so that our observation wanders from one to another of the apparent objects each barring the other from existence.

It can now be argued that while the original perceptual presentation does not achieve an entirely detached existence, but appears in conjunction with the new percept of the wax-figure, it does not serve to found a genuine percept: only the wax-figure is perceived, it alone is believed to be really there. The isolation is achieved after a fashion, which suffices for the present purpose. But it would only really suffice if we could truly speak of isolation in this case, if we could, in other words, assume the presentation of the lady in the second case to be really contained in the original percept of the same lady. But, when the fraud is exposed, presentation amounts to perceptual consciousness resolved in conflict. But a consciousness qualified in this fashion is naturally not part of the original percept. Certainly both have something in common: they are as like one another in our illustration, which cannot in this respect be improved upon, as percept and corresponding presentation can possibly be. Certainly both share the same *matter*, for which such far-reaching likeness is by no means needed. It is the same lady who appears on both occasions, and who appears endowed with the same set of phenomenal properties. But in the one case she stands before us as real, in the other case as a fiction, with a full-bodied appearance which yet amounts to nothing. The difference lies in the qualities of our acts. It is almost exactly as if she herself were present, a genuine, actual person: the unusual likeness in matter and other non-qualitative constituents of our acts certainly inclines us to slip from a representational into a perceptual mode of consciousness. It is only the contradiction which this tendency towards believing perception encounters, as it directs itself upon the beckoning lady, that prevents us from really yielding to it, a contradiction due to the percept of the mere wax-doll, which in part coincides with our lady and in other respects rules her out, and due especially to the note of belief which informs this latter percept. The difference is, however, plainly of a sort that excludes the thought that the presentation should be contained in the percept. The same matter is at one time matter for a percept, and at another time matter for a mere perceptual fiction, but both can evidently not be combined. A percept cannot also fictitiously construct what it perceives, and a fiction cannot also perceive what it constructs.

Descriptive analysis does not, therefore, favour the view, so obvious to many, that each percept is a compound, in which a moment of belief, the characteristic quality of perception, is imposed on a *complete* act of perceptual presentation, endowed with its own independent quality.

Chapter 4

Study of founding presentations with special regard to the theory of judgement

§32 An ambiguity in the word 'presentation', and the supposed self-evidence of the principle that every act is founded on an act of presentation

If we may take the results of our last chapter as assured, we must distinguish *two* concepts of Presentation. Presentation in Sense One is an act (or a peculiar act-quality) on a level with Judgement, Wish, Question etc. We have examples of this concept in all cases where isolated words, or where complete sentences not functioning normally, are merely understood: we understand indicative, interrogative and optative sentences without ourselves judging, asking or wishing. The same applies to any unexpressed, merely floating thoughts where no 'attitude' is taken up, or any mere imaginations etc.

In Sense Two, 'Presentation' is no act, but the matter for an act, constituting one side of the intentional essence of each complete act, or, more concretely, this matter united with the remaining moments needed for full concreteness – what we shall later call 'representation'. This 'presentation' underlies every act, and so also underlies the act of presentation (in Sense One). If this happens, the matter which can function as self-identical in acts of different sorts, is given with the peculiar act-quality of ('presentation', in a peculiar 'mode of consciousness'.

If we model the meaning of talk about acts of mere presentation on the above examples, we can in the case of such acts undoubtedly carry out a phenomenological analysis in terms of quality and matter just as we could in the case of other acts. In the case of judgement we distinguish between the specific character of conviction, and the contents of the conviction: here we distinguish between the peculiar mental state of mere understanding, pure entertainment, and the determination which lays down what we understand. The same plainly holds whatever set of examples one selects to elucidate Mere Presentation or to bring out its notion. It must always be kept in mind that our present analysis attempts no resolution of acts into parts, only a distinction of *abstract* moments or 'sides' in them. These appear as acts are compared, they are moments contained in the essence of the acts themselves, they condition the possibility of arranging acts serially according to their likeness and difference. The likeness and difference intuitively shown in such a series plainly are the 'sides' in question, e.g. quality and matter. In the same way no one can break up a motion into direction, acceleration etc.: he can only distinguish these properties in it.

That each intentional experience is either itself a (mere) presentation, or is based on such a presentation, is a proposition that our previous investigations have shown to have a merely *pretended self-evidence*. The mistake rested on the just discussed ambiguity of 'presentation'. In its first half, the proposition, correctly interpreted, speaks of 'presentation' in the sense of a certain *sort of act*, in its second half in the sense of the mere *matter of acts* (completed in the manner indicated above). This second half by itself, i.e. *every intentional experience is based on a presentation*, has genuine self-evidence, if 'presentation' is interpreted as completed matter. The false proposition we reject arises if 'presentation' is here given the sense of an act as well.

An objection here warns us to take care. Is there only one way in which 'presentation' can be interpreted as an act? The questionable proposition perhaps admits of other interpretations which are not open to our objection. In that case our treatment would be right as regards the concept of presentation taken over from ordinary explanations of the word, but not right in regard to other concepts of presentation, nor to the consequently arising new interpretations of our proposition, with its ever shifting senses.

Further contributions to the theory of judgement. 'Presentation' as a qualitatively unitary genus of nominal and propositional acts

§37 The aim of the following investigation. The concept of an objectifying act

The investigations just completed have not done with the question raised at the beginning of §34 (excised from this edition). Our result was that presentations and judgements are essentially different acts. Since the ambiguity of words again needs the help of standard-setting concepts, we mean by 'presentations' nominal acts, and by 'judgements' assertions that are normally performed and complete. Naming and asserting do not merely differ grammatically, but 'in essence', which means that the acts which confer or fulfil meaning for each, differ in *intentional essence*, and therefore in *act-species*. Have we thereby shown that presentation and judgement, the acts which lend meaning and semantic fulfilment to naming and assertion, belong to different *basic classes* of intentional experience?

Obviously our answer must be negative: nothing points to such a thing. We must recall that intentional essence is made up of the two aspects of *matter* and *quality*, and that a distinction of 'basic class' obviously relates only to act-qualities. We must further recall that our exposition does not at all entail that nominal and propositional acts *differ in quality*, much less that they differ *generically* as regards quality.

This latter point should not arouse objection. The matter of acts is in our sense no alien, external attachment, but an internal moment, an inseparable side of the act-intention, of the intentional essence itself. Talk about the differing 'ways of consciousness', in which we can be aware of the same state of affairs, should not mislead us. It points to a distinction of acts, but not one of act-qualities. Quality may remain identical – so much has guided us since we formed the Idea of matter – while the same object remains differently present to consciousness. One may think, e.g., of equivalent positing presentations, which point by way of differing matters to the same object. The essential change of meaning which an assertion undergoes when it passes over into the nominal (or other parallel) function, a point whose proof we found so important above, may involve no more than a *change of matter; quality or at least qualitative genus* (according to the kind of nominal modification) *may remain unchanged.*

That this describes the actual situation becomes plain if we carefully attend to the matters themselves. Completion by nominally significant articles like 'the circumstance that', 'the fact that', where a propositional meaning is made to function as subject, has been shown by the above examples to be necessary. The examples introduce us to contexts where transformed sense goes with a transfer of unchanged, essential, material content, and where, therefore, interpretative functions are present which the original assertion lacks, or for which it has substitutes. The essential moments which agree in the two cases, also undergo, as we can see in each case, a different 'categorial structuring'. One may compare, e.g., the form '*S* is *P*' with its nominal modification '*S* which is *P*'.

The following treatments will show, on the other hand, that there is a *qualitative* community between nominal and propositional acts; we shall therefore end by *demarcating yet another new concept of presentation, wider and more significant than the former*, which will give us a new, most important interpretation of the principle that each act has its basis in presentations.

To keep our present two concepts of 'presentation' apart, we shall – without making final recommendations as to terminology – speak of 'nominal acts' in the case of the narrower concept, and of 'objectifying acts' in the case of the wider. We need hardly stress, after our whole introduction of the concept of 'nominal presentation' in the last chapter, that the expression does not merely cover acts attached to nominal expressions, and conferring or fulfilling their meaning, but also all acts that function analogously, even if not performing the same grammatical role.

§38 Qualitative and material differentiation of objectifying acts

Among nominal acts we distinguish positing from non-positing acts. The former were after a fashion existence-meanings: they were either sensuous percepts, or percepts in the wider sense of pretended apprehensions of what is, or other acts which, without claiming to seize an object 'itself', in 'full-bodied' or intuitive fashion, yet refer to it as *existent*.[1] The other acts leave the existence of their object unsettled: the object may, objectively considered, exist, but it is not referred to as existent in them, it does not *count* as actual, but rather as 'merely presented'. In all this there is a law to the effect that to each positing nominal act a non-positing act, a 'mere presentation' of like matter, corresponds, and vice versa, this correspondence being understood in the sense of the ideally possible.

A certain *modification*, as we may also express the matter, makes each positing nominal act pass over into a mere presentation with like matter. We find exactly the same modification in the case of judgements. Each judgement has its modified form, an act which merely presents what the judgement takes to be true, which has an object without a decision as to truth and falsity.[2] Phenomenologically regarded, this modification of judgements is quite of the same sort as that of positing nominal acts. Judgements as *positing propositional acts* have therefore their merely presentative correlates in *non-positing propositional acts*. The corresponding acts have in both cases the same matter and a differing quality. But just as we count positing and non-positing nominal acts as *one* genus of quality, we do the same for propositional acts in regard to judgements and their modified counterparts. The qualitative differences are in both cases the same, and not to be regarded as differentiations of any higher genera of quality. To pass from the positing to the modified act is not to pass to a heterogeneous class, as in the case of passing from any nominal act to a desire or act of will. But in the passage from a positing nominal act to an act of affirmative assertion, we are not tempted to see a qualitative difference; the same holds if we compare the corresponding 'mere presentations'. Matter alone, in the sense fixed for the present investigation, constitutes both differences: it alone determines the unity of the nominal, and the unity of the propositional acts.

This suffices to mark off a comprehensive class of intentional experiences which includes all the acts hitherto dealt with in their qualitative essence, and determines the widest concept that the term 'presentation' can stand for within the total class of intentional experiences. We ourselves would like to call this qualitatively unitary class, taken in its natural width, the class of *objectifying acts*. It yields (to put the matter clearly in front of us):

1. through qualitative differentiation, the division into positing acts – acts of belief or judgement in the sense of Mill and Brentano respectively – and non-positing acts, acts 'modified' as regards positing, the corresponding 'mere presentations'. How far the concept of positing belief extends, and how it is specified, remains undetermined;

2. through differentiation of matter, it yields the difference of nominal and propositional acts, though we still must consider whether this difference is not merely one of many equally valid material differences.

A glance over the analyses of the last chapter,[3] makes us aware of the truly pervasive opposition between *synthetic, many-rayed act-unifies* and *single-rayed acts, acts which posit or entertain something in a single thesis*. We must note, however, that predicative synthesis is only an especially favoured form (or complete system of forms) of synthesis, to which other frequently inwoven forms stand opposed, e.g. the form of conjunctive or disjunctive synthesis. We have, for example, in the plural predication '*A* and *B* and *C* are *P*' a unitary predication terminating in three predicative layers on the same predicate *P*. 'Upon' the basic positing of *A*, the secondary positing of *B*, and the tertiary positing of *C*, the predicate *P*, kept identical throughout, is posited in a single, three-layered act. Our act of judgement is as it were articulated by a 'caesura' into a subject- and a predicate-positing, but so that the one subject-member is in its turn a unitary conjunction of three nominal members. These are united in the conjunction, but they do not come together in one nominal presentation. But it is true of the 'conjunctive' (or better 'collective') synthesis, as it is true of the predicative synthesis, that it permits of nominalization, in which case the collective object constituted by the synthesis, becomes the simply presented object of a new 'single-rayed' act, and so is made 'objective' in the pregnant sense of the word. The nominal presentation of the collection now again refers back in its own sense (in the matter from the original act that it takes over and modifies) to the matter (or the consciousness) which originally constituted it. Closer examination reveals in all synthesis what we noted in the case of the predicative synthesis – when we kept, moreover, to the basic predicative form of categorical synthesis – that we can always perform the *fundamental operation of nominalization, the transformation of many-rayed synthesis into single-rayed naming with an appropriate backward reference in our material.*

Our general treatment of ideally possible objectifying acts therefore brings us back to the basic distinction of 'thetic' and 'synthetic' acts, of 'single-rayed' and 'many-rayed' acts. The single-rayed acts are not articulate, the many-rayed acts are articulate. Each member has its objectifying quality (its peculiar stance towards being, or the corresponding qualitative modification of this stance) and its matter. The whole synthesis as a single objectifying act has likewise a quality and a matter, the latter articulate. To analyse such a whole is, on the one hand, to come upon members and, on the other, upon syntactical forms of synthesis. The members in their turn may be simple or complete. They may themselves be articulate and synthetically unified, as in our above example of the conjunctive subjects of plural predications, or as in the case of conjoined antecedents in hypothetical predications, or as in the corresponding disjunctions in either case etc.

We at length come down to simple members, *single-rayed in their objectification, but not necessarily primitive in some ultimate sense.* For such single-rayed members may still be nominalized syntheses, nominal presentations of states of affairs or *collectiva* or *disjunctiva*, whose members may again be states of affairs etc. Our matter will therefore contain *backward references* of a more or less complex sort, and therefore, in a peculiarly modified, indirect sense, *implicit* articulations and synthetic forms. If the members no longer refer back, they are also simple in this respect. This is, e.g., plainly true of all proper name-presentations, and of single-membered percepts, imaginations, etc., which are not split up by explanatory syntheses. Such wholly straightforward objectifications are free from all 'categorial forms'. Plainly the analysis of each act that is *not* straightforward in its objectifications, must pursue the series of backward references contained in its nominalizations, until it comes down upon *such straightforward act-members, simple both in form and in matter.* We may finally note that the general treatment of possible articulations and synthetic formations leads to the pure *logico-grammatical laws* discussed in our Fourth Investigation. In this respect only *matters* (objectifying act-senses) are relevant, and in these all forms of structured objectifying synthesis express themselves. Here the principle obtains that our self-contained objectifying matter (and therefore any possible non-dependent meaning) can function as a member in every synthesis of every possible form. This entails the particular principle that each such matter is either a complete propositional (predicative) matter or a possible member of such a matter. If we now bring in qualities, we can affirm the principle that, ideally regarded, any objectifying matter can be combined with any quality.

If we now look at the special difference between nominal and propositional acts, which is of such particular interest in our present Investigation, the just-mentioned possibility of combining any quality with any matter can be readily confirmed. In the analyses of previous sections, it has not been made universally plain, since we confined ourselves to modifications of the judgement, i.e. a *positing* propositional act, into a nominal act. Undeniably, however, each judgement modified into a 'mere' presentation can be transformed into a corresponding nominal act. Thus '2 × 2 = 5', uttered to express understanding and not to take up an assertive stance, can be changed into the name 'that 2 × 2 = 5'. Since 'modifications' are spoken of in the case of such transformations of propositions into names as leave qualities unaffected, i.e. in the case of mere transformations of propositional or other synthetic *matters*, it will be well to reserve the name 'qualitative modification' for the quite different type of modification which affects *qualities* (transforming of positing names and statements into non-positing ones). Where the matter, which alone gives form or underlies formal distinctions, either remains, or is meant to remain constant, where a name stays a name, a proposition a proposition, in all their internal articulations and forms, we shall also have to speak of *conformative modifications* of positing acts. But if the notion of conformative modification is widened, by a natural extension, so as to cover *every modification not affecting act-material*, then (as we shall presently see) it will be a *wider* notion than our present concept of qualitative modification.

§39 Presentation in the sense of an objectifying act, and its qualitative modification

When we grouped objectifying acts into a single class, we were decisively moved by the fact that this whole class is characterized by one qualitative opposition: just as there is a 'merely presentative' counterpart to each nominal belief, so there is one in the case of each propositional belief, each complete judgement. We may now doubt, however, whether this qualitative modification really characterizes a *class*, whether it does not rather govern the whole sphere of such experiences, and provide a basis for dividing them.

An obvious argument favours this last: there is a mere presentation corresponding to every intentional experience, to a wish the mere idea of a wish, to a hate the mere idea of a hate, to a volition the mere idea of willing etc. – just as there are mere presentations corresponding to actual cases of naming and assertion.

One should not, however, mix up quite different things. To each possible act, to each possible experience, to each possible object in general, there is a presentation which relates to it, and which can as readily be qualified as positing as non-positing (as 'mere' presentation). Fundamentally, however, we have not here one, but a whole multitude of presentations of different sorts: this is true even if we restrict ourselves (as we would seem tacitly to have done) to presentations of nominal type. Such a presentation can present its object intuitively or notionally, directly or by way of attributes, and can do so very differently. But it suffices for our purposes to speak of *one* presentation, or to high-light any one variety of presentation, e.g. the imaginative, since all varieties of presentation are in each case and in the same way possible.

To each object, therefore, corresponds the presentation of that object, to a house the presentation of a house, to a presentation the presentation of the presentation, to a judgement the presentation of a judgement etc. Here we must note, however, as indicated above, that the presentation of the judgement is not the presentation of the state of affairs judged. Just so, more generally, the presentation of a positing is not the presentation of the positingly presented object. Different objects are presented in each case. The will, e.g., to realize a state of affairs, differs from the will to realize a judgement or the nominal positing of this state of affairs. A positing act's qualitative counterpart corresponds to it in quite different fashion from the fashion in which its presentation, or any act's presentation, corresponds to that act. *Modifying an act qualitatively is quite a different 'operation', as it were, from producing a presentation 'of' this act.* The true difference between these operations comes out in the fact that the *operation of presentative objectification*, shown symbolically in the sequence O, $P(O)$, $P(P(O))$ . . . where O is any object and $P(O)$ its presentation, admits of iteration, *whereas qualitative modification does not*, and in the further fact that *presentative objectification applies to all objects whatever, whereas qualitative modification only makes sense in the case of acts*. It also comes out in the fact that, in the one order of modifications, 'presentations' are exclusively *nominal*, whereas the other order is not so restricted, and in the further fact that, in the first order, *qualities remain irrelevant*, and modification only affects *matters*, whereas, in the other order of modification, it is precisely *quality* that is modified. Each act of belief has a 'mere presentation' as its counterpart, which presents the same object in precisely the same manner, i.e. on the ground of the same matter, and only differs from the former act in that it leaves the presented object *in suspense*, and does not refer to it positively as existent. Such a modification can of course not be repeated, as little as it makes sense in the case of acts not ranged under the notion of belief. It therefore creates a quite peculiar connection between acts of this quality and their counterparts. A positing percept or recollection, e.g., has its counterpart in a corresponding act of 'mere' imagination having the same matter, as in, e.g., the intuitive percept of an image, the consideration of a painting that we allow to influence us purely artistically, without in any way responding to the existence or non-existence of what is represented, or the intuition of some mental picture where we drop all stances towards existence and lose ourselves in fantasy. 'Mere' presentation has here no further counterpart: it is unintelligible what such a presentation could mean or achieve. If belief has been transformed into mere presentation, we can at best *return* to belief: There is no modification that can be repeated in the *same* sense, and carried on further.

The case is different if we pass from the operation of qualitative modification to that of nominalizing, presentative objectification. Here there is an evident possibility of iteration. This is most simply shown in the relation of acts to the ego, and their division among different persons and points of time. At one time I perceive something, at another I present to myself that I am perceiving it, at yet another I present to myself that I am presenting to myself that I am perceiving it etc.[4] Or another example: *A* is painted, a second painting represents the first painting, a third the second etc. The differences are obvious in these cases, and they are of course not merely differences in sense-contents, but in the interpretative act-characters (and their intentional 'matters') without which it would be quite senseless to talk of mental images, paintings etc. These differences are immanently apprehended, are *phenomenologically* certain, as soon as the corresponding experiences have been had, and their intentional differences reflected upon. This happens, e.g., when a man draws distinctions and says: I am now perceiving *A*, picturing *B*, while *C* is represented in this painting etc. A man who has become clear regarding these relations, will not fall into the error of those who think *presentations of presentations* phenomenologically undiscoverable, in fact mere *fictions*. Such judgements confuse the two operations distinguished here: they substitute the presentation *of* a mere presentation for the utterly impossible qualitative modification of this presentation.

We may now, it seems, assume a community of *kind*[5] among qualities coordinated by conformative modification, and may think it true that one or other of these qualities pertains to all acts, entering essentially into the unitary structure of each qualitatively unmodified or modified judgement, whether we consider acts of mere significant intention or acts which fulfil meaning. It is obvious, further, that the mere presentations of any act whatever, which we distinguished above from the qualitative counterparts possible only in the case of positing acts, are, as mere presentations, themselves qualitative counterparts, but not to their acts of origin, which are rather their presented objects. The mere presentation of a wish is no counterpart of a wish, but of any positing act, e.g. a percept, directed upon this wish. This pair, percept and mere presentation of a wish, are of one kind, whereas the wish and its percept or imagination or any other presentation which relates to it, differ in kind.

§40 Continuation. Qualitative and imaginative modification

One is readily led to call positing acts *affirmative* (*fürwahrhaltende*), their counterparts *imaginative*. Both expressions have at first blush their objections, which especially impede the terminological fixation of the latter. The discussion of these objections will prompt us to make certain not unimportant additions.

The whole tradition of logic only speaks of affirmation in the case of judgements, i.e. the meanings of statements, but now we wish to call all percepts, recollections, anticipations, and all acts of normally expressed positing, 'affirmations'. The word 'imagination', likewise, normally means a non-positing act, but we should have to extend its original meaning beyond the sphere of sensuous imagination, so as to cover all possible counterparts of affirmations. Its meaning will also require restriction, since we must exclude all thought of imaginations as conscious fictions, as objectless presentations or false opinions. Often enough we understand narrations without decision as to their truth or falsity. Even when we read novels, this is normally the case: we know we are dealing with aesthetic fictions, but this knowledge remains inoperative in the purely aesthetic effect.[6] In such cases all expressions express non-positing acts, 'imaginings' in the sense of our proposed terminology, both in respect of significant intentions and of fancied fulfilments. This also affects complete assertions. Judgements are passed in a certain manner, but they lack the character of genuine judgements: we neither believe, deny or doubt what is told us – mere 'imaginings' replace genuine judgements. Such talk must not be taken to mean that *imagined judgements here take the place of actual ones*. We rather enact, instead of a judgement affirming a state of affairs, the *qualitative* modification, the neutral putting in suspense of the same state of affairs, which cannot be identified with any picturing of it.

The name 'imagination' has an inconvenience which seriously blocks its use as a term: it suggests an imaginative or fanciful conception, pictorial in the stricter sense, while we can by no means say that *all non-positing acts involve imagining*, and that *all positing acts are non-imagining*. This last is immediately clear. A pictured sensuous object can as readily come before us posited as existent, as merely imagined in modified fashion. This can be so, while the representative content of its intuition remains identical, the content which not merely gives the intuition its determinate relation to *this object*, but also the character of imaginative, i.e. of fanciful or pictorial representation, of it.

The phenomenal content of a painting, with its painted figures etc., remains, e.g., the same, whether we regard these as representing real objects, or allow them to influence us aesthetically without positing anything. It is most doubtful whether anything similar occurs in its purity in normal perception: whether perception can preserve the rest of its phenomenological features, but be qualitatively modified, so as to lose its normal positing character. It may be doubted whether the characteristic perceptual view of the object as *itself* present in full-bodied reality, would not at once pass over into a picture-view, where the object, much as in the case of normal perceptual picture-consciousness (paintings and the like) appears portrayed rather than as itself given. Yet one might here point to many sensible appearances, e.g. stereoscopic phenomena, which one can treat, like aesthetic objects, as 'mere phenomena', without adopting an existential stance, and yet treat as 'themselves', and not as portraits of something else. It suffices that perception can pass over into a corresponding picturing (an act with like 'matter' differently interpreted) yet without change in its positing character.

We see that two conformative modifications may here be distinguished: one *qualitative* and one *imaginative*. In both the 'matter' remains unchanged. But with matter unchanged, more than quality can alter in an act. Quality and matter we took to be absolutely essential to acts, since inseparable from them, and relevant to their meaning, but we originally pointed out that other aspects could be distinguished in them. Our next investigation will show more precisely the relevance of these last two distinctions between non-intuitive objectification and intuition, and between perception and imagination.

When the descriptive relations are clarified, it is plainly a purely terminological issue whether one limits the word 'judgement', in the sense of tradition, to the unmodified meaning of statements, or applies it throughout the sphere of acts of belief. In the former case no 'ground-class' of acts, not even a lowest qualitative difference, is completely covered, since the 'matter' – which for us covers the 'is not' as well as the 'is' – assists in the demarcation. All this is, however, irrelevant. Since 'judgement' is a logical term, it is for logical interests and logical tradition alone to decide what concept will be its meaning. It has to be said, in this connection, that a notion so fundamental as that of an (ideal) propositional meaning, being the ultimate point of unity to which all things logical must relate, must retain its natural, traditional expression. The term 'act of judging' must therefore be confined to corresponding types of act, to the significant intentions behind complete statements, and to the fulfilments which fit in with these and share their semantic essence. To call all positing acts 'judgements' tends to obscure the essential distinction, despite all qualitative community, between nominal and propositional acts, and so to confuse an array of important relationships. The case of the term 'presentation' resembles that of the term 'judgement'. Logical requirements must decide what logic is to mean by it. Heed must be paid to the (mutually) exclusive separation of presentation and judgement, and to the fact that a 'presentation' claims to be something from which a complete judgement may possibly be built up. Shall one then accept the notion of presentation, as comprehending *all possible part-meanings of logical judgement*, which Bolzano made basic for his treatment of *Wissenschaftslehre*? Or shall one limit one's notion to what are, phenomenologically speaking, relatively independent meanings of this type, complete members of judgements and, in particular, *nominal acts*? Or shall one not follow another route of division, and treat as presentations the mere *representations*, i.e. the total content of all acts that survives the abstraction of quality, and only preserves the 'matter' out of their intentional essence? These are difficult questions which can certainly not be decided here.

§41 New interpretation of the principle that makes presentations the bases of all acts. The objectifying act as the primary bearer of 'matter'

Several thinkers in olden and more modern times have interpreted the term 'presentation' so widely as to include 'affirmative' acts, particularly judgements, as well as 'merely presentative' acts, in its purview, and so to include in this *the whole sphere of objectifying acts*. If we now base ourselves on this important concept which sums up a closed class of quality, our proposition regarding basic presentations gains a highly significant, novel sense – as pointed out above – of which the former sense based on the nominal concept of presentation, is merely a secondary offshoot. For we may say: *Each intentional experience is either an objectifying act or has its basis in such an act*, i.e. it must, in the latter case, contain an objectifying act among its constituents, whose total matter is individually the same as *its* total matter. What we previously said,[7] in expounding the sense of this as yet unclarified proposition, can now be practically used word for word in justification of the term 'objectifying act'. If no act, or act-quality, not objectifying by nature, can acquire 'matter' except through an objectifying act that is inwoven with it in unity, objectifying acts have the unique function of first providing other acts with presented objects, to which they may then refer in their novel ways. The reference to an object is, in general terms, constituted in an act's 'matter'. But all matter, according to our principle, *is the matter of an objectifying act*, and only through the latter can it become matter for a new act-quality founded upon this. We must after a fashion distinguish between *secondary* and *primary intentions*, the latter owing their intentionality to their foundation on the former. Whether primary objectifying acts are of a positing, affirming, believing character, or of a non-positing, merely presenting, neutral character, does not affect this function. Many secondary acts invariably require affirmations, as, e.g. joy and sorrow: for others mere modifications suffice, e.g. for wishes or aesthetic feelings. Quite often there is a complex underlying objectifying act, including acts of both sorts.

Summing-up of the most important ambiguities in the terms 'presentation' and 'content'

§44 'Presentation'

In the last chapter we have encountered a fourfold or fivefold ambiguity attaching to the word 'presentation'.

1. Presentation as *act-material* or *matter*, which can be readily completed into: Presentation as the *representation* underlying the act, i.e. the full content of the act exclusive of quality. This concept also played a part in our treatment, though our special interest in the relation between quality and matter made it important for us to lay special stress on the latter. The matter tells us, as it were, what object is meant in the act, and in what sense it is there meant. 'Representation' brings in the additional moments lying outside of the intentional essence which determine whether the object is referred to in, e.g., a perceptually intuitive or imaginatively intuitive fashion, or in a merely non-intuitive mode of reference. Comprehensive analyses will be devoted to all this in the first section of the next Investigation.

2. Presentation as 'mere presentation', as qualitative modification of any form of belief, e.g. as *mere* understanding of propositions, without an inner decision leading to assent or dissent, surmise or doubt etc.

3. Presentation as *nominal act*, e.g. as the subject-presentation of an act of assertion.

4. Presentation as *objectifying act*, i.e. in the sense of an act-class necessarily represented in every complete act since every 'matter' (or 'representation') must be given primarily as the matter of such an act. This qualitative ground-class includes acts of belief, whether nominal or propositional, as well as their counterparts, so that all presentations in the second and third of our above senses are included here.

The more precise analysis of these concepts of presentation or the experiences they comprise, and the final determination of their mutual relations, will be a task for further phenomenological investigations. Here we shall only try to add some further equivocations to those affecting the term under discussion. To keep them sharply apart is of fundamental importance in our logical and epistemological endeavours. The phenomenological analyses indispensably needed to resolve these equivocations, have only been partially encountered in our previous expositions. What is missing has, however, often been touched upon, and indicated to an extent that makes a brief list of headings possible. We therefore continue our enumeration as follows:

5. Presentation is often opposed to mere thinking. The same difference is then operative that we also call the difference between *intuition* and *concept*. Of an ellipsoid I have a presentation, though not of a surface of Kummer: through suitable drawings, models or theoretically guided flights of fancy I can also achieve a presentation of the latter. A round square, a regular icosahedron[1] and similar *a priori* impossibilia are in this sense 'unpresentable'. The same holds of a completely demarcated piece of a Euclidean manifold of more than three dimensions, of the number π, and of other constructs quite free from contradiction. In all these cases of non-presentability 'mere concepts' are given to us: more precisely, we have nominal expressions inspired by significant intentions in which the objects of our reference are 'thought' more or less indefinitely, and particularly in the indefinite attributive form of *an A* as the mere bearer of definitely named attributes. To mere thinking 'presentation' is opposed: plainly this means the intuition which gives fulfilment, and adequate fulfilment, to the mere meaning-intention. The new class of cases is favoured because in it 'corresponding intuitions' are added member by member and from all sides to thought-presentations – whether these are purely symbolic meaning-intentions or fragmentarily and inadequately mixed with intuitions – presentations which leave our deepest cognitive cravings unsatisfied. What we intuit stands *before our eyes in perception or imagination* just as we intended it in our thought. To *present something to oneself means therefore to achieve a corresponding intuition of what one merely thought of or what one meant but only at best very inadequately intuited.*

6. A very common concept of presentation concerns the opposition of *imagination* to perception. This notion of presentation dominates ordinary discourse. If I see St Peter's Church, I do not have an 'idea', a presentation of it. But I do have the latter, when I picture it in my memory, or when it stands before me in a painting or drawing etc.

7. A presentation has just been identified with the *concrete act of imagination*. But, looked at more narrowly, a physical thing-image is also called a presentation or representation of what it depicts, as, e.g., in the words 'This photograph represents St Peter's Church'. The word 'presentation' is also applied to the apparent image-object, in distinction from the image-subject or thing represented. This is here the thing appearing in photographic colours, not the photographed church (image-subject), and it only presents (represents) the latter. These ambiguities carry over into the straightforward pictured presence of *memory* or *mere imagination*. The appearance of the fancied object as such in experience is naïvely interpreted as the real containment of an image in consciousness. What appears, in its mode of

appearing, counts as an inner picture, like a painted picture presenting the imagined object. In all this it is not realized that the inner 'picture' is *intentionally* constituted, and that so is the way in which it and other possible pictures present one and the same thing, and that it cannot be counted as a real moment in the imaginative experience.[2]

8. In all cases of this ambiguous talk of presentation, where a picturing relation is supposed, the following thought also seems active. A very inadequate picture 'represents' a thing and also recalls it, is a sign of it, and this last in the sense that it is able to introduce a direct presentation of it that is richer in content. A photograph recalls an original, and also is its representative, in a manner its surrogate. Its pictorial presentation makes many judgements possible, that would otherwise need a basis in a percept of the original. A sign remote in content from a thing often fulfils similar functions, e.g. an algebraic symbol. It arouses the presentation of what it stands for, even if this is something non-intuitive, an integral etc.; it turns our thought towards this, as when we represent to ourselves the complete definitory sense of the integral. At the same time, the sign functions 'representatively', surrogatively, in a context of mathematical operations: one operates with it in additions, multiplications etc., as if the symbolized were directly given in it. Previous discussions have shown this mode of expression to be rather crude,[3] but it expresses the governing notion in our use of 'presentation', which here means representation in *the double sense of provoking presentations and doing duty for them*. Thus the mathematician drawing on the blackboard says: 'Let OX represent (present) the asymptote of the hyperbola', or, calculating, 'Let x represent (present) the root of the equation $f(x) = O$'. A sign, whether it depicts or names, is called the 'representation' ('presentation') of what it stands for.

Our present talk of representation (which we do not wish to erect into a fixed terminology) relates to *objects*. These 'representative objects' are constituted in certain acts, and acquire a representative character for *new objects* in certain new acts of transcendent (*hinausdeutenden*) presentation. Another, more primitive sense of 'representation' was mentioned under (1): this made 'representatives' experienced contents receiving an objectifying *interpretation* in such representation, and in this manner helping to present objects, without becoming objective themselves.

This leads to a new ambiguity.

9. The distinction between *perception* and *imagination* (which latter itself shows important descriptive differences) is always confused with the distinction between *sensations* and *images*. The former is a distinction of acts, the latter of non-acts, which receive interpretation in acts of perception or imagination. (If one wishes to call *all* contents which are in this sense 'representative', 'sensations', we shall have to have the distinct terms 'impressional' and 'reproductive sensations'.) If there are essential descriptive differences between sensations and images, if the usually mentioned

differences of liveliness, constancy, elusiveness etc., are sufficient, or if a varying mode of consciousness must be brought in, cannot be discussed here. Anyhow we are sure that possible distinctions of content do not make up the difference between *perception* and *imagination*, which analysis shows, with indubitable clarity, to be a difference of acts *qua* acts. We cannot regard what is descriptively given in perception or imagination as a mere complex of experienced sensations or images. The all too common confusion between them is, however, grounded in the fact that at one time a 'presentation' is understood as an imaginative idea (in the sense of (6) and (7)), at another time as a corresponding image (the complex of representative contents or imagery), so that a new ambiguity arises.

10. The confusion between an appearance (e.g., a concrete imaginative experience or a 'mental picture'), and what appears in it, leads us to call the presented object a presentation (idea). This applies to perceptions, and generally to presentations in the sense of mere intuitions or logically interpreted intuitions, e.g. 'The world is my idea'.

11. The notion that all conscious experiences (contents in the real (*reellen*)[4] phenomenological sense) are 'in consciousness', in the sense of inner perception or some other inner orientation (consciousness, original apperception), and that with this orientation a presentation is *eo ipso* given (consciousness or the ego represents the content to itself), led to all contents of consciousness being called 'presentations'. These are the 'ideas' of the English empiricist philosophy since Locke. (Hume calls them 'perceptions'.) *To have an experience and to experience a content*: these expressions are often used as equivalent.

In logic it is very important to separate the specifically logical concepts of presentation (idea) from other concepts of it. That there are several such concepts has already been indicated in passing. We may again mention one not included in our list so far, Bolzano's notion of the 'presentation in itself', which we interpreted as equal to every independent or dependent part-meaning within a complete assertion.

In connection with all purely logical concepts of presentation, we must, on the one hand, distinguish the ideal presentation from the real (*realen*)[4] one, e.g. the nominal presentation in the purely logical sense and the *acts* in which it is realized. And, on the other hand, we must distinguish between the mere *meaning-intentions* and the experiences which fulfil them more or less adequately, i.e. presentations in the sense of intuitions.

13. Beside the aforementioned ambiguities, whose danger is obvious to all who seriously absorb themselves in the phenomenology of the thought-experiences, there are others which are in part less important. We may for instance mention talk of presentation (idea) in the sense of Opinion (δόξα). This is an ambiguity which arose through gradual transformations as occurs in all similar terms. I recall the verbally manifold, but always equivalent phrases: It is a widely held opinion, idea, view, conception etc.

§45 The 'presentational content'

Expressions correlative to 'presentation' naturally have a correspondent ambiguity. This is particularly the case in regard to talk about 'what is presented in a presentation', i.e. about the 'content' of a presentation. That a mere distinction between content and object of presentations, like the one recommended by Twardowski following Zimmerman, will not remotely suffice – however meritorious it may have been to dig down to any form-differences in this field – is clear from our analyses up to this point. In the logical sphere – to which these authors limit themselves without being aware of their limitation – there is not *one* thing which can be distinguished as 'content' from the *object named*; there are several things which can and must be so distinguished. Above all, we can mean by 'content', in the case, e.g., of a nominal presentation, its *meaning* as an ideal unity: the presentation in the sense of pure logic. To this corresponds, as a real (*reelles*) moment in the *real* (*reellen*) *content* of the presentative act, the *intentional essence* with its presentative quality and matter. We can further distinguish, in this real (*reellen*) content, the separable contents not belonging to the intentional essence: the 'contents' which receive their interpretation in the act-consciousness (in the intentional essence), i.e. the *sensations* and *images*. To these are again added, in the case of many presentations, variously meant differences of *form* and *content*: particularly important is here the difference of *matter* (in a totally new sense) and *categorial form*, with which we shall have to concern ourselves a great deal. With this is connected the by no means univocal talk concerning the *content of concepts*: content = sum total of 'properties', in distinction from their mode of combination. How dubious 'blanket' talk about 'content' can be, when we merely oppose act, content and object, is shown by the difficulties and confusions into which Twardowski fell, and which have in part been exposed above. We may point particularly to his talk of 'presentative activity moving in two directions', his complete ignoring of meaning in the ideal sense, his psychologistic elimination of plain differences of meaning by recourse to etymological distinctions and, lastly, his treatment of the doctrine of 'intentional inexistence' and the doctrine of universal objects.

Note. In recent times a view has often been expressed which denies the difference between presentation and presented content, or at least denies its phenomenological ostensibility. One's attitude to this rejection naturally depends on one's interpretation of the words 'presentation' and 'content'. If these are interpreted as the mere having of sensations and images, and the phenomenological moment of interpretation is ignored or discounted, it is right to deny a distinct act of presentation: presentation and presented are one and the same. The mere having of the content, as a mere experiencing of an experience, is no intentional experience, directing itself upon an object by way of an interpretative sense: it is, in particular, not an introspective percept. For this reason we identified a sensation with a sensational content. But can anyone doubt, once he has distinguished the various concepts of presentation, that a concept so delimited is impossible to sustain, and has arisen merely through a misinterpretation of original, intentional notions of presentation? However the notion of presentation is defined, it is universally seen as a pivotal concept, not only for psychology, but also for epistemology and logic, and particularly for pure logic. A man who admits this, and yet bases himself on the above rejection, has *eo ipso* involved himself in confusion. For this concept has no part to play in epistemology and pure logic.

Only through this confusion can I explain how a thinker as pentrating as v. Ehrenfels, on occasion maintained (*Zeitschr. f. Psychologie u. Physiologie der Sinnesorgane, XVI*, 1898) that we cannot dispense with a distinction between act and content of presentation since without it we should be unable to state the psychological difference between the presentation of an object *A*, and the presentation of a presentation of this object. For the rest, he informs us, he has no direct assurance of the existence of such a phenomenon. I myself should say that an act of presentation is as such directly intuited, precisely where this distinction between a presentation and a presentation of this presentation is *phenomenologically* drawn. Were there no such cases, no earthly argument could possibly provide an indirect justification of the distinction in question. Just so, I believe, we have directly established the existence of an act of presentation in becoming clear as to the difference between a mere sound-pattern and the same pattern understood as a name etc.

Foreword to the Second Edition (1921)

The present new edition of the final part of my *Logical Investigations* does not correspond, unfortunately, with the notice in the Preface added in 1913 to the first volume of the Second Edition. I was forced to a decision to publish the old text, only essentially improved in a few sections, instead of the radical revision of which a considerable portion was already in print at the time. Once again the old proverb came true: that books have their destinies. The exhaustion naturally consequent on a period of overwork first forced me to interrupt the printing. Theoretical difficulties that had made themselves felt as the printing progressed, called for revolutionary transformations of the newly planned text, for which fresher mental powers were necessary. In the war years which followed, I was unable to muster, on behalf of the phenomenology of logic, that passionate engagement without which fruitful work is impossible for me. I could only bear the war and the ensuing 'peace' by absorption in the most general philosophical reflections, and by again taking up my works devoted to the methodological and material elaboration of the Idea of a phenomenological philosophy, to the systematic sketch of its foundations, to the arrangement of its work-problems and the continuation of such concrete investigations as were in these connections indispensable. My new teaching activity at Freiburg favoured a direction of my interest to dominant generalities and to system. Only very recently have these systematic studies led me back into the territories where my phenomenological researches originated, and have recalled me to my old work on the foundations of pure logic which has so long awaited completion and publication. Divided as I am between intensive teaching and research, it is uncertain when I shall be in a position to adapt my old writings to the advances since made, and to recast their literary form. It is also uncertain whether I shall use the text of the Sixth Investigation for this purpose, or shall give my plans, whose content already goes far beyond the text, the form of an entirely new book.

As things stand, I have yielded to the pressures of the friends of the present work, and have decided to make its last part once more accessible, at least in its old form.

The First Section, that I could not revise in detail without endangering the style of the whole, I have allowed to be reprinted practically *verbatim*. But in the Second Section on *Sense and understanding* by which I set particular store, I have, on the other hand, continually intervened to improve the form of the text. I remain of the opinion that the chapter on 'Sensuous and categorial intuitions', together with the preparatory arguments of the preceding chapters, has opened the way for a phenomenological clarification of *logical* self-evidence (and *eo ipso* of its parallels in the axiological and practical sphere). Many misunderstandings of my *Ideas towards a Pure Phenomenology* would not have been possible had these chapters been attended to. Quite obviously, the *immediacy* of the vision of universal essences spoken of in the *Ideas*, implies, like the immediacy of any other categorial intuition, an opposition to the mediacy of a non-intuitive, e.g. an emptily symbolic thought. But people have substituted for *this* immediacy, the immediacy of intuition in the ordinary sense of the word, just because they were unacquainted with the distinction, fundamental to any theory of reason, of sensible and categorial intuition. I think it shows something about the contemporary state of philosophical science that straightforward statements of such incisive meaning, presented in a work that for nearly two decades has been much attacked, but also much used, should have remained without noticeable literary effect.

The position is similar in the case of the textually improved chapter on 'The *A priori* laws of authentic and inauthentic thinking'. It at least offers a blueprint for the first radical worsting of psychologism in the theory of Reason. This blueprint makes its 'breakthrough' within the framework of an Investigation exclusively concerned with formal logic, and is therefore restricted to the Reason of formal logic. With how little deep attention this chapter is read, is shown by the often heard, but to my mind grotesque reproach, that I may have rejected psychologism sharply in the first volume of my work, but that I fell back into psychologism in the second. It does not affect what I have said to add that, after twenty years of further work, I should not write at many points as I then wrote, and that I do not approve of much that I then wrote, e.g. the doctrine of categorial representation. Nonetheless, I think I can say that even the immature and misguided elements in my work deserve a close pondering. For everything and all that is there said, derives from a research which actually reaches up to the things themselves, which orients itself towards their intuitive self-givenness, and which also has that eidetic-phenomenological attitude to pure consciousness through which alone a fruitful theory of reason becomes possible. Anyone who here, as also in the *Ideas*, wishes to grasp the *sense* of my arguments, must not be afraid of considerable efforts, including the efforts of 'bracketing' his own notions and convictions upon the same, or the putatively same, themes. These efforts are demanded by the nature of the things themselves.

One who is not afraid, will find sufficient opportunity for improving on my positions and, if he cares to, for censuring their imperfections. Only if he entrenches himself in a superficial reading drawn from an extra-phenomenological sphere of thought, will he refuse to attempt this, if he is not to be disavowed by all who truly understand the matter. How readily many authors employ critical rejections, with what conscientiousness they read my writings, what nonsense they have the audacity to attribute to me and to phenomenology, are shown in the *Allgemeine Erkenntnislehre* of Moritz Schlick. On page 121 of this work it is said that my *Ideas* 'asserts the existence of a peculiar intuition, that is *not a real psychical act*, and that if someone fails to find *such an "experience", which does not fall within the domain of psychology*, this indicates that he has not understood the doctrine, that he has not yet penetrated to the correct attitude of experience and thought, for this requires "peculiar, strenuous studies"''. The total impossibility that I should have *been able* to utter so insane an assertion as that attributed to me by Schlick in the above italicized sentences, and the falsity of the rest of his exposition of the meaning of phenomenology, must be plain to anyone familiar with this meaning. Of course I have always repeated my demand for 'strenuous studies'. But not otherwise than, e.g., the mathematician demands them of anyone who wishes to *share in talk* of mathematical matters, or who even presumes to criticize the value of mathematical science. In any case, to devote less study to a doctrine than is necessary to master its meaning, and yet to criticize it, surely violates the eternal laws of the literary conscience. No amount of learning in natural science or psychology or historical philosophies, will make it unnecessary to make these efforts in penetrating into phenomenology, or can do more than lighten them. Everyone, however, who has made these efforts, and who has risen to a very seldom exercised lack of prejudice, has achieved an indubitable certainty regarding the givenness of its scientific *foundation* and the inherent justification of the *method* demanded by it, a method which here, as in other sciences, renders possible a common set of conceptually definite work-problems, as well as definite decisions as to truth or falsehood. I must expressly observe that, in the case of M. Schlick, one is not dealing with irrelevant slips, but with sense-distorting substitutions on which all his criticism is built up.

After these words of defence, I must also observe, in regard to Section 111, that I changed my position on the problem of the phenomenological interpretation of interrogative and optative sentences shortly after the first edition of the work, and that there would be no place for small revisions, which were all that could be undertaken at the time. The text therefore remained unaltered. I could be less conservative as regards the much used *Appendix* on 'External and Internal Perception'. Though the text's essential content has been preserved, it now appears in a considerably improved form.

The desideratum of an Index for the whole work could unfortunately not be realized, since my promising pupil, Dr Rudolf Clemens, who had undertaken to prepare it, had died for his country.

E. HUSSERL

Freiburg-im-Breisgau, October 1920

Elements of a phenomenological elucidation of knowledge

Introduction

Our last Investigation may have seemed at first to lose itself in remote questions of descriptive psychology: it has, however, been of considerable help in our attempted elucidation of knowledge. All thought, and in particular all theoretical thought and knowledge, is carried on by way of certain 'acts', which occur in a context of expressive discourse. In these acts lies the source of all those unities-of-validity which confront the thinker as objects of thought and knowledge, or as the explanatory grounds and principles, the theories or sciences of the latter. In these acts, therefore, lies the source, also, of the pure, universal Ideas connected with such objects, whose ideally governed combinations pure logic attempts to set forth, and whose elucidation is the supreme aim of epistemological criticism. Plainly we shall have gone far in our elucidation of knowledge, once we have established the phenomenological peculiarities of *acts* as such, that much debated, little understood class of experiences. By putting our logical experiences into this class, we shall have taken an important step towards the demarcation of an analysis which will 'make sense' of the logical sphere and of the fundamental concepts which concern knowledge. In the course of our Investigation we were led to distinguish various concepts of *content* which tend to become confusedly mixed up whenever acts, and the ideal unities pertaining to acts, are in question. Differences which had already struck us in our First Investigation, in the narrower context of meanings and of acts conferring meaning, appeared once more in a wider context and in the most general forms. Even the highly noteworthy notion of content, that of 'intentional essence', which emerged as a novel gain from our last Investigation, was not without this relation to the logical sphere: for the same series of identities, previously employed to illustrate the unity of meaning, now yielded, suitably generalized, a certain identity, that of 'intentional essence', which applied to all acts whatsoever. By thus linking up, or subordinating, the ideal unities and phenomenological characters of the logical realm, to the quite general characters and unities of the sphere of acts, we importantly deepened our phenomenological and critical understanding of the former.

The investigations carried out in the last chapter, basing themselves on the distinction of act-quality and act-material within the unity of intentional essence, again led us far into the zone of logical interest. We were forced to enquire into the relation of such intentional material to the presentational foundation essential to every act, and were compelled to hold apart several important, constantly confounded concepts of presentation, and so to work out a fundamental part of the 'theory of judgement'. Here as elsewhere a vast amount remains to be done: we have barely made a beginning.

We have not yet even been successful in our more immediate task, that of laying bare the source of the Idea of Meaning. Undeniably and importantly, the meaning of expressions must lie in the intentional essence of the relevant acts, but we have not at all considered the sorts of acts that can thus function in meaning, and whether all types of acts may not be in this respect on a level. But when we seek to tackle this question, we at once encounter – as the next paragraphs will demonstrate – *the relation between meaning-intention and meaning-fulfilment*, or to speak traditionally, and in fact ambiguously, the relation between 'concept' or 'thought' on the one hand, understood as mere meaning without intuitive fulfilment, and 'corresponding intuition', on the other.

It is most important that this distinction, touched on even in our First Investigation, should be most minutely explored. In carrying out the appropriate analyses and, in the first instance, attaching them to the simplest naming-intentions, we at once perceive that our whole treatment calls for a *natural extension and general circumscription*. The widest class of acts, in which we meet with distinctions between intention and intention-fulfilment (or intention-frustration), extends far beyond the logical sphere. This is itself demarcated by a peculiarity in the relation of fulfilment. A class of acts – those known as 'objectifying' – are in fact marked off from all others, in that the fulfilment-syntheses appropriate to their sphere have the character of *knowings*, of *identifications*, of a 'putting-together' of things congruent, while their syntheses of frustration, similarly, have the correlative character of a setting apart of things conflicting. Within this widest sphere of objectifying acts, we shall have to study *all the relations relevant to the unity of knowledge*. We shall not have to limit ourselves to the fulfilment of such peculiar meaning-intentions as attach to our verbal expressions, since similar intentions also turn up without grammatical support. Our intuitions, further, themselves mostly have the character of intentions, which both require, and very often sustain a further fulfilment.

We shall provide a phenomenological characterization of the quite general notions of *signification* and *intuition* in relation to the phenomena of fulfilment, and we shall pursue the analysis of *various sorts of intuition*, starting with sensuous intuition, an enquiry basic to the elucidation of knowledge. We shall then embark upon the phenomenology of the varying degrees of knowledge, giving clearness and definite form to a related series of fundamental epistemological concepts. Here certain novel notions of content, barely glanced at in our previous analyses, will take the centre of the stage: the concept of *intuitive content* and the concept of *representing (interpreted)* content. We shall range the notion of *epistemic essence* alongside of our previous notion of intentional essence, and within the former we shall draw a distinction between intentional quality and intentional matter, the latter being divided into *interpretative sense, interpretative form* and interpreted (apperceived, or representing) content. We shall thereby pin down the concept of *Interpretation (Auffassung)* or *Representation*, as the unity of material and representing content by way of interpretative form.

In connection with the graded transition from intention to fulfilment, we shall recognize distinctions of greater or less *mediacy in an intention itself*, which exclude straightforward fulfilment, and which require rather a graded sequence of fulfilments: this will lead to an understanding of the all-important, hitherto unclarified sense of talk about 'indirect presentations'. We then follow up the differences of greater or lesser adequacy of intention to the intuitive experiences which fuse with it, and which fulfil it in knowledge, and point to the case of an *objectively complete adequacy* of the one to the others. In this connection we strive towards an ultimate phenomenological clarification of the concepts of Possibility and Impossibility (harmony, compatibility – conflict, incompatibility), and of the ideal axioms relating to these. Bringing back into consideration the act-qualities that we have for a while neglected, we then deal with the distinction, applicable to thetic acts, of a *provisional* and a *final fulfilment*. This final fulfilment represents an ideal of perfection. It always consists in a corresponding percept (we of course take for granted a necessary widening of the notion of perception beyond the bounds of sense). The synthesis of fulfilment achieved in this limiting case is *self-evidence or knowledge in the pregnant sense of the word*. Here we have *being in the sense of truth*, 'correspondence' rightly understood, the *adaequatio rei ac intellectus*: here this *adaequatio* is itself given, to be directly seized and gazed upon. The *varying notions of truth*, which all must be built up on one single, selfsame phenomenological situation, here reach complete clearness. The same holds of the correlative ideal of imperfection and therefore of the case of *absurdity*, and as regards the 'conflict' and the non-being, experienced therewith, of falsehood.

The natural course of our Investigation, which at first only concerns itself with such intentions as are meanings, has as a consequence that our treatments all begin with the simplest meanings, and in so doing abstract from *formal differences* among such meanings. The complementary Investigations of our Second Section will then make these differences their main theme, and will at once lead to *a totally new concept of matter or material*, to a basic contrast between *sensuous stuff* and *categorial form* or – abandoning an objective for a phenomenological stance – to a contrast between *sensuous* and *categorial acts*. In close connection with this last, we have the important distinction between sensuous (real) and categorial objects, determinations, combinations etc., regarding which last it becomes clear that they can only be 'perceptually' given in acts *which are founded* upon other acts, and in the last resort, on acts of sensibility. In general we may say that the intuitive, and accordingly likewise the imaginative, fulfilment of categorial acts, is founded on acts of sense. *Mere* sense, however, never fulfils categorial acts, or intentions which include categorial forms: fulfilment lies rather, in every case, in a sensibility structured by categorial acts. With this goes an *unavoidable extension of the originally sense-turned concepts of intuition and perception*, which permits us to speak of *categorial* and, in particular, of *universal intuition*. The distinction between *sensuous* and *purely categorial* abstraction then leads to a distinction between *sensuous concepts* and *categories*. The old epistemological contrast between *sensibility* and *understanding* achieves a much-needed clarity through a distinction between straightforward or sensuous, and founded or categorial intuition. The same is true of the contrast between *thinking* and *seeing* (intuiting), which confuses philosophical parlance by confounding the relations of signification to fulfilling intuition, on the one hand, with the relations of sensuous and categorial acts, on the other. All talk of *logical form* concerns what is purely categorial in the meanings and meaning-fulfilments in question. But the 'matter' of logic, the 'intention' of terms, itself admits, through a graded superimposition of categorial intentions, of distinctions of *matter* and *form*, so that the *logical* antithesis of matter and form points the way to a readily understandable 'relativization' of our absolute distinction.

We shall end the main body of this Investigation by discussing the factors which limit freedom in the actual categorial shaping of given matter. We shall become aware of the *analytic rules of authentic thinking* which, grounded in pure categories, do not depend on the specificity of their materials. Similar factors limit thought *in the inauthentic sense*, i.e. pure acts of meaning to the extent that they might lend themselves to authentic cases of expression, resting on *a priori* principles and not dependent on subject-matters to be expressed. From this demand springs the function of the laws of authentic thinking to provide norms for our acts of mere meaning.

We raised a question at the beginning of this Investigation as to the natural circumscription of sense-giving and sense-fulfilling acts: this is answered by ranging such acts under objectifying acts, and by subdividing the latter into acts of signification and acts of intuition. Having successfully clarified the phenomenological relations which concern fulfilment, we are at last in a position to evaluate the arguments for, and the arguments against, Aristotle's view of optative and imperative sentences as special cases of predication. The last section of the present Investigation is devoted to clearing up this controversial issue.

The aims just sketched are not the final, highest aims of a phenomenological elucidation of knowledge in general. Our analyses, comprehensive as they are, leave untilled the extremely fruitful field of *mediate* thought and knowledge: the nature of *mediate* evidence, and of its correlated *idealia*, remains insufficiently illuminated. We consider, however, that our aims have not been too trivial, and we hope that we may have dug down to the genuinely first, underlying foundations of a critique of knowledge. Even such a critique demands of us an exercise of the modesty essential to all strict, scientific research. If this last aims at a real, full completion of the tasks at hand, if it has given up the dream of solving the great problems of knowledge by merely criticizing traditional philosophemes assertions or by probable argumentation, if it has at last seen that matters can be advanced and transformed only by getting to close grips with them, it must then also reconcile itself to tackling the problems of knowledge, not in their higher or their highest, and therefore their most interesting developments, but in their comparatively simplest forms, in the lowest grades of development accessible to us. That even such a modest epistemological enquiry has vastly many difficulties to surmount, that it has in fact still got all its achievements ahead of it, will become clear in the course of the ensuing analyses.

Objectifying intentions and their fulfilments: knowledge as a synthesis of fulfilment and its gradations

Chapter 1

Meaning-intention and meaning-fulfilment

§1 Whether every type of mental act, or only certain types, can function as carriers of meaning

We shall now go on with the question raised in our Introduction: whether meaning-something is exclusively the prerogative of certain restricted sorts of mental acts. It might seem at first plain that no such restrictions can exist, and that any and every act might operate in sense-giving fashion. For it seems plain that we can verbally *express* acts of every kind – whether presentations, judgements, surmises, questions, wishes etc. – and that, when we do this, they yield us the meanings of the forms of speech in question, the meanings of names, of statements, of interrogative or optative sentences etc.

The opposite view can, however, lay claim to the same obviousness, particularly in a form that restricts meanings to a single, narrow class of acts. All acts are certainly expressible, if language is sufficiently rich, each has its own appropriate speech-form: sentence-forms, e.g., differentiate themselves into indicative, interrogative, imperative etc., and among the first of these we have categorical, hypothetical, disjunctive and other sentence-forms. In each case the act, in so far as it achieves *expression* in this or that speech-form, must be known for the sort of act it is, the question as a question, the wish as a wish, the judgement as a judgement etc. This will apply also to the partial acts constitutive of such acts, in so far as these too are expressed. Acts cannot, it seems, find their own appropriate expressive forms till their form and content have been apperceived and known. The expressive role in speech lies, accordingly, not in mere words, but in *expressive acts*: these create for the correlated acts to be expressed by them a new expressive material in which they can be given *thinking expression*, the general essence of which constitutes the meaning of the speech-form in question.

A striking confirmation of this view seems to lie in the possibility of a purely symbolic functioning of expressions. The mental (*geistige*) expression, the thinking counterpart of the act to be expressed, attaches to the verbal expression, and can be brought to life by the latter even when the act itself is not performed by the person who understands the expression. We understand the expression of an act of perception without ourselves perceiving anything, of a question without ourselves asking anything etc. We experience more than the mere words, we enjoy the thought-forms or the expressions. In the opposed case, where the intended acts are themselves actually present, the expression comes to coincidence with what it has to express, the meaning which clings to the words fits itself into what it means, its thought-intention finds in the latter its fulfilling intuition.

It is plainly in close connection with these opposed viewpoints that we have the old dispute as to whether or not the peculiar forms of interrogative, optative, imperative and similar sentences are to count as statements, and their meanings as *judgements*. Aristotle's doctrine places the meaning of all complete sentences in the varied array of psychic experiences, experiences of judging, wishing, commanding and so forth. As against this, another more modern and increasingly influential doctrine locates meaning exclusively in our judgements (or in their purely presentative modifications). An interrogative sentence in a sense expresses a question, but only in so far as this question is realized to be a question, in so far as it is referred in thought to a speaker, and so judged to be *his* experience. And so similarly in other cases. Each meaning is, on this view, either a name-meaning or a propositional meaning, i.e. either the meaning of a complete indicative sentence or a possible part of such a meaning. Indicative sentences are here to be understood as predicative sentences, since judgements are, on this view, generally thought of as *predicative acts*: we shall see, however, that the controversy still has a sense even when judgements are looked on as *positing acts in general*.

To find the right stance towards the questions here raised would call for more exact discussion than the above, superficial argumentations have attempted. It will become plain, when we look at the matter more closely, that the appeals to sheer obviousness on one side or the other conceal obscurity and even error.

§2 That all acts may be expressed does not decide the issue. There are two senses to talk about expressing an act

All acts it has been agreed are *expressible*. This cannot, of course, be questioned, but it does not therefore follow, as might be surreptitiously suggested, that all acts for that reason also function as *carriers of meaning*. Talk of 'expressing' is, as we argued earlier,[1] ambiguous, and it remains so even when we connect it with the *acts* to be expressed. What are expressed may be, on the one hand, said to be the sense-*giving* acts, to which, in the narrower sense, 'voice' is given. But there are other acts which can also be said to be expressed, though this is the case, naturally, in a different sense. I refer here to the very frequent cases in which we *name acts we are now experiencing*, and through such naming manage *to say that we are experiencing them*. In this sense I 'express' a wish through the words 'I wish that . . .', a question through the words 'I am asking whether . . .', a judgement through the words 'I judge that . . .', and so on. Naturally we can pass judgement on our own inner experiences just as we can pass judgement on outward things and, when we do the former, the meanings of the relevant sentences will reside in our *judgements* upon such experiences, and not in the experiences themselves, our wishes, questions etc. Just so, the meanings of statements about external things do not reside in these things (the horses, houses etc.), but in the judgements we inwardly pass upon them (or in the presentations that help to build up such judgements). That the objects judged about in one case transcend consciousness (or purport to do so), in another case are taken to be immanent in consciousness, makes no real difference. Naturally when I express the wish that now fills me, it is concretely one with my act of judgement, but it does not really contribute to the latter. The wish is apprehended in an act of reflex perception, subsumed under the concept of wishing, and named by way of this concept and of the further determining presentation of the wish-content. Thus the conceptual *presentation* makes the same sort of direct contribution to the judgement about the wish (and the corresponding wish-*name* to the wish-statement), that the presentation of Man makes to a judgement about Man (or the name 'Man' to a statement about Man). Substitute for the subject word 'I' in the sentence 'I wish that . . .' the relevant proper name, and the sense of the sentence remains unaffected in its remaining parts. It is, however, undeniable that the wish-statement can now be understood without change of sense by someone who hears it, and can be imitatively re-judged by him, even though he *does not share the wish at all*. We see, therefore, that, even when a wish chances to form a unity with an act of judgement directed upon it, it does not really form part of the meaning of the latter. A truly sense-giving experience can never be absent if the living sense of the expression is to survive change.

It becomes clear, therefore, that the expressibility of all acts is without relevance to the question whether all acts can function in sense-giving fashion, so far, that is, as such 'expressibility' means no more than the possibility of making certain statements about such acts. For in this connection acts are just not functioning as carriers of meaning at all.

§3 A third sense of talk about the 'expression' of acts. Formulation of our theme

We have just distinguished two senses in which there can be talk about 'acts expressed'. Either they are acts in which the sense, the meaning of the relevant expression is constituted, or they are acts that the speaker attributes to himself as items in his recent experience. This latter conception may be appropriately widened. Plainly the situation that it covers would not differ in any essential respect, were an expressed act *not* to be attributed to the experiencing ego, but to other objects, and it would not differ for any conceivable form of expression that really (*reell*) named this act as something experienced, even if it did not do it so as to mark the act off as the subject- or object-member of a predication. The main point is that the act, whether directly named or otherwise 'expressed', should appear as the actually present *object of discourse* (or of the objectifying, positing activity behind discourse), whereas this is *not* the case in regard to our sense-giving acts.

There is a *third* sense of the same talk of 'expression' in which we deal, as in our second sense, with a judgement or other objectification related to the acts in question, but not with a judgement *about* the latter – not, therefore, with an objectification of these acts by way of presentations and naming-acts which refer to them; we have rather a judgement *grounded* upon such acts, which does not demand their objectification. That I express my percept of something may, e.g., mean that I attribute this or that content to it: it may also mean that I derive my judgement from my percept, that I do not merely assert but also perceive the matter of fact in question, and that I assert it as I perceive it. My judgement is not here concerned with the perceiving but with the thing perceived. By 'judgements of perception' *tout court* we generally mean judgements belonging to this last class.

In a similar manner we can give expression to other intuitive acts, whether imaginings, remembering or expectations.

In the case of utterances grounded on imagination we may indeed doubt whether a genuine judgement is present: it is in fact plain that this is *not* then present. We are here thinking of cases where we allow our imagination to 'run away' with us, and where we employ ordinary statements, appropriate to things perceived, in giving a name to what then appears to us, or of the narrative form in which story-tellers, novelists etc., 'express', not real circumstances, but the creations of their artistic fancy. As we saw in our last Investigation, we are here dealing with conformably modified acts which serve as *counterparts* which correspond to the actual judgements that might be expressed in the same words, just as intuitive imaginations correspond to perceptions, and perhaps also to rememberings and expectations. We shall leave aside all such distinctions for the present.

In connection with the above class of cases, and in connection with the thereby defined new sense of 'expressed act', we wish to make clear the whole relation between meaning and expressed intuition. We wish to consider whether such an intuition may not itself be the act constitutive of meaning, or if this is not the case, how the relation between them may be best understood and systematically classified. We are now heading towards a more general question: Do the acts which *give* expression in general, and the acts which in general are capable of *receiving* expression, belong to essentially different spheres, and thereby to firmly delimited act-species? And do they nonetheless take their tone from an overarching, unifying genus of acts, in which all acts *capable of functioning 'meaningfully', in the widest sense of the word* – whether as meanings proper, or as 'fulfilments' of meanings – can be brought together and set apart, so that all other genera of acts can *eo ipso*, in law-governed fashion, be excluded from such functions? This, we may say, is the immediate aim of our Investigation. And as our considerations advance, there will be an obvious widening of our sphere of treatment so as to render self-evident the relation of the questions here raised to a general 'sense-making' of knowledge. New and higher aims will then enter our field of view.

§4 The expression of a percept ('judgement of perception'). Its meaning cannot lie in perception, but must lie in peculiar expressive acts

Let us consider an example. I have just looked out into the garden and now give expression to my percept in the words: 'There flies a blackbird!' *What is here the act in which my meaning resides?* I think we may say, in harmony with points established in our First Investigation, that it does not reside in perception, at least not in perception alone. It seems plain that we cannot describe the situation before us as if there were nothing else in it – apart from the sound of the words – which decides the meaningfulness of the expression, but the percept to which it attaches. For we could base different statements on the *same percept*, and thereby unfold *quite different senses*. I could, e.g., have remarked: 'That is black!', 'That is a black bird!', 'There flies that black bird!', 'There it soars!', and so forth. And conversely, the sound of my words and their sense might have remained the same, though my percept varied in a number of ways. Every chance alteration of the perceiver's relative position alters his percept, and different persons, who perceive the same object simultaneously, never have exactly the same percepts. No such differences are relevant to the meaning of a perceptual statement. One may at times pay special attention to them, but one's statement will then be correspondingly different.

One might, however, maintain that this objection only showed meaning to be unaffected by such differences in *individual* percepts: it might still be held to reside in something *common* to the whole multitude of perceptual acts which centre in a single object.

To this we reply, that percepts may not only vary, but may also vanish altogether, without causing an expression to lose all its meaning. A listener may understand my words, and my sentence as a whole, without looking into the garden: confident in my veracity, he may bring forth the same judgement without the percept. Possibly he is helped by an imaginative re-enactment, but perhaps this too is absent, or occurs in so mutilated, so inadequate a form, as to be no fit counterpart of what appears perceptually, at least not in respect of the features 'expressed' in my statement.

But if the sense of a statement survives the elimination of perception, and is the same sense as before, we cannot suppose that perception is the act in which the sense of a perceptual statement, its expressive intention, is achieved. The acts which are united with the sound of our words are phenomenologically quite different according as these words have a purely symbolic, or an intuitively fulfilled significance, or according as they have a merely fancied or a perceptually realizing basis: we cannot believe that signification is now achieved in *this* sort of act, and now in *that*. We shall rather have to conceive that the function of meaning pertains in all cases to one and the same sort of act, a type of act free from the limitations of the perception or the imagination which so often fail us, and which, in all cases where an expression authentically 'expresses', merely becomes one with the act expressed.

It remains, of course, incontestable that, in 'judgements of perception', perception is internally related to our statements' sense. We have good reason to say: the statement *expresses the percept*, i.e. brings out what is perceptually '*given*'. The same percept may serve as a foundation for several statements, but, however the sense of such statements may vary, it addresses itself to the phenomenal content of perception. It is now one, now another, part of our unified, total percept – a part, no doubt, in a non-independent, attributive sense – which gives our judgement its specific basis, without thereby becoming the true carrier of its meaning, as the possibility of eliminating percepts has just shown us.

We must accordingly say: *This 'expression' of percept* – more objectively phrased, of a perceived thing as such – *is no affair of the sound of words, but of certain expressive acts*. 'Expression' in this context means verbal expression informed with its full sense, which is here put in a certain relation to perception, through which relation the latter is in its turn said to be 'expressed'. This means, at the same time, that *between* percept and sound of words another act (or pattern of acts) is *intercalated*. I call it an act, since the expressive experience, whether or not accompanied by a percept, always has an intentional direction to something objective. This mediating act must be the true giver of meaning, must pertain to the significantly functioning expression as its essential constituent, and must determine its possession of an identical sense, whether or not this is associated with a confirming percept.

The rest of our investigation will show ever more clearly that our conception is workable.

§5 Continuation. Perception as an act which determines meaning, without embodying it

We can go no further without discussing a doubt which crops up at this point. Our treatment seems to demand a definite narrowing down: it appears to cover more than can be fully justified. If perception never constitutes the full meaning of a statement grounded on perception, it seems nonetheless to make a contribution to this meaning, and to do so in cases of the sort just dealt with. This will become clearer if we slightly modify our example, and instead of speaking quite indefinitely of *a* blackbird, proceed to speak of *this* blackbird. 'This' is an essentially occasional expression which only becomes fully significant when we have regard to the circumstances of utterance, in this case to an actually performed percept. The perceived object, as it is given in perception, is what the word 'this' signifies. The present tense in the grammatic form of a verb likewise expresses a relation to what is actually *present*, and so again to perception. Plainly the same holds of our original example: to say 'There flies a blackbird' is not to say that some blackbird in general is flying by, but that a blackbird is flying by here and now.

It is clear, of course, that the meaning in question is not attached to the word-sound of 'this'; it does not belong among the meanings firmly and generally bound up with this word. We must, however, allow that the sense of a unified statement is to be found in the total act of meaning which in a given case underlies it – whether or not this may be completely expressed through the universal meanings of its words. It seems, therefore, that we must allow that perception contributes to the significant content of a judgement, in all cases where such perception gives intuitive presence to the fact to which our statement gives judgemental expression. It is of course a contribution that can perhaps also be made by other acts, in an essentially similar manner. The listener does not perceive the garden, but he is perhaps acquainted with it, has an intuitive idea of it, places the imagined blackbird and reported event in it, and so, through the mere picture-work of fantasy, achieves an understanding which follows the intention and which agrees in sense with the speaker's.

The situation permits, however, of another reading. Intuition may indeed be allowed to contribute to the meaning of a perceptual statement, but only in the sense that the meaning could not acquire a *determinate* relation to the object it means without some intuitive aid. But this does not imply that the intuitive act is itself a carrier of meaning, or that it really makes *contributions* to this meaning, contributions *discoverable* among the constituents of the completed meaning. Genuinely occasional expressions have no doubt a meaning which varies from case to case, but in all such changes a common element is left over, which distinguishes *their* ambiguity from that of a casual equivocation.[2] The addition of intuition has as effect that this common element of meaning, indeterminate in its abstraction, can determine itself. Intuition in fact gives it complete determinateness of objective reference, and thereby its last difference. This achievement does not entail that a part of the meaning must itself lie in the intuitive sphere.

I say 'this', and now mean the paper lying before me. Perception is responsible for the relation of my word to *this* object, but my meaning does not lie in perception. When I say 'this', I do not merely perceive, but a *new act of pointing (of this-meaning) builds itself on my perception, an act directed upon the latter and dependent on it, despite its difference. In this pointing reference, and in it alone, our meaning resides.* Without a percept – or some correspondingly functioning act – the pointing would be empty, without definite differentiation, impossible in the concrete. For of course the indeterminate thought of the *speaker as pointing to something* – which the hearer may entertain before he knows *what* object we wish to indicate by our 'this' – is not the thought we enact in the actual pointing, with which the determinate thought of the thing pointed to has been merely associated. One should not confuse the general character of actual pointing as such with the indefinite presentation of 'a certain' act of pointing.

Perception accordingly *realizes the possibility* of an unfolding of my act of this-meaning with its definite relation to the object, e.g. to this paper before my eyes. But it does not, on our view, itself constitute this meaning, nor even part of it.

In so far as the act-character of a pointing act is oriented to intuition, it achieves a definiteness of intention which fulfils itself in intuition, in accordance with a general feature of acts which may be called their *intentional essence*. For a pointing reference remains the same, whichever out of a multitude of mutually belonging percepts may underlie it, in all of which the same, and *recognizably* the same, object appears. The meaning of 'this' is again the same when, instead of a percept, some act from our range of imaginative presentation is substituted for it, an act presenting the same object through a picture in a recognizably identical manner. It changes, however, when intuitions from other perceptual or imaginative spheres are substituted. We are once more referring to a *this*, but the general character of the reference which obtains here, that of direct, attributively unmediated aiming at an object, is otherwise differentiated: the intention to another object attaches to it, just as physical pointing becomes spatially different with each change in spatial direction.

We hold, therefore, that *perception is an act which determines, but does not embody meaning.* This view is confirmed by the fact that essentially occasional expressions like 'this' can often be used and understood without an appropriate intuitive foundation. Once the intention to an object has been formed on a suitable intuitive basis, it can be revived and exactly reproduced *without* the help of a suitable act of perception or imagination.

Genuinely occasional expressions are accordingly much like *proper names*, in so far as the latter function with their authentic meaning. For a proper name also names an object 'directly'. It refers to it, not attributively, as the bearer of these or those properties, but without such 'conceptual' mediation, as what it *itself* is, just as perception might set it before our eyes. The meaning of a proper name lies accordingly in a direct reference-to-this-object, a reference that perception only *fulfils*, as imagination does provisionally and illustratively, but which is not identical with these intuitive acts. It is just in this manner that perception gives an object to the word 'this' (where it is directed to objects of possible perception): our reference to 'this' is fulfilled in perception, but is not perception itself. And naturally the meaning of both types of directly naming expressions has an intuitive origin, from which their naming intentions first orient themselves towards an individual object. In other respects they are different. As 'this' is infected with the thought of a pointing, it imports (as we showed) a mediation and a complication, i.e. a peculiar form absent from the proper name. The proper name also belongs as a fixed appellation to its object; to this constant pertinence corresponds something in the manner of its relation to that object. This is shown in the fact of our knowing a person or thing by name, as something *called* so-and-so: I know Hans as *Hans*, Berlin as *Berlin*. We have, in our treatment, no doubt ignored the case of all those proper names which are *significant in derivative fashion*. When proper names have once been formed in direct application (and so on a basis of intuitions which *give* things to us), we can, by employing the concept of 'being called', itself formed by reflection on the use of proper names, give proper names to objects, or take cognizance of their proper names, even though such objects are not directly given or known to us, but are only described indirectly as the bearers of certain properties. *The capital of Spain*, e.g., *is called* (i.e. has the proper name) *'Madrid'*. A person unacquainted with the town Madrid itself, thereby achieves both knowledge of its name and the power to name it correctly, and yet not thereby the individual meaning of the word 'Madrid'. Instead of the direct reference, which only an actual seeing of the city could arouse, he must make do with an indirect pointing to this reference, operating through characteristic ideas of properties and the conception of 'being called' such and such.

If we may trust our arguments, we must not only draw a general distinction between the perceptual and the significant element in the statement of perception; we must also locate *no part of the* meaning *in the percept itself.* The percept, *which presents the object, and the statement which, by way of the judgement* (or by the thought-act inwoven into the unity of the judgement) *thinks and expresses it, must be rigorously kept apart*, even though, in the case of the perceptual judgement now being considered, they stand to each other in the most intimate relation of mutual *coincidence*, or in the unity of fulfilment.

We need not dwell on the fact that a like result applies also to other intuitive judgements, and thus also to statements which, in a sense analogous to that which applies to perceptual judgements, 'express' the intuitive content of an imagination, a remembering, an expectation etc.

Addendum. In the exposition of §26 of Investigation I we began with the understanding of the hearer, and drew a distinction between the 'indicating' (*anzeigende*) and the 'indicated' (*angezeigte*) meaning of an essentially occasional expression and, in particular, of the word 'this'. For the hearer, in whose momentary field of vision the thing that we wish to point out is perhaps not present, only this indefinitely general thought is at first aroused:

Something is being pointed out. Only when a presentation is added (an intuitive presentation if the thing dealt with demands an intuitive pointing out), is a definite reference constituted for him, and so a full, authentic meaning for the demonstrative pronoun. For the speaker there is no such sequence: he has no need of the indefinitely referential idea which functions as 'index' for the hearer. Not the idea of an indication, but an indication itself, is given in his case, and it is *eo ipso* determinately directed thingward: from the first the speaker enjoys the 'indicated' meaning, and enjoys it in a presentative intention immediately oriented towards intuition. If the thing meant cannot be intuitively picked out, as in a reference to a theorem in a mathematical proof, the conceptual thought in question plays the part of an intuition: the indicative intuition could derive fulfilment from an actual re-living of this past thought. In each case we observe a *duplicity* in the indicative intention: the character of the indication seems in the first case to espouse the directly objective intention, as a result of which we have an intention directed upon a definite object that we are intuiting here and now. Our other case does not differ. If the previous conceptual thought is not now being performed, an intention which corresponds to it survives in memory; this attaches itself to the act-character of the indication, thereby lending it definiteness of direction.

What we have just said about *indicating* and *indicated meaning* can have *two* meanings. It can mean (1) the two mutually resolving thoughts which characterize the hearer's successive understanding: *first* the indeterminate idea of something or other referred to by 'this', *then* the act of definitely directed indication into which a completing presentation transforms it. In the latter act we have the indicated, in the former the indicating meaning. (2) If we confine ourselves to the complete, definitely directed indication which the speaker has from the beginning, we can again see something double about it: the general character of indication as such, and the feature which determines this, which narrows it down to an indication of 'this thing there'. The former can again be called an indicating meaning, or rather the indicating element in the indissoluble unity of meaning, in so far as it is what the hearer can immediately grasp by virtue of its expressive generality, and can use to indicate what is referred to. If I say 'this', the hearer at least knows that something is being pointed at. (Just so in the case of other essentially occasional expressions. If I say 'here', I have to do with something in my nearer or further spatial environment, etc.) On the other hand, the true aim of my talk lies not in this general element, but in the direct intending of the object in question. Towards it and its fulness of content I am directed, and these empty generalities do little or nothing towards determining the latter. In this sense a direct intention is the primary, indicated meaning.

This second distinction is the one laid down by our definition in our previous exposition. (*Inv.* I, §26). The distinctions achieved in this section, and our much clearer treatment, will probably have helped towards a further clarification of this difficult matter.

§6 The static unity of expressive thought and expressed intuition. Recognition (*das Erkennen*)

We shall now absorb ourselves in a closer investigation of the relations holding among intuitive acts, on the one hand, and expressive acts, on the other. We shall confine ourselves, in the present section entirely, to the range of the simplest possible cases, and so naturally to expressions and significant intentions which belong to the sphere of *naming*. We shall make, for the rest, no claim to treat this field exhaustively. We are concerned with nominal expressions, which refer themselves in the most perspicuous of possible fashions to 'corresponding' percepts and other forms of intuition.

Let us first glance in this field at a *relationship of static union, where a sense-giving thought has based itself on intuition, and is thereby related to its object*. I speak, e.g., of my *inkpot*, and my inkpot also stands before me: I see it. The name names the object of my percept, and is enabled to name it by the significant act which expresses its character and its form in the form of the name. The relation between name and thing named, has, in this state of union, a certain *descriptive character*, that we previously noticed: the name 'my inkpot' seems to *overlay* the perceived object, to belong *sensibly* to it. This belonging is of a peculiar kind. The words do not belong to the objective context of physical thinghood that they express: in this context they have no place, they are not referred to as something in or attaching to the things that they name. If we turn to the experiences involved, we have, on the one hand, as said before,[3] the acts in which the words appear, on the other hand, the similar acts in which the things appear. As regards the latter, the inkpot confronts us in perception. Following our repeated demonstration of the descriptive essence of perception, this means no more phenomenologically then that we undergo a certain sequence of experiences of the class of sensations, sensuously unified in a peculiar serial pattern, and informed by a certain act-character of 'interpretation' (*Auffassung*), which endows it with an objective sense. This act-character is responsible for the fact that an *object*, i.e. this inkpot, is perceptually apparent to us. In similar fashion, the appearing word is constituted for us in an act of perception or imaginative presentation.

Not word *and* inkpot, therefore, but the act-experiences just described, in which they make their appearance, are here brought into relation: in these word and inkpot appear, while yet being nothing whatever *in* the acts in question. But how does this happen? What brings these acts into unity? The answer seems clear. The relation, as one of naming, is mediated, not merely by acts of meaning, but by acts of recognition (*Erkennen*), which are here also acts of *classification*. The perceived object is *recognized* for an inkpot, known as one, and in so far as the act of meaning is most intimately one with an act of classification, and this latter, as recognition of the perceived object, is again intimately one with the act of perception, the expression seems to be *applied* to the thing and to clothe it like a garment.

Ordinarily we speak of recognizing and classifying the object of perception, as if our act busied itself with this *object*. But we have seen that there is no object in the experience, only a perception, a thus and thus determinate mindedness (*Zumutesein*): *the recognitive act in the experience must accordingly base itself on the act of perception.* One must not of course misunderstand the matter, and raise the objection that we are putting the matter as if perception was classified rather than its object. We are not doing this at all. Such a performance would involve acts of a quite different, much more complex constitution, expressible through expressions of corresponding complexity, e.g. 'the perception of the inkpot'. It follows that the recognitive experience of this thing as 'my inkpot', is nothing but a recognition which, in a definite and direct fashion, fuses an expressive experience, on the one hand, with the relevant percept, on the other.

The same holds of cases in which *picture-presentations* serve in place of percepts. The imaginatively apparent object, e.g. the identical inkpot in memory or in fancy, is felt to bear the expression which names it. This means, phenomenologically speaking, that a recognitive act in union with an expressive experience is so related to an imaginative act as to be, in objective parlance, spoken of as the recognition of an imaginatively presented object as, e.g., our inkpot. The imagined object, too, is absolutely nothing in our presentation of it, our experience is rather a certain blend of images, fancied sensations, informed by a certain interpretative act-character. To live through this act, and to have an imaginative presentation of the object, are one and the same. If we therefore express the situation in the words 'I have before me an image, the image of an inkpot', we have plainly coupled *new* acts with our expressions and, in particular, a *recognitive* act which is intimately one with our act of imagining.

§7 Recognition as a character of acts, and the 'generality of words'

The following more exact argument would seem to show conclusively that, in all cases where a name is applied to a thing intuitively given, we may presume the presence of a recognitive act-character mediating between the appearance of the word-sounds, on the one hand (or the complete sense-informed word), and the intuition of the thing on the other. One often hears of the *generality of words*, and usually understands by this highly ambiguous phrase that a word is not bound to an individual intuition, but belongs rather to an endless array of possible intuitions.

In what, however, does this belonging consist?

Let us deal with an extremely simple example, that of the name 'red'. In so far as it names an appearing object as red, it belongs to this object in virtue of the moment of red that appears in this object. And each object that bears a moment of like sort in itself, justifies the same appellation: the same name belongs to each, and does so by way of an identical sense.

But in what does this appellation by way of an identical sense consist?

We observe first that the word does not attach externally, and merely through hidden mental mechanisms, to the individual, specifically similar traits of our intuitions. It is not enough, manifestly, to acknowledge the bare fact that, wherever such and such an individual trait appears in our intuition, the word also *accompanies* it as a mere pattern of sound. A mere concomitance, a mere external going with or following on one another would not forge any internal bond among them, and certainly not an intentional bond. Yet plainly we have here such an intentional bond, and one of quite peculiar phenomenological character. The word *calls* the red thing red. The red appearing before us is what is *referred* to by the name, and is referred to as '*red*'. In this mode of naming reference, the name appears as *belonging* to the named and as *one* with it.

On the other hand, however, the word has its sense quite apart from an attachment to this intuition, and without attachment to *any* 'corresponding' intuition. Since this sense is everywhere the same, it is plain that it is not the mere phoneme, rather the true, complete word, endowed on all occasions with the constant character of its sense, that must be held to underlie the naming relation. Even then it will not be enough to describe the union of meaningful word and corresponding intuition in terms of mere concomitance. Take the word, present in consciousness and *understood as a mere symbol* without being actually used to name anything, and set the corresponding intuition beside it: these two phenomena may at once, for genetic reasons, be brought together in the phenomenological unity of naming. Their mere togetherness is, however, not as yet this unity, which *grows out of it* with plain novelty. It is conceivable, *a priori*, that no such unity should emerge, that the coexistent phenomena should be phenomenologically disjoined, that the object before us should not be the thing meant or named by the meaningful word, and that the word should not *belong* to the object as its name, and so name it.

Phenomenologically we find before us no mere aggregate, but an intimate, in fact intentional, unity: we can rightly say that the two acts, the one setting up the complete word, and the other the thing, are intentionally combined in a single *unity of act*. What here lies before us can be naturally described, with equal correctness, by saying that the *name 'red' calls the object red*, or that *the red object is recognized (known) as red, and called 'red' as a result of this recognition*. To 'call something red' – in the fully actual sense of 'calling' which presupposes an underlying intuition of the thing so called – and to 'recognize something as red', are in reality *synonymous* expressions: they only differ in so far as the latter brings out more clearly that we have here no mere duality, but a unity engineered by a single act-character. In the intimacy of this fusion, we must nonetheless admit, the various factors implicit in our unity – the physical word-phenomenon with its ensouling meaning, the aspect of recognition and the intuiting of what one names – do not separate themselves off clearly, but our discussion compels us to presume them all to be there. We shall have more to say on this point later on.

It is plain that the recognitive character of certain acts, which gives them their significant relation to objects of intuition, does not pertain to words as noises, but to words in their meaningful, their *semantic* (*bedeutungsmässigen*) essence. Very different verbal sounds, e.g. the 'same' word in different languages, may involve an identical recognitive relation: the object is essentially known for the same, though with the aid of quite different noises. Naturally the complete recognition of something red, being equivalent to the actually used name, must include the noise 'red' as a part. The members of different speech-communities feel different verbal sounds to be fitting, and include these in the unity of 'knowing something'. But the meaning attaching to such words, and the recognitive act actually attaching this meaning to its object, remains everywhere the same, so that these verbal differences are rightly regarded as irrelevant.

The 'generality of the word' means, therefore, that the unified sense of one and the same word covers (or, in the case of a nonsense-word, purports to cover) an ideally delimited manifold of possible intuitions, each of which could serve as the basis for an act of recognitive naming endowed with the same sense. To the word 'red', e.g., corresponds the possibility of both knowing as, and calling 'red', all red objects that might be given in possible intuitions. This possibility leads on, with an *a priori* guarantee, to the further possibility of becoming aware, through an *identifying synthesis* of all such naming recognitions, of a sameness of meaning of one with the other: this *A* is red, and that *A* is *the same*, i.e. *also* red: the two intuited singulars belong under the same 'concept'.

A dubious point emerges here. We said above that a word could be understood even if not actually used to name anything. Must we not, however, grant that a word must at least have the *possibility* of functioning as the actual name of something and so of achieving an actual recognitive relation to corresponding intuition? Must we not say that without such a possibility it could not be a word at all? The answer, of course, is that this possibility depends on the possibility of the recognitions, the 'knowings', in question. Not all intended knowing is possible, not all nominal meaning can be *realized*. 'Imaginary' names may be names, but they cannot *actually* be used to name anything, they have, properly speaking, no extension, they are *without generality in the sense of the possible and the true*. Their generality is *empty pretension*. But how these last forms of speech are themselves to be made clear, what phenomenological facts lie behind them, will be a matter for further investigation.

What we have said applies to *all* expressions, and not merely to such as have generality of meaning in the manner of a *class-concept*. It applies also to expressions having *individual reference*, such as proper names. The fact spoken of as the 'generality of verbal meaning' does not point to the generality accorded to generic, as opposed to individual concepts, but, on the contrary, embraces either indifferently. The 'recognition', the 'knowing', of which we speak when a significantly functioning expression encounters corresponding intuition, must not, therefore, be conceived as an actual *classification*, the ranging of an intuitively or cogitatively presented object in a *class*, a ranging necessarily based on general concepts and verbally mediated by general names. Proper names, too, have their generality, though, when actually used to name anything, they can *eo ipso* not be said to classify it. Proper names, like other names, cannot name anything, without thereby also 'knowing' it. That their relation to corresponding intuition is, in fact, as indirect as that of any other expression, can be shown by a treatment exactly analogous to the one conducted above. Each and every name obviously belongs to no definite percept, nor to a definite imagination nor to any other pictorial illustration. The same person can make his appearance in countless possible intuitions, and all these appearances have no merely intuitive but also a recognitive unity. Each appearance from such an intuitive manifold will justify a precisely synonymous use of the proper name. Whichever appearance is given, the man using the name means one and the same person or thing. And he means this not merely in being intuitively oriented to it, as when he deals with an object personally strange to him; he knows it as this definite person or thing. He knows Hans as *Hans*, Berlin as *Berlin*. To recognize a person as this person, or a city as this city, is again an act not tied to the particular sensuous content of this or that word-appearance. It is identically the same act in the case of a variety (in possibility of an infinite variety) of verbal noises, as, e.g., when several different proper names apply to the same thing.

This generality of the proper name, and of the peculiar meaning which corresponds to it, is plainly quite different in kind from that of the *general name*.

The former consists in the fact that a synthesis of possible intuitions belongs to a *single* individual object, intuitions made one by the common intentional character imparted by every relation to the same object, despite all phenomenal differences among individual intuitions. On this unified basis, the particular unity of recognitive knowing reposes, which belongs to the 'generality of verbal meaning', to its range of ideally possible realizations. In this way the naming word has a recognitive relation to a boundless multitude of intuitions, whose identical object it both knows and thereby names.

The case of the *class-name* is quite different. Its generality covers a *range of objects*, to each of which, *considered apart*, a possible synthesis of percepts, a possible individual meaning and proper name belongs. The general name 'covers' this range through being able to name each item in the whole range in general fashion, i.e. not by individually recognizing it in the manner of the proper name, but by classifying it, in the manner of the common name. The thing that is either directly given, or known in its authentic self-being (*Eigenheit*), or known through its properties, is now known as *an A* and named accordingly.

§8 The dynamic unity of expression and expressed intuition. The consciousness of fulfilment and that of identity

From the tranquil, as it were *static* coincidence of meaning and intuition, we now turn to that *dynamic* coincidence where an expression first functions in merely symbolic fashion, and then is accompanied by a 'more or less' corresponding intuition. Where this happens, we experience a descriptively peculiar *consciousness of fulfilment:*[4] the act of pure meaning, like a goal-seeking intention, finds its fulfilment in the act which renders the matter intuitive. In this transitional experience, the *mutual belongingness* of the two acts, the act of meaning, on the one hand, and the intuition which more or less corresponds to it, on the other, reveals its phenomenological roots. We experience how *the same* objective item which was 'merely thought of' in symbol is now presented in intuition, and that it is intuited as being precisely the determinate so-and-so that it was at first merely thought or meant to be. We are merely expressing the same fact if we say that *the intentional essence of the act of intuition* gets more or less perfectly *fitted into the semantic essence of the act of expression.*

In the previously considered static relation among acts of meaning and intuition, we spoke of a *recognition*, a *knowing*. This represents the sense-informed relation of the name to the intuitive datum that it names. But the element of meaning is not here itself the act of recognition. In the purely symbolic understanding of a word, an act of meaning is performed (the word means something to us) but nothing is thereby known, recognized. The difference lies, as the foregoing paragraphs have established, not in the mere accompanying presence of the intuition of the thing named, but in the phenomenologically peculiar form of unity. What is characteristic about this unity of knowing, of recognition, is now shown up by the dynamic relationship before us. In it there is at first the meaning-intention, quite on its own: then the corresponding intuition comes to join it. At the same time we have the phenomenological unity which is now stamped as a consciousness of fulfilment. Talk about recognizing objects, and talk about fulfilling a meaning-intention, therefore express the same fact, merely from differing standpoints. The former adopts the standpoint of the object meant, while the latter has the two acts as its foci of interest. Phenomenologically the acts are always present, while the objects are sometimes non-existent. Talk of fulfilment therefore characterizes the phenomenological essence of the recognitive relation more satisfactorily. It is a primitive phenomenological fact, that acts of signification[5] and acts of intuition can enter into this peculiar relation. Where they do so, where some act of meaning-intention fulfils itself in an intuition, we also say: 'The object of intuition is known through its concept' or 'The correct name has been applied to the object appearing before us'.

We can readily do justice to the obvious phenomenological difference between the static and the dynamic fulfilment or recognition. In the dynamic relationship the members of the relation, and the act of recognition which relates them, are disjoined in time: they unfold themselves in a temporal pattern. In the static relationship, which represents the lasting outcome of this temporal transaction, they occur in temporal and material (*sachlicher*) coincidence. *There* we have a first stage of mere thought (of pure conception or mere signification), a meaning-intention wholly unsatisfied, to which a second stage of more or less adequate fulfilment is added, where thoughts repose as if satisfied in the sight of their object, which presents itself, *in virtue of* this consciousness of unity, as what is thought of in this thought, what it refers to, as the more or less perfectly attained goal of thinking. In the static relationship, on the other hand, we have this consciousness of unity alone, perhaps with no noticeably marked-off, precedent stage of unfulfilled intention. The fulfilment of the intention is not here an event of self-fulfilment, but a tranquil state of being-fulfilled, not a coming into coincidence, but a being coincident.

From an objective point of view we may here also speak of a *unity of identity*. If we compare both components of a unity of fulfilment – whether treating them in dynamic transition into one another, or holding them apart analytically in their static unity, only to see them at once flowing back into one another – we assert their *objective identity*. For we said, and said with self-evidence, that the object of intuition is the *same* as the object of the thought which fulfils itself in it and, where the fit is exact, that the object is seen as being exactly the same as it is thought of or (what always says the same in this context) meant. Identity, it is plain, is not first dragged in through comparative, cogitatively mediated reflection: it is there from the start as experience, as unexpressed, unconceptualized experience. In other words, the thing which, from the point of view of our acts is phenomenologically described as fulfilment, will also, from the point of view of the two objects involved in it, the intuited object, on the one hand, and the thought object, on the other, be expressively styled 'experience of identity', 'consciousness of identity', or 'act of identification'. A more or less complete *identity* is the *objective datum which corresponds to the act of fulfilment*, which 'appears in it'. This means that, not only signification and intuition, but also their mutual adequation, their union of fulfilment, can be called an act, since it has its own peculiar intentional correlate, an objective something to which it is 'directed'. Another side of the same situation is again, we saw above, expressed in talk about *recognizing* or *knowing*. The fact that our meaning-intention is united with intuition in a fulfilling manner, gives to the *object* which appears in such intuition, when it primarily concerns us, the character of a thing known. If we try to say more exactly 'as what' we recognize something, our objective reflection points, not to our *act* of meaning (*Bedeutens*), but to the meaning (*Bedeutung*), the self-identical 'concept' itself; talk of recognition therefore expresses our view of the same unified state from the standpoint of the object of intuition (or of the fulfilling act), in its relations to the meaning-concept of the signitive act. Conversely we say, though perhaps in more special contexts, that our thought 'grasps' (*begreife*) the matter, that it is the latter's concept (*Begriff*) or 'grasp'. After our exposition it is obvious that recognition, like fulfilment – the former is in fact only another name for the latter – can be called an act of identification.

Addendum. I cannot here suppress a difficulty connected with the otherwise illuminating notion of the unity of identity or recognition, as an *act* of identification or recognition. This is particularly the case, since this difficulty will reveal itself as a serious one as our clarifications proceed and progress, and will inspire fruitful discussions. Closer analysis makes it plain that, in the cases detailed above, where a name is actually applied to an object of intuition, we refer to the intuited and named *object*, but not to the *identity* of this object, as something at once intuited and named. Shall we say that an emphasis of attention decides the matter? Or ought we not rather to grant that there is not here a fully constituted act of identification: the nucleus of this act, the connective union of significant intention and corresponding intuition is really present, but it 'represents' no objectifying interpretation (*Auffassung*). On the experienced unity of coincidence *no act of relational identification* is founded, no intentional consciousness of identity, in which identity, as a unity referred to, first gains objective status. In our reflection on the unity of fulfilment, in analysing and opposing its mutually connected acts, we naturally, and indeed necessarily, also framed that relational interpretation which the form of its union, with *a priori* necessity, permits. Our second section will deal with this question in its widest form which concerns the categorial characters of acts (see Chapter VI, §48, and the whole of Chapter VII). Meanwhile we shall continue to treat the sort of unity in question as a full act, or we shall at least not differentiate it expressly from a full act. This will not affect the essential point in our treatment, in so far as the passage from a consciousness of unity to a relational identification always remains open, has a possibility guaranteed *a priori*, so that we are entitled to say that an identifying coincidence has been *experienced*, even if there is no *conscious intention* directed to identity, and no *relational* identification.

§10 The wider class of experiences of fulfilment. Intuitions as intentions which require fulfilment

We may now further characterize the consciousness of fulfilment by seeing in it an experiential form which plays a part in many other fields of mental life. We have only to think of the opposition between wishful intention and wish-fulfilment, between voluntary intention and execution, of the fulfilment of hopes and fears, the resolution of doubts, the confirmation of surmises etc., to be clear that essentially the same opposition is to be found in very different classes of intentional experiences: the opposition between significant intention and fulfilment of meaning is merely a special case of it. We have dealt with this point previously,[6] and delimited a class of intentional experience under the more pregnant name of 'intentions': their peculiarity lies in being able to provide the basis for relations of fulfilment. In this class are ranged all the acts which are in a narrower or wider sense 'logical', including the *intuitive*, whose role it is to fulfil other intuitions in knowledge.

When, e.g., a familiar melody begins, it stirs up definite intentions which find their fulfilment in the melody's gradual unfolding. The same is the case even when the melody is unfamiliar. The regularities governing melody as such, determine intentions, which may be lacking in complete objective definiteness, but which nonetheless find or can find their fulfilments. As concrete experiences, these intentions are of course fully definite: the 'indefiniteness' of what they intend is plainly a descriptive peculiarity pertaining to their character. We may say, in fact, with correct paradox (as we did before in a similar case) that 'indefiniteness' (i.e. the peculiarity of demanding an incompletely determined completion, which lies in a 'sphere' circumscribed by a law) is a definite feature of such an intention. Such an intention has not merely a range of possible fulfilment, but imports a common fulfilment-character into each actual fulfilment from this range. The fulfilment of acts which have definite or indefinite intentions is phenomenologically different, and the same holds of fulfilments of intentions whose indefiniteness points in this or that direction of possible fulfilment.

In our previous example there is also a relation between *expectation* and *fulfilment of expectation*. It would, however, be quite wrong to think, conversely, that every relation of an intention to its fulfilment was a relationship involving expectation. *Intention is not expectancy*, it is not of its essence to be directed to future appearances. If I see an incomplete pattern, e.g. in this carpet partially covered over by furniture, the piece I see seems clothed with intentions pointing to further completions – we feel as if the lines and coloured shapes go on 'in the sense' of what we see – but we expect nothing. It would be possible for us to expect something, if movement promised us further views. But possible expectations, or occasions for possible expectations, are not themselves expectations.

The external perceptions of the senses offer us an indefinite number of relevant examples. The features which enter into perception always point to completing features, which themselves might appear in other possible percepts, and that definitely or more or less indefinitely, according to the degree of our 'empirical acquaintance' with the object. Every percept, and every perceptual context, reveals itself, on closer analysis, as made up of components which are to be understood as ranged under two standpoints of intention and (actual or possible) fulfilment. The same applies to the parallel acts of imagining and picture-thought in general. In the normal case intentions lack the character of expectancy, they lack it in all cases of tranquil perceiving or picturing, and they acquire it only when perception is in flux, when it is spread out into a continuous series of percepts, all belonging to the perceptual manifold of one and the same object. Objectively put: the object then shows itself from a variety of sides. What was pictorially suggested from one side, becomes confirmed in full perception from another; what was merely adumbrated or given indirectly and subsidiarily as background, from one side, at least receives a portrait-sketch from another, it appears perspectivally foreshortened and projected, only to appear 'just as it is' from another side. All perceiving and imagining is, on our view, a web of partial intentions, fused together in the unity of a single total intention. The correlate of this last intention is the thing, while the correlate of its partial intentions are *the thing's parts and moments*. Only in this way can we understand how consciousness reaches out beyond what it actually experiences. It can so to say mean beyond itself, and its meaning can be fulfilled.

§11 Frustration and conflict. The synthesis of distinction

In the wider sphere of the acts to which distinctions of intention and fulfilment apply, *frustration* may be set beside fulfilment, as its incompatible contrary. The negative expression that we normally use in this case, e.g. even the term 'non-fulfilment', has no merely privative meaning: it points to a new descriptive fact, a form of synthesis as peculiar as fulfilment. This is so even in the narrower case of significant intentions as they stand to intuitive intentions. The synthesis of recognition, of 'knowing', is the consciousness of a certain agreement. The possibility correlated with agreement is, however, 'disagreement' or 'conflict': intuition may not accord with a significant intention, but may 'quarrel' with it. Conflict 'separates', but the experience of conflict puts things into relation and unity: it is a form of *synthesis*. If the previously studied synthesis was one of *identification*, this new synthesis is one of *distinction* (unfortunately we possess no other positive name). This 'distinction' must not be confused with the other 'distinction' which stands opposed to a positive likening. The oppositions between 'identification and distinction' and between 'likening and distinction' are not the same, though it is clear that a close phenomenological affinity explains our use of the same word. In the 'distinction' which is here in question, the *object* of the frustrating act appears *not the same as*, '*distinct from* the object of the intending act. These distinctions point to wider classes of cases than we have hitherto preferred to deal with. Not only significative, but even intuitive intentions are fulfilled in identifications and frustrated in conflicts. We shall have to explore the whole question of the natural circumscription of the acts to which the terms 'same' and 'other' (we can as well say 'is' and 'is not') have application.

The two syntheses are not, however, completely parallel. Each conflict presupposes something which directs its intention to the object of the conflicting act; only a synthesis of fulfilment can give it this direction. Conflict, we may say, presupposes a certain basis of agreement. If I think A to be *red*, when it shows itself to be 'in fact' green, an intention to red quarrels with an intention to green in this showing forth, i.e. in this application to intuition. Undeniably, however, this can only be the case because A has been identified in the two acts of signification and intuition. Were this not so, the intention would not relate to the intuition. The total intention points to an A which is red, and intuition reveals an A which is green. It is in the coincidence of meaning and intuition in their direction to an identical A, that the moments intended in union with A in the two cases, come into conflict. The presumed red (i.e. red of A) fails to agree with the intuited green. It is through identity that such non-coincident aspects *correspond* with each other: instead of being 'combined' by fulfilment, they are 'sundered' by conflict. An intention is referred to an appropriate aspect in intuition from which it is also turned away.

What we have here said with special regard to significant intentions and the frustrations they encounter, applies also to our whole previously sketched class of objectifying intentions. We may generally say: *An intention can only be frustrated in conflict in so far as it forms part of a wider intention whose completing part is fulfilled.* We can therefore not talk of conflict in the case of simple, i.e. isolated, acts.

Indirect characterization of objectifying intentions and their essential varieties through differences in the syntheses of fulfilment

§13 The synthesis of knowing (recognition) as the characteristic form of fulfilment for objectifying acts. Subsumption of acts of meaning under the class of objectifying acts

We have, in the above treatment, classed meaning-intentions in the wider class of 'intentions' in the pregnant sense of the word. All intentions have corresponding possibilities of fulfilment (or of opposed frustration): these themselves are peculiar transitional experiences, characterizable as acts, which permit each act to 'reach its goal' in an act specially correlated with it. These latter acts, inasmuch as they fulfil intentions, may be called 'fulfilling acts', but they are called so only on account of the synthetic act of fulfilment, or rather of self-fulfilment. *Such transitional experience is not always the same in character*. In the case of meaning-intentions, and not less clearly in the case of intuitive intentions, such experiences are unities of knowing, or unities of identification in respect of their objects. This need not be so in the wider class of intentions in general. Everywhere we may speak of coincidences, and everywhere we shall meet with identifications. But the latter often depend on an inwrought act of a sort which permits of a unity of identification and also serves as the foundation of one in the contexts in question.

An example will clarify the matter. The self-fulfilment of a wish is achieved in an act which includes an identification, and includes it as a necessary component. For there is a law which ties the quality of wishing to an underlying presentation, i.e. to an objectifying act, and more precisely to a 'mere presentation', and this leads to a complementary law tying a wish-fulfilment to an underlying act, which incorporates this presentation in its identifying grasp. A wishful intention can only find its fulfilling satisfaction in so far as the underlying mere presentation of the thing wished for becomes transformed into the corresponding percept. What we have, however, is not this mere transformation, the mere fact of imagination dissolved in perception: both enter in unity into the character of an act of identifying coincidence. In this synthetic character, we have it constituted that *a thing is really and truly so* (i.e. as we had previously merely pictured and wished): this of course does not exclude the possibility that such 'really being so' is merely putative, and especially, in most cases, that it is inadequately presented. If a wish is based on a purely signitive presentation, this identification can of course involve the more special coincidence described above, in which meaning is fulfilled by an intuition that fits it. The same could plainly be said of all intentions that, as objectifying acts, are based on presentations, and what applies to fulfilment carries over, *mutatis mutandis*, to the case of frustration.

It is clear accordingly, to stick to our example, that even if the fulfilment of a wish is founded on an identification, and perhaps on an act of intuitive recognition, this latter act never exhausts the fulfilment of the wish, but merely provides its basis. The self-satisfaction of the specific wish-quality is a peculiar, act-character, different in kind. It is by a mere analogy that we extend talk of satisfaction, and even of fulfilment, beyond the sphere of emotional intentionality.

The peculiar character of an intention accordingly goes with the peculiar character of its fulfilling coincidence. Not only does *every nuance of an intention correspond to some nuance of the correlated fulfilment*, and likewise of the self-fulfilling activity in the sense of a synthetic act, but to the *essentially different classes of intention there also correspond pervasive class-differences in fulfilment* (in the twofold sense mentioned above). And obviously *the members which belong to these parallel series belong also to a single class of acts.* The syntheses of fulfilment in the case of wish- and will-intentions certainly show close affinities, and differ deeply from those occurring, e.g., in the case of meaning-intentions. On the other hand, the fulfilments of meaning-intentions and of intuitive acts are definitely of the same character, and so in the case of all acts that we classed as 'objectifying'. We may say of this class of acts which alone concerns us here, *that in them unity of fulfilment has the character of unity of identification*, possibly the narrower character of a unity of knowing, i.e. of an act to which objective identity is the corresponding correlate.

We must here emphasize the following point: As pointed out above, every fulfilment of a 'signitive' by an intuitive act has the character of a synthesis of identification. But it is not the case, conversely, that, in each synthesis of identification, a meaning-intention is fulfilled, and fulfilled by a corresponding intuition. In the widest sense, certainly, we do ordinarily speak of every actual identification as a recognition. But, in a narrower sense, what is clearly felt to be at issue is an approach to a goal of knowledge and, in the narrowest sense of a critique of knowledge, the arrival at that goal. To turn this mere feeling into clear insight, and to define the precise sense of this approach or arrival, will yet be our task. Meanwhile we shall maintain that the *unity of identification*, and thereby all *unity of knowing* in the narrower and the narrowest sense, has *its place of origin in the sphere of objectifying acts.*

Their peculiar manner of fulfilment will therefore suffice to characterize the unified class of acts to which it essentially belongs. We can accordingly *define* objectifying acts as those whose syntheses of fulfilment have a character of identification, while their synthesis of frustration has a character of distinction. We can also define them as acts which can function phenomenologically as members of possible syntheses of identification and distinction. Lastly, presuming a law as yet unformulated, we can define them as the intending, fulfilling or frustrating acts which have a possible knowledge-function. *To this class belong also the synthetic acts of identification and distinction themselves*: they are themselves either a merely *putative* grasp of identity or non-identity, or a corresponding *real* grasp of the one or the other. This putative grasp can be either 'confirmed' or 'refuted' in an act of knowing (in the pregnant sense of the word): identity is really grasped, i.e. 'adequately perceived', in the former case, as non-identity in the latter.

Our analyses have been lightly sketched rather than thoroughly executed, but they lead to the result that *both meaning-intentions and acts of meaning-fulfilment*, acts of 'thought' and acts of intuition, *belong to a single class of objectifying acts*. We establish thereby *that acts of another sort can never exercise any sense-giving function*, and that they can be 'expressed' only in so far as the meaning-intentions which attach to words are fulfilled in percepts or imaginations which have as *objects* the acts requiring expression. While, therefore, where acts function meaningfully, and achieve expression in this sense, a 'signitive' or intuitive relation to objects is constituted in them, in the other cases *the acts are mere objects*, and objects, of course, for other acts which here function as the authentic carriers of meaning.

Before we discuss this matter more closely, and seek to refute many plausible counter-arguments – see the final Section of this Investigation – we must explore the remarkable facts of fulfilment somewhat more carefully, and in the sphere of objectifying acts.

§14 Phenomenological characterization of the distinction between signitive and intuitive intentions through peculiarities of fulfilment

(a) Sign, image and self-presentation

In the course of the last discussion we have been led to note how the generic character of an intention closely coheres with that of its synthesis of fulfilment, so that the whole class of objectifying acts can be defined through the identification generically characteristic of their syntheses of fulfilment, whose nature we take to be familiar. This thought leads us on to ask whether the specific differences *within* this class of objectifications, may not likewise rest upon corresponding differences in the mode of fulfilment. Objectifying intentions are basically divided into *significative* and *intuitive* intentions: let us try to give an account of the difference between these types of act.

Since the starting point of our treatment lay in expressed acts, we took *signitive intentions* to be the significations, the meanings of expressions. If we leave aside the question whether the same acts which give sense to expressions can also function outside of the sphere of meaning, these signitive intentions always have intuitive support in the sensuous side of the expression, but not on that account intuitive *content*. Though in a manner one with intuitive acts, they yet differ from them in kind.

We can readily grasp the distinction between expressed and purely intuitive intentions if we contrast *signs* with *likenesses* or *images*.

The sign has in general no community of content with the thing it signifies; it can stand as readily for what is heterogeneous, as for what is homogeneous with itself. The likeness on the other hand is related to the thing by *similarity*: where there is no similarity, there can be no talk of a likeness, an image. The sign as object is constituted for us in an act of appearing. This act is not significant: it needs, as we held in former analyses, to be tied up with a new intention, a new way of taking things, through which a novel, signified object takes the place of the old, intuitively apparent one. The likeness similarly, e.g. the marble bust, is as much a thing as anything else: the new way of regarding it first makes it a *likeness*. Not merely a thing of marble appears before us, but we have, based on this appearance, a reference to a person through a likeness.

The intentions attaching to the phenomenal content are, in either case, not externally tied up with it, but essentially based upon it, and in such a way that the character of the intention is determined thereby. It would be a descriptively wrong notion of the matter, to think of the whole difference as lying in the fact that the same intention which, in the one case is tied to the appearance of an object *like* the object referred to, is in the other case tied to the appearance of an object *unlike* it. For the sign, too, can be like what it signifies, even entirely like it: the sign-presentation is not thereby made into a presentation by way of a likeness. A photograph of the sign A is immediately taken to be a picture of the sign. But when we use the sign A as a sign of the sign A, as when we write 'A is a letter of the Latin written alphabet', we treat A, despite its representational similarity, as a sign, and not as a likeness.

The objective fact of similarity between what appears and what is meant, is accordingly irrelevant: it is not, however, irrelevant where something is presented by way of a likeness. This shows itself in the possibility of fulfilment: it was only the recollection of this possibility which allowed us to bring in 'objective' similarity in this context. The likeness-presentation plainly has the peculiarity that, when it achieves fulfilment, the object which appears before it as likeness gets identified through similarity with the object *given* in the fulfilling act. Having held this to be the peculiarity of a presentation by way of likeness, we have admitted that *fulfilment of like by like internally fixes the character of a synthesis of fulfilment as imaginative*. But, when, on the other hand, casual likeness between sign and thing signified leads to a knowledge of their mutual resemblance, this knowledge is not at all a case of the peculiar consciousness of identity, when similar is referred to similar and made to coincide with it in the manner of likeness and original thing. It is rather of the very essence of a *significative* intention, that in it the apparent objects of intending and fulfilling acts (e.g. name and thing named in their fully achieved unity) 'have nothing to do with one another'. It is clear, therefore, that descriptively distinct modes of fulfilment, being rooted in the descriptively distinct character of our intention, can help us to detect these latter differences, and to find definitions for them.

We have so far only considered the difference between signitive and imaginative intentions. If we ignore less weighty distinctions within the wider sphere of imaginative acts – we have preferred to consider representation by way of physical images, instead of stressing those of fantasy – we must still consider the case of *percepts*.

As opposed to imagination, perception is characterized by the fact that in it, as we are wont to express the matter, the object 'itself' appears, and does not merely appear 'in a likeness'. In this we at once recognize characteristic differences in *syntheses of fulfilment*. Imagination fulfils itself through the peculiar synthesis of image-resemblance, perception through the *synthesis of identical thinghood* (*sachlichen Identität*). The thing establishes itself through its very self, in so far as it shows itself from varying sides while remaining one and the same.

(b) The perceptual and imaginative adumbration of the object

We must, however, pay heed to the following distinction. Perception, so far as it claims to give us the object 'itself', really claims thereby to be no mere intention, but an act, which may indeed be capable of offering fulfilment to other acts, but which itself requires no further fulfilment. But generally, and in all cases of 'external' perception, this remains a mere pretension. The object is not actually given, it is not given wholly and entirely as that which it itself is. It is only given 'from the front', only 'perspectivally foreshortened and projected' etc. While many of its properties are illustrated in the nuclear content of the percept, at least in the (perspectival) manner which the last expressions indicate, many others are not present in the percept in such illustrated form: the elements of the invisible rear side, the interior etc., are no doubt subsidiarily intended in more or less definite fashion, symbolically suggested by what is primarily apparent, but are not themselves part of the intuitive, i.e. of the perceptual or imaginative content, of the percept. On this hinges the possibility of indefinitely many percepts of the same object, all differing in content. If percepts were always the actual, genuine self-presentations of objects that they pretend to be, there could be only a single percept for each object, since its peculiar essence would be exhausted in such self-presentation.

We must, however, note that the object, as it is *in itself* – in the only sense relevant and understandable in our context, the sense which the fulfilment of the perceptual intention would carry out – is *not wholly different* from the object realized, however imperfectly, in the percept. It is part so-to-say of a percept's inherent sense to be the self-appearance of the object. Even if, for phenomenological purposes, ordinary perception is composed of countless intentions, some purely perceptual, some merely imaginative, and some even signitive, it yet, as a *total act*, grasps the object itself, even if only by way of an adumbration. If we may conceive of a percept put into a relation of fulfilment to the adequate percept that would *offer us the object itself*, in the ideally strict and most authentic sense, then we may say that a percept so intends its object that this ideal synthesis would have the character of a *partial coincidence* of the purely perceptual contents of intending and fulfilling acts, and also the character of a complete coincidence of both complete perceptual intentions. The 'purely perceptual' content in 'external' perception is what remains over when we abstract from all purely imaginative and symbolic components: it is the 'sensed' content to which its own, immediate, purely perceptual interpretation is given, which evaluates all its parts and moments as self-projections of corresponding parts and moments of the perceptual object, and so imparts to its total content the character of a 'perceptual picture', a perceptual adumbration of the object. In the ideal, limiting case of adequate perception, this self-presenting sensed content coincides with the perceived object. This common relation to the object 'in itself', i.e. to the ideal of adequation, enters into the sense of all perception, and is also manifest in the phenomenological mutual belongingness of the manifold percepts pertaining to a single object. In one percept the object appears from this side, in another from that side; now it appears close, now at a distance etc. In each percept, despite these differences, one and the same object is 'there', in each it is intended in the complete range of its familiar and of its perceptually present properties. To this corresponds phenomenologically a continuous flux of fulfilment or identification, in the steady serialization of the percepts 'pertaining to the same object'. Each individual percept is a mixture of fulfilled and unfulfilled intentions. To the former corresponds that part of the object which is given in more or less perfect projection in *this* individual percept, to the latter that part of the object that is not yet given, that new percepts would bring to actual, fulfilling presence. All such syntheses of fulfilment are marked by a common character: they are identifications binding self-manifestations of an object to self-manifestations of the same object.

It is at once clear that similar distinctions apply in the case of imaginative presentation. Here too the same object is pictured, now from this and now from that side. Corresponding to the synthesis of manifold perceptions, where the same object always presents *itself*, we have the parallel synthesis of manifold imaginations, in which the same object appears *in a likeness*. To the changing perceptual adumbrations of the object there are corresponding imaginative adumbrations, and in the ideal of perfect copying the projection would coincide with the complete likeness. If imaginative acts are at one time fulfilled in imaginative contexts, and at another time through corresponding percepts, the difference lies plainly in the character of their synthesis of fulfilment: the passage from likeness to likeness has a different character from the passage from likeness to original thing.

The above analysis will be of use for the further investigations to be carried on in the next chapter; they also show the mutual affinity of percepts and imaginations, and their common opposition to 'signitive' intentions. In all cases we distinguish between an actually given, appearing content, which is *not* what we mean, and an object which *is* what we mean – whether we signify, represent or perceive it – or between a sign-content on the one hand, and the imaginative or perceptual projection of the object on the other. But while sign and thing signified 'have nothing to do with one another', there are inner affinities between a thing's imaginative and perceptual projections and the thing itself, affinities which are part of the very sense of our use of such words. These relationships are phenomenologically documented in differences in their constitutive intentions, and not less in their syntheses of fulfilment.

This account does not, of course, affect our interpretation of *every* fulfilment as being an identification. *In all cases* an intention comes into coincidence with the act which offers it *fulness*, i.e. the object which is meant in it is the same as the object meant in the fulfilling act. We were not, however, comparing these objects of meaning-reference, but signs and adumbrations in their relations to such objects, or to what corresponds phenomenologically to these relationships.

Our interest in the preceding paragraphs was primarily directed to peculiarities in syntheses of fulfilment: these enable us to differentiate intuitive and signitive acts in a merely *indirect* manner. Only in the further course of our investigation – in §26 – shall we be able to give a *direct* characterization, based on an analysis of the intentions, and without regard to their possible fulfilments.

§15 Signitive intentions beyond the limits of the meaning-function

In our last discussion we have pinned down certain components of intuitive acts as signitive intentions. But in the whole of our investigations up to this point, signitive acts were for us acts of *meaning*, sense-giving factors attached to expressions. The terms 'signification' and 'signitive intention' were for us synonymous. It is now time to ask ourselves whether the same acts, or acts essentially similar to those found to function in meaning, may not occur quite divorced from this function and from all expressions.

That this question must be answered affirmatively, is shown by certain cases of wordless recognition, which exhibit the precise character of verbal recognition, although words, in their sensuous-signitive content, are not actually present at all. We recognize an object, e.g. as an ancient Roman milestone, its scratchings as weather-worn inscriptions, although no words are aroused at once, or indeed at all. We recognize a tool as a drill, but its name will not come back to us etc. Genetically expressed, present intuitions stir up an associative disposition directed to the significant expression. But the meaning-component of this last alone is actualized, and this now radiates backwards into the intuition which aroused it, and overflows into the latter with the character of a fulfilled intention. These cases of wordless recognition are none other than fulfilments of meaning-intentions, but phenomenologically divorced from the signitive contents which otherwise pertain to them. Comparable examples are furnished by reflection on the normal interweavings of scientific pondering. We observe here how trains of thought sweep on to a large extent without bondage to appropriate words, set off by a flood of intuitive imagery or by their own associative interconnections.

With this is connected the further fact that *expressive* speech goes so far beyond the intuitive data necessary for the actual appropriateness of the expression of acquaintance. This has, no doubt, an opposed ground in the extraordinary ease with which verbal images are revived by intuitions, and can themselves then revive symbolic thoughts without corresponding intuitions. But we must also observe, contrariwise, how the reproduction of imaged words often lags quite far behind the trains of thought revived by each present intuition. In both these ways a large number of inadequate expressions arise, which do not apply in a straightforward manner to the primary intuitions actually present, nor to the synthetic formations actually built upon them, but range far beyond what is thus given. Curious mixtures of acts result. Objects are, strictly speaking, only 'known', as they are given in their actual intuitive foundation, but, since the unity of our intention ranges further, objects appear to be known as what they are for this total intention. *The character of knowing is accordingly somewhat broadened.* Thus we recognize (know) a person as an adjutant of the Kaiser, a handwriting as Goethe's, a mathematical expression as the Cardanian formula, and so on. Here our recognition can of course not apply itself to what is given in perception, at best it permits possible application to intuitive sequences, which need not themselves be actualized at all. In this manner recognitions, and sequences of recognitions, are possible on a basis of partial intuitions, which would on *a priori* grounds, not at all be possible on a basis of complete actual intuitions, since they combine incompatibles in themselves. There are, and are only too many, *false and even absurd recognitions.* But 'really' they are not recognitions, i.e. not logically worthwhile, complete 'knowings', not recognitions in the strong sense. To say this is to anticipate later discussions. For we have not yet clarified the ordering of the levels of knowledge (a matter here touched upon), nor the ideals which limit these.

So far we had to do with signitive intentions, which exist identically, and just as they are, both within and without the function of meaning. But countless signitive intentions lack either a fixed or a passing tie with expressions, though their essential character puts them in a class with meaning-intentions. I here recur to the perceptual or imaginative course of a melody, or of some other familiar type of event, and to the definite or indefinite intentions and fulfilments which arise in such a course. I refer likewise to the empirical arrangement and connection of things in their phenomenal coexistence, in regard to whatever gives the things appearing in this order, and especially the parts in each unified individual thing, the character of a *unity involving precisely this order and this form.* Representation and recognition through analogy may unite likeness and original (analogon and analogizatum), and may make them seem to belong together, but they cannot unite what is not merely contiguously given together, but what appears as belonging together. And even if, in the realization of representations through contiguity, images anticipating what is signitively represented are confirmed by their fulfilling originals, the unity among such contiguous representatives and what is represented through them can be given by no relation of picturing (since such a relation is not operative among them) but only through the entirely peculiar relation of signitive representation by way of contiguity.

We may therefore rightly see, in inadequate percepts and imaginations, interwoven masses of primitive intentions, among which, in addition to perceptual and imaginative elements, there are also intentions of a signitive kind. We may therefore maintain, in general, that all phenomenological differences in objectifying acts reduce to their constituent elementary intentions and fulfilments, the former bound to the latter through syntheses of fulfilment. On the side of intentions, the only last differences are those between signitive intentions, as intentions by way of contiguity, and imaginative intentions, as intentions by way of analogy, each plain and pure in their own kind. On the side of fulfilment, intentions of either sort again function as components, but on occasion (as in the case of perception) we have components which cannot be called intentions, since they only fulfil but require no fulfilment, *self*-presentations of the object meant by them in the strictest sense of the word. The character of the elementary acts then determines the characters of the syntheses of fulfilment, which in their turn determine the homogeneous unity of the complex act. The emphatic power of attention helps to transfer the character of this or that elementary act to the unity of the act as a whole: this whole act becomes imagination or signification or pure perception. And where two such unified acts enter into relation, relationships of agreement and conflict arise, whose character is determined by the total acts underlying such relations, and ultimately by their elements.

In the next chapter these relationships will be further tracked down, within the limits in which they can be phenomenologically ascertained and epistemologically evaluated. We shall keep strictly to phenomenologically given unities, and to the sense inherent in these and declared in their fulfilment. We shall thus avoid the temptation to embark on hypothetical construction, with whose doubts a clarification of knowledge should in no way be burdened.

Chapter 3

The phenomenology of the levels of knowledge

§16 Simple identification and fulfilment

In describing the relation of significant intention to fulfilling intuition we began with the verbal expression of a percept, and said that the intentional essence of the intuitive act fitted in with, or *belonged* to, the semantic essence of the significative act. This is plainly so in every case of total identification, where acts of like quality, i.e. *both* assertive or *both* unassertive, are synthetically unified; where the acts are of unlike quality, the identification is solely based on their *materials*. This carries over, *mutatis mutandis*, to cases of partial identification, so that we may hold that the *material* or *matter* is the aspect of the character of each act which comes up for synthesis, that is essential for identification (and naturally also for distinction).

In the case of identification, the 'matters' are the special carriers of the synthesis, without themselves being identified. For talk of identification is, in virtue of its sense, concerned with the *objects* presented by such 'matters'. On the other hand, in the act of identification, the matters themselves achieve coincidence. Every example shows, however, that even where qualities are alike, the acts need not become quite alike: this is due to the fact that an act is not exhausted by its intentional essence. What remains over will reveal its importance in a careful phenomenological investigation of the levels of knowledge, which will be our task. It is clear from the start that, if knowledge admits of degrees of perfection, even when matter is constant, matter cannot be responsible for such differences of perfection, and cannot therefore determine the peculiar essence of knowledge as against any identification whatever. We shall tie our further investigation to a discussion of the previously studied difference of *mere identification and fulfilment*.

We equated[1] fulfilment with knowledge (in the narrower sense of the word) indicating that we were only talking of certain forms of identification which brought us nearer to the *goal of knowledge*. What this means may be elucidated by saying: In each fulfilment there is more or less complete *intuitive illustration* (*Veranschaulichung*). What the intention means, but presents only in more or less inauthentic and inadequate manner, the fulfilment – the act attaching itself to an intention, and offering it 'fulness' in the synthesis of fulfilment – *sets directly before us*, or at least more directly than the intention does. In fulfilment our experience is represented by the words: 'This is the thing *itself*'. This 'itself' must not be understood too strictly, as if there must be some percept bringing the object itself to actual phenomenal presence. It is possible that, in the progress of knowledge, in the gradual ascent from acts of poorer, to acts of ever richer epistemic fulness, we must at length always reach fulfilling percepts: this does not mean that each step, each individual identification that we call a fulfilment, need contain a percept as its fulfilling act. The relative manner in which we speak of 'more or less direct' and of 'self', indicates the main point: that the synthesis of fulfilment involves an *inequality in worth* among its related members. The fulfilling act has a *superiority* which the mere intention lacks: *it imparts to the synthesis the fulness of 'self', at least leads it more directly to the thing itself*. The relativity of this 'directness', this 'self', points further to the fact that the relation of fulfilment is of a sort that admits of degrees. A concatenation of such relations seems accordingly possible where the epistemic superiority steadily increases. Each such ascending series points, however, to an *ideal limit*, or includes it as a final member, a limit setting an unsurpassable goal to all advances: *the goal of absolute knowledge, of the adequate self-presentation of the object of knowledge.*

We have thereby achieved, at least in preliminary fashion,[2] the *characteristic differentiating mark of fulfilments* within the wider class of identifications. For not every identification represents such an approach to a goal of knowledge: there can well be a purposeless infinity of ever further identifications. There are, e.g., indefinitely many arithmetical expressions having the same numerical value 2, which permit us to add identification to identification *in infinitum*. Just so there may be infinitely many images of one and the same thing, determining again the possibility of endless chains of identifications tending to no goal of knowledge. The same holds for the endlessly many percepts of one and the same thing.

If we pay heed to the constitutive elementary intentions in these intuitive examples, we shall of course find moments of true fulfilment entering into the total act of identification. This happens when we set image-presentations side by side which are not of completely equal intuitive content, so that the new image brings out many things much more clearly, and perhaps sets something before us 'just as it is', while a former image merely 'projects' it or denotes it symbolically. If we imaginatively envisage an object turning itself to every side, our sequence of images is constantly linked by syntheses of fulfilment in respect of its partial intentions, but each new image-presentation does not, as a whole, fulfil its predecessor, nor does the whole series progressively approach any goal. Just so in the case of the manifold percepts belonging to the same external thing. Gain and loss are balanced at every step: a new act has richer fulness in regard to certain properties, for whose sake it has lost fulness in regard to others. But against this we may hold that the *whole synthesis* of the series of imaginations or percepts represents an increase in fulness in comparison with an act singled out from the series: the imperfection of the one-sided representation is, relatively speaking, overcome in the all-sided one. We say 'relatively speaking', since the all-sided representation is not achieved in such a synthetic manifold in the single flash which the ideal of adequation requires, as a pure self-presentation without added analogizing or symbolization: it is achieved piecemeal and always blurred by such additions. Another example of an intuitive fulfilment-series is the transition from a rough drawing to a more exact pencil-sketch, then from the latter to the completed picture, and from this to the living finish of the painting, all of which present the same, visibly the same, object.

Such examples from the sphere of mere imagination show that the character of fulfilment does not require that assertive quality in the intending and fulfilling acts which is part of the logical concept of knowledge. We prefer to speak of 'knowledge' where an opinion, in the normal sense of a *belief*, has been confirmed or attested.

§17 The question of the relation between fulfilment and intuitive illustration

We must now enquire into the part played in knowledge by the various kinds of objectifying acts – signitive and intuitive acts – and, under the latter rubric, acts of perception and imagination. Here intuitive acts plainly seem to be preferred, so much so, in fact, as to incline one to call all fulfilment *intuitive illustration* (*Veranschaulichung*) – as we did above in passing – or to describe the work of fulfilment, wherever one deals with intuitive intentions, as a mere increase in intuitive fulness. The relation between intention and fulfilment plainly underlies the formation of the conceptual couple: *thought* (more narrowly, *concept*), on the one hand, and *corresponding intuition*, on the other. But we must not forget that a notion of intuition oriented towards this relation does not at all coincide with that of an *intuitive act*, although, through the inherent tendency towards intuition which enters into the sense of all fulfilment, it closely depends on the latter and even pre-supposes it. To make a thought clear to oneself means, primarily, to give epistemic fulness to the content of one's thought. This can, however, be achieved, *in a certain fashion*, even by a signitive presentation. Of course, if we ask for a clearness which will make matters self-evident, which will make 'the thing itself' clear, render its possibility and its truth knowable, we are referred to intuition in the sense of our intuitive acts. For this reason talk of 'clearness' in epistemological contexts plainly has this narrower sense, it indicates recourse to fulfilling intuition, to the 'originative source' of concepts and propositions in their subject-matters themselves.

Carefully analysed examples are now needed if we are to confirm and develop what has just been suggested. These will help us to clear up the relation between fulfilment and intuitive illustration, and to render quite precise the part played by intuition in *every* fulfilment. Differences between authentic and inauthentic illustration (or fulfilment) will distinguish themselves clearly, and the difference between mere identification and fulfilment will also therewith reach final clarity. The work of intuition will be shown to be that of contributing to the intended act, when authentically fulfilled, a genuinely novel element, to which the name 'fulness' may be given. We are thereby made aware of a hitherto unstressed side of the phenomenological content of acts, which is fundamental for knowledge. 'Fulness' must take its place as a new 'moment' in an intuitive act alongside of its quality and its matter, a moment specially belonging to the matter which it in some manner completes.

§22 Fullness and 'intuitive substance' (*Gehalt*)

Closely regarded, the concept of fulness is still fraught with an ambiguity. The above mentioned moments can be looked at in respect of their own existential content, without regard to the functions of pure imagination or perception, which first confer on them the value of being a picture or a perspectivally slanted self-revelation, and so a value for the function of fulfilment. On the other hand, one can consider these moments *in* their interpretation, i.e. not these moments alone, but the full pictures or slanted self-revelations in question. Ignoring only intentional qualities, one can deal with purely intuitive acts as wholes, which include these moments in themselves, since they give them an objective significance. These 'purely intuitive' acts we conceive as mere constituents of the intuitions just mentioned, being the element in them which gives to the moments previously mentioned, a relation to corresponding objective properties which are represented through them. We ignore therewith (in addition to the qualities) the yet further attached *signitive* relations to further parts or sides of the object *which are not, properly speaking (intuitively), represented*.

It is plainly these purely intuitive constituents which impart to total acts the character of percepts or imaginings, i.e. their intuitive character, and which function in the system of serially ordered fulfilments as the element which confers 'fulness', or which enriches or increases the same when already present. To deal with this ambiguity in our talk of 'fulness' we shall introduce the following distinguishing terms:

By *intuitively presentative or intuitively representative contents* (*Inhalten*) we understand those contents of intuitive acts which, owing to the purely imaginative or perceptual interpretations that they sustain, point unambiguously to definitely corresponding contents in the object, represent these in imagined or perceived perspectival slantings. The act-aspects which characterize them in this manner, we ignore. Since the character of imagination lies in analogical picturing, in 'representation' in a narrower sense, while the character of perception can be called strictly presentative, the following distinctive names suggest themselves: For the intuitively presentative contents in either case – *analogizing* or *picturing* contents, on the one hand, and *strictly presentative* or *self-presentative* contents, on the other. The expressions 'imaginatively slanted contents' and 'perceptively slanted contents' are also very apt. The intuitively presentative contents of outer perception define the concept of *sensation* in the ordinary, narrow sense. The intuitively presentative contents of external fantasy are *sensory phantasms* or images.

The intuitively presentative or intuitively representative contents in and with the interpretation put upon them, we call the *intuitive substance* (*Gehalt*) *of the act*: in this we still ignore the quality of the act (whether assertive or not), as being indifferent to the distinctions in question. On the above, all signitive components of an act are excluded from its intuitive 'substance'.[3]

§23 Relationships of weight between the intuitive and signitive 'substance' (*Gehalt*) of one and the same act. Pure intuition and pure signification. Perceptual and imaginal content, pure perception and pure imagination. Gradations of fulness

To increase the clearness of the concepts just marked off, and to aid in the marking off of a new set of concepts, rooted in the same soil, we embark on the following discussion:

In an intuitive presentation (*Vorstellung*) an object is meant in the manner of perception or imagination: in this manner it is more or less perfectly made apparent. To each part and each property of the object, including its reference to a *here* and a *now*, there must necessarily be a corresponding part or moment of the conscious act. What we do not mean, is simply not there for our presentation (*Vorstellung*). We now find in general that it is possible to draw the following phenomenological distinction between

(1) *The purely intuitive 'substance'* (*Gehalt*) of the act, i.e. all that corresponds in the act to the sum total of the object's properties that 'become apparent',

(2) *The signitive 'substance'* of the act, which corresponds to the sum total of the remaining, subsidiarily given properties of the object, which do not themselves become apparent.

We all draw such a distinction, in purely phenomenological fashion, in the intuition involved in the percept or image of a thing, between whatever in the object is truly made apparent, the mere 'side' from which the object is shown to us, and whatever lacks intuitive presentation (*Darstellung*), is hidden by other phenomenal objects etc. Such talk plainly implies, what phenomenological analysis within certain limits definitely proves, that even what is *not* presented (*Nicht-Dargestelltes*) in an intuitive presentation (*Vorstellung*) is subsidiarily meant, and that an array of signitive components must accordingly be ascribed to the latter, from which we have to abstract, if we wish to keep our *intuitive* content pure. This last gives the intuitively presenting (*darstellende*) content its direct relation to corresponding objective moments: other novel and, to that extent, mediate, signitive intentions, are attached to these by contiguity.

If we now define the *weight* of the intuitive (or signitive) content as the sum total of the intuitively (or signitively) presented (*vorgestellte*) moments of the object, both 'weights' in each presentation (*Vorstellung*) will add up to a single total weight, i.e. the sum total of the object's properties. Always therefore the symbolic equation holds: $i + s = 1$. The weights i and s can plainly vary in many regards: the same, intentionally same, object can be intuitively given with more or less numerous, ever varying properties. The signitive content also alters correspondingly, it is increased or diminished.

Ideally we now have the possibility of two limiting cases:

$$i = 0 \quad s = 1$$
$$i = 1 \quad s = 0.$$

In the former, the presentation (*Vorstellung*) would have only signitive content: no property of its intentional object would remain over which was brought to intuitive presentation (*Darstellung*) in its content. The special case of purely signitive presentations, well-known to us as pure meaning-intentions, therefore appears here as a limiting case of intuition.

In the second case the presentation (*Vorstellung*) has *no* signitive content whatever. In it all is fulness: no part, no side, no property of its object fails to be intuitively presented (*dargestellt*), none is merely indirectly and subsidiarily meant. Not only is everything that is intuitively presented also meant – so much is analytically true – but whatever is meant is also intuitively presented. This new class of presentations may be defined as *pure intuitions*, the term here used with innocuous ambiguity, at times to cover complete acts, at times such acts in abstraction from their quality. We may speak distinguishingly of *qualified* and *unqualified* pure intuitions.

In each presentation (*Vorstellung*) we can therefore surely abstract from all signitive components, and limit ourselves to what is really represented in its representative content. By so doing we form a *reduced* presentation, with a reduced object in regard to which it is purely intuitive. We can accordingly say that the *intuitive substance* (*Gehalt*) of a presentation comprises *all that is pure intuition in it*, just as we may also speak of *the object*'s purely intuitive content, of all that is rendered intuitive in this presentation. The like applies to the signitive substance of the presentation: this can be said to be all that is *pure signification* in it.

Each total act of intuition has either the character of a percept or an imagination: its intuitive substance is then either *perceptual* or *imaginative* substance or content. This must not be confused with the perceptually or imaginatively presenting content in the sense defined in §22.

Perceptual content comprises (though not in general exclusively) strictly presentative contents: imaginative contents comprise only analogizing contents. It is not to the point that these latter contents permit of *another* interpretation (as in the case of physical images), in which they function strictly presentatively.

On account of the mixture of perceptual and imaginative components which the intuitive substance of a percept permits and usually exhibits, we can again consider adopting a division of perceptual content into *pure perceptual content*, on the one hand, and *supplementary image-content*, on the other.

If then, in each pure intuition we take P_p and I_p to be the weights of its *purely* perceptual and *purely* imaginative components, we can write down the symbolic equation

$$P_p + I_p = 1$$

where 1 symbolizes the weight of the total intuitive content of the pure intuition, and thus the total content of its object. If $I_p = 0$, i.e. if the pure intuition is free from all imaginal content, it should be called a *pure perception*: we shall here ignore the qualitatively assertive character usually embraced in the sense of the term 'perception'. But if $P_p = 0$, the intuition is called *pure imagination*. The 'purity' of pure perception relates, therefore, not merely to signitive, but also to imaginative supplements. The narrowing of an impure percept which throws out symbolic components yields the pure intuition which is immanent in it: a further reductive step then throws out everything imagined, and yields the substance of pure perception.

Can the intuitively presentative content in the case of pure perception be identified with the object itself? The essence of pure presentation (in the strict sense) surely consists in being a pure self-presentation of the object, one which means the intuitively presentative content *directly* (in the manner of 'self') as its object. This would, however, be a paralogism. The percept, as presentation in the strict sense, so interprets the intuitively presentative content, that the object appears as itself given with and in this content. Presentation (in the strict sense) is *pure*, when each part of the object is actually and intuitively presented in the content, and none is merely imagined or symbolized. As there is nothing in the object not strictly presented, so there is nothing in the content not strictly presentative. Despite such exact correspondence, self-presentation may still have the character of the mere, even if all-sided perspectivity (of a completed perceptual picture): it need not attain the ideal of adequation, where the intuitively presenting content is also the intuitively presented content. The pure picture-presentation, which completely depicts its object through its freedom from all signitive additions, holds in its intuitively presentative content a complete likeness of the object. This likeness can approach the object more or less closely, to a limit of complete resemblance. The same may be true in the case of pure perception, with the sole difference, that imagination treats the content as a likeness or image, whereas perception looks on it as a self-revelation of the object. Pure perception no less than pure imagination admits, accordingly, of differing degrees of fulness, without thereby altering its intentional object. Regarding the *degrees of fulness of intuitive content*, to which degrees of fulness of representative content run *eo ipso* parallel, we may distinguish:

1. The *extent* or *richness* of the fulness, according as the content of the object achieves intuitive presentation with greater or less completeness.

2. The *liveliness* of this fulness, i.e. the degree of approximation of the primitive resemblances of the intuitive presentation to the corresponding moments of content in the object.

3. The reality-level (*Realitätsgehalt*) of the fulness, the greater or less number of its strictly presentative contents.

In all these regards, adequate perception represents an ideal: it has a maximum of extent, liveliness and reality: it is the self-apprehension of the whole, full object.

§25 Fullness and intentional matter

We now wish to discuss the relation between the new concept of presentational content covered by the name 'fulness', with content in the sense of 'matter', which last has played such a large part in our investigation up to this point. 'Matter' was classed as that moment in an objectifying act which makes the act present *just this object in just this manner*, i.e. in just these articulations and forms, and with special relation to just these properties or relationships. Presentations which agree in their matter do not merely present the same object in some general fashion: they mean it in the most complete fashion *as* the same, as having exactly the same properties. The one presentation confers nothing on the object in its intention which the other presentation does not likewise confer. To each objectifying articulation and form on one side there is a corresponding articulation and form on the other, in such a manner that the agreeing elements of the presentations have an identical objective reference. In this sense we said in our Fifth Investigation, in elucidating the concepts of 'matter' and 'semantic essence': 'Two judgements are in essence the same judgement (i.e. judgements with the same 'matter'), if everything that would hold of the state of affairs judged according to one, would likewise hold of it according to the other, and nothing different would hold of it in either case. The truth-value of the judgements is the same'. They *mean* the same in regard to the object, even if they are otherwise quite different, if the one, e.g., is achieved signitively, while the other is more or less illustrated by intuition.

I was led to form this notion through a consideration of what is identical in the assertive and understanding use of the same expression, where one may 'believe' the content of some statement, while another leaves it unde-cided, without disturbing this content's identity, in which case it also makes no difference whether expression occurs in connection with correspondent intuition, and whether it can so occur or not. One might therefore be tempted – I myself hesitated long on this point – to define meaning as this very 'matter', which would, however, have the inconvenience that the moment of *assertion* in, e.g., a predicative statement, would fall outside of that state-ment's meaning. (One could no doubt limit the concept of meaning in this fashion, and then distinguish between qualified and unqualified meanings.) Our comparison of meaning-intentions with their correlative intuitions, in the static and dynamic unity of identifying coincidence, showed us, however, that the very thing that we marked off as the 'matter' of meaning, reap-peared once more in the corresponding intuition, and furnished the means for an identification. Our freedom, therefore, to add to or take away intuit-ive elements, and even all correspondent intuitions, wherever we limited our concern to the abiding meaningfulness of a given expression, was based on the fact that the whole act attaching to the sound of our words had the same 'matters' on the intuitive as on the meaning side, in respect, that is, of such elements of meaning as receive intuitive illustration at all.

It is clear, therefore, that the concept of 'matter' must be defined by way of the unity of total identification as *the element in our acts which serves as a basis for identification*, and that all differences of fulness which go beyond mere identification, and which variously determine peculiarities of fulfilment and increase of fulfilment, have no relevance in the formation of this con-ception. However the fulness of a presentation may vary within its possible gradients of fulfilment, its intentional object, intended as it is intended, remains the same: its 'matter', in other words, stays the same. Matter and fulness are, however, by no means unrelated and, when we range an intuitive act along-side a signitive act to which it brings fulness, the former act does not differ from the latter merely by the joining on of a third distinct moment of fulness to the quality and matter common to the two acts. This at least is not the case where we mean by 'fulness' the intuitive content of intuition. For intuit-ive content itself already includes a complete 'matter', the matter of an act *reduced* to a pure intuition. If the intuitive act in question was already *purely* intuitive, its matter also would be a constituent of its intuitive content.

The relations which obtain here will be best set forth by establishing the following parallelism between signitive and intuitive acts.

A purely *signitive* act would be a mere complex of quality and matter, if indeed it could exist by itself at all, i.e. be a concrete experiential unity 'on its own'. This it cannot be: we always find it clinging to some intuitive basis. This intuition of a sign may have 'nothing at all to do' with the object of the significative act, it may stand to it in no relation of fulfilment, but it realizes its possibility *in concreto* of being an altogether unfulfilled act. The follow-ing proposition therefore seems to hold: An act of signification is only possible in so far as an intuition becomes endued with a new intentional essence, whereby its intuitive object points beyond itself in the manner of a sign (whether as a sign regularly or fleetingly used). More closely considered, this proposition does not, however, seem to express the necessities of connection which obtain here with the needed analytic clearness, and perhaps says more than is justified. For we can, it seems, say that *it is not our founding intuition as a whole, but only its representational content*, which really assists the signitive act. For what goes beyond this content, what pins down the sign as a natural object, *can be varied at will* without disturbing the sign's signitive function. Whether the letters of a verbal sign are of wood, iron or printer's ink etc., or seem to be such objectively, makes no difference. Only their repeatedly recognizable shape is relevant, not as the objective shape of the thing of wood etc., but as the shape actually present in the intuitively presentative sensuous content of intuition. If there is only a connection between the signitive act and the intuitively presentative content of our intuition, and if the quality and matter of this intuition mean nothing to this signitive function, then we ought not to say that each signitive act requires a founding intuition, but only that it requires a founding content. It would seem that *any* content can function in this fashion, just as any content can function as the intuitively presentative content of an intuition.

If we now turn our regard to the parallel case of the *purely intuitive act*, its quality and matter (its intentional essence) are not capable of separate existence on their own: here too a supplement is required. This is furnished by the representative content, i.e. the content – sensuous in the case of a sensuous intuition – which in its present fusion with an intentional essence has acquired the character of being an intuitive representative. If we bear in mind the fact that the same (e.g. sensuous) content can at one time carry a meaning, and at another time an intuition – denoting in one case and picturing in the other – we are led to widen the notion of a representative content, and to distinguish between *contents which represent signitively* (signitive representatives) and *contents which represent intuitively* (intuitive representatives).

Our division is, however, incomplete. We have so far considered only the purely intuitive or purely signitive acts. If we bring in the *mixed* acts as well, those we ordinarily class as intuitive, we find them peculiar in the fact that their representative content is pictorial or self-presentative in respect of one part of what it objectively presents, while being merely denotative as to the remaining part. We must accordingly range *mixed* representatives beside purely signitive and purely intuitive representatives: *these represent signitively and intuitively at the same time, and in regard to the same intentional essence.* We may now say:

Each concretely complete objectifying act has three components: its quality, its matter and its representative content. To the extent that this content functions as a purely signitive or purely intuitive representative, or as both together, the act is a purely signitive, a purely intuitive or a mixed act.

§26 Continuation. Representation or interpretation (*Auffassung*). Matter as the interpretative sense, the interpretative form and the interpreted content. Differentiating characterization of intuitive and signitive interpretation

We may now ask *what this 'functioning' really stands for*, since we have it as an *a priori* possibility that the same content, bound up with the same quality and matter, should function in this threefold manner. It is plain that it can only be *the phenomenological peculiarity of the relevant form of unity* that can give a phenomenologically discoverable content to our distinction. This form specially unites the *matter* to the representative content, since the representative function is unaffected by change in the quality. Whether, e.g., an imaginative picturing claims to be the calling up of a real object or to be merely imaginative, makes no difference to its pictorially presentative character, that its content bears the function of an image-content. We therefore call *the phonomenological union of matter with representative content*, in so far as it lends the latter its representative character, the *form of representation*, and the *whole* engendered by these two moments the representation *pure and simple*. This designation expresses the relation between representing and represented content (latter = the object or part of the object represented) by going back to its phenomenological foundation. Leaving aside the object as something not phenomenologically given, and endeavouring merely to express the fact that, when a content functions representatively, we are always differently 'minded', we may speak of a change in *interpretation (Auffassung)*. We may also call the form of representation the *interpretative form*. Since the matter after a manner fixes the *sense* in which the representative content is interpreted, we may also speak of the *interpretative sense*. If we wish to recall the older term, and at the same time indicate an opposition to form, we may also speak of the *interpretative matter*. In each interpretation we must therefore distinguish phenomenologically between: *interpretative matter* or *sense, interpretative form* and *interpreted content*; this last is to be distinguished from *the object of the interpretation*. The term 'apperception' is unsuitable despite its historical provenance, on account of its misleading terminological opposition to 'perception'; 'apprehension' would be more usable.

Our next question concerns the distinguishing marks of the various modes of representation or interpretation which, as we saw, can be different even when the interpretative matter – the 'as what' of interpretation – is constant. In the previous chapter we characterized differences of representations through differences in forms of fulfilment, in the present context we have regard to an internal characterization limited to the proper descriptive stuff of intentions. If we may make use of the beginnings of an analytical clarification which our previous treatment suggested, as well as of our subsequent advances in the general grasp of 'representation', the following train of ideas suggests itself:

We begin with the observation that *signitive representation* institutes a *contingent, external* relation between matter and representative content, whereas intuitive representation institutes one that is *essential, internal*. The contingency of the former consists in the fact that an identical signification can be thought of as attached to every content whatsoever. *Significative matter has a general need for supporting content, but between the specific nature of the former and the specific being of the latter no bond of necessity can be found.* Meaning cannot, as it were, hang in the air, but for what it means, the sign, whose meaning we call it, is entirely indifferent.

The case of *purely intuitive representation* is quite different. Here *there is an internal, necessary connection between matter and representing content*, fixed by the specific stuff of both. Only those contents can be intuitively representative of an object that resemble it or are like it. Phenomenologically put: we are not wholly free to interpret a content *as* this or *as* that (or in this or that interpretative sense) and this has more than an empirical foundation – *every* interpretation including a significative one is empirically necessary – since the content to be interpreted sets limits to us through a certain sphere of similarity and exact likeness, i.e. through its specific substance. The internality of the relation does not merely forge a link between *the interpretative matter as a whole* and *the whole content*: it links their parts on each side *piece by piece*. This occurs in the presupposed case of pure intuition. In the case of *impure intuition* the specific union is partial: a part of the matter – the matter of the reduced, and therefore, of course, pure, intuition – provides the intuitive sense in which the content is interpreted, while the remainder of the matter undergoes no representation through similarity or exact likeness, but merely through contiguity, i.e. in mixed intuition the representative content functions as intuitive representative for one part of the matter, but as signitive representative for the remaining part.

If one finally asks how one and the same content (in the sense of 'same matter') can at times be 'taken up' in the manner of an intuitive, and at times in the manner of a signitive representative, in what the differing nature of these interpretative forms consists, I can give them no further answer. We are facing a difference that cannot be phenomenologically reduced.

In these discussions we have treated representation independently as a union of matter and representative content. If we go back again to the complete acts, these reveal themselves as combinations of act-quality with either intuitive or signitive representation. The whole acts are called intuitive or signitive, a difference determined by these inwrought representations. The study of relations of fulfilment led us above to the concept of intuitive substance or fulness. If we compare that case of concept-formation with the present one, it sets bounds to the purely intuitive representation (i.e. pure intuition) that belongs to an act of impure intuition. 'Fulness' was a notion specially framed for the comparative treatment of acts in their fulfilling function. The limiting case opposed to pure intuition, pure signification, is of course the same as purely signitive representation.

§29 Complete and defective intuitions. Adequate and objectively complete intuitive illustrations. *Essentia (Essenz)*

In an intuitive presentation a *varying amount of intuitive fulness* is possible. This talk of a varying amount points, as we argued, to possible gradients of fulfilment: proceeding along these, we come to know the object better and better, by way of a presentative content that resembles it ever more and more closely, and grasps it more and more vividly and fully. We know also that intuition can occur where whole sides and parts of the object meant are not apparent at all, i.e. the presentation has an intuitive content not containing pictorial representatives of these sides and parts, so that they are only presented 'inauthentically', through inwrought signitive intentions. In connection with these differences, which result in very different modes of presentation for one and the same object, with meaning governed by the same matter, we spoke above of differences in the *extent* of fulness. Here two important possibilities must be distinguished.

1. The intuitive presentation presents its object *adequately*, i.e. with an intuitive substance (*Gehalt*) of such fulness, that to each constituent of the object, as it is meant in this presentation, a representative constituent of the intuitive content corresponds.

2. Or this is *not* the case. The presentation contains no more than an incomplete projection of the object: it presents it *inadequately*.

Here we are talking of the adequacy or inadequacy of a presentation *to its object*. Since, however, we speak more widely of adequacy in contexts of fulfilment, we introduce yet another set of terms. We shall speak of *complete* and *defective intuitions* (more particularly of complete and mutilated percepts or imaginations). All pure intuitions are complete. The following considerations will at once show that the converse does not hold, and that our proposed division does not simply coincide with that of *pure* and *impure* intuitions.

Whether presentations are simple or complex is a matter regarding which nothing is presupposed in the distinction just drawn. Intuitive presentations may, however, be complex in two ways:

(*a*) The relation to the object may be simple in so far as the act (more specifically, its matter) has no constituent acts (or no separate matters) that *independently present the same total object*. This does not preclude the possibility that an act should be made up of partial intentions homogeneously fused, which relate to the individual parts or sides of its object. One can scarcely avoid assuming such complexity in the case of 'external' percepts and imaginations, and we have proceeded on this assumption. But, on the other hand we have

(*b*) the kind of complexity in which the total act is built out of constituent acts, *each of which independently is a full intuitive presentation of the same object.* This we have in those extremely remarkable *continuous syntheses* which bind together a multitude of percepts which pertain to the same object, into a single 'many-sided' or 'all-sided' percept, which deals with the object continuously in 'varying positions'. There are the corresponding syntheses of imagination. In the continuity of a prolonged fusion-into-sameness not broken up into isolated acts, the same single object appears singly, not as often as individual acts can be distinguished. It appears, however, with *altering* fulness of content, though the matters, and likewise *the qualities remain steadfastly the same,* at least when the object is known from all angles, and repeatedly comes to light in its unenriched familiarity.

The distinction between adequacy and inadequacy relates also to these continuous syntheses. An adequate presentation of, e.g., an external thing is possible in synthetic form in respect of its all-sided surface-contours: in the form of an objectively simple presentation, it is impossible.

Of complete intuitions it is plain that objectively simple ones, but by no means always objectively complex ones, are *pure* intuitions. The pure intuition which corresponds to an empirical thing is denied to us, it lies hidden after a fashion in the complete synthetic intuition itself, but as it were dispersedly, with a perpetual admixture of signitive representation. If we reduce this synthetic intuition to its pure form, we do not have the pure intuition possible in an objectively simple presentation, but a continuum of intuitive contents, in which each aspect of the object quite often achieves intuitive representation, achieves ever varied perspectival projection, and in which only the continuous fusion of identity constitutes the phenomenon of objective unity.

When an intuitive fact serves to give fulness in connection with a signitive intention, perhaps in connection with a meaning-intention expressed in words, similar possibilities arise. The object as it is meant can receive an adequate or an inadequate intuitive illustration. The former possibility covers two separable possibilities in the case of complex meanings:

First, that to all parts (members, moments, forms) of the meaning, which themselves have a meaning-character, fulfilment should accrue through corresponding parts of the fulfilling intuition.

Secondly, that the fulfilling intuition, to the extent that its object is meant in any articulations and forms which have been drawn into the function of fulfilment, is intrinsically adequate to its object.

The first determines the completeness of the adaptation of signitive acts to *corresponding intuitions*; the second the completeness of the adaptation of signitive acts – through *complete* intuitions – *to the object itself.*

The expression 'a green house' can thus be intuitively illustrated if a house is really present to our intuition as green. This is a case of the first perfection. The second requires an adequate presentation of a green house. We generally only have the former in mind when we speak of an adequate illustration of expressions. To find distinct terms for this *double* perfection we shall speak of an *objectively perfect* intuitive illustration of our signitive presentation as opposed to its adequate, but *objectively defective*, intuitive illustration.

Similar relationships obtain in the case of an intuitive illustration which *conflicts with, rather than fulfilling a meaning*. When a signitive intention encounters frustration from an intuition, because perhaps it refers to a *green A*, though the same *A*, perhaps any *A* at all, is red, and is now intuited as red, the *objective completeness* of the intuitive realization of conflict requires that *all* constituents of the meaning-intention should find an objectively complete intuitive illustration. It is therefore necessary, not merely that the *A*-intention should receive complete objective fulfilment in the intuition in question, but also that the green-intuition should be fulfilled, though naturally in another intuition which cannot be united to the intuition of the *red A*. It is not then merely the signitive green-intention, but the same intention in its objectively complete fulfilment, which is at odds with the red-intuition: these two intuitive moments are in total 'rivalry', while the correlative intuitive wholes are in partial rivalry. This rivalry especially touches, as one might say, the *intuitive* or *intuitively presentative* contents of these fulfilling acts.

If nothing special is prefaced we shall in future speak of 'intuitive illustrations' only in the case of fulfilments (not frustrations).

Distinctions of fulness in cases where quality and matter are identical, prompt us to frame one further important concept:

We shall say that two intuitive acts have the same *essentia (Essenz)*, *if their pure intuitions have the same matter*. A percept, and the whole possibly existent infinity of imaginative presentations, which all present the same object with the same breadth of fulness, have one and the same *essentia*. All objectively complete intuitions with one and the same matter have the same *essentia*.

A signitive presentation has no *essentia* in its own right. But a certain *essentia* may, in an inauthentic sense, be ascribed to it, if it permits of complete fulfilment through one of the possible manifold of intuitions pertaining to this *essentia*, or, what is the same, if it has a 'fulfilling sense'.

This probably clarifies the true meaning of the scholastic term *essentia*, which certainly hinges on the possibility of a 'concept'.

Chapter 5

The ideal of adequation.
Self-evidence and truth

§36 Introduction

In our discussions up to this point we have said nothing of the *qualities* of acts, nor presumed anything in regard to them. Possibility and impossibility have indeed no special relation to these qualities. It makes no difference, e.g., to the possibility of a proposition, whether we realize the propositional matter as matter for an act of *assertion* (not of an act that assents to something in the accepting or recognizing manner of approval, but in the manner of a simple act of belief or taking for true), or whether we use it, in qualitatively modified fashion, as the matter of a pure presentation. A proposition is always 'possible', when the concrete act of propositional meaning permits of a fulfilling identification with an objectively complete intuition of matching material. It is likewise irrelevant if this fulfilling intuition is a percept, or a pure construction of fantasy, etc. Since the summoning up of imaginative pictures is more subject, in varying degrees, to our will, than that of percepts and assertions, we incline to relate possibility specially to the picture-life of fantasy. A thing counts as possible, if it allows itself, objectively speaking, to be realized in the form of an adequate imaginative picture, whether we ourselves, as particular empirical individuals, succeed in thus realizing it or not. But through the ideal linkage between perception and imagination, which assures us *a priori* that to each percept a possible image corresponds, this proposition is equivalent to our own, and the limitation of the concept to imagination not essential.

What we have now to do, quite briefly, is to discuss the effect of these just indicated differences upon relationships of fulfilment, so that our treatments may at least reach a provisional term, as well as a view over further researches.

§37 The fulfilling function of perception. The ideal of ultimate fulfilment

We have seen that differences in the completeness of 'fulness' have an important bearing on the manner in which objects are made present in presentations. Signitive acts constitute the lowest step: they possess no fulness whatever. Intuitive acts have fulness, in graded differences of more and less, and this is already the case within the sphere of imagination. The perfection of an imagination, however great, still leaves it different from a perception: it does not present the object itself, not even in part, it offers only its image, which, as long as it is an image at all, never is the thing itself. The latter we owe to perception. Even this, however, 'gives' us the object in varied gradations of perfection, in differing degrees of 'projection'. The intentional character of perception, as opposed to the mere representation of imagination, is that of direct presentation. This is, as we know, an *internal* difference of acts, more precisely of their interpretative form. But 'direct' presentation does not in general amount to a true being-present, but only to an appearance of presence, in which objective presence, and with it the perfection of veridicity (*Wahr-nehmung*, perception) exhibits degrees. This is shown by a glance at the corresponding scale of fulfilment, to which all exemplification of perfection in presentation is here, as elsewhere, referred. We thereby become clear that a difference extends over the fulness of perception that we sought to cover by our talk of perceptual *projection*, a difference that does not concern fulness in respect of its sensuous stuff, its internal character, but means a graded extension of its character *as* fulness, i.e. of the interpretative character of the act. From this point of view many elements of fulness count for us – quite apart from anything genetic, for we know full well that these, like all similar differences, have an associative origin – as *final presentations* of the corresponding objective elements. They offer themselves as identical with these last, not as their mere representatives: they are *the thing itself* in an absolute sense. Other cases again count as mere adumbrations of colour, perspectival foreshortenings etc., in which case it is clear that to such locutions something corresponds in the phenomenological content of the act prior to all reflection. We have already dealt with these 'projective' differences, and found them, pictorially transferred, in the case of imagination. Every projection is representative in character, and represents by way of similarity, but the manner of this representation by similarity differs according as the representation takes the projected content as picture or self-presentation (self-projection) of the object.[1] The ideal limit, which an increase of fulness of projection permits, is, in the case of perception, the absolute self of the thing (as in imagination it is its absolutely resembling image), and that for every side and for every presented element of the object.

The discussion of possible relationships of fulfilment therefore points to *a goal in which increase of fulfilment terminates, in which the complete and entire intention has reached its fulfilment*, and that not intermediately and partially, but ultimately and finally. The intuitive substance of this last fulfilment is the absolute sum of possible fulness; the intuitive representative is the object itself, as it is in itself. Where a presentative intention has achieved its last fulfilment, the genuine *adaequatio rei et intellectus* has been brought about. *The object is actually 'present' or 'given', and present as just what we have intended it*; no partial intention remains implicit and still lacking fulfilment.

And so also, *eo ipso*, the ideal of every fulfilment, and therefore of a *significative* fulfilment, is sketched for us; the *intellectus* is in this case the thought-intention, the intention of meaning. And the *adaequatio* is realized when the object meant is in the strict sense *given* in our intuition, and given as just what we think and call it. No thought-intention could fail of its fulfilment, of its last fulfilment, in fact, in so far as the fulfilling medium of intuition has itself lost all implication of unsatisfied intentions.

One sees that the perfection of the adequation of thought to thing is twofold: on the one hand there is a perfect adaptation to intuition, since the thought means nothing that the fulfilling intuition does not completely present as belonging to the thought. In this the two previously (§29) distinguished 'perfections' are plainly comprehended: they yield what we called the 'objective completeness' of the fulfilment. On the other hand the complete intuition itself involves a perfection. The intuition fulfils the intention which terminates in it as not itself again being an intention which has need of further fulfilment, but as offering us the *last* fulfilment of our intention. We must therefore draw a distinction between the perfection of the *adaptation to intuition*, which is 'adequation' in the natural, wider sense, and the perfection of final fulfilment which presupposes this fulfilment, and which is an adequation with the 'thing itself'. Each faithful, unalloyed description of an intuitive object or event provides an example of the former perfection. If the object is something in interior experience, and is grasped as it is in reflex perception, then the second perfection may be added, as when, for instance, looking back on a categorical judgement just made, we speak of the subject-presentation in this judgement. The first perfection is, however, lacking, when we call the tree standing before us a 'cultivated' variety of apple-tree, or when we speak of the 'vibratory frequency' of the note just dying away, or, in general, when we speak of such properties of perceptual objects as, however much they may be marginally meant in our perceiving intention, are not even more or less projectively present in what actually appears.

The following observation is also in place. Since an ultimate fulfilment may contain absolutely no unfulfilled intentions, it must issue out of a *pure* percept. An objectively complete percept, but one achieved by the continuous synthesis of impure percepts, will not fill the bill.

Against our mode of treatment, which places the final fulfilment of all intentions in perception, it may be objected that the realized consciousness of the universal, the consciousness which gives fulness to conceptually general presentations, and which sets the 'universal object itself' before our eyes, rests on a ground of mere imagination, or is at least indifferent to the difference between perception and imagination. The same is obviously true, as a consequence of what has just been said, of all self-evident general assertions, which make themselves plain to us, in axiomatic fashion, 'from our very notions alone'.

This objection points to a gap in our investigation that has already been touched on from time to time. We first took perception, with immediate obviousness, as being the same as *sense*-perception, intuition as being the same as sensuous intuition. Tacitly, without any clear consciousness, we have frequently gone beyond the bounds of these notions, e.g. in connection with our discussions of compatibility. We regularly did this, when, e.g., we spoke of intuiting a conflict or a union, or some other synthesis as such. In our next chapter, which deals generally with categorial forms we shall show the need to widen the concepts of perception and other sorts of intuition. To remove our objection, we shall now only say that the imagination, which serves as basis for generalizing abstraction, does not therefore exercise an actual, authentic function of fulfilment, and so does not play the part of a 'corresponding' intuition. What is individually singular in phenomena, is not itself, as we have several times stressed, the universal, nor does it contain the universal as a real (*reell*) 'piece' of itself.

§38 Positing acts in the function of fulfilment. Self-evidence in the loose and strict sense

Under the rubric of 'intentions', positing and non-positing acts have so far been indiscriminately ranged. Nonetheless, though the general character of fulfilment essentially depends on the 'matter' of acts, which alone is relevant to an array of most important relationships, the quality of acts shares in the determination of others, and to such a degree that talk of intention, of directed aiming, really only seems to suit assertive acts. Our *thought (Meinung)* aims at a thing, and it hits its mark, or does not hit it, according as it agrees or does not agree in a certain way with perception (which is here an assertive act). Positing then agrees with positing: the intending and fulfilling act are alike in this quality. Mere presentation, however, is passive: it leaves matters 'in suspense'. Where by chance an adequate percept accompanies a mere presentation, a fulfilling coincidence certainly issues from the mutually fitting 'matters' of the acts: in the transition, however, the presentation acquires an assertive note, and the unity of coincidence itself certainly has this note quite homogeneously. *Each actual identification or differentiation is an assertive act*, whether itself founded on assertions or not. This last briefly-worded proposition adds an all-important characterization to the results of our last chapter, a characterization determining all relationships of compatibility: the theory of identifications and differentiations thereby reveals itself, with more clearness than before, as a chapter in the theory of judgement. For according as positing or non-positing acts function in our intentions or their fulfilments, they illuminate distinctions like that between *illustration*, perhaps *exemplification*, on the one hand, and *verification or confirmation* and its opposite *refutation*, on the other. The concept of verification relates exclusively to *positing acts in relation to their positing fulfilment*, and ultimately to their *fulfilment through percepts*.

To this last pre-eminent case we now give closer consideration. It is a case in which the ideal of adequation yields us *self-evidence* (*Evidenz*). We speak somewhat loosely of self-evidence wherever *a positing* intention (a statement in particular) finds verification in a corresponding, fully accommodated percept, even if this be no more than a well-fitting synthesis of coherent single percepts. To speak of *degrees and levels of self-evidence* then has a good sense. Here are relevant all approximations of percepts to the objective completeness of their presentation of their object, all further steps towards the final ideal of perfection, the ideal of adequate perception, of the complete self-manifestation of the object, however it was referred to in the intention to be fulfilled. But the *epistemologically pregnant sense* of self-evidence is exclusively concerned with this last unsurpassable goal, *the act of this most perfect synthesis of fulfilment*, which gives to an intention, e.g. the intention of judgement, the absolute fulness of content, the fulness of the object itself. The object is not merely meant, but in the strictest sense *given*, and given as it is meant, and made one with our meaning-reference. It does not matter, for the rest, whether one is dealing with an individual or a universal object, with an object in the narrower sense or with a state of affairs, the correlate of an identifying or distinguishing synthesis.

Self-evidence itself, we said, is the act of this most perfect synthesis of coincidence. Like every identification, it is an objectifying act, its objective correlate being called *being in the sense of truth,* or simply *truth* – if one does not prefer to award this term to another concept of the many that are rooted in the said phenomenological situation. Here, however, a closer discussion is needed.

§39 Self-evidence and truth

1. If we at first keep to the notion of truth just suggested, *truth* as the correlate of an identifying act is a *state of affairs* (*Sachverhalt*), as the correlate of a coincident identity it is an *identity: the full agreement* of what is meant with what is *given as such.* This agreement we *experience* in self-evidence, in so far as self-evidence means the actual carrying out of an adequate identification. The proposition that self-evidence is the 'experience' of truth cannot, however, be simply interpreted as telling us that the self-evidence is the perception (in a sufficiently wide sense) of truth and, in the case of strict self-evidence, the *adequate perception of truth.* For, to recur to a previously voiced doubt (see the addendum to §8 and chapter 7), we must allow that the carrying out of an identifying coincidence is not as yet an actual perception of objective agreement, but becomes so only through its own act of objectifying interpretation, its own looking towards present

truth. Truth is indeed 'present'. Here we have always the *a priori* possibility of looking towards this agreement, and of laying it before our intentional consciousness in an adequate percept.

2. A second concept of truth concerns the *ideal relationship* which obtains in the unity of coincidence which we defined as self-evidence, *among the epistemic essences of the coinciding acts.* While truth in sense 1 was the *objective* item corresponding to the act of self-evidence, truth in *this* sense is the Idea which belongs to the act-form: *the epistemic essence interpreted as the ideal essence of the empirically contingent act of self-evidence, the Idea of absolute adequation as such.*

3. We also experience in self-evidence, from the side of the act which furnishes 'fulness', *the object given in the manner* of *the object meant*: so given, the object is fulness itself. This object can also be called being, truth, the 'truth' in so far as it is here not experienced as in the merely adequate percept, but as the ideal fulness for an intention, as that which makes an intention true (or as the ideal fulness for the intention's *specific* epistemic essence).

4. Lastly, considered from the standpoint of the intention, the notion of the relationship of self-evidence yields us truth as the *rightness of our intention* (and especially that of our judgement), its adequacy to its true object, or *the rightness of the intention's epistemic essence in specie.* We have, in the latter regard, the rightness, e.g., of the judgement in the logical sense of the proposition: the proposition 'directs' itself to the thing itself, it says that it is so, and it really is so. In this we have the expression of the ideal, and therefore general, possibility that a proposition of such and such a 'matter' admits of fulfilment in the sense of the most rigorous adequation.

We must further particularly note that the 'being' here in question in our first objective sense of truth, is not to be confused with the 'being' covered by the *copula* in the affirmative categorical judgement. Self-evidence is a matter of *total coincidence,* whereas the 'being' of the copula corresponds generally, if not invariably to partial identifications (i.e. judgements of quality).

But even where total identification is predicated, the two 'beings' will not coincide. For we must observe that in the case of a self-evident judgement, i.e. of a self-evident predicative assertion, *being in the sense of truth is experienced but not expressed,* and so never coincides with the being meant and experienced in the 'is' of the assertion. This second 'being' is the synthetic moment in what *is* in the sense of *is true* – how could it express the fact that the latter is true ? There are in fact *several agreements* which are here brought to synthesis: *one* of these, the partial, predicative one, is meant assertively and perceived adequately, and so self-presented. (What this means will become clearer in the next chapter by way of the more general doctrine of categorial objectification.) This is the *agreement of subject with predicate,* the suiting of predicate to subject. We have, in the second place, *the agreement which constitutes the synthetic form of the act of self-evidence,* and therefore of the total coincidence of the meaning-intention of our assertion with the percept of the state of affairs itself, a coincidence naturally achieved in stages, which do not here concern us further. *This* agreement is plainly not asserted, it is not objective like the first agreement, which belongs to the state of affairs judged. No doubt it *can* always be asserted and asserted with self-evidence. It then becomes the verifying state of affairs for a new self-evidence, of which the like is true, and so on. At each step, however, one must distinguish the verifying state of affairs from the state of affairs constitutive of the self-evidence itself, we must distinguish the objectified from the not-objectified state of affairs.

The distinctions just drawn lead to the following general discussion.

In our exposition of the relationships of the concepts of self-evidence and truth, we have not drawn a distinction which touches the *objective* side of the acts which, whether functioning as intentions or fulfilments, find their absolute adequation in self-evidence: we have not, that is, distinguished between states of affairs, on the one hand, and other objects, on the other. We have paid no heed, correspondingly, to the phenomenological difference between acts which relate, on the one hand – acts of agreement and disagreement, predicative acts – and acts which do not relate, on the other. We have paid no need, therefore, to the difference between relational and non-relational meanings, or to the relational-non-relational distinction among ideally apprehended essences in general. Strict adequation can bring non-relating as much as relating intentions into union with their complete fulfilments. If we now particularly consider the field of expressions, we need not concern ourselves with judgements as assertive intentions or assertive fulfilments; acts of naming can also achieve their adequation. The concepts of truth, rightness, the true, are generally interpreted more narrowly than we have done: they are connected with judgements and propositions, or with the states of affairs which are their objective correlates. 'Being' is meanwhile mainly spoken of in relation to absolute objects (not states of affairs), though no definite lines are drawn. Our right to our more general interpretation of these concepts is unassailable. The very nature of the case demands that the concepts of truth and falsehood, should, in the first instance at least, be fixed so widely as to span the whole sphere of objectifying acts. It seems therefore most suitable that the concepts of truth and being should be so distinguished, that our concepts of truth – a certain range of equivocation remaining inevitable but hardly dangerous once our concepts are clarified – are applied *from the side of the acts themselves* and their ideally graspable moments, whereas the concepts of *being* (genuine being) are applied to the corresponding *objective correlates*. Truth would then have to be defined in the manner of (2) and (4) as the Idea of adequation, or as the rightness of objectifying assertion and meaning. Being would then have to be pinned down according to (1) and (3) as the identity of the object at once meant and given in adequation, or (in conformity with the natural sense of words) as the adequately perceivable thing as such, in an indefinite relation to an intention that it is to make true or fulfil adequately.

After our concepts have been thus widely fixed and assured phenomenologically, we may pass on, having regard to the distinction between relational and non-relational acts (predications versus absolute assertions) to define *narrower concepts of truth and being*. The narrower concept of truth would be limited to the ideal adequation of a *relational* act to the corresponding adequate percept of a state of affairs: just so the narrower concept of being would concern the being of absolute objects, and would separate this off from the 'subsistence' of the state of affairs.

The following is accordingly clear: if one defines a judgement as an assertive act in general, then the sphere of judgement, subjectively speaking, coincides with the joint spheres of the concepts *true* and *false* in the widest sense of these words. But if one defines it by way of the statement and its possible fulfilment, and ranges under judgements only the sphere of relational assertions, then the same coincidence obtains again, provided that the *narrower* concepts of truth and falsehood are again used as a basis.

In one-sided fashion we have hitherto favoured the case of self-evidence, the act described as one of total coincidence. But, turning to the correlated case of conflict, we encounter *absurdity*, the experience of the total conflict between intention and quasi-fulfilment. To the concepts of truth and being the correlated concepts of *falsehood* and *non-being* then correspond. The phenomenological clarification of these concepts can be carried out without particular difficulty, once all foundations have been prepared. The negative ideal of an *ultimate frustration* would first have to be exactly circumscribed.

When self-evidence is conceived strictly, in the manner made basic here, it is plain that such doubts as have from time to time been expressed in modern times are absurd, doubts as to whether the experience of self-evidence might not be associated with the matter *A* for one man, while absurdity is associated with it for another. Such doubts are only possible as long as self-evidence and absurdity are interpreted as peculiar (positive or negative) *feelings* which, contingently attaching to the act of judgement, impart to the latter the specific features which we assess logically as truth and falsehood. If someone experiences the self-evidence of *A*, it is *self-evident* that no second person can experience the absurdity of this same *A*, for, that *A* is self-evident, means that *A* is not merely meant, but also genuinely given, and given as precisely what it is thought to be. In the strict sense it is itself present. But how could a second person refer in thought to this same thing *A*, while the thought that it is *A* is genuinely excluded by a genuinely given non-*A*? One is, it is plain, dealing with a matter of essence, the same matter, in fact, that the law of contradiction (into whose ambiguities the correlations discussed in §39, naturally enter) successfully expresses.

It is reliably clear, as a result of our analyses, that being and non-being are not concepts which in their origin express opposition among the *qualities* of our judgements. Following our interpretation of the phenomenological relationships involved, every judgement is assertive: this assertion does not characterize the 'is' of which the 'is not' is the *qualitative* contrary. The qualitative contrary of a judgement is a mere presentation having the same 'matter'. Differences between 'is' and 'is not' are differences in intentional 'matter'. Just as an 'is' expresses predicative agreement after the manner of a meaning-intention, so an 'is not' expresses a predicative conflict.

Sense and understanding

Chapter 6

Sensuous and categorial intuitions

§40 The problem of the fulfilment of categorial meaning-forms, with a thought leading towards its solution

In our discussions up to this point we have repeatedly and strongly felt a large gap. It had to do with the categorial objective forms, or with the synthetic functions in the sphere of objectifying acts through which these objective forms come to be constituted, through which they may come to 'intuition' and thereby also to 'knowledge'. We shall now attempt to some extent to fill in this gap, taking our point of departure from the investigation of our first chapter; this was concerned with one limited aim of epistemological clarification: the relation of a meaning-intention as the thing to be expressed, with an expressed sensuous intuition. We shall for the time being again build on the simplest cases of perceptual and other intuitive statements, and shall use them to shed light on the theme of our next treatments, in the following manner:

In the case of a perceptual statement, not only the inwrought nominal presentations are fulfilled: the whole sense of the statement finds fulfilment through our underlying percept. We say likewise that the whole statement gives utterance to our percept: we do not merely say 'I see this paper, an inkpot, several books', and so on, but also 'I see that the paper has been written on, that there is a bronze inkpot standing here, that several books are lying open', and so on. If a man thinks the fulfilment of nominal meanings clear enough, we shall ask him how we are to understand the fulfilment of total statements, especially as regards that side of them that stretches beyond their 'matter', in this case beyond their nominal terms. What may and can furnish fulfilment for those aspects of meaning which make up propositional form as such, the aspects of *'categorial form'* to which, e.g., the copula belongs?

Looked at more narrowly, this question also applies to nominal meanings, in so far as these are not totally formless like the meanings for individuals. The name, like the statement, even in its grammatical appearance, possesses both 'matter' and 'form'. If it comprises words, the form lies partly in the way these words are strung together, partly in its own form-words, partly in the mode of construction of the individual words, which allows us to draw a distinction between its moments of 'matter' and its moments of 'form'. Such grammatical distinctions refer us back to distinctions of meaning. There is at least a rough expression of the articulations and forms which are rooted in our meaning's essence and the articulations and forms of grammar. In our meanings, therefore, parts of very different kinds are to be found, and among these we may here pay special attention to those expressed by formal words such as 'the', 'a', 'some', 'many', 'few', 'two', 'is', 'not', 'which', 'and', 'or' etc., and further expressed by the substantival and adjectival, singular and plural inflection of our words etc.

How does all this stand as regards fulfilment? Can the ideal of completely adequate fulfilment formulated by us in our third chapter still be maintained? *Are there parts and forms of perception corresponding to all parts and forms of meaning?* In that case we should have the *parallelism* between meaningful reference and fulfilling intuition that talk of 'expression' suggests. The expression would be an image-like counterpart of the percept (i.e. in all its parts and forms to be expressed) but reconstituted in a new stuff – an *ex-pression* in the *stuff of meaning.*

The prototype for interpreting the relation between meaning and intuiting would then be the relation of the 'proper' individual meaning to corresponding percepts. The man who knows Cologne itself, and therefore possesses the genuine 'proper meaning' of the word 'Cologne', has in his contemporary actual experience something exactly corresponding to the future confirming percept. It is not, properly speaking, a representation of the percept, as, e.g., the corresponding imagination would be. But just as the city is thought to be itself present to us in the percept, so the proper name 'Cologne', in its 'proper meaning', refers, as previously argued, to the same city 'directly': it means that city itself, and as it is. The straightforward percept here renders the object apparent without the help of further, superordinate acts, the object *which* the meaning-intention means, and *just as* the latter means it. The meaning-intention therefore finds in the mere percept the act which fulfils it with complete adequacy.

If instead of considering directly naming, unstructured expressions, we rather consider structured, articulated expressions, the matter seems quite the same. I *see* white paper and *say* 'white paper', thereby expressing, with precise adequacy, only what I see. The same holds of complete judgements. I *see* that this paper is white, and express just this by saying: 'This paper is white'.

We are not to let ourselves be led astray by such ways of speaking; they are in a certain manner correct, yet are readily misunderstood. One might try to use them to show that meaning here has its seat in perception, which, as we have shown, is not so. The word 'white' certainly means something attaching to the white paper itself; this 'meaning' therefore coincides, in the state of fulfilment, with the partial percept which relates to the 'white-aspect' of the object. But the assumption of a mere coincidence with this part-percept is not enough: we are wont to say here that the *white* thus apparent is known *as white* and is called so. In our normal talk of 'knowledge', we are, however, more inclined to call the object which is our (logical) subject the thing 'known'. In *such* knowledge another act plainly is present, which perhaps includes the former one, but is nonetheless different from it: the *paper* is known as white, or rather as a white thing, whenever we express our percept in the words 'white paper'. The intention of the word 'white' only partially coincides with the colour-aspect of the apparent object; a surplus of meaning remains over, a form which finds nothing in the appearance itself to confirm it. White paper is paper which *is* white. Is this form not also repeated, even if it remains hidden, in the case of the noun 'paper'? Only the quality-meanings contained in its 'concept' terminate in perception. Here also the whole object is known as paper, and here also a supplementary form is known which includes being, though not as its sole form, in itself. The fulfilment effected by a straight percept obviously does not extend to such forms.

We have but to ask, further, what corresponds in perception to the difference between the two expressions 'this white paper' and 'this paper is white', which are both realized on the same perceptual basis, we have but to ask what side of perception is really brought out by this difference – the difference, that is, of the attributive and the predicative mode of statement – and what, in the case of adequate adaptation, this difference brings out with peculiar exactness, and we experience the same difficulty. Briefly we see that the case of structured meanings is not so simple as the case of a 'proper' individual meaning, with its straightforward relation of coincidence with perception. Certainly one can tell one's auditors, intelligibly and unambiguously that 'I see that this paper is white', but the thought behind such talk need not be that the meaning of this spoken sentence expresses *a mere act of seeing*. It may also be the case that the epistemic essence of our seeing, in which the apparent object announces itself as self-given, serves to base certain connective or relational or otherwise formative acts, and that it is to *these* that our expression in its changing forms is adjusted, and that it is in such acts, performed on a basis of actual perception, that our expression, in respect of such changing forms, finds fulfilment. If we now combine these founded acts or rather act-forms with the acts which serve as their foundation, and give the comprehensive name 'founded act' to the whole act-complexes that result from such formal 'founding', we may say: Granted the possibility just sketched, our parallelism may be re-established, but it is no longer a parallelism between the meaning-intentions of expressions and the mere percepts which correspond to them: it is a parallelism between meaning-intentions and the above mentioned *perceptually founded acts*.

§41 Continuation. Extension of our sphere of examples

If we suppose our range of examples widened so as to cover the whole field of predicative thinking, we shall encounter similar difficulties and similar possibilities of resolving them. Judgements in particular will come up which have no definite relation to anything individual which ought to be given through any intuition: they will give *general* expression to relations among ideal unities. The general meanings embodied in such judgements can also be realized on a basis of corresponding intuition, since they have their origin, mediately or immediately, in intuition. The intuited individual is not, however, what we mean here; it serves at best only as an individual case, an example, or only as the rough analogue of an example, for the universal which alone interests us. So, for instance, when we speak generically of 'colour' or specifically of 'red', the appearance of a single red thing may furnish us with a documenting intuition.

It also at times happens, that one calls such a general statement an expression of intuition. We say, e.g., that an arithmetical axiom expresses what we find in intuition, or we raise objection to a geometrician that he merely expresses what he sees in his figure without deducing it formally, that he borrows from his drawing and omits steps in his proof. Such talk has its good sense (as when the objection scores no mean hit against the formal validity of Euclidean geometry) but 'expression' here means something different from the previous cases. Even in *their* case expression was not a mere counterpart of intuition: this is even less the case here, where our thought's intention is not aimed at intuitively given phenomena nor at their intuitive properties or relationships, and *can* in our case not be aimed at them. For a figure understood geometrically is known to be an ideal limit incapable in principle of intuitive exhibition in the concrete. Even in our case, nonetheless, and in the generic field as such, intuition has an essential relation to expression and to its meaning: these, therefore, constitute an experience of general knowledge related to intuition, no mere togetherness of them all, but a unity of felt belongingness among them. Even in our case, concept and proposition are oriented towards intuition, through which alone, after corresponding adjustment, self-evidence, the crown of knowledge, emerges. It requires little reflection, on the other hand, to see that the meaning of the expressions in question is not found in intuition at all, that such intuition only gives them a filling of clarity and in the favourable case of self-evidence. We in fact know only too well that the overwhelming majority of general statements, and in particular those of science, behave meaningfully without any elucidation from intuition, and that only a vanishing section, even of the true and the proven, are and remain open to complete intuitive illumination.

Even in the general realm, as in the realm of individuals, our natural talk has a relation to intuitively founded acts of thought. Should intuition fall wholly away, our judgement would cease to know anything. It means, in all cases, in cogitative style, just what could be known by the aid of intuition, if such judgement is indeed true at all. Knowledge always has the character of a fulfilment and an identification: this may be observed in every case where we confirm a general judgement through subsequent intuition, as in every other case of knowledge.

Our difficulty then is how identification can arise where the form of the general proposition, and in particular its form of universality, would vainly seek sympathetic elements in individual intuition. To remove this difficulty, as in the previous case, the possibility of 'founded acts' suggests itself. This possibility, carried out more fully, would run more or less as follows:

Where general thoughts find fulfilment in intuition, certain new acts are built on our percepts and other appearances of like order, acts related quite differently to our appearing object from the intuitions which constitute it. This difference in mode of relation is expressed by the perspicuous turn of phrase employed above: that the intuited object is not here itself the thing meant, but serves only as an elucidatory example of our true general meaning. But if *expressive* acts conform to these differences, their significative intention will not move towards what is to be intuitively presented, but towards what is universal, what is merely documented in intuition. Where this new intention is adequately fulfilled by an underlying intuition, it reveals its own objective possibility (or the possibility or 'reality' of the universal).

§42 The distinction between sensuous stuff and categorial form throughout the whole realm of objectifying acts

After these provisional treatments have shown us our difficulty, and have provided us with a thought leading to its possible removal, we shall embark upon our actual discussion.

We started by assuming that, in the case of structured expressions, the notion of a more or less mirror-like mode of expression was quite unavailing in describing the relation which obtains between meanings to be expressed, on the one hand, and expressed intuitions, on the other. This is doubtless correct and need now only be made more precise. We need only earnestly ponder what things can be possible matter for perception, and what things possible matter for meaning, to become aware that, *in the mere form of a judgement, only certain antecedently specifiable parts of our statement can have something which corresponds to them in intuition, while to other parts of the statement nothing intuitive possibly can correspond.*

Let us consider this situation a little more closely.

Perceptual statements are, completely and normally expressed, articulate utterances of varying pattern. We have no difficulty in distinguishing such types as '*A* is *P*' (where '*A*' serves as index for a proper name), 'An *S* is *P*',

'This S is P, 'All S are P' etc. Many complications arise through the modifying influence of negation, through the introduction of distinctions between
absolute and relative predicates (attributes), through conjunctive, disjunctive and determinative connectives etc. In the diversity of these types certain
sharp distinctions of meaning make themselves clear. To the various letters
(variables) and words in these types correspond sometimes *members*, sometimes *connective forms*, in the meanings of the actual statements which
belong to these types. Now it is easy to see that *only at the places indicated
by letters (variables)* in such 'forms of judgement', *can* meanings be put
that are themselves fulfilled in perception, whereas it is hopeless, even quite
misguided, to look directly in perception for what could give fulfilment to
our supplementary formal meanings. The letters (variables) on account of
their merely functional meaning, can doubtless take complex thoughts as
their values: statements of high complexity can be seen from the standpoint
of very simple judgement-types. The same difference between 'matter' and
'form' therefore repeats itself in what is looked upon, in unified fashion, as
a 'term'. But eventually, in the case of each perceptual statement, and likewise, of course, in the case of every other statement that in a certain primary
sense, gives expression to intuition, we shall come down to certain final
elements of our terms – we may call them elements of stuff – which find
direct fulfilment in intuition (perception, imagination etc.), while the supplementary *forms*, which as forms of meaning likewise crave fulfilment,
can find nothing that ever could fit them in perception or acts of like order.

This fundamental difference we call, in a natural extension of its application
over the whole sphere of objectifying presentation, the *categorial* and *absolute* distinction between the *form* and *matter* of *presentation*, and at the same
time separate it off from the *relative* or *functional* difference which is closely
bound up with it, and which has just been subsidiarily touched on above.

We have just spoken of a natural extension of our distinction over the
whole sphere of objectifying presentation. We take the constituents of the
fulfilment which correspond to the material or formal constituents of our
meaning-intentions as being material or formal constituents respectively, so
making clear what is to count as 'material' or 'formal' in the general sphere
of objectifying acts.

Of matter (stuff) and form we often talk in many other senses. We must
expressly point out that our present talk of 'matter', which has its contrast
in categorial form, has nothing whatever to do with the 'matter' which
contrasts with the quality of acts, as when, e.g., we distinguish the 'matter'
in our meanings from their assertive or merely presentative quality, this
'matter' being what tells *us as what*, or as *now* determined and interpreted,
an object is meant in our meanings. To make the distinction easier, we shall
not speak of 'matter' in our categorial contrast, but of 'stuff', while wherever 'matter' is meant in our previous sense, we shall talk pointedly of
'intentional matter' or of 'interpretative sense'.

§43 The objective correlates of categorial forms are not 'real' (*realen*) moments

It is now time to illuminate the distinction to which we have just given a name. We shall link on, for this purpose, to our previous examples.

The form-giving flexion *Being*, whether in its attributive or predicative function, is not fulfilled, as we said, in any percept. We here remember Kant's dictum: *Being is no real predicate.* This dictum refers to being *qua* existence, or to what Herbart called the being of 'absolute position', but it can be taken to be no less applicable to predicative and attributive being. In any case it precisely refers to what we are here trying to make clear. I can see colour, but not *being*-coloured. I can feel smoothness, but not *being*-smooth. I can hear a sound, but not that something *is* sounding. Being is nothing *in* the object, no part of it, no moment tenanting it, no quality or intensity of it, no figure of it or no internal form whatsoever, no constitutive feature of it however conceived. But being is also nothing attaching *to* an object: as it is no real (*reales*) internal feature, so also it is no real external feature, and therefore not, in the *real* sense, a 'feature' at all. For it has nothing to do with the *real* forms of unity which bind objects into more comprehensive objects, tones into harmonies, things into more comprehensive things or arrangements of things (gardens, streets, the phenomenal external world). On these real forms of unity the external features of objects, the right and the left, the high and the low, the loud and the soft etc., are founded. Among these anything like an 'is' is naturally not to be found.

We have just been speaking of *objects*, their constitutive features, their factual connection with other objects, through which more comprehensive objects are created, and also, at the same time, external features in the partial objects. We said that something corresponding to *being* was not to be sought among them. For all these are perceptible, and they exhaust the range of possible percepts, so that we are at once saying and maintaining *that being is absolutely imperceptible.*

Here, however a clarifying supplement is necessary. *Perception* and *object* are concepts that cohere most intimately together, which mutually assign sense to one another, and which widen or narrow this sense conjointly. But we must emphasize that we have here made use of a certain naturally delimited, natural, but also *very narrow concept of perception (or of object).* It is well-known that one also speaks of 'perceiving', and in particular of 'seeing', in a greatly widened sense, which covers the grasping of whole states of affairs, and even ultimately the *a priori* self-evidence of laws (in the case of 'insight'). In the *narrower* sense of perception (to talk roughly and popularly) we perceive everything objective that we see with our eyes, hear with our ears or can grasp with any 'outer' or even 'inner sense'. In ordinary speech, no doubt, only *external* things and connective forms of things (together with their immediate qualities) can count as 'perceived by the senses'.

But once talk of an 'inner sense' had been introduced, one should in consistency have widened the notion of sense-perception suitably, so as to include 'inner perception', and so as to include under the name 'sense-object' the correlated sphere of 'inner objects', the ego and its internal experiences.

In the sphere of sense-perception thus understood, and in the sphere, likewise, of sensuous intuition in general – we adhere to our much widened talk of the 'sensuous' – a meaning like that of the word 'being' can find no possible *objective correlate*, and so no possible fulfilment in the acts of such perception. What holds of 'being' is plainly true of the remaining categorial forms in our statements, whether these bind the constituents of terms together, or bind terms themselves together in the unity of the proposition. The 'a' and the 'the', the 'and' and the 'or', the 'if' and the 'then', the 'all' and the 'none', the 'something' and the 'nothing', the forms of quantity and the determinations of number etc. – all these are meaningful propositional elements, but we should look in vain for their objective correlates (if such may be ascribed to them at all) in the sphere of *real* objects, which is in fact no other than the sphere of *objects of possible sense-perception*.

§44 The origin of the concept of Being and of the remaining categories does not lie in the realm of inner perception

This holds – we stress it expressly – both of the sphere of outer sense, and of that of 'inner sense'. It is a natural but quite misguided doctrine, universally put about since the time of Locke, that the meanings in question (or the corresponding substantivally hypostatized meanings) – the *logical categories* such as being and non-being, unity, plurality, totality, number, ground, consequence etc. – arise through *reflection upon certain mental acts, and so fall in the sphere of 'inner sense', of 'inner perception'*. In this manner, indeed, concepts like Perception, Judgement, Affirmation, Denial, Collecting, Counting, Presupposing and Inferring arise, which are all, therefore, 'sensuous' concepts, belonging, that is, to the sphere of 'inner sense'. The previous series of concepts do not arise in this manner, since they cannot at all be regarded as concepts of mental acts, or of their real constituents. The thought of a Judgement fulfils itself in the inner intuition of an actual judgement, but the thought of an 'is' does not fulfil itself in this manner. Being is not a judgement nor a constituent of a judgement. Being is as little a real constituent of some inner object as it is of some outer object, and so not of a judgement. In a judgement, a predicative statement, 'is' functions as a side of our meaning, just as perhaps, although otherwise placed and functioning, 'gold' and, 'yellow' do. The *is* itself does not enter into the judgement, it is merely meant, signitively referred to, by the little word 'is'. It is, however, *self-given*, or at least putatively given, in the *fulfilment* which at times invests the judgement, the *becoming aware* of the state of affairs supposed. Not only what is meant in the partial meaning *gold*, nor only what is meant in the partial meaning *yellow*, itself appears before us, but also *gold-being-yellow* thus appears. Judgement and judgemental intuition are therefore at one in the self-evident judgement, and pre-eminently so if the judgement is self-evident in the ideally limiting sense.

If one now understands by 'judging', not merely meaning-intentions connected with actual assertions, but the fulfilments that in the end fit them completely, it is indeed correct that *being can only·be apprehended through judging*, but this does not *at all mean* that the concept of being must be arrived at 'through reflection' on certain judgements, or that it can ever be arrived at in this fashion. 'Reflection' is in other respects a fairly vague word. In epistemology it has at least the relatively fixed sense that Locke gave it, that of internal perception: we can only adhere to this sense in interpreting a doctrine which imagines it can find the origin of the concept of *Being* through reflecting on judgements. The relational being expressed in predication, e.g. through 'is', 'are' etc., lacks independence: if we round it out to something fully concrete, we get the *state of affairs* in question, the objective correlate of the complete judgement. We can then say: *As the sensible object stands to sense-perception so the state of affairs stands to the 'becoming aware' in which it is* (more or less adequately) *given* – we should like to say simply: so the state of affairs stands to the *perception* of it. As the concept *Sensuous Object* (*Real Object*) cannot arise through reflection upon perception, since this could only yield us the concept *Perception* (or a concept of certain real constituents of Perception), so the concept of State of Affairs cannot arise out of reflection on judgements, since this could only yield us concepts of judgements or of real constituents of judgements.

That percepts in the one case, and judgements (judgemental intuitions, percepts of states of affairs) in the other, must be *experienced*, in order that each such act of abstraction should get started, goes without saying, but to be experienced is not to he made objective. 'Reflection', however, implies that what we reflect upon, the phenomenological experience, is rendered objective to us (is inwardly perceived by us), and that the properties to be generalized are really given in this objective content.

Not in reflection upon judgements, nor even upon fulfilments of judgements, but in the fulfilments of judgements themselves lies the true source of the concepts State of Affairs and Being (in the copulative sense). Not in these *acts as objects*, but in *the objects of these acts*, do we have the abstractive basis which enables us to realize the concepts in question. And naturally the appropriate modifications of these acts yield just as good a basis.

It is in fact obvious from the start that, just as any other concept (or Idea, Specific Unity) can only 'arise', i.e. become *self-given* to us, if based on an act which at least sets some individual instance of it imaginatively before our eyes, so the concept of Being can arise only when *some being, actual or imaginary, is set before our yes*. If 'being' is taken to mean predicative being, some *state of affairs* must be given to us, and this by way of an *act which gives it, an analogue of common sensuous intuition*.

The like holds of all *categorial forms* (or of all *categories*). An aggregate, e.g., is given, and can only be given, in an actual act of assembly, in an act, that is, expressed in the conjunctive form of connection *A and B and C . . .* But the concept of *Aggregate* does not arise through reflection on this act: instead of paying heed to the act which presents an aggregate, we have rather to pay heed to what it presents, to the *aggregate* it renders apparent *in concreto*, and then to lift the universal form of our aggregate to conceptually universal consciousness.

§45 Widening of the concept of Intuition, and in particular of the concepts Perception and Imagination. Sensible and categorial intuition

If we now ask: 'Where do the categorial forms of our meanings find their fulfilment, if not in the "perception" or "intuition which we tried provisionally to delimit in talking of "sensibility"', our answer is plainly prefigured in the discussions just completed.

We have taken it for granted that forms, too, can be genuinely fulfilled, or that the same applies to variously structured total meanings, and not merely to the 'material' elements of such meanings, and our assumption is put beyond doubt by looking at each case of faithful perceptual assertion. This will explain also why we call the whole perceptual assertion an expression of perception and, in a derivative sense, of whatever is intuited or itself presented in perception. But if the 'categorial forms' of the expression, present together with its material aspects, have no terminus in perception, if by the latter we understand merely *sense*-perception, then talk of expressing a percept must here rest on a different meaning: there must at least be an act which renders identical services to the categorial elements of meaning that merely sensuous perception renders to the material elements. The essential homogeneity of the function of fulfilment, as of all the ideal relationships necessarily bound up with it, obliges us to give the name 'perception' to each fulfilling act of confirmatory self-presentation, to each fulfilling act whatever the name of an 'intuition', and to its intentional correlate the name of '*object*'. If we are asked what it means to say that *categorially structured meanings* find fulfilment, confirm themselves in perception, we can but reply: it means only that they relate to the object itself *in its categorial structure*. The object with these categorial forms is not merely referred to, as in the case where meanings function purely symbolically, but it is set before our very eyes in just these forms. In other words: it is not merely thought of, but intuited or perceived. When we wish, accordingly, to set forth what this talk of 'fulfilment' is getting at, what structured meanings and their structural elements express, what unitary or unifying factor corresponds to them objectively, we unavoidably come on 'intuition' (or on 'perception' and 'object'). We cannot manage without these words, whose widened sense is of course evident. What shall we call the correlate of a non-sensuous subject-presentation, one involving non-sensuous structure, if the word 'object' is not available to us? How shall we speak of its actual givenness, or apparent givenness, when the word 'perception' is denied us? In common parlance, therefore, *aggregates, indefinite pluralities, totalities, numbers, disjunctions, predicates* (right-ness), *states of affairs*, all count as 'objects', while the acts through which they seem to be given count as 'percepts'.

Plainly the connection between the wider and narrower, the *supersensuous* (i.e. raised above sense, or categorial) and *sensuous concept of perception,* is no external or contingent matter, but one rooted in the whole business on hand. It falls within the great class of acts whose peculiarity it is that in them something appears as 'actual', as 'self-given'. Plainly this appearance of actuality and self-givenness (which may very well be delusive) is throughout characterized by its difference from essentially related acts through which alone it achieves full clarity – its difference from an imaginative 'making present', or from a merely significative 'thinking of', which both exclude 'presence' (so to say appearance 'in person'), though not excluding the belief in being. As regards the latter, imaginal or symbolic representation is possible in two manners: in an assertive manner, asserting something's being in imaginal or symbolic fashion, and in a non-assertive manner, as 'mere' imagination or thinking without taking something to be. We need not enter more closely into the discussion of these differences after the analyses of the previous section, which permit of a sufficiently general interpretation. It is clear, in any case, that the concept of imagination must be *widened in correspondence with* the concept of perception. We could not speak of something super-sensuously or categorially *perceived,* if we could not *imagine* this thing 'in the same manner' (i.e. not merely sensuously). We must therefore draw a quite general distinction between *sensuous* and *categorial* intuition (or show the possibility of such a distinction).

Our extended concept of Perception permits, further, of a narrower and a wider interpretation. In the widest sense even universal states of affairs can be said to be perceived ('seen', 'beheld with evidence'). In the narrower sense, perception terminates upon individual, and so upon temporal being.

§46 Phenomenological analysis of the distinction between sensuous and categorial perception

In our next treatments we shall first only discuss individual percepts, then widen our treatment to take in individual intuitions of the same order.

The division between 'sensuous' and 'supersensuous' percepts was only very superficially indicated and quite roughly characterized above. Antiquated talk of external and internal senses, plainly stemming from the naïve metaphysic and anthropology of daily life, may be useful in pointing out the sphere to be excluded, but a true determination and circumscription of the sensory sphere is not thereby reached, so depriving the concept of categorial perception of its descriptive underpinning. To ascertain and clarify the said distinction is all the more important, since such fundamental distinctions as that between categorial form and sensuously founded matter, and the similar distinction between categories and all other concepts, depends wholly on it. Our concern is therefore to seek more profound descriptive character-izations, which will give us some insight into the essentially different con-stitution of sensuous and categorial percepts (or intuitions in general).

For our immediate purposes it is, however, unnecessary to carry out an exhaustive analysis of the phenomena involved. That would be a task that would require extraordinarily comprehensive treatments. Here it is sufficient to concentrate on some weightier points, which may help to mark off both sorts of acts in their mutual relation.

It is said of every percept that it grasps its object *directly*, or grasps this object *itself*. But this direct grasping has a different sense and character according as we are concerned with a percept in the narrower or the wider sense, or according as the directly grasped object is *sensuous* or *categorial*. Or otherwise put, according as it is a *real* or an *ideal* object. Sensuous or real objects can in fact be characterized as *objects of the lowest level of possible intuition*, categorial or ideal objects as *objects of higher levels*.

In the sense of the *narrower, 'sensuous' perception*, an object is directly apprehended or is itself present, if it is set up in an act of perception *in a straightforward (schlichter) manner*. What this means is this: that the object is also an *immediately given object* in the sense that, as *this object perceived with this definite objective content*, it is not *constituted* in relational, con-nective, or otherwise articulated acts, *acts founded on other acts which bring other objects to perception*. Sensuous objects are present in perception *at a single act-level*: they do not need to be constituted in many-rayed fashion in acts of higher level, whose objects are set up for them by way of other objects, already constituted in other acts.

Each straightforward act of perception, by itself or together with other acts, can serve as basic act for new acts which at times include it, at times merely presuppose it, acts which in their new mode of consciousness like-wise bring to maturity *a new awareness of objects which essentially presup-poses the old*. When the new acts of conjunction, of disjunction, of definite and indefinite individual apprehension (that – something), of generalization, of straightforward, relational and connective knowledge, arise, we do not then have *any* sort of subjective experiences, nor just acts connected with the original ones. What we have are acts which, as we said, *set up new objects*, acts in which something *appears as actual and self-given*, which was not given, and could not have been given, as what it now appears to be, in these foundational acts alone. *On the other hand, the new objects are based on the older ones, they are related to what appears in the basic acts.* Their manner of appearance is essentially determined by this relation. We are here dealing with a sphere of objects, *which can only show themselves 'in person' in such founded acts.* In such founded acts we have the categorial element in intuition and knowledge, in them assertive thought, functioning expressively, finds fulfilment; the possibility of complete accord with such acts determines the truth, the rightness, of an assertion. So far we have of course only considered the sphere of perception, and only its most elementary cases. But one sees at once that the distinction of straightforward and founded acts can be extended from percepts to all intuitions. We clearly envisage the possibility of complex acts which in mixed fashion have a part-basis in straightforward percepts and a part-basis in straightforward imaginations, and the further possibility of setting up new foundations on intuitions which themselves have foundations, and so building up whole series of foundings upon foundings. We further see that signitive intentions have structures patterned on such foundings whether of lower or higher order, and that again mixtures of signitive and intuitive acts emerge out of such 'founding', founded acts, in short, that are built on acts of one or the other sort. Our first task, however, is to deal with the elementary cases and elucidate them completely.

§47 Continuation. Characterization of sense-perception as 'straightforward' perception

We shall now scrutinize the acts in which sensuous concreta and their sensuous constituents are presented as given; as opposed to these we shall later consider the quite different acts in which concretely determinate States of Affairs, Collections and Disjunctions are given as complex thought-objects, or as objects of higher order, *which include their foundational objects as real parts* (*reell*) *in themselves.* We shall then deal with acts of the type of generalizing or indefinitely individual apprehension, whose objects certainly are of higher level, but which do *not* include their foundational objects in themselves.

In *sense*-perception, the 'external' thing appears 'in one blow', as soon as our glance falls upon it. The manner in which it makes the thing appear present is *straightforward*: it requires no apparatus of founding or founded acts. To what complex mental processes it may trace back its origin, and in what manner, is of course irrelevant here.

We are not ignoring the obvious complexity that can be shown to exist in the phenomenological content of the straightforward perceptual act, and particularly in its unitary intention.

Many constitutive properties certainly pertain to the thing when it appears with a given content, some of them themselves 'falling under perception', others merely intended. But we certainly do not live through all the articulated acts of perception which *would* arise were we to attend to all the details of the thing, or, more precisely, to the properties of the 'side turned to us', were we to make them objects in their own right. No doubt ideas of such supplementary properties, not given in perception, are 'dispositionally excited', no doubt intentions which relate to them contribute to perception, and determine its total character. But, just as the thing does not appear before us as the mere sum of its countless individual features, which a later preoccupation with detail may distinguish, and as even the latter does not dirempt the thing into such details, but takes note of them only in the ever complete, unified thing, so the act of perception also is always a homogeneous unity, which gives the object 'presence' in a simple, immediate way. The unity of perception does *not* therefore arise through *our own synthetic activity*, as if only a form of synthesis, operating by way of founded acts, could give unity of objective reference to part-intentions. It requires no articulation and hence no actual linkage. The unity of perception comes into being as a *straightforward* unity, *as an immediate fusion of part-intentions, without the addition of new art-intentions.*

We may also be unsatisfied with a single glance, we may handle the thing from all sides in a *continuous perceptual series*, feeling it over as it were with our senses. But each single percept in this series is already a percept of the thing. Whether I look at this book from above or below, from inside or outside, I always see *this book*. It is always one and the same thing, and that not merely in some purely physical sense, but in the view of our percepts themselves. If individual properties dominate variably at each step, the thing itself, as a perceived unity, is not in essence set up by some overreaching act, founded upon these separate percepts.

Considering things more closely, we should not present the matter as if the one sensible object *could* be presented in a founded act (in a continuously developing act of perceiving), while it merely does not *need* to be presented in such an act. Closer analysis shows that even a continuous perceptual flux involves a *fusion* of part-acts in one act, *rather than a peculiar act founded upon such part-acts.*

To prove this we embark on the following discussion.

The individual percepts of our series have a continuous unity. Such continuity does not amount to the mere fact of temporal adjunction: the series of individual acts rather has the character of a phenomenological unity, in which the individual acts are fused. In this unity, our manifold acts are not merely fused into a phenomenological whole, but into *one act*, more precisely, into *one concept*. In the continuous running on of individual percepts we continuously perceive the single, selfsame object. Can we now call this continuous percept, since it is built out of individual percepts, a percept *founded* upon them? It is of course founded upon them in the sense in which a whole is founded on its parts, not however in the sense here relevant, according to which a founded act manifests a new act-character, grounded in the act-characters that underlie it and unthinkable apart from these. In the case before us perception is merely, as it were, extended: it allows parts to be broken off from itself which can function as complete, independent percepts. But the unification of these percepts into a continuous percept is not the performance of some peculiar act, through which a new consciousness of something objective is set up. We find, instead, that absolutely nothing new is objectively meant in the extended act, but that the same object is continuously meant in it, the very object that the part-percepts, *taken singly*, were already meaning.

One might lay stress on this sameness, and say that our unity is plainly a *unity of identification*, that the intention of the serially arranged acts coincides continuously, and that so the unity arises. This is certainly right. But *unity of identification* is unavoidably distinct, *does not say the same as the unity of an act of identification*. An act *means* something, an act of identification means identity, presents it. In our case an identification is performed, but no identity is meant. The object meant in the differing acts of the continuous perceptual series is indeed always the same, and the acts are one through coincidence, but what is perceived in the series, what is rendered objective in it, is solely the sensible object, never its identity with self. Only when we use the perceptual series to found a novel act, only when we articulate our individual percepts, and relate their objects to each other, does the unity of continuity holding among these individual percepts – the unity of fusion through their coinciding intentions – provide a *point d'appui* for a consciousness of identity. Identity itself is now made objective, the moment of coincidence linking our act-characters with one another, serves as *representative content for a new percept, founded upon* our articulated individual percepts. This brings to intentional awareness that what we now see and what we saw before are one and the same. Naturally we have then to do with a regular act of our second group. Our act of identification is in sober fact a new awareness of objectivity, which causes a new 'object' to appear to us, an object that can only be apprehended or given in its very selfhood in a founded act of this sort.

Before we penetrate further into our new class of acts and objects, we must, however, first round off our treatment of straightforward percepts. If we may presume to have cleared up the sense of the concept of a *straightforward* percept, or, what we take for the same, of sense-perception, then we have also cleared up the concept of a *sensible* or *real object* (in the most basic sense of 'real'). We define a real object as the possible object of a straightforward percept. There is a necessary parallelism between perception and *imagination*, which guarantees that a possible imagination (or more precisely a whole series of imaginations) having the same essence, corresponds to each possible percept, a *straightforward* imagination is correlated with each straightforward percept, thereby giving certainty to the wider concept of *sensible intuition*. We can then define *sensible* objects as the possible objects of sensible imagination and sensible intuition in general: this of course involves no essential generalization of our previous definition. The parallelism just stressed makes both definitions equivalent.

Through the concept of a real object, the concept of a *real* part, or more particularly, the concepts of a *real piece*, and a *real* moment (real feature), and a *real form*, are determined. Each part of a real object is a real part.

In straightforward perception we say that the whole object is explicitly given, while each of its parts (in the widest sense of 'parts') is implicitly given. The sum total of objects that can be *explicitly or implicitly given* in straightforward percepts constitutes *the most widely conceived sphere of sensible objects.*

Each concrete sensible object is perceptible in explicit fashion, and so also every piece of such an object. How does the matter stand in regard to abstract moments? Their nature makes them incapable of separate being: their representative content, even where there is merely representation by way of analogy, cannot be experienced alone, but only in a more comprehensive concrete setting. But this does not mean that their intuition need be a founded act. It would be one, if the apprehension of an abstract moment was necessarily preceded by the *apprehension* of the concrete whole or of its complementary moments, such an apprehension being an act of intuitive turning towards its object. This I do not find obvious. It is clear, *per contra*, that the apprehension of a moment and of a part generally *as* a part of the whole in question and, in particular, the apprehension of a sensuous feature *as* a feature, or of a sensuous form *as* a form, point to acts which are all founded: these acts are in our case of a relational kind. This means that the sphere of 'sensibility' has been left and that of 'understanding' entered. We shall now subject the just mentioned group of founded acts to a closer consideration.

§48 Characterization of categorial acts as founded acts

A sensible object can be apprehended by us in a variety of ways. It can, first of all, of course, be apprehended in 'straightforward' fashion. It is this possibility, which like all the other possibilities here in question must be throughout interpreted as 'ideal', which characterizes the sensible object as a sensible object. Understood in this manner, it stands as it were simply before us: the parts which constitute it are indeed in it, but are not made our explicit objects in the straightforward act. The same object can, however, be grasped by us in explicating fashion: acts of articulation can put its parts 'into relief', relational acts bring the relieved parts into relation, whether to one another or to the whole. Only through such new modes of interpretation will the connected and related members assume the character of 'parts' (or of 'wholes'). The articulating acts and, taken in retrospect, the act we call 'straightforward', are not merely experienced one after the other:

overreaching unities of act are rather always present, in which, *as new objects*, the *relationships of the parts* become constituted.

Let us first look at the relationships of parts and wholes: limiting ourselves to the simplest cases, let us consider the relationships *A is or has α* and *α is in A*. To point to the founded acts in which these typical states of affairs become constituted as data, and to clear up the just employed forms of categorical statement (to lead them back to their intuitive origin and adequate fulfilment) are one and the same. We are not, however, here concerned with the qualities of acts, but only with the constitution of their interpretative forms: to that extent our analysis, if regarded as an analysis of judgement, will be defective.

An act of perception grasps *A* as a whole, at one 'blow' and in straightforward fashion. A second act of perception is trained upon *α*, the part or dependent moment, that belongs constitutively to *A*. These two acts are not merely performed together, or after one another, in the manner of disjoined experiences; rather are they bound together in a single act in whose synthesis *A* is first given as containing *α* in itself. Just so, *α* can, with a reversal of the direction of relational perception, achieve self-givenness as pertaining to *A*.

Let us now try to penetrate a little deeper.

The total intuitive reference to our object implicitly contains an intention to *α*. For perception purports to grasp the object itself: its 'grasping' must therefore reach to all its constituents in and with the whole object. (Naturally we are here only concerned with what constitutes the object *as* it appears in perception, and *as what* it appears in perception, and not with such constituents as may pertain to it in 'objective reality', and which only later experience, knowledge and science will bring out.)

In the narrowing down of our total percept to one specific percept, the part-intention to *α* will not be torn out of the total appearance of *A*, so as to break up the latter's unity, but an *independent* act will have *α* as its own perceptual object. At the same time one's continuously operative total percept will coincide with this specific percept in respect of one implicit part-intention. The 'content' which represents *α*, will be functioning as the same content in a twofold fashion and, in so far as it does this, it will effect a coincidence, a peculiar unity of the two representative functions; we shall, in other words, have two coincident interpretations, both sustained by the representative content in question. But this unity of these two representative functions will now itself take on a representative role. It will not itself count in its own right as an experienced bond among acts: it will not set itself up as our object, but will help to set up another object. It will act representatively, and to such effect, that *A* will now appear to contain *α* in itself (or, with a reversed direction, *α* will appear as contained in *A*).

According, therefore, to our 'interpretative standpoint', or to the 'sense of our passage' from part to whole or contrariwise – which are both *novel phenomenological characters* making their contribution to the total intentional matter of the relating act – there will be two possibilities, marked off in *a priori* fashion, in which the 'same relation' can achieve actual givenness. To these correspond two *a priori* possibilities of relation, objectively different, yet tied together by an ideal law, possibilities *which can only be directly constituted in founded acts of the sort in question*, which can achieve 'self-givenness to perception' only in acts built up in this manner.

Our exposition obviously applies to all specific forms of the relation between a *whole* and its *parts*. All such relationships are of categorial, ideal nature. It would be a mistake to try to locate them in the straightforwardly given whole, to discover them in this whole by analysis. The part certainly lies hidden in the whole before all division into members, and is subsidiarily apprehended in our perceptual grasp of this whole. But this fact, that it thus lies hidden in the whole, is at first merely the ideal possibility of bringing the part, and the fact that it is a part, to perception in correspondingly articulated and founded acts.

The matter is plainly similar in the case of *external* relations, from which predications such as '*A* is to the right of *B*', '*A* is larger, brighter, louder than *B* etc.', take their rise. Wherever sensible objects – directly and independently perceptible – are brought together, despite their mutual exclusion, into more or less intimate unities, into what fundamentally are more comprehensive objects, then a possibility of such external relations arises. They all fall under the general type of the relation of *part to parts within a whole. Founded acts are once more the media in which the primary appearance of the states of affairs in question*, of such external relationships, is achieved. It is clear, in fact, that neither the straightforward percept of the complex whole, nor the specific percepts pertaining to its members, are in themselves the relational percepts which alone are possible in such a complex. Only when one member is picked out as principal member, and is dwelt on while the other members are still kept in mind, does a determination of members by members make its appearance, a determination which varies with the kind of unity that is present and plainly also with the particular members set in relief. In such cases also the choice of a principal member, or of a direction of relational apprehension, leads to phenomenologically distinct forms of relationship, correlatively characterized, which forms are not genuinely present in the unarticulated percept of the connection as a straightforward phenomenon, but which are in it only as *ideal possibilities*, the possibilities, that is, of fulfilling relevant founded acts.

A real (*reelle*) location of these relations of parts in the whole would be a confusion of distinct things: of *sensuous* or *real* (*realen*) forms of combination, with *categorial* or *ideal* ones. Sensible combinations are aspects of the real (*realen*) object, its actual moments, present in it, if only implicitly, and capable of being 'lifted out of it' by an abstractive percept. As against this, forms of categorial combination go with the manner in which acts are synthesized: they are constituted as objects in the synthetic acts built upon our sensibility. In the formation of external relations sensuous forms may serve as foundations for the categorial forms which correspond to them, as when, in the face of the sensuously intuited contact of the contents *A* and *B* within a comprehensive whole *W*, we, observe, and perhaps verbally express our observation, in the synthetic forms '*A* is in contact with *B*', or '*B* is in contact with *A*'. But, in constituting the latter forms, we bring new objects into being, objects belonging to the class of 'states of affairs', which includes none but 'objects of higher order'. In the sensible whole, the parts *A* and *B* are made one by the sensuously combinatory form of contact. The abstraction of these parts and moments, the formation of intuitions of *A*, *B* and *contact*, will not yet yield the presentation *A in contact with B*. This demands a novel act which, taking charge of such presentations, shapes and combines them suitably.

§52 Universal objects constituting themselves in universal intuitions

The simple synthetic acts with which we have so far concerned ourselves were so founded upon straightforward percepts that the *synthetic intention was subsidiarily directed to the objects of these founding percepts*, inasmuch as it held them together in ideal 'contents' or brought them to a relational unity. This is a *universal* character of synthetic acts as such. We now turn to examples from *another set of categorial acts*, in which the objects of the founding acts do not *enter into* the intention of the founded one, and would only reveal their close relation to it in relational acts. Here we have the field of the *universal intuition* – an expression which no doubt will not seem better to many than 'wooden iron'.

Abstraction gets to work on a basis of primary intuitions, and with it a new categorial act-character emerges, in which a new style of objectivity becomes apparent, an objectivity which can *only* become apparent – whether given as 'real' or as 'merely imagined' – in just such a founded act. Naturally I do not here mean 'abstraction' merely in the sense of a setting-in-relief of some non-independent moment in a sensible object, but Ideational Abstraction, where no such non-independent moment, but its Idea, its Universal, is brought to consciousness, and achieves *actual givenness*. We must presuppose such an act in order that the Very Sort, to which the manifold single moments 'of one and the same sort' stand opposed, may *itself* come before us, and may come before us *as one and the same*. For we become aware of the identity of the universal through the repeated performance of such acts upon a basis of several individual intuitions, and we plainly do so in an overreaching act of identification which brings all such single acts of abstraction into one synthesis. Through such acts of abstraction, woven into new act-forms, there arise, further, acts of universal determination, acts, that is, which determine objects *generally* as subsumed under certain species *A*, or acts in which *unspecified* objects *of a sort A* become present to us.

In an act of abstraction, which need not necessarily involve the use of an abstract name, the universal *itself is given to us*; we do not think of it merely in significative fashion as when we merely understand general names, but we apprehend it, *behold* it. Talk of an *intuition* and, more precisely, of a *perception of the universal* is in this case, therefore, well-justified.

Difficulties arise, however, from another quarter. Talk of 'perception' presupposes the possibility of correspondent imagination: a distinction between them, we held, is part of the natural sense of our ordinary talk about 'intuition'. But it is just this distinction that we cannot here draw. This seems to stem from the fact that abstractive acts do not differ in consonance with the character of the straightforward intuitions which underlie them; they are quite unaffected by the assertive or non-assertive character of such underlying acts, or by their perceptual or imaginative character. The *Red*, the *Triangle* exemplified in mere phantasy is specifically the same as the *Red*, the *Triangle* exemplified in our percepts. Our consciousness of the universal has as satisfactory a basis in perception as it has in parallel imagination, and, wherever it arises, the Idea *Red*, the Idea *Triangle*, is *itself* apprehended, is intuited in the one unique way which permits no distinction between image and original.

We must, however, note that the examples adduced were all cases of the *adequate* perception of the universal. The universal was here truly grasped and given on the basis of truly correspondent instances. Where this is the case, there seems in fact to be no parallel imagination having the same intuitive content, and this is so in *every* case of adequate perception. For how, we may ask, even in the realm of individuals, could a content pattern itself on itself, since, taken as itself, it cannot also be meant as its own analogon? And how can the note of *assertion* be wanting, where the meant content is the one experienced and given? It is quite different in, e.g., the case where mathematical analysis has given us an indirectly conceived Idea of a certain class of curves of the third order, though we have never *seen* any curve of this sort. In such a case an intuitive figure, e.g. of a familiar third-order curve, perhaps actually drawn, perhaps merely pictured, may very well serve as an intuitive image, an analogon, of the universal we are intending: our consciousness of the universal is here intuitive, but analogically intuitive, in its use of an individual intuition. And does not an ordinary rough drawing function analogically in comparison with an ideal figure, thereby helping to condition the *imaginative character of the universal presentation*? This is how we contemplate the Idea of a steam-engine, basing ourselves on a model of a steam-engine, in which case there can naturally be no talk of an adequate abstraction or conception. In such cases we are not concerned with significations, but with universal representations by way of analogy, with universal imaginations, in short. If, however, the consciousness of mere analogy lapses, as may happen, e.g., in the intuition of a model, we have a case of the *perception of the universal*, even if it is one of *inadequate* perception.

In the same way we may now discover the previously missing differences between *an assertive, and a merely contemplative, consciousness of the universal.* Where we contemplate a universal object in a merely analogizing, imaginative fashion, we may also mean it assertively, and this act, like any assertive reference, may be confirmed or refuted by adequate future perception. The former happens wherever the universal meaning is fulfilled by an adequate percept, i.e. by a new consciousness of the universal which constitutes itself on the basis of a 'true' abstraction from the corresponding individual percept. The universal object is then not merely presented and posited, but is itself given to us. Again we can have an analogizing presentation of the universal, without actually positing it. We conceive it, but leave it in suspense. The intention to the universal which here rests on an intuitive basis makes no decision regarding 'being' or 'non-being', only one regarding the *possibility* or impossibility of the universal, and of its presentation through adequate abstraction.

Chapter 7

A study in categorial representation

§53 Backward reference to the researches of our first section

The founded acts analysed by us in select examples were considered by us to be intuitions, and intuitions of the new types of object that they brought to light, objects which can only be given in founded acts of a sort and form which corresponds to each of them. The explanatory value of this extended use of the concept Intuition can only lie in the fact that we are not here dealing with some inessential, merely disjunctive widening of a concept, which permits us to extend the sphere of that concept over the spheres of any heterogeneous concepts whatsoever,[1] but with an authentic generalization, which rests on a community of essential features. We call the new acts 'intuitions' in that, with a mere surrender of a 'straightforward' relation to their object – the peculiar sort of immediacy defined by us as 'straightforwardness' – they yet have all the essential peculiarities of intuitions: we find in their case the same essential divisions, and they show themselves capable of achieving the same fully performed *fulfilments*. This last mentioned capacity is particularly important for our purposes, for it was with a view to such performances that this whole investigation has been conducted. Knowledge as the unity of fulfilment is not achieved on a mere basis of straightforward acts, but in general, on a basis of categorial acts: when, accordingly, we oppose *intuition* to *thought* (as meaning), we cannot mean by 'intuition' merely sensuous intuition.

The conception of categorial acts as intuitions, first brings true perspicuity into the relation of thought to intuition – a relation that no previous critique of knowledge has made tolerably clear: it is the first to render knowledge itself intelligible, in its essence and its achievement. Through such a conceptual extension the theses of our first section first gain adequate confirmation. To all intuitions, in our present widest sense, however near or far they may stand from sensibility, expressive meanings correspond – as their possible ideal counterparts. The divisions drawn by us within 'epistemic essence', and the concepts framed in close connection therewith, retain their validity in this wider sphere, though marked off by us in relation to a narrower one.

Each categorial act of intuition has therefore:

1. its quality;
2. its (intentional) material, or interpretative sense;
3. its representing contents.

These distinctions do not reduce to distinctions among *founding* acts. The quality of a total act may differ from that of a basic act, just as basic acts, when many, may be differently qualified, as, e.g., in an idea of a relation between a fictitious object and one taken to be real.

Not only has each of the founding acts its own material, but the founded act imports its own material: it is true to say that this *novel material*, or, where this includes the materials of basic acts, the *newly added part* of it, is *founded on the materials of the basic act*.

Finally, also, the new act has *representing contents* in regard to which there are serious difficulties. *Must new representing contents be assumed for this new material*, and *what* can these be?

Chapter 8

The *a priori* laws of authentic and inauthentic thinking

§59 The complication into ever new forms. The pure theory of the forms of possible intuitions

The varied forms of founded acts where, instead of straightforward, sensuously-intuitive objects, categorially formed and synthetically connected objects are constituted, permit manifold complications into new forms: in consequence of certain *a priori* categorial laws, categorial unities may again and again become the objects of new connecting, relating or ideating acts. Universal objects, e.g., can be collectively connected, the collections thus formed can in their turn be collectively connected with other collections of similar or different type, and so on *in infinitum*. The possibility of unlimited complication is here self-evident and *a priori*. Just so, within certain law-bound limits, one can unify states of affairs in new states of affairs, pursue an indefinitely extended search for internal and external relations among all such possible unities, use the results of such discovery as terms for novel relations etc. Obviously such complication is achieved in founded acts of ever higher level. The governing legality in this field is the intuitive counterpart of the grammatical legality of pure logic. In this case, also, we are not concerned with laws which seek to assess the real being of the objects presented at different levels. These laws at all events say nothing directly about the ideal conditions of possibilities of adequate fulfilment. To the pure theory of the forms of meanings we here have a corresponding pure theory of the forms of intuitions, in which the possibility of the primitive types of simple and complex intuitions must be established by intuitive generalization, and the laws of their successive complication into ever new and more complex intuitions must be laid down. To the extent that adequate intuition itself represents a type of intuition, the pure theory of intuitive forms embraces all the laws which concern the forms of adequate intuition: these have a peculiar relevance to the laws of the adequate *fulfilment* of significative intentions, or of intentions already intuitive.

§60 The relative or functional difference between matter and form. Pure acts of understanding, and those mixed with sense. Sensuous concepts and categories

The *relative, merely functional* difference of matter and form hangs together with the possibility of making categorial intuitions the foundations for new categorial intuitions, and thereupon of expressing them in corresponding expressions and meanings. This difference was indicated above in passing (§42). In an absolute sense, a founding sensibility provides the matter for all acts of categorial form which are built upon it. In a relative sense, *the objects of founding acts furnish this matter*, relatively, that is, to the *newly* emergent forms of the founded acts. If we relate two objects already categorial, e.g. two states of affairs, these states of affairs are our matter relatively to the relation which brings them together. To this definite use of the concepts of matter and form the traditional distinction between *the matter and form of statements* corresponds exactly. The terms of a statement express the founding acts of the whole 'relational presentation', or, what is the same, they are names for its founding objects, and therefore represent the place in which alone contributions of sense may be sought. But founding objects may themselves be categorial in type. Plainly *fulfilment is carried out in a chain of acts which take us down a whole ladder of 'foundations'*. Indirect presentations here play an essential part, whose exact investigation is an important task in a clarification of the complex forms of cognitive thought.

Acts of straightforward intuitions we called 'sensuous'; founded acts, whether leading back immediately or mediately to sense, we called 'categorial'. But it is worth our while to draw a distinction, within the sphere of categorial acts, between those acts that are *purely categorial*, acts of 'pure understanding', and *mixed acts of understanding that are blended with sense*. It lies in the nature of the case that everything categorial ultimately rests upon sensuous intuition, that a 'categorial intuition', an intellectual insight, a case of thought in the highest sense, without any foundation of sense, is a piece of nonsense. *The idea of a pure intellect*, interpreted as a faculty of pure thinking (= categorial action), *quite cut off* from a 'faculty of sensibility', could only be conceived *before* there had been an elementary analysis of knowledge in the irrefragable evidence of its being. Nonetheless, the distinctions just indicated, and with them the concept of a purely categorial act and, if one likes, the further concept of a pure understanding, all have a good sense. If we ponder on the peculiarity of eidetic abstraction, that it necessarily rests on individual intuition, but does not for that reason mean what is individual in such intuition, if we pay heed to the fact that it is really a new way of conceiving, constitutive of generality instead of individuality – *then the possibility of universal intuitions arises, intuitions which not merely exclude all individuality, but also all sensibility from their intentional purview*. In other words, we distinguish between *sensuous abstraction*, which yields *sensuous concepts* – purely sensuous or mixed with categorial forms – and *purely categorial abstraction*, which yields *purely categorial concepts*. *Colour, house, judgement, wish* are purely sensuous concepts; *colouredness, virtue, the axiom of parallels* etc., have a categorial admixture, while *unity, plurality, relation, concept* are purely categorial. Where we speak absolutely of categorial concepts, purely categorial ones are always meant. Sensuous concepts find their immediate basis in the data of sensuous intuition, categorial concepts in the data of categorial intuition, purely with regard to the categorial form of the whole categorially formed object. If, e.g., the intuition of a relation underlies an abstraction, the abstractive consciousness may direct itself to the relational form *in specie*, so that everything sensuous in what underlies the relation is discounted. So arise *categories*, which rubric, understood pointedly, merely covers the *primitive* concepts in our present context.

We have just identified concept and *Species*: this was implicit in the whole sense of our completed discussion. But, if one understands by 'concepts' *universal presentations* instead of universal objects, whether these be *universal intuitions* or the *universal meanings* which correspond to them, our distinction carries over simply to these. It carries over similarly to presentations of the form *an A*, having regard to the fact that the Species *A* may include or exclude what is sensible. All *logical forms* and *formulae* such as *All S are P, No S is P* etc., are purely categorial. Here the letters '*S*', '*P*' etc., merely point indirectly to 'certain', indefinite concepts, variable 'at will'; in the total formula a complex thought, made up of purely categorial elements, corresponds to them. Like all *pure logic*, so all *pure arithmetic*, the *pure theory of manifolds, pure mathematics*, in short, in the widest sense, are *pure in the sense that they contain no sensuous concept in their whole theoretical fabric*.

§61 Categorial forming involves no real reshaping of the object

Our talk of categorial form, as has been clear from our last set of discussions, is naturally and harmlessly ambiguous, since we have drawn a thoroughgoing distinction between act and object. We mean by categorial form, on the one hand, the *characters of founded acts*, which give form to acts of straightforward or of already founded intuition, and transform them into new presentations of objects. These latter presentations, as opposed to the acts on which they are founded, set up for us a peculiarly modified objectivity: the original *objects* are now seen in certain interpretative and connective forms which are *our categorial forms in the second, objective sense*. The conjunctive connection *A and B*, which as a unified act means a *categorial unity of objects* (the aggregate of them both), will serve as an example.

The expression '*A and B*' illustrates, particularly in relation to the meaning of 'and', a further sense of our talk of categorial form, according to which *significative* forms, forms which find possible fulfilment in founded types of act, are called categorial forms, or, more cautiously, categorial forms in a *loose* sense of the word.

This being premised, we now wish to bring to explicit clearness, for the sake of its importance, a proposition that we have already enunciated and which is really obvious in the light of our whole exposition. This is the proposition that categorial functions, in 'forming' sensible objects, leave their real essence untouched. The object is intellectually grasped by the intelligence, and especially by 'knowledge' (itself a categorial function), but it is not thereby falsified. To clarify this, let us remember the difference mentioned in passing between categorial unities in the objective sense, and real unities such as the unity of the parts of a thing, or of trees in an avenue etc. The unity of the real elements in a mental experience, or the unity of all experiences which coexist in a single individual consciousness, likewise count among such real unities. All such unities, treated as wholes, resemble their parts in being objects in the straightforward, primary sense: they can be intuited in possible straightforward intuitions. They are not merely categorially unified, constituted through a being-considered-together, through collection, disjunction, relation etc. They are intrinsically unified: they have a form of union, perceivable in the whole as a real property, a real moment of unity, and perceivable in the same sense in which any of their connected members and *their* intrinsic properties are perceivable.

It is quite different in the case of categorial forms. The new objects they create are not objects in the primary, original sense. Categorial forms do not glue, tie or put parts together, so that a real, sensuously perceivable whole emerges. They do not form in the sense in which the potter forms. Otherwise the original datum of sense-perception would be modified in its own objectivity: relational and connective thought and knowledge would not be of what is, but would be a falsifying transformation into something else. Categorial forms leave primary objects untouched: they can do nothing to them, cannot change them in their own being, since the result would otherwise be a new object in the primary, real sense. Evidently the outcome of a categorial act, e.g. one of collection or relation, consists in an objective 'view' (*Fassung*) of what is primarily intuited, a 'view' that can only be given in such a founded act, so that the thought of a straightforward percept of the founded object, or of its presentation through some other straightforward intuition, is a piece of nonsense.

§62 Our freedom in the categorial forming of given material and its limits. Purely categorial laws (laws of 'authentic' thinking)

Real, sensuous forms of unity, whether external or internal, are determined by a law governing the essential nature of the parts to be connected; if the individuation of these parts is taken in its full extent, they are absolutely determined. All unity points to governing legality, as real unity points to real governing legality. What is really one, must also really be made one. Where we speak of *our freedom to unite* or *not to unite*, we are not speaking of contents in their full reality, which includes their spatio-temporal properties. While in this field the consciousness, and especially the direct intuition, of real contents, is *eo ipso* the consciousness of their real connections and forms, the position is quite different in regard to categorial forms. With real contents none of the categorial forms which fit them is necessarily given: there is abundant freedom to connect and relate, to generalize and subsume etc. There are many arbitrary ways to divide up a sensuously unified group into part-groups: we may at will arrange these diversely divisible part-groups, and effect same-level connections among them, we can also build collections of the second, third . . . order upon one another. Many possibilities of categorial shaping therefore arise on the foundation of the same sensuous stuff. Just so, we can compare any item from one and the same sense-complex with any other of its members, or distinguish it from them. We can make either of them the subject-term, or, by arbitrary conversion, the object-term of some relation in question. We can put these relations into relation with one another, connect them collectively, classify them etc.

Great, however, as this *freedom of categorial union and formation* may be, it still has its *law-governed limits*. The very fact that categorial forms constitute themselves in founded characters of acts, and in these alone, involves a certain necessity of connection. For how else could we speak of categorial *perception* and *intuition*, if any conceivable matter could be put into any conceivable form, and the underlying straightforward intuitions therefore permitted themselves to be arbitrarily combined with categorial characters? Where, e.g., we carry out a whole-part relationship intuitively, we can normally convert it, but not in such a manner that the part, with unchanged real content, can be looked on as the whole, and the whole as the part. It is also not open to us to treat this relation as one of total identity or of total exclusion etc. We can no doubt 'think' any relation between any set of terms, and any form whatever on the basis of any matter – think them, that is, in the sense of merely meaning them. But we cannot really carry out 'foundings' on every foundation: we cannot *see* sensuous stuff in any categorial form we like, let alone *perceive* it thus, and above all not perceive it *adequately*.

In framing our widened concept of perception, we found, *eo ipso*, a certain *tied character* in it. This does not mean that the character of perception is really (*reell*) bound up with sensuous content. This is never the case, for this would mean that nothing existed unperceived, or could exist unperceived. Certainly, however, nothing exists that cannot be perceived. This means that the actual performance of actual acts on the ground of just these straightforward intuitions is in the ideal sense *possible*. And these possibilities, like ideal possibilities in general, are limited by law to the extent that certain impossibilities, ideal incompatibilities, are by law ranged alongside of them.

The *ideal laws* governing the connection of such possibilities and impossibilities, belong among *categorial forms in specie*, i.e. among categories in the objective sense of the word. They determine *what variations in any given categorial forms there can be in relation to the same definite, but arbitrarily chosen, matter.* They circumscribe the ideally closed manifold of the rearrangements and transformations of categorial forms on the basis of constant, selfsame matter. This matter is here only relevant in so far as it must be kept intentionally identical. But, to the extent that the species of this matter are quite freely variable, and are only subject to the obvious ideal condition of capacity to sustain the forementioned forms, the laws in question are of an entirely pure and *analytic* character, and *quite independent of the particularity of their matter.* Their general expression, therefore, contains no reference to material species, but makes exclusive use of algebraical symbols as bearers of indeterminately general presentations of certain matters, variable in all but the identity they must keep with themselves.

To gain insight into these laws, does not therefore require an actual carrying out of a categorial intuition, which makes its matters truly intuitive: any categorial intuition suffices, which puts the *possibility* of the *categorial formation* in question before one's eyes. In the generalizing abstraction of this comprehensive possibility the unitary, intuitive 'insight' into the law is achieved: this insight has, in the sense used in our doctrine, the character of an *adequate general percept*. The general object, which is itself present in it, is the categorial law. We may assert: *The ideal conditions of categorial intuition in general are, correlatively regarded, the conditions of the possibility of the objects of categorial intuition*, and of the possibility of *categorial objects simpliciter*. That an object thus and thus categorially formed is possible, is essentially related to the fact that a categorial intuition – a mere imagination – can set such an object completely before one's eyes, to the fact, in other words, that *the requisite categorial syntheses and other categorial acts can be really performed on the basis of the founding intuitions concerned* (even if the latter are imaginary).

What categorial formations are in fact permitted by given materials of perception or imagination, what categorial acts can be really carried out on the basis of their constitutive sensuous intuitions: on this point our analytic laws, which are here our ideal conditions, say nothing. That boundless arbitrariness does not here obtain, that 'actual' performability has not here the character of empirical actuality, but of ideal possibility, is shown by our above examples. These also make plain that it is the particularity of the matter which, from case to case, circumscribes possibility, so that we can, e.g., say that W is really a whole as regards w, or that g is really a property of G etc. In such cases, of course, the categorial form (unlike its real counterpart) is not limited to the kinds of content covered by *W*, *w*, *G*, *g*, so as to have no bearing on contents of other kinds. Contrariwise it is evident that *contents of all kinds can be formed by all categories*. For categorial forms are not founded on material contents, as we have already explained above (cf. §57 excised from this edition). These pure laws can therefore not prescribe what forms a *given* matter can assume, but can only tell us that, when it, and any matter in general, assumes a certain form, or is capable of assuming it, a definitely limited circle of further forms remains open to the same matter. There is, i.e., *an ideally closed circle of possible transformation of a functioning form, into ever new forms*. The ideal *possibility* of these new forms in relation to the same matter, has its *a priori* guarantee in the before mentioned analytic laws which embody the presuppositions in question.

These are the pure laws of *authentic thinking*, the laws, that is, of *categorial intuitions in virtue of their purely categorial forms*. For categorial intuitions function in the thought of theory as actual or possible fulfilments (or frustrations) of meanings, and impart to statements (according to their mode of functioning) the logical values of truth and falsehood. On the laws here considered the normative regulation of purely signitive, or admixedly signitive, thought depends.

To expound this matter more precisely, and to clear up the special sense implied in talk of the laws of *authentic* thinking, we must take a closer look into the sphere of meanings and of meaning-fulfilments.

§63 The new laws of the validity of signitive and admixedly signitive acts (laws of inauthentic thinking)

In our discussions up to this point we have thought of categorial acts as free from all significative side-structures, as carried out, but not as founding acts of knowing or naming. Every unprejudiced analyst will concede that we can, e.g., intuit aggregates, or many primitive states of affairs, without expressing them nominally or propositionally. We now oppose the case of mere signification to the case of mere intuition: we note that to all acts of categorial intuition, with their categorially formed objects, purely significative acts may correspond. This is an obvious *a priori* possibility. There is no act-form relevant here, to which there is not a corresponding possible form of meaning, and each meaning can be thought of as carried out without a correlated intuition. The ideal of a logically adequate language is that of a language which can give unambiguous expression to all possible matters and all possible categorial forms. To its words certain significative intentions unambiguously pertain, which can come alive even in the absence of 'corresponding', i.e. of fulfilling, intuition. There is therefore, running parallel to all possible primary and founded intuitions, a system of primary and founded meanings which could possibly express them.

The realm of meaning is, however, much wider than that of intuition, i.e. than the total realm of possible fulfilment. For, on the meaning-side, an endless host of *complex meanings* arises, which lack 'reality' or 'possibility'. They are patterns of meanings assembled together into *unitary meanings*, to which, however, *no possible unitary correlate of fulfilment* can correspond.

For this reason there is *no complete parallelism between categorial types*, i.e. types of categorial intuition, and *types of meaning*. To each categorial type of lower or higher level a meaning-type corresponds, but to every type formed by free significative welding to complex types, there is not a corresponding type of categorial objectivity. We recall types of analytic contradiction such as 'an *A* which is not an *A*', 'All *A*'s are *B*'s and some *A*'s are not *B*'s' etc. Only in connection with primitive types can and must such parallelism obtain, since all primitive meanings 'originate' in the fulness of correlated intuition, or, to put the matter more plainly, since talk of compatibility and incompatibility applies only in the sphere of what is put together, or is to be put together, simple meanings, as expressions of what is simple, can never be 'imaginary'. This applies also to every simple *form* of meaning. While 'Something that is at once *A* and not-*A*' is impossible, 'an *A* and a *B*' is possible, since the and-form, being simple, has a 'real' sense.

If we transfer the term 'categorial' to the realm of meaning, a peculiar significative form (and a peculiar meaning-form *in specie*) will correspond to each *authentic* categorial form, whether to one authentic in the objective sense, or to the corresponding categorial form of intuition (in which what is categorially objective is *perceptually or imaginatively* constituted). In this form of signification we achieve significative reference to a collection or a disjunction, an identity or a non-identity etc. Whenever one opposes presentation in the *authentic*, to presentation in an *inauthentic* sense, one normally has the intuitive-significative antithesis in mind (though occasionally, no doubt, one is thinking of the other antithesis of adequate-inadequate). Our present cases would accordingly be cases of collection, disjunction, identification, abstraction etc., *in an inauthentic sense*.

If one includes under the rubric of 'acts of thinking', all the categorial acts through which judgements, as predicative significations, gain fulness and their whole value for knowledge, we must distinguish between *authentic acts of thinking* and *inauthentic* ones. The inauthentic acts of thinking would be the significant intentions behind statements and, by a natural extension, all significative acts which could possibly function as parts of such predicative intentions: all significative acts can plainly function in this fashion. The *authentic acts of thinking* would lie in the corresponding fulfilments, i.e. the intuitions of states of affairs, and all intuitions which function as possible parts of such intuitions. All intuitions can function in this manner: there is, in particular, no categorial form that could not be a constituent of the form of a state of affairs. The *general doctrine of the form of symbolic judgements* (the meanings of statements) includes that of the forms of meaning in general (the pure logico-grammatical forms). Just so the *general doctrine of the pure forms of the intuitions of states of affairs* (and of the pure forms of states of affairs) includes that of the *categorial forms of intuitions* (and of objective categorial forms) *in general*.

If, as often happens, *thinking* is identified with *judging*, we should have to distinguish between *authentic* and *inauthentic judging. The* concept of judging would then be pinned down by the element common to statement-intention and statement-fulfilment, i.e. by the intentional essence compounded of quality and intentional material. As acts of thinking in the widest sense, not only acts of judging, but also all possible part-acts in judgements, would have to count: we should be brought back to a definition equivalent to our previous definition of the concept Act of Thinking.

In the sphere of inauthentic thinking, of pure signification, we are beyond all bounds of categorial laws. Here anything and everything can be brought together in unity. We spoke of this in our Fourth Investigation: we pointed to the *purely logico-grammatical laws* which, as laws of complication and modification, distinguish the spheres of sense and nonsense. In inauthentic categorial formation and transformation, we are free as long as our meanings are not nonsensically conglomerated. But if we wish to avoid formal and real nonsense, the widest sphere of inauthentic thought, of the significatively combinable, is very much narrowed. We are now concerned with the *objective* possibility of complex meanings, with the possibility of their application to an intuition which fulfils them totally and singly. *The pure laws of the validity of meanings, of the ideal possibility of their adequate intuitive illustration,* obviously runs parallel to the pure laws governing the combination and transformation of *authentic* categorial forms.

In the pure laws of the validity of meanings, we are again not dealing with laws from which the validity of any given meaning can be read off, but with the possibilities, determined in purely categorial fashion, of the combination and transformation of meanings, that can be undertaken, *salva veritate,* in each possible given case, i.e. without prejudicing the possibility of a fulfilment of meaning, to the extent that this previously existed. If, e.g., the statement 'w is a part of W' is valid, then a statement of the form 'W is a whole relatively to w' is also valid. If it is true that there is an A which is B, then it is also true that a certain A is B, or that not all A's are not B's etc. In such propositions, what is material is boundlessly variable; hence all material meanings are replaced by algebraical signs of indirect and wholly unfixed significance. For this reason such propositions are characterized as *analytic*. In this situation, it is again irrelevant whether the matter is constituted in percepts or in imaginations. The possibilities and impossibilities concern the setting up of acts giving adequate intuitive illustration to the form of a meaning whatever its material substratum: we are concerned, in short, with the *pure conditions of the possibility of completely adequate signification in general*, which, in their turn, depend on the *pure conditions of the possibility of categorial intuition in general.* These laws of the validity of meanings are not, of course, themselves identical with the authentic categorial laws, but they follow the latter faithfully, in virtue of the law which regulates the connection of significant intentions with fulfilments of meaning.

The whole treatment that we have just completed requires a natural, obvious extension. We have simplified the matter to the extent of confining our discussion to two extremes only: we opposed completely intuitive, i.e. actually executed categorial act-forms, on the one hand, to purely signitive, i.e. not authentically executed act-forms, on the other, forms only to be realized in processes of possible fulfilment. The ordinary cases are, however, mixtures: thought proceeds intuitively in many stretches, in many stretches signitively, here a categorial synthesis, a predication, a generalization is really carried out, there a merely signitive intention directed to such a categorial synthesis attaches to the intuitively, or to the only verbally presented members. The complex acts arising in this manner have, taken as a whole, the character of inauthentic categorial intuitions: their total objective correlate is not actually, only inauthentically, presented. Its 'possibility', i.e. the objective possibility of its correlate, is not guaranteed. The sphere of inauthentic thinking must accordingly be made wide enough for it to take in these mixed act-forms also. Everything we have said then holds, *mutatis mutandis*, for such an extension. Instead of talking of the laws of the validity of mere meanings, merely symbolic judgements etc., we shall also have to speak of the laws of the validity of signitively admixed presentations or judgements. Where there is talk of merely symbolic thinking, it is generally these mixed cases that one has in mind.

§64 The pure logico-grammatical laws are laws for any understanding whatever, and not merely for any human understanding. Their psychological meaning and normative function in relation to inadequate thought

Both sorts of laws are, of course, of an *ideal* nature. That a piece of sensory stuff can only be apprehended in certain forms, and bound together according to certain forms, that the possible transformation of these forms is subject to pure laws, in which the material element varies freely, that the meanings to be expressed are likewise limited to certain forms, which they can change only in prescribed manners, if they are not to lose their true expressibility – all this does not depend on the empirical contingencies of the course of consciousness, not even on the contingencies of our intellectual or common-human organization. It depends on the *specific nature of the acts in question*, on their intentional and epistemic essence; it belongs not to the nature of just our (individual or common-human) sensibility, nor just our understanding, but rather to the *Ideas of Sensibility and Understanding in general*. An understanding governed by other than the purely logical laws would be an understanding without understanding. If we define understanding, as opposed to sensibility, as the capacity for categorial acts, also, perhaps, as a capacity for expression and meaning directed upon such acts, and made 'right' by them, then the general laws rooted in the specific nature of these acts belong to the definitory essence of understanding. Other beings may gaze upon other 'worlds', they may also be endowed with 'faculties' other than ours, but, if they are minded creatures at all, possessing some sort of intentional experiences, with the relevant differences between perception and imagination, straightforward and categorial intuition, meaning and intuition, adequate and inadequate knowledge – then such creatures have both sensibility and understanding, and are 'subject' to the pertinent laws.

The laws of authentic thinking naturally, therefore, belong *also* to the nature of human consciousness, to our common human 'psychic organization'. But they are not characteristic of this organization in respect of its *peculiar* character. The laws are rooted, we said, in the purely specific character of certain acts: this means that they concern these acts not just in so far as they occur together in a human organization. They pertain rather to all possible organizations which can be made up of acts of this sort. The differentiating peculiarities of each type of mental organization, all that distinguishes, e.g., the *human* consciousness as such, in the manner of a natural historical species, is not at all affected by such *pure* laws as are the laws of thought.

A relation to 'our' mental organization, or to 'consciousness in general' (understood as the aspects of consciousness *common to men in general*), does not define the pure and genuine, but a grossly distorted *a priori*. The notion of a common mental organization, like that of a physical organization, clearly has a merely 'empirical' meaning, the meaning of a mere 'matter of fact'. But pure laws are precisely pure of matter of fact, they tell us not what is generally wont to be in this or that province of the real, but what absolutely goes beyond all wont and all divisions into spheres of reality, and that for the reason that what is in question belongs to the *essential* make-up of what is. The *true logical a priori*, therefore concerns all that pertains to the ideal essence of understanding as such, to the essence of its act-species and act-forms, to that, accordingly, which cannot be eliminated, as long as the understanding, and the acts definitory of it, are what they are, i.e. thus and thus natured, maintaining their selfsame conceptual essence.

The extent, accordingly, to which the logical laws and, in the first instance, the ideal laws of authentic thinking, also claim a *psychological* meaning, and the extent to which they govern the course of actual mental happenings, is at once clear. Each genuine 'pure' law, expressing a compatibility or an incompatibility grounded in the nature of a given species, will, in relation to species of mentally realizable contents, limit the empirical possibilities of psychological (phenomenological) coexistence and succession. What is seen to be incompatible *in specie*, cannot be brought together, be rendered compatible, in empirical instances. In so far as the logical thought of experience is, to an incomparably major extent, conducted inadequately and signitively, we can think, believe, many things which in *truth*, in the manner of authentic thought, the actual carrying out of merely intended syntheses, cannot be brought together at all. Just for this reason *the a priori laws of authentic thinking and authentic expression become norms for merely opinion-forming, inauthentic thought and expression.* Put somewhat differently: on the laws of authentic thinking other laws are founded, formulable too as practical norms, which express in a manner suited to the sphere of signitive or admixedly signitive presentation, the ideal conditions of a possible truth (or *right*ness in general), the ideal conditions, that is, of 'logical' compatibility (logical, since related to possible adequation) within this sphere of admixedly signitive thinking. The laws of inauthentic thinking do not hold *psychologically* like empirical laws governing the origin and change of such thought, but as the possibilities or impossibilities of adequation founded in their ideal purity in the variously formed acts of inauthentic thinking in relation to corresponding acts of authentic thinking.

§65 The senseless problem of the real meaning of the logical

We now also completely understand why the notion of a course of the world violating the laws of logic – the analytic laws of authentic thinking and the consequent norms of inauthentic thinking – or of the need or possibility of first grounding these laws in experience, the 'matter of fact' of sense, and fixing for them their limits of validity – is a piece of pure nonsense. We ignore the fact that even a probabilistic grounding on facts is a grounding which, as such, obeys ideal principles, principles which by anticipation we see to rest upon 'authentic' experiences of probability, both as regards their specific content and their status as laws. Here we must rather stress that the so-to-say facticity of a fact belongs to sensibility, and that to call in sensibility to help provide a basis for purely categorial laws – laws whose very meaning excludes all sensibility and facticity, which make pure assertions of essence about categorial *forms*, as forms of possible correctness and truth as such – represents a most obvious μετάβασις εἰς ἄλλο γένος. Laws which refer to no fact cannot be confirmed or refuted by a fact. The problem, earnestly and profoundly treated by great philosophers, as to the 'real or formal meaning of the logical', is therefore a nonsensical problem. *One requires no metaphysical or other theories to explain the agreement of the course of nature and the 'native' regularities of the understanding.* Instead of an explanation, one needs only a phenomenological clarification of meaning, thinking and knowing, and of the ideas and laws which spring from these.

The world constitutes itself as a sensuous unity: its very meaning is to be the unity of actual and possible straightforward percepts. Its true being, however, precludes its being adequately given, or given without qualification, in any closed process of perception. It is for us always a quite inadequately meant unity for theoretical research, in part intended through straightforward and categorial intuition, in part through signification. The further our knowledge progresses, the better and more richly will the idea of the world be determined, the more, too, will inconsistencies be excluded from it. To doubt whether the world really is as it appears to us to be, or as it is thought of in contemporary theoretical science, and as it counts for the well-grounded belief of the latter, has a good sense, since inductive science can never construct an adequate world-picture, however far it may carry us. But it is also nonsensical to doubt whether the true course of the world, the true structure of the world in itself, could conflict with the forms of thinking. For this would mean that a definite, hypothetically assumed sensibility, which would bring the world to adequate representation in an ideally complete set of unending perceptual processes, would be capable of assuming categorial forms, while forcing syntheses upon them that are generically ruled out by the universal nature of such forms. That they are thus ruled out, and that the laws of the categories hold as pure laws in abstraction from all sensuous stuff, and are accordingly unaffected by limitless variation of such stuff, this *we do not merely think, but we see it to be true.* It is given to us in fullest adequacy. This insight is of course achieved subjectively on the basis of any casual empirical intuition, but it is a generic insight relating purely to form. The basis of abstraction contains in this case, as in others, nothing presupposed by the ideal possibility and validity of the Idea abstracted from it.

It would further be possible to demonstrate *ad nauseam* the absurdity involved in considering the *possibility* of an illogical course of the world in signitive thought, thereby making this possibility *hold*, and destroying in one breath, so to say, the laws which make this or any other possibility hold at all. We could also point out that a correlation with perceivability, intuitability, meanability and knowability, is inseparable from the sense of being in general, and that the ideal laws, therefore, which pertain to these possibilities *in specie*, can never be set aside by the contingent content of what itself happens to be at the moment. But enough of such argumentations, which merely ring the changes on one and the same position, and have already given us guidance in the *Prolegomena*.

§66 Distinction between the most important differences mixed up in the current opposition of 'intuiting' and 'thinking'

The above investigations should have imported a satisfactory, general clearness into the much used, but little clarified, relation between *thinking* and *intuiting*. We here list the following oppositions, whose confusion has vexed epistemological research so inordinately, and whose distinctness has become quite clear to ourselves.

1. The opposition between *intuition* and *signification*. Intuition as perception or imagination – it is irrelevant whether categorial or sensuous, adequate or inadequate – is opposed to *mere thinking*, as *merely significative reference*. Our parenthetically noted differences are, of course, generally ignored. We consider them very important, and now specially stress them.

2. The opposition between *sensuous* and *categorial intuition*. We therefore oppose *sensuous intuition* in the ordinary, straightforward sense, to *categorial intuition*, or intuition in the extended sense. The founded acts, characteristic of the latter, now count as the thought which 'intellectualizes' sensuous intuition.

3. The opposition between *inadequate* and *adequate* intuition, or, more generally, between adequate and inadequate presentation (since we are classing intuitive and significative presentation together). In an inadequate representation we merely *think* that something is so (appears so), in adequate presentation we look at the matter itself, and are *for the first time made acquainted with its full selfhood*.

4. The opposition between *individual intuition* (usually conceived, with what is plainly baseless narrowness, as sensuous intuition) and *universal intuition*. A new concept of intuition is fixed by means of this opposition. It is opposed to generalization, and so, further, to the categorial acts implying generalization, and also, in unclear admixture, to the significative counterparts of such acts. 'Intuition', we now say, *merely presents the individual*, while 'thought' points to the *universal*, is carried out by way of 'concepts'. One generally speaks in this context of the opposition between 'intuition and concept'.

How strongly we tend to let these oppositions shade into one another would be shown by a criticism of Kant's theory of knowledge, which throughout bears the impress of the failure to draw any clear distinction among these oppositions. In Kant's thought categorial (logical) functions play a great role, but he fails to achieve our fundamental extension of the concepts of perception and intuition over the categorial realm, and this because he fails to appreciate the deep difference between intuition and signification, their possible separation and their usual commixture. And so he does not complete his analysis of the difference between the inadequate and adequate adaptation of meaning to intuition. He therefore also fails to distinguish between concepts, as the universal meanings of words, and concepts as species of *authentic* universal presentation, and between both, and concepts as universal objects, as the intentional correlates of universal presentations. Kant drops from the outset into the channel of a metaphysical epistemology in that he attempts a critical 'saving' of mathematics, natural science and metaphysics, before he has subjected knowledge as such, the whole sphere of acts in which pre-logical objectivation and logical thought are performed, to a clarifying critique and analysis of essence, and before he has traced back the primitive logical concepts and laws to their phenomenological sources. It was ominous that Kant (to whom we nonetheless feel ourselves quite close) should have thought he had done justice to the domain of pure logic in the narrowest sense, by saying that it fell under the principle of contradiction. Not only did he never see how little the laws of logic are all analytic propositions in the sense laid down by his own definition, but he failed to see how little his dragging in of an evident principle for analytic propositions really helped to clear up the achievements of analytic thinking.

Additional note to the Second Edition

All the main obscurities of the Kantian critique of reason depend ultimately on the fact that Kant never made clear to himself the peculiar character of pure Ideation, the adequate survey of conceptual essences, and of the laws of universal validity rooted in those essences. He accordingly lacked the phenomenologically correct concept of the *a priori*. For this reason he could never rise to adopting the only possible aim of a strictly scientific critique of reason: the investigation of the pure, essential laws which govern acts as *intentional* experiences, in all their modes of sense-giving objectivation, and their fulfilling constitution of 'true being'. Only a perspicuous knowledge of these laws of essence could provide us with an absolutely adequate answer to all the questions regarding our understanding, questions which can be meaningfully raised in regard to the 'possibility of knowledge'.

Clarification of our introductory problem

Chapter 9

Non-objectifying acts as apparent fulfilments of meaning

§67 That not every act of meaning includes an act of knowing

Having gone far enough in our investigation of the relation between meaning and corresponding intuition in regard to much more general problems, and having thus done enough to lay bare the essence of authentic and inauthentic expression, we have reached clearness on the difficult issues which troubled us at the beginning of this Investigation, and which first prompted us to undertake it.

We have, above all, rid ourselves of the temptation to conceive of the meaning-function of expressions as in some sense a case of knowing, and in fact a case of classification, a temptation which springs from a line of thought touched on above (§1), and which always crops up in important epistemological contexts. One says: An expression must surely give expression to some act of the speaker, but in order that this act should find its appropriate speech-form, it must be suitably apperceived and known, a presentation as a presentation, an attribution as an attribution, a negation as a negation etc.

Our reply is that talk of knowledge refers to a relationship between acts of thought and fulfilling intuitions. Acts of thought are not, however, brought to expression in statements and parts of statements, e.g. names, in such a manner that they in their turn are thought of and known. Otherwise these last acts would be the carriers of meaning, it would be *they* primarily that were expressed, they would accordingly be in need of other new acts of thought, and so on *in infinitum*. If I call this intuited object a 'watch', I complete, in naming it, an act of thought and knowledge, but I know the watch, and not my knowledge. This is naturally so in the case of all acts that confer meaning. Should I utter the word 'or' in a context of expressive speech, I carry out a disjunction, but my thought (of which the disjoining is a part) is not trained upon the disjoining but upon the (objective) *disjunctivum*, in so far as this last enters into the unitary state of affairs. This *disjunctivum* is known and objectively denominated. The word 'or' is accordingly no name, and likewise no non-independent appellation of disjoining; it merely gives voice to this act. Naturally this applies also to complete judgements. If I assert something, I think of *things*, that things stand in this or that manner: this is what I express, and perhaps also know. But I do not think and know my act of judging, as if I were also making it into my object, and were classifying it as a judgement and naming it through this form of expression.

But does not the grammatical adaptation of expression to expressed act point to an act of knowing in which such adaptation is performed? In a certain manner or in certain cases it does, in all those cases, that is, where the sense of 'expression' dealt with by us at the beginning of the present Investigation is relevant. This is not the case where we are dealing with expression as a mere 'voice-giving', in which case all meaning-conferring counts as expressed by our words (as verbal noises), and again not where 'expression' means the same as 'meaning', and what is expressed is one and the same meaning. In the two latter senses, every statement, whether merely significative or intuitively fulfilled, expresses something: it expresses the judgement (our conviction), or that 'judgement's content' (the selfsame propositional meaning). But in the former sense only the intuitively fulfilled statement (or the statement which is *to be* intuitively fulfilled) expresses something, in which case not the verbal noise, but the already sense-enlivened locution represents the 'expression' of the corresponding intuition. It is the function that lends meaning to our words which is primarily and universally responsible for the unitary interweaving of the signitive intentions attaching to those words. The latter merely make up a signitive judgement, in which they lack all fulfilling intuition: the synthesis of agreement or disagreement, which our total signitive intention expresses (or claims to express) is here not authentically carried out, only signitively meant. But if, contrariwise, the indicated synthesis is authentically carried out, the authentic synthesis will coincide with the non-authentic one (the synthesis in signification). Both are one and the same intentional essence, representing one and the same meaning, the simple, selfsame judgement, whether carried out intuitively or merely signitively. Similar things plainly hold for cases where only some of our verbalized intentions enjoy intuitive 'fulness'. The signitive acts involve the same meaning as the intuitive, though without the latter's fulness; they merely '*ex*press' this meaning. The suggestions of this word are the more fitting, since signitive acts likewise preserve the sense of an intuition after the latter has disappeared, like an empty shell without the intuitive kernel. The unity of coincidence is, in the case of the intuitive judgement, a true unity of knowledge (if not a unity of relational cognition): we know, however, that, in the unity of knowledge, it is not the fulfilling act (here the authentic synthesis of judgement) that we know, but the *fact* which is its objective correlate. In intuiting things we carry out a judging synthesis, *an intuitive thus it is* or *thus it is not*. Because our expressive intention, with its associated word-sounds (the grammatical expression) applies itself to this act of fact-envisagement, we achieve knowledge of the intuited fact in question.

§68 The controversy regarding the interpretation of the peculiar grammatical forms which express non-objectifying acts

We now turn to a final discussion of the seemingly trivial, but, correctly regarded, most important and difficult point at issue (see above, §1 *ff.*) whether the familiar grammatical forms used in our speech for wishes, questions, voluntary intentions – acts, generally speaking, we do not class as 'objectifying' – are to be regarded as *judgements* concerning our acts, or whether these acts themselves, and not merely such as are 'objectifying', can function as 'expressed', whether in a sense-giving or sense-fulfilling fashion. We are dealing with sentences like 'Is π a transcendental number?' 'May heaven help us!' etc.

The teasing character of the question is shown by the fact that pre-eminent logicians since Aristotle have been unable to agree on its answer. Statements express the fact that something is, or that something is not, they assert, they judge about something. In their case alone can one talk of true and false. A wish or a question asserts nothing. We cannot object to one who utters them: 'What you say is untrue'. He would not even understand our objection.

Bolzano thought this argument invalid. He said: 'A question like "What is the relation of the diameter of a circle to its circumference?" asserts nothing about what it enquires into, but it asserts something nonetheless: our desire, in fact, to be informed concerning the object asked about. It is indeed capable of truth and falsehood, and is false when our desire is mis-stated by it' (Bolzano, *Wissenschaftslehre* 1, §22, p. 88).

We may doubt, however, whether Bolzano has not here confused two things: the adequacy or inadequacy of an expression – here a word-sound – to our thought, and the truth or falsehood which relates it to the content of that thought, and its adequacy to the thing. Regarding the adequacy of an expression (as word-sound) to our thought, we can speak in two senses, one which relates to *unsuitability* – as when a speaker chooses to express the thoughts which fill his mind in words whose customary meaning conflicts with the latter – and one relating to *untruthfulness*, i.e. to deliberately deceptive, lying speech – as when the speaker does not wish to express the thoughts actually filling his mind, but others at variance with these, and merely imagined by him: he wishes to express these thoughts *as if* they were filling his mind. A suitable, sincerely employed expression can still state both what is true and what is false, according as *through its sense* it expresses what is or is not, or, what is the same, according as its sense can be adequately fulfilled or frustrated by a possible adequate percept.

One might now counter Bolzano as follows. One can talk of sincerity and insincerity, of suitability and unsuitability, in the case of *every* expression, but one can only talk of truth and falsehood in the case of statements. A speaker can, accordingly, be objected to in different ways. 'What you say is false': this is the *factual objection*. And 'You are not speaking sincerely' or 'You are expressing yourself unsuitably': this is the objection of *insincerity* or *inadequacy* of speech. Objections of the latter sort are the only ones that can be made to a questioner. He is perhaps pretending, or is using his words incorrectly, and saying something different from what he intends to say. But one can raise no factual objection to him, since he is making no factual claim. If one treats the objection concerned with unsuitability of expression as showing that a question expresses a judgement, one, i.e., that would be completely expressed in the form 'I am asking whether . . .', one would have in consistency to treat each expression in the same manner, and so to treat the true sense of each statement whatever as being what we adequately express in the word-form 'I am asserting that . . .'. But the same would have to hold of these restatements, which would accordingly land us in an infinite regress. In all this it is easily seen that this abundance of ever new statements is no mere abundance of words, but yields new statements by no means equivalent to the original ones, let alone identical in meaning. Does such nonsensical consistency not compel us to acknowledge an essential difference between one order of sentence-forms and another? (How this difference really must be interpreted is explained in our next section: cf. the final paragraph.)

Here two positions can be taken up. Either one can say: The question of sincerity affects every utterance: a judgement accordingly pertains to each utterance as such, a judgement relating to the experience of the speaker which is to be intimated. A man who speaks, intimates something, and to this the intimating judgement corresponds. But what is intimated or expressed differs from case to case: the interrogative sentence intimates a question, the imperative sentence a command, the indicative sentence a judgement. Each indicative sentence therefore implies a double judgement, a judgement, namely, about this or that fact, and a second judgement, passed by the speaker as such, upon this first judgement as his own experience.

This appears to be Sigwart's position. We read (*Logik*, 1, 2nd edn, 17 *f*. Note):

> The imperative undoubtedly includes an assertion, to the effect, namely, that the speaker wills the action he is demanding, the optative that he wishes what he utters. This assertion is involved in *the fact of speech*, not in the content of what he utters; every statement of the form *A* is *B* accordingly involves the assertion, based on the mere fact of speech, that the thinker thinks and believes what he says. *These assertions regarding the subjective state of the speaker, involved in the fact that he speaks*, and valid on the assumption of his sincerity, *accompany all speech in the same fashion*, and can accordingly not serve as a basis for differentiating our various sentence-forms.

Another way of conceiving the matter would be to reject the 'intimating judgement', and to regard the consequent duplication of judgement in the case of indicative sentences as a contingent complication, only exceptionally present, and first brought into the picture, moreover, by descriptive reflection. Against this one might hold that, in each case of adequate, not contextually elliptical speech what was expressed was essentially one, in the interrogative sentence a question, in the optative sentence a wish, in the indicative sentence a judgement. Before I had completed these Investigations, I myself thought this position unavoidable, hard as it was to reconcile with the phenomenological facts. I thought myself compelled by the following arguments, that I now accompany with suitable criticism.

§69 Arguments for and against the Aristotelian conception

According to the doctrine which is opposed to that of Aristotle, a man who, e.g., utters a question will be communicating to another his wish to be informed regarding the state of affairs in question. This communication regarding the speaker's actual experience is, it is held, a statement like any communication. In the form of the question itself there is no express saying that one is asking whether . . . ; this form only marks off the question as a question. Our speech, therefore, is a case of contextual ellipticity. The circumstances of utterance make it obvious that it is the speaker himself who asks the question. The complete meaning of the sentence does not, accordingly lie in what its mere word-sounds suggest, but is determined by the occasion, the context, the relation to the person speaking at the moment.

In favour of the Aristotelian conception, many replies could now be given.

(*a*) The argument ought to apply equally to indicative sentences, so that we have to interpret the sentence '*S* is *P*' as a contextual ellipsis for the new expression 'I judge that *S* is *P*', and so on *in infinitum.*

(*b*) The argument is based on the view that the expressed sense of the interrogative sentence differs from its real sense. For, undeniably, in the interrogative or wish-sentence, the relation of the wish to the wisher does not need to be brought out, as little as, in the case of the indicative sentence, the relation of the judgement to the judging person. If this relation is not part of the explicit sense of the sentence, but only of its contextually variable part, this concession gives one all that one could want. The explicit meaning can be altered in certain circumstances, but there will surely also be circumstances where it will be just what we mean. In such cases the mere question (and similarly the mere request or command etc.) will receive wholly adequate expression.

(*c*) More careful comparison with the indicative sentences of ordinary speech favours the Aristotelian conception. In verbal communication such a sentence intimates that one is judging, and it is the grammatical form of the indicative sentence which brings out the judgement as such. On the utterance of such grammatically framed speech, the effect forthwith attends, that the person addressed takes the speaker to be judging. This effect cannot, however, constitute the meaning of the expression, which surely means the same in soliloquy as in communicative speech. The meaning lies rather in the act of judging as the identical judgement-content.

The same could be the case in regard to interrogative sentences. The meaning of an interrogative sentence is unchanged whether we deal with an internal question or an overt one. The relation of speaker to person addressed belongs here, as in the case compared, to the merely communicative function. And just as in that case the 'content of judgement', i.e. a certain specific character of judgement, determined in this or that manner as regards content, constituted the meaning of the indicative sentence, so here the content of the question constitutes the meaning of the interrogative sentence. In both cases the ordinary meaning can undergo circumstantial modifications. We may utter an indicative sentence with the primary intention, not of communicating the relevant state of affairs, but the fact that we have the conviction in question, and mean to put it forward. This intention, buttressed, perhaps, by non-grammatical aids (stress, gesture), may be understood. Here what underlies our words is a judgement relating to our explicit judgement. Just so, in the case of an interrogative or wish-sentence, our primary intention may lie, not in our mere wish, but in the fact that we wish to express the wish to a hearer. Naturally this interpretation could not hold in all cases. It could not hold, e.g., where a burning wish bursts spontaneously from the heart. The expression then is intimately one with the wish, it clings to it immediately and directly.

Criticism. Regarded more closely, this argument only proves that a thought relating to the communicative function cannot be part of the sense of every sentence. The opposing argument is refuted: it rests on the false assumption that all expression is communicative, and that communication is always a judgement regarding the internal (intimated) experiences of the speaker. But its thesis is unrefuted, at least when suitably modified. For we cannot exclude the possibility that the controversial wish-, request-, and command-sentences etc., are still judgements about the relevant experienced acts of wishing, asking and willing, and that it is only as being so, that they can give these experiences adequate expression. If there is no place for judgements here in the narrower sense of predications – Aristotle certainly had this conception of the controversial sentences – perhaps there is place for them in a wider sense of assertive objectivations in general.

1. As regards (*a*) we note, further, that the case of statements is not the same as, e.g., that of questions. If we transform the sentence '*S* is *P*' into the sentence 'I judge that *S* is *P*', or into any related sentence, which expresses a relation to the judging person, however indefinitely, we obtain not merely altered meanings, but such as are not equivalent to the original ones: for the straightforward sentence may be true, the subjectivized sentence false, and conversely. The situation is wholly different in the case compared. Even if

one refuses to speak of true and false in this case, one can surely always find a statement that 'in essence says the same' as the original question or wish-form, e.g. 'Is *S P*?' = 'I should like to know . . .' or 'One would like to know whether *S* is *P*' etc. May such sentence-forms not imply a relation to the speaker, even if only indefinitely and subsidiarily? Does the preservation of 'essential meaning' in the transformed indicative forms not point to the fact that the meaning-giving acts are at least of the same general sort as judgements? These considerations also deal with (*b*): not the mere experience of wishing or willing, but the inner intuition of these experiences (and the signification adapted to this intuition) will be relevant to our meaning. This conception is, however, affected by the following argument:

2. There is another way in which one might try to interpret the expressed forms in question as judgements. If we utter a wish, even in soliloquy, we put it, and the wished-for content, into words, we accordingly have a presentation of it, and of what constitutes it. The wish is, however, not *any* merely presented wish, but the living wish that we have just taken note of. And it is this wish, and this wish as such, that we want to intimate. It is not, accordingly, our mere presentation, but our inner percept, i.e. really a judgement, that achieves expression. It is not, indeed, a judgement of the same sort as our ordinary assertions, that predicate something of something. In the expression of a wish, it is only our concern to grasp the internally noted experience conceptually (significatively) in straightforward affirmation, and to express its simple existence. It is not our concern to make a relational predication about such an experience, connecting it with the experiencing subject.

Against this conception it may be objected that the situation is exactly the same for expressed judgements as for all other expressed experiences. If we state something, we judge, and our words cover not only the presentation underlying our judgement, but also our judgement itself (i.e. in the form of an assertion). We should, therefore, also conclude here that the judgement is internally perceived, and that the meaning of our statement lies in the straight-forwardly affirmative judgement about what we perceive, i.e. about our judgement. If no one finds such a conception acceptable in the case of a statement, it cannot be seriously entertained in the case of other independent sentences. We recall what was said in our last section. The expressions which fit themselves to the expressed experiences, are not related to them in the way that names are, nor in any analogous manner. Our experiences are not first *objectively* presented, and then brought under concepts, as if, together with each new word, a subsumption or predication had taken place. A person who judges gold to be yellow, does not judge that the presentation which accompanies his use of the word 'gold' is yellow: he does not judge that the manner of judging he carries out when he utters the word 'is' falls under the concept 'is' etc. The word 'is' does not in fact symbolize judgement, but the being which is found in a state of affairs. 'Gold', likewise, does not name a presentative experience: it names a metal. Expressions name experiences only when such experiences have been made objects of presentation or judgement in reflection. The same holds for all words, even syncategorematic ones, in their relation to what is objective: they mean this in their fashion even when they do not name it.

Expressions are not therefore associated as names with the acts which fill our minds at each moment, acts in which we live without judging about them reflectively: such expressions belong rather to the concrete being of the acts themselves. To judge expressly is to judge, to wish expressly is to wish. To name a judgement or wish is not to judge or wish, but merely to name. A judgement named need never be judged by the man who names it, a wish named never wished by him. And, even when this is not so, the naming expresses no judgement or no wish, but a presentation related to one or the other.

Criticism. This objection also exposes the weakness of our at first attractive preliminary argument. It is clear from it, as from our previous discussions, that not every expression (*qua* the expression it is) presupposes a judgement or other act, which makes the intimated experience its object. This again does not dispose of the thesis: we have not shown, just in the case of the sentence-forms under discussion, that they are not judgements about momentary wishing, questioning or requesting experiences, or that they do not express their straightforward existence in the speaker. True, to name a wish is not *therefore* to wish, but is experiencing a wish and naming it in the same breath, not *also* a case of wishing? So that, even if expressed wishing is necessarily a wishing which involves naming and stating, the proposition still holds, that expressed wishing is wishing and not mere naming.

3. The controversial expressions have the form of sentences, and at times the form of categorical sentences with subjects and predicates. From this it follows that they can also be treated as having predication in their content, and not merely as predications in relation to one, same, unmentioned subject 'I'. E.g. 'May God protect the Kaiser', 'The coachman should harness the horses'. A 'may' or a 'should' is uttered: the subject in question is apprehended as standing under a requisition or an obligation.

One could here rejoin: Where a 'should' counts as an objective predicate and is actually attributed as such, the should-sentence has not merely the force of a wish or a command, or not this alone. An objective obligation can be said to hold, though the man stating it need experience no act of the kind which constitutes an actual consciousness of obligation. If I know that someone's will is bound by a relationship of service or by custom or morality, I can judge that he should and must do something. But this expresses no living wish, desire or obligation. Statements of obligation may indeed serve in appropriate contexts to express acts of this sort, e.g. 'John must harness the horses!' But it is clear that here no mere objective obligation is expressed, but my own will, and this not in my words, but rather in my tone and in the circumstances. In such circumstances the predicative form doubtless does duty for an imperative or optative form, i.e. the thought-predication implied by the words is either not carried out at all, or is merely subsidiary. It is undeniable, lastly, that the predicative interpretation only is plausible in certain cases, and not in the case in question. B. Erdmann, who otherwise leans towards it, does not favour it in this case. (See B. Erdmann, *Logic*, 1[1], §45, pp. 271 *ff.*)

Criticism. It may be questioned whether this refutation suffices. That a should-predicate has an objective sense and value cannot be doubted. But that, where this is not true, nothing is predicated or at least judged, is by no means proved. One might maintain: When we issue a command to someone, e.g. a command to the coachman John to harness the horses, he counts for us as someone subordinate to our will: he is apprehended as such by us and accordingly addressed in this form of expression. We say: 'John, harness the horses!' That he is one who should harness horses is here predicated of him, naturally in the expectation of corresponding practical results, and not merely to attest that he counts as such for me. The expression of the command is relative. We can think of no one commanded, without at the same time thinking, definitely or indefinitely, of someone who commands him. This being wholly obvious requires no explicit expression. Instead of the cumbrous form 'I command etc.', we employ the brief imperative, whose form points to a communicative relation. The speech-forms 'should' and 'must' were not originally used by a commander in face of the commanded to express his actual voluntary intent, but only when a more objective expression of his own or someone else's voluntary intent was needed, e.g. when there was a third person relaying someone else's command or when a legislating will found expression in a law. When communication between commander and commanded lapses, the imperative, which fits the conscious situation of the former, loses application. This conception can be applied generally. One can say: In the optative, what we wish is presented as wished, and stated to be such. Just so, in a requesting form, what we request is presented as requested, in a question what we ask presented as asked etc. These acts are related in our presentation to their intentional objects, and are so themselves made objective as reflexive predicates attaching to the latter.

In the communicative situation, many others of the expressions in question have, like commands, the role of telling the hearer (like essentially occasional expressions) that the speaker is performing certain intimated acts (of request, congratulation, condolence etc.) with an intentional regard to his auditor. To the extent that expressions of all sorts may in full consciousness be informed by the wish to communicate with others, and to acquaint others with one's own convictions, doubts, hopes etc., they are perhaps all accompanied by reflex acts directed upon such inner experiences and, more precisely, by acts which intuitively relate the latter to the speaker and to the person addressed. This accordingly holds of communicative statements as well. These acts of reflection and reference do not on that account form part of the meaning of a statement and of all other expressions, but this may very well be said of expressions of our controversial class, in virtue of which they are in all cases directed to inner experiences of the speaker.

In solitary mental life – if we disregard exceptional cases of talking to oneself, asking oneself questions, desiring or commanding oneself – relation to an auditor falls away, and the subjective expressions in question, which are still applicable, express the simple being of inner experiences in more or less definite relation to the subject. In a monologue a question is either of the form 'I ask myself whether . . .', or relation to the subject vanishes entirely: the interrogative expression becomes a mere name, or not really even that. For the normal use of a name is in a context of predicative or attributive relation, of which there is here no question. Since the expression becomes one with the intuited inner experience as a knowing of the latter, an interweaving of factors arises having the character of a self-enclosed phenomenon. To the extent that, in such interweaving, we live principally in an interrogative act, with which our expression merely fits in, and to which it gives articulate voice, the whole interweaving is called a question. Knowledge is not here a theoretical function – this is the case only in predication, while here nothing is predicated. The question is known and expressed, without being 'subjectivized', in the sense of being made either the subject or the object of predicative acts. Plainly this directly expressive sense of the interrogative sentence helps to constitute the predicative interrogation – I ask myself whether etc. – or the meaning which corresponds to such altered circumstances.

§70 Decision

If by a 'judgement' one means a predicative act, then our discussions have shown that our disputed sentences *do not invariably express judgements*. Even in these cases, however, an unbridgeable gulf separates us from the logicians who side with Aristotle. On their view, names, statements, optative sentences, interrogations, commands etc., are *coordinated* expressive forms, and coordinated in the following manner: names express presentations, statements express judgements, optative sentences express wishes etc. Presentations, judgements, questions etc., in short, acts of all sorts, can serve to confer meaning in exactly the same fashion, for to 'express acts' means the same in all cases, i.e. to have one's meaning in such acts. We, on the other hand, see a *fundamental difference* between names and statements, on the one hand, and the expressions of our controversial group, on the other. The acts of presentation or judging expressed by names or statements may confer or fulfil meaning, but are not therefore meant; they do not become objects of naming and predication, but are *constitutive of such objects*. On the other hand we find, in flat contrast, that the acts 'expressed' by our controversial expressions, though seeming to confer meanings, are made into *objects*. This may happen, as we saw, through inner intuition reflectively directed upon such acts, and generally also through relational acts based on such intuitions. It may also happen by way of certain acts of signification, perhaps only partially uttered, which attach as cognitions to these inner intuitions and acts of relating, thereby making their objects, the acts, namely, of asking, wishing, commanding etc., into objects named and otherwise talked of, and perhaps into components of predicated states of affairs. In these acts of objectification lie the true meanings of our controversial expressions. We are not in their case concerned with acts which confer meaning in some fundamentally new manner, but only with contingent specifications of the one, unique class of meaning-intentions. And, just so, the acts which fulfil meaning do not fall into different classes, but belong to the one, unique class of intuitions. It is not the wishes, commands etc., *themselves* that are expressed by these grammatical patterns and their significations; it is rather the intuitions of these acts that serve as fulfilments. When we compare indicative with optative sentences, we must not coordinate judgements with wishes, but *states of affairs* with wishes.

What results accordingly is the fact that:

The ostensible expressions of non-objectifying acts are really contingent specifications of statements and other expressions of objectifying acts which have an immense practical and communicative importance.

The contentious issue here dealt with is of fundamental importance, since on its solution depends, on the one hand, whether we accept a doctrine which makes all meaning, whether in intention or fulfilment, of a single kind – the genus of objectifying acts, with their fundamental division into the significative and the intuitive – or whether, on the other hand, we decide to permit acts of all sorts to confer or fulfil meaning. The issue is, of course, not less important because it is the first to call our attention to the fundamental triplicity of the ambiguity of talk about 'expressed acts', on whose analysis our present Investigation first embarked (cf. §2 above). There it was said that we may mean by 'expressed acts':

1. The *significative acts* which give expressions meaning, and which have, in their significative fashion, a certain objectivity of reference.

2. The *intuitive acts*, which frequently fulfil the significant intent of an expression, and so represent the significantly meant objects intuitively, and in a parallel intuitive 'sense'.

3. The acts which are the *objects* of signification, and likewise of intuition, in all cases where an expression (in sense 2) expresses the speaker's *own experiences of the moment*. If these are not objectifying acts, their nature will not permit them to function under the rubrics 1 and 2.

The root of all our difficulties lies in the fact that, in the direct application of expressions (or acts to be expressed) to intuitively grasped inner experiences, our significative acts are completely fulfilled by the inner intuition which attaches to them, so that both are most intimately blended, while these same intuitions, being internal, exhaust themselves in the straightforward presentation of the acts that they mean.

Finally we must observe that the distinction made above as against Bolzano – between cases where only the *subjective* objection can be raised – the objection to the expression's sincerity or adequacy – and cases where the *factual objection* can be raised – the objection related to objective truth and falsity – that this distinction has, on a closer survey, no true connection with our controversial question. For it has a quite general concern with the difference between expressions relating to intuitively envisaged act-experiences, and experiences not so relating. In the first class there are many quite uncontroversial predications, e.g. all statements of the form 'I ask whether . . .', 'I command, wish that . . .' etc. And, be it noted, there can be no factual objections to subjective judgements thus formulated: they are true or false, but *truth here coincides with sincerity*. In the case of other statements which aim at what is 'objective' (i.e. not at the self-expressing subject and his experiences) the factual question concerns our meaning. The question of sincerity depends on the possibility of seeming assertions, from which the genuine, normal act of meaning is absent. Really there is no judgement; the meaning of a statement is presented in the context of an intent to deceive.

External and internal perception: physical and psychical phenomena

I

The concepts of *external perception* and *perception of self*, of *sensuous* and *internal perception*, have for the naïve man the following content. *External perception* is the perception of external things, their qualities and relationships, their changes and interactions. *Perception of self* is the perception that each can have of his own ego and its properties, its states and activities. Asked who this perceived ego may be, the naïve man would reply by pointing to his bodily appearance, or would recount his past and present experiences. To the further question whether all this is included in his percept of self, he would naturally reply that, just as the perceived external thing has many properties, and has had many in the course of its changes, which are not for the moment 'open to perception', so a corresponding fact holds for his perceived ego. In the changing acts of *self*-perception appear, on occasion, such and such presentations, feelings, wishes and bodily activities of the ego, just as the exterior or the interior of a house, or such and such sides and parts of it, enter from time to time into *outer* perception. Naturally, however, the ego remains the perceived object in the one case, as the house is in the other.

For the naïve man our second pair of notions, that of *sensuous* and *internal* perception, does not altogether coincide with the pair just discussed, that of outward perception and perception of self. We perceive sensuously what we perceive by the eye and the ear, by smell and taste, in brief, through the organs of sense. In this field everyone locates, not only external things, but his own body and bodily activities, such as walking, eating, seeing, hearing etc. What we call 'inner perception', on the other hand, concerns mainly such 'spiritual' experiences as thinking, feeling and willing, but also everything that we locate, like these, in the interior of our bodies, do not connect with our outward organs.

In philosophical diction, both pairs of terms – we usually prefer the pair of 'internal and external perception' – express only one pair of concepts. After Descartes had sharply separated *mens* and *corpus*, Locke, using the terms 'sensation' and 'reflection', introduced the two corresponding classes of perception into modern philosophy. This division has remained in force till today. External perception was regarded, following Locke, as our perception of bodies, while inner perception was the perception that our 'spirits' or 'souls' have of their own activities (their *cogitationes* in the Cartesian sense). A *division of perceptions is accordingly mediated by a division among the objects of perception*, though a difference in *origin* is likewise set beside it. In one case perception arises from the effects of physical things operating through the senses on our spirits, in the other case out of a reflection on the activities carried out by the mind on the basis of 'ideas' won through sensation.

2

In quite recent times men have been much concerned to achieve an adequate overhaul and a deepening of Locke's obviously vague and rough positions.

General epistemological interests were, on the one hand, responsible for this move. We recall the traditional estimate of the relative value for knowledge of the two forms of perception: *external perception is deceptive, inner perception evident.* In this evidence lies one of the basic pillars of knowledge, which scepticism cannot shake. Inner perception is also the only case of perception where the object truly corresponds to the act of perception, is, in fact, immanent in it. It is also, to speak pointedly, the one type of perception that deserves the name. In the interest of perceptual theory, we must therefore enter more exactly into the essence of inner, as opposed to outer perception.

Psychological interests were, on the other hand, involved. Men were concerned with the much-debated *fixing of the domain of empirical psychology* and, particularly, with establishing for it its own justification as against the natural sciences, by marking out for it a peculiar territory of phenomena. Even the prime place in epistemology readily accorded to psychology as basic philosophical discipline, required that its objects be defined with as few epistemological commitments as possible; it should not, therefore, concern itself with transcendent realities of so controversial a type as soul and body as if they were obvious data. Locke's classification of perceptions had just such a presupposition: it was therefore at once unsuited, and not in fact designed, to serve as a basis for a definition of psychology, and to do justice to the interests mentioned. It is clear, further, that if a distinction of perceptions is set up on the basis of an anticipated distinction between bodily and spiritual matters, then the former distinction cannot be used as a basis of distinction between the science of bodily and the science of spiritual phenomena. The matter would be different if one could succeed in finding *purely descriptive marks* for a division of percepts, marks which left our classes unaltered in extent, and which, while lacking all epistemological presuppositions, would serve to demarcate the corresponding bodily phenomena from psychic phenomena.

A possible path seemed here to be opened by the Cartesian approach through doubt, with its emphasis on the epistemological position of inner perception. We have already touched on this above. The line of thought, which develops here, runs as follows:

However widely I may extend my critical doubts regarding knowledge, I cannot doubt that I exist and am doubting, or again, while I experience them, that I am having presentations, am judging, feeling or however else I may designate such inwardly perceived appearances: to doubt in such a case would evidently be irrational. We accordingly have absolute 'evidence' regarding the existence of the objects of inner perception, we have that clearest cognition, that unassailable certainty which distinguishes knowledge in the strictest sense. It is quite different in the case of outer perception. It lacks 'evidence', and the frequent conflicts in statements relying upon it point, in fact, to its capacity to deceive. We have therefore no right to assume from the outset that the objects of outer perception really and truly exist as they seem to us to be. We have, in fact, many reasons to think that they do not really exist at all, but can at best lay claim to a phenomenal or 'intentional' existence. If one makes the reality of a perceived object part of the notion of perception, then outer perception is not, in this strict sense, perception at all. This *evident character* will in any case give us a *descriptive mark*, free from presuppositions regarding metaphysical realities, which will enable us to sort out our various classes of perceptions. It is a character given with, or absent from, the perceptual experience itself, and this alone determines our division.

If we now consider the *phenomena* presented by these various classes of perceptions, they unmistakably constitute *essentially distinct classes*. This is not to assert that the objects in themselves, i.e. the souls and bodies, that we rightly or wrongly range under them, differ essentially: a purely *descriptive treatment* that avoids all transcendence establishes an unbridgeable gulf between these phenomena. On the one side we have the *sensory qualities*, which in themselves form a descriptively closed class, whether there are such things as senses and sense-organs or not. They form a Kind in the strict Aristotelian sense of the word. To these are added features necessarily attaching, either to sense-qualities in general, or to single ranges of such qualities (again strict Aristotelian species), or, conversely, features themselves necessarily presupposing qualities, and only able to achieve concrete being in association with them. Here well-known propositions come up for treatment, e.g. no intuited spatiality without quality. Many would say that the converse obtained also: No quality without something spatial. Others would here only approve particular cases: No colour, no tactile quality without something spatial. Further propositions of the same class would be: No tone-quality without intensity, no timbre without tone-qualities etc.[1]

On the other side we have phenomena such as having presentations, judgements, surmises, wishes, hopes etc. We here enter, as it were, another world.

These phenomena have relation to what is sensible, but are not themselves to be compared with the latter: they do not belong to one and the same (genuine) kind. When we have first clearly seen the descriptive unity of this class through examples, one finds, with a little attention, a positive mark which characterizes them all: the mark of 'intentional inexistence'.

One can of course use the above descriptive distinction of inner and outer perception to arrive at just such a distinction of the two classes of phenomena. It becomes now a good definition to say: Psychic phenomena are the phenomena of inner perception, physical phenomena those of outer perception.[2]

In this manner a closer treatment of the two sorts of perceptions leads, not merely to a descriptive, epistemologically important characterization of these perceptions themselves, but also to a fundamental, descriptive division of phenomena into two classes, the physical and the psychical. And we seem to have achieved, for psychological and scientific purposes, a metaphysically uncommitted definition, not oriented towards supposed data in some transcendent world, but to what is truly given phenomenally.

Physical phenomena are no longer defined as the phenomena which arise out of the operation of bodies on our minds through our sense-organs, psychic phenomena as the phenomena discovered by us in perceiving the activities of our minds. In both cases the descriptive character of the phenomena, as experienced by us, alone furnishes our criterion. Psychology can now be defined as the science of psychic phenomena, as natural science is of physical phenomena.

These definitions require certain limitations in order to correspond truly to our actual sciences, limitations which point to explanatory metaphysical hypotheses, whereas the phenomena, as descriptively differentiated, remain the true starting-points of our treatments, and the objects to be explained.

> The definition of natural science is particularly in need of limiting conditions, for it is not concerned with all physical phenomena, not with the phenomena of imagination, but only with those which come before sense-perception. And, even in their case, it only sets up laws to the extent that these depend on the physical stimulation of the sense-organs. One might express the scientific task of natural science, by saying that natural science is the science which seeks to explain the sequence of the physical phenomena of normal, pure sensations – sensations uninfluenced by peculiar psychical conditions and events – by assuming the action on our sense-organs of a world extended in three space-like dimensions, and taking place in one time-like dimension. Without settling the absolute character of this world, it is satisfied to attribute to it powers provocative of our sensations and influencing each other in their operation, and to set up laws of coexistence and succession for such powers. In stating these, it indirectly states the laws of sequence of the physical phenomena of our sensations, laws conceived in their purity, in scientific abstraction from

concomitant mental conditions, as things taking place for an invariant sensibility. The expression 'science of physical phenomena' must be interpreted in this rather complicated way, if it is to be equated with the meaning of 'natural science'.

(Brentano, *Psychologie*, 1, pp. 127–128)

In regard to the conceptual demarcation of psychology, it might appear that the concept of the psychic phenomenon should be widened rather than narrowed, since the physical phenomena of imagination fall as entirely in its field of reference as do psychic phenomena in the previously defined sense, and since even the physical phenomena appearing in sensation cannot be disregarded in the doctrine of sensation. But it is plain that such physical phenomena only enter into descriptions of the peculiarities of psychic phenomena as the content of the latter. The same holds of all psychic phenomena which exist only phenomenally. The true subject-matter of psychology can be regarded as consisting solely of psychic phenomena in the sense of actual states. It is exclusively in regard to the latter that we call psychology the science of psychic phenomena.

(Ibid. pp. 129 *f.*)

3

The interesting line of thought that I have just expounded represents, as my longer quotations have made plain, the standpoint of Brentano,[3] and also that of a whole succession of thinkers who are theoretically close to him. There are further respects, as is well known, in which 'inner perception' plays an important role in Brentano's psychology. I am here only concerned with his doctrine of inner consciousness. Every psychic phenomenon is not merely a consciousness, but itself the *content* of a consciousness; we are conscious of it in the narrower sense of perceiving it. The flux of inner experience is therefore also a continuous flux of inner percepts, which are most intimately united with the psychic experiences in question. For inner perception is no second, independent act supervening upon a relevant psychic phenomenon; the latter rather involves, in addition to its relation to a primary object, e.g. an externally perceived content, 'itself in all its completeness as presented and known' (ibid. p. 182). In so far as the act directly intends its primary object, it is also subsidiarily directed upon itself. In this way one avoids the endless complication seemingly threatened by the consciousness which accompanies all psychic phenomena (since their multiple division into three 'ground-classes' itself involves an inner perception). The 'evidence' and infallibility of inner perception will also be rendered possible in this manner (ibid. II, ch. 3, pp. 182 *ff.*). Brentano is here, in one of his main views, i.e. in his interpretation of consciousness as a continuous stream of internal perception, in harmony with the great thinkers of the past. Even Locke, a true student of experience, defines consciousness as the perception of what goes on in a man's own mind.[4]

Brentano's theories have aroused much opposition. This has not only been directed to the doctrines of inner perception just mentioned, whose subtly constructed complexity still certainly requires a phenomenological foundation, but also against his distinction between perceptions and phenomena and, in particular, against the laying down of the tasks of psychology and natural science which is based upon this.[5] The relevant questions have repeatedly been made the theme of serious discussion in the past decade, and it is sad that, despite its fundamental importance for psychology and epistemology, agreement has not been reached.

Criticism, it would appear, has not penetrated far enough, to hit upon the decisive points, and to separate what is indubitably significant in Brentano's thought-motivation from what is erroneous in its elaboration. This is due to the fact that the fundamental psychological and epistemological questions which cause controversy in these dimensions of enquiry, have not been sufficiently clarified, a natural consequence of defective phenomenological analysis. On both sides the conception with which men operated remained ambiguous, on both sides there was a consequent falling into delusive confusions. This will be clear from the following criticism of the illuminating views of Brentano.

4

According to Brentano inner perception distinguishes itself from outer perception:

1. by its evidence and its incorrigibility, and

2. by essential differences in phenomena. In inner perception we experience exclusively psychic phenomena, in outer perception physical phenomena. This exact parallelism makes it possible for the first-named distinction to serve as a characteristic distinguishing mark of the perceivable phenomena as well.

As opposed to this, *inner and outer perception* seem to me, *if the terms are naturally interpreted*, to be of an entirely similar epistemological *character*. More explicitly: there is a well-justified distinction between *evident* and *non-evident*, or between infallible and fallible perception. But, if one understands by *outer* perception (as one naturally does, and as Brentano also does) the perception of physical things, properties, events etc., and classes all other perceptions as *inner* perceptions, then such a division will not coincide at all with the division previously given. For not every perception of the ego, nor every perception of a psychic state referred to the ego, is certainly evident, if by the 'ego' we mean what we all mean by it, and what we all think we perceive in perceiving ourselves, i.e. our own empirical personality. It is clear, too, that most perceptions of psychic states cannot be evident, since these are perceived with a bodily location. That anxiety tightens my throat, that pain bores into my tooth, that grief gnaws at my heart: I perceive these things as I perceive that the wind shakes the trees, or that this box is square and brown in colour, etc. Here, indeed, outer perceptions go with inner perceptions, but this does not affect the fact that the psychic phenomena perceived are, *as they are perceived*, non-existent. Surely it is clear that *psychic* phenomena, also, can be perceived transcendently? Exactly regarded, all psychic phenomena seen in natural or empirical-scientific attitudes are perceived transcendently. The pure presentedness of experience presupposes a purely phenomenological attitude which will inhibit all transcendent assertions.

I know what will here be objected: that we have forgotten the difference between *perception* and *apperception*. Inner perception means the directly-conscious living-through of mental acts, they are here taken as what they *are*, and not as what they are *apprehended* or *apperceived as*. One must, however, reflect that what is true for the case of inner perception must be true also for the case of outer perception. If the essence of perception does not lie in apperception, then all talk of perception in regard to external things, mountains, woods, houses etc., is misguided, and this, the normal sense of the word 'perception', surely illustrated in these cases above all others, must be abandoned. Outer perception is apperception, and the unity of the concept demands that inner perception should be so too. It is of the essence of perception that something should appear in it: *apperception, however, constitutes what we call appearance*, whether veridical or not, and whether it remains faithfully and adequately in the frame of the immediately given, or anticipates future perception in going beyond it. The *house* appears to me – in no other manner than that I apperceive actually experienced sense-contents in a certain fashion. I hear a *barrel organ* – the tones sensed are interpreted *as those of a barrel organ*. In the same way I apperceivingly perceive my own psychic phenomena, the blessedness quivering through 'me', the grief in my heart etc. They are called 'appearances', or rather apparent contents, being contents of apperception.

5

The term 'appearance' is, of course, beset with ambiguities, whose extreme dangers are seen precisely in this case. It will not be useless at this point to list these equivocations explicitly: we have already touched on them in passing in the text of these Investigations. Talk of 'appearance' has a preferred application to acts of intuitive presentation, to acts of *perception*, on the one hand, and to acts of *representation*, on the other, e.g. acts of remembering, imagining, or pictorially representing (in the ordinary sense), on a basis mixed with perception. 'Appearance' accordingly means:

1. The concrete intuitive experience (the intuitive presentedness or rep-resentedness of a given object for us); the concrete experience, e.g., when we perceive the lamp standing before us. Since the qualitative character of the act, whether the object is regarded as real or not, is irrelevant, it can also be ignored entirely, and 'appearance' then coincides with what we defined as 'representation' in the last Investigation (cf. VI, §26).

2. The intuited (appearing) object, taken as it appears *here* and *now*, e.g. this lamp as it counts for some percept we have just performed.

3. In misleading fashion we also call the *real* (*reellen*) *constituents* of ap-pearances in sense 1, i.e. those of the concrete acts of appearing or intuiting, 'appearances'. Such appearances are, above all, the presentative *sensations*, the experienced moments of colour, form etc., which we fail to distinguish from *apparent properties* of the (coloured, formed) *objects* corresponding to them, and apparent in the act which 'interprets' them. That it is import-ant to distinguish between them, that it does not do to confuse a colour-sensation with an apparent bodily colouring, the sensation of form with bodily form etc., we have often stressed. Uncritical theories certainly ignore the distinction. But even those who would refuse to say with Schopenhauer that 'the world is my idea', are accustomed to speak as if apparent things were compounded out of sense-contents. One could certainly say that *apparent* things as such, the mere things of sense, are composed of a stuff analogous to that which as sensation is counted a content of conscious-ness. This does not affect the fact that the thing's apparent properties are not themselves sensations, but only appear as analogues of sensations. For they are not present, as sensations are, in consciousness, but are merely represented in it, as properties which *appear* in it, which are transcend-ently referred to. For this reason perceived external things, likewise, are not complexes of sensations: they are rather objects of appearances, objects appearing as complexes of properties, whose types stand in a peculiar *ana-logy* to types found among sensations. We could put what we have just said somewhat differently. Under the rubric of 'sensations', we range cer-tain sorts of *experiences* of this or that actual kind belonging to a unity of consciousness. If it now happens that, in a unity of consciousness, real properties of analogous kinds appear as external to, and transcending such sensations, we may then call them after these sensational classes, but they are no longer sensations. We emphasize the word 'external', which must of course not be understood spatially. However we may decide the ques-tion of the existence or nonexistence of phenomenal external things, we cannot doubt that the reality of each such perceived thing cannot be under-stood as the reality of a perceived complex of sensations in a perceiving consciousness. For it is plain, and confirmable by phenomenological ana-lysis in each instance, that the thing of perception, this so-called sensa-tional complex, differs in every circumstance, both as a whole and in every

distinct moment of property, from the sensational complex actually lived through in the percept in question, whose objective apperception first constitutes the perceptual sense, and thereby the apparent thing, in intentional fashion.

It may indeed be said that the original concept of appearance was the one given in our second place above: the concept of what appears, or of what could appear, of the intuitive as such. Having regard to the fact that all sorts of experiences (including the experiences of outer intuition, whose objects are therefore called *outer* appearances) can be made objects of reflective, inner intuition, we call all experiences in an ego's experiential unity 'phenomena'. *Phenomenology* is accordingly the theory of experiences in general, inclusive of all matters, whether real (*reellen*) or intentional, given in experiences, and evidently discoverable in them. Pure phenomenology is accordingly the theory of the essences of 'pure phenomena', the phenomena of a 'pure consciousness' or of a 'pure ego': it does not build on the ground, given by transcendent apperception, of physical and animal, and so of psycho-physical nature, it makes no empirical assertions, it propounds no judgements which relate to objects transcending consciousness: it establishes no truths concerning natural realities, whether physical or psychic – no psychological truths, therefore, in the historical sense – and borrows no such truths as assumed premises. It rather takes all apperceptions and judgemental assertions which point beyond what is given in adequate, purely immanent intuition, which point beyond the pure stream of consciousness, and treats them purely as the experiences they are in themselves: it subjects them to a purely immanent, purely descriptive examination into essence. This examination of essence is also pure in a second sense, in the sense of Ideation; it is an *a priori* examination in the true sense. So understood, all the Investigations of the present work have been purely phenomenological, in so far, that is, as they did not have ontological themes, and did not, as in the Third and Sixth Investigation, seek to make *a priori* assertions regarding the *objects* of possible consciousness. They did not speak of psychological facts and laws in an 'objective' nature, only of pure possibilities and necessities, which belong to any form of the pure 'cogito': they spoke of these as regards their real (*reellen*) and their intentional contents, or as regards their *a priori* possibilities of connection with other such patterns in an ideally possible conscious context.

As the term 'appearance' is ambiguous, so also, and consequently, is the term 'perception', and so are all further terms used in connection with perception. These ambiguities fill theories of perception with confused errors. The 'perceived' is, e.g., what appears in perception, i.e. its object (the house) and, further, the sense-content experienced in it, i.e. the sum of the presenting contents, which in their interconnection are 'interpreted' as the house, and singly 'interpreted' as its properties.

5*a*

Excerpt from the First Edition which was replaced by the first two paragraphs of the third note in the preceding §5 in Edition II.

3. If we are only clear that we have to draw a distinction in our intuition between sensations as lived experiences, which are accordingly components of the subject, and phenomenal determinations, as components of the intentional object, and that both only coincide in the ideal case of adequate intuition (which does not come into question for us), then we readily see that our inwoven sensations cannot themselves count as appearances, whether in the sense of acts or of apparent objects. Not in the former, since under the rubric of sensations we sum up certain non-acts, which perhaps receive an objectifying interpretation in acts; not in the latter, since acts would have to be part of the phenomenal objectivity of sensations, acts which would have to direct their intention to them. Such acts are indeed possible, but that they are part of the stock-in-trade of every percept, and this in relation to the percept's presentative sensations, cannot be shown to be necessary either by descriptive analysis or on genetic grounds. All this goes without saying for imaginative intuitions as well, in relation to their imaginatively representative contents.

If one has once got to the point of regarding all components of appearances in sense 1 as themselves appearances, then it is a further, almost unconscious step to regard everything psychic, all lived experiences in the experiential unity of the ego, as phenomena.

6

How misleading such ambiguities show themselves to be appears in Brentano's theory, with its division into inner and outer perception according to evidential character and separate phenomenal class. We are told that:

Outer perception is not evident, and is even delusive. This is undoubtedly the case if we mean by the 'physical phenomena' what such perception perceives, physical things, their properties and changes etc. But when Brentano exchanges this authentic, and alone permissible sense of the word 'perceive', for an improper sense which relates, not to external objects, but to presenting contents, contents, i.e., present as real parts (*reell angehörigen*) in perception, and when he consequently gives the name of 'physical phenomena', not merely to outer objects, but also to these contents, these latter seem infected with the fallibility of outer perception. I believe that stricter divisions are necessary here. If an external object (a house) is perceived, presenting sensations are experienced in *this* perception, but they are not perceived. When we are deluded regarding the existence of the house, we are not deluded regarding the existence of our experienced sense-contents, since we do not pass judgement on them at all, do not perceive them in this perception. If we afterwards take note of these contents – our ability to do this is, within certain limits, undeniable – and if we abstract from all that we recently or usually meant by way of them, and take them simply as they are, then we certainly perceive them, but perceive no external object through them. This new perception has plainly the same claim to inerrancy and evidence as any 'inner' perception. To doubt what is immanent (in consciousness), and is meant precisely as it is, would be quite evidently irrational. I may doubt whether an outer object exists, and so whether a percept relating to such objects is correct, but I cannot doubt the now experienced sensuous content of my experience, whenever, that is, I reflect on the latter, and simply *intuit it as being what it is*. There are, therefore, evident percepts of 'physical' contents, as well as of 'psychical'.

If it were now objected that sensuous contents are invariably and necessarily interpreted objectively, that they are always bearers of outer intuitions, and can only be attended to as contents of such intuitions, the point need not be disputed: it would make no difference to the situation. The evidence of the existence of these contents would be as indisputable as before, and would also not be our evidence for 'psychic phenomena' in the sense of acts. The evidence for the being of the whole psychic phenomenon implies that for each of its parts, but the perception of the part is a new perception with a new evidence, which is by no means that of the whole phenomenon.

An analogous ambiguity to that which affects the notion of a physical phenomenon, will also be found, if our conception is consistent, in the case of the notion of the psychic phenomenon. This is not the case for Brentano. He understands by a psychic phenomenon only an actually present act-experience, and by an inner perception a perception which simply apprehends such an experience, just as it is there. Brentano ignores the fact that he has only done justice to one class of percepts of psychic phenomena under the name of 'inner perception', and that it is not possible to divide all percepts into the two groups of outer and inner. He also ignores the fact that the whole evidential prerogative accorded to his 'inner perception' hangs upon the fact that he has employed an essentially distorted concept of perception in the case of inner perception, and that it does not depend on the peculiarity of inwardly perceived 'phenomena'. Had he treated as genuine percepts of physical phenomena only such objective interpretations and apprehensions as survey their objects adequately, he could have attributed evidence to that perception of sense-experiences which was by him assigned to outer perception, and he could not have said of inner perception (in his sense) that it is 'really the only sort of perception in the true sense of the word' (ibid. p. 119).

It is absolutely clear that the conceptual pairs of inner and outer, and of evident and non-evident perception, need not coincide at all. The first pair is determined by the concepts of physical and psychical, however these may be demarcated; the second expresses the epistemologically fundamental anti-thesis studied in our Sixth Investigation, the opposition between *adequate* perception (or intuition in the narrowest sense, whose perceptual intention is exclusively directed to a content truly present to it) and the merely sup-posing, *inadequate* perception, whose intention does not find fulfilment in present content, but rather goes through this to constitute the lively, but always one-sided and presumptive, presentedness of what is transcendent. In the first case the experienced *content* is also the *object* of perception, in the second, content and object fall asunder. The content represents what it does not itself have, what is, however, made manifest in it, and what is, in a certain sense, its analogue (if we confine ourselves to what is immediately intuited), as body-colour is an analogue of sense-colour.

In this separation we have the essence of the *epistemological* difference that men look for between inner and outer perception. It is the operative factor in the Cartesian treatment of doubt. I can doubt the truth of an inadequate, merely projective perception: the intended, or, if one likes, in-tentional, object is not immanent in the act of appearing. The intention is there, but the object itself, that is destined finally to fulfil it, is not one with it. How could its existence be evident to me? But I cannot doubt an adequate, purely immanent perception, since there are no residual intentions in it that must yet achieve fulfilment. The whole intention, or the intention in all its aspects, is fulfilled. Or, as we also expressed it: the object is not in our percept merely believed to exist, but is also itself truly given, and as what it is believed to be. It is of the essence of adequate perception that the intuited object itself really and truly dwells in it, which is merely another way of saying that *only the perception of one's own actual experiences is indubitable and evident.* Not every such percept is evident. In the percept of toothache, e.g., a real experience is perceived, and yet our perception often deceives: the pain appears to bore a sound tooth. The possibility of our error is plain. The perceived object is not the pain as experienced, but the pain in a transcendent reference as connected with the tooth. Adequate perception involves, however, that in it the perceived is experienced *as* it is perceived (as the perception thinks or conceives it). In this sense we obvi-ously only have an adequate percept of our own experiences, and of these only to the extent that we apprehend them purely, without going apperceptively beyond them.

7

It might now be objected: An experience is surely the same as a psychic phenomenon. What, then, is the dispute all about? I answer: If one means by 'psychic phenomena' the real (*realen*) constituents of our conscious-ness, the experiences themselves that are there, and if one further means by *inner* percepts, or percepts of psychic phenomena, adequate percepts, whose intention finds immanent fulfilment in the experiences in question, *then* the scope of *inner perception* will of course coincide with that of *adequate* perception. It is important, however, to note:

1. That psychic phenomena in this sense are not the same as psychic phenomena in Brentano's sense, nor as Descartes's *cogitationes*, nor as Locke's *acts or operations of mind*, since in the sphere of experiences as such all sense-contents, all sensations, also belong.

2. That the *non-inner* perceptions (the remainder class) *will not then coincide with outer perceptions* in the ordinary sense of the word, but with the much wider class of *transcendent, inadequate* perceptions. If a sense-content, or sense-complex or sequence of sense-contents is apprehended as a thing out there, as a multitude, an articulated connection of several things, or as a change in things, an external happening etc., we have an outer percept in the ordinary sense. But a non-sensuous content can also belong to the representative stuff of a transcendent percept, particularly in association with sense-contents. Our perceived object can then as readily be an *external* object with perceived *mental* properties (this happens in differing fashion in the apprehension of one's own and other men's bodily being as 'persons') or, as in psycho-physical apperception, an *inner* object, a subjective experience, perceived with *physical* properties attaching to it.

3. When in psychology, as the objective science of animal mentality, we mean by perceptions of psychic phenomena the perceptions that a man has of his own experiences, which the perceiver apprehends as belonging to himself, this particular person, all inner perceptions are no less cases of transcendent apperception than are outer perceptions. Among these there are some which (with some abstraction) count as *adequate*, in so far as they seize the man's own (relevant) experiences in their very selves. But in so far as even such 'adequate' inner perceptions apperceive the experiences they apprehend as those of a percipient, psycho-physical, personal ego, and so as belonging to the presented objective world, they are in this respect infected with an essential inadequacy. There are, further, cases of inner perception, as there are cases of outer perception, where the perceived object, in the sense given to it in our percept, has no existence. *The distinction, fundamental even for psychology, between adequate and inadequate perception – psychological adequateness being understood as the abstraction we mentioned – intersects the distinction between inner and outer perception,* and therefore pervades the sphere of the former.

8

The ambiguities of the word 'phenomenon' allow us first to call apparent objects and their properties 'phenomena', then to apply the term to the experiences which constitute their act of appearing (particularly to the experienced contents in the sense of sensations) and, lastly, to all experiences whatever. These ambiguities explain why we tend to confuse *two essentially different types of psychological division of 'phenomena'*.

1. Divisions of experiences, e.g. the division of experiences into *acts* and *non-acts*. Such divisions naturally fall into the sphere of psychology, which accordingly has to deal with all experiences, which it of course apperceives in transcendent fashion as experiences of animal beings in nature.

2. The division of *phenomenal objects* into, e.g., such as seem to belong to *the consciousness of an ego* and such as *do not seem to do so*, i.e. the division into psychical and physical objects (contents, properties, relations etc.).

In Brentano these two divisions are confused. He simply opposes physical to psychical phenomena, and defines them unmistakably as a division of *experiences* into acts and non-acts. But he at once mixes up, under the rubric of physical phenomena the contents of sense,[6] and apparent external objects (or their phenomenal properties), so that the division now becomes a division of *phenomenal* objects into physical and psychical (in an ordinary or near-ordinary sense), in which the latter division furnishes the names.

Closely connected with this confusion is the erroneous criterion, also used by Brentano, to divide the two classes of phenomena: that physical phenomena only exist 'phenomenally and intentionally, while psychical phenomena also 'have an *actual* existence as well as an intentional one'.[7] If we understand by 'physical phenomena' phenomenal things, it is at least sure that they do not need to exist. The forms of productive fancy, most of the objects of artistic representation in paintings, statues, poems etc., hallucinatory and illusory objects, exist only in a phenomenal and intentional manner, i.e. they do not exist in the *authentic* sense at all; only the relevant *acts of appearing* exist with their real (*reellen*) and intentional contents. The matter is quite different in the case of physical phenomena interpreted as sensed contents. The sensed (experienced) colour-contents, shape-contents etc., which we enjoy when we look at Böcklin's picture of the Elysian Fields, and which, informed by an imaginative act-character, are made into the consciousness of the pictured objects, are real (*reelle*) constituents of this experience. And they do not exist in merely phenomenal, intentional fashion (as apparent, merely intended contents) but in actuality. One must not forget, of course, that 'actual' does not here mean the same as 'external to consciousness', but the same as 'not merely putative'.

Notes

Prolegomena to pure logic

1 Logic as a normative and, in particular, as a practical discipline

1 Bergmann, *Die Grundlagen der Logik* (1895), p. 78. Cf. also Bolzano's *Wissenschaftslehre* (Sulzbach 1837), 1, p. 24: 'Is the question whether coriander helps to strengthen memory a logical question? It surely should be if logic is an *ars rationis formandae* in the complete meaning of the words'.

2 Bolzano, *Wissenschaftslehre*, 1, p. 7. The fourth volume of the *Wissenschaftslehre* is indeed specially devoted to the task which the definition expresses. But it strikes one as strange that the incomparably more important disciplines which the first three volumes treat of, should be represented merely as aids to a technology of scientific textbooks. Naturally, too, the value of this by no means as yet sufficiently valued work, which is, in fact, almost unused, rests on the researches of these earlier volumes.

3 Psychologism, its arguments and its attitude to the usual counter-arguments

1 I use the expressions 'psychologist', 'psychologism' and so on without any evaluative 'colouring', similar to Stumpf in his *Psychology and Theory of Knowledge.*

2 'Logic is a psychological discipline just as surely as knowing only arises in the mind, and as thinking which terminates in knowledge is a mental happening.' Lipps, *op. cit.*

3 Cf., e.g. W. Hamilton's Lectures III, p. 78, Drobisch, *Neue Darstellung der Logik*, ed. IV, §2; cf. also B. Erdmann, *Logik* I, p. 18.

4 *Logik*, vol. I, p. 10. Sigwart's own way of treating logic (as we shall see in Ch. VIII) is altogether on psychologistic lines.

5 This point of view is expressed with increasing clearness in the works of Mill, Sigwart, Wundt, and Höfler-Meinong. Cf. on this the quotations and criticisms in Ch. VIII, §49 *f.*

6 Cf. Lotze's *Logik*, ed. II, §332, pp. 543–4; Natorp 'Über objektive und subjektive Begründungen der Erkenntnis', *Philos. Monatshefte* XXIII, p. 264; Erdmann's *Logik*, vol. I, p. 18. As against this cf. Stumpf 'Psychologie und Erkenntnistheorie', p. 5 (*Proceedings of Kais. Bay. Akad. d. Wiss.*, I Kl., vol. XIX, Section II, p. 469). That Stumpf is discussing epistemology, not logic, obviously makes no essential difference.

4 Empiricistic consequences of psychologism

1 I mean by these the senses of the propositions '*A* and *B*', i.e. both hold, and '*A* or *B*', i.e. one holds – which does not imply that *only* one holds.
2 Cf. the systematic discussions of Ch. VIII of this work regarding the sceptical-relativistic absurdity of all conceptions which make logical principles depend on facts.

7 Psychologism as a sceptical relativism

1 Please note that the term 'knowledge' is, in this work, not restricted, as it usually is restricted, to objects that are real.
2 See Ch. V, Appendix to §§25–6.
3 His view should recommend itself to those who think to separate subjective from objective truths by denying an objective character to judgements of introspection. They assume that the being-for-me of a conscious content cannot at the same time be a being-in-itself, that subjectivity in the psychological sense excludes objectivity in the logical sense.

8 The psychologistic prejudices

1 A mark of a mark is, generally speaking, plainly *not* a mark of the thing. If the principle meant what it literally says, we could infer: This blotting-paper is red, Red is a colour, therefore this blotting-paper is a colour.
2 In this view, that the normative notion of 'ought' does not form part of the content of logical laws, I am glad to find myself in agreement with Natorp, who has recently made the brief and clear remark in his *Sozialpädagogik* (Stuttgart, 1899), §4, that 'logical principles, we maintain, are as little about what people actually think in such and such circumstances, as they are about what they ought to think'. He says of the equational reasonings 'If $A = B$ and $B = C$, $A = C$' that 'I perceive its truth when only the terms to be compared, and the relations given together with them, are before me, without having to think in the least of the actual or proper conduct of some corresponding act of thought' (pp. 20–1). There are certain other equally important *rapprochements* between these Prolegomena and the distinguished thinker's present work, which unhappily came too late to assist in forming and expounding these thoughts. Two previous writings of Natorp, the above quoted article from *Phil. Monatshefte*, XXIII and the *Einleitung in die Psychologie*, stimulated me, however – though other points in them provoked me to controversion.
3 'Pure' or 'formal' mathematics, as I use the term, includes all pure arithmetic and theory of manifolds, but not geometry. Geometry corresponds in pure mathematics to the theory of a three-dimensional Euclidean manifold. This manifold is the generic Idea of space, but not space itself.
4 See in addition the fine statement of Natorp 'Über objektive und subjektive Begründung der Erkenntnis', *Philos. Monatshefte*, XXIII, p. 265 *f.* Cf. also G. Frege's stimulating work *Die Grundlagen der Arithmetik* (1884), p. vi *f.* (I need hardly say that I no longer approve of my own fundamental criticisms of Frege's antipsychologistic position set forth in my *Philosophie der Arithmetik*, I, pp. 129–32.) I may here take the opportunity, in relation to all of the discussions of these Prolegomena, to refer to the Preface of Frege's later work *Grundgesetze der Arithmetik*, vol. I (Jena, 1893).

5 Wundt, *Logik*, I, 2nd ed., p. 91. Wundt regularly couples inner evidence with universal validity in this passage. As regards the latter, he distinguishes between a subjective form of universal validity, a mere consequence of inner evidence, and an objective form, which also covers the postulate of the intelligibility of experience. But as the justification and adequate fulfilment of this postulate itself rests on inner evidence, it does not seem feasible to drag in 'universal validity' into discussions of basic principles.

6 If we really had to interpret the theory of inner evidence in the manner of Höfler on p. 133, *op. cit.*, it would have been corrected by our previous critique of empiricistic misunderstandings of logical principles (see §23). Höfler's statement 'that an affirmative and a negative judgement about the same object are incompatible', is, as an exact statement, false, and can even less count as a statement of the logical principle. A similar mistake slips into the definition of the correlatives 'ground' and 'consequence': if it were correct, it would falsify all syllogistic rules. It runs: 'A judgement C is the consequence of a ground G, if the *belief* in the falsity of C is incompatible with the (imagined) *belief* in the truth of G' (*op. cit.* p. 136). Note that Höfler explains incompatibility in terms of evident non-coexistence (*op. cit.* p. 129). He plainly confuses the ideal non-coexistence (i.e. lack of joint truth) of the propositions in question, with the real non-coexistence of the corresponding acts of affirmation, presentation etc.

10 End of our critical treatments

1 Ueberweg can find as much to mention about both of them: their titles. Some day men will regard an historical treatment of logic, oriented, like Ueberweg's, to the 'great philosophy', an extraordinary anomaly.

11 The idea of pure logic

1 Cf. §6. We were there no doubt concerned under the rubric of 'science', with a narrower concept, that of theoretical explanatory abstract science. This, however, makes no essential difference, especially in view of the eminent position of the abstract sciences, that we shall be discussing immediately below.

2 We are therefore not concerned with a subjective psychological character of the judgement in question, e.g. a feeling of necessitation, etc. How ideal objects, and with them ideal predicates of such objects, stand to our subjective acts has been more or less indicated in §39 (excised from this edition). More in the following Investigations.

3 Cf. above §32. Above, when I pinned down the pointed notion of scepticism, there was no place for so subtle a distinction, and I merely opposed the noetic conditions of *theoretical knowledge* to the objectively logical conditions of *theory itself*. But here, where all relevant relationships must be brought to complete clearness, it seems proper to treat the logical conditions, in the first place, as being conditions of *knowledge* as well, and then only to give them a direct relation to *objective theory* itself. This of course has no effect on anything essential to our conception, which rather achieves a clearer unfolding. The like holds in regard to the inclusion in our scope of the empirical, subjective conditions of knowledge together with the noetic, purely logical ones. We are profited in all this by our treatment of logical self-evidence: see above, §50. Self-evidence is indeed nothing other than the character of knowledge as such.

Investigations into phenomenology and the theory of knowledge

Introduction

1 *Logic*, Book I, ch. I, §1.
2 See the final chapter of the Prolegomena, §§66–7 in particular.
3 Cf. §11 of Investigation I.

Investigation I: Expression and meaning

I Essential distinctions

1 I often make use of the vaguer expression 'objective correlate' (*Gegenständlichkeit*, 'objectivity') since we are here never limited to objects in the narrower sense, but have also to do with states of affairs, properties, and non-independent forms etc., whether real or categorial.
2 Cf. with this Twardowski's assumption of a 'presentative activity moving in two directions' in his work *Zur Lehre vom Ihbalt und Gegenstand der Vorstellungen* (Vienna 1894), p. 14.
3 G. Frege, *Über Sinn und Bedeutung, Zeitschr. f. Philos. u. philos. Kritik*, vol. 100, p. 25.
4 *Die Impersonalien*, p. 62.
5 B. Erdmann, *Logik*, I, p. 233.
6 A. Marty, 'Über subjektlose Sätze und das Verhältnis der Grammatik zur Logik und Psychologie', Art. VI, *Vierteljahrschrift f. wiss. Phil.* XIX, 80 *f.*
7 Ibid. p. 81 note. Cf. Art. V, Vol. XVIII, p. 464.

3 Fluctuation in meaning and the ideality of unities of meaning

1 Husserl's example is of the German word *Hund* meaning both a dog and a truck used in mines.
2 The restriction to concreta is not essential. Demonstratives, e.g., can also refer to abstracta.
3 More on this point in Investigation IV.

Investigation II: The ideal unity of the species and modern theories of abstraction

I Universal objects and the consciousness of universality

1 For more detailed treatment of the intuitive apprehensions of collections see my *Philosophie der Arithmetik* (1891), ch. XI, on the intuitive cognition of likeness, p. 233 in particular.
2 It is not suitable to speak of a theory when, as the following treatments will show, there is nothing at all to be theoretically treated, i.e. to be explained.

2 The psychological hypostatization of the universal

1 [It would have been possible for Husserl here to have used his other term *reellen*, signifying an actual part, not something intended or meant.]

2 As against this see B. Erdmann, *Logik*, I, pp. 81–5, and K. Twardowski, *Zur Lehre vom Inhalt und Gegenstand der Vorstellungen*, p. 106.

3 Abstraction and attention

1 See A. v. Meinong, *Hume-Studien*, I, p. 68.
2 The word symbolized by letter '*A*' in such combinations, must count as syncategorematic. The expressions: 'the lion', 'a lion', 'this lion' 'all lions, etc. certainly and evidently have a common element of meaning, but the word can have no independent sense except as occurring in one of these forms. If we are asked whether one of these meanings is not *contained* in all the reset, whether the direct idea of the Species corresponding to *A* does not lie hidden in the other meanings, we must answer 'No'. The Species *A* 'lies hidden' in these meanings, but only potentially and not as a meant object.
3 It is easy to see that as a result of this supposed 'unconsciousness' the absurd χωρισμός, of Locke's general idea returns. What is not 'conscious' cannot be a differentia of what is conscious. If exclusive attention to the moment of triangularity was possible, in a manner which made the differentiating characters vanish from consciousness, then the 'conscious', intuitive object would be the triangle as such and no more.

4 Abstraction and representation

1 Cf. also the end of the quotation in §9 of the present Investigation. Among modern philosophers I may mention Rickert, 'Zur Theorie der naturwissenschaftlichen Begriffsbildung', *Vierteljahreschrift für wiss. Philos.* XVIII.
2 Cf. the Prolegomena to Pure Logic, ch. IX.

Investigation III: On the theory of wholes and parts

Introduction

1 As regards these 'formal objective categories' and the formal ontological truths of essence pertaining to them, see the statements of the last chapter of the Prolegomena, (1 §§67 *f*).

I The difference between independent and non-independent objects

1 The two Husserlian terms, *real* and *reell*, here occur in the same sentence, the former connoting what is actually there in the space-time world, and not abstract or ideal, the latter what is actually immanent in an experience, and not merely 'meant' by it. [Translator's note]
2 In the present discussion, there is no danger of confusion between 'presented content', in the sense of any presented object (in the psychological sphere: any psychological datum), and 'presented content' in the sense of 'what' the presentation signifies.
3 *Principles*, Introduction §10.
4 Almost exactly as formulated by C. Stumpf in *Über den psychologischen Ursprung der Raumvorstellung* (1873), p. 109.

5 Stumpf previously used the expression 'partial content', but now prefers to speak of an 'attributive moment'.
6 In the following expositions, I employed my essay 'On Abstract and Concrete Concepts', (No. I of the 'Psychological Studies in the Elements of Logic', *Philos. Monatshefte*, 1894, Vol. XXX).
7 Loc. cit. p. 112.
8 Loc. cit. p. 113.
9 Cf. Ehrenfels, '*Über Gestaltqualitäten*', *Vierteljahrsschrift für Wiss. Philosophie* (1890); my *Philosophie der Arithmetik* (1891), particularly the whole of ch. XI, Meinong, '*Beiträge Zur Theorie der psychischen Analyse*', *Zeitschrift f. Psychologie u. Physiologie d Sinnesorgane, VI* (1893).

2 Thoughts towards a theory of the pure forms of wholes and parts

1 In the sense namely of the abbreviated mode of speech defined in the last section, which must everywhere be remembered here.
2 One must certainly distinguish the *sensuous moment of likeness* from *likeness as a categorial unity*: the former is related to the latter as the sensuous characters of plurality, which serve us as direct indications of multiplicity and diversity, stand to multiplicity and diversity themselves. See my *Phil. der Arithmetik*, p. 233. This first work of mine (an elaboration of my *Habilitationsschrift*, never published and only partially printed, at the University of Halle, 1887) should be compared with all assertions of the present work on aggregates, moments of unity, combinations, wholes and objects of higher order. I am sorry that in many recent treatments of the doctrine of 'form-qualities', this work has mostly been ignored, though quite a lot of the thought-content of later treatments by Cornelius, Meinong etc., of questions of analysis, apprehension of plurality and combination, is already to be found, differently expressed, in my *Philos. der Arithm.* I think it would still be of use today to consult this work on the phenomenological and ontological issues in question, especially since it is the first work which attached importance to acts and objects of higher order and investigated them thoroughly.
3 See §11, above.
4 See *Prolegomena*, Vol. 1 (§§67–72) on the role of formalization for constituting the idea of a pure logic as *mathesis universalis*. We must emphasize again that where we speak simply of 'abstraction', as we have done so far, we mean the emphasis on a non-independent 'moment' of content, or the corresponding ideation under the title of 'ideating abstraction', but *not* formalization.
5 See §19, above.
6 Prop. 3 in §19 above.

Investigation IV: The distinction between independent and non-independent meanings and the idea of pure grammar

Introduction

1 B. Bolzano, *Wissenschaftslehre* (Sulzbach, 1837), I, §57. 'Presentation' means for Bolzano 'presentations-in-themselves', which corresponds to our concept of meaning.

2 A. Marty, 'Über subjektlose Sätze', *Vierteljahrschrift fur wis. Philos.*, viiith year, p. 293, note.

3 Marty, 'Über das Verhältnis von Grammatik und Logik', *Symbolae Pragenses* (1893), p. 121, n. 2.

4 In his last-mentioned article Marty defines a categorematic sign as one which independently arouses a *complete presentation*, through which an object is named. But the definition of the syncategorematic sign which follows (see above) does not clearly bring out that the grammatical division rests on an essential division in the field of meaning, as Marty certainly thought.

5 The word 'presentation', carefully regarded, does not here mean 'act of presentation', but merely what is presented as such, together with the articulations and forms with which it is present in consciousness. The 'presentational form' is therefore the form of what is presented as such; we must keep this in mind in what follows.

6 A. Marty recently wrote, in his 'Untersuchungen zur Grundlegung der allgemeinen Grammatik und Sprachphilosophie' (Halle, 1908) of 'autosemantic' and 'synsemantic' signs (pp. 205 *ff.*).

7 The mode of speech need not be taken as literally as Marty has done in his Untersuchungen, pp. 211 *f.*, as meaning that we build total meanings out of 'bricks' of partial meaning that could also exist separately. That this is a wrong conception is precisely the theme of my further argued doctrine of non-independent meanings. I cannot see how the exposition above can bear such an interpretation, and that it is in any way touched by Marty's objections. See the further discussions below regarding the understanding of isolated syncategorematica.

8 In so far as these and the rest have not lost their articulate meanings in the evolution of speech.

9 We dealt with an analogous, closely related question in §2.

10 §15.

11 The genuine contribution traditional logic makes to pure logic including the whole logic of the syllogism, is part of the logic of propositional meanings (or 'apophantic' logic).

Investigation V: On intentional experiences and their 'contents'

1 Consciousness as the phenomenological subsistence of the ego and consciousness as inner perception

1 See my *Ideas towards a Pure Phenomenology, etc.*, in the *Jahrbuch für Philos. u. phänom. Forschung*, 1 (1913), Section 2. [The present paragraph is an insertion in the Second Edition.]

2 Which is only in question *qua* phenomenal, since we exclude all questions regarding its existence or non-existence, and that of the empirical ego which appears in it, if we wish our treatments to have, not a descriptive-psychological, but a purely phenomenological value. One should note how, up to this point and for the future, each analysis can be first conducted as mere psychology, but there really permits of that 'purification' which gives it value as 'pure' phenomenology. [Second Edition comment.]

3 Or what we also call its 'appearance' in the sense given above, which will also be employed in future, the sense in which a (phenomenologically understood) experience is itself styled an 'appearance'.

4 In the First Edition the name 'phenomenological ego' was given to the stream of consciousness as such.

5 The opposition to the doctrine of a 'pure' ego, already expressed in this paragraph, is one that the author no longer approves of, as is plain from his *Ideas* cited above (see *ibid* §57, p. 107; §80, p. 159).

6 The text as here set forth is taken over without essential change from the First Edition. It fails to do justice to the fact that the empirical ego is as much a case of transcendence as the physical thing. If the elimination of such transcendence, and the reduction to pure phenomenological data, leaves us with no residual pure ego, there can be no real (adequate) self-evidence attaching to the 'I am'. But if there is really such an adequate self-evidence – who indeed could deny it? – how can we avoid assuming a pure ego? It is precisely the ego apprehended in *carrying out* a self-evident *cogito*, and the pure carrying out *eo epso* grasps it in phenomenological purity, and necessarily grasps it as the subject of a pure experience of the type *cogito*.

7 Cf. the whole of §4 in Natorp's *Einleitung in die Psychologie nach kritischer Methode*, pp. 11 *f.*

8 I have since managed to find it, i.e. have learnt not to be led astray from a pure grasp of the given through corrupt forms of ego-metaphysic cf. note to §6.

2 Consciousness as intentional experience

1 My deviations from Brentano are not on the same lines as the qualifications that he found necessary to add to the inadequate simplifications of which he was clearly conscious (See *Psychologie*, I, pp. 127 *ff.*). This will be plain from the discussions in App. 2 at the end of this volume.

2 We could not say 'experiencing contents', since the concept of 'experience' has its prime source in the field of 'psychic acts'. Even if this concept has been widened to include non-acts, these for us stand connected with, ranged beside and attached to acts, in a unity of consciousness so essential that, were it to fall away, talk of 'experiencing' would lose its point.

3 See further the *Appendix* referred to above.

4 *Psychologie*, I, 115.

5 We are not therefore troubled by such vexed questions as to whether all mental phenomena, e.g. the phenomena of feeling, have the peculiarity in question. We must ask instead whether the phenomena in question *are* mental phenomena. The oddness of the question springs from the unsuitability of its wording. More about this later.

6 Within the framework of psychological apperception, the purely phenomenological concept of experience fuses with that of mental reality, or rather, it turns into the concept of the mental state of an animal being (either in actual nature or in an ideally possible nature with ideally possible animals, i.e. without existential implications). Later on the pure *phenomenological* generic Idea *intentional experience* transforms itself into the parallel, nearly related *psychological* generic concept. According as psychological apperception is kept out or kept in, the same sort of analysis has phenomenological or psychological import.

7 *Psychologie*, p. 111 (end of §3).

8 *Psychologie*, p. 104.

9 Cf. Brentano, *Psychologie*, pp. 266–7, 295 and *passim*.

10 No reference to selective attention or notice is included in the sense of the 'reference' involved in our 'intention'. See also §13.

11 We may here ignore the various possible assertive traits involved in the believed being of what is presented. One should again recall that it is possible to leave out all presupposing of natural reality, persons and other conscious animals included therein in our completed studies, so that they are understood as discussions of *ideal* possibilities. One finally sees them in the light of methodological exclusions, which cut out whatever is matter of transcendent apperception and assertion, so as to bring out what is *really* part of an experience and of its essence. Experience has then become the pure experience of phenomenology, from which psychological apperception has likewise dropped away.

12 As regards the seemingly obvious distinction between immanent and transcendent objects, modelled on the traditional schema of inner conscious image *v.* extraconscious being-in-itself, cf. the Appendix at the end of this chapter.

13 Cf. the additional note to ch. I above, and my *Ideen zu einer reinen Phänomenologie*, l.c.

14 Cf. §19 (excised from this edition).

15 We are in complete agreement with Natorp (*Einleitung in die Psychologie*, 1st edn, p. 21) when he objects to fully serious talk about 'mental activities', or 'activities of consciousness', or 'activities of the ego', by saying that 'consciousness only appears as a doing, and its subject as a doer, because it is often or always accompanied by conation'. We too reject the 'mythology of activities': we define 'acts' as intentional experiences, not as mental activities.

16 P. Natorp, *Einleitung in die Psychologie*, 1st edn, p. 18.

17 Last three sentences added in Edition II.

18 Cf. my 'Psychological Studies . . .', *Philos. Monatshefte* XXX (1894), p. 182.

19 The much discussed dispute as to the relation between perceptual and imaginative presentation can have no satisfactory outcome in default of a properly prepared phenomenological foundation and consequent clarity in concepts and questions. The like holds of enquiries as to the relation of simple perception to representational or sign-consciousness. It can be readily shown, I think, that act-characters differ in such cases in pictorial representation, e.g. an essentially new mode of intention, is experienced.

20 *Psychologie*, I, pp. 116 *ff.*

21 [Paragraph added in Edition II.]

22 Here as elsewhere I identify the pain-sensation with its 'content', since I do not recognize peculiar sensing acts. Naturally I reject Brentano's doctrine that presentative acts, in the term of acts of feeling-sensation, underlie acts of feeling.

23 I point here, for purposes of comparison, and perhaps completion, to H. Schwarz's *Psychologie des Willens* (Leipzig, 1900) which in §12 (excised from this edition) deals with similar questions.

24 In the First Edition I wrote 'real *or* phenomenological' for 'real'. The word 'phenomenological' like the word 'descriptive' was used in the First Edition only in connection with *real* (*reelle*) elements of experience, and in the present edition it has so far been used predominately in this sense. This corresponds to one's natural starting with the psychological point of view. It became plainer and plainer, however, as I reviewed the completed Investigations and pondered on their themes more deeply – particularly from this point onwards – that the description of intentional objectivity as such, as we are conscious of it in the concrete act-experience, represents a distinct descriptive dimension where purely intuitive description may be adequately practised, a dimension opposed to that of real (*reellen*) act-constituents, but which also deserves to be called 'phenomenological'. These methodological extensions lead to important extensions of the field of problems now opening before us and considerable improvements due to a fully conscious separation of descriptive levels. Cf. my *Ideen zu einer reinen Phänomenologie*, Book I, and particularly what is said of *Noesis and Noema* in Section III.

25 Paragraph added in the Second Edition.

26 *Real* would sound much better alongside 'intentional' but it definitely keeps the notion of thinglike transcendence which the reduction to *real* (*reell*) immanence in experience is meant to exclude. It is well to maintain a conscious association of the *real* with the thinglike.

27 We have here a case of 'foundation' in the strict sense of our Third Investigation. We only use the term in this strict sense.

28 Cf. the Appendix to this chapter.

29 Confusion results from unavoidable ambiguities in talk of the definite and the indefinite. One speaks, e.g., of the indefiniteness of perceptual judgements, which consists in the fact that the rear side of a perceived object is subsidiarily meant, but indefinitely, whereas the clearly seen front side seems definite. Or one speaks of the indefiniteness of 'particular' assertions, e.g. *An A is B, Some A's are B's*, as opposed to the definiteness of the singular assertion 'This *A* is *B*'. Such definitenesses and indefinitenesses differ in sense from those in the text: they belong among the particularities of possible 'matters', as will be plainer in what follows.

30 One constantly notices that all the empirical psychological aspects of the examples fall out and become irrelevant with the ideational grasp of the phenomenological difference of essence.

31 Cf. §17 (excised from this edition).

32 For the moment we permit ourselves this improper mode of expression, which in its proper interpretation assorts ill with the image-theory.

33 Which does not mean, we must repeat, that the object is noticed, or that we are thematically occupied with it, though such things are included in our ordinary talk about 'referring'.

3 The matter of the act and its underlying presentation

1 At the time, of course, of the appearance of this work's First Edition.

5 Further contributions to the theory of judgement. 'Presentation' as a qualitatively unitary genus of nominal and propositional acts

1 Cf. the examples in §34 (excised from this edition).

2 It must be noted that this mode of expression is a circumlocution.

3 [§38, from this point onwards, is mainly a Second Edition supplement.]

4 All this must of course not be understood in an empirical-psychological manner. We are concerned here (as everywhere in this investigation) with *a priori* possibilities rooted in pure essence, which are as such grasped by us with apodictic self-evidence.

5 Cf. however the interpretation of a 'community of kind' as a peculiar relation of 'essence and counter-essence' in my *Ideas*, p. 233. The further pursuit of the results of this investigation has generally led to many essential deepenings and improvements. Cf. in particular, *Ideas*, §§109–14, 117 on the neutrality modification.

6 The same is of course true of other act-products, e.g. the aesthetic consideration of pictures.

7 §23.

6 Summing-up of the most important ambiguities in the terms 'presentation' and 'content'

1 Not a good example of the impossible, but a slip. *Translator.*
2 See the criticism of the picture-theory in §21, Appendix to §11 and §20 (p. 238 of this book).
3 Cf. Inv. I, §20 (excised from this edition). Also Inv. II, §20 (excised from this edition), and the chapter on 'Abstraction and Representation'.
4 *Reell* applies to a thing's actual parts as opposed to what it merely intends or means. *Real* is the being of real things in the world. [Translator]

Investigation VI: Elements of a phenomenological elucidation of knowledge

First Section: Objectifying intentions and their fulfilments: knowledge as a synthesis of fulfilment and its gradations

1 Meaning-intention and meaning-fulfilment

1 *Log. Inv.* I, §12.
2 See *Log. Inv.* I, §26.
3 *Log. Inv.* I, §§9, 10.
4 Cf. my *Psych. Studies of elementary Logic*, II, 'Concerning Intuitions and Representations', *Philos. Monatshefte*, 1894, p. 176. I have given up the concept of intuition supported there, as the present work makes plain.
5 I use this expression without specially introducing it as a term, since it is the mere translation of 'meaning'. I shall accordingly often speak of *significative* or *signitive acts*, instead of acts of meaning-intention, of meaning etc. 'Meaning-acts' can scarcely be talked of, since *expressions* are used as the normal subjects of meaning. 'Signitive' also offers us a suitable terminological opposite to 'intuitive'. A synonym for 'signitive' is 'symbolic', to the extent that the modern abuse of a word 'symbol' obtains – an abuse already denounced by Kant – which equates a symbol with a 'sign', quite against its original and still indispensable sense.
6 Cf. §13 of the previous Investigation.

3 The phenomenology of the levels of knowledge

1 See above §14.
2 Cf. the deeper analyses of §24.
3 In the above paragraph, the German terms '*darstellen*', '*Darstellung*' etc. are translated by 'intuitively present', 'intuitive presentation' etc. The terms 'strictly present' etc. are used to translate '*präsentieren*' etc. 'Presentation' *simpliciter* still translates '*Vorstellung*'. [Translator]

5 The ideal of adequation. Self-evidence and truth

1 Cf. §23.

Second Section: Sense and understanding

7 A study in categorial representation

1 If α represents the constitutive features in a concept and β those of any other concept *whatever*, one can always construct the form: Something that is *either* α or β. This external sort of conceptual extension which I call 'disjunctive', can at times prove very useful. It plays, e.g., an important role in the development of artificial mathematical techniques not sufficiently appreciated by logicians. The logic of mathematics is in fact in its infancy: few logicians have even seen that here is a field of great problems, fundamental for the understanding of mathematics and of mathematicizing natural science, and admitting of strict solution despite all their difficulty.

Appendix: External and internal perception: physical and psychical phenomena

1 It is remarkable that no one has tried to found a positive determination of 'physical phenomena' on these intuitive interconnections. In pointing to them, I depart from my role as a reporter. To employ them seriously, one must, of course, have due regard to the ambiguity of talk about 'physical phenomena', an ambiguity we shall immediately discuss.

2 Brentano (*Psychologie*, I, pp. 118 *f.*) says it is a distinguishing mark of all psychic phenomena 'that they are only perceived in an inner consciousness, whereas outer perception alone is possible in the case of physical phenomena'. It is emphatically said on p. 119 that this determination characterizes psychic phenomena adequately. 'Inner consciousness' is here merely another expression for inner perception.

3 Up to the positive mark of physical phenomena given in 2 above. I hope, further, to have achieved accuracy in restating the main points of view which have been governing factors in the doctrines of the thinkers I value so highly.

4 Locke's *Essay*, II. i. 19. Locke is not perfectly consistent in so far as he expressly makes 'perception' an apprehension of ideas, and yet makes the apprehension of the ideas of mental activities depend on *special* acts of reflection, that only at times supervene on these activities. This is obviously due to the wretched dual concept 'idea' which promiscuously covers the *presentations* of contents that may be experienced, and also the experienced contents themselves. See our Inv. II, §10.

5 Criticism, as it strikes me, generally stops at the first provisional theses of Brentano – psychology as a science of psychic phenomena, natural science of physical phenomena – without thinking of the 'tacit limitations' which Brentano himself expounded with characteristic clarity and acuteness. I have been all the more happy, therefore, to recall them by the full citations given above.

6 Brentano understands by 'sensations' *acts* of sensing, and opposes them to sensed contents. In our mode of speech, as expounded above, no such distinction obtains. We call 'sensations' the mere fact that a sense-content and, further, that a non-act in general, is present in the experiential complex. In relation to appearing, talk of 'sensing' only serves to point to the apperceptive function of such contents (that they function as bearers of an interpretation, in which the appearance in question is carried out perceptually or imaginatively).

7 Cf. Brentano, loc. cit. §7, p. 120. In detailed examples he says: 'Knowledge, joy, desire, exist actually, colour, tone, warmth only phenomenally and intentionally.' On p. 104 he lists as examples of physical phenomena: 'A figure, *landscape* that I *see* . . . warmth, cold, smell that I *sense*.'

Index

CPSIA information can be obtained at www.ICGtesting.com
Printed in the USA
LVOW072107191212

312222LV00002B/16/P